RANDOM
HOUSE

LARGE
PRINT

A PROMISED LAND

A
PROMISED
LAND

BARACK
OBAMA

RANDOM HOUSE
LARGE PRINT

The letter from Nicole Brandon on page 405 has been edited and condensed for clarity.

Cover design: Christopher Brand
Cover photograph: Pari Dukovic

The Library of Congress has established a Cataloging-in-Publication record for this title.

ISBN: 978-0-525-63376-1

www.penguinrandomhouse.com/large-print-format-books

FIRST LARGE PRINT EDITION

Printed in the United States of America

10 9 8 7 6 5 4 3 2 1

This Large Print edition published in accord with the standards of the N.A.V.H.

To Michelle—my love and life's partner
and
Malia and Sasha—whose dazzling light makes
everything brighter

O, fly and never tire,
Fly and never tire,
Fly and never tire,
There's a great camp-meeting in the Promised Land.

—FROM AN AFRICAN AMERICAN SPIRITUAL

Don't discount our powers;
We have made a pass
At the infinite.

—ROBERT FROST, "KITTY HAWK"

CONTENTS

PREFACE

I BEGAN WRITING THIS BOOK shortly after the end of my presidency—after Michelle and I had boarded Air Force One for the last time and traveled west for a long-deferred break. The mood on the plane was bittersweet. Both of us were drained, physically and emotionally, not only by the labors of the previous eight years but by the unexpected results of an election in which someone diametrically opposed to everything we stood for had been chosen as my successor. Still, having run our leg of the race to completion, we took satisfaction in knowing that we'd done our very best—and that however much I'd fallen short as president, whatever projects I'd hoped but failed to accomplish, the country was in better shape now than it had been when I'd started. For a month, Michelle and I slept late, ate leisurely dinners, went for long walks, swam in the ocean, took stock, replenished our friendship, rediscovered our love, and planned for a less eventful but hopefully no less satisfying second act. And by the time I was ready to get back to work and sat down with a pen and yellow pad (I still like writing things out in longhand, finding that a computer gives even my roughest drafts too smooth a gloss and lends half-baked thoughts the mask of tidiness), I had a clear outline of the book in my head.

First and foremost, I hoped to give an honest rendering of my time in office—not just a historical record of key events that happened on my watch and important figures with whom I interacted but also an account of some of the political, economic, and cultural crosscurrents that helped determine the challenges my administration faced and the choices my team and I made in response. Where possible, I wanted to offer readers a sense of what it's like to **be** the president of the United States; I wanted to pull the curtain back a bit and remind people that, for all its power and pomp, the presidency is still just a job and our federal government is a human enterprise like any other, and the men and women who work in the White House experience the same daily mix of satisfaction, disappointment, office friction, screw-ups, and small triumphs as the rest of their fellow citizens. Finally, I wanted to tell a more personal story that might inspire young people considering a life of public service: how my career in politics really started with a search for a place to fit in, a way to explain the different strands of my mixed-up heritage, and how it was only by hitching my wagon to something larger than myself that I was ultimately able to locate a community and purpose for my life.

I figured I could do all that in maybe five hundred pages. I expected to be done in a year.

It's fair to say that the writing process didn't go exactly as I'd planned. Despite my best intentions, the book kept growing in length and scope—the reason why I eventually decided to break it into two volumes. I'm painfully

aware that a more gifted writer could have found a way
to tell the same story with greater brevity (after all, my
home office in the White House sat right next to the
Lincoln Bedroom, where a signed copy of the 272-word
Gettysburg Address rests beneath a glass case). But each
time that I sat down to write—whether it was to describe
the early phases of my campaign, or my administration's
handling of the financial crisis, or negotiations with the
Russians on nuclear arms control, or the forces that led
to the Arab Spring—I found my mind resisting a simple
linear narrative. Often, I felt obliged to provide context
for the decisions I and others had made, and I didn't
want to relegate that background to footnotes or endnotes (I hate footnotes and endnotes). I discovered that I
couldn't always explain my motivations just by referencing reams of economic data or recalling an exhaustive
Oval Office briefing, for they'd been shaped by a conversation I'd had with a stranger on the campaign trail, a
visit to a military hospital, or a childhood lesson I'd
received years earlier from my mother. Repeatedly my
memories would toss up seemingly incidental details
(trying to find a discreet location to grab an evening
smoke; my staff and I having a laugh while playing cards
aboard Air Force One) that captured, in a way the public
record never could, my lived experience during the eight
years I spent in the White House.

Beyond the struggle to put words on a page, what I
didn't fully anticipate was the way events would unfold
during the three and a half years after that last flight on Air
Force One. As I sit here, the country remains in the grips
of a global pandemic and the accompanying economic
crisis, with more than 178,000 Americans dead, businesses

shuttered, and millions of people out of work. Across the nation, people from all walks of life have poured into the streets to protest the deaths of unarmed Black men and women at the hands of the police. Perhaps most troubling of all, our democracy seems to be teetering on the brink of crisis—a crisis rooted in a fundamental contest between two opposing visions of what America is and what it should be; a crisis that has left the body politic divided, angry, and mistrustful, and has allowed for an ongoing breach of institutional norms, procedural safeguards, and the adherence to basic facts that both Republicans and Democrats once took for granted.

This contest is not new, of course. In many ways, it has defined the American experience. It's embedded in founding documents that could simultaneously proclaim all men equal and yet count a slave as three-fifths of a man. It finds expression in our earliest court opinions, as when the chief justice of the Supreme Court bluntly explains to Native Americans that their tribe's rights to convey property aren't enforceable since the court of the conqueror has no capacity to recognize the just claims of the conquered. It's a contest that's been fought on the fields of Gettysburg and Appomattox but also in the halls of Congress, on a bridge in Selma, across the vineyards of California, and down the streets of New York—a contest fought by soldiers but more often by union organizers, suffragists, Pullman porters, student leaders, waves of immigrants, and LGBTQ activists, armed with nothing more than picket signs, pamphlets, or a pair of marching shoes. At the heart of this long-running battle is a simple question: Do we care to match the reality of America to its ideals? If so, do we really believe that our notions of self-government and individual freedom, equality of opportunity and equality before the law, apply to everybody? Or are we instead committed, in practice if not in statute, to reserving those things for a privileged few?

I recognize that there are those who believe that it's time to discard the myth—that an examination of America's past and an even cursory glance at today's headlines show that this nation's ideals have always been secondary to conquest and subjugation, a racial caste system and rapacious capitalism, and that to pretend otherwise is to be complicit in a game that was rigged from the start. And I confess that there have been times during the course of writing this book, as I've reflected on my presidency and all that's happened since, when I've had to ask myself whether I was too tempered in speaking the truth as I saw it, too cautious in either word or deed, convinced as I was that by appealing to what Lincoln called the better angels of our nature I stood a greater chance of leading us in the direction of the America we've been promised.

I don't know. What I can say for certain is that I'm not yet ready to abandon the possibility of America— not just for the sake of future generations of Americans but for all of humankind. For I'm convinced that the pandemic we're currently living through is both a manifestation of and a mere interruption in the relentless march toward an interconnected world, one in which peoples and cultures can't help but collide. In that world—of global supply chains, instantaneous capital transfers, social media, transnational terrorist networks, climate change, mass migration, and ever-increasing complexity—we will learn to live together, cooperate with one another, and recognize the dignity of others, or we will perish. And so the world watches America—the only great power in history made up of people from every corner of the planet, comprising every race and faith and cultural practice—to see if our experiment in democracy can work. To see if we can do what no other nation has ever done. To see if we can actually live up to the meaning of our creed.

The jury's still out. By the time this first volume is published, a U.S. election will have taken place, and while I believe the stakes could not be higher, I also know that no single election will settle the matter. If I remain hopeful, it's because I've learned to place my faith in my fellow citizens, especially those of the next generation, whose conviction in the equal worth of all people seems to come as second nature, and who insist on making real those principles that their parents and teachers told them were true but perhaps never fully believed themselves. More than anyone, this book is for those young people— an invitation to once again remake the world, and to bring about, through hard work, determination, and a big dose of imagination, an America that finally aligns with all that is best in us.

August 2020

PART ONE

THE BET

CHAPTER 1

OF ALL THE ROOMS and halls and landmarks that make up the White House and its grounds, it was the West Colonnade that I loved best.

For eight years that walkway would frame my day, a minute-long, open-air commute from home to office and back again. It was where each morning I felt the first slap of winter wind or pulse of summer heat; the place where I'd gather my thoughts, ticking through the meetings that lay ahead, preparing arguments for skeptical members of Congress or anxious constituents, girding myself for this decision or that slow-rolling crisis.

In the earliest days of the White House, the executive offices and the First Family's residence fit under one roof, and the West Colonnade was little more than a path to the horse stables. But when Teddy Roosevelt came into office, he determined that a single building couldn't accommodate a modern staff, six boisterous children, and his sanity. He ordered construction of what would become the West Wing and Oval Office, and over decades and successive presidencies, the colonnade's current configuration emerged: a bracket to the Rose Garden north and west—the thick wall on the north side, mute and unadorned save for high half-moon windows; the stately white columns on the west side, like an honor guard assuring safe passage.

As a general rule, I'm a slow walker—a Hawaiian walk, Michelle likes to say, sometimes with a hint of impatience. I walked differently, though, on the colonnade, conscious of the history that had been made there and those who had preceded me. My stride got longer, my steps a bit brisker, my footfall on stone echoed by the Secret Service detail trailing me a few yards back. When I reached the ramp at the end of the colonnade (a legacy of FDR and his wheelchair—I picture him smiling, chin out, cigarette holder clenched tight in his teeth as he strains to roll up the incline), I'd wave at the uniformed guard just inside the glass-paned door. Sometimes the guard would be holding back a surprised flock of visitors. If I had time, I would shake their hands and ask where they were from. Usually, though, I just turned left, following the outer wall of the Cabinet Room and slipping into the side door by the Oval Office, where I greeted my personal staff, grabbed my schedule and a cup of hot tea, and started the business of the day.

Several times a week, I would step out onto the colonnade to find the groundskeepers, all employees of the National Park Service, working in the Rose Garden. They were older men, mostly, dressed in green khaki uniforms, sometimes matched with a floppy hat to block the sun, or a bulky coat against the cold. If I wasn't running late, I might stop to compliment them on the fresh plantings or ask about the damage done by the previous night's storm, and they'd explain their work with quiet pride. They were men of few words; even with one another they made their points with a gesture or a nod, each of them focused on his individual task but all of them moving with synchronized grace. One of the oldest was Ed Thomas, a tall, wiry Black man with sunken cheeks who had worked at the White House for forty years. The first time I met him, he reached into his back pocket for a cloth to wipe off the dirt before shaking my hand. His hand, thick with veins and knots like the roots of a tree, engulfed mine. I asked how much longer he intended to stay at the White House before taking his retirement.

"I don't know, Mr. President," he said. "I like to work. Getting a little hard on the joints. But I reckon I might stay long as you're here. Make sure the garden looks good."

Oh, how good that garden looked! The shady magnolias rising high at each corner; the hedges, thick and rich green; the crab apple trees pruned just so. And the flowers, cultivated in greenhouses a few miles away, providing a constant explosion of color—reds and yellows and pinks and purples; in spring, the tulips massed in bunches, their heads tilted toward the sun; in summer, lavender heliotrope and geraniums and lilies; in fall, chrysanthemums and daisies and wildflowers. And always a few roses, red mostly but sometimes yellow or white, each one flush in its bloom.

Each time I walked down the colonnade or looked out the window of the Oval Office, I saw the handiwork of the men and women who worked outside. They reminded me of the small Norman Rockwell painting I kept on the wall, next to the portrait of George Washington and above the bust of Dr. King: five tiny figures of varying skin tones, workingmen in dungarees, hoisted up by ropes into a crisp blue sky to polish the lamp of Lady Liberty. The men in the painting, the groundskeepers in the garden—they were guardians, I thought, the quiet priests of a good and solemn order. And I would tell myself that I needed to work as hard and take as much care in my job as they did in theirs.

With time, my walks down the colonnade would accumulate with memories. There were the big public events, of course—announcements made before a phalanx of cameras, press conferences with foreign leaders. But there were also the moments few others saw—Malia and Sasha racing each other to greet me on a surprise afternoon visit, or our dogs, Bo and Sunny, bounding through the snow, their paws sinking so deep that their chins were bearded white. Tossing footballs on a bright fall day, or comforting an aide after a personal hardship.

Such images would often flash through my mind, interrupting whatever calculations were occupying me. They reminded me of time passing, sometimes filling me with longing—a desire to turn back the clock and begin again. This wasn't possible on my morning walk, for time's arrow moved only forward then; the day's work beckoned; I needed to focus on only those things to come.

The night was different. On the evening walk back to the residence, my briefcase stuffed with papers, I would try to slow myself down, sometimes even stop. I'd breathe air laced with the scent of soil and grass and pollen, and listen to the wind or the patter of rain. I sometimes stared at the light against the columns, and the regal mass of the White House, its flag aloft on the roof, lit bright, or I'd look toward the Washington Monument piercing the black sky in the distance, occasionally catching sight of the moon and stars above it, or the twinkling of a passing jet.

In moments like these, I would wonder at the strange path—and the idea—that had brought me to this place.

I DON'T COME from a political family. My maternal grandparents were midwesterners from mostly Scots-Irish stock. They would have been considered liberal, especially by the standards of the Depression-era Kansas towns they were born in, and they were diligent about keeping up with the news. "It's part of being a well-informed citizen," my grandmother, whom we all called Toot (short for Tutu, or Grandma, in Hawaiian), would tell me, peering over the top of her morning **Honolulu Advertiser**. But she and my grandfather had no firm ideological or partisan leanings to speak of, beyond what they considered to be common sense. They thought about work—my grandmother was vice president of escrow at one of the local banks, my grandfather a life insurance salesman—and paying the bills, and the small diversions that life had to offer.

And anyway, they lived on Oahu, where nothing seemed that urgent. After years spent in places as disparate as Oklahoma, Texas, and Washington State, they'd finally moved to Hawaii in 1960, a year after its statehood was established. A big ocean now separated them from riots and protests and other such things. The only political conversation I can recall my grandparents having while I was growing up had to do with a beachside bar: Honolulu's mayor had torn down Gramps's favorite watering hole in order to renovate the beachfront at the far end of Waikiki.

Gramps never forgave him for it.

My mother, Ann Dunham, was different, full of strong opinions. My grandparents' only child, she rebelled against convention in high school—reading beatnik poets and French existentialists, joyriding with a friend to San Francisco for days without telling anyone. As a kid, I'd hear from her about civil rights marches, and why the Vietnam War was a misguided disaster; about the women's movement (yes on equal pay, not as keen on not shaving her legs) and the War on Poverty. When we moved to Indonesia to live with my stepfather, she made sure to explain the sins of government corruption ("It's just stealing, Barry"), even if everyone appeared to be doing it. Later, during the summer I turned twelve, when we went on a month-long family vacation traveling across the United States, she insisted we watch the Watergate hearings every night, providing her own running commentary ("What do you expect from a McCarthyite?").

She didn't just focus on headlines either. Once, when she discovered I had been part of a group that was teasing a kid at school, she sat me down in front of her, lips pursed with disappointment.

"You know, Barry," she said (that's the nickname she and my grandparents used for me when I was growing up, often shortened to "Bar," pronounced "Bear"), "there are people in the world who think only about themselves. They don't care what happens to other people so long as they get what they want. They put other people down to make themselves feel important.

"Then there are people who do the opposite, who are

able to imagine how others must feel, and make sure that they don't do things that hurt people.

"So," she said, looking me squarely in the eye. "Which kind of person do you want to be?"

I felt lousy. As she intended it to, her question stayed with me for a long time.

For my mother, the world was full of opportunities for moral instruction. But I never knew her to get involved in a political campaign. Like my grandparents, she was suspicious of platforms, doctrines, absolutes, preferring to express her values on a smaller canvas. "The world is complicated, Bar. That's why it's interesting." Dismayed by the war in Southeast Asia, she'd end up spending most of her life there, absorbing the language and culture, setting up micro-lending programs for people in poverty long before micro-credit became trendy in international development. Appalled by racism, she would marry outside her race not once but twice, and go on to lavish what seemed like an inexhaustible love on her two brown children. Incensed by societal constraints put upon women, she'd divorce both men when they proved overbearing or disappointing, carving out a career of her own choosing, raising her kids according to her own standards of decency, and pretty much doing whatever she damn well pleased.

In my mother's world, the personal really was political—although she wouldn't have had much use for the slogan.

None of this is to say that she lacked ambition for her son. Despite the financial strain, she and my grandparents would send me to Punahou, Hawaii's top prep school.

The thought of me not going to college was never entertained. But no one in my family would ever have suggested I might hold public office someday. If you'd asked my mother, she might have imagined that I'd end up heading a philanthropic institution like the Ford Foundation. My grandparents would have loved to see me become a judge, or a great courtroom lawyer like Perry Mason.

"Might as well put that smart mouth of his to use," Gramps would say.

Since I didn't know my father, he didn't have much input. I vaguely understood that he had worked for the Kenyan government for a time, and when I was ten, he traveled from Kenya to stay with us for a month in Honolulu. That was the first and last I saw of him; after that, I heard from him only through the occasional letter, written on thin blue airmail paper that was preprinted to fold and address without an envelope. "Your mother tells me you think you may want to study architecture," one letter might read. "I think this is a very practical profession, and one that can be practiced anywhere in the world."

It was not much to go on.

As for the world beyond my family—well, what they would see for most of my teenage years was not a budding leader but rather a lackadaisical student, a passionate basketball player of limited talent, and an incessant, dedicated partyer. No student government for me; no Eagle Scouts or interning at the local congressman's office. Through high school, my friends and I didn't discuss much beyond sports, girls, music, and plans for getting loaded.

Three of these guys—Bobby Titcomb, Greg Orme,

and Mike Ramos—remain some of my closest friends. To this day, we can laugh for hours over stories of our misspent youth. In later years, they would throw themselves into my campaigns with a loyalty for which I will always be grateful, becoming as skilled at defending my record as anyone on MSNBC.

But there were also times during my presidency—after they had watched me speak to a big crowd, say, or receive a series of crisp salutes from young Marines during a base tour—when their faces would betray a certain bafflement, as if they were trying to reconcile the graying man in a suit and tie with the ill-defined man-child they'd once known.

That guy? they must have said to themselves. **How the hell did that happen?**

And if my friends had ever asked me directly, I'm not sure I'd have had a good answer.

I DO KNOW that sometime in high school I started asking questions—about my father's absence and my mother's choices; about how it was I'd come to live in a place where few people looked like me. A lot of the questions centered on race: Why did Blacks play professional basketball but not coach it? What did that girl from school mean when she said she didn't think of me as Black? Why were all the Black men in action movies switchblade-wielding lunatics except for maybe the one decent Black guy—the sidekick, of course—who always seemed to end up getting killed?

But I wasn't concerned only with race. It was class as well. Growing up in Indonesia, I'd seen the yawning chasm between the lives of wealthy elites and impoverished masses. I had a nascent awareness of the tribal tensions in my father's country—the hatred that could exist between those who on the surface might look the same. I bore daily witness to the seemingly cramped lives of my grandparents, the disappointments they filled with TV and liquor and sometimes a new appliance or car. I noticed that my mother paid for her intellectual freedom with chronic financial struggles and occasional personal chaos, and I became attuned to the not-so-subtle hierarchies among my prep school classmates, mostly having to do with how much money their parents had. And then there was the unsettling fact that, despite whatever my mother might claim, the bullies, cheats, and self-promoters seemed to be doing quite well, while those she considered good and decent people seemed to get screwed an awful lot.

All of this pulled me in different directions. It was as if, because of the very strangeness of my heritage and the worlds I straddled, I was from everywhere and nowhere at once, a combination of ill-fitting parts, like a platypus or some imaginary beast, confined to a fragile habitat, unsure of where I belonged. And I sensed, without fully understanding why or how, that unless I could stitch my life together and situate myself along some firm axis, I might end up in some basic way living my life alone.

I didn't talk to anyone about this, certainly not my friends or family. I didn't want to hurt their feelings or stand out more than I already did. But I did find refuge in books. The reading habit was my mother's doing, instilled early in my childhood—her go-to move anytime I complained of boredom, or when she couldn't afford to send me to the international school in Indonesia, or when I had to accompany her to the office because she didn't have a babysitter.

Go read a book, she would say. **Then come back and tell me something you learned.**

There were a few years when I lived with my grandparents in Hawaii while my mother continued her work in Indonesia and raised my younger sister, Maya. Without my mother around to nag me, I didn't learn as much, as my grades readily attested. Then, around tenth grade, that changed. I still remember going with my grandparents to a rummage sale at the Central Union Church, across the street from our apartment, and finding myself in front of a bin of old hardcover books. For some reason, I started pulling out titles that appealed to me, or sounded vaguely familiar—books by Ralph Ellison and Langston Hughes, Robert Penn Warren and Dostoyevsky, D. H. Lawrence and Ralph Waldo Emerson. Gramps, who was eyeing a set of used golf clubs, gave me a confused look when I walked up with my box of books.

"Planning to open a library?"

My grandmother shushed him, finding my sudden interest in literature admirable. Ever practical, she did suggest I might want to focus on my class assignments before digging into **Crime and Punishment.**

I ended up reading all those books, sometimes late, after I got home from basketball practice and a six-pack with my friends, sometimes after bodysurfing on a Saturday afternoon, sitting alone in Gramps's rickety old Ford Granada with a towel around my waist to avoid getting the upholstery wet. When I finished with the first set of books, I went to other rummage sales, looking for more. Much of what I read I only dimly understood; I took to circling unfamiliar words to look up in the dictionary, although I was less scrupulous about decoding pronunciations—deep into my twenties I would know the meaning of words I couldn't pronounce. There was no system to this, no rhyme or pattern. I was like a young tinkerer in my parents' garage, gathering up old cathode-ray tubes and bolts and loose wires, not sure what I'd do with any of it, but convinced it would prove handy once I figured out the nature of my calling.

MY INTEREST IN books probably explains why I not only survived high school but arrived at Occidental College in 1979 with a thin but passable knowledge of political issues and a series of half-baked opinions that I'd toss out during late-night bull sessions in the dorm.

Looking back, it's embarrassing to recognize the degree to which my intellectual curiosity those first two years of college paralleled the interests of various women I was attempting to get to know: Marx and Marcuse so I had something to say to the long-legged socialist who lived in my dorm; Fanon and Gwendolyn Brooks for the smooth-skinned sociology major who never gave me a second look; Foucault and Woolf for the ethereal bisexual who wore mostly black. As a strategy for picking up girls, my pseudo-intellectualism proved mostly worthless; I found myself in a series of affectionate but chaste friendships.

Still, these halting efforts served a purpose: Something approaching a worldview took shape in my mind. I was helped along by a handful of professors who tolerated my iffy study habits and my youthful pretensions. I was helped even more by a handful of mostly older students—Black kids from the inner city, white kids who had scratched their way into college from small towns, first-generation Latino kids, international students from Pakistan or India or countries in Africa that teetered on the edge of chaos. They knew what mattered to them; when they spoke in class, their views were rooted in actual communities, actual struggles. **Here's what these budget cuts mean in my neighborhood. Let me tell you about my school before you complain about affirmative action. The First Amendment is great, but why does the U.S. government say nothing about the political prisoners in my country?**

The two years I spent at Occidental represented the start of my political awakening. But that didn't mean I believed in politics. With few exceptions, everything I observed about politicians seemed dubious: the blow-dried hair, the wolfish grins, the bromides and self-peddling on TV while behind closed doors they curried the favor of corporations and other monied interests. They were actors in a rigged game, I decided, and I wanted no part of it.

What did capture my attention was something broader and less conventional—not political campaigns but social movements, where ordinary people joined together to make change. I became a student of the suffragists and early labor organizers; of Gandhi and Lech Wałesa and the African National Congress. Most of all I was inspired by the young leaders of the civil rights movement—not just Dr. King but John Lewis and Bob Moses, Fannie Lou Hamer and Diane Nash. In their heroic efforts—going door-to-door to register voters, sitting down at lunch counters, and marching to freedom songs—I saw the possibility of practicing the values my mother had taught me; how you could build power not by putting others down but by lifting them up. This was true democracy at work—democracy not as a gift from on high, or a division of spoils between interest groups, but rather democracy that was earned, the work of everybody. The result was not just a change in material conditions but a sense of dignity for people and communities, a bond between those who had once seemed far apart.

This, I decided, was an ideal worth pursuing. I just needed focus. After my sophomore year I transferred to Columbia University, figuring it would be a new start. For three years in New York, holed up in a series of dilapidated apartments, largely shorn of old friends and bad habits, I lived like a monk—reading, writing, filling up journals, rarely bothering with college parties or even eating hot meals. I got lost in my head, preoccupied with questions that seemed to layer themselves one over the next. What made some movements succeed where others failed? Was it a sign of success when portions of a cause were absorbed by conventional politics, or was it a sign that the cause had been hijacked? When was compromise acceptable and when was it selling out, and how did one know the difference?

Oh, how earnest I was then—how fierce and humorless! When I look back on my journal entries from this time, I feel a great affection for the young man that I was, aching to make a mark on the world, wanting to be a part of something grand and idealistic, which evidence seemed to indicate did not exist. This was America in the early 1980s, after all. The social movements of the

previous decade had lost their vibrancy. A new conservatism was taking hold. Ronald Reagan was president; the
economy was in recession; the Cold War was in full
swing.

If I were to travel back in time, I might urge the young
man I was to set the books aside for a minute, open the
windows, and let in some fresh air (my smoking habit
was then in full bloom). I'd tell him to relax, go meet
some people, and enjoy the pleasures that life reserves for
those in their twenties. The few friends I had in New
York tried to offer similar advice.

"You need to lighten up, Barack."

"You need to get laid."

"You're so idealistic. It's great, but I don't know if what
you're saying is really possible."

I resisted these voices. I resisted precisely because I
feared they were right. Whatever I was incubating during
those hours spent alone, whatever vision for a better
world I'd let flourish in the hothouse of my youthful
mind, it could hardly withstand even a simple conversa-
tional road test. In the gray light of a Manhattan winter
and against the overarching cynicism of the times, my
ideas, spoken aloud in class or over coffee with friends,
came off as fanciful and far-fetched. And I knew it. In
fact, it's one of the things that may have saved me from
becoming a full-blown crank before I reached the age of
twenty-two; at some basic level I understood the absurdity of my vision, how wide the gap was between my
grand ambitions and anything I was actually doing in
my life. I was like a young Walter Mitty; a Don Quixote
with no Sancho Panza.

This, too, can be found in my journal entries from

that time, a pretty accurate chronicle of all my short-comings. My preference for navel-gazing over action. A certain reserve, even shyness, traceable perhaps to my Hawaiian and Indonesian upbringing, but also the result of a deep self-consciousness. A sensitivity to rejection or looking stupid. Maybe even a fundamental laziness.

I took it upon myself to purge such softness with a regimen of self-improvement that I've never entirely shed. (Michelle and the girls point out that to this day I can't get into a pool or the ocean without feeling com-pelled to swim laps. "Why don't you just wade?" they'll say with a snicker. "It's fun. Here . . . we'll show you how.") I made lists. I started working out, going for runs around the Central Park Reservoir or along the East River and eating cans of tuna fish and hard-boiled eggs for fuel. I stripped myself of excess belongings—who needs more than five shirts?

What great contest was I preparing for? Whatever it was, I knew I wasn't ready. That uncertainty, that self-doubt, kept me from settling too quickly on easy answers. I got into the habit of questioning my own assumptions, and this, I think, ultimately came in handy, not only because it prevented me from becoming insufferable, but because it inoculated me against the revolutionary formulas embraced by a lot of people on the left at the dawn of the Reagan era.

Certainly that was true when it came to questions of race. I experienced my fair share of racial slights and could see all too well the enduring legacy of slavery and Jim Crow anytime I walked through Harlem or parts of the Bronx. But, by dint of biography, I learned not to claim my own victimhood too readily and resisted the notion held by some of the Black folks I knew that white people were irredeemably racist.

The conviction that racism wasn't inevitable may also explain my willingness to defend the American idea: what the country was, and what it could become.

My mother and grandparents had never been noisy in their patriotism. Reciting the Pledge of Allegiance in class, waving small flags on the Fourth of July—these were treated as pleasant rituals, not sacred duties (their attitudes toward Easter and Christmas were pretty much the same). Even Gramps's service in World War II was downplayed; he told me more about eating K rations— "Terrible!"—than he ever told me about the glory of marching in Patton's army.

And yet the pride in being American, the notion that America was the greatest country on earth—that was always a given. As a young man, I chafed against books that dismissed the notion of American exceptionalism; got into long, drawn-out arguments with friends who insisted the American hegemon was the root of oppression worldwide. I had lived overseas; I knew too much. That America fell perpetually short of its ideals, I readily conceded. The version of American history taught in schools, with slavery glossed over and the slaughter of Native Americans all but omitted—that, I did not defend. The blundering exercise of military power, the rapaciousness of multinationals—yeah, yeah, I got all that.

But the **idea** of America, the **promise** of America: this I clung to with a stubbornness that surprised even me. "We hold these truths to be self-evident, that all men are created equal"—**that** was my America. The America Tocqueville wrote about, the countryside of Whitman and Thoreau, with no person my inferior or my better; the America of pioneers heading west in search of a better life or immigrants landing on Ellis Island, propelled by a yearning for freedom.

It was the America of Thomas Edison and the Wright brothers, making dreams take flight, and Jackie Robinson stealing home. It was Chuck Berry and Bob Dylan, Billie Holiday at the Village Vanguard and Johnny Cash at Folsom State Prison—all those misfits who took the scraps that others overlooked or discarded and made beauty no one had seen before.

It was the America of Lincoln at Gettysburg, and Jane Addams toiling in a Chicago settlement home, and weary GIs at Normandy, and Dr. King on the National Mall summoning courage in others and in himself.

It was the Constitution and the Bill of Rights, crafted by flawed but brilliant thinkers who reasoned their way to a system at once sturdy and capable of change.

An America that could explain me.

"Dream on, Barack" is how those arguments with my college friends would usually end, as some smug bastard dropped a newspaper in front of me, its headlines trumpeting the U.S. invasion of Grenada or cuts in the school lunch program or some other disheartening news. "Sorry, but **that's** your America."

SUCH WAS MY state when I graduated in 1983: big ideas and nowhere to go. There were no movements to join, no selfless leader to follow. The closest I could find to what I had in mind was something called "community organizing"—grassroots work that brought ordinary people together around issues of local concern. After bouncing around in a couple of ill-fitting jobs in New York, I heard about a position in Chicago, working with a group of churches that were trying to stabilize communities racked by steel plant closures. Nothing grand, but a place to start.

I've recorded elsewhere my organizing years in Chicago. Victories were small and transitory in the mostly Black working-class neighborhoods where I spent my time; my organization was a bit player in its attempts to address the changes that were sweeping not just Chicago but cities across the country—the decline of manufacturing, white flight, the rise of a discrete and disconnected underclass even as a new knowledge class began to fuel gentrification in the urban core.

But if my own impact on Chicago was small, the city changed the arc of my life.

For starters, it got me out of my own head. I had to listen to, and not just theorize about, what mattered to people. I had to ask strangers to join me and one another on real-life projects—fixing up a park, or removing asbestos from a housing project, or starting an after-school program. I experienced failure and learned to buck up so I could rally those who'd put their trust in me. I suffered rejections and insults often enough to stop fearing them.

In other words, I grew up—and got my sense of humor back.

I came to love the men and women I worked with: the single mom living on a ravaged block who somehow got all four children through college; the Irish priest who threw open the church doors every evening so that kids had an option other than gangs; the laid-off steelworker who went back to school to become a social worker. Their stories of hardship and their modest victories confirmed for me again and again the basic decency of people. Through them, I saw the transformation that took place when citizens held their leaders and institutions to account, even on something as small as putting in a stop sign on a busy corner or getting more police patrols. I noticed how people stood up a little straighter, saw themselves differently, when they learned that their voices mattered.

Through them, I resolved the lingering questions of my racial identity. For it turned out there was no single way to be Black; just trying to be a good man was enough.

Through them, I discovered a community of faith— that it was okay to doubt, to question, and still reach for something beyond the here and now.

And because I heard in church basements and on bungalow porches the very same values—honesty, and hard work, and empathy—that had been drilled into me by my mother and grandparents, I came to trust the common thread that existed between people.

I can't help but wonder sometimes what would have happened if I had stayed with organizing, or at least some version of it. Like many local heroes I've met over the years, I might have managed to build up an institution that could reshape a neighborhood or a portion of the city. Anchored deep in a community, I might have steered money and imagination to change not the world but just that one place or that one set of kids, doing work that touched the lives of neighbors and friends in some measurable and useful way.

But I didn't stay. I left for Harvard Law School. And

here's where the story gets murkier in my mind, with my motives open to interpretation.

I TOLD MYSELF THEN—and like to tell myself still—that I left organizing because I saw the work I was doing as too slow, too limited, not able to match the needs of the people I hoped to serve. A local job-training center couldn't make up for thousands of steel jobs lost by a plant closing. An after-school program couldn't compensate for chronically underfunded schools, or kids raised by their grandparents because both parents were doing time. On every issue, it seemed, we kept bumping up against somebody—a politician, a bureaucrat, some distant CEO—who had the power to make things better but didn't. And when we did get concessions from them, it was most often too little, too late. The power to shape budgets and guide policy was what we needed, and that power lay elsewhere.

Moreover, I came to realize that just two years before I arrived, there **had** been a movement for change in Chicago, one that was both social and political—a deep swift current that I had failed to fully appreciate because it hadn't conformed to my theories. It was the movement to elect Harold Washington as the city's first Black mayor.

It seemed like it sprang out of nowhere, as grassroots a political campaign as anything modern politics had ever seen. A small band of Black activists and business leaders, tired of the chronic bias and inequities of America's most segregated big city, decided to register a record number of voters, and then drafted a rotund congressman of prodigious talent but limited ambition to run for an office that appeared well out of reach.

Nobody thought it had a chance; even Harold was skeptical. The campaign operated hand to mouth, staffed largely by inexperienced volunteers. But then it happened—some form of spontaneous combustion. People who had never thought about politics, people who had never even voted, got swept up in the cause. Seniors and schoolchildren started sporting the campaign's blue buttons. A collective unwillingness to keep putting up with a steady accumulation of unfairness and slights—all the bogus traffic stops and secondhand textbooks; all the times Black folks walked past a Park District field house on the North Side and noticed how much nicer it was than the one in their neighborhood; all the times they'd been passed over for promotions or denied bank loans— gathered like a cyclone and toppled city hall.

By the time I arrived in Chicago, Harold was halfway through his first term. The city council, once a rubber stamp for Old Man Daley, had divided into racial camps, a controlling majority of white aldermen blocking every reform that Harold proposed. He tried to wheedle and cut deals, but they wouldn't budge. It was riveting television, tribal and raw, but it limited what Harold could deliver for those who'd elected him. It took a federal court redrawing a racially gerrymandered aldermanic map for Harold to finally get the majority and break the deadlock. And before he could realize many of the changes he'd promised, he was dead of a heart attack. A scion of the old order, Rich Daley, ultimately regained his father's throne.

Far from the center of the action, I watched this drama unfold and tried to absorb its lessons. I saw how the tremendous energy of the movement couldn't be sustained without structure, organization, and skills in governance. I saw how a political campaign based on racial redress, no matter how reasonable, generated fear and backlash and ultimately placed limits on progress. And in the rapid collapse of Harold's coalition after his death, I saw the danger of relying on a single charismatic leader to bring about change.

And yet what a force he was for those five years. Despite the roadblocks, Chicago changed on his watch. City services, from tree trimming to snow removal to road repair, came to be spread more evenly across wards. New schools were built in poor neighborhoods. City jobs were no longer subject solely to patronage, and the business community at long last started paying attention to the lack of diversity in their ranks.

Above all, Harold gave people hope. The way Black Chicagoans talked about him in those years was reminiscent of how a certain generation of white progressives talked about Bobby Kennedy—it wasn't so much what he did as how he made you feel. Like anything was possible. Like the world was yours to remake.

For me, this planted a seed. It made me think for the first time that I wanted to someday run for public office. (I wasn't the only one thus inspired—it was shortly after Harold's election that Jesse Jackson would announce he was running for president.) Wasn't this where the energy of the civil rights movement had migrated—into electoral politics? John Lewis, Andrew Young, Julian Bond—hadn't they run for office, deciding this was the arena where they could make the most difference? I knew there were pitfalls—the compromises, the constant money chase, the losing track of ideals, and the relentless pursuit of winning.

But maybe there was another way. Maybe you could generate the same energy, the same sense of purpose, not just within the Black community but across racial lines. Maybe with enough preparation, policy know-how, and management skills, you could avoid some of Harold's mistakes. Maybe the principles of organizing could be marshaled not just to run a campaign but to govern—to encourage participation and active citizenship among those who'd been left out, and to teach them not just to trust their elected leaders, but to trust one another, and themselves.

That's what I told myself. But it wasn't the whole story. I was also struggling with narrower questions of my own ambitions. As much as I'd learned from organizing, I didn't have much to show for it in terms of concrete accomplishments. Even my mother, the woman who'd always marched to a different drummer, worried about me.

"I don't know, Bar," she told me one Christmas. "You can spend a lifetime working outside institutions. But you might get more done trying to change those institutions from the inside.

"Plus, take it from me," she said with a rueful laugh. "Being broke is overrated."

And so it was that in the fall of 1988, I took my ambitions to a place where ambition hardly stood out. Valedictorians, student body presidents, Latin scholars, debate champions—the people I found at Harvard Law School were generally impressive young men and women who, unlike me, had grown up with the justifiable conviction that they were destined to lead lives of consequence. That I ended up doing well there I attribute mostly to the fact that I was a few years older than my classmates. Whereas many felt burdened by the workload, for me days spent in the library—or, better yet, on the couch of my off-campus apartment, a ball game on with the sound muted—felt like an absolute luxury after three years of organizing community meetings and knocking on doors in the cold.

There was also this: The study of law, it turned out, wasn't so different from what I'd done during my years of solitary musing on civic questions. What principles should govern the relationship between the individual and society, and how far did our obligations to others extend? How much should the government regulate the market? How does social change happen, and how can rules ensure that everybody has a voice?

I couldn't get enough of this stuff. I loved the back-and-forth, especially with the more conservative students, who despite our disagreements seemed to appreciate the fact that I took their arguments seriously. In classroom discussions, my hand kept shooting up, earning me some well-deserved eye rolls. I couldn't help it; it was as if, after years of locking myself away with a strange obsession—like juggling, say, or sword swallowing—I now found myself in circus school.

Enthusiasm makes up for a host of deficiencies, I tell my daughters—and at least that was true for me at Harvard. In my second year, I was elected the first Black head of the **Law Review,** which generated a bit of national press. I signed a contract to write a book. Job offers arrived from around the country, and it was assumed that my path was now charted, just as it had been for my predecessors at the **Law Review:** I'd clerk for a Supreme

Court justice, work for a top law firm or the Office of the United States Attorney, and when the time was right, I could, if I wanted to, try my hand at politics.

It was heady stuff. The only person who questioned this smooth path of ascent seemed to be me. It had come too quickly. The big salaries being dangled, the attention—it felt like a trap.

Luckily I had time to consider my next move. And anyway, the most important decision ahead would end up having nothing to do with law.

CHAPTER 2

MICHELLE LAVAUGHN ROBINSON was already practicing law when we met. She was twenty-five years old and an associate at Sidley & Austin, the Chicago-based firm where I worked the summer after my first year of law school. She was tall, beautiful, funny, outgoing, generous, and wickedly smart—and I was smitten almost from the second I saw her. She'd been assigned by the firm to look out for me, to make sure I knew where the office photocopier was and that I generally felt welcome. That also meant we got to go out for lunches together, which allowed us to sit and talk—at first about our jobs and eventually about everything else.

Over the course of the next couple of years, during school breaks and when Michelle came to Harvard as part of the Sidley recruiting team, the two of us went out to dinner and took long walks along the Charles River, talking about movies and family and places in the world we wanted to see. When her father unexpectedly died of complications arising from multiple sclerosis, I flew out to be with her, and she comforted me when I learned that Gramps had advanced prostate cancer.

In other words, we became friends as well as lovers, and as my law school graduation approached, we gingerly circled around the prospect of a life together. Once, I took her to an organizing workshop I was conducting, a favor for a friend who ran a community center on the South Side. The participants were mostly single moms, some on welfare, few with any marketable skills. I asked them to describe their world as it was and as they would like it to be. It was a simple exercise I'd done many times, a way for people to bridge the reality of their communities and their lives with the things they could conceivably change. Afterward, as we were walking to the car, Michelle laced her arm through mine and said she'd been touched by my easy rapport with the women.

"You gave them hope."

"They need more than hope," I said. I tried to explain to her the conflict that I was feeling: between working for change within the system and pushing against it; wanting to lead but wanting to empower people to make change for themselves; wanting to be in politics but not of it.

Michelle looked at me. "The world as it is, and the world as it should be," she said softly.

"Something like that."

Michelle was an original; I knew nobody quite like her. And although it hadn't happened yet, I was starting to think I might ask her to marry me. For Michelle, marriage was a given—the organic next step in a relationship as serious as ours. For me, someone who'd grown up with a mother whose marriages didn't last, the need to formalize a relationship had always felt less pressing. Not only that, but in those early years of our courtship, our arguments could be fierce. As cocksure as I could be, she never gave ground. Her brother, Craig, a basketball star at Princeton who had worked in investment banking before getting into coaching, used to joke that the family didn't think Michelle ("Miche," they called her) would ever get married because she was too tough—no guy could keep up with her. The weird thing was, I liked that about her; how she constantly challenged me and kept me honest.

And what was Michelle thinking? I imagine her just before we met, very much the young professional, tailored and crisp, focused on her career and doing things the way they're supposed to be done, with no time for nonsense. And then this strange guy from Hawaii with a scruffy wardrobe and crazy dreams wanders into her life. That was part of my appeal, she would tell me, how different I was from the guys she'd grown up with, the men she had dated. Different even from her own father, whom she adored: a man who had never finished community college, who had been struck by MS in his early thirties, but who had never complained and had gone to work every single day and made all of Michelle's dance recitals and Craig's basketball games, and was always present for his family, truly his pride and joy.

Life with me promised Michelle something else, those things that she saw she had missed as a child. Adventure. Travel. A breaking of constraints. Just as her roots in Chicago—her big, extended family, her common sense, her desire to be a good mom above all else—promised an anchor that I'd been missing for much of my youth. We didn't just love each other and make each other laugh and share the same basic values—there was symmetry there, the way we complemented each other. We could have each other's back, guard each other's blind spots. We could be a team.

Of course, that was another way of saying we were very different, in experience and in temperament. For Michelle, the road to the good life was narrow and full of hazards. Family was all you could count on, big risks weren't taken lightly, and outward success—a good job, a nice house—never made you feel ambivalent because failure and want were all around you, just a layoff or a shooting away. Michelle never worried about selling out, because growing up on the South Side meant you were always, at some level, an outsider. In her mind, the road-blocks to making it were plenty clear; you didn't have to go looking for them. The doubts arose from having to prove, no matter how well you did, that you belonged in the room—prove it not just to those who doubted you but to yourself.

AS LAW SCHOOL was coming to an end, I told Michelle of my plan. I wouldn't clerk. Instead, I'd move back to Chicago, try to keep my hand in community work while also practicing law at a small firm that specialized in civil rights. If a good opportunity presented itself, I said, I could even see myself running for office.

None of this came as a surprise to her. She trusted me, she said, to do what I believed was right.

"But I need to tell you, Barack," she said, "I think what you want to do is really hard. I mean, I wish I had your optimism. Sometimes I do. But people can be so selfish and just plain ignorant. I think a lot of people don't want to be bothered. And I think politics seems like it's full of people willing to do anything for power, who just think about themselves. Especially in Chicago. I'm not sure you'll ever change that."

"I can try, can't I?" I said with a smile. "What's the point of having a fancy law degree if you can't take some risks? If it doesn't work, it doesn't work. I'll be okay. We'll be okay."

She took my face in her hands. "Have you ever noticed that if there's a hard way and an easy way, you choose the hard way every time? Why do you think that is?"

We both laughed. But I could tell Michelle thought she was onto something. It was an insight that would carry implications for us both.

AFTER SEVERAL YEARS of dating, Michelle and I were married at Trinity United Church of Christ on October 3, 1992, with more than three hundred of our friends, colleagues, and family members crammed happily into the pews. The service was officiated by the church's pastor, Reverend Jeremiah A. Wright, Jr., whom I'd come to know and admire during my organizer days. We were joyful. Our future together was officially beginning.

I had passed the bar and then delayed my law practice for a year to run Project VOTE! in advance of the 1992 presidential race—one of the largest voter-registration drives in Illinois history. After returning from our honeymoon on the California coast, I taught at the University of Chicago Law School, finished my book, and officially joined Davis, Miner, Barnhill & Galland, a small civil rights firm that specialized in employment discrimination cases and did real estate work for affordable housing groups. Michelle, meanwhile, had decided she'd had enough of corporate law and made a move to the City of Chicago's Department of Planning and Development, working there for a year and a half before agreeing to direct a nonprofit youth leadership program called Public Allies.

Both of us enjoyed our jobs and the people we worked with, and as time went on, we got involved with various civic and philanthropic efforts. We took in ball games and concerts and shared dinners with a widening circle of friends. We were able to buy a modest but cozy condo in Hyde Park, right across from Lake Michigan and Promontory Point, just a few doors down from where Craig and his young family lived. Michelle's mother, Marian, still lived in the family's South Shore house, less than fifteen minutes away, and we visited often, feasting on her fried chicken and greens and red velvet cake and barbecue made by Michelle's Uncle Pete. Once we were stuffed, we'd sit around the kitchen and listen to her uncles tell stories of growing up, the laughter louder as the evening wore on, while cousins and nephews and nieces bounced on the sofa cushions until they were sent out into the yard.

Driving home in the twilight, Michelle and I some-times talked about having kids of our own—what they might be like, or how many, and what about a dog?—and imagined all the things we'd do together as a family.

A normal life. A productive, happy life. It should have been enough.

BUT THEN IN the summer of 1995, a political opportunity arose suddenly, through a strange chain of events. The sitting congressman from the Second District of Illinois, Mel Reynolds, had been indicted on several charges, including allegedly having sex with a sixteen-year-old campaign volunteer. If he was convicted, a special election would be promptly held to replace him.

I didn't live in the district, and I lacked the name recognition and base of support to launch a congressional race. The state senator from our area, Alice Palmer, however, was eligible to run for the seat and, not long before the congressman was convicted in August, she threw her hat into the ring. Palmer, an African American former educator with deep roots in the community, had a solid if unremarkable record and was well liked by progressives and some of the old-time Black activists who had helped Harold get elected; and although I didn't know her, we had mutual friends. Based on the work I'd done for Project VOTE! I was asked to help her nascent campaign, and as the weeks went by, several people encouraged me to think about filing to run for Alice's soon-to-be-vacant senate seat.

Before talking to Michelle, I made a list of pros and cons. A state senator wasn't a glamorous post—most people had no idea who their state legislators were—and Springfield, the state capital, was notorious for old-style pork-barreling, logrolling, payola, and other political mischief. On the other hand, I had to start somewhere and pay my dues. Also, the Illinois state legislature was in session only a few weeks out of the year, which meant I could continue teaching and working at the law firm.

Best of all, Alice Palmer agreed to endorse me. With Reynolds's trial still pending, it was difficult to know how the timing would work. Technically it would be possible for Alice to run for Congress while keeping the option of retaining her state seat if she lost the bigger race, but she insisted to me and others that she was done with the senate, ready to move on. Along with an offer of support from our local alderman, Toni Preckwinkle, who boasted the best organization in the area, my chances looked better than good.

I went to Michelle and made my pitch. "Think of it as a test run," I said.

"Hmph."

"Dipping our toes in the water."

"Right."

"So what do you think?"

She pecked me on the cheek. "I think this is something you want to do, so you should do it. Just promise me I won't have to spend time in Springfield."

I had one last person to check in with before I pulled the trigger. Earlier in the year, my mother had fallen sick and had been diagnosed with uterine cancer.

The prognosis wasn't good. At least once a day, the thought of losing her made my heart constrict. I'd flown to Hawaii right after she'd gotten the news and had been relieved to find that she looked like herself and was in good spirits. She confessed she was scared but wanted to be as aggressive as possible with her treatment.

"I'm not going anywhere," she said, "until you give me some grandchildren."

She received the news of my possible state senate run with her usual enthusiasm, insisting I tell her every detail. She acknowledged it would be a lot of work, but my mother was never one to see hard work as anything but good.

"Make sure Michelle's all right with it," she said. "Not that I'm the marriage expert. And don't you dare use me as an excuse not to do it. I've got enough to deal with without feeling like everybody's putting their lives on hold. It's morbid, understand?"

"Got it."

Seven months after her diagnosis, the situation would turn grim. In September, Michelle and I flew to New York to join Maya and my mother for a consultation with a specialist at Memorial Sloan Kettering. Midway through chemo now, she was physically transformed. Her long dark hair was gone; her eyes looked hollow. Worse, the specialist's assessment was that her cancer was at stage four and that treatment options were limited. Watching my mother suck on ice cubes because her saliva glands had shut down, I did my best to put on a brave face. I told her funny stories about my work and recounted the plot of a movie I'd just seen. We laughed as Maya— nine years younger than me and then studying at New York University—reminded me what a bossy big brother I'd been. I held my mother's hand, making sure she was comfortable before she settled in to rest. Then I went back to the hotel room and cried.

It was on that trip to New York that I suggested my mother come stay with us in Chicago; my grandmother was too old to care for her full-time. But my mother, forever the architect of her own destiny, declined. "I'd rather be someplace familiar and warm," she said, looking out the window. I sat there feeling helpless, thinking about the long path she had traveled in her life, how unexpected each step along the way must have been, so full of happy accidents. I'd never once heard her dwell on the disappointments. Instead she seemed to find small pleasures everywhere.

Until this.

"Life is strange, isn't it?" she said softly.

It was.

FOLLOWING MY MOTHER'S advice, I threw myself into my maiden political campaign. It makes me laugh to think back on what a bare-bones operation it was—not much more sophisticated than a campaign for student council. There were no pollsters, no researchers, no TV or radio buys. My announcement, on September 19, 1995, was at the Ramada Inn in Hyde Park, with pretzels and chips and a couple hundred supporters— probably a quarter of whom were related to Michelle. Our campaign literature consisted of an eight-by-four-inch card with what looked like a passport picture of me, a few lines of biography, and four or five bullet points that I'd tapped out on my computer. I'd had it printed at Kinko's.

I did make a point of hiring two political veterans I'd met working on Project VOTE! Carol Anne Harwell, my campaign manager, was tall and sassy, in her early forties and on loan from a West Side ward office. Although she came off as irrepressibly cheerful, she knew her way around Chicago's bare-knuckle politics. Ron Davis, a big grizzly bear of a man, was our field director and petition expert. He had a gray-flecked Afro, scraggly facial hair, and thick wire-rimmed glasses, his bulk hidden by the untucked black shirt he seemed to wear every single day.

Ron proved to be indispensable: Illinois had strict ballot access rules, designed to make life hard on challengers who didn't have party support. To get on the ballot, a candidate needed more than seven hundred registered voters who lived in the district to sign a petition that was circulated and attested to by someone who also lived in the district. A "good" signature had to be legible, accurately linked to a local address, and from a registered voter. I still remember the first time a group of us gathered around our dining room table, Ron huffing and puffing as he passed out clipboards with the petitions attached, along with voter files and a sheet of instructions. I suggested that before we talked about petitions, we should organize some meet-the-candidate forums, maybe draft some position papers. Carol and Ron looked at each other and laughed.

"Boss, let me tell you something," Carol said. "You can save all that League of Women Voters shit for after the election. Right now, the only thing that matters is these petitions. The folks you're running against, they're gonna go through these things with a fine-tooth comb to see if your signatures are legit. If they're not, you don't get to play. And I guarantee you, no matter how careful we are, about half of the signatures will end up being bad, which is why we got to get at least twice as many as they say we do."

"Four times as many," Ron corrected, handing me a clipboard.

Duly chastened, I drove out to one of the neighborhoods Ron had selected to gather signatures. It felt just like my early organizing days, going from house to house, some people not home or unwilling to open the door; women in hair curlers with kids scampering about, men doing yard work; occasionally young men in T-shirts and do-rags, breath thick with alcohol as they scanned the block. There were those who wanted to talk to me about problems at the local school or the gun violence that was creeping into what had been a stable, working-class neighborhood. But mostly folks would take the clipboard, sign it, and try as quickly as possible to get back to what they'd been doing.

If knocking on doors was pretty standard fare for me, the experience was new to Michelle, who gamely dedicated part of every weekend to helping out. And while she'd often collect more signatures than I did—with her megawatt smile and stories of growing up just a few blocks away—there were no smiles two hours later when we'd get back into the car to drive home.

"All I know," she said at one point, "is that I must really love you to spend my Saturday morning doing this."

Over the course of several months, we managed to collect four times the number of required signatures. When I wasn't at the firm or teaching, I visited block clubs, church socials, and senior citizen homes, making my case to voters. I wasn't great. My stump speech was stiff, heavy on policy speak, short on inspiration and humor. I also found it awkward to talk about myself. As an organizer, I'd been trained to always stay in the background.

I did get better, though, more relaxed, and slowly the ranks of my supporters grew. I rounded up endorsements from local officials, pastors, and a handful of progressive organizations; I even got a few position papers drafted. And I'd like to say that this is how my first campaign ended—the plucky young candidate and his accomplished, beautiful, and forbearing wife, starting with a few friends in their dining room, rallying the people around a new brand of politics.

But that's not how it happened. In August 1995, our disgraced congressman was finally convicted and sentenced to prison; a special election was called for late November. With his seat empty and the timeline officially set, others besides Alice Palmer jumped into the congressional race, among them Jesse Jackson, Jr., who had drawn national attention for the stirring introduction of his father at the 1988 Democratic National Convention. Michelle and I knew and liked Jesse Jr. His sister Santita had been one of Michelle's best friends in high school and the maid of honor at our wedding. He was popular enough that his announcement immediately changed the dynamics of the race, putting Alice at an enormous disadvantage.

And because the special congressional election was now going to take place a few weeks before petitions for Alice's senate seat had to be filed, my team started to worry.

"You better check again to make sure Alice isn't going to mess with you if she loses to Jesse Jr.," Ron said.

I shook my head. "She promised me she wasn't running. Gave me her word. And she's said it publicly. In the papers, even."

"That's fine, Barack. But can you just check again, please?"

I did, phoning Alice and once again getting her assurance that regardless of what happened with her congressional run, she still intended to leave state politics.

But when Jesse Jr. handily won the special election, with Alice coming in a distant third, something shifted.

Stories started surfacing in the local press about a "Draft Alice Palmer" campaign. A few of her longtime supporters asked for a meeting, and when I showed up they advised me to get out of the race. The community couldn't afford to give up Alice's seniority, they said. I should be patient; my turn would come. I stood my ground—I had volunteers and donors who had already invested a lot in the campaign, after all; I had stuck with Alice even when Jesse Jr. got in—but the room was unmoved. By the time I spoke to Alice, it was clear where events were headed. The following week she held a press conference in Springfield, announcing that she was filing her own last-minute petitions to get on the ballot and retain her seat.

"Told ya," Carol said, taking a drag from her cigarette and blowing a thin plume of smoke to the ceiling.

I felt disheartened and betrayed, but I figured all was not lost. We had built up a good organization over the previous few months, and almost all the elected officials who'd endorsed me said they'd stick with us. Ron and Carol were less sanguine.

"Hate to tell you, boss," Carol said, "but most folks still have no idea who you are. Shit, they don't know who she is either, but—no offense, now—'Alice Palmer' is a hell of a lot better ballot name than 'Barack Obama.'"

I saw her point but told them we were going to see things through, even as a number of prominent Chicagoans were suddenly urging me to drop out of the race. And then one afternoon Ron and Carol arrived at my house, breathless and looking like they'd won the lottery.

"Alice's petitions," Ron said. "They're terrible. Worst

I've ever seen. All those Negroes who were trying to bully you out of the race, they didn't bother actually doing the work. This could get her knocked off the ballot."

I looked through the informal tallies Ron and our campaign volunteers had done. It was true; the petitions Alice had submitted appeared to be filled with invalid signatures: people whose addresses were outside the district, multiple signatures with different names but the same handwriting. I scratched my head. "I don't know, guys . . ."

"You don't know what?" Carol said.

"I don't know if I want to win like this. I mean, yeah, I'm pissed about what's happened. But these ballot rules don't make much sense. I'd rather just beat her."

Carol pulled back, her jaw tightening. "This woman gave you her **word,** Barack!" she said. "We've all been busting our asses out here, based on that promise. And now, when she tries to screw you, and can't even do **that** right, you're going to let her get away with it? You don't think they would knock you off the ballot in a second if they could?" She shook her head. "Naw, Barack. You're a good guy . . . that's why we believe in you. But if you let this go, you might as well go back to being a professor and whatnot, 'cause politics is not for you. You will get chewed up and won't be doing anybody a damn bit of good."

I looked at Ron, who said quietly, "She's right."

I leaned back in my chair and lit a cigarette. I felt suspended in time, trying to decipher what I was feeling in my gut. How much did I want this? I reminded myself about what I believed I could get done in office, how hard I was willing to work if I got the chance.

"Okay," I said finally.

"Okay!" Carol said, her smile returning. Ron gathered up his papers and put them in his bag.

It would take a couple of months for the process to play out, but with my decision that day, the race was effectively over. We filed our challenge with the Chicago Board of Election Commissioners and when it became clear the board was going to rule in our favor, Alice dropped out. While we were at it, we knocked several other Democrats with bad petitions off the ballot as well. Without a Democratic opponent and with only token Republican opposition, I was on my way to the state senate.

Whatever vision I had for a more noble kind of politics, it would have to wait.

I suppose there are useful lessons to draw from that first campaign. I learned to respect the nuts and bolts of politics, the attention to detail required, the daily grind that might prove the difference between winning and losing. It confirmed, too, what I already knew about myself: that whatever preferences I had for fair play, I didn't like to lose.

But the lesson that stayed with me most had nothing to do with campaign mechanics or hardball politics. It had to do with the phone call I received from Maya in Hawaii one day in early November, well before I knew how my race would turn out.

"She's taken a bad turn, Bar," Maya said.

"How bad?"

"I think you need to come now."

I already knew that my mother's condition had been deteriorating; I'd spoken to her just a few days before.

Hearing a new level of pain and resignation in her voice, I had booked a flight to Hawaii for the following week.

"Can she talk?" I asked Maya now.

"I don't think so. She's fading in and out."

I hung up the phone and called the airline to reschedule my flight for first thing in the morning. I called Carol to cancel some campaign events and run through what needed to be done in my absence. A few hours later, Maya called back.

"I'm sorry, honey. Mom's gone." She had never regained consciousness, my sister told me; Maya had sat at her hospital bedside, reading out loud from a book of folktales as our mother slipped away.

We held a memorial service that week, in the Japanese garden behind the East-West Center at the University of Hawaii. I remembered playing there as a child, my mother sitting in the sun and watching me as I tumbled in the grass, hopped over the rock steps, and caught tadpoles in the stream that ran down one side. Afterward, Maya and I drove out to the lookout near Koko Head and scattered her ashes into the sea, the waves crashing against the rocks. And I thought about my mother and sister alone in that hospital room, and me not there, so busy with my grand pursuits. I knew I could never get that moment back. On top of my sorrow, I felt a great shame.

UNLESS YOU LIVE at the southern tip of Chicago, the quickest route to Springfield is via I-55. During rush hour, heading out of downtown and through the western suburbs, traffic slows to a crawl; but once you get past Joliet things open up, a straight, smooth spread of asphalt cutting southwest through Bloomington (home of State Farm insurance and Beer Nuts) and Lincoln (named after the president, who helped incorporate the town when he was still just a lawyer) and taking you past miles and miles of corn.

For almost eight years I made this drive, usually alone, usually in about three and a half hours, trekking back and forth to Springfield for a few weeks in the fall and through much of the winter and early spring, when the Illinois legislature did the bulk of its work. I'd drive down Tuesday night after dinner and get back home Thursday evening or Friday morning. Cell phone service dropped about an hour outside of Chicago, and the only signals that registered on the dial after that were talk radio and Christian music stations. To stay awake, I listened to audiobooks, the longer the better—novels mostly (John le Carré and Toni Morrison were favorites) but also histories, of the Civil War, the Victorian era, the fall of the Roman Empire.

When asked, I'd tell skeptical friends how much I was learning in Springfield, and, for the first few years at least, it was true. Of all fifty states, Illinois best represented the demographics of the nation, home to a teeming metropolis, sprawling suburbs, farm country, factory towns, and a downstate region considered more southern than northern. On any given day, under the high dome of the capitol, you'd see a cross section of America on full display, a Carl Sandburg poem come to life. There were inner-city kids jostling one another on a field trip, well-coiffed bankers working their flip phones, farmers in seed caps looking to widen the locks that allowed industrial barges to take their crops to market.

You'd see Latina moms looking to fund a new day-care center and middle-aged biker crews, complete with muttonchops and leather jackets, trying to stop yet another legislative effort to make them wear helmets.

I kept my head down in those early months. Some of my colleagues were suspicious of my odd name and Harvard pedigree, but I did my homework and helped raise money for other senators' campaigns. I got to know my fellow legislators and their staffers not just in the senate chamber but also on the basketball court and at golf outings and during the weekly bipartisan poker games we organized—with a two-dollar, three-raise limit, the room thick with smoke, trash talk, and the slow fizz of yet another beer can being opened.

It helped that I already knew the senate minority leader, a hefty Black man in his sixties named Emil Jones. He'd come up through the ranks of one of the traditional ward organizations under Daley Sr. and represented the district where I'd once organized. That's how we first met: I'd brought a group of parents to his office, demanding a meeting to get a college prep program funded for area youth. Rather than stiff-arm us, he invited us in.

"You may not know it," he said, "but I been waiting for y'all to show up!" He explained how he'd never had the chance to graduate from college himself; he wanted to make sure more state money was steered to neglected Black neighborhoods. "I'm gonna leave it up to you to figure out what we need," he told me with a slap on the back as my group left his office. "You leave the politics to me."

Sure enough, Emil got the program funded, and our friendship carried over to the senate. He took an odd

pride in me and became almost protective of my reformist ways. Even when he badly needed a vote on a deal he
was cooking up (getting riverboat gambling licensed in
Chicago was a particular obsession), he would never
squeeze me if I told him I couldn't do it—though he
wasn't above uttering a few choice curses as he charged
off to try someone else.

"Barack's different," he once told a staffer. "He's going
places."

For all my diligence and Emil's goodwill, neither of us
could change one stark fact: We were in the minority
party. Republicans in the Illinois senate had adopted the
same uncompromising approach that Newt Gingrich
was using at the time to neuter Democrats in Congress.
The GOP exercised absolute control over what bills got
out of committee and which amendments were in order.
Springfield had a special designation for junior members
in the minority like me—"mushrooms," because "you're
fed shit and kept in the dark."

On occasion, I found myself able to shape significant
legislation. I helped make sure Illinois's version of the
national welfare reform bill signed by Bill Clinton provided sufficient support for those transitioning to work.
In the wake of one of Springfield's perennial scandals,
Emil assigned me to represent the caucus on a committee
to update the ethics laws. Nobody else wanted the
job, figuring it was a lost cause, but thanks to a good
rapport with my Republican counterpart, Kirk Dillard,
we passed a law that curbed some of the more embarrassing practices—making it impossible, for example, to use
campaign dollars for personal items like a home addition

or a fur coat. (There were senators who didn't talk to us for weeks after that.)

More typical was the time, toward the end of the first session, when I rose from my seat to oppose a blatant tax giveaway to some favored industry when the state was cutting services for the poor. I had lined up my facts and prepared with the thoroughness of a courtroom lawyer; I pointed out why such unjustified tax breaks violated the conservative market principles Republicans claimed to believe in. When I sat down, the senate president, Pate Philip—a beefy, white-haired ex-Marine notorious for insulting women and people of color with remarkably casual frequency—wandered up to my desk.

"That was a hell of a speech," he said, chewing on an unlit cigar. "Made some good points."

"Thanks."

"Might have even changed a lot of minds," he said. "But you didn't change any votes." With that, he signaled to the presiding officer and watched with satisfaction as the green lights signifying "aye" lit up the board.

That was politics in Springfield: a series of transactions mostly hidden from view, legislators weighing the competing pressures of various interests with the dispassion of bazaar merchants, all the while keeping a careful eye on the handful of ideological hot buttons—guns, abortion, taxes—that might generate heat from their base.

It wasn't that people didn't know the difference between good and bad policy. It just didn't matter. What everyone in Springfield understood was that 90 percent of the time the voters back home weren't paying attention. A complicated but worthy compromise, bucking party orthodoxy to support an innovative idea—that could cost you a key endorsement, a big financial backer, a leadership post, or even an election.

Could you get voters to pay attention? I tried. Back in the district, I accepted just about any invitation that came my way. I started writing a regular column for the **Hyde Park Herald,** a neighborhood weekly with a readership of less than five thousand. I hosted town halls, setting out refreshments and stacks of legislative updates, and then usually sat there with my lonesome staffer, looking at my watch, waiting for a crowd that never came.

I couldn't blame folks for not showing up. They were busy, they had families, and surely most of the debates in Springfield seemed remote. Meanwhile, on the few high-profile issues that my constituents did care about, they probably agreed with me already, since the lines of my district—like those of almost every district in Illinois—had been drawn with surgical precision to ensure one-party dominance. If I wanted more funding for schools in poor neighborhoods, if I wanted more access to primary healthcare or retraining for laid-off workers, I didn't need to convince my constituents. The people I needed to engage and persuade—they lived somewhere else.

By the end of my second session, I could feel the atmosphere of the capitol weighing on me—the futility of being in the minority, the cynicism of so many of my colleagues worn like a badge of honor. No doubt it showed. One day, while I was standing in the rotunda after a bill I'd introduced went down in flames, a well-meaning lobbyist came up and put his arm around me.

"You've got to stop beating your head against the wall, Barack," he said. "The key to surviving this place is understanding that it's a business. Like selling cars. Or the dry cleaner down the street. You start believing it's more than that, it'll drive you crazy."

SOME POLITICAL SCIENTISTS argue that everything I've said about Springfield describes exactly how pluralism is supposed to work; that the horse trading between interest groups may not be inspiring, but it keeps democracy muddling along. And maybe that argument would have gone down easier with me at the time if it weren't for the life I was missing at home.

The first two years in the legislature were fine—Michelle was busy with her own work, and although she kept her promise not to come down to the state capital except for my swearing in, we'd still have leisurely conversations on the phone on nights I was away. Then one day in the fall of 1997, she called me at the office, her voice trembling.

"It's happening."

"What's happening?"

"You're going to be a daddy."

I was going to be a daddy. How full of joy the months that followed were! I lived up to every cliché of the expectant father: attending Lamaze classes, trying to figure out how to assemble a crib, reading the book **What to Expect When You're Expecting** with pen in hand to underline key passages. Around six a.m. on the Fourth of July, Michelle poked me and said it was time to go to the hospital. I fumbled around and gathered the bag I'd set by the door, and just seven hours later was introduced to Malia Ann Obama, eight pounds and fifteen ounces of perfection.

Among her many talents, our new daughter had good timing; with no session, no classes, and no big pending cases to work on, I could take the rest of the summer off. A night owl by nature, I manned the late shift so Michelle could sleep, resting Malia on my thighs to read to her as she looked up with big questioning eyes, or dozing as she lay on my chest, a burp and good poop behind us, so warm and serene. I thought about the generations of men who had missed such moments, and I thought about my own father, whose absence had done more to shape me than the brief time I'd spent with him, and I realized that there was no place on earth I would rather be.

But the strains of young parenthood eventually took their toll. After a blissful few months, Michelle went back to work, and I went back to juggling three jobs. We were lucky to find a wonderful nanny who cared for Malia during the day, but the addition of a full-time employee to our family enterprise squeezed the budget hard.

Michelle bore the brunt of all this, shuttling between mothering and work, unconvinced that she was doing either job well. At the end of each night, after feeding and bath time and story time and cleaning up the apartment and trying to keep track of whether she'd picked up the dry cleaning and making a note to herself to schedule an appointment with the pediatrician, she would often fall into an empty bed, knowing the whole cycle would start all over again in a few short hours while her husband was off doing "important things."

We began arguing more, usually late at night when the two of us were thoroughly drained. "This isn't what I signed up for, Barack," Michelle said at one point. "I feel like I'm doing it all by myself."

I was hurt by that. If I wasn't working, I was home—and if I was home and forgot to clean up the kitchen after dinner, it was because I had to stay up late grading exams or fine-tuning a brief. But even as I mounted my defense, I knew I was falling short. Inside Michelle's anger lay a more difficult truth. I was trying to deliver a lot of things to a lot of different people. I was taking the hard way, just as she'd predicted back when our burdens were lighter, our personal responsibilities not so enmeshed. I thought now about the promise I'd made to myself after Malia was born; that my kids would **know** me, that they'd grow up knowing my love for them, feeling that I had always put them first.

Sitting in the dim light of our living room, Michelle no longer seemed angry, just sad. "Is it worth it?" she asked.

I don't recall what I said in response. I know I couldn't admit to her that I was no longer sure.

IT'S HARD, in retrospect, to understand why you did something stupid. I don't mean the small stuff—ruining your favorite tie because you tried to eat soup in the car or throwing out your back because you got talked into playing tackle football on Thanksgiving. I mean dumb choices in the wake of considerable deliberation: those times when you identify a real problem in your life, analyze it, and then with utter confidence come up with precisely the wrong answer.

That was me running for Congress. After numerous conversations, I had to concede that Michelle was right to question whether the difference I was making in Springfield justified the sacrifice. Rather than lightening my load, though, I went in the opposite direction, deciding I needed to step on the gas and secure a more influential office. Around this same time, veteran congressman Bobby Rush, a former Black Panther, challenged Mayor Daley in the 1999 election and got trounced, doing poorly even in his own district.

I thought Rush's campaign had been uninspired, without a rationale other than the vague promise to continue Harold Washington's legacy. If this was how he operated in Congress, I figured I could do better. After talking it over with a few trusted advisors, I had my staff jerry-rig an in-house poll to see whether a race against Rush would be viable. Our informal sampling gave us a shot. Using the results, I was able to persuade several of my closest friends to help finance the race. And then, despite warnings from more experienced political hands that Rush was stronger than he looked, and despite Michelle's incredulity that I would somehow think she'd feel better with me being in Washington instead of Springfield, I announced my candidacy for congressman from the First Congressional District.

Almost from the start, the race was a disaster. A few weeks in, the rumblings from the Rush camp began: **Obama's an outsider; he's backed by white folks; he's a Harvard elitist. And that name—is he even Black?**

Having raised enough money to commission a proper poll, I discovered that Bobby had 90 percent name recognition in the district and a 70 percent approval rating, whereas only 11 percent of voters even knew who I was. Shortly thereafter, Bobby's adult son was tragically shot and killed, eliciting an outpouring of sympathy. I effectively suspended my campaign for a month and watched television coverage of the funeral taking place at my own church, with Reverend Jeremiah Wright presiding. Already on thin ice at home, I took the family to Hawaii for an abbreviated Christmas break, only to have the governor call a special legislative session to vote on a gun control measure I supported. With eighteen-month-old Malia sick and unable to fly, I missed the vote and was roundly flayed by the Chicago press.

I lost by thirty points.

When talking to young people about politics, I sometimes offer this story as an object lesson of what **not** to do. Usually I throw in a postscript, describing how, a few months after my loss, a friend of mine, worried that I'd fallen into a funk, insisted that I join him at the 2000 Democratic National Convention in L.A. ("You need to get back on the horse," he said.) But when I landed at LAX and tried to rent a car, I was turned down because my American Express card was over its limit. I managed to get myself to the Staples Center, but then learned that the credential my friend had secured for me didn't allow entry to the convention floor, which left me to haplessly circle the perimeter and watch the festivities on mounted TV screens. Finally, after an awkward episode later that evening in which my friend couldn't get me into a party he was attending, I took a cab back to the hotel, slept on the couch in his suite, and flew back to Chicago just as Al Gore was accepting the nomination.

It's a funny story, especially in light of where I ultimately ended up. It speaks, I tell my audience, to the unpredictable nature of politics, and the necessity for resilience.

What I don't mention is my dark mood on that flight

back. I was almost forty, broke, coming off a humiliating defeat and with my marriage strained. I felt for perhaps the first time in my life that I had taken a wrong turn; that whatever reservoirs of energy and optimism I thought I had, whatever potential I'd always banked on, had been used up on a fool's errand. Worse, I recognized that in running for Congress I'd been driven not by some selfless dream of changing the world, but rather by the need to justify the choices I had already made, or to satisfy my ego, or to quell my envy of those who had achieved what I had not.

In other words, I had become the very thing that, as a younger man, I had warned myself against. I had become a politician—and not a very good one at that.

CHAPTER 3

A FTER GETTING DRUBBED BY Bobby Rush, I allowed myself a few months to mope and lick my wounds before deciding that I had to reframe my priorities and get on with things. I told Michelle I needed to do better by her. We had a new baby on the way, and even though I was still gone more than she would have preferred, she at least noticed the effort I was making. I scheduled my meetings in Springfield so that I'd be home for dinner more often. I tried to be more punctual and more present. And on June 10, 2001, not quite three years after Malia's birth, we experienced the same blast of joy—the same utter amazement—when Sasha arrived, as plump and lovely as her sister had been, with thick black curls that were impossible to resist.

For the next two years, I led a quieter life, full of small satisfactions, content with the balance I'd seemingly struck. I relished wriggling Malia into her first ballet tights or grasping her hand as we walked to the park; watching baby Sasha laugh and laugh as I nibbled her feet; listening to Michelle's breath slow, her head resting against my shoulder, as she drifted off to sleep in the middle of an old movie. I rededicated myself to my work in the state senate and savored the time spent with my students at the law school. I took a serious look at our finances and put together a plan to pay down our debts. Inside the slower rhythms of my work and the pleasures of fatherhood, I began to consider options for a life after politics—perhaps teaching and writing full-time, or returning to law practice, or applying for a job at a local charitable foundation, as my mother had once imagined I'd do.

In other words, following my ill-fated run for Congress, I experienced a certain letting go—if not of my desire to make a difference in the world, then at least of the insistence that it had to be done on a larger stage. What might have begun as a sense of resignation at whatever limits fate had imposed on my life came to feel more like gratitude for the bounty it had already delivered.

Two things, however, kept me from making a clean break from politics. First, Illinois Democrats had won the right to oversee the redrawing of state districting maps to reflect new data from the 2000 census, thanks to a quirk in the state constitution that called for a dispute between the Democrat-controlled house and the Republican senate to be settled by drawing a name out of one of Abraham Lincoln's old stovepipe hats. With this power, Democrats could reverse the Republican gerrymandering of the previous decade and vastly better the odds that senate Democrats would be in the majority after the 2002 election. I knew that with one more term, I'd finally get a chance to pass some bills, deliver something meaningful for the people I represented— and perhaps end my political career on a higher note than it was currently on.

The second factor was an instinct rather than an event. Since being elected, I'd tried to spend a few days each summer visiting various colleagues in their home districts across Illinois. Usually I'd go with my chief senate aide, Dan Shomon—a former UPI reporter with thick glasses, boundless energy, and a foghorn voice. We'd throw our golf clubs, a map, and a couple of sets of clothes in the back of my Jeep and head south or west, winding our way to Rock Island or Pinckneyville, Alton or Carbondale.

Dan was my key political advisor, a good friend, and an ideal road trip companion: easy to talk to, perfectly fine with silence, and he shared my habit of smoking in the car. He also had an encyclopedic knowledge of state politics. The first time we made the trip, I could tell he was a little nervous about how folks downstate might react to a Black lawyer from Chicago with an Arab-sounding name.

"No fancy shirts," he instructed before we left.

"I don't have fancy shirts," I said.

"Good. Just polos and khakis."

"Got it."

Despite Dan's worries that I'd be out of place, what struck me most during our travels was how familiar everything felt—whether we were at a county fair or a union hall or on the porch on someone's farm. In the way people described their families or their jobs. In their modesty and their hospitality. In their enthusiasm for high school basketball. In the food they served, the fried chicken and baked beans and Jell-O molds. In them, I heard echoes of my grandparents, my mother, Michelle's mom and dad. Same values. Same hopes and dreams.

These excursions became more sporadic once my kids

were born. But the simple, recurring insight they offered stayed with me. As long as the residents of my Chicago district and districts downstate remained strangers to one another, I realized, our politics would never truly change. It would always be too easy for politicians to feed the stereotypes that pitted Black against white, immigrant against native-born, rural interests against those of cities.

If, on the other hand, a campaign could somehow challenge America's reigning political assumptions about how divided we were, well then just maybe it would be possible to build a new covenant between its citizens. The insiders would no longer be able to play one group against another. Legislators might be freed from defining their constituents' interests—and their own—so narrowly. The media might take notice and examine issues based not on which side won or lost but on whether our common goals were met.

Ultimately wasn't this what I was after—a politics that bridged America's racial, ethnic, and religious divides, as well as the many strands of my own life? Maybe I was being unrealistic; maybe such divisions were too deeply entrenched. But no matter how hard I tried to convince myself otherwise, I couldn't shake the feeling that it was too early to give up on my deepest convictions. Much as I'd tried to tell myself I was done, or nearly done, with political life, I knew in my heart that I wasn't ready to let go.

As I gave the future more thought, one thing became clear: The kind of bridge-building politics I imagined wasn't suited to a congressional race. The problem was structural, a matter of how district lines were drawn: In an overwhelmingly Black district like the one I lived in, in a community that had long been battered by discrimination and neglect, the test for politicians would more often than not be defined in racial terms, just as it was in many white, rural districts that felt left behind. **How well will you stand up to those who are not like us,** voters asked, **those who have taken advantage of us, who look down on us?**

You could make a difference from such a narrow political base; with some seniority, you could secure better services for your constituents, bring a big project or two back to your home district, and, by working with allies, try to influence the national debate. But that wouldn't be enough to lift the political constraints that made it so difficult to deliver healthcare for those who most needed it, or better schools for poor kids, or jobs where there were none; the same constraints that Bobby Rush labored under every day.

To really shake things up, I realized, I needed to speak to and for the widest possible audience. And the best way to do that was to run for a statewide office—like, for example, the U.S. Senate.

WHEN I THINK back now on the brashness—the sheer chutzpah—of me wanting to launch a U.S. Senate race, fresh as I was off a resounding defeat, it's hard not to admit the possibility that I was just desperate for another shot, like an alcoholic rationalizing one last drink. Except that's not how it felt. Instead, as I rolled the idea around in my head, I experienced a great clarity—not so much that I **would** win, but that I **could** win, and that if I did win, I could have a big impact. I could see it, feel it, like a running back who spots an opening at the line of scrimmage and knows that if he can get to that hole fast enough and break through, there will be nothing but open field between him and the end zone. Along with this clarity came a parallel realization: If I didn't pull it off, it would be time to leave politics— and so long as I had given it my best effort, I could do so without regret.

Quietly, over the course of 2002, I began to test the proposition. Looking at the Illinois political landscape, I saw that the notion of a little-known Black state legislator going to the U.S. Senate wasn't totally far-fetched. Several African Americans had won statewide office before, including former U.S. senator Carol Moseley Braun, a talented but erratic politician whose victory had electrified the country before she was dinged up by a series of self-inflicted wounds involving financial ethics. Meanwhile, the Republican who'd beaten her, Peter Fitzgerald, was a wealthy banker whose sharply conservative views had made him relatively unpopular across our increasingly Democratic state.

I began by talking to a trio of my state senate poker buddies—Democrats Terry Link, Denny Jacobs, and Larry Walsh—to see whether they thought I could compete in the white working-class and rural enclaves they represented. From what they'd seen during my visits, they thought I could, and all agreed to support me if I ran. So did a number of white progressive elected officials along Chicago's lakefront and a handful of independent Latino legislators as well. I asked Jesse Jr. if he had any interest in running, and he said no, adding that he was prepared to lend me his support. Congressman Danny

Davis, the genial third Black congressman in the Illinois delegation, signed on too. (I could hardly fault Bobby Rush for being less enthusiastic.)

Most important was Emil Jones, now poised to be state senate president and hence one of the three most powerful politicians in Illinois. At a meeting in his office, I pointed out that not a single current U.S. senator was African American, and that the policies that we'd fought for together in Springfield really could use a champion in Washington. I added that if he were to help get one of his own elected to the U.S. Senate, it would surely gall some of the old-guard white Republicans in Springfield who he felt had always sold him short, which was a rationale I think he particularly liked.

With David Axelrod, I took a different tack. A media consultant who'd previously been a journalist and whose clients included Harold Washington, former U.S. senator Paul Simon, and Mayor Richard M. Daley, Axe had developed a national reputation for being smart, tough, and a skilled ad maker. I admired his work and knew that having him on board would lend my nascent campaign credibility not just around the state but with national donors and pundits.

I knew, too, that he'd be a tough sell. "It's a reach," he said on the day we met for lunch at a River North bistro. Axe had been one of many who'd warned me against taking on Bobby Rush. Between hearty bites of his sandwich, he told me I couldn't afford a second loss. And he doubted a candidate whose name rhymed with "Osama" could get downstate votes. Plus, he'd already been approached by at least two other likely Senate candidates— state comptroller Dan Hynes and multimillionaire hedge fund manager Blair Hull—both of whom seemed in much stronger positions to win, so taking me on as a client was likely to cost his firm a hefty sum.

"Wait till Rich Daley retires and then run for mayor," he concluded, wiping mustard off his mustache. "It's the better bet."

He was right, of course. But I wasn't playing the conventional odds. And in Axe I sensed—beneath all the poll data and strategy memos and talking points that were the tools of his trade—someone who saw himself as more than just a hired gun; someone who might be a kindred spirit. Rather than argue campaign mechanics, I tried to appeal to his heart.

"Do you ever think about how JFK and Bobby Kennedy seemed to tap into what's best in people?" I asked. "Or wonder how it must have felt to help LBJ pass the Voting Rights Act, or FDR pass Social Security, knowing you'd made millions of people's lives better? Politics doesn't have to be what people think it is. It can be something more."

Axe's imposing eyebrows went up as he scanned my face. It must have been clear that I wasn't just trying to convince him; I was convincing myself. A few weeks later, he called to say that after talking it over with his business partners and his wife, Susan, he'd decided to take me on as a client. Before I could thank him, he added a proviso.

"Your idealism is stirring, Barack . . . but unless you raise five million bucks to get it on TV so people can hear it, you don't stand a chance."

With this, I finally felt ready to test the waters with Michelle. She was now working as the executive director for community affairs at the University of Chicago hospital system, a job that gave her more flexibility but still required her to juggle high-level professional responsibilities with coordinating the girls' playdates and school pickups. So I was a little surprised when instead of responding with a "Hell no, Barack!" she suggested we talk it through with some of our closest friends, including Marty Nesbitt, a successful businessman whose wife, Dr. Anita Blanchard, had delivered both our girls, and Valerie Jarrett, a brilliant and well-connected attorney who'd been Michelle's boss at the city's planning department and become like an older sister to us. What I didn't know at the time was that Michelle had already gotten to Marty and Valerie and assigned them the job of talking me out of my foolishness.

We gathered at Valerie's Hyde Park apartment, and over a long brunch, I explained my thought process, mapping out the scenarios that would get us to the Democratic nomination and answering questions about how this race would be different from the last. With Michelle, I didn't sugarcoat the amount of time I'd be away. But this was it, I promised, up or out; if I lost this one, we were done with politics for good.

By the time I finished, Valerie and Marty had been persuaded, no doubt to Michelle's chagrin. It wasn't a question of strategy for her, aside from the fact that the thought of another campaign appealed to her about as much as a root canal. She was most concerned with the effect on our family finances, which still hadn't fully recovered from the last one. She reminded me that we had student loans, a mortgage, and credit card debt to think about. We hadn't started saving for our daughters' college educations yet, and on top of that, a Senate run would require me to stop practicing law in order to avoid conflicts of interest, which would further diminish our income.

"If you lose, we'll be deeper in the hole," she said. "And what happens if you win? How are we supposed to maintain two households, in Washington and Chicago, when we can barely keep up with one?"

I'd anticipated this. "If I win, hon," I said, "it will draw national attention. I'll be the only African American in the Senate. With a higher profile, I can write another book, and it'll sell a lot of copies, and that will cover the added expenses."

Michelle let out a sharp laugh. I'd made some money on my first book, but nothing close to what it would take to pay for the expenses I was now talking about incurring. As my wife saw it—as most people would see it, I imagine—an unwritten book was hardly a financial plan.

"In other words," she said, "you've got some magic beans in your pocket. That's what you're telling me. You have some magic beans, and you're going to plant them, and overnight a huge beanstalk is going to grow high into the sky, and you'll climb up the beanstalk, kill the giant who lives in the clouds, and then bring home a goose that lays golden eggs. Is that it?"

"Something like that," I said.

Michelle shook her head and looked out the window. We both knew what I was asking for. Another disruption. Another gamble. Another step in the direction of something I wanted and she truly didn't.

"This is it, Barack," Michelle said. "One last time. But

don't expect me to do any campaigning. In fact, you shouldn't even count on my vote."

AS A KID, I had sometimes watched as my salesman grandfather tried to sell life insurance policies over the phone, his face registering misery as he made cold calls in the evening from our tenth-floor apartment in a Honolulu high-rise. During the early months of 2003, I found myself thinking of him often as I sat at my desk in the sparsely furnished headquarters of my newly launched Senate campaign, beneath a poster of Muhammad Ali posed triumphantly over a defeated Sonny Liston, trying to pep-talk myself into making another fundraising call.

Aside from Dan Shomon and a Kentuckian named Jim Cauley we'd recruited as campaign manager, our staff consisted mostly of kids in their twenties, only half of whom were paid—and two of whom were still under-graduates. I felt especially sorry for my lone full-time fundraiser, who had to push me to pick up the phone and solicit donations.

Was I getting better at being a politician? I couldn't say. In the first scheduled candidates' forum in February 2003, I was stiff and ineffectual, unable to get my brain to operate in the tidy phrases such formats required. But my loss to Bobby Rush had given me a clear blueprint for upping my game: I needed to interact more effectively with the media, learning to get my ideas across in pithy sound bites. I needed to build a campaign that was less about policy papers and more about connecting one-on-one with voters. And I needed to raise money—lots of it. We'd conducted multiple polls, which seemed to confirm that I could win, but only if I managed to improve my visibility with costly TV ads.

And yet, as snakebit as my congressional race had been, this one felt charmed. In April, Peter Fitzgerald decided not to run for reelection. Carol Moseley Braun, who would probably have locked up the Democratic nomination for her old seat, had inexplicably chosen to run for president instead, leaving the contest wide open. In a primary race against six other Democrats, I went about lining up endorsements from unions and popular members of our congressional delegation, helping to shore up my downstate and liberal bases. Aided by Emil and a Democratic majority in the state senate, I spearheaded the passage of a slew of bills, from a law requiring the videotaping of interrogations in capital cases to an expansion of the Earned Income Tax Credit, reinforcing my credentials as an effective legislator.

The national political landscape tilted in my favor as well. In October 2002, before even announcing my candidacy, I'd been invited to speak against the impending U.S. invasion of Iraq, addressing an antiwar rally held in downtown Chicago. For a soon-to-be Senate candidate, the politics were muddy. Both Axe and Dan thought that taking a clear, unequivocal stand against the war would help in a Democratic primary. Others cautioned that, given the post-9/11 mood of the country (at the time, national polls showed as many as 67 percent of Americans in favor of taking military action against Iraq), the likelihood of at least short-term military success, and my already challenging name and lineage, opposition to the war could cripple my candidacy by election time.

"America likes to kick ass," one friend warned.

I mulled over the question for a day or so and decided this was my first test: Would I run the kind of campaign that I'd promised myself? I typed out a short speech, five or six minutes long, and—satisfied that it reflected my honest beliefs—went to bed without sending it to the team for review. On the day of the rally, more than a thousand people had gathered at Federal Plaza, with Jesse Jackson as the headliner. It was cold, the wind gusting. There was a smattering of applause muffled by mittens and gloves as my name was called and I stepped up to the microphone.

"Let me begin by saying that although this has been billed as an antiwar rally, I stand before you as someone who is not opposed to war in all circumstances."

The crowd grew quiet, uncertain of where I was going. I described the blood spilled to preserve the Union and usher in a new birth of freedom; the pride I had in my grandfather volunteering to fight in the wake of Pearl Harbor; my support for our military actions in Afghanistan and my own willingness to take up arms to prevent another 9/11. "I don't oppose all wars," I said. "What I **am** opposed to is a dumb war." I went on to argue that Saddam Hussein posed no imminent threat to the United States or its neighbors, and that "even a successful war against Iraq will require a U.S. occupation of undetermined length, at undetermined cost, with undetermined consequences." I ended with the suggestion that if President Bush was looking for a fight, he should finish the job against al-Qaeda, stop supporting repressive regimes, and wean America off Middle Eastern oil.

I took my seat. The crowd cheered. Leaving the plaza,

I assumed my remarks would be little more than a foot-note. News reports barely mentioned my presence at the rally.

ONLY A FEW months after a U.S.-led military coali-tion began bombing Baghdad, Democrats started turning against the Iraq War. As casualties and chaos mounted, the press began asking questions that should have been posed from the outset. A groundswell of grassroots activism lifted a little-known Vermont governor, Howard Dean, to challenge 2004 presidential candidates like John Kerry who had voted in support of the war. The short speech I'd given at the antiwar rally suddenly looked prescient and began to circulate on the internet. My young staff had to explain to me what the hell "blogs" and "MySpace" had to do with the flood of new volun-teers and grassroots donations we were suddenly getting.

As a candidate, I was having fun. In Chicago, I spent Saturdays plunging into ethnic neighborhoods—Mexican, Italian, Indian, Polish, Greek—eating and dancing, marching in parades, kissing babies and hugging grandmas. Sundays would find me in Black churches, some of them modest storefronts wedged between nail salons and fast-food joints, others expansive megachurches with parking lots the size of football fields. I hopscotched through the suburbs, from the leafy, mansion-filled North Shore to towns just south and west of the city, where poverty and abandoned buildings made some of them indistinguishable from Chicago's roughest neighborhoods. Every couple of weeks, I'd head downstate—sometimes driving myself but more often traveling with Jeremiah

Posedel or Anita Decker, the two talented staffers running my operations there.

Talking to voters in the early days of the campaign, I tended to address the issues I was running on—ending tax breaks for companies that were moving jobs overseas, or promoting renewable energy, or making it easier for kids to afford college. I explained why I had opposed the war in Iraq, acknowledging the remarkable service of our soldiers but questioning why we had started a new war when we hadn't finished the one in Afghanistan while Osama bin Laden was still at large.

Over time, though, I focused more on listening. And the more I listened, the more people opened up. They'd tell me about how it felt to be laid off after a lifetime of work, or what it was like to have your home foreclosed upon or to have to sell the family farm. They'd tell me about not being able to afford health insurance, and how sometimes they broke the pills their doctors prescribed in half, hoping to make their medicine last longer. They spoke of young people moving away because there were no good jobs in their town, or others having to drop out of college just short of graduation because they couldn't cover the tuition.

My stump speech became less a series of positions and more a chronicle of these disparate voices, a chorus of Americans from every corner of the state.

"Here's the thing," I would say. "Most people, wherever they're from, whatever they look like, are looking for the same thing. They're not trying to get filthy rich. They don't expect someone else to do what they can do for themselves.

"But they **do** expect that if they're willing to work, they should be able to find a job that supports a family. They expect that they shouldn't go bankrupt just because they get sick. They expect that their kids should be able to get a good education, one that prepares them for this new economy, and they should be able to afford college if they've put in the effort. They want to be safe, from criminals or terrorists. And they figure that after a lifetime of work, they should be able to retire with dignity and respect.

"That's about it. It's not a lot. And although they don't expect government to solve all their problems, they do know, deep in their bones, that with just a slight change in priorities government could help."

The room would be quiet, and I'd take a few questions. When a meeting was over, people lined up to shake my hand, pick up some campaign literature, or talk to Jeremiah, Anita, or a local campaign volunteer about how they could get involved. And I'd drive on to the next town, knowing that the story I was telling was true; convinced that this campaign was no longer about me and that I had become a mere conduit through which people might recognize the value of their own stories, their own worth, and share them with one another.

WHETHER IN SPORTS or politics, it's hard to understand the precise nature of momentum. But by the beginning of 2004 we had it. Axe had us shoot two television ads: The first had me speaking directly to the camera, ending with the tagline "Yes we can." (I thought this was corny, but Axe immediately appealed to a higher power, showing it to Michelle, who deemed it "not corny at all.") The second featured Sheila Simon, daughter of the state's beloved former senator Paul Simon, who had died following heart surgery days before he'd planned to publicly endorse me.

We released the ads just four weeks before the primaries. In short order, my support almost doubled. When the state's five largest newspapers endorsed me, Axe recut the ads to highlight it, explaining that Black candidates tended to benefit more than white candidates from the validation. Around this time, the bottom fell out of my closest rival's campaign after news outlets published details from previously sealed court documents in which his ex-wife alleged domestic abuse. On March 16, 2004, the day of the Democratic primary, we ended up winning almost 53 percent of the vote in our seven-person field—not only more than all the other Democratic candidates combined, but more than all the Republican votes that had been cast statewide in their primary.

I remember only two moments from that night: the delighted squeals from our daughters (with maybe a little fear mixed in for two-year-old Sasha) when the confetti guns went off at the victory party; and an ebullient Axelrod telling me that I'd won all but one of the majority white wards in Chicago, which had once served as the epicenter of racial resistance to Harold Washington. ("Harold's smiling down on us tonight," he said.)

I remember the next morning as well, when after almost no sleep I went down to Central Station to shake hands with commuters as they headed for work. A gentle snow had begun to fall, the flakes thick as flower petals, and as people recognized me and shook my hand, they all seemed to wear the same smile—as if we had done something surprising together.

"BEING SHOT FROM a cannon" was how Axe would describe the next few months, and that's exactly how it felt. Our campaign became national news overnight, with networks calling for interviews and elected officials from around the country phoning with congratulations. It wasn't just that we had won, or even the unexpectedly large margin of our victory; what interested observers was the way we'd won, with votes from all demographics, including from southern and rural white counties. Pundits speculated on what my campaign said about the state of American race relations—and because of my early opposition to the Iraq War, what it might say about where the Democratic Party was headed.

My campaign didn't have the luxury of celebration; we just scrambled to keep up. We brought on additional, more experienced staff, including communications director Robert Gibbs, a tough, quick-witted Alabaman who had worked on the Kerry campaign. While polls showed me with a nearly twenty-point lead over my Republican opponent, Jack Ryan, his résumé made me cautious about taking anything for granted—he was a Goldman Sachs banker who had quit to teach at a parochial school serving disadvantaged kids and whose matinee-idol looks sanded the edges off his very conventional Republican platform.

Fortunately for us, none of this translated on the campaign trail. Ryan was flogged by the press when, in an attempt to tag me as a big-spending, tax-hiking liberal, he used a series of charts showing numbers that turned out to be wildly and obviously wrong. He was later pilloried for having dispatched a young staffer who aggressively tailed me with a handheld camcorder, following me into lavatories and hovering even while I tried to talk to Michelle and the girls, hoping to catch me in a gaffe. The final blow came when the press got hold of sealed records from Ryan's divorce, in which his ex-wife alleged that he had pressured her to visit sex clubs and tried to coerce her into having sex in front of strangers. Within a week, Ryan withdrew from the race.

With just five months to go until the general election, I suddenly had no opponent.

"All I know," Gibbs announced, "is after this thing is all over, we're going to Vegas."

Still, I maintained a grueling schedule, often finishing the day's business in Springfield and then driving to nearby towns for campaign events. On the way back from one such event, I got a call from someone on John Kerry's staff, inviting me to give the keynote address at the Democratic National Convention being held in Boston in late July. That I felt neither giddy nor nervous said something about the sheer improbability of the year I'd just had. Axelrod offered to pull together the team to begin the process of drafting a speech, but I waved him off.

"Let me take a crack at it," I told him. "I know what I want to say."

For the next several days, I wrote my speech, mostly in the evenings, sprawled on my bed at the Renaissance Hotel in Springfield, a ball game buzzing in the background, filling a yellow legal pad with my thoughts. The words came swiftly, a summation of the politics I'd been searching for since those early years in college and the inner struggles that had prompted the journey to where I was now. My head felt full of voices: of my mother, my grandparents, my father; of the people I had organized with and folks on the campaign trail. I thought about all those I'd encountered who had plenty of reason to turn bitter and cynical but had refused to go that way, who kept reaching for something higher, who kept reaching for one another. At some point, I remembered a phrase I'd heard once during a sermon by my pastor, Jeremiah Wright, one that captured this spirit.

The audacity of hope.

Axe and Gibbs would later swap stories about the twists and turns leading up to the night I spoke at the convention. How we had to negotiate the time I would be allotted (originally eight minutes, bargained up to seventeen). The painful cuts to my original draft by Axe and his able partner John Kupper, all of which made it better. A delayed flight to Boston as my legislative session in Springfield dragged into the night. Practicing for the first time on a teleprompter, with my coach, Michael Sheehan, explaining that the microphones worked fine, so "you don't have to yell." My anger when a young Kerry staffer informed us that I had to cut one of my favorite lines because the nominee intended to poach it for his own speech. ("You're a state senator," Axe helpfully reminded me, "and they've given you a national stage. . . . I don't think it's too much to ask.") Michelle backstage, beautiful in white, squeezing my hand, gazing lovingly into my eyes, and telling me "Just don't screw it up, buddy!" The two of us cracking up, being silly, when our love was always best, and then the introduction by the senior senator from Illinois, Dick Durbin, "Let me tell you about this Barack Obama . . ."

I've only watched the tape of my 2004 convention speech once all the way through. I did so alone, well after the election was over, trying to understand what happened in the hall that night. With stage makeup, I look impossibly young, and I can see a touch of nerves at the beginning, places where I'm too fast or too slow, my gestures slightly awkward, betraying my inexperience.

But there comes a point in the speech where I find my cadence. The crowd quiets rather than roars. It's the kind of moment I'd come to recognize in subsequent years, on certain magic nights. There's a physical feeling, a current of emotion that passes back and forth between you and the crowd, as if your lives and theirs are suddenly spliced together, like a movie reel, projecting backward and forward in time, and your voice creeps right up to the edge of cracking, because for an instant, you feel them deeply; you can see them whole. You've tapped into some collective spirit, a thing we all know and wish for—a sense of connection that overrides our differences and replaces them with a giant swell of possibility—and like all things that matter most, you know the moment is fleeting and that soon the spell will be broken.

BEFORE THAT NIGHT, I thought I understood the power of the media. I'd seen how Axelrod's ads had catapulted me into a lead in the primary, how strangers would suddenly honk and wave from their cars, or how children would rush up to me on the street and say with great seriousness, "I saw you on TV."

But this was exposure of a different magnitude—an unfiltered, live transmission to millions of people, with clips cycled to millions more via cable news shows and across the internet. Leaving the stage, I knew the speech had gone well, and I wasn't all that surprised by the crush of people greeting us at various convention events the following day. As satisfying as the attention I got in Boston was, though, I assumed it was circumstantial. I figured these were political junkies, people who followed this stuff minute by minute.

Immediately after the convention, though, Michelle and I and the girls loaded up our stuff and set out for a weeklong RV trip in downstate Illinois designed to show voters I remained focused on Illinois and hadn't gotten too big for my britches. We were a few minutes from our first stop, rolling down the highway, when Jeremiah, my downstate director, got a call from the advance staff.

"Okay . . . okay . . . I'll talk to the driver."

"What's wrong?" I asked, already a little worn-out by sleep deprivation and the hectic schedule.

"We were expecting maybe a hundred people at the park," Jeremiah said, "but right now they're counting at least five hundred. They asked us to slow down so they have time to deal with the overflow."

Twenty minutes later, we pulled up to see what looked like the entire town crammed into the park. There were parents with kids on their shoulders, seniors on lawn chairs waving small flags, men in plaid shirts and seed caps, many of them surely just curious, there to see what the fuss was about, but others standing patiently in quiet anticipation. Malia peered out the window, ignoring Sasha's efforts to shove her out of the way.

"What are all the people doing in the park?" Malia asked.

"They're here to see Daddy," Michelle said.

"Why?"

I turned to Gibbs, who shrugged and just said, "You're gonna need a bigger boat."

At every stop after that, we were met by crowds four or five times larger than any we'd seen before. And no matter how much we told ourselves that interest would fade and the balloon deflate, no matter how much we tried to guard against complacency, the election itself became almost an afterthought. By August, the Republicans—unable to find a local candidate willing to run (although former Chicago Bears coach Mike Ditka publicly flirted with the idea)—bafflingly recruited conservative firebrand Alan Keyes. ("See," Gibbs said with a grin, "they've got their own Black guy!") Aside from the fact that Keyes was a Maryland resident, his harsh moralizing about abortion and homosexuality didn't sit well with Illinoisans.

"Jesus Christ would not vote for Barack Obama!" Keyes would proclaim, deliberately mispronouncing my name every time.

I beat him by more than forty points—the biggest margin for a Senate race in the state's history.

Our mood on election night was subdued, not only because our race had become a foregone conclusion but because of the national results. Kerry had lost to Bush; Republicans had retained control of the House and the Senate; even the Democratic Senate minority leader, Tom Daschle of South Dakota, had lost in an upset. Karl Rove, George Bush's political mastermind, was crowing about his dream of installing a permanent Republican majority.

Meanwhile, Michelle and I were exhausted. My staff calculated that over the previous eighteen months, I had taken exactly seven days off. We used the six weeks before my swearing in as a U.S. senator to tend to mundane household details that had been largely neglected. I flew to Washington to meet with my soon-to-be colleagues, interview potential staff, and look for the cheapest apartment I could find. Michelle had decided that she and the kids would stay in Chicago, where she had a support circle of family and friends, not to mention a job she really loved. Though the thought of living apart three days a week for much of the year made my heart sink, I couldn't argue with her logic.

Otherwise, we didn't dwell much on what had happened. We spent Christmas in Hawaii with Maya and Toot. We sang carols, built sandcastles, and watched the girls unwrap gifts. I tossed a flower lei into the ocean at the spot where my sister and I had scattered my mother's ashes and left one at the National Memorial Cemetery of the Pacific, where my grandfather was interred. After New Year's, the whole family flew to Washington. The night before my swearing in, Michelle was in the bedroom of our hotel suite getting ready for a welcome dinner for new members of the Senate when I got a call from my book editor. The convention speech had lifted my reissued book, which had been out of print for years, to the top of the bestseller list. She was calling to congratulate me on its success and the fact that we had a deal for a new book, this time with an eye-popping advance.

I thanked her and hung up just as Michelle came out of the bedroom in a shimmery formal dress.

"You look so pretty, Mommy," Sasha said. Michelle did a twirl for the girls.

"Okay, you guys behave yourselves," I said, kissing them before saying goodbye to Michelle's mother, who was babysitting that night. We were headed down the hall toward the elevator when suddenly Michelle stopped.

"Forget something?" I asked.

She looked at me and shook her head, incredulous. "I can't believe you actually pulled this whole thing off. The campaign. The book. All of it."

I nodded and kissed her forehead. "Magic beans, baby. Magic beans."

TYPICALLY THE BIGGEST challenge for a freshman senator in Washington is getting people to pay attention to anything you do. I ended up having the opposite problem. Relative to my actual status as an incoming senator, the hype that surrounded me had grown comical. Reporters routinely pressed me on my plans, most often asking if I intended to run for president. When on the day I was sworn in a reporter asked, "What do you consider your place in history?" I laughed, explaining that I had just arrived in Washington, was ranked ninety-ninth in seniority, had yet to cast a vote, and didn't know where the restrooms were in the Capitol.

I wasn't being coy. Running for the Senate had felt like a reach as it was. I was glad to be there, and eager to get started on the work. To counteract any inflated expectations, my team and I looked to the example set by Hillary Clinton, who'd entered the Senate four years earlier to a lot of fanfare and had gone on to develop a reputation for diligence, substance, and attention to her constituents. To be a workhorse, not a show horse—that was my goal.

No one was temperamentally more suited to implement such a strategy than my new chief of staff, Pete Rouse. Almost sixty years old, graying, and built like a panda bear, Pete had worked on Capitol Hill for nearly thirty years. His experience, most recently as chief of staff to Tom Daschle, and his wide-ranging relationships around town led people to fondly refer to him as the 101st senator. Contrary to the stereotype of Washington political operatives, Pete was allergic to the spotlight, and—beneath a droll, gruff exterior—he was almost shy, which helped explain his long-term bachelorhood and doting affection for his cats.

It had required considerable effort to convince Pete to take on the job of setting up my rookie office. He was less concerned, he said, with the big step down in status than he was with the possibility that it wouldn't leave him enough time to help find jobs for all the junior staffers who, in the aftermath of Daschle's defeat, were now unemployed.

It was this unfailing decency and rectitude, as much as his knowledge, that made Pete a godsend. And it was on the basis of his reputation that I was able to recruit a topflight staff to fill out the ranks in my office. Along with Robert Gibbs as communications director, we enlisted veteran Hill staffer Chris Lu as legislative director; Mark Lippert, a sharp young naval reservist, as a foreign policy staffer; and Alyssa Mastromonaco, a top lieutenant on the Kerry presidential campaign whose baby face belied an unmatched talent for troubleshooting and organizing events, as director of scheduling. Finally we added a thoughtful, good-looking twenty-three-year-old named Jon Favreau. Favs, as he came to be known, had also worked on the Kerry campaign and was both Gibbs's and Pete's number one choice as our speechwriter.

"Haven't I met him before?" I asked Gibbs after the interview.

"Yep . . . he's the kid who showed up and told you that Kerry was stealing one of your lines at the convention."

I hired him anyway.

Under Pete's supervision, the team set up offices in Washington, Chicago, and several downstate locations. To emphasize our focus on voters back home, Alyssa put together an ambitious schedule of town hall meetings in Illinois—thirty-nine in the first year. We instituted a strict policy of avoiding national press and the Sunday morning shows, instead devoting our attention to Illinois papers and TV affiliates. Most important, Pete worked out an elaborate system for handling mail and constituent requests, spending hours with young staffers and interns who worked in the correspondence office, obsessively editing their responses and making sure they were familiar with all the federal agencies that dealt with lost Social Security checks, discontinued veterans' benefits, or loans from the Small Business Administration.

"People may not like your votes," Pete said, "but they'll never accuse you of not answering your mail!"

With the office in good hands, I could dedicate most of my time to studying the issues and getting to know my fellow senators. My task was made easier by the generosity of Illinois's senior senator, Dick Durbin, a friend and disciple of Paul Simon's, and one of the most gifted debaters in the Senate. In a culture of big egos, where senators generally didn't take kindly to a junior partner soaking up more press than them, Dick was unfailingly helpful. He introduced me around the Senate chambers, insisted that his staff share credit with us on various Illinois projects, and maintained his patience and good humor when—at the Thursday morning constituent breakfasts we jointly hosted—visitors spent much of the time asking me for pictures and autographs.

The same could be said for Harry Reid, the new Democratic leader. Harry's path to the Senate had been at least as unlikely as mine. Born dirt-poor in the small town of Searchlight, Nevada, to a miner and a laundress, he spent his early years in a shack without indoor plumbing or a telephone. Somehow, he had scratched and clawed his way into college and then George Washington University Law School, working as a uniformed United States Capitol Police officer between classes to help pay his way, and he was the first to tell you that he had never lost that chip on his shoulder.

"You know, Barack, I boxed when I was a kid," he said in his whispery voice the first time we met. "And gosh, I wasn't a great athlete. I wasn't big and strong. But I had two things going for me. I could take a punch. And I didn't give up."

That sense of overcoming long odds probably explained why, despite our differences in age and experience, Harry and I hit it off. He wasn't one to show much emotion and in fact had a disconcerting habit of forgoing the normal niceties in any conversation, especially on the phone. You might find yourself in mid-sentence only to discover he'd already hung up. But much as Emil Jones had done in the state legislature, Harry went out of his way to look out for me when it came to committee assignments and kept me apprised of Senate business, regardless of my lowly rank.

In fact, such collegiality seemed to be the norm. The old bulls of the Senate—Ted Kennedy and Orrin Hatch, John Warner and Robert Byrd, Dan Inouye and Ted Stevens—all maintained friendships across the aisle, operating with an easy intimacy that I found typical of the Greatest Generation. The younger senators socialized less and brought with them the sharper ideological edge that had come to characterize the House of Representatives after the Gingrich era. But even with the most conservative members, I often found common ground: Oklahoma's Tom Coburn, for example, a devout Christian and an unyielding skeptic of government spending, would become a sincere and thoughtful friend, our staffs working together on measures to increase transparency and reduce waste in government contracting.

In many ways, my first year in the Senate felt a bit like a reprise of my early years in the Illinois legislature, though the stakes were higher, the spotlight brighter, and the lobbyists more skilled at wrapping their clients' interests in the garb of grand principles. Unlike the state legislature, where many members were content to keep their heads down, often not knowing what the hell was going on, my new colleagues were well briefed and not shy with their opinions, which caused committee meetings to drag on interminably and made me far more sympathetic to those who'd suffered through my own verbosity in law school and Springfield.

In the minority, my fellow Democrats and I had little say on which bills emerged from committee and got a vote on the Senate floor. We watched as Republicans put forward budgets that underfunded education or watered down environmental safeguards, feeling helpless beyond the declamations we made before a largely empty chamber and the unblinking eye of C-SPAN. Repeatedly we agonized over votes that were not designed to advance a policy so much as to undermine the Democrats and provide fodder for upcoming campaigns. Just as I had in Illinois, I tried to do what I could to influence policy at the margins, pushing modest, nonpartisan measures—funding to safeguard against a pandemic outbreak, say, or the restoration of benefits to a class of Illinois veterans.

As frustrating as certain aspects of the Senate could be, I didn't really mind its slower pace. As one of its youngest members and with a 70 percent approval rating back in Illinois, I knew I could afford to be patient. At some point, I thought I'd consider running for governor or, yes, even president, steered by the belief that an executive position would give me a better chance to set an agenda. But for now, forty-three years old and just starting out on the national scene, I figured I had all the time in the world.

My mood was further buoyed by improvements on the home front. Barring bad weather, the commute from D.C. to Chicago took no longer than the trip to and from Springfield. And once I was home, I wasn't as busy or distracted as I'd been during the campaign or while juggling three jobs, leaving me more time to shuttle Sasha to dance class on Saturdays or read a chapter of **Harry Potter** to Malia before I tucked her into bed.

Our improved finances also relieved a whole lot of stress. We bought a new house, a big, handsome Georgian across from a synagogue in Kenwood. For a modest price, a young family friend and aspiring chef named Sam Kass agreed to do grocery shopping and cook healthy meals that could stretch through the week. Mike Signator—a retired Commonwealth Edison manager who had served as a volunteer during the campaign—chose to stay on as my part-time driver, practically becoming a member of our family.

Most important, with the financial backstop we now could provide, my mother-in-law, Marian, agreed to reduce her hours at work and help look after the girls. Wise, funny, still young enough to chase after a four- and seven-year-old, she made everyone's life easier. She also happened to love her son-in-law and would rise to my defense whenever I was late, messy, or otherwise not up to scratch.

The additional help gave me and Michelle that extra bit of time together we'd been missing for too long. We laughed more, reminded once again that we were each other's best friend. Beyond that, though, what surprised us both was how little we felt changed by our new circumstances. We continued to be homebodies, shying away from glitzy parties and career-advancing soirees, because we didn't want to give up evenings with the girls, because we felt silly getting gussied up too often, and because Michelle, a perennial early riser, got sleepy after ten o'clock. Instead, we spent weekends as we always had, me playing basketball or taking Malia and Sasha to a nearby pool, Michelle running errands at Target and organizing playdates for the girls. We had dinners or afternoon barbecues with family and our tight circle of friends—especially Valerie, Marty, Anita, and Eric and Cheryl Whitaker (a pair of doctors whose children were the same ages as ours), along with Kaye and Wellington Wilson, affectionately known as "Mama Kaye" and "Papa Wellington," an older couple (he was a retired community college administrator; she was a program officer at a local foundation and a magnificent cook) whom I'd known from my organizing days and who considered themselves my surrogate parents in Chicago.

That's not to say that Michelle and I didn't have to make adjustments. People now recognized us in crowds, and as supportive as they generally were, we found the sudden loss of anonymity disconcerting. One evening, shortly after the election, Michelle and I went to see the biopic **Ray**, starring Jamie Foxx, and were surprised when our fellow patrons burst into applause as we walked into the movie theater. Sometimes when we went out to dinner, we noticed that people at adjoining tables either wanted to strike up long conversations or got very quiet, in a not-so-subtle effort to hear what we were saying.

The girls noticed as well. One day during my first summer as a senator, I decided to take Malia and Sasha to the Lincoln Park Zoo. Mike Signator warned me that the crowds on a beautiful Sunday afternoon might be a little overwhelming, but I insisted we make the trip, confident that sunglasses and a baseball cap would shield me from any attention. And for the first half hour or so, everything went according to plan. We visited the lions prowling behind the glass in the big-cat house and made funny faces at the great apes, all without a disturbance.

Then, as we stopped to look at the visitors' guide for directions to the sea lions, we heard a man shout.

"Obama! Hey, look . . . it's Obama! Hey, Obama, can I take a picture with you?"

The next thing I knew, we were surrounded by families, people reaching for a handshake or an autograph, parents arranging their kids next to me for a photo. I signaled to Mike to take the girls to see the sea lions without me. For the next fifteen minutes, I gave myself over to my constituents, appreciative of their encouraging words, reminding myself that this was part of what I'd signed up for, but feeling my heart sink a little at the thought of my daughters wondering what happened to their daddy.

I finally rejoined my kids, and Mike suggested we leave the zoo and find a quiet place to get ice cream instead. As we drove, Mike stayed mercifully quiet—the girls, not so much.

"I think you need an alias," Malia declared from the backseat.

"What's an alias?" Sasha asked.

"It's a fake name you use when you don't want people to know who you are," Malia explained. "Like 'Johnny McJohn John.'"

Sasha giggled. "Yeah, Daddy . . . you should be Johnny McJohn John!"

"And you need to disguise your voice," Malia added. "People recognize it. You have to talk with a higher voice. And faster."

"Daddy talks **so** slow," Sasha said.

"Come on, Daddy," Malia said. "Try it." She shifted

into the highest-pitched, fastest voice she could muster, saying, "Hi! I'm Johnny McJohn John!"

Unable to contain himself, Mike burst out laughing. Later, when we got home, Malia proudly explained her scheme to Michelle, who patted her on the head.

"That's a great idea, honey," she said, "but the only way for Daddy to disguise himself is if he has an operation to pin back his ears."

ONE FEATURE OF the Senate that excited me was the ability it gave me to influence foreign policy, something that the state legislature didn't afford. Since college, I'd been particularly interested in nuclear issues, and so even before my swearing in, I'd written to Dick Lugar, the chair of the Foreign Relations Committee, whose signature issue was nuclear nonproliferation, to let him know that I hoped to work with him.

Dick's response was enthusiastic. A Republican from Indiana and a twenty-eight-year veteran of the Senate, he was reliably conservative on domestic issues like taxes and abortion, but on foreign policy he reflected the prudent, internationalist impulses that had long guided mainstream Republicans like George H. W. Bush. In 1991, shortly after the breakup of the Soviet Union, Dick had teamed up with Democrat Sam Nunn to design and pass legislation that allowed America to aid Russia and former Soviet states in securing and deactivating weapons of mass destruction. Nunn-Lugar, as it came to be known, proved a bold and durable achievement— more than 7,500 nuclear warheads would be deactivated over the next two decades—and its implementation helped facilitate relationships between U.S. and Russian national security officials that were critical in managing a dangerous transition.

Now, in 2005, intelligence reports indicated that extremist groups like al-Qaeda were scouring poorly guarded outposts throughout the former Soviet bloc, searching for remaining nuclear, chemical, and biological materials. Dick and I began discussing how to build on the existing Nunn-Lugar framework to further protect against such threats. Which is how in August that year I found myself with Dick on a military jet, headed for a weeklong visit to Russia, Ukraine, and Azerbaijan. Though the need to monitor Nunn-Lugar's progress had made such visits routine for Dick, this was my first official foreign trip, and over the years I had heard stories about congressional junkets—the less than strenuous schedules, the lavish dinners and shopping sprees. If that was supposed to be the deal, though, Dick had not gotten the memo. Despite being in his seventies, he maintained a relentless pace. After a day full of meetings with Russian officials in Moscow, we flew a couple of hours southeast to Saratov and then drove another hour to visit a secret nuclear storage site where American funding had helped upgrade the security surrounding Russian missiles. (We were also treated to a meal of borscht and a type of fish gelatin, which Dick gamely ate while I spread it around my plate like a six-year-old.)

Visiting the city of Perm near the Ural Mountains, we wandered through a graveyard of SS-24 and SS-25 missile casings, the last remnants of tactical nuclear warheads once aimed at Europe. In Donetsk, in the eastern part of Ukraine, we toured an installation where warehouses of conventional weapons—ammunition, high-grade explosives, surface-to-air missiles, and even tiny bombs hidden in children's toys—had been collected from around the country and were now slated for destruction. In Kiev, we were taken by our hosts to a dilapidated, unguarded three-story complex in the center of town, where Nunn-Lugar was funding the installation of new storage systems for Cold War–era biological research samples, including anthrax and bubonic plague. It was sobering, all of it, proof of people's capacity to harness ingenuity in the service of madness. But for me, after so many years spent focused on domestic issues, the trip was also invigorating—a reminder of just how big the world was and of the profound human consequences of decisions made in Washington.

Watching Dick operate would leave a lasting impression. His gnomish face always fixed in a placid smile, he was tireless in answering my questions. I was struck by the care, precision, and mastery of facts he demonstrated anytime he spoke in meetings with foreign officials. I observed his willingness to endure not only travel delays but also endless stories and noontime vodka shots, knowing that common courtesy spoke across cultures and ultimately could make a difference in advancing American interests. For me, it was a useful lesson in diplomacy, an example of the real impact a senator could have.

Then a storm hit, and everything changed.

OVER THE COURSE of the week I'd spent traveling with Dick, a tropical weather system that had formed over the Bahamas crossed Florida and deposited itself in the Gulf of Mexico, picking up energy over the warmer waters and aiming itself ominously at the southern shores of the United States. By the time our Senate delegation landed in London to meet with Prime Minister Tony Blair, a ferocious and full-blown catastrophe was under way. Making landfall with 125 mph winds, Hurricane Katrina had leveled entire communities along the Gulf Coast, overwhelmed levees, and left much of New Orleans underwater.

I stayed up half the night watching the news coverage, stunned by the murky, primordial nightmare washing across the television screen. There were floating corpses, elderly patients trapped in hospitals, gunfire and looting, refugees huddled and losing hope. To see such suffering was bad enough; to see the slow government response, the vulnerability of so many poor and working-class people, made me ashamed.

A few days later, I joined George H. W. and Barbara Bush, along with Bill and Hillary Clinton, in a visit to Houston, where thousands of people displaced by the hurricane had been bused to emergency shelters set up inside the sprawling Astrodome convention complex. Together with the Red Cross and FEMA, the city had been working around the clock to provide basic necessities, but it struck me as I moved from cot to cot that many of the people there, most of whom were Black, had been abandoned long before the hurricane—scratching out a living on the periphery without savings or insurance. I listened to their stories about lost homes and loved ones missing in the flood, about their inability to evacuate because they had no car or couldn't move an ailing parent, people no different from those I'd worked to organize in Chicago, no different from some of Michelle's aunts or cousins. I was reminded that no matter how my circumstances may have changed, theirs had not. The politics of the country had not. Forgotten people and forgotten voices remained everywhere, neglected by a government that often appeared blind or indifferent to their needs.

I felt their hardship as a rebuke, and as the only African American in the Senate, I decided it was time to end my moratorium on national media appearances. I hit the network news shows, arguing that while I didn't believe racism was the reason for the botched response to the Katrina disaster, it did speak to how little the ruling party, and America as a whole, had invested in tackling the isolation, intergenerational poverty, and lack of opportunities that persisted in large swaths of the country.

Back in Washington, I worked with my colleagues drafting plans to help rebuild the Gulf region as part of the Homeland Security and Governmental Affairs Committee. But life in the Senate felt different. How many years in that chamber would it take to actually make a difference in the lives of the people I'd met in Houston? How many committee hearings, failed amendments, and budget provisions negotiated with a recalcitrant chairman would be required to offset the misguided actions of a single FEMA director, Environmental Protection Agency functionary, or Department of Labor appointee?

Such feelings of impatience were compounded when, a few months later, I joined a small congressional delegation on a visit to Iraq. Nearly three years after the U.S.-led invasion, the administration could no longer deny the disaster the war had become. In disbanding the Iraqi military and allowing the Shiite majority to aggressively remove large numbers of Sunni Muslims from government positions, U.S. officials had created a situation that was chaotic and increasingly perilous—a bloody sectarian conflict marked by escalating suicide assaults, roadside explosions, and car bombs detonating on crowded market streets.

Our group visited U.S. military bases in Baghdad, Fallujah, and Kirkuk, and from the Black Hawk helicopters that carried us the entire country looked exhausted, the cities pockmarked by mortar fire, the roads eerily quiet, the landscape coated with dust. At each stop, we met commanders and troops who were smart and courageous, driven by the conviction that with the right amount of military support, technical training, and elbow grease, Iraq could someday turn the corner. But my conversations with journalists and with a handful of high-ranking Iraqi officials told a different story. Wicked spirits had been unleashed, they said, with the killings and reprisals between Sunnis and Shiites making the prospect of reconciliation distant, if not unattainable. The only thing holding the country together appeared to be the thousands of young soldiers and Marines we'd deployed, many of them barely out of high school. More than two thousand of them had been killed already, and many thousands more injured. It seemed clear that the longer the war dragged on, the more our troops would become targets of an enemy they often could not see and did not understand.

Flying back to the United States, I couldn't shake the thought of those kids paying the price for the arrogance of men like Dick Cheney and Donald Rumsfeld, who'd rushed us into war based on faulty information and refused, still, to fully consider the consequences. The fact that more than half of my Democratic colleagues had approved this fiasco filled me with an altogether different kind of worry. I questioned what might happen to me the longer I stayed in Washington, the more embedded and comfortable I became. I saw now how it could happen—how the incrementalism and decorum, the endless positioning for the next election, and the group-think of cable news panels all conspired to chip away at your best instincts and wear down your independence, until whatever you once believed was utterly lost.

If I'd been on the edge of feeling content, thinking I was in the right job, doing the right thing at an acceptable pace, Katrina and my Iraq visit put a stop to all that. Change needed to come faster—and I was going to have to decide what role I would play in bringing it about.

CHAPTER 4

RARELY DOES A WEEK GO by when I don't run into somebody—a friend, a supporter, an acquaintance, or a total stranger—who insists that from the first time they met me or heard me speak on TV, they knew I'd be president. They tell me this with affection, conviction, and a certain amount of pride in their political acumen, talent spotting, or soothsaying. Sometimes they will cloak it in religious terms. God had a plan for you, they'll tell me. I'll smile and say that I wish they had told me this back when I was thinking about running; it would have saved me a lot of stress and self-doubt.

The truth is, I've never been a big believer in destiny. I worry that it encourages resignation in the down-and-out and complacency among the powerful. I suspect that God's plan, whatever it is, works on a scale too large to admit our mortal tribulations; that in a single lifetime, accidents and happenstance determine more than we care to admit; and that the best we can do is to try to align ourselves with what we feel is right and construct some meaning out of our confusion, and with grace and nerve play at each moment the hand that we're dealt.

I know that by the spring of 2006, the idea of me running for president in the next election, while still unlikely, no longer felt outside the realm of possibility. Each day, our Senate office was inundated with media requests. We were getting twice as much mail as other senators. Every state party and candidate for the November midterm elections wanted me to headline their events. And our rote denials that I was planning to run seemed only to fuel speculation.

One afternoon, Pete Rouse walked into my office and closed the door behind him.

"I want to ask you something," he said.

I looked up from the constituent letters I'd been signing. "Shoot."

"Have your plans changed for 2008?"

"I don't know. Should they?"

Pete shrugged. "I think the original plan to stay out of the limelight and focus on Illinois made sense. But your profile's not going down. If there's even a remote chance you're considering it, I'd like to write a memo outlining what we need to do to keep your options open. You all right with that?"

I leaned back in my chair and stared at the ceiling, knowing the implications of my answer. "Makes sense," I finally said.

"Okay?" Pete asked.

"Okay." I nodded, returning to my paperwork.

"The Memo Master" is how some on the staff referred to Pete. In his hands, the lowly memorandum approached an art form, each one efficient and oddly inspiring. A few days later, he distributed a revised road map for the remainder of the year for my senior team to consider. It called for an expanded travel schedule to support more Democratic candidates in the midterms, meetings with influential party officials and donors, and a retooled stump speech.

For months to come, I followed this plan, putting myself and my ideas before new audiences, lending my support to Democrats in swing states and swing districts, and traveling to parts of the country I'd never been to before. From the West Virginia Jefferson-Jackson Dinner to the Nebraska Morrison Exon Dinner, we hit them all, packing the house and rallying the troops. Anytime someone asked if I was going to run for president, though, I continued to demur. "Right now, I'm just focused on getting Ben Nelson back to the Senate, where we need him," I'd say.

Was I fooling them? Was I fooling myself? It's hard to say. I was testing, I suppose, probing, trying to square what I was seeing and feeling as I traveled around the country with the absurdity of my launching a national campaign. I knew that a viable presidential candidacy wasn't something you just fell into. Done right, it was a deeply strategic endeavor, built slowly and quietly over time, requiring not only confidence and conviction but also piles of money and enough commitment and good-will from others to carry you through all fifty states and two straight years of primaries and caucuses.

Already, a number of my fellow Democratic senators—Joe Biden, Chris Dodd, Evan Bayh, and, of course, Hillary Clinton—had laid the groundwork for a possible run. Some had run before; all had been preparing for years and had a seasoned cadre of staff, donors, and local officials lined up to help. Unlike me, most could point to a record of meaningful legislative accomplishments. And I liked them. They had treated me well, broadly shared my views on the issues, and were more than capable of running an effective campaign and, beyond that, an effective White House. If I was becoming convinced that I could excite voters in ways that they couldn't—if I suspected that only a wider coalition than they could build, a different language than they used, could shake up Washington and give hope to those in need—I also understood that my favored status was partly an illusion, the result of friendly media coverage and an over-stoked appetite for anything new. The infatuation could reverse itself in an instant, I knew, the rising star transformed into the callow youth, presumptuous enough to think he could run the country less than halfway through his first term.

Better to hold off, I told myself. Pay dues, collect chits, wait my turn.

On a bright spring afternoon, Harry Reid asked me to stop by his office. I trudged up the wide marble stairs from the Senate chamber to the second floor, the unsmiling, dark-eyed portraits of long-dead men staring down upon me with each step. Harry greeted me in the reception area and led me into his office, a big, high-ceilinged room with the same intricate moldings, tile work, and spectacular views that other senior senators enjoyed, but short on memorabilia or photos of handshakes with the famous that adorned other offices.

"Let me get to the point," Harry said, as if he were known for small talk. "We've got a lot of people in our caucus planning to run for president. I can hardly count them all. And they're good people, Barack, so I can't be out there publicly, taking sides . . ."

"Listen, Harry, just so you know, I'm not—"

"But," he said, cutting me off, "I think you need to consider running this cycle. I know you've said you wouldn't do it. And sure, a lot of people will say you need more experience. But let me tell you something. Ten more years in the Senate won't make you a better president. You get people motivated, especially young people, minorities, even middle-of-the-road white people. That's different, you see. People are looking for something different. Sure, it will be hard, but I think you can win. Schumer thinks so too."

He stood up and headed toward the door, making it clear the meeting was over. "Well, that's all I wanted to tell you. So think about it, okay?"

I left his office stunned. As good a relationship as I'd developed with Harry, I knew him to be the most practical of politicians. Walking down the stairs, I wondered if there was some angle to what he had said, some sophisticated game he was playing that I was too dim to recognize. But when I later talked to Chuck Schumer, and then to Dick Durbin, they delivered the same message: The country was desperate for a new voice. I would never be in a better position to run than I was now, and with my connection with young voters, minorities, and independents, I might broaden the map in a way that could help other Democrats down the ballot.

I didn't share these conversations beyond my senior staff and closest friends, feeling as if I had stepped into a minefield and shouldn't make any sudden moves. As I mulled it all over with Pete, he suggested I have one more conversation before I considered taking a more serious look at what a race would entail.

"You need to talk to Kennedy," he said. "He knows all

the players. He's run himself. He'll give you some perspective. And at the very least, he'll tell you if he plans to support anyone else."

Heir to the most famous name in American politics, Ted Kennedy was by then the closest thing Washington had to a living legend. During more than four decades in the Senate, he'd been at the forefront of every major progressive cause, from civil rights to the minimum wage to healthcare. With his great bulk, huge head, and mane of white hair, he filled every room he walked into, and was the rare senator who commanded attention whenever he gingerly rose from his seat in the chamber, searching his suit pocket for his glasses or his notes, that iconic Boston baritone launching each speech with "Thank you, Madam President." The argument would unspool—the face reddening, the voice rising—building to a crescendo like a revivalist sermon, no matter how mundane the issue at hand. And then the speech would end, the curtain would come down, and he would become the old, avuncular Teddy again, wandering down the aisle to check on the roll call or sit next to a colleague, his hand on their shoulder or forearm, whispering in their ear or breaking into a hearty laugh—the kind that made you not care that he was probably softening you up for some future vote he might need.

Teddy's office on the third floor of the Russell Senate Office Building was a reflection of the man—charming and full of history, its walls cluttered with photographs of Camelot and models of sailboats and paintings of Cape Cod. One painting in particular caught my attention, of dark, jagged rocks curving against a choppy, white-capped sea.

"Took me a long time to get that one right," Teddy said, coming up beside me. "Three or four tries."

"It was worth the effort," I said.

We sat down in his inner sanctum, with the shades drawn and a soft light, and he began telling stories—about sailing, his children, and various fights he'd lived through on the Senate floor. Ribald stories, funny stories. Occasionally he drifted along some unrelated current before tacking back to his original course, sometimes uttering just a fragment of a thought, all the while both of us knowing that this was a performance—that we were just circling the real purpose of my visit.

"So . . ." he finally said, "I hear there's talk of you running for president."

I told him it was unlikely, but that I nevertheless wanted his counsel.

"Yes, well, who was it who said there are one hundred senators who look in the mirror and see a president?" Teddy chuckled to himself. "They ask, 'Do I have what it takes?' Jack, Bobby, me too, long ago. It didn't go as planned, but things work out in their own way, I suppose . . ."

He trailed off, lost in his thoughts. Watching him, I wondered how he took the measure of his own life, and his brothers' lives, the terrible price each one of them had paid in pursuit of a dream. Then, just as suddenly, he was back, his deep blue eyes fixed on mine, all business.

"I won't be wading in early," Teddy said. "Too many friends. But I can tell you this, Barack. The power to inspire is rare. Moments like this are rare. You think you may not be ready, that you'll do it at a more convenient time. But you don't choose the time. The time chooses

you. Either you seize what may turn out to be the only
chance you have, or you decide you're willing to live with
the knowledge that the chance has passed you by."

MICHELLE WAS HARDLY oblivious to what was
happening. At first she simply ignored the fuss. She
stopped watching political news shows and waved off all
the overeager questions from friends and co-workers
about whether I planned to run. When one evening at
home I mentioned the conversation I'd had with Harry,
she just shrugged, and I did not press the issue.

As the summer wore on, though, the chatter began to
seep through the cracks and crevices of our home life.
Our evenings and weekends appeared normal so long as
Malia and Sasha were swirling about, but I felt the tension whenever Michelle and I were alone. Finally, one
night after the girls were asleep, I came into the den
where she was watching TV and muted the sound.

"You know I didn't plan any of this," I said, sitting
down next to her on the couch.

Michelle stared at the silent screen. "I know," she said.

"I realize we've barely had time to catch our breath.
And until a few months ago, the idea of me running
seemed crazy."

"Yep."

"But given everything that's happened, I feel like we
have to give the idea a serious look. I've asked the team
to put together a presentation. What a campaign schedule would look like. Whether we could win. How it
might affect the family. I mean, if we were ever going to
do this—"

Michelle cut me off, her voice choked with emotion.

"Did you say **we**?" she said. "You mean **you**, Barack. Not **we**. This is **your** thing. I've supported you the whole time, because I believe in you, even though I **hate** politics. I hate the way it exposes our family. You **know** that. And now, finally, we have some stability . . . even if it's still not normal, not the way I'd choose for us to live . . . and now you tell me you're going to run for **president**?"

I reached for her hand. "I didn't say I **am** running, honey. I just said we can't dismiss the possibility. But I can only consider it if you're on board." I paused, seeing that none of her anger was dissipating. "If you don't think we should, then we won't. Simple as that. You get the final say."

Michelle lifted her eyebrows as if to suggest she didn't believe me. "If that's really true, then the answer is no," she said. "I don't want you to run for president, at least not now." She gave me a hard look and got up from the couch. "God, Barack . . . When is it going to be enough?"

Before I could answer, she'd gone into the bedroom and closed the door.

How could I blame her for feeling this way? By even suggesting the possibility of a run, by involving my staff before I'd asked for her blessing, I had put her in an impossible spot. For years now, I'd asked Michelle for fortitude and forbearance when it came to my political endeavors, and she'd given it—reluctantly but with love. And then each time I'd come back again, asking for more.

Why would I put her through this? Was it just vanity? Or perhaps something darker—a raw hunger, a blind ambition wrapped in the gauzy language of service? Or was I still trying to prove myself worthy to a father who had abandoned me, live up to my mother's starry-eyed expectations of her only son, and resolve whatever self-doubt remained from being born a child of mixed race? "It's like you have a hole to fill," Michelle had told me early in our marriage, after a stretch in which she'd watched me work myself to near exhaustion. "That's why you can't slow down."

In truth, I thought I'd resolved those issues long ago, finding affirmation in my work, security and love in my family. But I wondered now if I could ever really escape whatever it was in me that needed healing, whatever kept me reaching for more.

Maybe it was impossible to disentangle one's motives. I recalled a sermon by Dr. Martin Luther King, Jr., called "The Drum Major Instinct." In it, he talks about how, deep down, we all want to be first, celebrated for our greatness; we all want "to lead the parade." He goes on to point out that such selfish impulses can be reconciled by aligning that quest for greatness with more selfless aims. You can strive to be first in service, first in love. For me, it seemed a satisfying way to square the circle when it came to one's baser and higher instincts. Except now I was also confronting the obvious fact that the sacrifices were never mine alone. Family got dragged along for the ride, put in the line of fire. Dr. King's cause, and his gifts, might have justified such sacrifice. But could mine?

I didn't know. Whatever the nature of my faith, I couldn't take refuge in the notion of God calling me to run for president. I couldn't pretend to be simply responding to some invisible pull of the universe. I couldn't claim I was indispensable to the cause of freedom and justice, or deny responsibility for the burden I'd be placing on my family.

Circumstances may have opened the door to a presidential race, but nothing during these months had prevented me from closing it. I could easily close the door still. And the fact that I hadn't, that instead I had allowed the door to open wider, was all Michelle needed to know. If one of the qualifications of running for the most powerful office in the world was megalomania, it appeared I was passing the test.

SUCH THOUGHTS COLORED my mood as I left in August for a seventeen-day tour through Africa. In South Africa, I took the boat ride out to Robben Island and stood in the tiny cell where Nelson Mandela had passed most of his twenty-seven years in prison, keeping his faith that change would come. I met with members of the South African Supreme Court, spoke with doctors at an HIV/AIDS clinic, and spent time with Bishop Desmond Tutu, whose joyful spirit I had gotten to know during his visits to Washington.

"So is it true, Barack," he said with an impish smile, "that you are going to be our first African president of the United States? Ah, that would make us all verrry proud!"

From South Africa, I flew to Nairobi, where Michelle and the girls—accompanied by our friend Anita Blanchard and her children—joined me. Abetted by wall-to-wall coverage in the local press, the Kenyan response to our presence was over the top. A visit to Kibera, one of Africa's largest shantytowns, drew thousands who packed themselves along the winding paths of red dirt, chanting my name. My half sister Auma had thoughtfully organized a family trip to Nyanza Province, so we could introduce

Sasha and Malia to our father's ancestral home in the western region of the country. Traveling there, we were surprised to see people lined up and waving alongside miles of highway. And when Michelle and I stopped at a mobile health clinic to publicly take an HIV test as a means of demonstrating its safety, a crowd of thousands showed up, swamping our vehicle and giving the diplomatic security team a real scare. Only when we went on safari, parked among the lions and wildebeests, did we escape the commotion.

"I swear, Barack, these folks think you're already president!" Anita joked one evening. "Just reserve me a seat on Air Force One, okay?"

Neither Michelle nor I laughed.

While the family headed back to Chicago, I continued on, traveling to the Kenya-Somalia border to get briefed on U.S.-Kenyan cooperation against the terrorist group al-Shabaab; taking a helicopter from Djibouti into Ethiopia, where U.S. military personnel were assisting flood relief efforts; and finally flying into Chad to visit refugees from Darfur. At each stop, I saw men and women engaged in heroic work, in impossible circumstances. At each stop, I was told how much more America could be doing to help relieve the suffering.

And at each stop, I was asked if I was running for president.

Just days after my return to the States, I flew to Iowa to give the keynote speech at Senator Tom Harkin's Annual Steak Fry, a ritual that took on added importance in the run-up to presidential elections, given that Iowa was always the first state to vote in the primary process. I'd accepted the invitation months earlier—Tom had asked me to speak precisely to avoid having to choose between all the presidential aspirants who coveted the slot—but now my appearance only fueled speculation. As we were leaving the fairgrounds following my speech, I was pulled aside by Steve Hildebrand, a former political director for the Democratic Senatorial Campaign Committee and an old Iowa hand who'd been enlisted by Pete to show me around.

"That's the hottest reception I've ever seen here," Steve said. "You can win Iowa, Barack. I can feel it. And if you win Iowa, you can win the nomination."

It felt sometimes as if I'd been caught in a tide, carried along by the current of other people's expectations before I'd clearly defined my own. The temperature rose even higher when, a month later, just a few weeks before the midterm elections, my second book was released. I'd labored on it all year, in the evenings in my D.C. apartment and on weekends after Michelle and the girls had gone to sleep; even in Djibouti, where I'd scrambled for several hours trying to fax corrected page proofs to my editor. I had never intended the book to serve as a campaign manifesto; I just wanted to present my ideas about the current state of American politics in an interesting way and sell enough copies to justify my sizable advance.

But that wasn't how it was received, by the political press or the public. Promoting it meant I was on television and radio practically nonstop, and combined with my very visible barnstorming on behalf of congressional candidates, I looked more and more like a candidate myself.

On a drive down from Philly to D.C., where I was scheduled to appear the next morning on **Meet the Press,**

Gibbs and Axe, along with Axe's business partner, David Plouffe, asked me what I planned to say when the show's host, Tim Russert, inevitably grilled me about my plans.

"He's going to run back the old tape," Axe explained. "The one where you say unequivocally you will not run for president in 2008."

I listened for a few minutes as the three of them began hashing out various ways to sidestep the question before I interrupted.

"Why don't I just tell the truth? Can't I just say that I had no intention of running two years ago, but circumstances have changed and so has my thinking, and I plan to give it serious thought after the midterms are over?"

They liked the idea, admitting that it said something about the strangeness of politics that such a straightforward answer would be considered novel. Gibbs also advised that I give Michelle a heads-up, predicting that a direct suggestion that I might run would cause the media frenzy to immediately intensify.

Which is exactly what happened. My admission on **Meet the Press** made headlines and the evening news. On the internet, a "Draft Obama" petition took off, gathering thousands of signatures. National columnists, including several conservative ones, penned op-eds urging me to run, and **Time** magazine published a cover story titled "Why Barack Obama Could Be the Next President."

Apparently, though, not everyone was sold on my prospects. Gibbs reported that when he stopped at a kiosk on Michigan Avenue to get a copy of **Time,** the Indian American vendor looked down at my picture and offered a two-word response: "**Fuuuuck** that."

We had a good laugh over this. And as the speculation about my candidacy grew, Gibbs and I would repeat the phrase like an incantation, one that helped maintain our grasp on reality and ward off the growing sense that events were moving beyond our control. The crowd at my final stop before the midterm elections, an evening rally in Iowa City in support of the Democratic candidate for governor, was especially raucous. Standing on the stage and looking out at the thousands of people gathered there, their breath rising like mist through the klieg lights, their faces turned up in expectation, their cheers drowning out my haggard voice, I felt as if I were watching a scene in a movie, the figure onstage not my own.

When I got home late that night, the house was dark and Michelle was already asleep. After taking a shower and going through a stack of mail, I slipped under the covers and began drifting off. In that liminal space between wakefulness and sleep, I imagined myself stepping toward a portal of some sort, a bright and cold and airless place, uninhabited and severed from the world. And behind me, out of the darkness, I heard a voice, sharp and clear, as if someone were right next to me, uttering the same word again and again.

No. No. No.

I jolted out of bed, my heart racing, and went downstairs to pour myself a drink. I sat alone in the dark, sipping vodka, my nerves jangled, my brain in sudden overdrive. My deepest fear, it turned out, was no longer of irrelevance, or being stuck in the Senate, or even losing a presidential race.

The fear came from the realization that I could win.

. . .

RIDING A WAVE of antipathy toward the Bush administration and the war in Iraq, Democrats swept just about every important contest in November, winning control of both the House and the Senate. As hard as we'd worked to help achieve these results, my team and I had no time to celebrate. Instead, starting the day after the election, we began charting a possible path to the White House.

Our pollster, Paul Harstad, went through the numbers and found me already among the first tier of candidates. We discussed the primary and caucus calendar, understanding that for an upstart campaign like mine, everything would depend on winning the early states, especially Iowa. We ran through what a realistic budget might look like, and how we'd go about raising the hundreds of millions of dollars it would take just to win the Democratic nomination. Pete and Alyssa presented plans for juggling my Senate duties with campaign travel. Axelrod wrote a memo outlining the themes of a potential campaign, and how—given voters' utter contempt for Washington—my message of change could compensate for my obvious lack of experience.

Despite how little time they'd had, everyone had carried out their assignments with thoroughness and care. I was especially impressed by David Plouffe. In his late thirties, slight and intense, with sharp features and a crisp yet informal manner, he had dropped out of college to work on a series of Democratic campaigns and also ran the Democratic Congressional Campaign Committee before joining Axelrod's consulting firm. I sat listening one day as he mapped out how we might power a grassroots state-by-state organizing effort using both our volunteer base and the internet, and later I told Pete that if we did this, Plouffe seemed like the clear choice for campaign manager.

"He's excellent," Pete said. "It might take some convincing, though. He's got a young family."

This was one of the more striking things about our discussions that month: The entire team displayed an ambivalence that matched my own. It wasn't just that my candidacy remained a long shot; both Plouffe and Axelrod were blunt in saying that for me to beat Hillary Clinton, a "national brand," we would have to pitch close to a perfect game. No, what gave them more pause was the fact that, unlike me, they had seen presidential campaigns up close. They knew all too well the grueling nature of the enterprise. They understood the toll it would take not just on me and my family but on them and their families as well.

We'd be on the road constantly. The press would be merciless in its scrutiny—"a nonstop colonoscopy" I believe Gibbs called it. I'd see very little of Michelle or the kids for a year at least—two years if we were lucky enough to win the primary.

"I'll be honest, Barack," Axe told me after one meeting. "The process can be exhilarating, but it's mostly misery. It's like a stress test, an EKG on the soul. And for all your talent, I don't know how you'll respond. Neither do you. The whole thing is so crazy, so undignified and brutal, that you have to be a little pathological to do what it takes to win. And I just don't know if you've got that hunger in you. I don't think you'll be unhappy if you never become president."

"That's true," I said.

"I know it is," Axe said. "And as a person, that's a strength. But for a candidate, it's a weakness. You may be a little too normal, too well-adjusted, to run for president. And though the political consultant in me thinks it would be a thrill to see you do this, the part of me that's your friend kind of hopes you don't."

Michelle, meanwhile, was also sorting out her feelings. She listened quietly during meetings, occasionally asking questions about the campaign calendar, what would be expected of her, and what it might mean for the girls. Gradually her resistance to the idea of me running had subsided. Perhaps it helped to hear the unvarnished truth of what a campaign entailed, her worst fears rendered concrete and specific and therefore more manageable. Maybe it was the conversations she'd had with Valerie and Marty, two of our most loyal friends, people whose judgment she implicitly trusted. Or the nudge she got from her brother, Craig—someone who had pursued his own unlikely dreams, first to play professional basketball and later to become a coach, even though it meant giving up a lucrative career in banking.

"She's just scared," he had told me over a beer one afternoon. He'd gone on to describe how Michelle and her mother used to watch his high school basketball games, but if the score got even a little close, they'd leave and go wait in the tunnel, the two of them too tense to stay in their seats. "They didn't want to see me lose," Craig said. "They didn't want to see me hurt or disappointed. I had to explain that it's part of competition." He was in favor of me taking my shot at the presidency and said he planned to talk it over with his sister. "I want her to see the bigger picture," he said. "The chance to compete at this level isn't something you can pass up."

One day in December, just ahead of our holiday trip to Hawaii, our team held what was to be the final meeting before I decided whether to move forward or not. Michelle patiently endured an hour-long discussion on staffing and the logistics of a potential announcement before cutting in with an essential question.

"You've said there are a lot of other Democrats who are capable of winning an election and being president. You've told me the only reason for you to run is if you could provide something that the others can't. Otherwise it's not worth it. Right?"

I nodded.

"So my question is why you, Barack? Why do **you** need to be president?"

We looked at each other across the table. For a moment, it was as if we were alone in the room. My mind flipped back to the moment seventeen years earlier when we first met, me arriving late to her office, a little damp from the rain, Michelle rising up from her desk, so lovely and self-possessed in a lawyerly blouse and skirt, and the easy banter that followed. I had seen in those round, dark eyes of hers a vulnerability that I knew she rarely let show. I knew even then that she was special, that I would need to know her, that this was a woman I could love. How lucky I had been, I thought.

"Barack?"

I shook myself out of the reverie. "Right," I said. "Why me?" I mentioned several of the reasons we'd talked about before. That I might be able to spark a new kind of politics, or get a new generation to participate, or bridge the divisions in the country better than other candidates could.

"But who knows?" I said, looking around the table. "There's no guarantee we can pull it off. Here's one thing I know for sure, though. I know that the day I raise my right hand and take the oath to be president of the United States, the world will start looking at America differently. I know that kids all around this country— Black kids, Hispanic kids, kids who don't fit in—they'll see themselves differently, too, their horizons lifted, their possibilities expanded. And that alone . . . that would be worth it."

The room was quiet. Marty smiled. Valerie was tearing up. I could see different members of the team conjuring it in their minds, the swearing in of the first African American president of the United States.

Michelle stared at me for what felt like an eternity. "Well, honey," she said finally, "that was a pretty good answer."

Everyone laughed, and the meeting moved on to other business. In years to come, those who'd been in the room would sometimes make reference to that meeting, understanding that my answer to Michelle's question had been an impromptu articulation of a shared faith, the thing that had launched us all on what would be a long, rough, and improbable journey. They would remember it when they saw a little boy touch my hair in the Oval Office, or when a teacher reported that the kids in her inner-city class had started studying harder after I was elected.

And it's true: In answering Michelle's question, I was anticipating the ways in which I hoped that even a credible campaign might shake loose some vestiges of

America's racial past. But privately I knew that getting there also meant something more personal.

If we won, I thought, it would mean that my U.S. Senate campaign hadn't just been dumb luck.

If we won, it would mean that what had led me into politics wasn't just a pipe dream, that the America I believed in was possible, that the democracy I believed in was within reach.

If we won, it would mean that I wasn't alone in believing that the world didn't have to be a cold, unforgiving place, where the strong preyed on the weak and we inevitably fell back into clans and tribes, lashing out against the unknown and huddling against the darkness.

If these beliefs were made manifest, then my own life made sense, and I could then pass on that promise, that version of the world, to my children.

I had made a bet a long time ago, and this was the point of reckoning. I was about to step over some invisible line, one that would inexorably change my life, in ways I couldn't yet imagine and in ways I might not like. But to stop now, to turn back now, to lose my nerve now—that was unacceptable.

I had to see how this whole thing played out.

PART TWO

YES WE CAN

CHAPTER 5

ON A BRIGHT FEBRUARY MORNING in 2007, I stood on a stage before the Old State Capitol in Springfield—the same spot where Abe Lincoln had delivered his "House Divided" speech while serving in the Illinois state legislature—and announced my candidacy for president. With temperatures in the low teens, we'd been worried that the cold might scare people off, but by the time I stepped up to the microphone, more than fifteen thousand people had gathered in the plaza and adjoining streets, all of them in a festive mood, bundled in parkas, scarves, ski caps, and earmuffs, many of them hoisting handmade or campaign-provided OBAMA signs, their collective breath hovering like patches of clouds.

My speech, carried live on cable TV, captured our campaign's big themes—the need for fundamental change; the need to tackle long-term problems like healthcare and climate change; the need to move past the tired Washington partisan divide; the need for an engaged and active citizenry. Michelle and the girls joined me onstage to wave at the roaring crowd when I was finished, the massive American flags hanging across nearby buildings making for a spectacular backdrop.

From there, my team and I flew to Iowa, where in eleven months the nation's first contest for the nomination would take place, and where we were counting on an early victory to catapult us past more seasoned opponents. At a series of town hall meetings, we were once again greeted by thousands of supporters and curiosity seekers. Backstage at an event in Cedar Rapids, I overheard a veteran Iowa political operative explain to one of the fifty or so national reporters who were following us that "this is not normal."

Looking at the footage from that day, it's hard not to get swept up in the nostalgia that still holds sway over my former staff and supporters—the feeling that we were kick-starting a magical ride; that over the course of two years we would catch lightning in a bottle and tap into something essential and true about America. But while the crowds, the excitement, the media attention of that day, all foreshadowed my viability in the race, I have to remind myself that nothing felt easy or predestined at the time, that again and again it felt as if our campaign would go entirely off the rails, and that, at the outset, it seemed not just to me but to many who were paying attention that I wasn't a particularly good candidate.

In many ways, my problems were a direct outgrowth of the buzz we'd generated, and the expectations that came with it. As Axe explained, most presidential campaigns by necessity start small—"Off-Broadway," he called it; small crowds, small venues, covered by local networks and small papers, where the candidate and his or her team could test lines, smooth out kinks, commit a pratfall, or work through a bout of stage fright without attracting much notice. We didn't have that luxury. From day one, it felt like the middle of Times Square, and under the glare of the spotlight my inexperience showed.

My staff's biggest fear was that I'd make a "gaffe," the expression used by the press to describe any maladroit phrase by the candidate that reveals ignorance, carelessness, fuzzy thinking, insensitivity, malice, boorishness, falsehood, or hypocrisy—or is simply deemed to veer sufficiently far from conventional wisdom to make said candidate vulnerable to attack. By this definition, most humans will commit five to ten gaffes a day, each of us counting on the forbearance and goodwill of our family, co-workers, and friends to fill in the blanks, catch our drift, and generally assume the best rather than the worst in us.

As a result, my initial instincts were to dismiss some of my team's warnings. On our way to our final stop in Iowa on announcement day, for example, Axe glanced up from his briefing book.

"You know," he said, "the town we're going to, it's pronounced 'Waterloo.'"

"Right," I said. "Waterloo."

Axe shook his head. "No, it's Water-**loo**. Not **Water**-loo."

"Do that for me again."

"Water-**loo**," Axe said, his lips pursing just so.

"One more time."

Axe frowned. "Okay, Barack . . . this is serious."

It didn't take long, though, to appreciate that the minute you announced your candidacy for president, the normal rules of speech no longer applied; that microphones were everywhere, and every word coming out of your mouth was recorded, amplified, scrutinized, and dissected. At the town hall in Ames, Iowa, on that first post-announcement tour, I was explaining my opposition to the war in Iraq when I got sloppy and said that the Bush administration's poorly-thought-out decision had resulted in more than three thousand of our young troops' lives being "wasted." The second I uttered the word, I regretted it. I'd always been careful to distinguish between my views on the war and my appreciation for the sacrifices of our troops and their families. Only a few press outlets picked up my blunder, and a quick mea culpa tamped down any controversy. But it was a reminder that words carried a different weight than before, and as I imagined how my carelessness might impact a family still grieving over the loss of a loved one, my heart sank.

By nature I'm a deliberate speaker, which, by the standards of presidential candidates, helped keep my gaffe quotient relatively low. But my care with words raised another issue on the campaign trail: I was just plain wordy, and that was a problem. When asked a question, I tended to offer circuitous and ponderous answers, my mind instinctively breaking up every issue into a pile of components and subcomponents. If every argument had two sides, I usually came up with four. If there was an exception to some statement I just made, I wouldn't just point it out; I'd provide footnotes. "You're burying the lede!" Axe would practically shout after listening to me drone on and on and on. For a day or two I'd obediently focus on brevity, only to suddenly find myself unable to resist a ten-minute explanation of the nuances of trade policy or the pace of Arctic melting.

"What d'ya think?" I'd say, pleased with my thorough-ness as I walked offstage.

"You got an A on the quiz," Axe would reply. "No votes, though."

These were issues I could fix with time. Of greater concern, as we rolled into the spring, was the fact that I was grumpy. One reason for that, I realize now, was the toll of a two-year Senate campaign, a year of town halls as a senator, and months of travel on behalf of other candidates. Once the adrenaline of the announcement wore off, the sheer magnitude of the grind now before me struck with full force.

And it was a grind. When not in Washington for Senate business, I soon found myself in Iowa or one of the other early states, putting in sixteen-hour days, six and a half days a week—sleeping in a Hampton Inn or a Holiday Inn or an AmericInn or a Super 8. I'd wake up after five or six hours and try to squeeze in a workout at whatever facility we could find (the old treadmill in the back of a tanning salon was memorable), before packing up my clothes and gulping down a haphazard breakfast; before hopping into a van and making fundraising calls on the way to the first town hall meeting of the day; before interviews with the local paper or news station, several meet-and-greets with local party leaders, a bath-room stop, and maybe a swing by a local eatery to shake hands; before hopping back in the van to dial for more dollars. I'd repeat this three or four times, with a cold sandwich or a salad wedged in there somewhere, before finally staggering into another motel around nine p.m., trying to catch Michelle and the girls by phone before they went to bed, before reading the next day's briefing materials, the binder gradually slipping out of my hands as exhaustion knocked me out.

And that's not even counting the flights to New York or L.A. or Chicago or Dallas for fundraisers. It was a life of not glamour but monotony, and the prospect of eighteen continuous months of it quickly wore down my spirit. I'd staked my claim in the presidential race, involved a big team of people, begged strangers for money, and propagated a vision I believed in. But I missed my wife. I missed my kids. I missed my bed, a consistent shower, sitting at a proper table for a proper meal. I missed not having to say the exact same thing the exact same way five or six or seven times a day.

Fortunately, along with Gibbs (who had the constitution, experience, and general orneriness to keep me focused while on the road), I had two other companions to help me push through my initial funk.

The first was Marvin Nicholson, a half Canadian with an easy charm and unflappable demeanor. In his mid-thirties and a towering six foot eight, Marvin had held a variety of jobs, from golf caddy to bartender at a strip club, before landing work as John Kerry's body man four years earlier. It's a strange role, the body man: a personal assistant and jack-of-all-trades responsible for making sure that the candidate has everything he or she needs to function, whether a favorite snack or a couple of Advil, an umbrella when it's wet or a scarf when it's cold, or the name of the county chairman who's striding your way for a handshake. Marvin operated with such skill and finesse, he'd become something of a cult figure in political circles, which had led us to hire him as our trip director, working with Alyssa and the advance team to coordinate travel, make sure I had the appropriate materials, and keep me at least close to on schedule.

Then there was Reggie Love. Raised in North Carolina, the son of middle-class Black parents, six foot four and powerfully built, Reggie had starred in both basketball and football at Duke University before Pete Rouse hired him as an assistant in my Senate office. (An aside: People often express surprise at how tall I am, a bit over six foot one, something I attribute in part to years of being dwarfed by Reggie and Marvin in photographs.) Under Marvin's tutelage, twenty-five-year-old Reggie took over as body man, and though he had a rough go of it at first—somehow managing to forget my briefcase in Miami and my suit jacket in New Hampshire during the same week—his serious work ethic and goofy good humor quickly made him a favorite of everyone on the campaign.

For the better part of two years, Gibbs, Marvin, and Reggie would be my caretakers, my anchors to normalcy, and a steady source of comic relief. We played cards and shot pool. We argued about sports and swapped music. (Reggie helped me update a hip-hop playlist that had stopped at Public Enemy.) Marvin and Reggie told me about their social lives on the road (complicated) and their adventures in various local stops after our work was done (tattoo parlors and hot tubs were sometimes featured). We teased Reggie about his youthful ignorance (once, when I mentioned Paul Newman, Reggie said, "That's the salad dressing guy, right?") and Gibbs about his appetites (at the Iowa State Fair, Gibbs would have trouble choosing between the deep-fried Twinkie and the deep-fried Snickers bar, until the woman behind the counter helpfully said, "Honey, why should you have to choose?").

Anytime we could, we played basketball. Even the smallest town had a high school gym, and if there wasn't time for a proper game, Reggie and I would still roll up our sleeves and get in a round of H-O-R-S-E while waiting for me to go onstage. Like any true athlete, he remained fiercely competitive. I sometimes woke up the day after a game of one-on-one barely able to walk, though I was too proud to let my discomfort show. Once we played a group of New Hampshire firefighters from whom I was trying to secure an endorsement. They were standard weekend warriors, a bit younger than me but in worse shape. After the first three times Reggie stole the ball down the floor and went in for thunderous dunks, I called a time-out.

"What are you doing?" I asked.

"What?"

"You understand that I'm trying to get their support, right?"

Reggie looked at me in disbelief. "You want us to lose to these stiffs?"

I thought for a second.

"Nah," I said. "I wouldn't go that far. Just keep it close enough that they're not too pissed."

Spending time with Reggie, Marvin, and Gibbs, I found respite from the pressures of the campaign, a small sphere where I wasn't a candidate or a symbol or a generational voice or even a boss, but rather just one of the guys. Which, as I slogged through those early months, felt more valuable than any pep talk. Gibbs did try to go the pep-talk route with me at one point as we were boarding another airplane at the end of another interminable day, after a particularly flat appearance. He told me that I needed to smile more, to remember that this was a great adventure and that voters loved a happy warrior.

"Are you having any fun?" he asked.

"No," I said.

"Anything we can do to make this more fun?"

"No."

Sitting in the seat in front of us, Reggie overheard the conversation and turned back to look at me with a wide grin. "If it's any consolation," he said, "I'm having the time of my life."

It was—although I didn't tell him that at the time.

ALL THE WHILE, I was learning a lot and quickly. I spent hours dutifully poring over the fat briefing books prepared by my staff, inhaling the latest studies on the value of early childhood education, new developments in battery technology that would make clean energy more accessible, and China's manipulation of its currency to boost its exports.

Looking back, I realize I was doing what most of us tend to do when we're uncertain or floundering: We reach for what feels familiar, what we think we're good at. I knew policy; I knew how to consume and process information. It took a while to figure out that my problem wasn't a lack of a ten-point plan. Rather, it was my general inability to boil issues down to their essence, to tell a story that helped explain an increasingly uncertain world to the American people and make them feel that I, as president, could help them navigate it.

My more seasoned opponents already understood

this. I embarrassed myself early in their presence at a healthcare forum sponsored by the Service Employees International Union, held in Las Vegas on a Saturday evening late in March 2007. Plouffe had resisted my participation. In his view, such "cattle calls," where the candidates appeared before this or that Democratic interest group, played to the strengths of insiders and took time away from direct voter contact. I disagreed. Healthcare was an issue I felt strongly about—not only because I'd heard many devastating personal stories while campaigning but because I'd never forget my mother in her waning days, fretting not just about her chances of survival but about whether her insurance would keep her solvent during treatment.

As it turned out, I should have listened to Plouffe. My head was crammed with too many facts and too few answers. Before a large audience of health workers, I stumbled, mumbled, hemmed and hawed onstage. Under pointed questioning, I had to confess that I didn't yet have a definitive plan for delivering affordable healthcare. You could hear crickets in the auditorium. The Associated Press ran a story critiquing my showing at the forum— one that would promptly get picked up by outlets across the country—under the painful headline IS OBAMA ALL STYLE AND LITTLE SUBSTANCE?

My performance stood in sharp contrast to those of John Edwards and Hillary Clinton, the two leading contenders. Edwards, the handsome and polished former vice presidential candidate, had left the Senate in 2004 to be John Kerry's running mate, then made a show of starting a poverty center but really never stopped campaigning full-time for president. Though I didn't know him well, I'd never been particularly impressed with Edwards: Despite the fact that he had working-class roots, his newly minted populism sounded synthetic and poll-tested to me, the political equivalent of one of those boy bands dreamed up by a studio marketing department. But in Las Vegas I was chastened as I watched him lay out a crisp proposal for universal coverage, displaying all the gifts that had made him a successful trial lawyer back in North Carolina.

Hillary was even better. Like many people, I'd spent the 1990s observing the Clintons from afar. I'd admired Bill's prodigious talent and intellectual firepower. If I wasn't always comfortable with the specifics of his so-called triangulations—signing welfare reform legislation with inadequate protections for those who couldn't find jobs, the tough-on-crime rhetoric that would contribute to an explosion in the federal prison population—I appreciated the skill with which he had steered progressive policy making and the Democratic Party back toward electability.

As for the former First Lady, I found her just as impressive, and more sympathetic. Maybe it was because in Hillary's story I saw traces of what my mother and grandmother had gone through: all of them smart, ambitious women who had chafed under the constraints of their times, having to navigate male egos and social expectations. If Hillary had become guarded, perhaps overly scripted—who could blame her, given the attacks she'd been subjected to? In the Senate, my favorable opinion of her had been largely confirmed. In all our interactions, she came across as hardworking, personable, and always impeccably prepared. She also had a good, hearty laugh that tended to lighten the mood of everyone around her.

That I'd decided to run despite Hillary's presence in the race had less to do with any assessment of her personal shortcomings and more to do with my feeling that she just couldn't escape the rancor, grudges, and hardened assumptions arising out of the Clinton White House years. Fair or not, I didn't see how she could close America's political divide, or change how Washington did business, or provide the country with the fresh start it needed. Yet watching her speak passionately and knowledgeably about healthcare onstage that evening at the SEIU forum and hearing the crowd cheer enthusiastically after she was done, I wondered if I'd miscalculated.

That forum would hardly be the last time Hillary—or, for that matter, half the primary field—outperformed me, for it soon seemed as if we were gathered for a debate once every two or three weeks. I had never been particularly good in these formats myself: My long windups and preference for complicated answers worked against me, particularly onstage with seven savvy pros and a single timed minute to answer a question. During our first debate in April, the moderator called time at least twice before I was done speaking. Asked about how I'd handle multiple terrorist attacks, I discussed the need to coordinate federal help but neglected to mention the obvious imperative to go after the perpetrators. For the next several minutes, Hillary and the others took turns pointing out my oversight. Their tones were somber, but the gleam in their eyes said, **Take that, rookie.**

Afterward, Axe was gentle in his postgame critique.

"Your problem," he said, "is you keep [...] the question."

"Isn't that the point?" I said.

"No, Barack," Axe said, "that is **not** the point. [...] point is to get your message across. What are your values? What are your priorities? That's what people care about. Look, half the time the moderator is just using the question to try to trip you up. Your job is to avoid the trap they've set. Take whatever question they give you, give 'em a quick line to make it seem like you answered it . . . and then talk about what **you** want to talk about."

"That's bullshit," I said.

"Exactly," he said.

I was frustrated with Axe and even more frustrated with myself. But I realized his insight was hard to deny after watching a replay of the debate. The most effective debate answers, it seemed, were designed not to illuminate but to evoke an emotion, or identify the enemy, or signal to a constituency that you, more than anyone else on that stage, were and would always be on their side. It was easy to dismiss the exercise as superficial. Then again, a president wasn't a lawyer or an accountant or a pilot, hired to carry out some narrow, specialized task. Mobilizing public opinion, shaping working coalitions—that was the job. Whether I liked it or not, people were moved by emotion, not facts. To elicit the best rather than the worst of those emotions, to buttress those better angels of our nature with reason and sound policy, to perform while still speaking the truth—that was the bar I needed to clear.

AS I WAS working to curb my screw-ups, Plouffe was running a seamless operation from our Chicago

.eadquarters. I didn't see him often but was coming to realize that the two of us had much in common. We were both analytical and even-keeled, generally skeptical of convention and pretense. But whereas I could be absentminded, indifferent to small details, incapable of maintaining an orderly filing system, constantly misplacing memos, pens, and cell phones that had just been handed to me, Plouffe turned out to be a managerial genius.

From the start, he focused unapologetically and unswervingly on winning Iowa. Even when cable pundits and some of our supporters were calling us idiots for being so single-minded, he wouldn't let anyone waver an inch from the strategy, certain it was our only path to victory. Plouffe imposed a martial discipline, giving everyone on our team—from Axe to our most junior organizer—a level of autonomy while also demanding accountability and a strict adherence to process. He capped salaries as a way of eliminating needless staff dissent. He pointedly directed resources away from bloated consulting contracts and media budgets in order to give our field organizers what they needed on the ground. Obsessive about data, he recruited a team of internet savants who designed a digital program that was light-years ahead of those not just of other campaigns but many private corporations as well.

Add it all up, and in six months, from a standing start, Plouffe built a campaign operation strong enough to go toe-to-toe with the Clinton machine. It was a fact he quietly relished. This was another thing I came to realize about Plouffe: Beneath the low-key persona and deep convictions, he just plain liked the combat. Politics was his sport, and in his chosen endeavor he was as competitive as Reggie was in basketball. Later, I'd ask Axe if he'd anticipated just how good a campaign architect his then junior partner would turn out to be. Axe shook his head.

"A fucking revelation," he said.

In presidential politics, the best strategy means little if you don't have the resources to execute it, and this was the second thing we had going for us: money. Given that the Clintons had been cultivating a national donor base for nearly three decades, our working assumption had been that Hillary would have a tremendous fundraising advantage over us. But the hunger for change in America was proving to be stronger than even we had anticipated.

Early on, our fundraising followed a traditional pattern: Big donors from big cities wrote and collected big checks. Penny Pritzker, a businesswoman and longtime friend from Chicago, served as our campaign's national finance chair, bringing both organizational acumen and a vast network of relationships to the effort. Julianna Smoot, our tough-talking and experienced finance director, built an expert team and had a gift for alternately sweet-talking, shaming, and sometimes scaring me into engaging in the endless hustle for dollars. She had a great smile, but the eyes of a killer.

I grew accustomed to the drill, partly out of necessity, but also because as time went on, our donors came to understand and even appreciate my terms. This was about building a better country, I'd tell them, not about egos or prestige. I would listen to their take on an issue, especially if they had some expertise, but I wouldn't shade my positions to satisfy them. If I had a spare minute, the thank-you notes I wrote and the birthday calls I made would be directed not to them but to our volunteers and young staff out in the field.

And if I won, they could count on me raising their taxes.

This attitude lost us a few donors but helped develop a culture among supporters that wasn't about perks or status. And anyway, with each successive month, the makeup of our donor base was shifting. Small donations—in ten- or twenty- or hundred-dollar increments—started pouring in, most coming through the internet, from college students who pledged their Starbucks budget for the duration of the campaign, or grandmas who'd taken up a sewing circle collection. All told during primary season, we would raise millions from small donors, allowing us to compete in every state for every vote. More than the money itself, the spirit behind the giving, the sense of ownership that the accompanying letters and email messages conveyed, infused the campaign with grassroots energy. **This is not all up to you,** these donations told us. **We are here, on the ground, millions of us scattered across the country— and we believe. We are all in.**

More than a strong operations strategy and effective grassroots fundraising, a third element kept both the campaign and our spirits afloat that first year: the work of our Iowa team and their indefatigable leader, Paul Tewes.

PAUL GREW UP in Mountain Lake, a farm town tucked into the southwest corner of Minnesota, a place where everyone knew and looked out for one another, where kids biked everywhere and nobody locked their doors, and where every student played every sport because in order to field a full team, none of the coaches could afford to cut anybody.

Mountain Lake was also a conservative place, which made the Tewes family stand out a little. Paul's mom instilled in him early an allegiance to the Democratic Party that was second only to the family's allegiance to the Lutheran faith. When he was six years old, he patiently explained to a classmate that he shouldn't support the Republicans "'cause your family ain't rich." Four years later, he cried bitterly when Jimmy Carter lost to Ronald Reagan. Paul's father was proud enough of his son's passion for politics that he shared the episode with a friend, the town's high school civics teacher, who in turn—perhaps hoping that a ten-year-old's interest in public affairs might inspire sullen teenagers—relayed it to his class. For the next several days, older kids teased Paul mercilessly, scrunching up their faces like crybabies whenever they spotted him in the halls.

Paul was undeterred. In high school, he organized a dance to raise money for Democratic candidates. In college, he interned for the local state representative, and—in a feat that gave him particular pride—somehow managed to deliver one of Mountain Lake's two precincts to his favored candidate, Jesse Jackson, in the 1988 presidential primary.

By the time I met him in 2007, Paul had worked on just about every type of campaign imaginable: from mayoral races to congressional races. He'd served as Al Gore's Iowa state caucus director and as the director of field operations across the country for the Democratic

Senatorial Campaign Committee. He was thirty-eight by then but looked older, stocky and slightly balding, with a pale blond mustache and pale skin to match. There was nothing fancy about Paul Tewes; his demeanor could be gruff, and his clothes never seemed to match, especially in the winter, when, like a true Minnesotan, he'd sport all manner of flannel shirts, down jackets, and ski caps. He was the kind of guy more comfortable talking to farmers in a cornfield or drinking in a corner saloon than mingling with high-paid political consultants. But sitting with him, you quickly realized he knew his stuff. More than that: Beneath the tactical insights, detailed district voting histories, and political anecdotes, you might hear—if you listened carefully enough—the heart of the ten-year-old boy who cared enough, who believed enough, to cry over an election.

Anyone who's ever run for president will likely tell you that there's nothing simple about winning Iowa. It's one of a number of U.S. states that hold a caucus to determine which candidates their delegates will support. As opposed to a traditional primary election in which citizens cast votes privately and largely at their convenience, a caucus is more of a throwback to town hall–style democracy, when voters showed up at an appointed hour, usually at a school gym or a library in their precinct, and debated the merits of each candidate in a neighborly manner for as long as it took to come up with a winner. Such participatory democracy had much to commend it, but it was time-consuming—a caucus could last three hours or more—and required participants to be well informed, willing to vote publicly, and committed enough to make an evening of it.

Unsurprisingly caucuses tended to attract a small and static cross section of the Iowa electorate, made up of older voters, party functionaries, longtime partisans—those who hewed, in general, to the tried-and-true. This meant that Democratic caucus-goers were more likely to support a known quantity like Hillary Clinton than someone like me.

From the start, Tewes impressed upon Plouffe, and Plouffe in turn impressed upon me, that if we wanted to win Iowa, we needed to run a different kind of campaign. We'd have to work harder and longer, face-to-face, to win over traditional caucus-goers. More important, we'd have to convince a whole lot of likely Obama supporters—young people, people of color, independents—to overcome the various hurdles and hang-ups and participate in the caucus for the very first time. To do it, Tewes insisted on opening offices right away, covering all ninety-nine Iowa counties; and for each office we'd hire a young staffer who, with little pay or day-to-day supervision, would be responsible for engineering their own local political movement.

It was a big investment and an early gamble, but we gave Tewes the green light. He went to work, with an outstanding team of deputies who helped develop his plan: Mitch Stewart, Marygrace Galston, Anne Filipic, and Emily Parcell, all of them smart, disciplined, with experience on multiple campaigns—and under thirty-two years old.

I spent the most time with Emily, who was an Iowa native and had worked for former governor Tom Vilsack. Tewes figured she'd be especially helpful to me as I navigated local politics. She was twenty-six, one of the youngest in the group, with dark hair and sensible clothes, and diminutive enough to pass for a high school senior. I quickly discovered she knew just about every Democrat in the state and had no qualms about giving me very specific instructions at every stop, covering whom I should talk to and which issues the local community most cared about. This information was delivered in a deadpan monotone, along with a look that suggested a low tolerance for foolishness—a quality Emily may have inherited from her mom, who'd worked at the Motorola plant for three decades and still managed to put herself through college.

During the long hours we spent traveling between events in a rented campaign van, I made it my mission to coax a smile out of Emily—jokes, wisecracks, puns, stray observations about the size of Reggie's head. But my charm and wit invariably crashed on the rocks of her steady, unblinking gaze, and I settled on trying to do exactly what she told me to do.

Mitch, Marygrace, and Anne would later describe the particulars of their work—which included collectively screening all the unorthodox ideas Tewes routinely pitched at meetings.

"He'd have ten a day," Mitch would explain. "Nine were ridiculous, one would be genius." Mitch was a gangly South Dakotan who'd worked in Iowa politics before but had never encountered someone as passionately eclectic as Tewes. "If he brought up the same idea to me three times," he'd recall, "I figured there might be something there."

Enlisting Norma Lyon, Iowa's "Butter Cow Lady," who at the state fair each year sculpted a life-sized cow out of salted butter, to make a prerecorded call announcing her support for us, which we then blasted across the state—genius. (She later created a twenty-three-pound "butter bust" of my head—also likely a Tewes idea.)

Insisting that we put up billboards along the highway, with rhyming phrases unfolding in sequence like the old 1960s Burma-Shave ads (TIME FOR CHANGE . . . LET'S SHIFT GEARS . . . VOTE 4 THE GUY . . . WITH BIG EARS . . . OBAMA 08)—not so genius.

Promising to shave his eyebrows if the staff reached the unreachable goal of collecting one hundred thousand supporter cards—not genius, until very late in the campaign, when the team actually hit the mark, at which point it became genius. ("Mitch shaved his too," Marygrace would explain. "We have pictures. It was horrible.")

Tewes would set the tone for our Iowa operation—grassroots, no hierarchies, irreverent, and slightly manic. No one—including senior staff, donors, or dignitaries—was exempt from doing some door knocking. In the early weeks, he hung signs on every wall in every office with a motto he'd authored: RESPECT, EMPOWER, INCLUDE. If we were serious about a new kind of politics, he explained, then it started right there on the ground, with every organizer committed to listening to people, respecting what they had to say, and treating everybody—including our opponents and their supporters—the way we wanted to be treated. Lastly he stressed the importance of encouraging voters to get involved instead of just selling them a candidate like a box of laundry detergent.

Anyone who breached these values got scolded and sometimes pulled from the field. When, during our team's weekly conference call, a new organizer made a

joke about why he'd joined the campaign, saying something about "hating pantsuits" (a reference to Hillary's
favorite campaign attire), Tewes admonished him in a
lengthy rant for all the other organizers to hear. "It's not
what we stand for," he said, "not even in private."

The team took this to heart, particularly because
Tewes practiced what he preached. Despite the occasional
intemperate outburst, he never failed to show people
how much they mattered. When Marygrace's uncle died,
Tewes declared National Marygrace Day, and had everyone in the office wear pink. He also had me record a
message announcing that for that one day, he would have
to do everything Marygrace said. (Of course, Marygrace
had to put up with three hundred days of Tewes and
Mitch chewing tobacco in the office, so the ledger never
fully balanced.)

This kind of camaraderie permeated the Iowa operation. Not just at headquarters but, more important,
among the close to two hundred field organizers we'd
deployed across the state. All told, I would spend eighty-
seven days in Iowa that year. I would sample each town's
culinary specialty, shoot hoops with schoolkids on any
court we could find, and experience every possible
weather event, from funnel clouds to sideways sleet.
Through it all, those young men and women, working
endless hours for subsistence wages, were my able guides.
Most were barely out of college. Many were on their first
campaigns and far away from home. Some had grown up
in Iowa or the rural Midwest, familiar with the attitudes
and way of life of midsized towns like Sioux City or
Altoona. But that wasn't typical. Assemble our organizers
in a room and you'd find Italians from Philly, Jews from

Chicago, Blacks from New York, and Asians from California; children of poor immigrants and children of the rich suburbs; engineering majors, former Peace Corps volunteers, military veterans, and high school dropouts. On the surface, at least, there seemed no way to connect their wildly varied experiences to the meat-and-potatoes folks whose votes we desperately needed.

And yet they did connect. Arriving in town with a duffel bag or a small suitcase, living in the spare bedroom or basement of some early local supporter, they would spend months getting to know a place—visiting the local barbershop, setting up card tables in front of the grocery store, speaking at the Rotary Club. They helped coach Little League, assisted local charities, and called their moms for a banana pudding recipe so they wouldn't show up to the potluck empty-handed. They learned to listen to their local volunteers—most of whom were much older, with their own jobs, families, and concerns— and got good at recruiting new ones too. They worked each day to exhaustion and fought off bouts of loneliness and fear. Month by month, they won people's trust. They were no longer strangers.

What a tonic these young kids in Iowa were! They filled me with optimism and gratitude and a sense of coming full circle. In them, I saw myself at twenty-five, arriving in Chicago, confused and idealistic. I remembered the precious bonds I'd made with families on the South Side, the mistakes and small victories, the community I found—similar to what our field organizers were now forging for themselves. Their experiences pointed me back to why I'd gone into government in the first place, toward the taproot idea that maybe politics could be less about power and positioning and more about community and connection.

Our volunteers across Iowa might believe in me, I thought to myself. But they were working as hard as they were mainly because of those young organizers. Just as those kids may have signed up to work for the campaign because of something I'd said or done, but now they belonged to the volunteers. What drove them, what sustained them, independent of their candidate or any particular issue, were the friendships and relationships, the mutual loyalty and progress born of joint effort. That and their cantankerous boss back in Des Moines, the one who was promising to shave his eyebrows if they succeeded.

BY JUNE, OUR campaign had turned a corner. Thanks to skyrocketing internet donations, our financial performance continued to far outstrip our projections, allowing us to go up early on Iowa TV. With school out for the summer, Michelle and the girls were able to join me more often on the road. Rumbling across Iowa in an RV, the sound of their chatter in the background as I made calls; seeing Reggie and Marvin taking on Malia and Sasha in marathon games of UNO; feeling the gentle weight of one daughter or another sleeping against me on an afternoon leg; and always the obligatory ice cream stops—all of it filled me with a joy that carried over into my public appearances.

The nature of those appearances changed as well. As the initial novelty of my candidacy wore off, I found myself speaking to more manageable crowds, a few hundred rather than thousands, which gave me the chance once again to meet people one-on-one and listen to their stories. Military spouses described the day-to-day struggles of running a household and fighting off the terror of possibly hearing bad news from the front. Farmers explained the pressures that led them to surrender their independence to big agribusiness concerns. Laid-off workers talked me through the myriad ways that existing job-training programs had failed them. Small-business owners detailed the sacrifices they'd made to pay for their employees' health insurance, until just one employee fell sick and everyone's premiums became unaffordable, including their own.

Informed by these stories, my stump speech became less abstract, less a matter of the head and more a matter of the heart. People heard their own lives reflected in these stories, learning that they were not alone in their hardship, and with that knowledge, more and more of them signed up to volunteer on my behalf. Campaigning on this more retail, human scale also offered the opportunity for chance encounters that made the campaign come alive.

That's what happened when I visited Greenwood, South Carolina, one day in June. Though most of my time was spent in Iowa, I was also paying regular visits to other states like New Hampshire, Nevada, and South Carolina, whose primaries and caucuses would follow in quick succession. The trip to Greenwood was the result of a rash promise I'd made to an influential legislator who'd offered to endorse me, but only if I visited her hometown. As it turned out, my visit was poorly timed, coming during an especially rough week, amid bad poll numbers, bad stories in the papers, bad moods, and bad sleep. It didn't help that Greenwood was more than an hour from the nearest major airport, we were driving through torrential rains, and when I finally arrived at the municipal building where the event was supposed to be held, I found only twenty people or so gathered inside— all of them as damp as I was from the storm.

A wasted day, I thought to myself, mentally ticking off all the other work I could have been doing. I was going through the motions, shaking hands, asking people what they did for a living, quietly trying to calculate how fast I could get out of there, when suddenly I heard a piercing voice shout out.

"Fired up!"

My staff and I were startled, thinking maybe it was a heckler, but without missing a beat, the rest of the room responded in unison.

"Ready to go!"

Again, the same voice shouted, "Fired up!" And once again the group responded, "Ready to go!"

Unsure of what was happening, I turned to look behind me, my eyes landing on the source of the commotion: a middle-aged Black woman, dressed like she had just come from church, with a colorful dress, a big hat, and an ear-to-ear grin that included a shiny gold tooth.

Her name was Edith Childs. In addition to serving on the Greenwood County Council and in the local NAACP chapter while also being a professional private eye, it turned out she was well known for this particular call-and-response. She started it at Greenwood's football games, Fourth of July parades, community meetings, or whenever the spirit happened to move her.

For the next few minutes, Edith led the room in hollering "Fired up! Ready to go!" back and forth, again and again. I was confused at first, but figured it would be impolite of me not to join in. And pretty soon, I started to feel **kinda fired up**! I started to feel like I was **ready to go**! I noticed everybody at the meeting suddenly was smiling too, and after the chanting was done we settled down and talked for the next hour about the community and the country and what we could do to make it better. Even after I left Greenwood, for the rest of the day, every so often, I'd point to someone on my staff and ask, "You fired up?" Eventually it became a campaign rallying cry. And that, I suppose, was the part of politics that would always give me the most pleasure: the part that couldn't be diagrammed, that defied planning or analytics. The way in which, when it works, a campaign—and by extension a democracy—proved to be a chorus rather than a solo act.

ANOTHER LESSON I learned from voters: They weren't interested in hearing me parrot conventional wisdom. During the first few months of campaigning, I'd worried at least subconsciously about what Washington opinion makers thought. In the interest of being deemed sufficiently "serious" or "presidential," I'd become stiff and self-conscious, undermining the very rationale that had led me to run in the first place. But by the summer, we went back to first principles and actively looked for opportunities to challenge the Washington playbook and tell hard truths. Before a teachers' union gathering, I argued not only for higher salaries and more flexibility in the classroom but also for greater accountability—that last bit eliciting a deafening silence and then a smattering of boos in the hall. At the Detroit Economic Club, I told auto executives that as president I would push hard for higher fuel economy standards, a position ardently opposed by the Big Three automakers. When a group called Iowans for Sensible Priorities, sponsored by Ben and Jerry of ice cream fame, gathered ten thousand signatures from people committing to caucus for a candidate who promised to cut the Pentagon's defense budget, I had to call either Ben or Jerry—I don't remember which—to say that although I agreed with the objective and very much wanted their support, I couldn't as president be hamstrung by any pledge I'd made when it came to our national security. (The group eventually opted to endorse John Edwards.)

I was starting to look different from my Democratic rivals in more ways than the obvious one. During a debate in late July, I was shown images of Fidel Castro, Iranian president Mahmoud Ahmadinejad, North Korean leader Kim Jong Il, and a couple of other despots and asked if I'd be prepared to meet with any of them during my first year in office. Without hesitation, I said yes—I'd meet with any world leader if I thought it could advance U.S. interests.

Well, you would have thought I had said the world was flat. When the debate was over, Clinton, Edwards, and a bunch of the other candidates pounced, accusing me of being naïve, insisting that a meeting with the American president was a privilege to be earned. The press corps in large part seemed to agree. Perhaps even a few months earlier I might have gotten wobbly, second-guessing my choice of words and issuing a clarifying statement afterward.

But I had my legs beneath me now and was convinced I was right, particularly on the more general principle that America shouldn't be afraid to engage its adversaries or push for diplomatic solutions to conflict. As far as I was concerned, it was this disregard for diplomacy that had led Hillary and the rest—not to mention the mainstream press—to follow George W. Bush into war.

Another foreign policy argument arose just a few days later, when during a speech I mentioned that if I had Osama bin Laden in my sights within Pakistani territory, and the Pakistani government was unwilling or unable to capture or kill him, I would take the shot. This shouldn't have been particularly surprising to anyone; back in 2003, I had premised my opposition to the Iraq War partly on my belief that it would distract us from destroying al-Qaeda.

But such blunt talk ran counter to the Bush administration's public position; the U.S. government maintained the dual fiction that Pakistan was a reliable partner in the war against terrorism and that we never encroached on Pakistani territory in the pursuit of terrorists. My statement threw Washington into a bipartisan tizzy, with Joe Biden, the chair of the Senate Foreign Relations Committee, and Republican presidential candidate John McCain both expressing the view that I was not ready to be president.

In my mind, these episodes indicated the degree to which the Washington foreign policy establishment got things backward—taking military action without first testing diplomatic options, observing diplomatic niceties in the interest of maintaining the status quo precisely when action was called for. It also indicated the degree to which decision makers in Washington consistently failed to level with the American people. I would never fully convince the national pundits that I was right on these arguments, but a funny trend began to show up in the polls after each of these dustups—Democratic primary voters agreed with me.

Having such substantive arguments felt liberating, a reminder of why I was running. They helped me regain my voice as a candidate. That confidence showed a few debates later, at an early-morning affair at Drake University in Iowa. The moderator, George Stephanopoulos of ABC, quickly gave Joe Biden the chance to explain why exactly I was not ready to be president. By the time I got an opportunity to respond, five minutes later, I'd had to listen to practically every other candidate onstage knock me around.

"Well, you know, to prepare for this debate, I rode in the bumper cars at the state fair," I said, using a line Axe had come up with, referencing my well-publicized excursion with Malia and Sasha to the state fair earlier that week. The audience laughed, and for the next hour I happily jousted with my opponents, suggesting that any Democratic voter who was trying to figure out who represented a real change from the failed policies of George Bush need look no further than the respective positions of those of us onstage. For the first time since the debates had begun, I enjoyed myself, and the consensus among the pundits that morning was that I had won.

It was a gratifying result, if for no other reason than not having to endure any dour looks from the team.

"You killed it!" Axe said, clapping me on the back.

"I guess we'll be pushing to have all the debates at eight in the morning!" Plouffe joked.

"That's not funny," I said. (I was not, and am not, a morning person.)

We piled into the car and started driving to our next stop. Along the route, our supporters, several rows deep, could be heard shouting long after they had disappeared from sight.

"Fired up!"

"Ready to go!"

PART OF THE reason I'd received so much attention from the moderators during the Drake University debate was the release of an ABC poll showing me leading in Iowa for the first time, albeit by just 1 percent, over both Clinton and Edwards. The race was close, clearly (later polls would put me right back in third place), but there was no denying that our Iowa organization was having an impact, especially among younger voters. You could feel it in the crowds—in their size, their energy, and, most important, the number of supporter cards and volunteer sign-ups we were collecting at every stop. With less than six months to go before the caucus, our strength was only building.

Unfortunately none of our progress showed up in national polling. Our focus on Iowa and to a lesser extent New Hampshire meant we'd made minimal TV buys and appearances elsewhere, and by September we remained around twenty points behind Hillary. Plouffe did his best to educate the press as to why national polls were meaningless at this early stage, but to no avail. Increasingly I found myself fielding anxious phone calls from supporters around the country, many offering policy advice, advertising suggestions, complaints that we'd neglected this or that interest group, and general questions about our competence.

Two things finally flipped the narrative, the first one not of our making. At a late-October debate in Philadelphia, Hillary—whose performances until then had been nearly flawless—got tangled up, unwilling to provide a straight answer on the issue of whether undocumented workers should be allowed driver's licenses. Undoubtedly she'd been coached to hedge her response, since it was an issue that divided the Democratic base. Her efforts to straddle the fence only fed the already prevalent impression that she was a garden-variety Washington politician—sharpening the contrast we'd been hoping to make.

And then there was what happened at the Iowa Jefferson-Jackson Dinner on November 10, which **was** of our making. Traditionally the JJ Dinner signaled the final sprint to caucus day and offered a kind of barometric reading of where the race stood, with each candidate delivering a ten-minute speech without notes before an arena of eight thousand potential caucus-goers as well as the national media. As such, it was a key test of both our message's appeal and our organizational prowess going into the final few weeks.

We put everything we had into a successful showing, lining up buses to bring in supporters from all ninety-nine counties across the state and dwarfing turnout from the other campaigns. John Legend gave a short predinner concert on our behalf for more than a thousand people, and when it was done, Michelle and I led the entire procession down the street to the arena where the dinner was being held, a pumped-up local high school drum and drill corps called the Isiserettes performing beside us, their happy racket giving us the air of a conquering army.

The speech itself won the day for us. To that point in my political career, I had always insisted on writing the bulk of any important speech myself, but campaigning nonstop as I was, there was no way I'd have time to write the JJ Dinner remarks on my own. I had to trust Favs, with guidance from Axe and Plouffe, to produce a draft that effectively summarized my case for the nomination.

And Favs delivered. In that critical moment of our campaign, with only modest input from me, this guy just a few years out of college had produced a great speech, one that did more than show the distinction between me and my rivals, between Democrats and Republicans. It outlined the challenges we faced as a nation, from war to climate change to the affordability of healthcare, and the need for new and clear leadership, noting that the party had historically been strongest with leaders who led "not by polls, but by principle . . . not by calculation, but by conviction." It was true to the moment, true to my aspirations for getting into politics, and true, I hoped, to the aspirations of the country.

I memorized the speech over several late nights after we were done campaigning. And by the time I finished delivering it—as luck would have it, the last candidate to speak—I was as certain of its effect as I'd been after my address to the Democratic National Convention three and a half years earlier.

Looking back, the night of the JJ Dinner was when I became convinced we would win Iowa—and by extension the nomination. Not necessarily because I was the most polished candidate, but because we had the right message for the time and had attracted young people with prodigious talent to throw themselves behind the cause. Tewes shared my assessment, telling Mitch, "I think we won Iowa tonight." (Mitch, who had organized the entire evening and was generally a basket of nerves— he suffered from insomnia, shingles, and hair loss through much of the campaign—ran to the bathroom to throw up for at least the second time that day.) Emily was similarly bullish, although you couldn't tell. After I was finished, an ecstatic Valerie ran into Emily and asked what she thought.

"It was great," Emily said.

"You don't look very excited."

"This is my excited face."

THE CLINTON CAMPAIGN apparently felt the shifting tide. Up to that point, Hillary and her team had largely avoided engaging our campaign directly, content to stay above the fray and nurse their sizable lead in national polls. But over the next several weeks, they changed tack, deciding to go after us hard. It was mostly standard-issue stuff, raising questions about my lack of experience and ability to take on Republicans in Washington. Unfortunately for them, though, the two lines of attack that attracted the most attention backfired badly.

The first grew out of a standard line in my stump speech, in which I said I was running for president not because it was owed to me or because I'd wanted to be president all my life, but because the times called for something new. Well, the Clinton camp issued a memo citing a press clip in which one of my teachers in Indonesia claimed that I had written an essay in kindergarten about wanting to be president—proof, it seemed, that my professed idealism was merely a disguise for a ruthless ambition.

When I heard about this, I laughed. As I told Michelle, the idea that anyone outside my family remembered anything I said or did almost forty years earlier was a bit far-fetched. Not to mention the difficulty of squaring my apparent youthful plan for world domination with middling high school grades and drug consumption, an obscure stint as a community organizer, and associations with all kinds of politically inconvenient characters.

Of course, over the next decade we'd discover that absurdity, incoherence, or a lack of factual support didn't prevent various crackpot theories about me—peddled by political opponents, conservative news outlets, critical biographers, and the like—from gaining real traction. But in December 2007, at least, the Clinton team's opposition research into what I called "my kindergarten files" was viewed as a sign of panic and widely panned.

Less amusing was an interview in which Billy Shaheen, the co-chair of Clinton's campaign in New Hampshire, suggested to a reporter that my self-disclosed prior drug use would prove fatal in a matchup against the Republican nominee. I didn't consider the general question of my youthful indiscretions out of bounds, but

Shaheen went a bit further, implying that perhaps I had dealt drugs as well. The interview set off a furor, and Shaheen quickly resigned from his post.

All this happened just ahead of our final debate in Iowa. That morning, both Hillary and I were in Washington for a Senate vote. When my team and I got to the airport for the flight to Des Moines, Hillary's chartered plane turned out to be parked right next to ours. Before takeoff, Huma Abedin, Hillary's aide, found Reggie and let him know that the senator was hoping to speak to me. I met Hillary on the tarmac, Reggie and Huma hovering a few paces away.

Hillary apologized for Shaheen. I thanked her and then suggested we both do a better job of reining in our surrogates. At this, Hillary got agitated, her voice sharpening as she claimed that my team was routinely engaging in unfair attacks, distortions, and underhanded tactics. My efforts at lowering the temperature were unsuccessful, and the conversation ended abruptly, with her still visibly angry as she boarded her plane.

On the flight to Des Moines, I tried to appreciate the frustrations Hillary must have been feeling. A woman of enormous intelligence, she had toiled, sacrificed, endured public attacks and humiliations, all in service of her husband's career—while also raising a wonderful daughter. Out of the White House, she had carved a new political identity, positioning herself with skill and tenacity to become the prohibitive favorite to win the presidency. As a candidate, she was performing almost flawlessly, checking every box, winning most debates, raising scads of money. And now, to find herself suddenly in a close contest with a man fourteen years younger, who hadn't had to pay the same dues, who didn't carry the same battle scars, and who seemed to be getting every break and every benefit of the doubt? Honestly, who wouldn't be aggravated?

Moreover, Hillary wasn't entirely wrong about my team's willingness to give as good as it got. Compared to other modern presidential campaigns, we really were different, consistently emphasizing a positive message, highlighting what I stood for rather than what I was against. I policed our tone from top to bottom. More than once, I killed TV spots I felt were unfair or too harsh. Still, we sometimes fell short of our high-minded rhetoric. In fact, the angriest I ever got during the campaign involved a leaked memo drafted by our research team back in June, criticizing Hillary's tacit support of outsourcing jobs to India and with the snarky title "Hillary Clinton (D-Punjab)." My team insisted the memo was never meant for public consumption, but I didn't care—its shoddy argument and nativist tone had me ripshit for days.

In the end, I don't think it was any specific action on our part that caused the dustup with Hillary on the tarmac. Rather, it was the general fact of my challenge, the intensifying heat of our rivalry. There were six other candidates still in the race, but the polls were beginning to clarify where we were headed, with Hillary and me battling each other until the end. It was a dynamic we'd live with, day and night, weekends and holidays, for many months to come, our teams flanking us like miniature armies, each staffer fully indoctrinated into the fight. It was part of the brutal nature of modern politics, I was discovering, the difficulty of competing in a game where there were no clearly defined rules, a game in which your opponents are not merely trying to put a ball through a basket or push it across your goal line, but are instead trying to convince the broad public—at least implicitly, more often explicitly—that in matters of judgment, intelligence, values, and character, they are more worthy than you.

You may tell yourself it's not personal, but that's not how it feels. Not to you and certainly not to your family, your staff, or your supporters, who count up every slight and every insult, real or perceived. The longer the campaign goes on, the tighter the contest, the higher the stakes, the easier it is to justify hardball tactics. Until those basic human responses that normally govern our daily lives—honesty, empathy, courtesy, patience, goodwill—feel like weakness when extended to the other side.

I can't say all this was on my mind by the time I walked into the debate the evening after the tarmac incident. Mostly I read Hillary's irritation as a sign that we were pulling ahead, that the momentum was truly ours. During the debate, the moderator asked why, if I was so insistent on the need for change in America's approach to foreign policy, did I have so many former Clinton administration officials advising me. "I want to hear that," Hillary said into the microphone.

I paused, letting the chuckles die down.

"Well, Hillary, I'm looking forward to you advising me as well."

It was a good night for the team.

WITH A MONTH left before the caucuses, a **Des Moines Register** poll now showed me with a three-point lead over Hillary. The sprint was full-on, with candidates from both parties dashing around the state in the final weeks, trying to win over any uncommitted voter, to find and motivate hidden pockets of people who might not otherwise turn out on the appointed night. The Clinton campaign had started handing out free snow shovels to supporters in case the weather got bad, and in a move that would later be criticized as outlandishly expensive, Hillary embarked on a blitzkrieg tour, visiting sixteen Iowa counties in a chartered helicopter (which her campaign dubbed "the Hill-O-Copter"). John Edwards, meanwhile, was attempting to cover similar terrain in a bus.

We had a few high-profile moments of our own, including a series of rallies with Oprah Winfrey, who'd become a friend and supporter, and was as wise, funny, and gracious on the trail as she was in person, attracting nearly thirty thousand people between two rallies in Iowa, another eighty-five hundred in New Hampshire, and almost thirty thousand in South Carolina. These gatherings were electric, pulling in the kind of new voters we most needed. (Many on my staff, it must be said, were starstruck around Oprah, with the predictable exception of Emily; the only famous person she ever expressed an interest in meeting was Tim Russert.)

In the end, though, it wasn't the polls, or the size of the rallies, or the celebrities who flew in that I remember most. Instead, it was how, in those last days, the whole campaign took on the feeling of family. Michelle's openness and candor had proven to be an asset; she was a natural on the stump. The Iowa team came to call her "the Closer," because of how many people signed up once they'd heard her speak. Our siblings and closest friends all came to Iowa, Craig from Chicago and Maya from Hawaii and Auma from Kenya; the Nesbitts, the Whitakers, Valerie, and all their kids, not to mention Michelle's passel of aunts, uncles, and cousins. My childhood friends from Hawaii, buddies from my organizing days, law school classmates, former state senate colleagues, and many of our donors came, arriving in groups like big traveling reunions, often without me even knowing they were there. Nobody asked for any special attention; instead, they just reported to field offices where the kid in charge would hand them a map and a list of supporters to contact so they could then celebrate the week between Christmas and New Year's with a clipboard in hand, knocking on doors in the face-numbing cold.

It was more than just blood relatives or people we'd known for years. The people of Iowa whom I'd spent so much time with felt like family too. There were local party leaders like attorney general Tom Miller and treasurer Mike Fitzgerald, who had taken a flier on me when few would give me a shot. There were volunteers like Gary Lamb, a progressive farmer from Tama County who helped us with rural outreach; Leo Peck, who at eighty-two had knocked on more doors than just about anybody; Marie Ortiz, an African American nurse married to a Hispanic man in a mostly white town, who came into the office to make calls three or four times a week, sometimes cooking dinner for our organizer there because she thought he was too skinny.

Family.

And then, of course, there were the field organizers. As busy as they were, we decided to have them invite their parents to the JJ Dinner, and the next day we hosted a reception for them, just so that Michelle and I could say thank you to each of them, and to their parents for having produced such amazing sons and daughters.

To this day, there's nothing I wouldn't do for those kids.

On the big night, Plouffe and Valerie decided to join me, Reggie, and Marvin on a surprise visit to a high school in Ankeny, a suburb of Des Moines, where several precincts would be holding their caucuses. It was January 3, just after six p.m., less than an hour before the caucuses were scheduled to begin, and yet the place was already packed. People streamed toward the main building from every direction, a noisy festival of humanity. No age, race, class, or body type appeared unrepresented. There was even one ancient-looking character dressed as Gandalf from **The Lord of the Rings,** complete with a long white cloak, a pluming white beard, and a sturdy wooden staff on top of which he'd somehow managed to mount a small video monitor, looping a clip of my JJ Dinner speech.

We had no press with us then, and I took my time wandering through the crowd, shaking hands and thanking those who planned to support me, asking those who were caucusing for another candidate to please at least make me their second choice. A few had last-minute questions about my stance on ethanol or what I intended to do about human trafficking. Over and over again, people rushed up to tell me that they'd never caucused before—some had never even bothered to vote—and that our campaign had inspired them to get involved for the very first time.

"I didn't know I counted before," one woman said.

On the ride back to Des Moines, we were mostly quiet, processing the miracle of what we had just witnessed. I looked out the window at the passing strip malls and houses and streetlights, all fuzzy behind the frosty glass, and felt a kind of peace. We were hours, still, from knowing what would happen. The results, when they came in, showed us winning Iowa decisively, carrying just about every demographic group, our victory propelled by unprecedented turnout, including tens of thousands of people who'd participated for the first time. I knew none of this yet, but pulling away from Ankeny about fifteen minutes before the caucuses began, I knew we had accomplished, if even for just a moment, something real and noble.

Right there, in that high school in the middle of the country on a cold winter night, I had witnessed the community I had so long sought, the America I imagined, made manifest. I thought of my mom then, and how happy she would have been to see it, and how proud she would have been, and I missed her terribly, and Plouffe and Valerie pretended not to notice as I wiped away my tears.

CHAPTER 6

OUR EIGHT-POINT MARGIN OF VICTORY in Iowa made news across the country. The media used words like "stunning" and "seismic" to describe it, noting that the results were especially devastating for Hillary, who finished third. Both Chris Dodd and Joe Biden promptly dropped out of the race. Elected officials who'd stayed cautiously on the sidelines were now calling, ready to endorse. Pundits declared me the new Democratic front-runner, suggesting that the high level of voter engagement in Iowa signaled a broader appetite for change in America.

Having spent the previous year as David, I was suddenly cast as Goliath—and as happy as I was about our victory, the new role felt awkward. For a year, my team and I had avoided getting too high or too low, ignoring both the initial hype surrounding my candidacy and the subsequent reports of its imminent demise. With only five days between Iowa and the New Hampshire primary, it took everything we had to tamp down expectations. Axe considered the gushing stories and TV images of me before adoring crowds ("Obama the icon," he complained) especially unhelpful in a state like New Hampshire, where the electorate—many of them independents who liked to decide at the last minute between voting in the Democratic or Republican primary—had a reputation for being contrarian.

Still, it was hard not to feel like we were in the driver's seat. Our organizers in New Hampshire were just as tenacious and our volunteers just as spirited as those in Iowa; our rallies drew enthusiastic crowds, with lines to get in that would wind through parking lots and stretch around the block. Then, in the span of forty-eight hours, the contest took a couple of unexpected turns.

The first happened during the lone debate before the primary when, midway through, the moderator asked Hillary how she felt when people said she was not "likable."

Now, this was the type of question that drove me nuts on several levels. It was trivial. It was unanswerable—what's a person supposed to say to something like that? And it was indicative of a double standard that Hillary specifically and women politicians in general had to put up with, in which they were expected to be "nice" in ways that were never deemed relevant to their male counterparts.

Despite the fact that Hillary was handling the question just fine ("Well, that hurts my feelings," she said, laughing, "but I'll try to go on"), I decided to interject.

"You're likable enough, Hillary," I said, deadpan.

I assumed the audience understood my intentions—to make an overture to my opponent while indicating scorn for the question. But whether because of bad delivery, clumsy phrasing, or spin by the Clinton communications team, a story line emerged—that I had been patronizing toward Hillary, dismissive, even, yet another boorish male putting down his female rival.

In other words, the opposite of what I had meant.

Nobody on our team got too exercised about my remark, understanding that any attempt to clarify it would only fuel the fire. But no sooner had the story begun to die down than the media exploded yet again, this time over how Hillary was being perceived following a meeting she'd had with a group of undecided voters in New Hampshire, most of them women. Fielding an empathetic question about how she was managing the stresses of the race, Hillary had momentarily choked up, describing how personally and passionately invested she was—how she didn't want to see the country move backward and how she'd devoted her life to public service "against some pretty difficult odds."

It was a rare and genuine show of emotion on Hillary's part, one that ran counter to her steely, controlled image, enough so that it made headlines and sent the cable news pundits into orbit. Some interpreted the moment as compelling and authentic, a new point of human connection between Hillary and the public. Others deemed it either a manufactured bit of emotion or a sign of weakness that threatened to damage her candidacy. Running beneath it all, of course, was the fact that Hillary quite possibly could become the nation's first female president and—just as mine did with race—her candidacy surfaced all sorts of stereotypes about gender and how we expected our leaders to look and behave.

The frenzy around whether Hillary was trending up or down continued right into primary day in New

Hampshire. My team took comfort in the fact that we had a big cushion: Polls showed us with a ten-point lead. So when the midday rally we'd scheduled at a local college drew a sparse crowd, my speech interrupted by a fainting student and what seemed like an interminable response time by the medics, I didn't take it as a bad omen.

It wasn't until that evening, after the polls had closed, that I knew we had a problem. As Michelle and I were in our hotel room getting ready for what we expected to be a victory celebration, I heard a knock and opened the door to find Plouffe, Axe, and Gibbs standing sheepishly in the hall, looking like teenagers who had just crashed their dad's car into a tree.

"We're going to lose," Plouffe said.

They began offering various theories on what had gone wrong. It was possible that independents who supported us over Hillary had decided to vote en masse in the Republican primary to help John McCain, figuring that we had our race well in hand. Undecided women may have swung sharply in Hillary's direction during the campaign's final days. Or maybe it was the fact that when the Clinton team attacked us on TV and in campaign mailings, we hadn't done enough to highlight their negative tactics, allowing the punches to land.

The theories all sounded plausible. But for the moment, the whys didn't matter.

"Looks like winning this thing's going to take a while," I said with a rueful smile. "Right now, let's figure out how to cauterize the wound."

No hangdog looks, I told them; our body language had to communicate to everyone—the press, donors, and most of all our supporters—that setbacks were par for the course. I reached out to our distraught New Hampshire team to tell them how proud I was of their efforts. Then there was the matter of what to say to the seventeen hundred or so people who had gathered in a Nashua school gym in anticipation of victory. Fortunately I had already worked with Favs earlier in the week to tone down any triumphalist tones in the speech, asking him instead to emphasize the hard work that lay ahead. I now got him on the phone to instruct that—other than a tip of the hat to Hillary—we barely change the text.

The speech I gave to our supporters that evening would end up being one of the most important of our campaign, not just as a rallying cry for the disheartened, but as a useful reminder of what we believed. "We know the battle ahead will be long," I said, "but always remember that no matter what obstacles stand in our way, nothing can stand in the way of the power of millions of voices calling for change." I said that we lived in a country whose history was all but built on hope, by people—pioneers, abolitionists, suffragists, immigrants, civil rights workers—who'd been undeterred by seemingly impossible odds.

"When we've been told we're not ready," I said, "or that we shouldn't try, or that we can't, generations of Americans have responded with a simple creed that sums up the spirit of a people: **Yes we can.**" The crowd began to chant the phrase like a drumbeat, and for perhaps the first time since Axe had suggested it as a slogan for my Senate campaign, I fully believed the power of those three words.

.   .   .

THE NEWS COVERAGE following our loss in New Hampshire was predictably tough, the overall message being that order had been restored and Hillary was back on top. But a funny thing happened inside our campaign. Devastated as they were by the loss, our staff grew more unified and also more determined. Instead of a drop-off in volunteers, our offices reported a surge of walk-ins across the country. Our online contributions— particularly from new small-dollar donors—spiked. John Kerry, who'd previously been noncommittal, came out with an enthusiastic endorsement for me. This was followed by announcements of support from Governor Janet Napolitano of Arizona, Senator Claire McCaskill of Missouri, and Governor Kathleen Sebelius of Kansas, all hailing from states that leaned Republican and helping to send a message that despite the setback, we were strong and moving forward, our hopes intact.

All this was gratifying, and it confirmed my instinct that losing New Hampshire wasn't the disaster commentators thought it might be. If Iowa had shown me to be a real contender, and not simply a novelty act, the rush to anoint me had been artificial and premature. In that sense, the good people of New Hampshire had done me a favor by slowing down the process. Running for president is supposed to be hard, I told a group of supporters the next day, because being president is hard. Delivering change is hard. We were going to have to earn this thing, and that meant getting back to work.

And that's what we did. Nevada's caucus came on January 19, just a week and a half after New Hampshire, and we weren't surprised when we lost the raw vote to Hillary; polls there had shown us to be well behind her throughout the year. But in presidential primaries, what matters is not so much the number of individual votes you get but rather how many pledged convention delegates you win, with delegates apportioned based on a series of arcane rules unique to each state. Thanks to our organization's strength in rural Nevada, where we'd campaigned hard (Elko, a town that looked like a western movie set, complete with tumbleweeds and a saloon, was one of my all-time favorite stops), our more even distribution of votes across the state resulted in us winning thirteen delegates to Hillary's twelve. Improbably enough, we were able to emerge from Nevada claiming a draw and entered the next phase of the campaign—the South Carolina primary and the behemoth, twenty-two-state Super Tuesday—with at least a fighting chance.

My senior team would later say it was my optimism that carried them through the loss in New Hampshire. I don't know if that's actually the case, since my staff and supporters operated with admirable resilience and consistency throughout the campaign, independent of anything I did. At most, I had simply returned the favor, given all that others had done to drag me across the Iowa finish line. What is probably true is that New Hampshire showed my team and supporters a quality I had learned about myself, something that proved useful not just during the course of the campaign but for the eight years that followed: I often felt steadiest when things were going to hell. Iowa may have convinced me and my team that I could end up being president. But it was the New Hampshire loss that made us confident I'd be up to the job.

I've often been asked about this personality trait—

my ability to maintain composure in the middle of crisis. Sometimes I'll say that it's just a matter of temperament, or a consequence of being raised in Hawaii, since it's hard to get stressed when it's eighty degrees and sunny and you're five minutes from the beach. If I'm talking to a group of young people, I'll describe how over time I've trained myself to take the long view, about how important it is to stay focused on your goals rather than getting hung up on the daily ups and downs.

There's truth in all of this. But there's another factor at play. In tough spots, I tend to channel my grandmother.

She was eighty-five years old then, the last survivor of the trio who raised me. Her health was declining; cancer had spread through a body already ravaged by osteoporosis and a lifetime of bad habits. But her mind was still sharp, and because she was no longer able to fly and I'd missed our annual Christmas trip to Hawaii due to the demands of the campaign, I had taken to calling her every few weeks just to check in.

I placed such a call after New Hampshire. As usual, the conversation didn't last long; Toot considered long-distance calls an extravagance. She shared news from the Islands, and I told her about her great-granddaughters and their latest mischief. My sister Maya, who lived in Hawaii, reported that Toot watched every twist and turn of the campaign on cable TV, but she never brought it up with me. In the wake of my loss, she had just one piece of advice.

"You need to eat something, Bar. You look too skinny."

This was characteristic of Madelyn Payne Dunham, born in Peru, Kansas, in 1922. She was a child of the

Depression, the daughter of a schoolteacher and a book-keeper at a small oil refinery, themselves the children of farmers and homesteaders. These were sensible people who worked hard, went to church, paid their bills, and remained suspicious of bombast, public displays of emotion, or foolishness of any sort.

In her youth, my grandmother had pushed against these small-town constraints, most notably by marrying my grandfather Stanley Armour Dunham, who was prone to all the questionable qualities mentioned above. Together they'd had their fair share of adventures, during the war and after, but by the time I was born, all that remained of Toot's rebellious streak was her smoking, drinking, and taste for lurid thrillers. At the Bank of Hawaii, Toot had managed to rise from an entry-level clerical position to become one of its first female vice presidents, and by all accounts she'd been excellent at her job. For twenty-five years, there would be no fuss, no mistakes, and no complaints, even when she saw younger men that she'd trained promoted ahead of her.

After Toot retired, I sometimes ran into people back in Hawaii who told stories of how she'd helped them—a man insisting he'd have lost his company without her intervention, or a woman recalling how Toot waived an arcane bank policy requiring an estranged husband's signature to secure a loan for the real estate agency she was starting. If you asked Toot about any of these things, though, she'd maintain that she'd started working at the bank not because of any particular passion for finance or wish to help others, but because our family needed the money, and that's what had been available to her.

"Sometimes," she told me, "you just do what needs to be done."

It wasn't until I was a teenager that I understood just how far my grandmother's life had strayed from the path she'd once imagined; how much of herself she had sacrificed, first for her husband, then for her daughter, then for her grandchildren. It struck me as quietly tragic, how cramped her world seemed.

And yet even then it wasn't lost on me that it was because of Toot's willingness to carry the load in front of her—waking before sunup every day to stuff herself into a business suit and heels and take the bus to her downtown office, working all day on escrow documents before coming home too tired to do much else—that she and Gramps were able to retire comfortably, travel, and maintain their independence. The stability she provided allowed my mother to pursue a career she enjoyed, despite its sporadic pay and overseas postings, and was why Maya and I had been able to go to a private school and fancy colleges.

Toot showed me how to balance a checkbook and resist buying stuff I didn't need. She was the reason why, even in my most revolutionary moments as a young man, I could admire a well-run business and read the financial pages, and why I felt compelled to disregard overly broad claims about the need to tear things up and remake society from whole cloth. She taught me the value of working hard and doing your best even when the work was unpleasant, and about fulfilling your responsibilities even when doing so was inconvenient. She taught me to marry passion with reason, to not get overly excited when life was going well, and to not get too down when it went badly.

All this was instilled in me by an elderly, plainspoken white lady from Kansas. It was her perspective that often came to mind when I was campaigning, and her worldview that I sensed in many of the voters I encountered, whether in rural Iowa or in a Black neighborhood in Chicago, that same quiet pride in sacrifices made for children and grandchildren, the same lack of pretension, the same modesty of expectations.

And because Toot possessed both the remarkable strengths and stubborn limitations of her upbringing— because she loved me fiercely and would literally do anything to help me, and yet never fully shed the cautious conservatism that had made her quietly agonize the first time my mother brought my father, a Black man, home for dinner—she also taught me the tangled, multifaceted truth of race relations in our country.

"THERE IS NOT a Black America and a white America and a Latino America and an Asian America. There's the United States of America."

It was probably the line most remembered from my 2004 convention speech. I'd intended it more as a statement of aspiration than a description of reality, but it was an aspiration I believed in and a reality I strove for. The idea that our common humanity mattered more than our differences was stitched into my DNA. It also described what I felt was a practical view of politics: In a democracy, you needed a majority to make big change, and in America that meant building coalitions across racial and ethnic lines.

Certainly that had been true for me in Iowa, where African Americans constituted less than 3 percent of the population. Day to day, our campaign didn't consider this an obstacle, just a fact of life. Our organizers encountered pockets of racial animosity, at times voiced openly even by potential supporters ("Yeah, I'm thinking about voting for the nigger" was heard more than once). Every so often, though, the hostility went beyond a rude remark or a slammed door. One of our most beloved supporters had woken up the day before Christmas to find her yard strewn with torn-up OBAMA signs, her house vandalized and spray-painted with racial epithets. Obtuseness, rather than meanness, was more common, with our volunteers fielding the kinds of remarks that are familiar to any Black person who's spent time in a largely white setting, a variation on the theme of "I don't think of him as being Black, really. . . . I mean, he's so intelligent."

For the most part, though, I found white voters across Iowa to be much like those I had courted just a few years earlier in downstate Illinois—friendly, thoughtful, and open to my candidacy, concerned less about my skin color or even my Muslim-sounding name than they were about my youth and lack of experience, my plans to create jobs or end the war in Iraq.

As far as my political advisors were concerned, our job was to keep it that way. It wasn't that we ducked racial issues. Our website made my position clear on hot-button topics like immigration reform and civil rights. If asked in a town hall, I wouldn't hesitate to explain the realities of racial profiling or job discrimination to a rural, all-white audience. Inside the campaign, Plouffe and Axe listened to the concerns of Black and Latino team members, whether someone wanted to tweak a television ad ("Can we include at least one Black face other than Barack's?" Valerie gently asked at one point) or was reminding us to work harder to recruit more senior staff of color. (On this score, at least, the world of experienced, high-level political operatives wasn't so different from that of other professions, in that young people of color consistently had less access to mentors and networks—and couldn't afford to accept the unpaid internships that might put them on the fast track to run national campaigns. This was one thing I was determined to help change.) But Plouffe, Axe, and Gibbs made no apologies for de-emphasizing any topic that might be labeled a racial grievance, or split the electorate along racial lines, or do anything that would box me in as "the Black candidate." To them, the immediate formula for racial progress was simple—we needed to win. And this meant gaining support not just from liberal white college kids but also from voters for whom the image of me in the White House involved a big psychological leap.

"Trust me," Gibbs would wisecrack, "whatever else they know about you, people have noticed that you don't look like the first forty-two presidents."

Meanwhile, I'd felt no shortage of love from African Americans since my election to the U.S. Senate. Local NAACP chapters got in touch, wanting to give me awards. My photo regularly showed up in the pages of **Ebony** and **Jet**. Every Black woman of a certain age told me I reminded her of her son. And the love for Michelle was at a whole other level. With her professional credentials, sister-friend demeanor, and no-nonsense devotion to motherhood, she seemed to distill what so many Black families worked toward and hoped for their children.

Despite all this, Black attitudes toward my candidacy

were complicated—driven in no small part by fear. Nothing in Black people's experience told them that it might be possible for one of their own to win a major party nomination, much less the presidency of the United States. In the minds of many, what Michelle and I had accomplished was already something of a miracle. To aspire beyond that seemed foolish, a flight too close to the sun.

"I'm telling you, man," Marty Nesbitt said to me shortly after I announced my candidacy, "my mother worries about you the same way she used to worry about me." A successful entrepreneur, a former high school football star with the good looks of a young Jackie Robinson, married to a brilliant doctor and with five wonderful kids, Marty seemed the embodiment of the American Dream. He'd been raised by a single mom who worked as a nurse in Columbus, Ohio; it was only as a result of a special program designed to get more young people of color into prep schools and on to college that Marty had climbed the ladder out of his neighborhood, a place where most Black men could hope for little more than a lifetime on the assembly line. But when after college he decided to leave a stable job at General Motors for a riskier venture into real estate investments, his mother had fretted, afraid he might lose everything by reaching too far.

"She thought I was crazy to give up that kind of security," Marty told me. "So imagine how my mom and her friends are feeling about you right now. Not just **running** for president, but actually believing you can **be** president!"

This mindset wasn't restricted to the working class.

Valerie's mother—whose family had epitomized the Black professional elite of the forties and fifties—was the wife of a doctor and one of the guiding lights in the early childhood education movement. But she expressed the same skepticism toward my campaign at the start.

"She wants to protect you," Valerie said.

"From what?" I asked.

"From disappointment," she said, leaving unspoken her mother's more specific fear that I might get myself killed.

We heard it again and again, especially during the first months of the campaign—a protective pessimism, a sense in the Black community that Hillary was a safer choice. With national figures like Jesse Jackson, Jr. (and a more grudging Jesse Sr.), behind us, we were able to get a good number of early endorsements from African American leaders, especially from younger ones. But many more chose to wait and see how I fared, and other Black politicians, businesspeople, and pastors—whether out of genuine loyalty toward the Clintons or an eagerness to back the prohibitive favorite—came out for Hillary before I'd even had a chance to make my case.

"The country's not ready yet," one congressman told me, "and the Clintons have a long memory."

Meanwhile, there were activists and intellectuals who supported me but viewed my campaign in purely symbolic terms, akin to earlier races mounted by Shirley Chisholm, Jesse Jackson, and Al Sharpton, a useful if transitory platform from which to raise a prophetic voice against racial injustice. Unconvinced that victory was possible, they expected me to take the most uncompromising positions on everything from affirmative action to reparations and were continually on alert for any hints that I might be spending too much time and energy courting middle-of-the-road, less progressive white folks.

"Don't be one of those so-called leaders who take the Black vote for granted," a supporter told me. I was sensitive to the criticism, for it wasn't entirely wrong. A lot of Democratic politicians did take Black voters for granted—at least since 1968, when Richard Nixon had determined that a politics of white racial resentment was the surest path to Republican victory, and thereby left Black voters with nowhere else to go. It was not only white Democrats who made this calculation. There wasn't a Black elected official who relied on white votes to stay in office who wasn't aware of what Axe, Plouffe, and Gibbs were at least implicitly warning against—that too much focus on civil rights, police misconduct, or other issues considered specific to Black people risked triggering suspicion, if not a backlash, from the broader electorate. You might decide to speak up anyway, as a matter of conscience, but you understood there'd be a price—that Blacks could practice the standard special-interest politics of farmers, gun enthusiasts, or other ethnic groups only at their own peril.

Of course, that was part of the reason I was running, wasn't it—to help us break free of such constraints? To reimagine what was possible? I wanted to be neither a supplicant, always on the periphery of power and seeking favor from liberal benefactors, nor a permanent protester, full of righteous anger as we waited for white America to expiate its guilt. Both paths were well trodden; both, at some fundamental level, were born of despair.

No, the point was to win. I wanted to prove to Blacks,

to whites—to Americans of all colors—that we could transcend the old logic, that we could rally a working majority around a progressive agenda, that we could place issues like inequality or lack of educational opportunity at the very center of the national debate and then actually deliver the goods.

I knew that in order to accomplish that, I needed to use language that spoke to all Americans and propose policies that touched everyone—a topflight education for **every** child, quality healthcare for **every** American. I needed to embrace white people as allies rather than impediments to change, and to couch the African American struggle in terms of a broader struggle for a fair, just, and generous society.

I understood the risks. I heard the muted criticisms that came my way from not just rivals but friends. How an emphasis on universal programs often meant benefits were less directly targeted to those most in need. How appealing to common interests discounted the continuing effects of discrimination and allowed whites to avoid taking the full measure of the legacy of slavery, Jim Crow, and their own racial attitudes. How this left Black people with a psychic burden, expected as they were to constantly swallow legitimate anger and frustration in the name of some far-off ideal.

It was a lot to ask of Black folks, requiring a mixture of optimism and strategic patience. As I tried to lead voters and my own campaign through this uncharted territory, I was constantly reminded that this wasn't an abstract exercise. I was bound to specific communities of flesh and blood, filled with men and women who had their own imperatives and their own personal histories—including a pastor who seemed to embody all the contradictory impulses I was attempting to corral.

I FIRST MET Reverend Jeremiah A. Wright, Jr., during my organizing days. His church, Trinity United Church of Christ, was one of the largest in Chicago. The son of a Baptist minister and a school administrator from Philadelphia, he had grown up steeped in Black church tradition while also attending the most prestigious—and largely white—schools in the city. Rather than go straight into the ministry, he left college to join the Marines and then the U.S. Navy, training as a cardiopulmonary technician and serving as part of the medical team caring for Lyndon Johnson after his 1966 surgery. In 1967, he enrolled at Howard University and, like many Blacks during those turbulent years, soaked up the forceful rhetoric of Black Power, an interest in all things African, and leftist critiques of the American social order. By the time he graduated from seminary, he'd also absorbed the Black liberation theology of James Cone—a view of Christianity that asserted the centrality of the Black experience, not because of any inherent racial superiority but because, Cone claimed, God sees the world through the eyes of those most oppressed.

That Reverend Wright came to pastor in an overwhelmingly white denomination gives some indication of his practical side; not only did the United Church of Christ value serious scholarship—something he emphasized every Sunday—but it had the money and infrastructure to help him build his congregation. What was once a staid church with fewer than one hundred members grew to six thousand during his tenure, a rollicking, bustling place containing the multitudes that make up Black Chicago: bankers and former gang members, kente robes and Brooks Brothers suits, a choir that could rock classic gospel and the "Hallelujah Chorus" in a single service. His sermons were full of pop references, slang, humor, and genuine religious insight that not only prompted cheers and shouts from his members but burnished his reputation as one of the best preachers in the country.

There were times when I found Reverend Wright's sermons a little over the top. In the middle of a scholarly explication of the Book of Matthew or Luke, he might insert a scathing critique of America's drug war, American militarism, capitalist greed, or the intractability of American racism, rants that were usually grounded in fact but bereft of context. Often, they sounded dated, as if he were channeling a college teach-in from 1968 rather than leading a prosperous congregation that included police commanders, celebrities, wealthy businesspeople, and the Chicago school superintendent. And every so often, what he said was just wrong, edging close to the conspiracy theories one heard on late-night public-access stations or in the barbershop down the street. It was as if this erudite, middle-aged, light-skinned Black man were straining for street cred, trying to "keep it real." Or maybe he just recognized—both within his congregation and within himself—the periodic need to let loose, to release pent-up anger from a lifetime of struggle in the face of chronic racism, reason and logic be damned.

All this I knew. And yet for me, especially when I was a young man still sorting out my beliefs and my place inside Chicago's Black community, the good in Reverend Wright more than outweighed his flaws, just as my admiration for the congregation and its ministries outweighed my broader skepticism toward organized religion. Michelle and I eventually joined Trinity as members, though we proved to be spotty churchgoers. Like me, Michelle hadn't been raised in a particularly religious household, and what started as once-a-month attendance became less frequent over time. When we did go, though, it was meaningful, and as my political career took off, I made a point of inviting Reverend Wright to do an invocation or a benediction at key events.

This had been the plan for the day I announced my candidacy. Reverend Wright was to lead the assembled crowd in a prayer before I appeared onstage. On my way down to Springfield a day ahead of the event, though, I had received an urgent call from Axe, asking if I'd seen a **Rolling Stone** article that had just been published about my candidacy. Evidently the reporter had sat in on a recent service at Trinity, absorbing a fiery sermon from Reverend Wright and quoting it in his story.

"He's quoted saying . . . hold on, let me read this: 'We believe in white supremacy and black inferiority and believe it more than we believe in God.'"

"Seriously?"

"I think it's fair to say that if he gives the invocation tomorrow, he'll be the lead story . . . at least on Fox News."

The article itself offered a generally fair view of Jeremiah Wright and Trinity's ministry, and I wasn't surprised that my pastor would point out the gap between America's professed Christian ideals and its brutal racial history. Still, the language he'd used was more incendiary than anything I'd heard before, and although a part of me was frustrated with the constant need to soften for white folks' benefit the blunt truths about race in this country, as a matter of practical politics I knew Axe was right.

That afternoon, I called Reverend Wright and asked if he'd be willing to skip the public invocation and instead offer Michelle and me a private prayer before my speech. I could tell he was hurt, but ultimately—and to my team's great relief—he went along with the new plan.

For me the episode churned up all the doubts I still had about running for the highest office in the land. It was one thing to have integrated my own life—to learn over time how to move seamlessly between Black and white circles, to serve as translator and bridge among family, friends, acquaintances, and colleagues, making connections across an ever-expanding orbit, until I felt I could finally know the world of my grandparents and the world of a Reverend Wright as a single, unified whole. But to explain those connections to millions of strangers? To imagine that a presidential campaign, with all its noise and distortions and simplifications, could some-how cut through hurt and fear and suspicion that had been four hundred years in the making? The reality of American race relations was too complicated to reduce to a sound bite. Hell, I myself was too complicated, the contours of my life too messy and unfamiliar to the aver-age American, for me to honestly expect I could pull this thing off.

MAYBE IF THE Rolling Stone article had come out earlier, foreshadowing problems to come, I would have decided not to run. It's hard to say. I do know that—in a bit of irony, or perhaps providence—it was another pastor and close friend of Reverend Wright's, Dr. Otis Moss, Jr., who helped me push through my doubts.

Otis Moss was a veteran of the civil rights movement, a close friend and associate of Dr. King's, the pastor of one of the largest churches in Cleveland, Ohio, and a former advisor to President Jimmy Carter. I didn't know him well, but after the article was published he called me one evening to offer support. He had gotten wind of the difficulties with Jeremiah, he said, and heard those voices within the Black community arguing that I wasn't ready, or I was too radical, or too mainstream, or not quite Black enough. He expected the path would only get harder but urged me not to get discouraged.

"Every generation is limited by what it knows," Dr. Moss told me. "Those of us who were part of the movement, giants like Martin, lieutenants and foot soldiers like me . . . we are the Moses generation. We marched, we sat in, we went to jail, sometimes in defiance of our elders, but we were in fact building on what they had done. We got us out of Egypt, you could say. But we could only travel so far.

"You, Barack, are part of the Joshua generation. You and others like you are responsible for the next leg of the journey. Folks like me can offer the wisdom of our experience. Perhaps you can learn from some of our mistakes. But ultimately it will be up to you, with God's help, to build on what we've done, and lead our people and this country out of the wilderness."

It's hard to overstate how these words fortified me, coming as they did almost a year before our Iowa victory; what it meant to have someone so intimately linked to the source of my earliest inspiration say that what I was trying to do was worth it, that it wasn't just an exercise in vanity or ambition but rather a part of an unbroken chain of progress. More practically, it was thanks to the willingness of Dr. Moss and other former colleagues of Dr. King's—like Reverend C. T. Vivian of Atlanta and Reverend Joseph Lowery of the Southern Christian Leadership Conference—to lay their proverbial hands on me, vouching for me as an extension of their historic work, that more Black leaders didn't swing early into Hillary's camp.

Nowhere was this more evident than in March 2007, when I attended the march across the Edmund Pettus Bridge in Selma, Alabama, that Congressman John Lewis hosted each year. I'd long wanted to make the pilgrimage to the site of Bloody Sunday, which in 1965 became a crucible of the battle for civil rights, when Americans fully realized what was at stake. But my visit promised to be complicated. The Clintons would be there, I was told; and before participants gathered to cross the bridge, Hillary and I were scheduled to speak simultaneously at dueling church services.

Not only that, but our host, John Lewis, had indicated that he was inclined to endorse Hillary. John had become a good friend—he'd taken great pride in my election to the Senate, rightly seeing it as part of his legacy—and I knew he was tortured by the decision. As I listened to him explain his reasoning over the phone, how long he had known the Clintons, how Bill's administration had supported many of his legislative priorities, I chose not to press him too hard. I could imagine the pressure this kind and gentle man was under, and I also recognized that, at a time when I was asking white voters to judge me on the merits, a raw appeal to racial solidarity would feel like hypocrisy.

The Selma commemoration could have turned into an uncomfortable political spectacle, but when I arrived, I immediately felt at ease. Perhaps it was being in a place that had played such a large role in my imagination and the trajectory of my life. Perhaps it was the response of ordinary people who'd gathered to mark the occasion, shaking my hand or giving me a hug, some sporting Hillary buttons but saying they were glad I was there. But mostly it was the fact that a group of respected elders had my back. When I entered the historic Brown Chapel AME Church for the service, I learned that Reverend Lowery had asked to say a few words before I was introduced. He was well into his eighties by then but had lost none of his wit and charisma.

"Let me tell you," he began, "some crazy things are happening out there. People say certain things ain't happening, but who can tell? Who can tell?"

"Preach now, Reverend," someone shouted from the audience.

"You know, recently I went to the doctor and he said my cholesterol was a little high. But then he explained to me that there's two kinds of cholesterol. There's the bad cholesterol, and then there's the good cholesterol. Having good cholesterol—that's all right. And that got me thinking how there's a lot of things like that. I mean, when we started the movement, a lot of folks thought **we** were crazy. Ain't that right, C.T.?" Reverend Lowery nodded in the direction of Reverend Vivian, who was sitting onstage. "That there's another **crazy Negro** . . . and he'll tell you that everybody in the movement was a little crazy . . ."

The crowd laughed heartily.

"But like cholesterol," he continued, "there's **good** crazy and **bad** crazy, see? Harriet Tubman with the Underground Railroad, she was as crazy as she could be! And Paul, when he preached to Agrippa, Agrippa said, 'Paul, you crazy' . . . but it was a **good** crazy."

The crowd began to clap and cheer as Reverend Lowery brought it home.

"And I say to you today that we need more folks in this country who are a good crazy. . . . You can't tell what will happen when you get folks with some good crazy . . . going to the polls to vote!"

The churchgoers rose to their feet, and the pastors sitting next to me onstage chortled and clapped me on the back; and by the time I got up to speak, taking the words Dr. Moss had offered me as a point of departure—about the legacy of the Moses generation and how it had made my life possible, about the responsibility of the Joshua generation to take the next steps required for justice in this nation and around the world, not just for Black people but for all those who had been dispossessed—the church was in full revival mode.

Outside, after the service was done, I saw another colleague of Dr. King's, Reverend Fred Shuttlesworth, a legendary and fearless freedom fighter who had survived the Klan bombing his house and a white mob beating him with clubs, chains, and brass knuckles, and stabbing his wife as they attempted to enroll their two daughters in a previously all-white Birmingham school. He had recently been treated for a brain tumor, leaving him frail, but he motioned me over to his wheelchair to talk, and as the marchers gathered, I offered to push him across the bridge.

"I'd like that just fine," Reverend Shuttlesworth said.

And so we went, the morning sky a glorious blue, crossing the bridge over a muddy brown river, voices rising sporadically in song and prayer. With each step, I imagined how these now elderly men and women must have felt forty-some years earlier, their young hearts beating furiously as they faced down a phalanx of armed men on horseback. I was reminded of just how slight my burdens were in comparison. The fact that they were still engaged in the fight and, despite setbacks and sorrow, hadn't succumbed to bitterness showed me that I had no cause to be tired. I felt renewed in my conviction that I was where I was supposed to be and doing what needed to be done, that Reverend Lowery might be right in saying there was some kind of "good crazy" in the air.

TEN MONTHS LATER, as the campaign shifted to South Carolina during the second and third weeks of January, I knew that our faith would again be tested. We badly needed a win. On paper, the state looked good for us: African Americans made up a large percentage of Democratic primary voters, and we had a great mix of veteran politicians and young activists, both white and Black, in our corner. But polls showed our support among white voters lagging, and we didn't know whether African American voters would turn out in the numbers we needed. Our hope was to move toward Super Tuesday with a win that didn't break down strictly along racial lines. But if the Iowa effort had displayed the possibilities of a more idealistic kind of politics, the campaign in South Carolina ended up being decidedly different. It became a brawl, an exercise in old-style politics, set against a landscape heavy with memories of a bitter, bloody racial history.

Some of this was the result of the tight race, rising anxieties, and what seemed to be a sense within the Clinton camp that a negative campaign worked to their advantage. Their attacks, on the air and through surrogates, had taken on a sharper tone. With voters from around the country increasingly paying attention, all of us were aware of the stakes. Our one debate that week turned into an absolute slugfest between me and Hillary, with John Edwards (whose campaign was on its last legs and who would soon drop out) rendered a spectator as Hillary and I went after each other like gladiators in the ring.

Afterward, Hillary left the state to campaign elsewhere, but the intensity hardly let up, the campaigning on their side now left to a feisty, energized, and omnipresent William Jefferson Clinton.

I sympathized with the position Bill was in: Not only was his wife under constant scrutiny and attack, but my promise to change Washington and transcend partisan gridlock must have felt like a challenge to his own legacy. No doubt I'd reinforced that perception when, in a Nevada interview, I said that while I admired Bill Clinton, I didn't think he'd transformed politics the way Ronald Reagan had in the 1980s, when he'd managed to reframe the American people's relationship to government on behalf of conservative principles. After all the obstructionism and sheer venom that Clinton had had to contend with throughout his presidency, I could hardly fault him for wanting to knock a cocky young newcomer down a peg or two.

Clinton clearly relished being back in the arena. A larger-than-life figure, he traveled across the state offering astute observations and emanating folksy charm. His attacks on me were for the most part well within bounds, the same points I'd have made if I'd been in his shoes—that I lacked experience and that if I did manage to win the presidency, Republicans in Congress would have me for lunch.

Beyond that, though, lay the politics of race, something that Clinton had navigated deftly in the past but proved trickier against a credible Black candidate. When he'd suggested ahead of the New Hampshire primary that some of my positions on the Iraq War were a "fairy tale," there were Black folks who heard it as a suggestion that the notion of me as president was a fairy tale, which led Congressman Jim Clyburn, the majority whip—South Carolina's most powerful Black official and someone who until then had maintained a careful neutrality—to publicly rebuke him. When Clinton told white audiences that Hillary "gets you" in ways that her opponents did not, Gibbs—himself a son of the South—heard echoes of Republican strategist Lee Atwater and dog-whistle politics and had no qualms about deploying some of our supporters to say so.

Looking back, I don't know that any of this was fair; Bill Clinton certainly didn't think so. But it was hard in South Carolina to distinguish what was true from what was felt. All across the state, I was met with great warmth and hospitality from Blacks and whites alike. In cities like Charleston, I experienced the much-touted New South—cosmopolitan, diverse, and bustling with commerce. Moreover, as someone who had made Chicago his home, I hardly needed reminding that racial division wasn't unique to the South.

Still, as I traveled through South Carolina making my case for the presidency, racial attitudes seemed less coded, blunter—sometimes not hidden at all. How was I to interpret the well-dressed white woman in a diner I visited, grimly unwilling to shake my hand? How was I to understand the motives of those hoisting signs outside one of our campaign events, sporting the Confederate flag and NRA slogans, yelling about states' rights and telling me to go home?

It wasn't just shouted words or Confederate statues that evoked the legacy of slavery and segregation. At the suggestion of Congressman Clyburn, I visited J. V. Martin Junior High School, a largely Black public school in the rural town of Dillon in the northeastern section of the state. Part of the building had been constructed in 1896, just thirty years after the Civil War, and if repairs had been made over the decades, you couldn't tell. Crumbling walls. Busted plumbing. Cracked windows. Dank, unlit halls. A coal furnace in the basement still used to heat the building. Leaving the school, I alternated between feeling downcast and freshly motivated: What message had generations of boys and girls received as they arrived at this school each day except for the certainty that, to those in power, they did not matter; that whatever was meant by the American Dream, it wasn't meant for them?

Moments like this helped me see the wearying effects of long-term disenfranchisement, the jaded filter through which many Black South Carolinians absorbed our campaign. I began to understand the true nature of my adversary. I wasn't running against Hillary Clinton or John Edwards or even the Republicans. I was running against the implacable weight of the past; the inertia, fatalism, and fear it produced.

Black ministers and power brokers who were accustomed to getting payments to turn out voters complained about our emphasis on recruiting grassroots volunteers instead. For them, politics was less about principles and more a simple business proposition, the way things had always been done. While campaigning, Michelle—whose great-great-grandfather had been born into slavery on a South Carolina rice plantation—would hear well-meaning Black women suggesting that losing an election might be better than losing a husband, the implication being that if I was elected, I was sure to be shot.

Hope and change were a luxury, folks seemed to be telling us, exotic imports that would wilt in the heat.

ON JANUARY 25, the eve of the primary, NBC released a poll that showed my support among white South Carolinians had fallen to a paltry 10 percent. The news set the pundits spinning. It was to be expected, they intoned; even high African American turnout couldn't make up for deep-seated white resistance to any Black candidate, much less one named Barack Hussein Obama.

Axelrod, always in catastrophe mode, relayed this to me while scrolling through his BlackBerry. He added, unhelpfully, that if we lost South Carolina, our campaign would likely be over. Even more unhelpfully, he went on to say that even if we eked out a win, the paucity of white support would lead both the press and the Clintons to discount the victory and reasonably question my viability in a general election.

Our entire team was on pins and needles on primary day, aware of all that was on the line. But when evening finally arrived and the returns started rolling in, the results exceeded our most optimistic projections. We beat Hillary by a two-to-one margin, with nearly 80 percent of a massive Black turnout and 24 percent of the white vote. We even won by ten points among white voters under forty. Given the gauntlet we'd run and the hits we'd taken since Iowa, we were jubilant.

As I walked onstage in an auditorium in Columbia to give our victory speech, I could feel the pulse of stomping feet and clapping hands. Several thousand people had packed themselves into the venue, though under the glare of television lights, I could see only the first few rows—college students mostly, white and Black in equal measure, some with their arms interlocked or draped over one another's shoulders, their faces beaming with joy and purpose.

"Race doesn't matter!" people were chanting. "Race doesn't matter! Race doesn't matter!"

I spotted some of our young organizers and volunteers mixed in with the crowd. Once again, they'd come through, despite the naysayers. They deserved a victory lap, I thought to myself, a moment of pure elation. Which is why, even as I quieted the crowd and dove into my speech, I didn't have the heart to correct those well-meaning chanters—to remind them that in the year 2008, with the Confederate flag and all it stood for still hanging in front of a state capitol just a few blocks away, race still mattered plenty, as much as they might want to believe otherwise.

CHAPTER 7

WITH SOUTH CAROLINA BEHIND US, things once again seemed to start breaking our way. In a **New York Times** op-ed on January 27, Caroline Kennedy announced her support for me, generously suggesting that our campaign had made her understand, for the first time, the inspiration young Americans had once drawn from her father. Her uncle, Ted Kennedy, followed suit the next day, joining me for an appearance before several thousand students at American University. Teddy was absolutely electric, summoning all the old Camelot magic, batting down the argument of inexperience once used against his brother and now directed toward me. Axe would call it a symbolic passing of the torch, and I could see what it meant to him. It was as if, in our campaign, Teddy recognized a familiar chord, and was reaching back to a time before his brothers' assassinations, Vietnam, white backlash, riots, Watergate, plant closings, Altamont, and AIDS, back to when liberalism brimmed with optimism and a can-do spirit—the same spirit that had shaped my mother's sensibilities as a young woman, and that she had funneled into me.

The Kennedy endorsement added poetry to our campaign and helped set us up for Super Tuesday, on

February 5, when more than half the nation's delegates would be determined in a single day. We'd always known that Super Tuesday would present an enormous challenge; even with our wins in Iowa and South Carolina, Hillary remained far better known, and the face-to-face retail campaigning we'd done in the early states was simply not possible in bigger, more densely populated places like California and New York.

What we did have, though, was a grassroots infantry that expanded by the day. With the help of our veteran delegate expert, Jeff Berman, and our tenacious field director, Jon Carson, Plouffe developed a strategy that we would execute with the same single-minded focus that we'd applied to Iowa. Rather than trying to win the big primary states and spend heavily on TV ads there just to mitigate our losses, we instead focused my time and our field efforts on the caucus states—many of them small, rural, and overwhelmingly white—where the enthusiasm of our supporters could produce relatively large turnouts and lopsided victories, which would translate to big delegate hauls.

Idaho was a case in point. It hadn't made sense for us to send paid staff to such a tiny, solidly Republican state, but a determined band of volunteers called Idahoans for Obama had organized themselves. They'd spent the past year using social media tools like MySpace and Meetup to build a community, getting to know my positions on issues, creating personal fundraising pages, planning events, and strategically canvassing the state. When, a few days before Super Tuesday, Plouffe told me that I was scheduled to campaign in Boise instead of putting in an extra day in California—where we were rapidly making up ground—I confess that I had my doubts. But a Boise State arena filled with fourteen thousand cheering Idahoans quickly cured me of any skepticism. We ended up winning Idaho by such a large margin that we gained more delegates there than Hillary got from winning New Jersey, a state with more than five times the population.

This became the pattern. Thirteen of the twenty-two Super Tuesday contests went our way; and while Hillary won New York and California by a few percentage points each, overall we netted thirteen more delegates than she did. It was a remarkable achievement, a testament to the skill and resourcefulness of Plouffe, our field staff, and most of all our volunteers. And given the questions that both pundits and the Clinton campaign continued to raise about my potential appeal in a general election, I took extra satisfaction in having run the table across the so-called red part of the country.

What struck me as well was the growing role that technology played in our victories. The extraordinary youth of my team allowed us to embrace and refine the digital networks that Howard Dean's campaign had set in motion four years earlier. Our status as upstarts forced us to trust, again and again, the energy and creativity of our internet-savvy volunteers. Millions of small donors were helping to fuel our operation, emailed links helped to spread our campaign messaging in ways that Big Media couldn't, and new communities were forming among people who'd previously been isolated from one another. Coming out of Super Tuesday, I was inspired, imagining that I was glimpsing the future, a resurgence of bottom-up participation that could make our democracy work again.

What I couldn't fully appreciate yet was just how malleable this technology would prove to be; how quickly it would be absorbed by commercial interests and wielded by entrenched powers; how readily it could be used not to unify people but to distract or divide them; and how one day many of the same tools that had put me in the White House would be deployed in opposition to everything I stood for.

Such insights would come later. After Super Tuesday, we went on an absolute tear, winning eleven straight primaries and caucuses over the course of two weeks, by an average margin of 36 percent. It was a heady stretch, almost surreal, although the staff and I did our best not to get too far ahead of ourselves—"Remember New Hampshire!" was a common refrain—understanding that the battle would remain pitched, aware that there were still plenty of people out there who wanted to see us fail.

IN THE SOULS OF BLACK FOLK, the sociologist W.E.B. Du Bois describes the "double consciousness" of Black Americans at the dawn of the twentieth century. Despite having been born and raised on American soil, shaped by this nation's institutions and infused with its creed, despite the fact that their toiling hands and beating hearts contributed so much to the country's economy and culture—despite all this, Du Bois writes, Black Americans remain the perpetual "Other," always on the outside looking in, ever feeling their "two-ness," defined not by what they are but by what they can never be.

As a young man, I had learned a lot from Du Bois's writing. But whether because of my unique parentage and upbringing or because of the times in which I had come of age, this notion of "double consciousness" was not something I felt personally. I had wrestled with the meaning of my mixed-race status and the fact of racial discrimination. Yet at no point had I ever questioned—or had others question—my fundamental "American-ness."

Of course, I had never run for president before.

Even before I formally announced, Gibbs and our communications team had beaten back various rumors that bubbled up on conservative talk radio or fly-by-night websites before migrating to the **Drudge Report** and Fox News. There were reports that I had been schooled in an Indonesian madrassa, which gained enough traction that a CNN correspondent actually traveled to my old elementary school in Jakarta, where he found a bunch of kids wearing Western-style uniforms and listening to New Kids on the Block on their iPods. There were claims that I wasn't an American citizen (helpfully illustrated by a picture of me wearing an African outfit at my Kenyan half brother's wedding). As the campaign progressed, more lurid falsehoods were circulated. These had nothing to do with my nationality but everything to do with a "foreignness" of a more familiar, homegrown, dark-hued variety: that I had dealt drugs, that I had worked as a gay prostitute, that I had Marxist ties and had fathered multiple children out of wedlock.

It was hard to take any of this stuff seriously, and initially at least, not many people did—in 2008, the internet was still too slow, too spotty, and too removed from mainstream news operations to directly penetrate the minds of voters. But there were indirect, more genteel ways to question my affinities.

Following the terror attacks of 9/11, for example, I had taken to wearing an American flag lapel pin, feeling that it was one small way to express national solidarity in the face of enormous tragedy. Then, as the debate about Bush's war on terrorism and the Iraq invasion wore on— as I watched John Kerry get swift-boated and heard those who opposed the Iraq War have their patriotism questioned by the likes of Karl Rove, as I saw my colleagues wearing flag pins in the Senate blithely vote for budget cuts to funding for veterans' programs—I quietly set my own pin aside. It was less an act of protest and more a reminder to myself that the substance of patriotism mattered far more than the symbol. Nobody seemed to notice, especially since most of my fellow senators— including former navy POW John McCain—regularly sported flag-pin-less lapels.

So when back in October a local reporter in Iowa had asked me why I wasn't wearing a flag pin, I told the truth, saying that I didn't think the presence or absence of a token you could buy in a dime store measured one's love of country. Soon enough, conservative talking heads were hammering on the purported meaning of my bare lapel. **Obama hates the flag, Obama disrespects our troops.** Months later, they were still making an issue of it, which began to piss me off. Just why was it, I wanted to ask, that only my pin habits, and not those of any previous presidential candidates, had suddenly attracted so much attention? Not surprisingly, Gibbs discouraged me from any public venting.

"Why give them the satisfaction?" he counseled. "You're winning."

Fair enough. I was less easily persuaded, though, when I saw the same sort of innuendo directed toward my wife.

Since Iowa, Michelle had continued to light up the campaign trail. With the girls in school, we limited her appearances to tight races and her travel mostly to weekends, but wherever she went, she was funny and engaging, insightful and blunt. She talked about raising kids and trying to balance the demands of work and family. She described the values she'd been raised with—her father never missing a day of work despite his MS, her mother's deep attention to her education, the family never having had much money but always having plenty of love. It was Norman Rockwell, **Leave It to Beaver** stuff. My in-laws fully embodied the tastes and aspirations we tend to claim as uniquely American, and I didn't know anyone more mainstream than Michelle, whose favorite meal was a burger and fries, who liked to watch reruns of **The Andy Griffith Show,** and who relished any chance to pass a Saturday afternoon shopping at the mall.

And yet, at least according to some commentators, Michelle was . . . different, not First Lady material. She seemed "angry," they said. One Fox News segment described her as "Obama's Baby Mama." It wasn't just conservative media either. **New York Times** columnist Maureen Dowd wrote a column suggesting that when Michelle painted a teasing portrait of me in her speeches as a hapless dad who let bread go stale in the kitchen and left dirty laundry lying around (reliably getting an appreciative laugh from her audience), she wasn't humanizing me but rather "emasculating" me, hurting my chances at being elected.

This sort of commentary was infrequent, and some on our staff considered it on par with the usual nastiness of campaigns. But that's not how Michelle experienced it. She understood that alongside the straitjacket that political wives were supposed to stay in (the adoring and compliant helpmeet, charming but not too opinionated; the same straitjacket that Hillary had once rejected, a choice she continued to pay dearly for), there was an extra set of stereotypes applied to Black women, familiar tropes that Black girls steadily absorbed like toxins from the day they first saw a blond Barbie doll or poured Aunt Jemima syrup on their pancakes. That they didn't meet the prescribed standards of femininity, that their butts were too big and their hair too nappy, that they were too loud or hot-tempered or cutting toward their men—that they were not just "emasculating" but masculine.

Michelle had managed this psychic burden all her life, largely by being meticulous about her appearance, maintaining control of herself and her environment, and preparing assiduously for everything, even as she refused to be cowed into becoming someone she wasn't. That she had emerged whole, with so much grace and dignity, just as so many Black women had succeeded in the face of so many negative messages, was amazing.

Of course, it was the nature of presidential campaigns that control would occasionally slip. For Michelle, it happened right before the Wisconsin primary, when, during the course of a speech in which she described being awed by how many people were energized by our campaign, she said, "For the first time in my adult life-time, I'm really proud of my country . . . because I think people are hungry for change."

It was a textbook gaffe—a few ad-libbed words that could then be diced, clipped, and weaponized by the conservative media—a garbled version of what she'd said many times before in her speeches about being proud of the direction our country was headed in, the promising surge in political participation. My team and I largely deserved the blame; we'd put Michelle on the road without the speechwriting, prep sessions, and briefers that I had at all times, the infrastructure that kept me organized and on point. It was like sending a civilian into live fire without a flak jacket.

No matter. Reporters pounced, speculating as to how much Michelle's comments might hurt the campaign, and how much it revealed about the Obamas' true feelings. I understood this to be part of a larger and uglier agenda out there, a slowly accruing, deliberately negative portrait of us built from stereotypes, stoked by fear, and meant to feed a general nervousness about the idea of a Black person making the country's most important decisions with his Black family in the White House. But I was less concerned about what all this meant for the campaign than I was pained by seeing how much it hurt Michelle; how it caused my strong, intelligent, and beautiful wife to doubt herself. Following the misstep in Wisconsin, she reminded me that she'd never had a desire to be in the spotlight and said that if her presence on the campaign trail hurt more than it helped, she would just as soon stay home. I assured her that the campaign would provide her better support, insisting that she was a far more compelling figure to voters than I would ever be. But nothing I said seemed to make her feel better.

· · ·

THROUGHOUT ALL THESE emotional ups and downs, our campaign continued to grow. By the time we entered Super Tuesday, the scale of our organization had mushroomed, a modest start-up transformed into a more secure and better-funded operation. The hotel rooms we stayed in were a bit roomier, our travel smoother. After starting out flying commercial, we'd later gone through our share of misadventures on cut-rate charter flights. One pilot landed us in the wrong city not once but twice. Another tried to jump-start the plane's battery with an extension cord plugged into a standard socket in the airport lounge. (I was grateful when the experiment failed, though it meant we then waited two hours for a battery to be trucked in from a neighboring town on a flatbed.) With a bigger budget, we were now able to lease our own plane, complete with a flight attendant, meals, and seats that actually reclined.

But new growth brought with it rules, protocols, process, and hierarchy. Our staff had grown to more than a thousand people nationwide, and while those on our senior team did their best to maintain the campaign's scrappy, informal culture, gone were the days when I could claim to know the majority of the people who worked for me. In the absence of such familiarity, fewer and fewer of the people I met in the course of a day addressed me as "Barack." I was "sir" now, or "Senator." When I entered the room, staff would often get up out of their seats to move elsewhere, assuming that I didn't want to be disturbed. If I insisted they stick around, they would smile shyly and speak only in a low murmur.

It made me feel old, and increasingly lonely.

In an odd way, so did the crowds at our rallies. They

had swelled to fifteen, twenty, or even thirty thousand strong at a stop, people wearing the red, white, and blue Obama campaign logo on shirts and hats and overalls, waiting for hours to get into whatever arena we'd found. Our team developed something of a pregame ritual. Reggie, Marvin, Gibbs, and I would jump out of the car at a service entrance or loading dock, then follow our advance team through corridors and back ways. Usually I'd meet with local organizers; take pictures with a hundred or so key volunteers and supporters, full of hugs, kisses, and small requests; and sign books, magazines, baseballs, birth announcements, military commissions, and just about anything else. Then there'd be an interview with a reporter or two; a quick lunch in a holding room that had been prestocked with bottled iced tea, trail mix, protein bars, and any other item that I had ever mentioned wanting, no matter how incidentally, in quantities adequate for a survivalist's bomb shelter; followed by a bathroom break, with either Marvin or Reggie handing me a gel to put on my forehead and nose so my skin wouldn't shine on television, though one of our videographers insisted it was a carcinogen.

I'd hear the buzz of the crowd growing louder as I walked under the stands or bleachers to the staging area. There'd be a cue to the sound engineer for the announcement ("the Voice of God," I learned it was called), I'd listen quietly backstage as a local person introduced me, and then would come the words "the next president of the United States," a deafening roar, the sound of U2's "City of Blinding Lights," and, after a quick fist bump or a "Go get 'em, boss," a walk through the curtain and onto the stage.

I did this two or three times a day, traveling from city to city, state to state. And though the novelty wore off quickly, the sheer energy of those rallies never stopped filling me with wonder. "Like a rock concert" is how reporters described it, and in terms of noise at least, that was accurate. But that wasn't how it felt while I was onstage. I wasn't offering the crowd a solo performance so much as trying to be a reflector, reminding Americans— through the stories they'd told me—of all that they truly cherished, and the formidable power that, joined together, they possessed.

Once my speech was over and I walked off the stage to shake hands along the rope line, I often found people screaming, pushing, and grabbing. Some would cry or touch my face, and despite my best efforts to discourage it, young parents would pass howling babies across rows of strangers for me to hold. The excitement was fun and at times deeply touching, but it was also a little unnerving. At some basic level people were no longer seeing me, I realized, with all my quirks and shortcomings. Instead, they had taken possession of my likeness and made it a vessel for a million different dreams. I knew a time would come when I would disappoint them, falling short of the image that my campaign and I had helped to construct.

I realized, too, that if supporters could mold bits and pieces of me into an outsized symbol of hope, then the vague fears of detractors could just as readily congeal into hate. And it was in response to this disturbing truth that I'd seen my life change the most.

I had been assigned Secret Service protection in May 2007, just a few months after my campaign began—given the code name "Renegade" and a round-the-clock security detail. This wasn't the norm. Unless you were a sitting vice president (or, in the case of Hillary, a former First Lady), candidates typically weren't assigned coverage until they'd all but secured the nomination. The reason my case was handled differently, the reason Harry Reid and Bennie Thompson, chair of the House Homeland Security Committee, had publicly insisted the Service move early, was straightforward: The number of threats directed my way exceeded anything the Secret Service had ever seen before.

The head of my personal detail, Jeff Gilbert, was an impressive guy. African American, bespectacled, with an open, friendly manner, he could have passed for an executive at a Fortune 100 company. In our first meeting, he emphasized his desire to make the transition as seamless as possible, understanding that as a candidate, I had to freely interact with the public.

Jeff proved true to his word: At no point did the Service ever prevent us from pulling off an event, and the agents did what they could to downplay their presence (using bales of hay rather than metal bike racks, for example, to create a barrier in front of an outdoor stage). The shift leaders, most in their forties, were professional and courteous, with dry senses of humor. Often, we'd sit in the back of the plane or on a bus ride and rib one another about our respective sports teams or talk about our kids. Jeff's son was a star offensive lineman at Florida, and we all began monitoring his prospects in the NFL draft. Meanwhile, Reggie and Marvin hit it off with the younger agents, going to the same watering holes after campaign business was done.

Still, to suddenly have armed men and women

hovering around me wherever I went, posted outside every room I occupied, was a shock to my system. My view of the outside world started to shift, obscured by the veil of security. I no longer walked through the front entrance of a building when a back stairwell was available. If I worked out in a hotel gym, agents first covered the windows with cloth to prevent a potential shooter from getting a sight line. Bulletproof barriers were placed inside any room I slept in, including our bedroom at home in Chicago. And I no longer had the option of driving myself anywhere, not even around the block.

As we moved closer to the nomination, my world shrank even further. More agents were added. My movements became more restricted. Spontaneity vanished entirely from my life. It was no longer possible, or at least not easy, for me to walk through a grocery store or have a casual chat with a stranger on the sidewalk.

"It's like a circus cage," I complained to Marvin one day, "and I'm the dancing bear."

There were times when I went stir-crazy, so fed up with the highly scheduled regimen of town halls, interviews, photo ops, and fundraising that I would up and take off, suddenly desperate to search for a good taco or to follow the sounds of some nearby outdoor concert, sending the agents scrambling to catch up, whispering "Renegade on the move" into their wrist mics.

"The bear is loose!" Reggie and Marvin would shout a little gleefully during such episodes.

But by the winter of 2008, these impromptu outings occurred less and less often. I knew that unpredictability made my detail's job harder and increased the risk to the agents. And anyway, the tacos didn't taste as good as I'd imagined when I was surrounded by a circle of anxious agents, not to mention the crowds and reporters that quickly assembled the moment I was recognized. When I had downtime, I found myself spending it more often in my room—reading, playing cards, quietly watching a ball game on TV.

To the relief of his keepers, the bear became accustomed to captivity.

BY THE END of February, we had built what looked like an insurmountable lead over Hillary in pledged delegates. It was around this time that Plouffe, always cautious in his assessments, called from Chicago to tell me what at some level I already knew.

"I think it's safe to say that if we play our cards right these next few weeks, you will be the Democratic nominee for president of the United States."

After we hung up, I sat alone, trying to take the measure of my emotions. There was pride, I suppose, the jolt of satisfaction a mountain climber must feel looking back at the jagged ground that's been covered below. Mostly, though, I felt a certain stillness, without elation or relief, sobered by the thought that the responsibilities of governance were no longer a distant possibility. Axe, Plouffe, and I found ourselves wrangling more frequently about our campaign platform, with me insisting that all our proposals withstand scrutiny—less because of the need to defend them during the election season (experience had cured me of the notion that anyone else paid close attention to my plans for tax reform or environmental regulation) than because I might have to actually implement them.

Such projections into the future might have occupied even more of my time had it not been for the fact that, despite the math showing I was going to be the nominee, Hillary simply would not give up.

Anyone else would have. She was running out of money. Her campaign was in turmoil, with staff recriminations spilling out into the press. The only remaining chance Hillary had to win the nomination depended on convincing superdelegates—the several hundred Democratic elected officials and party insiders who were given a vote at the convention and could cast it any way they wanted—to choose her when the party convened in August. It was a slender reed to hang on: While Hillary had started with a big early lead in superdelegates (who tended to announce which way they would vote long before the convention), more and more had committed to us as the primary season dragged on.

And yet she soldiered on, embracing her underdog status. Her voice took on a greater urgency, especially when discussing working-class concerns, offering her willingness to campaign to the bitter end as proof that she'd fight just as hard for American families. With upcoming primaries in Texas and Ohio (states populated by older white and Hispanic voters who tended to lean her way), to be followed seven weeks later by Pennsylvania (a state where she also enjoyed a healthy lead), Hillary assured anyone who'd listen that she planned to take our contest all the way to the convention floor.

"She's like a fucking vampire," Plouffe groused. "You can't kill her off."

Her tenacity was admirable, but my sympathies extended only so far. Senator John McCain would soon wrap up the Republican nomination, and another two or three months of bitter Democratic primary contests would give him a big head start on laying the groundwork for November's general election. It also meant that after almost eighteen months of nonstop campaigning, nobody on my team would get a meaningful break, which was unfortunate because all of us were running on fumes.

That probably explains how we came to make the one big tactical error of our campaign.

Rather than set realistic expectations and effectively concede Ohio so that we could focus on Texas, we decided to go for the knockout punch and try to win both. We spent massively in each state. For a week, I shuttled back and forth, from Dallas to Cleveland to Houston to Toledo, my voice raw, my eyes bloodshot—hardly looking like a herald of hope.

Our efforts had a modest effect on the polls, but they lent credence to the Clinton campaign's claim that a victory for her in Texas and Ohio could fundamentally reset the race. Meanwhile, the political press, seeing these primaries as perhaps my final test before securing the nomination and eager to sustain a drama that had proven to be a cable news ratings bonanza, gave more prominent coverage to Hillary's attacks on me, including an ad she ran contending that I wasn't ready to handle the "three a.m. phone call" involving a crisis. When all was said and done, we lost Ohio (decisively) and Texas (just barely).

On the flight from San Antonio back to Chicago after the primary, my team's mood was grim. Michelle barely said a word. When Plouffe attempted to lighten things by announcing that we'd won Vermont, it barely elicited a shrug. When someone else offered up the theory that we had all died and entered purgatory, where we were destined to debate Hillary for all eternity, no one laughed. It felt too close to the truth.

Hillary's victories didn't change the delegate count in a meaningful way, but they put enough wind in her campaign's sails to guarantee at least two more months of bitter primaries. The results also gave her camp fresh ammunition for an argument that seemed to be gaining traction with reporters—that I couldn't connect with white working-class voters, that Latinos were lukewarm at best about me, and that in an election of this importance, these weaknesses could make me a very risky Democratic nominee.

Just one week later, I found myself wondering if they were right.

IT HAD BEEN more than a year since I'd given much thought to my pastor, Reverend Jeremiah Wright. But on March 13, we woke up to discover that ABC News had compiled a series of short clips culled from several years of his sermons, skillfully packaged to fit a two-minute segment on **Good Morning America**. There was Reverend Wright calling America "USA of KKK." There was Reverend Wright saying, "Not God **bless** America. God **damn** America." There was Reverend Wright, in living color, explaining how the tragedy of 9/11 might in part be explained by our record of military interventions and wanton violence overseas, a matter of "America's chickens . . . coming home to roost." The video offered no context or history; in fact, it could not have portrayed Black radicalism more vividly, or provided a more surgical tool to offend Middle America. It was like a Roger Ailes fever dream.

Within hours of its initial broadcast, the video was running everywhere. Inside my campaign, it felt as if a torpedo had blown through our hull. I issued a statement, forcefully denouncing the sentiments expressed in the video, while also emphasizing all the good work that Reverend Wright and Trinity did in Chicago. The next day, I appeared at an already scheduled meeting with the editorial boards of two newspapers and then did a round of network TV interviews, each time offering a condemnation of the views expressed in the video clips. But no sound bite could offset the harm. The image of Reverend Wright kept rolling across TV screens, the cable chatter continued nonstop, and even Plouffe admitted we might not survive this.

Later, Axe and Plouffe would fault themselves for not having had our researchers obtain the videos a year earlier, after the **Rolling Stone** article hit, which would have given us more time to do damage control. But I knew the blame lay squarely on my shoulders. I may not have been in church for any of the sermons in question or heard Reverend Wright use such explosive language. But I knew all too well the occasional spasms of anger within the Black community—my community—that Reverend Wright was channeling. I **did** know how differently Black and white folks still viewed issues of race in America, regardless of how much else they had in common. For me to believe that I could bridge those worlds had been pure hubris, the same hubris that had led me to assume that I could dip in and out of a complex institution like Trinity, headed by a complex man like Reverend Wright, and select, as if off a menu, only those things that I liked. Maybe I could do that as a private citizen, but not as a public figure running for president.

Anyway, it was too late now. And while there are moments in politics, as in life, when avoidance, if not retreat, is the better part of valor, there are other times when the only option is to steel yourself and go for broke.

"I need to make a speech," I told Plouffe. "On race. The only way to deal with this is to go big and put Reverend Wright in some kind of context. And I need to do it in the next few days."

The team was skeptical. We'd booked the next three days solid with events, without any real time to spend on what could end up being the most consequential speech of the campaign. But we had no choice. On a Saturday night, after a day of stumping in Indiana, I went home to Chicago and spent an hour on the phone with Favs, dictating the argument I'd formed in my mind. I wanted to describe how Reverend Wright and Trinity were representative of America's racial legacy, how institutions and individuals who embodied the values of faith and work, family and community, education and upward mobility, might still harbor bitterness toward—and feel betrayed by—a country they loved.

But I had to do more than that. I had to explain the other side, why white Americans might resist, or even resent, claims of injustice from Blacks—unhappy with any presumption that all whites were racist, or that their own fears and day-to-day struggles were less valid.

Unless we could recognize one another's reality, I'd argue, we would never solve the problems America faced. And to hint at what such a recognition might mean, I would include a story that I had told in my first book but had never spoken about in a political speech—the pain and confusion I had experienced as a teenager, when Toot expressed her fear of a panhandler at a bus stop—not only because he had been aggressive but because he was Black. It hadn't made me love her any less, for my grandmother was a part of me, just as, in a more indirect way, Reverend Wright was a part of me.

Just as they were both a part of the American family.

As I wrapped up the call with Favs, I remembered the one time Toot and Reverend Wright had met. It had been at my wedding, where Reverend Wright hugged my mother and grandmother and told them what a wonderful job they'd done raising me, how proud they should be. Toot had smiled in a way I rarely saw her smile, whispering to my mother how the pastor seemed quite charming—although she got a bit uncomfortable later, when during the ceremony Reverend Wright described the conjugal obligations of the newlyweds in terms far more vivid than anything Toot had ever heard in the Methodist church of her childhood.

Favs wrote the first draft, and for the next two nights, I stayed up late, editing and rewriting, finishing finally at three a.m. on the day I was to deliver it. In the holding room at Philadelphia's National Constitution Center, Marty, Valerie, and Eric Whitaker, as well as Axe, Plouffe, and Gibbs, joined me and Michelle to wish me luck.

"How you feel?" Marty asked.

"Good," I said, and it was true. "I figure if it works, we get through this. If it doesn't, we probably lose. But either way, I'll be saying what I believe."

It worked. The networks carried the speech live, and

within twenty-four hours, more than one million people had watched it on the internet—a record at the time. Reviews from pundits and editorial writers around the country were strong, and the effect on those in the hall—including Marty, who was photographed with a fat tear running down his cheek—indicated I had touched a chord.

But the most important review came that evening, when I placed a call to my grandmother in Hawaii.

"That was a very nice speech, Bar," she told me. "I know it wasn't easy."

"Thanks, Toot."

"You know I'm proud of you, don't you?"

"I know," I said. And it was only after I hung up that I allowed myself to cry.

THE SPEECH STANCHED the bleeding, but the Reverend Wright situation had taken a toll, particularly in Pennsylvania, where Democratic voters skewed older and more conservative. What kept us from an outright free fall was the hard work of our volunteers, an influx of money from small donors that helped us run ads for four weeks, and the willingness of some key state officials to vouch for me with their white working-class base. Chief among them was Bob Casey, the affable Irish Catholic son of the state's former governor and one of my colleagues in the U.S. Senate. There wasn't much upside for him—Hillary had broad support and was likely to win the state—and he hadn't announced his endorsement when the Reverend Wright video hit the news. And yet, when I called Bob before my speech and offered to free him from his commitment to endorse me in light of the changed circumstances, he insisted on going forward.

"The Wright stuff's not great," he said in a bit of world-class understatement. "But I still feel like you're the right guy."

Bob then backed up his endorsement with decency and courage, campaigning by my side for more than a week, up and down Pennsylvania. Slowly, our poll numbers began ticking back up. Although we knew a victory was not in the cards, we figured a three- or four-point loss remained within reach.

And then, on cue, I made my biggest mistake of the campaign.

We'd flown to San Francisco for a big-dollar fundraiser, the kind of event that I generally dreaded, taking place in a fancy house and involving a long photo line, shiitake mushroom hors d'oeuvres, and wealthy donors, most of them terrific and generous one-on-one but collectively fitting every stereotype of the latte-drinking, Prius-driving West Coast liberal. We were running late into the evening when, during the obligatory question-and-answer session, someone asked me to explain why I thought so many working-class voters in Pennsylvania continued to vote against their interests and elect Republicans.

I'd been asked a form of this question a thousand times. Normally I had no problem describing the mix of economic anxiety, frustration with a seemingly unresponsive federal government, and legitimate differences on social issues like abortion that pushed voters into the Republican column. But whether because I was mentally and physically worn-out, or because I was just impatient, that's not how my answer came across.

"You go into some of these small towns in Pennsylvania," I said, "and, like a lot of small towns in the Midwest, the jobs have been gone now for twenty-five years and nothing's replaced them. And they fell through the Clinton administration and the Bush administration, and each successive administration has said that somehow these communities are going to regenerate and they have not."

So far so good. Except I then added, "So it's not surprising then that they get bitter, they cling to guns or religion or antipathy toward people who aren't like them, or anti-immigrant sentiment, or anti-trade sentiment as a way to explain their frustrations."

I can provide the exact quote here, because in the audience that night was a freelance writer who was recording me. To her mind, my answer risked reinforcing negative stereotypes some Californians already had about working-class white voters and was therefore worth blogging about on **Huffington Post**. (It's a decision I respect, by the way, though I wish she had talked to me about it before writing the story. This is what separates even the most liberal writers from their conservative counterparts—the willingness to flay politicians on their own side.)

Even today, I want to take that sentence back and make a few simple edits. "So it's not surprising then that they get frustrated," I would say in my revised version, "and they look to the traditions and way of life that have been constants in their lives, whether it's their faith, or hunting, or blue-collar work, or more traditional notions of family and community. And when Republicans tell them we Democrats despise these things—or when we give these folks reason to believe that we do—then the best policies in the world don't matter to them."

That's what I believed. It's why I'd gotten votes from rural white voters in downstate Illinois and Iowa—because they sensed, even when we didn't agree on an issue like abortion or immigration, that I fundamentally respected and cared about them. In many ways they were more familiar to me than the people I spoke to that night in San Francisco.

And so I still brood about this string of poorly chosen words. Not because it subjected us to a whole new round of bludgeoning at the hands of the press and the Clinton campaign—although that was no fun—but because the words ended up having such a long afterlife. The phrases "bitter" and "cling to guns or religion" were easily remembered, like a hook in a pop song, and would be cited deep into my presidency as evidence that I failed to understand or reach out to working-class white people, even when the positions I took and policies I championed consistently indicated the contrary.

Maybe I'm overstating the consequences of that night. Maybe things were bound to play out as they did, and what nags at me is the simple fact that I screwed up and don't like being misunderstood. And maybe I'm bothered by the care and delicacy with which one must state the obvious: that it's possible to understand and sympathize with the frustrations of white voters without denying the ease with which, throughout American history, politicians have redirected white frustration about their economic or social circumstances toward Black and brown people.

One thing's for certain. The fallout from my gaffe that night provided my San Francisco questioner a better answer than any verbal response I might have given.

WE LIMPED THROUGH the remainder of the Pennsylvania campaign. There was the final debate in Philadelphia, a brutal affair consisting almost entirely of questions about flag pins, Wright, and "bitter." Campaigning across the state, an invigorated Hillary touted her newfound appreciation for gun rights— Annie Oakley, I called her. We lost by nine points.

As had been true of the Ohio and Texas primaries, the results had little impact on our delegate lead. But there was no denying we'd taken a serious hit. Political insiders speculated that if the results of the next two big contests (Indiana, where Hillary had a solid lead, and North Carolina, where we were heavily favored) showed any further erosion in our support, superdelegates might start running scared, giving Hillary a realistic chance of wresting away the nomination.

Such talk grew appreciably louder several days later, when Jeremiah Wright decided to make a round of public appearances.

I had spoken to him only once after the video came out, to let him know how strongly I objected to what he'd said, but also to say that I wanted to shield him and the church from any further fallout. I don't remember the details, just that the call was painful and brief, his questions full of hurt. Had any of these so-called reporters bothered to listen to the full sermons? he asked me. How could they selectively edit a lifetime of work down to two minutes? Listening to this proud man defend himself, I could only imagine his bewilderment. He'd been a sought-after speaker at America's leading universities and seminaries, a pillar of his community, a luminary within not just Black churches but many white ones as well. And then, in what felt like an instant, he'd become a national object of fear and derision.

I felt genuine remorse, knowing this was all because of his association with me. He was collateral damage in a struggle he'd played no part in choosing. And yet I had no meaningful way to salve his wounds, and when I made the practical—if transparently self-interested—suggestion that he lie low for a time and let things blow over, I knew he felt it as just one more affront.

When it was announced that Reverend Wright would be giving an interview on Bill Moyers's show and then a keynote address at a Detroit NAACP dinner and then an appearance before the National Press Club in Washington, all just ahead of the Indiana and North Carolina primaries in early May, I fully expected the worst. As it turned out, the first two appearances were notable mainly for their restraint, with the reverend coming across as more theologian and preacher than provocateur.

Then, at the National Press Club, the dam broke. Strafed by questions from the political press and flustered by their unwillingness to consider his answers, Reverend Wright unleashed a rant for the ages, gesticulating as if he were at a tent revival, eyes glistening with righteous fury. He pronounced America racist at its core. He suggested that the U.S. government was behind the AIDS epidemic. He praised Nation of Islam leader Louis Farrakhan. The attacks on him were all racially motivated, and my denunciation of his earlier statements he dismissed as just "what politicians do" in order to get elected.

Or, as Marty would later put it, "he went full ghetto on their ass."

I missed the live broadcast, but watching the replay, I knew what I had to do. The following afternoon, I found myself sitting on a bench in a high school locker room in Winston-Salem, North Carolina, with Gibbs, staring at walls painted industrial green, the stale smell of football uniforms wafting about, waiting to deliver the press statement in which I would permanently sever my relationship with someone who had played a small but significant part in making me the man that I was; someone whose words had once served as a tagline for the speech that put me on the national stage; someone who, for all his now inexcusable blind spots, had never shown me anything but kindness and support.

"You okay?" Gibbs asked me.

"Yep."

"I know this can't be easy."

I nodded, touched by Gibbs's concern. It wasn't the norm for the two of us to acknowledge the pressure we were under; Gibbs was a warrior first, a prankster second, and on the road we usually opted for easy banter and profanity-laced humor. But perhaps because he'd grown up in Alabama, he understood better than most the complications of race, religion, and family, and how good and bad, love and hate, might be hopelessly tangled in the same heart.

"You know, I'm not sure Hillary's wrong," I told him.

"About what?"

"About me being damaged goods. I think about it

sometimes, how this isn't supposed to be about my own ambition. It's supposed to be about making the country better," I said. "If the American people can't get past this Wright thing, and I stagger my way into the nomination, only to lose the general, what good have I done?"

Gibbs put a hand on my shoulder. "You're not going to lose," he said. "People are looking for something real, and they've seen it in you. Let's just get this shit behind us once and for all, so we can get back to reminding them why you should be president."

My brief statement, in which I unequivocally denounced and separated myself from Reverend Wright, served its purpose. If it didn't fully allay voter concerns, it at least convinced reporters I had nothing further to say on the matter. Back on the campaign trail, we refocused our attention on healthcare, jobs, the war in Iraq, unsure of exactly how things would all play out.

Then we got some help from an unexpected quarter.

Throughout the spring of 2008, gas prices had been skyrocketing, mostly the result of various supply disruptions. Nothing got voters in a bad mood like high gas prices, and eager to get out ahead of the issue, John McCain had proposed a temporary suspension of the federal gas tax. Hillary immediately endorsed the idea, and the team asked me what I wanted to do.

I told them I was against it. While it had some superficial appeal, I knew it would drain an already depleted federal highway fund, leading to fewer infrastructure projects and jobs. Based on my experience as an Illinois state senator, where I'd once voted for a similar proposal, I was sure that consumers wouldn't see much benefit. In fact, gas station owners were just as likely to keep prices high and boost their own profits as they were to pass the three-cents-a-gallon savings on to motorists.

Somewhat to my surprise, Plouffe and Axe agreed. In fact, Axe suggested that we highlight my opposition as more proof that I was willing to be straight with voters. The next day, I stood outside a gas station and made my argument before a gaggle of reporters, contrasting what I considered a serious, long-term energy policy with the typical Washington solution that both McCain and Hillary were proposing. It was a bit of political posturing, I said, designed to give the impression of action without actually solving the problem. Then, when both Hillary and McCain tried to paint me as out of touch and unconcerned with what a few hundred dollars might mean to America's working families, we doubled down, shooting a TV ad on the issue and running it nonstop throughout Indiana and North Carolina.

It was one of our prouder moments, taking a tough position without the benefit of polls and in the face of pundits who thought we were crazy. We began seeing signs in the polling data that voters were buying our argument, though none of us at this point—not even Plouffe—fully trusted data anymore. Like a patient awaiting the results of a biopsy, the campaign lived with the possibility of a bad outcome.

The night before the primaries, we held an evening rally in Indianapolis featuring a performance by Stevie Wonder. After my stump speech, Valerie, Marty, Eric, and I parked ourselves in a small room, enjoying the music, some beer, and a cold chicken dinner.

We were in a reflective mood, reminiscing about the joys of Iowa, the heartbreak of New Hampshire, volunteers we'd met and new friends we'd made. Eventually someone brought up Reverend Wright's appearance at the National Press Club, and Marty and Eric began taking turns acting out some of the more excruciating lines. Whether it was a sign of exhaustion, or anxious anticipation of the next day's voting, or maybe just us recognizing the absurdity of our circumstances—four longtime friends, African Americans from the South Side of Chicago, eating chicken and listening to Stevie Wonder while waiting to see if one of us would become the Democratic nominee for president of the United States— we all started to laugh and couldn't stop, the kind of deep, tear-inducing, falling-out-of-your-chair laughter that's a kissing cousin to despair.

Then Axe walked in, wearing his most forlorn look.

"What's the matter?" I said, still laughing and trying to catch my breath.

Axe shook his head. "I just got our overnight numbers . . . had us down twelve in Indiana. I just don't think we're going to make it."

For a moment, everyone grew quiet. Then I said, "Axe, I love you, but you're a downer. Either grab a drink and sit down with us or get the fuck out of here."

Axe shrugged and left the room, taking his worries with him. I looked around at my friends and raised my beer in a toast.

"To the audacity of hope," I said. Clinking our bottles, we started to laugh as hard as before.

TWENTY-FOUR HOURS LATER, in a Raleigh hotel room, Gibbs read me the election results. We'd won North Carolina by fourteen points. More surprisingly, we had pulled out an effective tie in Indiana, losing by just a few thousand votes. There would be six more contests before the official end of the Democratic primary season, and a few weeks would pass before Hillary's belated but gracious concession speech and endorsement, but the results that night told us that the race was basically over.

I would be the Democratic nominee for president of the United States.

In my speech that night, I began the pivot to the general election, knowing there wasn't a minute to waste, telling our audience that I was confident that Democrats would unite to prevent John McCain from continuing the legacy of George W. Bush. I spent some time talking to Axe about potential running mates and then phoned Toot to tell her the news. ("It really is something, Bar," she said.) Well past midnight, I called Plouffe back at our Chicago headquarters, and the two of us went over what we needed to do to get ready for the convention, less than three months away.

Lying in bed later, unable to sleep, I took a silent inventory. I thought about Michelle, who had put up with my absences, held down the home front, and overridden her reticence about politics to become effective and fearless on the stump. I thought about my daughters, as lively and cuddly and engaging as ever, even when I didn't see them for a week. I thought about the skill and focus of Axe and Plouffe and the rest of my senior team, how they never gave any indication of doing what they did for money or power, and how in the face of unrelenting pressure they'd proven loyal not just to me and to one another but to the idea of making America better. I thought about friends like Valerie, Marty, and Eric, who'd shared my joys and eased my burdens along every step, asking nothing in return. And I thought about the young organizers and volunteers who'd braved bad weather, skeptical voters, and their candidate's missteps without wavering.

I had asked something hard of the American people— to place their faith in a young and untested newcomer; not just a Black man, but someone whose very name evoked a life story that seemed unfamiliar. Repeatedly I'd given them cause not to support me. There'd been uneven debate performances, unconventional positions, clumsy gaffes, and a pastor who'd cursed the United States of America. And I'd faced an opponent who'd proven both her readiness and her mettle.

Despite all that, they'd given me a chance. Through the noise and chatter of the political circus, they'd heard my call for something different. Even if I hadn't always been at my best, they'd divined what was best in me: the voice insisting that for all our differences, we remained bound as one people, and that, together, men and women of goodwill could find a way to a better future.

I promised myself I would not let them down.

CHAPTER 8

ENTERING THE SUMMER OF 2008, our campaign's first order of business was unifying the Democratic Party. The prolonged and bruising primary had left hard feelings between Hillary's staff and mine, and some of her more ardent boosters threatened to withhold their support unless I put her on the ticket.

But despite speculation in the press of a possibly irreparable breach, our first post-primary meeting, held in early June at the Washington home of our colleague Senator Dianne Feinstein, proved to be courteous and businesslike, if not without tension. At the outset, Hillary felt obliged to get a few things off her chest, mainly having to do with what she considered unfair attacks by my campaign. As the winner, I felt obliged to keep my own complaints to myself. But it didn't take long to clear the air. The bottom line, she said, was that she wanted to be a team player—for the good of the Democratic Party, and for the good of the country.

It may have helped that she sensed my sincere admiration. Although I would ultimately decide that having her as a running mate posed too many complications (including the awkwardness of a former president roaming the West Wing without a clear portfolio), I was already considering a different role for her in an Obama administration. How Hillary felt about me, I couldn't say. But if she harbored any doubts about my readiness for the job ahead, she kept them to herself. From our first public appearance together a few weeks later, in a small New Hampshire town called Unity (corny, but effective), until the very end of the campaign, both she and Bill did everything we asked of them with energy and a smile.

With Hillary on board, the team and I got busy designing our broader electoral strategy. Like the primaries and caucuses, a presidential general election resembles a big math puzzle. Which combination of states do you need to win to get the requisite 270 electoral votes? For at least twenty years, nominees of both parties had come up with the same answer, assuming that the majority of states were inalterably Republican or Democratic, and therefore concentrating all their time and money on a handful of big battleground states like Ohio, Florida, Pennsylvania, and Michigan.

Plouffe had a different idea. One happy by-product of our interminable primary was that we'd campaigned in every nook and corner of the country. We had battle-tested volunteers in a number of states Democrats had historically ignored. Why not use that advantage to compete in traditionally Republican-leaning territory? Based on the data, Plouffe was convinced we could win western states like Colorado and Nevada. With a big boost in turnout among minority and younger voters, he believed we even had a chance in North Carolina, a state that hadn't gone Democratic in a presidential election since Jimmy Carter in 1976, and Virginia, which hadn't gone Democratic since Lyndon Johnson in 1964. Broadening the electoral map would give us multiple paths to victory, Plouffe argued, and would also help down-ballot Democratic candidates. At a minimum, it would force John McCain and the Republican Party to spend resources shoring up their vulnerable flanks.

Among the various Republicans who had competed for the presidential nomination, I had always considered John McCain to be most worthy of the prize. I had admired him from afar before I got to Washington—not only for his service as a navy pilot and the unimaginable courage he'd shown during five and a half harrowing years as a POW, but because of the contrarian sensibility and willingness to buck Republican Party orthodoxy on issues like immigration and climate change that he'd shown in his 2000 presidential campaign. While we were never close in the Senate, I often found him insightful and self-deprecating, quick to puncture pretension and hypocrisy on both sides of the aisle.

McCain did enjoy being something of a press corps darling ("my constituency," he once called them), never passing up a chance to be on the Sunday morning news shows, and among his colleagues he had a well-earned reputation for volatility—quick to explode over small disagreements, his pallid face reddening, his reedy voice rising at the first sign of a perceived slight. But he wasn't an ideologue. He respected not only the customs of the Senate but also the institutions of our government and our democracy. I never saw him display the race-tinged nativism that regularly infected other Republican politicians, and on more than one occasion, I'd seen him display real political courage.

Once, as the two of us stood in the well of the Senate waiting for a vote, John had confided to me that he couldn't stand a lot of the "crazies" in his own party. I knew this was part of his shtick—privately playing to Democrats' sensibilities while voting with his caucus about 90 percent of the time. But the disdain he expressed for the far-right wing of his party wasn't an act. And in an increasingly polarized climate, the political equivalent of a holy war, McCain's modest heresies, his unwillingness to profess the true faith, carried a real cost. The "crazies" in his party mistrusted him, they considered him a RINO—Republican in Name Only—and he was regularly attacked by the Rush Limbaugh crowd.

Unfortunately for McCain, it was precisely these voices of the hard Right that were exciting the core GOP voters most likely to vote in presidential primaries, rather than the business-friendly, strong-on-defense, socially moderate Republicans McCain appealed to and was most comfortable with. And as the Republican primary wore on, and McCain sought to win over some of the very people he professed to despise—as he abandoned any pretense of fiscal rectitude in favor of even bigger tax cuts than the Bush tax cuts he'd once voted against, and hedged his position on climate change to accommodate fossil fuel interests—I sensed a change taking place in him. He seemed pained, uncertain—the once jaunty, irreverent warrior transformed into a cranky Washington insider, lassoed to an incumbent president with an approval rating around 30 percent and a hugely unpopular war.

I wasn't sure I could beat the 2000 version of John McCain. But I was increasingly confident that I could beat the McCain of 2008.

. . .

THAT'S NOT TO say I thought the race would be easy. In a contest against an American hero, the election wouldn't be decided on issues alone. Indeed, we suspected that the central question was likely to be whether a majority of voters could get comfortable with the idea of a young, inexperienced African American senator—one who hadn't previously served in the military or even an executive office—filling the role of commander in chief.

I knew that if I was to earn Americans' trust on this front, I needed to speak from the most informed position possible, especially about the nation's role in Iraq and Afghanistan. Which is why, just a few weeks after I'd wrapped up the nomination, we decided I would embark on nine days of foreign travel. The proposed schedule was brutal: In addition to a brief stop in Kuwait and three days on the ground in Afghanistan and Iraq, I would meet with the leaders of Israel, Jordan, the United Kingdom, and France, and deliver a major foreign policy address in Berlin. If we pulled the trip off, we'd not only dispel concerns voters might have about my ability to operate effectively on the world stage but also highlight—at a time when voters were deeply troubled by the strained alliances of the Bush years—just what a new era of American leadership might look like.

Of course, with the political press sure to flyspeck my every move, there was a good chance something might go wrong. Even a single blunder might reinforce the notion that I wasn't ready for prime time and tank our campaign. My team figured it was worth the risk.

"Walking a tightrope without a net," Plouffe said. "That's when we're at our best."

I pointed out that it was me and not "we" perilously up in the air. Nevertheless, I left Washington in good spirits, eager to travel overseas after a year and a half with my nose to the campaign grindstone.

Joining me on the Afghanistan and Iraq legs of the trip were two of my favorite colleagues, both of whom were seasoned in foreign policy: Chuck Hagel, the ranking member of the Senate Foreign Relations Committee, and Jack Reed, who sat on the Armed Services Committee. In personality, the two men couldn't have been more different. Jack, a liberal Democrat from Rhode Island, was slightly built, studious, and understated. A proud West Point graduate, he had been one of the few senators to vote against authorizing the Iraq War. Chuck, a conservative Republican from Nebraska, was broad-shouldered, expansive, and full of good humor. A Vietnam veteran with two Purple Hearts, he had voted for the Iraq War. What the two shared was an abiding reverence for the U.S. military and a belief in the prudent use of American power. After almost six years, their views on Iraq had converged, and they were now two of the war's most incisive and credible critics. Their bipartisan presence on the trip helped deflect any criticism that it was a campaign stunt; and Chuck's willingness not only to travel with me but also to publicly praise aspects of my foreign policy, just four months before the election, was a bold and generous gesture.

On a Saturday in mid-July, we landed at Bagram Air Base, a six-square-mile installation north of Kabul, set against the jagged peaks of the Hindu Kush, that served as the largest U.S. military base in Afghanistan. The news wasn't good: The collapse of Iraq into sectarian violence, and the Bush administration's decision to reinforce our presence with a sustained troop surge, had siphoned military and intelligence capabilities out of Afghanistan (by 2008, we had five times as many troops in Iraq as we had there). The shift in focus had allowed the Taliban—the Sunni Islamic insurgents we'd been fighting since 2001—to go on the offensive, and that summer the monthly U.S. casualties in Afghanistan would exceed those in Iraq.

As usual, our military was doing all it could to make a tough situation work. The newly assigned commander of coalition forces, General Dave McKiernan, arranged for his team to brief us on the steps they were taking to push back against Taliban strongholds. The following day, dining in the mess hall at the U.S. coalition head-quarters in Kabul, we listened as a group of soldiers spoke of their mission with enthusiasm and pride. Hearing these earnest young men and women, most of them just a few years out of high school, talk about building roads, training Afghan soldiers, and setting up schools, only to see their work periodically interrupted or undone because they were understaffed or under-resourced, was both humbling and frustrating, and I vowed that, given the chance, I would get them more help.

That night we slept at the heavily fortified U.S. embassy, and in the morning we drove to the imposing nineteenth-century palace where President Hamid Karzai lived. In the 1970s, Kabul had been not so different from the capitals of other developing countries, ragged around the edges but peaceful and growing, full of elegant hotels, rock music, and college students intent on mod-ernizing their country. Karzai and his ministers were products of that era, but many had fled to Europe or the United States either during the Soviet invasion that began in 1979 or when the Taliban took over in the mid-1990s. After its assault on Kabul, the United States had brought Karzai and his advisors back and installed them in power—functional expatriates we hoped would serve as the Afghan face of a new, nonmilitant order. With their impeccable English and stylish dress, they fit the part, and as our delegation dined on a banquet of traditional Afghan fare, they did their best to persuade us that a modern, tolerant, and self-sufficient Afghanistan was within reach so long as American troops and cash continued to flow.

I might have believed Karzai's words were it not for reports of rampant corruption and mismanagement within his government. Much of the Afghan countryside was beyond the control of Kabul, and Karzai rarely ventured out, reliant not just on U.S. forces but on a patchwork of alliances with local warlords to maintain what power he possessed. I thought about his seeming isolation later that day as a pair of Black Hawk helicopters flew us over mountainous terrain on our way to a U.S. forward operating base (FOB) near Helmand on Afghanistan's southern plateau. The small villages of mud and wood that we saw from the air blended seamlessly into the dun-colored rock formations, with barely a paved road or an electrical line in sight. I tried to imagine what the people below thought of the Americans in their midst, or their own president in his sumptuous palace, or even the idea of a nation-state called Afghanistan. Not much, I suspected. They were just trying to survive, buffeted by forces as constant and unpredictable as the winds. And I wondered what it might take—beyond the courage and skill of our troops, despite the best-laid plans of analysts in Washington—to reconcile American ideas of what Afghanistan should be with a landscape that for hundreds of years had proven impervious to change.

Such thoughts stayed with me as we left Afghanistan and headed to Iraq, spending a night in Kuwait along the way. Trends had improved since my last visit to Iraq; a surge in U.S. troops, the internationally certified election of Shiite prime minister Nuri Kamal al-Maliki, and a brokered agreement with Sunni tribal leaders in the western province of Anbar had reversed some of the sectarian carnage unleashed by the original U.S. invasion and subsequent bungling by men like Donald Rumsfeld and Paul Bremer. John McCain interpreted the recent successes to mean we were winning the fight and would continue to so long as we stayed the course and—in what had become a common nostrum among Republicans—"listened to our commanders on the ground."

I drew a different conclusion. After five years of heavy U.S. involvement, with Saddam Hussein gone, no evidence of WMDs, and a democratically elected government installed, I believed phased withdrawal was in order: one that would build in the time needed to stand up Iraqi security forces and root out the last vestiges of al-Qaeda in Iraq; guarantee ongoing military, intelligence, and financial support; and begin bringing our troops home so that we could hand Iraq back to its people.

As in Afghanistan, we had a chance to mingle with troops and visit an FOB in Anbar, before meeting with Prime Minister Maliki. He was a dour figure, vaguely Nixonian with his long face, heavy five-o'clock shadow, and indirect gaze. He had cause to be stressed, for his new job was both difficult and dangerous. He was trying to balance the demands of the domestic Shiite power blocs that had elected him and the Sunni population that had dominated the country under Saddam; he also had to manage countervailing pressures from his U.S. benefactors and Iranian neighbors. Indeed, Maliki's ties to Iran, where he had lived in exile for many years, as well as his uneasy alliances with certain Shiite militias, made him anathema to Saudi Arabia and other U.S. allies in the Persian Gulf region, underscoring just how much the U.S. invasion had strengthened Iran's strategic position there.

Whether anyone in the Bush White House had discussed such a predictable consequence before ordering U.S. troops into Iraq was uncertain. But the administration sure wasn't happy about it now. My conversations with several high-ranking generals and diplomats made clear that the White House's interest in maintaining a sizable troop presence in Iraq was about more than a simple desire to ensure stability and reduce violence. It was also about preventing Iran from taking further advantage of the mess we'd made.

Given that the issue was dominating the foreign policy debate both in Congress and in the campaign, I asked Maliki through the interpreter whether he thought Iraq was ready for a withdrawal of U.S. troops. We were all surprised by his unequivocal response: Though he expressed deep appreciation for the efforts of U.S. and British forces and hoped that America would continue to help pay for the training and maintenance of Iraqi forces, he agreed with me that we set a time frame for a U.S. withdrawal.

It was unclear what was behind Maliki's decision to push an accelerated timetable for U.S. withdrawal. Simple nationalism? Pro-Iranian sympathies? A move to consolidate his power? But as far as the political debate in the United States was concerned, Maliki's position had big implications. It was one thing for the White House or John McCain to dismiss my calls for a timetable for withdrawal as weak and irresponsible, a version of "cut and run." It was quite another to dismiss the same idea coming from Iraq's newly elected leader.

Of course, at the time, Maliki still didn't really call the shots in his country. The commander of coalition forces in Iraq, General David Petraeus, did—and it was my conversation with him that foreshadowed some of the central foreign policy debates I'd have for much of my presidency.

Trim and fit, with a PhD in international relations and economics from Princeton and an orderly, analytical mind, Petraeus was considered the brains behind our improved position in Iraq and the individual to whom the White House had essentially contracted out its strategy. We took a helicopter together from the Baghdad airport to the heavily fortified Green Zone, talking all the way, and although the substance of our conversation wouldn't appear in any press write-ups, as far as my campaign team was concerned that was just fine. It was the photographs they cared about—images of me seated next to a four-star general aboard a Black Hawk helicopter, wearing a headset and aviator glasses. Apparently it proved a youthful, vigorous contrast to an unfortunate depiction of my Republican opponent that happened to surface on the very same day: McCain riding shotgun on a golf cart with former president George H. W. Bush, the two of them resembling a couple of pastel-sweatered grandpas on their way to a country club picnic.

Meanwhile, sitting together in his spacious office at coalition headquarters, Petraeus and I discussed everything from the need for more Arabic-language specialists in the military to the vital role development projects would play in delegitimizing militias and terrorist organizations and bolstering the new government. Bush deserved credit, I thought, for having selected this particular general to right what had been a sinking ship. If we had unlimited time and resources—if America's long-term national security interests absolutely depended on creating a functioning and democratic state allied to the United States in Iraq—then Petraeus's approach had as good a chance as any of achieving the goal.

But we did not have unlimited time or resources. When you boiled it down, that's what the argument over withdrawal was all about. How much did we continue to give, and when would it be enough? As far as I was concerned, we were approaching that line; our national security required a stable Iraq, but not a showcase for American nation-building. Petraeus, on the other hand, believed that without a more sustained U.S. investment, whatever gains we'd made were still easily reversed.

I asked how long it would take for them to feel permanent. Two years? Five? Ten?

He couldn't say. But announcing a fixed timetable for withdrawal, he believed, would only give the enemy the chance to wait us out.

But wouldn't that always be true?

He conceded the point.

And what about surveys indicating that a strong majority of Iraqis, both Shiite and Sunni, had wearied of the occupation and wanted us out sooner rather than later?

That was a problem we would have to manage, he said.

The conversation was cordial, and I couldn't blame Petraeus for wanting to finish the mission. If I were in your shoes, I told him, I'd want the same thing. But a president's job required looking at a bigger picture, I said, just as he himself had to consider trade-offs and constraints that officers under his command did not. As a nation, how should we weigh an additional two or three years in Iraq at a cost of nearly $10 billion a month against the need to dismantle Osama bin Laden and core al-Qaeda operations in northwestern Pakistan? Or against the schools and roads not built back home? Or the erosion of readiness should another crisis arise? Or the human toll exacted on our troops and their families?

General Petraeus nodded politely and said he looked forward to seeing me after the election. As our delegation took its leave that day, I doubted I'd persuaded him of the wisdom of my position any more than he had persuaded me.

WAS I PREPARED to be a world leader? Did I have the diplomatic skills, the knowledge and stamina, the authority to command? The balance of the trip was designed to answer such questions, an elaborate audition on the international stage. There were bilateral meetings with King Abdullah in Jordan, Gordon Brown in England, Nicolas Sarkozy in France. I met with Angela Merkel in Germany, where I also spoke to an audience of two hundred thousand people gathered in front of Berlin's historic Victory Column, declaring that just as an earlier generation had torn down the wall that once divided Europe, it was now our job to tear down other, less visible walls: between rich and poor, between races and tribes, between natives and immigrants, between Christians, Muslims, and Jews. Over a couple of marathon days in Israel and the West Bank, I met separately with Israeli prime minister Ehud Olmert and Palestinian president Mahmoud Abbas, and did my best to understand not only the logic but also the emotions behind an ancient and seemingly intractable conflict. In the town of Sderot, I listened as parents described the terror of rocket shells launched from nearby Gaza landing just a few yards from their children's bedrooms. In Ramallah, I heard Palestinians speak of the daily humiliations endured at Israeli security checkpoints.

According to Gibbs, the U.S. press thought I'd passed the "looking presidential" test with flying colors. But for me, the trip went beyond mere optics. Even more than back home, I felt the immensity of the challenges that awaited me if I won, the grace I'd need to do the job.

These thoughts were on my mind the morning of July 24, when I arrived at the Western Wall in Jerusalem, built two thousand years ago to protect the sacred Temple Mount and viewed as a gateway to divinity and a place where God accepted the prayers of all who visit. For centuries, pilgrims from around the world had made a custom of committing their prayers to paper and stuffing them into the cracks of the wall, so before coming that morning, I'd written my own prayer on a piece of hotel stationery.

In the gray light of dawn, surrounded by my Israeli hosts, aides, Secret Service agents, and the clatter of media cameras, I bowed my head before the wall as a bearded rabbi read a psalm calling for peace in the holy city of Jerusalem. As was the custom, I laid a hand on the soft limestone, stilling myself in silent contemplation, and then wadded up my piece of paper and pushed it deep into a crevice in the wall.

"Lord," I had written, "protect my family and me. Forgive me my sins, and help me guard against pride and despair. Give me the wisdom to do what is right and just. And make me an instrument of your will."

I had assumed those words were between me and God. But the next day they showed up in an Israeli newspaper before achieving eternal life on the internet. Apparently a bystander dug my scrap of paper out of the wall after we left—a reminder of the price that came with stepping onto the world stage. The line between my private and public lives was dissolving; each thought and gesture was now a matter of global interest.

Get used to it, I told myself. It's part of the deal.

RETURNING FROM MY overseas trip, I felt like an astronaut or an explorer just back from an arduous expedition, charged with adrenaline and vaguely disoriented by ordinary life. With only a month to go before the Democratic National Convention, I decided to try to normalize things a little by taking my family to Hawaii for a week. I told Plouffe the matter wasn't up for debate.

After campaigning for seventeen months, I needed to recharge, and so did Michelle. Also, Toot's health was deteriorating rapidly, and while we couldn't know exactly how long my grandmother might have, I didn't intend to repeat the mistake I had made with my mother.

Most of all, I wanted some time with my daughters. As far as I could tell, the campaign hadn't affected our bonds. Malia was as chatty and inquisitive with me as ever, Sasha as buoyant and affectionate. When I was on the road, I talked to them by phone every night, about school, their friends, or the latest **SpongeBob** episode; when I was home, I read to them, challenged them to board games, and occasionally snuck out with them for ice cream.

Still, I could see from week to week how fast they were growing, how their limbs always seemed an inch or two longer than I remembered, their conversations at dinner more sophisticated. These changes served as a measure of all that I had missed, the fact that I hadn't been there to nurse them when they were sick, or hug them when they were scared, or laugh at the jokes they told. As much as I believed in the importance of what I was doing, I knew I wouldn't ever get that time back, and often found myself questioning the wisdom of the trade.

I was right to feel guilty. It's hard to overstate the burden I placed on my family during those two years I ran for president—how much I relied on Michelle's fortitude and parenting skills, and how much I depended on my daughters' preternatural good cheer and maturity. Earlier that summer, Michelle had agreed to bring the girls and join me as I campaigned in Butte, Montana, on the Fourth of July, which also happened to be Malia's tenth birthday. My sister Maya and her family decided to come as well. We had our share of fun that day, visiting a mining museum and squirting one another with water guns, but much of my time was still devoted to vote getting. The girls trudged dutifully beside me as I shook hands along the town's parade route. They stood in the heat watching me speak at an afternoon rally. In the evening, after the fireworks I'd promised were canceled due to thunderstorms, we held an impromptu birthday party in a windowless conference room on the lower level of the local Holiday Inn. Our advance staff had done its best to liven up the place with a few balloons. There was pizza and salad and a cake from the local supermarket. Still, as I watched Malia blow out the candles and make her wish for the year ahead, I wondered whether she was disappointed, whether she might later look back on this day as proof of her father's misplaced priorities.

Just then, Kristen Jarvis, one of Michelle's young aides, pulled out an iPod and hooked it up to a portable speaker. Malia and Sasha grabbed my hands to pull me out of my chair. Pretty soon everyone was dancing to Beyoncé and the Jonas Brothers, Sasha gyrating, Malia shaking her short curls, Michelle and Maya letting loose as I showed off my best dad moves. After about half an hour, all of us happily out of breath, Malia came over and sat on my lap.

"Daddy," she said, "this is the best birthday ever."

I kissed the top of her head and held her tight, not letting her see my eyes get misty.

Those were my daughters. That's what I'd given up by being away so much. That's why the days we stole in Hawaii that August were worth it, even if we lost some ground against McCain in the polls. Splashing in the ocean with the girls, letting them bury me in sand without having to tell them I had to get on a conference call or leave for the airport—it was worth it. Watching the sun go down over the Pacific with my arms wrapped around Michelle, just listening to the wind and rustling palms—worth it.

Seeing Toot hunched over on her living room couch, barely able to raise her head but still smiling with quiet satisfaction as her great-granddaughters laughed and played on the floor, and then feeling her mottled, blue-veined hand squeeze mine for perhaps the last time.

A precious sacrament.

I COULDN'T LEAVE the campaign entirely behind while I was in Hawaii. There were updates from the team, thank-you calls to supporters, a preliminary outline of my convention speech that I drafted and sent to Favs. And there was the single most consequential decision I had to make now that I was the nominee.

Who would be my running mate?

I had narrowed it down to Governor Tim Kaine of Virginia and Senate colleague Joe Biden of Delaware. At the time, I was much closer to Tim, who had been the first prominent elected official outside of Illinois to endorse me for president and had worked hard as one of our top campaign surrogates. Our friendship came easily; we were roughly the same age, had similar midwestern roots, similar temperaments, and even similar résumés. (Tim had worked on a mission in Honduras while a student at Harvard Law School and had practiced civil rights law before going into politics.)

As for Joe, we couldn't have been more different, at least on paper. He was nineteen years my senior. I was running as the Washington outsider; Joe had spent thirty-five years in the Senate, including stints as chairman of the Judiciary Committee and the Foreign Relations Committee. In contrast to my peripatetic upbringing, Joe had deep roots in Scranton, Pennsylvania, and took pride in his working-class Irish heritage. (It was only later, after we were elected, that we discovered our respective Irish forebears, both boot makers, had left Ireland for America just five weeks apart.) And if I was seen as temperamentally cool and collected, measured in how I used my words, Joe was all warmth, a man without inhibitions, happy to share whatever popped into his head. It was an endearing trait, for he genuinely enjoyed people. You could see it as he worked a room, his handsome face always cast in a dazzling smile (and just inches from whomever he was talking to), asking a person where they were from, telling them a story about how much he loved their hometown ("Best calzone I ever tasted") or how they must know so-and-so ("An absolutely great guy, salt of the earth"), flattering their children ("Anyone ever tell you you're gorgeous?") or their mother ("You can't be a day over forty!"), and then on to the next person, and the next, until he'd touched every soul in the room with a flurry of handshakes, hugs, kisses, backslaps, compliments, and one-liners.

Joe's enthusiasm had its downside. In a town filled with people who liked to hear themselves talk, he had no peer. If a speech was scheduled for fifteen minutes, Joe went for at least a half hour. If it was scheduled for a half hour, there was no telling how long he might talk. His soliloquies during committee hearings were legendary. His lack of a filter periodically got him in trouble, as when during the primaries, he had pronounced me "articulate and bright and clean and a nice-looking guy," a phrase surely meant as a compliment, but interpreted by some as suggesting that such characteristics in a Black man were noteworthy.

As I came to know Joe, though, I found his occasional gaffes to be trivial compared to his strengths. On domestic issues, he was smart, practical, and did his homework. His experience in foreign policy was broad and deep. During his relatively short-lived run in the primaries, he had impressed me with his skill and discipline as a debater and his comfort on a national stage.

Most of all, Joe had heart. He'd overcome a bad stutter as a child (which probably explained his vigorous attachment to words) and two brain aneurysms in middle age. In politics, he'd known early success and suffered embarrassing defeats. And he had endured unimaginable tragedy: In 1972, just weeks after Joe was elected to the Senate, his wife and baby daughter had been killed—and his two young sons, Beau and Hunter, injured—in a car accident. In the wake of this loss, his colleagues and siblings had to talk him out of quitting the Senate, but he'd arranged his schedule to make a daily hour-and-a-half Amtrak commute between Delaware and Washington to care for his boys, a practice he'd continue for the next three decades.

That Joe had survived such heartbreak was a credit to his second wife, Jill, a lovely and understated teacher whom he'd met three years after the accident, and who had raised Joe's sons as her own. Anytime you saw the

Bidens together, it was immediately obvious just how much his family sustained Joe—how much pride and joy he took in Beau, then Delaware's attorney general and a rising star in state politics; in Hunter, a lawyer in D.C.; in Ashley, a social worker in Wilmington; and in their beautiful grandkids.

Family had sustained Joe, but so, too, had a buoyancy of character. Tragedy and setbacks may have scarred him, I would learn, but they hadn't made him bitter or cynical.

It was on the basis of those impressions that I had asked Joe to undergo the initial vetting process and meet me while I was campaigning in Minnesota. He was resistant at first—like most senators, Joe had a healthy ego and disliked the idea of playing second fiddle. Our meeting began with him explaining all the reasons why the job of vice president might be a step down for him (along with an explanation of why he'd be the best choice). I assured him that I was looking not for a ceremonial stand-in but for a partner.

"If you pick me," Joe said, "I want to be able to give you my best judgment and frank advice. You'll be the president, and I'll defend whatever you decide. But I want to be the last guy in the room on every major decision."

I told him that was a commitment I could make.

Both Axe and Plouffe thought the world of Tim Kaine, and like me, they knew he'd fit seamlessly into an Obama administration. But also like me, they wondered whether putting two relatively young, inexperienced, and liberal civil rights attorneys on a ticket might be more hope and change than the voters could handle.

Joe carried his own risks. We figured his lack of discipline in front of a microphone might result in unnecessary controversies. His style was old-school, he liked the limelight, and he wasn't always self-aware. I sensed that he could get prickly if he thought he wasn't given his due—a quality that might flare up when dealing with a much younger boss.

And yet I found the contrast between us compelling. I liked the fact that Joe would be more than ready to serve as president if something happened to me—and that it might reassure those who still worried I was too young. His foreign policy experience would be valuable during a time when we were embroiled in two wars; so would his relationships in Congress and his potential to reach voters still wary of electing an African American president. What mattered most, though, was what my gut told me—that Joe was decent, honest, and loyal. I believed that he cared about ordinary people, and that when things got tough, I could trust him.

I wouldn't be disappointed.

HOW THE DEMOCRATIC National Convention in Denver got put together is largely a mystery to me. I was consulted on the order of the program over the four nights it would take place, the themes that would be developed, the speakers scheduled. I was shown biographical videos for approval and asked for a list of family and friends who would need accommodations. Plouffe checked in to see if I was game to hold the convention's final night not in a traditional indoor arena, but at Mile High Stadium, home of the Denver Broncos. With a capacity of close to eighty thousand, it could accommodate the tens of thousands of volunteers from across the country who'd been the foundation of our campaign. It also had no roof, which meant we'd be exposed to the elements.

"What if it rains?" I asked.

"We pulled one hundred years' worth of weather reports for Denver on August 28 at eight p.m.," Plouffe said. "It's only rained once."

"What if this year's the second time? Do we have a backup plan?"

"Once we lock in the stadium," Plouffe said, "there's no going back." He gave me a slightly maniacal grin. "Remember, we're always at our best without a net. Why stop now?"

Why indeed.

Michelle and the girls traveled to Denver a couple of days ahead of me while I campaigned in a few states, so by the time I arrived, the festivities were in full swing. Satellite trucks and press tents surrounded the arena like an army laying siege; street vendors hawked T-shirts, hats, tote bags, and jewelry adorned with our rising sun logo or my jug-eared visage. Tourists and paparazzi clicked away at the politicians and occasional celebrity wandering the arena.

Unlike the 2000 convention, when I'd been the kid pressing his face against the candy store window, or the 2004 convention, when my keynote had placed me at the center of the spectacle, I now found myself both the starring attraction and on the periphery, trapped in a hotel suite or looking out the window of my Secret Service vehicle, arriving in Denver only on the second-to-last night of the convention. It was a matter of security,

I was told, as well as deliberate stagecraft—if I remained out of sight, anticipation would only build. But it made me feel restless and oddly removed, as if I were merely an expensive prop to be taken out of the box under special conditions.

Certain moments from that week do stand out in my mind. I remember Malia and Sasha and three of Joe's granddaughters rolling around on a pile of air mattresses in our hotel suite, all of them giggling, lost in their secret games and wholly indifferent to the hoopla below. I remember Hillary stepping up to the microphone representing the New York delegates and formally making the motion to vote me in as the Democratic nominee, a powerful gesture of unity. And I remember sitting in the living room of a very sweet family of supporters in Missouri, making small talk and munching on snacks before Michelle appeared on the television screen, luminescent in an aquamarine dress, to deliver the convention's opening night address.

I had deliberately avoided reading Michelle's speech beforehand, not wanting to meddle in the process or add to the pressure. Having seen her on the campaign trail, I had no doubt she'd be good. But listening to Michelle tell her story that night—seeing her talk about her mom and dad, the sacrifices they'd made and the values they'd passed on; hearing her trace her unlikely journey and describe her hope for our daughters; having this woman who had shouldered so much vouch for the fact that I'd always been true to my family and to my convictions; seeing the convention hall audience, the network anchors, and the people sitting next to me transfixed—well, I couldn't have been prouder.

Contrary to what some commentators said at the time, my wife didn't "find" her voice that night. A national audience finally had a chance to hear that voice unfiltered.

FORTY-EIGHT HOURS LATER, I found myself holed up with Favs and Axe in a hotel room, fine-tuning the acceptance speech I'd deliver the following evening. It had been tough to write. We felt the moment called for more prose than poetry, with a hard-hitting critique of Republican policies and an account of specific steps I intended to take as president—all without being too long, too dry, or too partisan. It had required countless revisions and I had little time to practice. As I stood behind a mock podium delivering my lines, the atmosphere was more workmanlike than inspired.

Only once did the full meaning of my nomination hit me. By coincidence, the last night of the convention fell on the forty-fifth anniversary of the March on Washington and Dr. King's historic "I Have a Dream" speech. We had decided not to draw too much attention to that fact, figuring that it was a poor idea to invite comparisons to one of the greatest speeches in American history. But I did pay tribute to the miracle of that young preacher from Georgia in the closing bars of my speech, quoting something he'd said to the people who'd gathered on the National Mall that day in 1963: "We cannot walk alone. And as we walk, we must make the pledge that we shall always march ahead. We cannot turn back."

"We cannot walk alone." I hadn't remembered these particular lines from Dr. King's speech. But as I read them aloud during practice, I found myself thinking about all the older Black volunteers I'd met in our offices around the country, the way they'd clutch my hands and tell me they never thought they'd see the day when a Black man would have a real chance to be president.

I thought about the seniors who wrote to me to explain how they had woken up early and been first in line to vote during the primaries, even though they were sick or disabled.

I thought about the doormen, janitors, secretaries, clerks, dishwashers, and drivers I encountered anytime I passed through hotels, conference centers, or office buildings—how they'd wave or give me a thumbs-up or shyly accept a handshake, Black men and women of a certain age who, like Michelle's parents, had quietly done what was necessary to feed their families and send their kids to school, and now recognized in me some of the fruits of their labor.

I thought of all the people who had sat in jail or joined the March on Washington forty, fifty years ago, and wondered how they would feel when I walked out onto that stage in Denver—how much they had seen their country transformed, and how far things still were from what they had hoped.

"You know what . . . give me a second," I said, my voice catching in my throat, my eyes starting to brim. I went to the bathroom to splash some water on my face. When I returned a few minutes later, Favs, Axe, and the teleprompter operator were all quiet, unsure of what to do.

"Sorry about that," I said. "Let's try it again from the top."

I had no trouble getting through the speech the second time around; the only interruption came about halfway through my oration, when we heard a knock on the door and found a hotel server with a Caesar salad standing in the hall ("What can I say?" Axe said with a sheepish grin. "I was starving"). And by the following evening, as I walked out onto the broad, blue-carpeted stage under a clear and open sky to address a stadium full of people and millions more across the country, all that I felt was calm.

The night was warm, the roar from the crowd infectious, the flash from thousands of cameras mirroring the stars overhead. When I was finished speaking, Michelle and the girls and then Joe and Jill Biden joined me to wave through a flurry of confetti, and across the stadium we could see people laughing and hugging, waving flags to the beat of a song by country artists Brooks & Dunn that had become a staple on the campaign trail: "Only in America."

HISTORICALLY, A PRESIDENTIAL candidate enjoys a healthy "bounce" in the polls after a successful convention. By all accounts, ours had been close to flawless. Our pollsters reported that after Denver, my lead over John McCain had indeed widened to at least five points.

It lasted about a week.

John McCain's campaign had been flailing. Despite the fact that he'd wrapped up the Republican nomination three months before I secured mine, he hadn't achieved much in the way of momentum. Swing voters remained unpersuaded by his proposal for further tax cuts on top of those Bush had already passed. In the new, more polarized climate, McCain himself appeared hesitant to even mention issues like immigration reform and climate change, which had previously burnished his reputation as a maverick inside his party. In fairness, he'd been dealt a bad hand. The Iraq War remained as unpopular as ever. The economy, already in recession, was rapidly worsening, and so were Bush's approval numbers. In an election likely to hinge on the promise of change, McCain looked and sounded like more of the same.

McCain and his team must have known they needed to do something dramatic. And I have to give them credit—they sure did deliver. The day after our convention ended, Michelle and I, along with Jill and Joe Biden, were on the campaign plane waiting to take off for a few days of events in Pennsylvania when Axe rushed up to tell us that word had leaked of McCain's running mate. Joe looked at the name on Axe's BlackBerry and then turned to me.

"Who the hell is Sarah Palin?" he said.

For the next two weeks, the national press corps would obsess over that question, giving McCain's campaign a much-needed shot of adrenaline and effectively knocking our campaign off the airwaves. After adding Palin to the ticket, McCain raked in millions of dollars in fresh donations in a single weekend. His poll numbers leapt up, essentially putting us in a dead heat.

Sarah Palin—the forty-four-year-old governor of Alaska and an unknown when it came to national politics—was, above all, a potent disrupter. Not only was she young and a woman, a potential groundbreaker in her own right, but she also had a story you couldn't make up: She'd been a small-town basketball player and pageant queen who'd bounced among five colleges before graduating with a journalism degree. She'd worked for a while as a sportscaster before getting elected mayor of Wasilla, Alaska, and then taking on the state's entrenched Republican establishment and beating the incumbent governor in 2006. She'd married her high school sweetheart, had five kids (including a teenage son about to be deployed to Iraq and a baby with Down syndrome), professed a conservative Christian faith, and enjoyed hunting moose and elk during her spare time.

Hers was a biography tailor-made for working-class white voters who hated Washington and harbored the not entirely unjustified suspicion that big-city elites—whether in business, politics, or the media—looked down on their way of life. If the **New York Times** editorial board or NPR listeners questioned her qualifications, Palin didn't care. She offered their criticism as proof of her authenticity, understanding (far earlier than many of her critics) that the old gatekeepers were losing relevance, that the walls of what was considered acceptable in a candidate for national office had been breached, and that Fox News, talk radio, and the budding power of social media could provide her with all the platforms she needed to reach her intended audience.

It helped, too, that Palin was a born performer. Her forty-five-minute speech at the Republican National Convention in early September was a masterpiece of folksy populism and well-aimed zingers. ("In small towns, we don't quite know what to make of a candidate who lavishes praise on working people when they're listening, and then talks about how bitterly they cling to their religion and guns when those people aren't listening." Ouch.) The delegates were ecstatic. Touring with Palin after the convention, McCain spoke to crowds three or four times larger than what he normally saw on his own. And while the Republican faithful cheered politely during his speeches, it became clear that it was his "hockey mom" running mate they were really there to see. She was new, different, one of them.

A "real American"—and fantastically proud of it.

In a different time and a different place—say, a swing-state Senate or gubernatorial race—the sheer energy Palin generated within the Republican base might have had me worried. But from the day McCain chose her and through the heights of Palin-mania, I felt certain the decision would not serve him well. For all of Palin's performative gifts, a vice president's most important qualification was the ability, if necessary, to assume the presidency. Given John's age and history of melanoma, this wasn't an idle concern. And what became abundantly clear as soon as Sarah Palin stepped into the spotlight was that on just about every subject relevant to governing the country she had absolutely no idea what the hell she was talking about. The financial system. The Supreme Court. The Russian invasion of Georgia. It didn't matter what the topic was or what form the question took—the Alaskan governor appeared lost, stringing words together like a kid trying to bluff her way through a test for which she had failed to study.

Palin's nomination was troubling on a deeper level. I noticed from the start that her incoherence didn't matter to the vast majority of Republicans; in fact, anytime she crumbled under questioning by a journalist, they seemed to view it as proof of a liberal conspiracy. I was even more surprised to witness prominent conservatives—including those who'd spent a year dismissing me as inexperienced, and who'd spent decades decrying affirmative action, the erosion of intellectual standards, and the debasement of Western culture at the hands of multiculturalists—suddenly shilling for Palin, tying themselves into knots as they sought to convince the public that in a vice presidential candidate, the need for basic knowledge of foreign policy or the functions of the federal government was actually overrated. Sarah Palin, like Reagan, had "good instincts," they said, and once installed, she'd grow into the job.

It was, of course, a sign of things to come, a larger, darker reality in which partisan affiliation and political expedience would threaten to blot out everything—your previous positions; your stated principles; even what your own senses, your eyes and ears, told you to be true.

CHAPTER 9

I N 1993, MICHELLE AND I purchased our first home, in a Hyde Park condominium complex called East View Park. It was a lovely location, across from Promontory Point and Lake Michigan, with dogwood trees in the ample courtyard that bloomed a bright pink every spring. The three-bedroom apartment, laid out like a railcar from front to back, wasn't large, but it had hardwood floors and decent light, and a proper dining room with walnut cabinets. Compared to the second floor of my mother-in-law's house, where we'd been living to save money, it felt absolutely lavish, and we furnished it as our budget allowed, with a combination of Crate & Barrel couches, Ace Hardware lamps, and yard-sale tables.

Next to the kitchen, there was a small study where I worked in the evenings. Michelle called it "the Hole" because of the way it was always filled with stacks of books, magazines, newspapers, legal briefs I was writing, and exams I was grading. Every month or so, prompted by my inability to find something I needed, I'd clean the Hole in an hour-long frenzy, and I would feel very proud of myself for the three days or so it would take for the books and papers and other clutter to spring back like weeds. The Hole was also the only room in the apartment where I smoked, although once the girls were born, I took my foul habit outside to the slightly rickety back porch, where I'd sometimes interrupt families of raccoons foraging through our trash cans.

Kids reshaped our home in all sorts of ways. Foam childproofing pads appeared on the table corners. The dining room slowly became less about dining and more a repository for the playpens and brightly colored mats and toys that I found myself stepping on at least once a day. But instead of feeling cramped, the apartment's modest size only amplified the joy and noise of our young family: splashy bath times and squeal-filled birthday parties and the sound of Motown or salsa coming from a boom box on the mantel as I spun the girls around in my arms. And while we noticed friends our age buying bigger houses in more well-off neighborhoods, the only time the idea of us moving came up was the summer when either one mouse or two (we couldn't be sure) repeatedly scampered down the long hallway. I would fix the problem with repairs to a kitchen floorboard, but only after—with remarkable foolishness and a wiseass grin on my face—I had disputed the notion that two mice really qualified as an "infestation," and Michelle in response had threatened to leave with the girls.

We paid $277,500 for the condo, with 40 percent down (thanks to some help from Toot) and a thirty-year fixed mortgage. On paper, our income should have comfortably supported our monthly payments. But as Malia and Sasha got older, the costs of childcare, school fees, and summer camps kept rising, while the principal on our college and law school loans never seemed to decrease.

Money was perpetually tight; our credit card balances grew; we had little in the way of savings. So when Marty suggested we consider refinancing our mortgage to take advantage of lower interest rates, I made a call the next day to a neighborhood mortgage broker.

The broker, an energetic young man with a buzz cut, confirmed that he could save us a hundred bucks or so a month by refinancing. But with home prices going through the roof, he asked if we had considered also using a portion of our equity to get some cash out of the transaction. It was routine, he said, just a matter of working with his appraiser. I was skeptical at first, hearing Toot's sensible voice ringing in my ears, but when I ran the numbers and considered what we'd save by paying off our credit card debt, the broker's logic was hard to dispute. With neither the appraiser nor the broker ever bothering to inspect our house, with me providing only three months of pay stubs and a handful of bank statements, I signed a few papers and walked out of the broker's office with a $40,000 check and the vague feeling that I'd just gotten away with something.

THAT'S HOW IT was in the early 2000s, a real estate gold rush. In Chicago, new developments seemed to pop up overnight. With home prices climbing at an unprecedented pace, with interest rates low and some lenders requiring just 10 or 5 percent—or even no money— down for a purchase, why pass up the extra bedroom, the granite countertops, and the finished basement that magazines and television shows insisted were standard measures of a middle-class life? It was a great investment, a sure thing—and once purchased, that same home could serve as your personal ATM, covering the right window treatments, that long-desired Cancún vacation, or making up for the fact that you didn't get a raise last year. Eager to get in on the action, friends, cabdrivers, and schoolteachers told me they'd started flipping houses, everyone suddenly fluent in the language of balloon payments, adjustable-rate mortgages, and the Case-Shiller Index. If I cautioned them gently—real estate can be unpredictable, you don't want to get in too deep—they'd assure me they had talked to their cousin or uncle who had made a killing, in a tone of mild amusement that implied I didn't know the score.

After I was elected to the U.S. Senate, we sold our East View Park condo at a price high enough to cover our mortgage and home equity loan and make a small profit. But I noticed, driving home one night, that my mortgage broker's storefront was now empty, with a big FOR SALE OR LEASE sign in the window. All those new condos in River North and the South Loop appeared unoccupied, even with developers offering buyers deeper and deeper discounts. A former staffer who'd left government to get her real estate license asked if I knew of any job openings—the new gig wasn't panning out as she'd hoped.

I was neither surprised nor alarmed by any of this, figuring it was just the cyclical ebb and flow of the market. But back in D.C., I happened to mention the softening Chicago real estate market to a friend of mine, George Haywood, while we were eating sandwiches in a park near the Capitol. George had dropped out of Harvard Law to play professional blackjack, parlayed his skill with numbers and tolerance for risk into a job as a

Wall Street bond trader, and had ultimately made a mint on personal investments. Being ahead of the curve was his business.

"This is just the start," he told me.

"What do you mean?"

"I mean the entire housing market," George said. "The entire financial system. It's all a house of cards waiting to topple."

As we sat in the afternoon sun, he gave me a quick tutorial on the burgeoning subprime mortgage market. Whereas banks had once typically held the mortgage loans they made in their own portfolios, a huge percentage of mortgages were now bundled and sold as securities on Wall Street. Since banks could now off-load their risk that any particular borrower might default on their loan, this "securitization" of mortgages had led banks to steadily loosen their lending standards. Credit rating agencies, paid by the issuers, had stamped these securities as "AAA," or least risky, without adequately analyzing the default risk on the underlying mortgages. Global investors, awash in cash and eager for higher returns, rushed in to buy these products, pumping more and more money into housing finance. Meanwhile, Fannie Mae and Freddie Mac, the two giant companies that Congress had authorized to purchase qualified mortgages to encourage homeownership—and which, by virtue of their quasi-governmental status, could borrow money much more cheaply than other companies—were knee-deep in the subprime market, with their shareholders making money hand over fist as the housing market swelled.

All of this had contributed to a classic bubble, George said. So long as housing prices kept going up, everybody was happy: the family who could suddenly buy their dream house with no money down; the developers that couldn't build houses fast enough to satisfy all these new customers; the banks that sold increasingly complex financial instruments at handsome profits; the hedge funds and investment banks that were placing bigger and bigger bets on these financial instruments with borrowed money; not to mention furniture retailers, carpet manufacturers, trade unions, and newspaper advertising departments, all of which had every incentive to keep the party going.

But with so many unqualified buyers propping up the market, George was convinced the party would eventually end. What I was noticing in Chicago was just a tremor, he told me. Once the earthquake came, the impact would be far worse in places like Florida, Arizona, and Nevada, where subprime lending had been most active. As soon as large numbers of homeowners started defaulting, investors would realize that a lot of mortgage-backed securities weren't so AAA after all. They'd likely rush for the exits, dumping the securities as fast as they could. Banks that held these securities would be vulnerable to runs, and would probably pull back on lending to cover losses or maintain capital requirements, making it hard for even qualified families to get a mortgage, which in turn would depress the housing market even further.

It would be a vicious cycle, likely to trigger a market panic, and because of the sheer amount of money involved, the result could be an economic crisis the likes of which we hadn't seen in our lifetimes.

I listened to all this with growing incredulity. George was not prone to exaggeration, especially when it came to money. He told me he had taken a hefty "short" position himself, essentially betting that the price of mortgage-backed securities would go way down in the future. I asked him why it was that if the risk of a full-blown crisis was so high, no one—not the Federal Reserve, or bank regulators, or the financial press—seemed to be talking about it.

George shrugged. "You tell me."

When I got back to my Senate office, I asked some of my staff to check with their counterparts on the Banking Committee to see if anyone saw any danger in the spiking of the subprime mortgage market. The reports came back negative: The Federal Reserve chairman had indicated that the housing market was a bit overheated and due for an eventual correction, but that given historical trends, he saw no major threat to the financial system or the broader economy. With all the other issues on my plate, including the start of the midterm campaigns, George's warning receded from my mind. In fact, when I saw him a couple of months later, in early 2007, both the financial and housing markets had continued to soften, but it didn't seem to be anything serious. George told me that he had been forced to abandon his "short" position after taking heavy losses.

"I just don't have enough cash to stay with the bet," he said calmly enough, adding, "Apparently I've underestimated how willing people are to maintain a charade."

I didn't ask George how much money he'd lost, and we moved on to other topics. We parted ways that day not knowing that the charade wouldn't last very much longer—or that its terrible fallout would, just a year and a half later, play a critical role in electing me president.

· · ·

"SENATOR OBAMA. This is Hank Paulson."

It was a week and a half after the Republican National Convention, eleven days before my first scheduled debate with John McCain. It was clear why the U.S. Treasury secretary had requested the call.

The financial system was in a meltdown and taking the American economy with it.

Although Iraq had been the biggest issue at the start of our campaign, I had always made the need for more progressive economic policies a central part of my argument for change. As I saw it, the combination of globalization and revolutionary new technologies had been fundamentally altering the American economy for at least two decades. U.S. manufacturers had shifted production overseas, taking advantage of low-cost labor and shipping back cheap goods to be sold by big-box retailers against which small businesses couldn't hope to compete. More recently, the internet had wiped out entire categories of office work and, in some cases, whole industries.

In this new, winner-take-all economy, those controlling capital or possessing specialized, high-demand skills—whether tech entrepreneurs, hedge fund managers, LeBron James, or Jerry Seinfeld—could leverage their assets, market globally, and amass more wealth than any group in human history. But for ordinary workers, capital mobility and automation meant an ever-weakening bargaining position. Manufacturing towns lost their lifeblood. Low inflation and cheap flat-screen TVs couldn't compensate for layoffs, fewer hours and temp work, stagnant wages and reduced benefits, especially when both healthcare and education costs (two sectors less subject to cost-saving automation) kept soaring.

Inequality also had a way of compounding itself. Even middle-class Americans found themselves increasingly priced out of neighborhoods with the best schools or cities with the best job prospects. They were unable to afford the extras—SAT prep courses, computer camps, invaluable but unpaid internships—that better-off parents routinely provided their kids. By 2007, the American economy was not only producing greater inequality than almost every other wealthy nation but also delivering less upward mobility.

I believed that these outcomes weren't inevitable, but rather were the result of political choices dating back to Ronald Reagan. Under the banner of economic freedom—an "ownership society" was the phrase President Bush used—Americans had been fed a steady diet of tax cuts for the wealthy and seen collective bargaining laws go unenforced. There had been efforts to privatize or cut the social safety net, and federal budgets had consistently underinvested in everything from early childhood education to infrastructure. All this further accelerated inequality, leaving families ill-equipped to navigate even minor economic turbulence.

I was campaigning to push the country in the opposite direction. I didn't think America could roll back automation or sever the global supply chain (though I did think we could negotiate stronger labor and environmental provisions in our trade agreements). But I was certain we could adapt our laws and institutions, just as we'd done in the past, to make sure that folks willing to work could get a fair shake. At every stop I made, in every city and small town, my message was the same. I promised to raise taxes on high-income Americans to pay for vital investments in education, research, and infrastructure. I promised to strengthen unions and raise the minimum wage as well as to deliver universal health-care and make college more affordable.

I wanted people to understand that there was a prec-edent for bold government action. FDR had saved capitalism from itself, laying the foundation for a post–World War II boom. I often talked about how strong labor laws had helped build a thriving middle class and a thriving domestic market, and how—by driving out unsafe products and fraudulent schemes—consumer protection laws had actually helped legitimate businesses prosper and grow.

I explained how strong public schools and state uni-versities and a GI Bill had unleashed the potential of generations of Americans and driven upward mobility. Programs like Social Security and Medicare had given those same Americans a measure of stability in their golden years, and government investments like those in the Tennessee Valley Authority and the interstate high-way system had boosted productivity and provided the platform for countless entrepreneurs.

I was convinced we could adapt these strategies to current times. Beyond any specific policy, I wanted to restore in the minds of the American people the crucial role that government had always played in expanding opportunity, fostering competition and fair dealing, and making sure the marketplace worked for everybody.

What I hadn't counted on was a major financial crisis.

. . .

DESPITE MY FRIEND George's early warning, it hadn't been until the spring of 2007 that I started noticing troubling headlines in the financial press. The nation's second-largest subprime lender, New Century Financial, declared bankruptcy after a surge in mortgage defaults in the subprime housing market. The largest lender, Countrywide, avoided the same fate only after the Federal Reserve stepped in and approved a shotgun marriage with Bank of America.

Alarmed, I had spoken to my economic team and delivered a speech at NASDAQ in September 2007, decrying the failure to regulate the subprime lending market and proposing stronger oversight. This may have put me ahead of the curve compared to other presidential candidates, but I was nonetheless well behind the pace at which events on Wall Street were beginning to spin out of control.

In the months that followed, financial markets saw a flight to safety, as lenders and investors moved their money into government-backed Treasury bonds, sharply restricted credit, and yanked capital out of any firm that might have significant risk when it came to mortgage-backed securities. Just about every major financial institution in the world was dangerously exposed, having either invested directly in such instruments (often taking on debt to finance their bets) or loaned money to firms that did. In October 2007, Merrill Lynch announced $7.9 billion in losses related to mortgages. Citigroup warned that its figure might be closer to $11 billion. In March 2008, the share price in the investment firm Bear Stearns dropped from $57 to $30 in a single day, forcing

the Fed to engineer a fire-sale purchase by JPMorgan
Chase. No one could say if or when Wall Street's three
remaining major investment banks—Goldman Sachs,
Morgan Stanley, and especially Lehman Brothers, all of
which were hemorrhaging capital at alarming rates—
would face a similar reckoning.

For the public, it was tempting to see all this as a
righteous comeuppance for greedy bankers and hedge
fund managers; to want to stand by as firms failed and
executives who'd drawn $20 million bonuses were forced
to sell off their yachts, jets, and homes in the Hamptons.
I'd encountered enough Wall Street executives personally
to know that many (though not all) lived up to the
stereotype: smug and entitled, conspicuous in their consumption, and indifferent to the impact their decisions
might have on everyone else.

The trouble was that in the midst of a financial panic,
in a modern capitalist economy, it was impossible to
isolate good businesses from bad, or administer pain only
to the reckless or unscrupulous. Like it or not, everybody
and everything was connected.

By spring, the United States had entered a full-blown
recession. The housing bubble and easy money had
disguised a whole host of structural weaknesses in the
American economy for a full decade. But with defaults
now spiking, credit tightening, the stock market declining, and housing prices plummeting, businesses large
and small decided to retrench. They laid off workers and
canceled orders. They deferred investments in new plants
and IT systems. And as people who had worked for
those companies lost their jobs, or saw the equity in
their homes or 401(k) plans dwindle, or fell behind on

their credit card payments and were forced to spend down their savings, they, too, retrenched. They put off new car purchases, stopped eating out, and postponed vacations. And with declining sales, businesses cut payrolls and spending even more. It was a classic cycle of contracting demand, one that worsened with each successive month. March's data showed that one in eleven mortgages was past due or in foreclosure and that auto sales had cratered. In May, unemployment rose a half point—the largest monthly increase in twenty years.

It had become President Bush's problem to manage. At the urging of his economic advisors, he had secured bipartisan agreement from Congress on a $168 billion economic rescue package providing tax breaks and rebates meant to stimulate consumer spending and give the economy a jolt. But any effect it may have had was dampened by high gas prices that summer, and the crisis only grew worse. In July, news stations across the country broadcast images of desperate customers lined up to pull their money out of IndyMac, a California bank that promptly went belly-up. The much larger Wachovia survived only after Secretary Paulson was able to invoke a "systemic risk exception" to prevent its failure.

Congress meanwhile authorized $200 billion to prevent Fannie Mae and Freddie Mac—the two privately owned behemoths that together guaranteed nearly 90 percent of America's mortgages—from going under. Both were placed in government conservatorship through the newly formed Federal Housing Finance Agency. Yet even with an intervention of that magnitude, it still felt as if the markets were teetering on the edge of collapse—as if the authorities were shoveling gravel into a crack in the earth that just kept on growing. And for the moment, at least, the government had run out of gravel.

Which was why Hank Paulson, the U.S. Treasury secretary, was calling me. I had first met Paulson when he was the CEO of Goldman Sachs. Tall, bald, and bespectacled, with an awkward but unpretentious manner, he'd spent most of our time talking about his passion for environmental protection. But his voice, typically hoarse, now sounded thoroughly frayed, that of a man fighting both exhaustion and fear.

That morning, Monday, September 15, Lehman Brothers, a $639 billion company, had announced it was filing for bankruptcy. The fact that the Treasury Department had not intervened to prevent what would be the largest bankruptcy filing in history signaled that we were entering a new phase in the crisis.

"We can expect a very bad market reaction," he said. "And the situation is likely to get worse before it gets better."

He explained why both Treasury and the Fed had determined that Lehman was too weak to prop up and that no other financial institution was willing to take on its liabilities. President Bush had authorized Paulson to brief both me and John McCain because further emergency actions would need bipartisan political support. Paulson hoped that both campaigns would respect and respond appropriately to the severity of the situation.

You didn't need a pollster to know that Paulson was right to be worried about the politics. We were seven weeks from a national election. As the public learned more about the enormity of the crisis, the idea of spending billions of taxpayer dollars to bail out reckless banks would surely rank in popularity somewhere between a bad case of shingles and Osama bin Laden. The following day, Paulson's Treasury would prevent catastrophes at Goldman Sachs and Morgan Stanley by redefining both institutions in a way that allowed them to create commercial banks eligible for federal protection. Still, even blue-chip companies with sterling ratings were suddenly unable to borrow the money needed to finance day-to-day operations, and money market funds, previously considered as safe and liquid as cash, were now starting to buckle.

For Democrats, it would be easy enough to lay blame for the fiasco at the foot of the administration, but the truth was that plenty of congressional Democrats had applauded rising homeownership rates throughout the subprime boom. For Republicans who were up for reelection and already saddled with an unpopular president and a tanking economy, the prospect of voting for more Wall Street "bailouts" looked like an invitation to dig their own graves.

"If you need to take further steps," I told Paulson, "I'm guessing your biggest problem will come from your side, not mine." Already, many Republicans were complaining that the Bush administration's interventions in the banking sector violated the core conservative principles of limited government. They accused the Federal Reserve of overstepping its mandate, and some had the gall to criticize government regulators for failing to catch the problems in the subprime market sooner—as if they themselves hadn't spent the past eight years working to weaken every financial regulation they could find.

John McCain's public comments up to that point had

been muted, and I urged Paulson to keep in close contact with my competitor as the situation developed. As the Republican nominee, McCain didn't have the luxury of distancing himself from Bush. His vow to continue most of Bush's economic policies, in fact, had always been one of his great vulnerabilities. During the primaries, he'd confessed that he didn't know much about economic policy. He'd more recently reinforced the impression that he was out of touch by admitting to a reporter that he wasn't sure how many homes he owned. (The answer was eight.) Based on what Paulson was telling me, McCain's political problems were about to get worse. I had no doubt his political advisors would urge him to improve his standing with voters by distancing himself from any financial rescue efforts the administration tried to make.

If McCain chose not to be supportive, I knew I'd be under fierce pressure from Democrats—and perhaps my own staff—to follow suit. And yet, as I wrapped up the conversation with Paulson, I knew that it didn't matter what McCain did. With the stakes this high, I would do whatever was necessary, regardless of the politics, to help the administration stabilize the situation.

If I wanted to be president, I told myself, I needed to act like one.

AS EXPECTED, John McCain had difficulty coming up with a coherent response to the rapidly unfolding events. On the day of the Lehman announcement, in an ill-timed attempt at reassuring the public, he appeared at a televised rally and declared that the "fundamentals of the economy are strong." My campaign absolutely roasted him for it. ("Senator, what economy are you talking about?" I asked, speaking later in the day at a rally of my own.)

In the ensuing days, the news of Lehman's bankruptcy sent financial markets into a full-blown panic. Stocks plunged. Merrill Lynch had already negotiated a desperation sale to Bank of America. Meanwhile, the Fed's $200 billion loan program to banks had proven to be insufficient. Along with all the money to shore up Fannie and Freddie, another $85 billion was now being consumed by an urgent government takeover of AIG, the massive insurance company whose policies underwrote the subprime security market. AIG was the poster child for "too big to fail"—so intertwined with global financial networks that its collapse would cause a cascade of bank failures—and even after the government intervened, it continued to hemorrhage. Four days after Lehman's collapse, President Bush and Secretary Paulson appeared on television alongside Ben Bernanke and Chris Cox, the respective chairs of the Federal Reserve and the Securities and Exchange Commission, and announced the need for Congress to pass a bill that would eventually be known as the Troubled Asset Relief Program, or TARP, establishing a new emergency fund of $700 billion. This was the price, they estimated, of staving off Armageddon.

Perhaps to compensate for his earlier blunder, McCain announced his opposition to the government bailout of AIG. A day later, he reversed himself. His position on TARP remained unclear, opposing bailouts in theory but maybe supporting this one in practice. With all the zigging and zagging, our campaign had no problem tying the crisis to a "Bush-McCain" economic agenda that prioritized the wealthy and powerful over the middle class, arguing that McCain was unprepared to steer the country through tough economic times.

Nevertheless, I did my best to stay true to the commitment I'd made to Paulson, instructing my team to refrain from making public comments that might jeopardize the Bush administration's chances at getting Congress to approve a rescue package. Along with our in-house economic advisors, Austan Goolsbee and Jason Furman, I had begun consulting with an ad hoc advisory group that included former Federal Reserve chairman Paul Volcker, former Clinton Treasury secretary Larry Summers, and legendary investor Warren Buffett. All had lived through major financial crises before, and each confirmed that this one was of a different order of magnitude. Without swift action, they told me, we faced the very real possibility of economic collapse: millions more Americans losing their homes and their life savings, along with Depression-era levels of unemployment.

Their briefings proved invaluable in helping me understand the nuts and bolts of the crisis and evaluate the various responses being proposed. They also scared the heck out of me. By the time I traveled to Tampa, where I would be preparing for my first debate with McCain, I felt confident that on the substance of the economy, at least, I knew what I was talking about— and I increasingly dreaded what a prolonged crisis might mean for families all across America.

EVEN WITHOUT THE distraction of a looming crisis, I probably wouldn't have looked forward to being holed up in a hotel for three days of debate prep. But given my inconsistency during the primary debates, I knew I needed the work. Fortunately, our team had recruited a pair of lawyers and political veterans—Ron Klain and Tom Donilon, who had served in similar roles prepping candidates like Al Gore, Bill Clinton, and John Kerry. The moment I arrived, they gave me a detailed breakdown of the debate format and an outline of every conceivable question that might be asked. Along with Axe, Plouffe, communications advisor Anita Dunn, and the rest of the team, they drilled me for hours on the precise answers they wanted to hear, down to the last word or turn of phrase. In the old Biltmore Hotel where we had set up shop, Ron and Tom had insisted on building an exact replica of the debate stage, and that first night they subjected me to a full ninety-minute mock debate, picking apart every aspect of my performance, from pace to posture to tone. It was exhausting but undeniably useful, and by the time my head hit the pillow, I was certain I would be dreaming in talking points.

Despite their best efforts, though, news from outside the Klain-Donilon bubble kept diverting my attention. In between sessions, I got updates on market developments and on the prospects for the administration's TARP legislation. To call it "legislation" was a stretch: The bill Hank Paulson had submitted to Congress consisted of three pages of boilerplate language authorizing the Treasury to use the $700 billion emergency fund to buy troubled assets or more generally take steps it deemed necessary to contain the crisis. With the press and the public howling at the price tag and representatives from both sides of the aisle balking at the lack of detail, Pete Rouse told me, the administration wasn't even close to having the votes it needed for passage.

Harry Reid and House Speaker Nancy Pelosi affirmed this when I spoke to them by phone. Both were hard-nosed politicians, not averse to bashing Republicans in order to solidify their majorities when the opportunity arose. But as I would see repeatedly over the next few years, both Harry and Nancy were willing (sometimes after a whole lot of grousing) to set politics aside when an issue of vital importance was at stake. On TARP, they were looking to me for direction. I shared my honest assessment: With some conditions attached to ensure it wasn't just a Wall Street giveaway, Democrats needed to help get it passed. And to their credit, the two leaders said they'd manage to drag in their respective caucuses and provide votes for passage—if Bush and GOP leaders delivered sufficient Republican votes as well.

I knew that was a hell of a big "if." Unpopular legisla-tion, an election fast approaching, and neither side wanting to hand ammunition to the other—it seemed a surefire recipe for gridlock.

To break the impasse, I started seriously considering a quixotic idea proposed by my friend Tom Coburn, a Republican senator from Oklahoma: that McCain and I put out a joint statement advocating that Congress pass some version of TARP. If both of us placed our hands on the bloody knife, Coburn reasoned, we could take the politics out of the vote and allow a nervous Congress to make a reasonable decision without obsessing over its Election Day impact.

I had no idea how McCain would respond to this. It

could come off as gimmicky, but knowing that unless a rescue package passed we'd be looking at what could turn into a full-blown depression, I figured it was worth a shot.

McCain and I spoke by phone as I rode back to my hotel after a short campaign event. His voice was soft, polite but cautious. He was open to a possible joint statement, he said, but had been mulling over a different idea: How about if we both suspended our campaigns? What if we postponed the debate, headed back to Washington, and waited until the rescue package passed?

Though I couldn't imagine how bringing the presidential campaign circus to Washington would be in any way helpful, I was encouraged by McCain's apparent interest in rising above the day-to-day scrum and getting a bill passed. Careful not to sound dismissive, I suggested—and John agreed—that our campaign managers work up a range of options for our consideration, and that we check back in with each other in an hour or two.

That's progress, I thought, hanging up. I then dialed Plouffe and instructed him to call Rick Davis, McCain's campaign manager, to follow up. Minutes later, I arrived at the hotel and found Plouffe scowling, having just hung up with Davis.

"McCain's about to hold a press conference," he said, "announcing his plan to suspend his campaign and fly back to Washington."

"What? I talked to him ten minutes ago."

"Yeah, well . . . it wasn't on the level. Davis says McCain won't even show at the debate unless a rescue package gets done in the next seventy-two hours. He says McCain's going to publicly call on you to join him in suspending campaigning since—get this—'Senator

McCain thinks politics should take a backseat right now.'" Plouffe spat out the words, looking like he wanted to hit somebody.

A few minutes later, we watched McCain make his announcement, his voice dripping with concern. It was hard not to feel both angry and disappointed. The charitable view was that John had reacted out of mistrust: Afraid that my suggestion of a joint statement was an attempt to one-up him, he'd decided to one-up me first. The less charitable view, shared unanimously by my staff, was that a desperate campaign was embarking on yet another poorly-thought-out political stunt.

Stunt or not, a whole passel of Washington political insiders considered McCain's move a masterstroke. As soon as he was off the air, we were bombarded with anxious messages from Democratic consultants and Beltway supporters saying we needed to suspend the campaign or risk ceding the high ground at a moment of national emergency. But by both temperament and experience we weren't inclined to follow the conventional wisdom. Not only did I think that the two of us posturing in Washington would lessen rather than improve the chances of getting TARP passed, but I felt that the financial crisis made it that much more important for the debate to take place, so that voters could hear directly from the two men vying to lead them through uncharted waters. Still, rejecting McCain's call felt like a huge gamble. With my team gathered around me, I asked if anyone disagreed with my assessment. Without hesitation, they all said no.

I smiled. "Okay, then."

An hour and a half later, I held my own press conference to say I would not be suspending my campaign. I pointed out that I was already in regular consultation with Paulson and congressional leaders and that I was available to fly to Washington at a moment's notice if needed. I then ad-libbed a line that would dominate the news coverage: "Presidents are going to have to deal with more than one thing at a time."

We had no idea how voters would respond, but we all felt good about my decision. As soon as we sat down to start gaming out next steps, though, Plouffe got an email from Josh Bolten, Bush's chief of staff, asking that he call. He darted out of the room; when he returned a few minutes later, his frown had deepened.

"Apparently McCain has asked Bush to host a meeting tomorrow at the White House with you, McCain, and the congressional leaders to try to hash out an agreement on TARP. Bush should be calling at any minute to invite you to the festivities."

Plouffe shook his head.

"This is absolute bullshit," he said.

ALTHOUGH IT'S NOT large, the Cabinet Room of the White House is stately, with a rich red carpet adorned with gold stars, and cream-colored walls with eagle-shaped sconces. On the north side of the room, marble busts of Washington and Franklin, sculpted in the classical style, gaze out from nooks on either side of a fireplace. At the center of the room sits an oval table made of gleaming mahogany and surrounded by twenty heavy leather chairs, a small brass plate affixed to the back of each one signifying where the president, vice president, and various cabinet members should sit. It's a place for sober deliberation, built to accommodate the weight of history.

On most days, light streams into the room through broad French doors that look out onto the Rose Garden. But on September 25, as I took my seat for the meeting Bush had called at McCain's behest, the sky was overcast. Around the table sat the president, Vice President Cheney, McCain, and me, along with Hank Paulson, Nancy Pelosi, Harry Reid, the Republican leaders John Boehner and Mitch McConnell, plus the chairpersons and ranking members of the relevant committees. A horde of White House and congressional staffers lined the walls, taking notes and leafing through thick briefing books.

No one looked like they wanted to be there.

The president certainly hadn't sounded enthusiastic when we'd spoken on the phone the previous day. I disagreed with just about every one of George W. Bush's major policy decisions, but I'd come to like the man, finding him to be straightforward, disarming, and self-deprecating in his humor.

"I can't tell you why McCain thinks this is a good idea," he'd said, sounding almost apologetic. He acknowledged that Hank Paulson and I were already communicating a couple of times daily and expressed appreciation for my behind-the-scenes help with congressional Democrats. "If I were you, Washington's the last place I'd want to be," Bush said. "But McCain asked, and I can't say no. Hopefully we can keep it short."

Only later would I learn that Paulson and the rest of Bush's team had been opposed to the meeting, and for good reason. Over the previous several days, congressional leaders had begun to narrow their differences on the TARP legislation. That very morning, there had been reports of a tentative agreement (although within a few hours, House Republicans pulled back from it). With negotiations at such a delicate stage, Bush's advisors rightly felt that inserting me and McCain into the process would likely hinder more than help.

Bush, though, had overruled his team, and I couldn't blame him. Given the increasing resistance to TARP within his own party, he could hardly afford to have the Republican nominee go south on him. Still, the entire proceeding had the air of an elaborate charade. Looking at the dour faces around the room, I understood we were gathered not for a substantive negotiation but rather a presidential effort to placate one man.

The president opened with a brief appeal for unity before turning the meeting over to Paulson, who updated us on current market conditions and explained how TARP funds would be used to buy up bad mortgages ("toxic assets," as they were called) from the banks, thereby shoring up balance sheets and restoring market confidence. "If Hank and Ben think this plan is going to work," Bush said after they were finished, "then that's what I'm for."

In accordance with protocol, the president next called on Speaker Pelosi. Rather than take the floor herself, though, Nancy politely informed the president that the Democrats would have me speak first, on their behalf.

It had been Nancy and Harry's idea that I serve as their point person, and I was grateful for it. Not only did it ensure that I wouldn't be outflanked by McCain during the deliberations, but it signaled that my fellow Democrats saw their political fortunes as wrapped up with mine. The move seemed to catch the Republicans by surprise, and I couldn't help noticing the president giving Nancy one of his patented smirks—as a shrewd politician, he recognized a deft maneuver when he saw one—before nodding my way.

For the next several minutes, I spoke about the nature of the crisis, the details of the emerging legislation, and the remaining points on oversight, executive compensation, and homeowner relief that Democrats believed still needed to be addressed. Noting that both Senator McCain and I had publicly pledged not to play politics with the financial rescue effort, I told the president that Democrats would deliver their share of the votes needed for passage. But I warned that if there was any truth to reports that some Republican leaders were backing away and insisting on starting from scratch with a whole new plan, it would inevitably bog down negotiations, and "the consequences would be severe."

Bush turned to McCain and said, "John, since Barack had a chance to speak, I think it's only fair if I let you go next."

Everyone looked at McCain, whose jaw tightened. He appeared to be on the verge of saying something, thought better of it, and briefly fidgeted in his chair.

"I think I'll just wait for my turn," he said finally.

There are moments in an election battle, as in life, when all the possible pathways save one are suddenly closed; when what felt like a wide distribution of probable outcomes narrows to the inevitable. This was one of those moments. Bush looked at McCain with a raised eyebrow, shrugged, and called on John Boehner. Boehner said he wasn't talking about starting from scratch but just wanted some modifications—including a plan he had trouble describing, which involved the federal government insuring banks' losses rather than purchasing their assets.

I asked Paulson if he'd looked at this Republican insurance proposal and determined whether it would work. Paulson said firmly that he had and it wouldn't.

Richard Shelby, the ranking member on the Senate Banking Committee, interjected to say he'd been told by a number of economists that TARP wouldn't work. He suggested that the White House give Congress more time to consider all its options. Bush cut him off and said the country didn't have more time.

As the discussion wore on, it became increasingly apparent that none of the Republican leaders were familiar with the actual content of the latest version of the TARP legislation—or for that matter the nature of their own proposed changes. They were simply trying to find a way to avoid taking a tough vote. After listening to several minutes of wrangling back and forth, I jumped in again.

"Mr. President," I said, "I'd still like to hear what Senator McCain has to say."

Once again, everyone turned to McCain. This time he studied a small note card in his hand, muttered something I couldn't make out, and then served up maybe two or three minutes of bromides—about how talks seemed to be making progress, how it was important to give Boehner room to move his caucus to yes.

And that was it. No plan. No strategy. Not even a smidgen of a suggestion as to how the different positions might be bridged. The room fell silent as McCain set down his note card, his eyes downcast, like a batter who knows he's just whiffed at the plate. I almost felt sorry for him; for his team to have encouraged such a high-stakes move and then sent their candidate into the meeting unprepared was political malpractice. When reporters got wind of his performance that day, the coverage would not be kind.

The more immediate effect of John's weirdness, though, was to set off a Cabinet Room free-for-all. Nancy and Spencer Bachus, the ranking Republican on the House Financial Services Committee, started arguing over who deserved credit for the stronger taxpayer protections in the most recent version of the legislation. Barney Frank, the tough and quick-witted Democrat from Massachusetts who knew his stuff and had probably worked harder than anyone to help Paulson get TARP across the finish line, started taunting the Republicans, yelling repeatedly, "What's your plan? What's your plan?" Faces reddened; voices rose; people talked over one another. And all the while, McCain remained silent, stewing in his chair. It got so bad that finally President Bush rose to his feet.

"I've obviously lost control of this meeting," he said. "We're finished."

With that, he wheeled around and charged out the south door.

The entire scene left me stunned.

As McCain and the Republican leadership quickly filed out of the room, I pulled Nancy, Harry, and the rest of the Democrats into a huddle in the adjacent Roosevelt Room. They were in various states of agitation, and because we'd already decided I wouldn't be giving any post-meeting comments to reporters, I wanted to make sure that none of them said anything that might make matters worse. We were discussing ways that they could constructively summarize the meeting when Paulson entered, looking absolutely shell-shocked. Several of my colleagues started shooing him away, as if he were an unpopular kid on the playground. A few even jeered.

"Nancy," Paulson said, towering next to the Speaker. "Please . . ." And then, in an inspired and somewhat sad blend of humor and desperation, he lowered his six-foot-five, sixty-two-year-old frame onto one knee. "I'm begging you. Don't blow this up."

The Speaker allowed a quick smile. "Hank, I didn't know you were Catholic," she said. Just as quickly her smile evaporated, and she added curtly, "You may not have noticed, but we're not the ones trying to blow things up."

I had to give Paulson credit; getting back to his feet, he stood there for several more minutes and let the Democrats vent. By the time they exited for press availability, everyone had calmed down and agreed to try to put the best spin they could on the meeting. Hank and I made plans to talk later that night. After leaving the White House, I put in a call to Plouffe.

"How'd it go?" he asked.

I thought for a moment.

"It went fine for us," I said. "But based on what I just saw, we better win this thing or the country is screwed."

I'M NOT BY NATURE a superstitious person. As a kid, I didn't have a lucky number or own a rabbit's foot. I didn't believe in ghosts or leprechauns, and while I might have made a wish when blowing out birthday candles or tossing a penny into a fountain, my mother had always been quick to remind me that there's a direct link between doing your work and having your wishes come true.

Over the course of the campaign, though, I found myself making a few concessions to the spirit world. One day in Iowa, for instance, a burly, bearded guy in biker garb and covered with tattoos strode up to me after an event and shoved something into my hand. It was his lucky metal poker chip, he explained; it had never failed him in Vegas. He wanted me to have it. A week later, a young blind girl in New Hampshire reached out to give me a small heart made of pink glass. In Ohio, it was a silver cross from a nun with an irrepressible smile and a face as grooved as a peach pit.

My assortment of charms grew steadily: a miniature Buddha, an Ohio buckeye, a laminated four-leaf clover, a tiny bronze likeness of Hanuman the monkey god, all manner of angels, rosary beads, crystals, and rocks. Each morning, I made a habit of choosing five or six of them and putting them in my pocket, half consciously keeping track of which ones I had with me on a particularly good day.

If my cache of small treasures didn't guarantee that the universe would tilt in my favor, I figured they didn't hurt. I felt comforted anytime I turned them over in my hand or felt their light jangling as I moved from event to event. Each charm was a tactile reminder of all the people I'd met, a faint but steady transmission of their hopes and expectations.

I also became particular about my debate-day rituals. The morning was always devoted to going over strategy and key points, the early afternoon to some light campaigning. But by four o'clock I wanted the schedule cleared. To shed excess adrenaline, I'd get in a quick workout. Then, ninety minutes before heading to the venue, I'd shave and take a long hot shower, before putting on the new shirt (white) and tie (blue or red) that Reggie had hung in the hotel closet beside my freshly pressed blue suit. For dinner, comfort food: steak cooked medium-well, roasted or mashed potatoes, steamed broccoli. And in the half hour or so ahead of the debate, while glancing at my notes, I'd listen to music delivered through earbuds or a small portable speaker. Eventually I became a tad compulsive about hearing certain songs. At first it was a handful of jazz classics—Miles Davis's "Freddie Freeloader," John Coltrane's "My Favorite Things," Frank Sinatra's "Luck Be a Lady." (Before one primary debate, I must have played that last track two or three times in a row, clearly indicating a lack of confidence in my preparations.)

Ultimately it was rap that got my head in the right place, two songs especially: Jay-Z's "My 1st Song" and Eminem's "Lose Yourself." Both were about defying the odds and putting it all on the line ("Look, if you had one shot or one opportunity, to seize everything you ever wanted in one moment, would you capture it? Or just let it slip . . ."); how it felt to spin something out of nothing; getting by on wit, hustle, and fear disguised as bravado. The lyrics felt tailored to my early underdog status. And as I sat alone in the back of the Secret Service van on the way to a debate site, in my crisp uniform and dimpled tie, I'd nod my head to the beat of those songs, feeling a whiff of private rebellion, a connection to something grittier and more real than all the fuss and deference that now surrounded me. It was a way to cut through the artifice and remember who I was.

Before my first debate with John McCain in late September, I followed the ritual to a T. I ate my steak, listened to my music, felt the weight of the charms in my pocket as I walked onto the stage. But frankly, I didn't need a lot of luck. By the time I arrived on the campus of the University of Mississippi—the place where less than fifty years earlier a Black man named James Meredith had been forced to obtain a Supreme Court order and the protection of five hundred federal law enforcement personnel simply to attend—I was no longer the underdog.

The race was now mine to lose.

As expected, the press covering the fiasco at the White House meeting had been merciless to McCain. His problems only grew worse when his campaign announced, just a few hours before the debate, that—because of the "progress" that had resulted from his intervention in congressional negotiations around TARP—he would lift the self-imposed suspension of his campaign and partici-pate after all. (We'd planned to show up regardless, even if it meant I had a nice, televised one-on-one conversa-tion with the moderator, Jim Lehrer.) Reporters saw McCain's latest move for what it was: a hasty retreat after a political stunt that had backfired.

The debate itself offered few surprises. McCain appeared relaxed onstage, patching together lines from his campaign speeches and standard Republican ortho-doxy, delivered with ample doses of humor and charm. Still, his spotty knowledge of the details of the financial crisis and his lack of answers for what he planned to do about it became more and more evident as we continued to joust. Meanwhile, I was on my game. No doubt my training regimen at the hands of drill sergeants Klain and Donilon had paid off; as much as I instinctively resisted canned answers to questions, there was no denying that both television audiences and the pundits found my more practiced responses compelling, and the preparation kept me from droning on too long.

More than that, though, my mood for the debate with McCain was noticeably different. Unlike my debates with Hillary and the rest of the Democratic field, which so often felt like an elaborate game, splitting hairs and notching style points, the differences between me and John McCain were real and deep; the stakes in choosing one of us over the other would reverberate for decades, with consequences for millions of people. Confident in my command of the facts, certain of why my ideas had a better chance than John's of meeting the challenges the country now faced, I felt energized by our exchanges and found myself (almost) enjoying our ninety minutes onstage.

The snap postdebate surveys of undecided voters showed me winning by a wide margin. My team was giddy, full of fist bumps, high fives, and probably a few private sighs of relief.

Michelle was happy but more subdued. She hated going to debates; as she described it, having to sit there looking serene, no matter what was said about me or how badly I screwed up, her stomach churning, was like getting a tooth drilled without novocaine. In fact, whether out of fear that it might jinx the outcome, or because of her own ambivalence about the prospect of my winning, she generally avoided talking to me about the horse-race aspect of the campaign. Which is why I was surprised when, in bed later that night, she turned to me and said, "You're going to win, aren't you?"

"A lot can still happen . . . but yeah. There's a pretty good chance I will."

I looked at my wife. Her face was pensive, as if she were working out a puzzle in her mind. Finally she nodded to herself and returned my gaze.

"You're going to win," she said softly. She kissed me on the cheek, turned off the bedside lamp, and pulled the covers over her shoulders.

ON SEPTEMBER 29, three days after the debate at Ole Miss, Bush's TARP legislation fell thirteen votes short of passage in the House of Representatives, with two-thirds of Democrats voting in support of it and two-thirds of Republicans voting against it. The Dow Jones immediately sustained a terrifying 778-point drop, and after a pounding in the press and no doubt a flood of calls from constituents watching their retirement accounts evaporate, enough members of both parties flipped to pass an amended version of the rescue package several days later.

Greatly relieved, I called Hank Paulson to congratulate him for his efforts. But while TARP's passage would prove to be critical in saving the financial system, the whole episode did nothing to reverse the public's growing impression that the GOP—and by extension their nominee for president—couldn't be trusted to responsibly handle the crisis.

Meanwhile, the campaign decisions that Plouffe had

pushed for months earlier were paying off. Our army of organizers and volunteers had fanned out across the country, registering hundreds of thousands of new voters and launching unprecedented operations in states that allowed early voting. Our online donations continued to flow, allowing us to play in whatever media markets we chose. When, a month ahead of the election, the McCain campaign announced it was halting its efforts in Michigan, historically a key battleground state, to concentrate its resources elsewhere, Plouffe was almost offended. "Without Michigan, they can't win!" he said, shaking his head. "They might as well raise a white flag!"

Instead of focusing energy on Michigan, the McCain campaign turned their attention to a man who'd become an unlikely cult figure: Joe Wurzelbacher.

I'd encountered Wurzelbacher a few weeks earlier as I did some old-fashioned door knocking in Toledo, Ohio. It was the kind of campaigning I enjoyed most, surprising people as they raked leaves or worked on their cars in the driveway, watching kids zoom up on bikes to see what the commotion was about.

That day, I was standing on a corner, signing autographs and talking with a group of people, when a man with a shaved head who looked to be in his late thirties introduced himself as Joe and asked about my tax plan. He was a plumber, he said, and he was worried that liberals like me would make it harder for him to succeed as a small-business owner. With the press pool cameras rolling, I explained that my plan would raise taxes only on the wealthiest 2 percent of Americans, and that by investing those revenues in things like education and infrastructure, the economy and his business would be more likely to prosper. I told him that I believed that this sort of redistribution of income—"when you spread the wealth around" were my words—had always been important in opening up opportunity to more people.

Joe was affable but unconvinced, and we agreed to disagree, shaking hands before I left. In the van headed back to our hotel, Gibbs—who like any great campaign communications director had an unerring nose for how a few seemingly innocuous words could trigger political silliness—told me my comment about spreading the wealth was problematic.

"What are you talking about?"

"The phrase doesn't poll well. People associate it with communism and shit."

I laughed it off, saying that the whole point of rolling back the Bush tax cuts was to redistribute income from people like me to folks like Joe. Gibbs looked at me like a parent whose child keeps making the same mistake over and over again.

Sure enough, as soon as the footage of me and Wurzelbacher, instantly dubbed "Joe the Plumber," surfaced, McCain started hammering on it during our debates. His campaign went all in, suggesting that this salt-of-the-earth guy in Ohio had unmasked my secret, socialist income-redistribution agenda, treating him like an oracle of Middle America. Broadcast news anchors were suddenly interviewing Joe. There were Joe the Plumber TV spots, and McCain brought Joe with him to a few campaign rallies. Joe himself seemed by turns amused, baffled, and occasionally put out by his new-found fame. But when all was said and done, most voters seemed to view Joe as not much more than a distraction from the serious business of electing the next president.

Most voters, but not all. For those who got their news from Sean Hannity and Rush Limbaugh, Joe the Plumber fit neatly into some larger narrative involving Reverend Wright; my alleged fealty to radical community organizer Saul Alinsky; my friendship with my neighbor Bill Ayers, who'd once been a leader of the militant group the Weather Underground; and my shadowy Muslim heritage. For these voters, I was no longer just a left-of-center Democrat who planned to broaden the social safety net and end the war in Iraq. I was something more insidious, someone to be feared, someone to be stopped. To deliver this urgent, patriotic message to the American people, they increasingly looked to their most fearless champion, Sarah Palin.

Since August, Palin had tanked during a number of high-profile media interviews, becoming a punch line on **Saturday Night Live** and other late-night comedy shows. But her power lay elsewhere. She'd spent the first week of October drawing big crowds and enthusiastically gassing them up with nativist bile. From the stage, she accused me of "palling around with terrorists who would target their own country." She suggested that I was "not a man who sees America the way you and I see America." People turned up at rallies wearing T-shirts bearing slogans like PALIN'S PITBULLS and NO COMMUNISTS. The media reported shouts of "Terrorist!" and "Kill him!" and "Off with his head!" coming from her audiences. Through Palin, it seemed as if the dark spirits that had long been lurking on the edges of the modern Republican

Party—xenophobia, anti-intellectualism, paranoid conspiracy theories, an antipathy toward Black and brown
folks—were finding their way to center stage.

It was a testament to John McCain's character, his
fundamental decency, that anytime a supporter approached
him spewing Palin-style rhetoric, he politely pushed back.
When a man at a Minnesota rally announced into the
microphone that he was afraid of having me as a president,
McCain wouldn't have it.

"I have to tell you, he is a decent person and a person
that you do not have to be scared of as president of the
United States," he said, causing his audience to boo lust-
ily. Answering another question, he said, "We want to
fight, and I will fight. But we will be respectful. I admire
Senator Obama and his accomplishments. I will respect
him. I want everyone to be respectful and let's make sure
we are because that's the way politics should be conducted
in America."

I wonder sometimes whether with the benefit of
hindsight McCain would still have chosen Palin—
knowing how her spectacular rise and her validation as a
candidate would provide a template for future politicians,
shifting his party's center and the country's politics overall in a direction he abhorred. I never posed the question
to him directly, of course. Over the next decade, our
relationship would evolve into one of grudging but genuine respect, but the 2008 election understandably
remained a sore point.

I like to think that, given the chance to do it over
again, he might have chosen differently. I believe he really
did put his country first.

.   .   .

THE CHANT THAT had started with Edith Childs and her big hat in a small room in Greenwood, South Carolina, more than a year earlier now rose spontaneously, rippling through crowds of forty or fifty thousand, as people filled up football fields and city parks, undaunted by the unseasonably hot October weather. **Fired up, ready to go! Fired up, ready to go!** We had built something together; you could feel the energy like a physical force. With just a few weeks to go before the election, our field offices were scrambling to find enough space to accommodate the numbers of people signing on to volunteer; Shepard Fairey's graphic art poster, titled HOPE, with a stylized red, white, and blue version of my face staring off into the distance, seemed suddenly ubiquitous. It felt as though the campaign had moved beyond politics and into the realm of popular culture. "You're the new 'in' thing," Valerie would tease.

That worried me. The inspiration our campaign was providing, the sight of so many young people newly invested in their ability to make change, the bringing together of Americans across racial and socioeconomic lines—it was the realization of everything I'd once dreamed might be possible in politics, and it made me proud. But the continuing elevation of me as a symbol ran contrary to my organizer's instincts, that sense that change involves "we" and not "me." It was personally disorienting, too, requiring me to constantly take stock to make sure I wasn't buying into the hype and remind myself of the distance between the airbrushed image and the flawed, often uncertain person I was.

I was also contending with the likelihood that if I was elected president, it would be impossible to meet the outsized expectations now attached to me. Since winning the Democratic nomination, I'd begun to experience reading the newspapers differently, in a way that gave me a jolt. Every headline, every story, every exposé, was another problem for me to solve. And problems were piling up quickly. Despite TARP's passage, the financial system remained paralyzed. The housing market was in a nosedive. The economy was shedding jobs at an accelerating rate, and there was speculation that the Big Three automakers would soon be in jeopardy.

The responsibility of tackling these problems didn't scare me. In fact, I relished the chance. But from everything I was learning, things were likely to get significantly worse before they got better. Resolving the economic crisis—not to mention winding down two wars, delivering on healthcare, and trying to save the planet from catastrophic climate change—was going to be a long, hard slog. It would require a cooperative Congress, willing allies, and an informed, mobilized citizenry that could sustain pressure on the system—not a solitary savior.

So what would happen when change didn't come fast enough? How would these cheering crowds respond to the inevitable setbacks and compromises? It became a running joke between me and the team: "Are we sure we want to win this thing? It's not too late to throw it." Marty expressed a more ethnic version of the same sentiment: "Two hundred and thirty-two years and they wait until the country's falling apart before they turn it over to the brother!"

MORE THAN ANYTHING campaign-related, it was news out of Hawaii that tempered my mood in

October's waning days. Maya called, saying the doctors didn't think Toot would last much longer, perhaps no more than a week. She was now confined to a rented hospital bed in the living room of her apartment, under the care of a hospice nurse and on palliative drugs. Although she had startled my sister with a sudden burst of lucidity the previous evening, asking for the latest campaign news along with a glass of wine and a cigarette, she was now slipping in and out of consciousness.

And so, twelve days before the election, I made a thirty-six-hour trip to Honolulu to say goodbye. Maya was waiting for me when I arrived at Toot's apartment; I saw that she had been sitting on the couch with a couple of shoeboxes of old photographs and letters. "I thought you might want to take some back with you," she said. I picked up a few photos from the coffee table. My grandparents and my eight-year-old mother, laughing in a grassy field at Yosemite. Me at the age of four or five, riding on Gramps's shoulders as waves splashed around us. The four of us with Maya, still a toddler, smiling in front of a Christmas tree.

Taking the chair beside the bed, I held my grandmother's hand in mine. Her body had wasted away and her breathing was labored. Every so often, she'd be shaken by a violent, metallic cough that sounded like a grinding of gears. A few times, she murmured softly, although the words, if any, escaped me.

What dreams might she be having? I wondered if she'd been able to look back and take stock, or whether she'd consider that too much of an indulgence. I wanted to think that she did look back; that she'd reveled in the memory of a long-ago lover or a perfect, sunlit day in her youth when she'd experienced a bit of good fortune and the world had revealed itself to be big and full of promise.

I thought back to a conversation I'd had with her when I was in high school, around the time that her chronic back problems began making it difficult for her to walk for long stretches.

"The thing about getting old, Bar," Toot had told me, "is that you're the same person inside." I remember her eyes studying me through her thick bifocals, as if to make sure I was paying attention. "You're trapped in this dog-gone contraption that starts falling apart. But it's still you. You understand?"

I did now.

For the next hour or so, I sat talking to Maya about her work and her family, all the while stroking Toot's dry, bony hand. But eventually the room felt too crowded with memories—colliding, merging, refracting, like images in a kaleidoscope—and I told Maya I wanted to take a quick walk outside. After consulting with Gibbs and my Secret Service detail, it was agreed that the press pool downstairs would not be informed, and I took the elevator to the basement level and went out through the garage, turning left down the narrow street that ran behind my grandparents' apartment building.

The street had barely changed in thirty-five years. I passed the rear of a small Shinto temple and community center, then rows of wooden homes broken up by the occasional three-story concrete apartment building. I had bounced my first basketball—a gift from my father when I was ten years old—down this street, dribbling the length of the uneven sidewalk on my way to and from the courts at the nearby elementary school. Toot used to say that she always knew when I was coming home for dinner because she could hear that darn ball bouncing from ten stories up. I had run down this street to the supermarket to buy her cigarettes, motivated by her promise that I could buy a candy bar with the change if I was back in ten minutes. Later, when I was fifteen, I'd walk this same street home from a shift at my first job, scooping ice cream at the Baskin-Robbins around the corner, Toot laughing heartily when I grumbled to her about my paltry paycheck.

Another time. Another life. Modest and without consequence to the rest of the world. But one that had given me love. Once Toot was gone, there would be no one left who remembered that life, or remembered me in it.

I heard a stampede of feet behind me; the press pool had somehow gotten wind of my unscheduled excursion and were gathering on the sidewalk across the street, cameramen jostling to set up their shots, reporters with microphones looking at me awkwardly, clearly conflicted about shouting a question. They were decent about it, really just doing their jobs, and anyway I had barely traveled four blocks. I gave the press a quick wave and turned around to go back to the garage. There was no point in going farther, I realized; what I was looking for was no longer there.

I left Hawaii and went back to work. Eight days later, on the eve of the election, Maya called to say Toot had died. It was my last day of campaigning. We were scheduled to be in North Carolina that evening, before flying to Virginia for our final event. Before heading to the venue, Axe asked me gently if I needed help writing a topper to my usual campaign remarks, to briefly acknowledge my grandmother's death. I thanked him and said no. I knew what I wanted to say.

It was a beautiful night, cool with a light rain. Standing on the outdoor stage, after the music and cheers and chants had died down, I spent a few minutes telling the crowd about Toot—how she'd grown up during the Depression and worked on an assembly line while Gramps was away in the war, what she had meant to our family, what she might mean to them.

"She was one of those quiet heroes that we have all across America," I said. "They're not famous. Their names aren't in the newspapers. But each and every day they work hard. They look after their families. They sacrifice for their children and their grandchildren. They aren't seeking the limelight—all they try to do is just do the right thing.

"And in this crowd, there are a lot of quiet heroes like that—mothers and fathers, grandparents, who have worked hard and sacrificed all their lives. And the satisfaction that they get is seeing that their children and maybe their grandchildren or their great-grandchildren live a better life than they did.

"That's what America's about. That's what we're fighting for."

It was as good a closing argument for the campaign as I felt that I could give.

IF YOU'RE THE CANDIDATE, Election Day brings a surprising stillness. There are no more rallies or town halls. TV and radio ads no longer matter; newscasts have nothing of substance to report. Campaign offices empty as staff and volunteers hit the streets to help turn out voters. Across the country millions of strangers step behind a black curtain to register their policy preferences and private instincts, as some mysterious collective alchemy determines the country's fate—and your own. The realization is obvious but also profound: It's out of your hands now. Pretty much all you can do is wait.

Plouffe and Axe were driven crazy by the helplessness, passing hours on their BlackBerrys scrounging for field reports, rumors, bad weather—anything that might be taken as a data point. I took the opposite tack, giving myself over to uncertainty as one might lie back and float over a wave. I did start the morning by calling into a round of drive-time radio shows, mostly at Black stations, reminding people to get out and vote. Around seven-thirty, Michelle and I cast our votes at the Beulah Shoesmith Elementary School, a few blocks from our home in Hyde Park, bringing Malia and Sasha with us and sending them on to school after that.

I then made a quick trip to Indianapolis to visit a field office and shake hands with voters. Later, I played basketball (a superstition Reggie and I had developed after we played the morning of the Iowa caucus but failed to play the day of the New Hampshire primary) with Michelle's brother, Craig, some old buddies, and a handful of my friends' sons who were fast and strong enough to keep us all working hard. It was a competitive game, filled with the usual good-natured trash talk, although I noticed an absence of hard fouls. This was per Craig's orders, I learned later, since he knew his sister would hold him accountable if I came home with a black eye.

Gibbs, meanwhile, was tracking news from the battle-ground states, reporting that turnout appeared to be shattering records across the country, creating problems in some polling places as voters waited four or five hours to cast their ballots. Broadcasts from the scenes, Gibbs said, showed people more jubilant than frustrated, with seniors in lawn chairs and volunteers passing out refreshments as if they were all at a neighborhood block party.

I spent the rest of the afternoon at home, puttering around uselessly while Michelle and the girls got their hair done. Alone in my study, I made a point of editing the drafts of both my victory and concession speeches. Around eight p.m. Axe called to say that the networks had called Pennsylvania in our favor, and Marvin said we should start heading to the downtown hotel where we'd be watching the returns before moving over to the public gathering at Grant Park.

Outside the front gate of our house, the number of Secret Service agents and vehicles seemed to have doubled over the past few hours. The head of my detail, Jeff Gilbert, shook my hand and pulled me into a brief embrace. It was unseasonably warm for Chicago at that time of year, almost in the mid-sixties, and as we drove down Lake Shore Drive, Michelle and I were quiet, staring out the window at Lake Michigan, listening to the girls horsing around in the backseat. Suddenly Malia turned to me and asked, "Daddy, did you win?"

"I think so, sweetie."

"And we're supposed to be going to the big party to celebrate?"

"That's right. Why do you ask?"

"Well, it doesn't seem like that many people might be coming to the party, 'cause there are no cars on the road."

I laughed, realizing my daughter was right; save for

our motorcade, the six lanes in both directions were completely empty.

Security had changed at the hotel as well, with armed SWAT teams deployed in the stairwells. Our family and closest friends were already in the suite, everyone smiling, kids racing around the room, and yet the atmosphere was still strangely muted, as if the reality of what was about to happen hadn't yet settled in their minds. My mother-in-law, in particular, made no pretense of being relaxed; through the din, I noticed her sitting on the couch, her eyes fixed on the television, her expression one of disbelief. I tried to imagine what she must be thinking, having grown up just a few miles away during a time when there were still many Chicago neighborhoods that Blacks could not even safely enter; a time when office work was out of reach for most Blacks, and her father, unable to get a union card from white-controlled trade unions, had been forced to make do as an itinerant tradesman; a time when the thought of a Black U.S. president would have seemed as far-fetched as a pig taking flight.

I took a seat next to her on the couch. "You okay?" I asked.

Marian shrugged and kept staring at the television. She said, "This is kind of too much."

"I know." I took her hand and squeezed it, the two of us sitting in companionable silence for a few minutes. Then suddenly a shot of my face flashed up on the TV screen and ABC News announced that I would be the forty-fourth president of the United States.

The room erupted. Shouts could be heard up and down the hall. Michelle and I kissed and she pulled back gently to give me the once-over as she laughed and shook her head. Reggie and Marvin rushed in to give everyone big bear hugs. Soon Plouffe, Axe, and Gibbs walked in, and I indulged them for several minutes as they rattled off state-by-state results before telling them what I knew to be true—that as much as anything I'd done, it was their skill, hard work, insight, tenacity, loyalty, and heart, along with the commitment of the entire team, that had made this moment possible.

The rest of the night is mostly a blur to me now. I remember John McCain's phone call, which was as gracious as his concession speech. He emphasized how proud America should be of the history that had been made and pledged to help me succeed. There were congratulatory calls from President Bush and several foreign leaders, and a conversation with Harry Reid and Nancy Pelosi, both of whose caucuses had had very good nights. I remember meeting Joe Biden's ninety-one-year-old mother, who took pleasure in telling me how she'd scolded Joe for even considering not being on the ticket.

More than two hundred thousand people had gathered in Grant Park that night, the stage facing Chicago's glittering skyline. I can see in my mind even now some of the faces looking up as I walked onstage, men and women and children of every race, some wealthy, some poor, some famous and some not, some smiling ecstatically, others openly weeping. I've reread lines from my speech that night and heard accounts from staff and friends of what it felt like to be there.

But I worry that my memories of that night, like so much else that's happened these past twelve years, are shaded by the images that I've seen, the footage of our family walking across the stage, the photographs of the crowds and lights and magnificent backdrops. As beautiful as they are, they don't always match the lived experience. In fact, my favorite photograph from that night isn't of Grant Park at all. Rather it's one I received many years later as a gift, a photograph of the Lincoln Memorial, taken as I was giving my speech in Chicago. It shows a small gathering of people on the stairs, their faces obscured by the darkness, and behind them the giant figure shining brightly, his marble face craggy, his eyes slightly downcast. They're listening to the radio, I am told, quietly contemplating who we are as a people— and the arc of this thing we call democracy.

PART THREE

RENEGADE

CHAPTER 10

ALTHOUGH I HAD VISITED THE White House several times as a U.S. senator, I had never been inside the Oval Office before I was elected president. The room is smaller than you might expect—less than thirty-six feet on its long axis, seven feet narrower along the other—but its ceiling is high and grand, and its features match up with the photos and newsreels. There's Washington's portrait above the mantel of an ivy-draped fireplace, and the two high-backed chairs, flanked by sofas, where the president sits with the vice president or visiting foreign dignitaries. There are two doors that blend seamlessly into the gently curved walls—one leading out to the hallway, the other to the "Outer Oval," where the president's personal aides are stationed—and a third leading to the president's small inner office and private dining room. There are the busts of long-dead leaders and Remington's famous bronze cowboy; the antique grandfather clock and the built-in bookcases; the thick oval carpet with a stern eagle stitched into its center; and the Resolute desk—a gift from Queen Victoria in 1880, ornately carved from the hull of a British ship that a U.S. whaling crew helped salvage after a catastrophe, full of hidden drawers and nooks and with a central panel that pops open, delighting any child who has a chance to crawl through it.

One thing cameras don't capture about the Oval Office is the light. The room is awash in light. On clear days, it pours through the huge windows on its eastern and southern ends, painting every object with a golden sheen that turns fine-grained, then dappled, as the late-afternoon sun recedes. In bad weather, when the South Lawn is shrouded by rain or snow or the rare morning fog, the room takes on a slightly bluer hue but remains undimmed, the weaker natural light boosted by interior bulbs hidden behind a bracketed cornice and reflecting down from the ceiling and walls. The lights are never turned off, so that even in the middle of the night the Oval Office remains luminescent, flaring against the darkness like a lighthouse's rounded torch.

I spent most of eight years in that room, grimly listening to intelligence reports, hosting heads of state, cajoling members of Congress, jousting with allies and adversaries, and posing for pictures with thousands of visitors. With staffers I laughed, cursed, and more than once fought back tears. I grew comfortable enough to put my feet up or sit on the desk, roll around on the floor with a child, or steal a nap on the couch. Sometimes I'd fantasize about walking out the east door and down the driveway, past the guardhouse and wrought-iron gates, to lose myself in crowded streets and reenter the life I'd once known.

But I would never fully rid myself of the sense of reverence I felt whenever I walked into the Oval Office, the feeling that I had entered not an office but a sanctum of democracy. Day after day, its light comforted and fortified me, reminding me of the privilege of my burdens and my duties.

MY FIRST VISIT to the Oval took place just days after the election, when, following a long tradition, the Bushes invited Michelle and me for a tour of our soon-to-be home. Riding in a Secret Service vehicle, the two of us traveled the winding arc of the South Lawn entrance to the White House, trying to process the fact that in less than three months we'd be moving in. The day was sunny and warm, the trees still flush with leaves, and the Rose Garden overflowing with flowers. Washington's prolonged fall provided a welcome respite, for in Chicago the weather had quickly turned cold and dark, an arctic wind stripping the trees bare of leaves, as if the unusually mild weather we had enjoyed on election night had been merely part of an elaborate set, to be dismantled as soon as the celebration was done.

The president and First Lady Laura Bush greeted us at the South Portico, and after the obligatory waves to the press pool, President Bush and I headed over to the Oval Office, while Michelle joined Mrs. Bush for tea in the residence. After a few more photographs and an offer of refreshments from a young valet, the president invited me to have a seat.

"So," he asked, "how's it feel?"

"It's a lot," I said, smiling. "I'm sure you remember."

"Yep. I do. Seems like yesterday," he said, nodding vigorously. "Tell you what, though. It's a heck of a ride you're about to take. Nothing like it. You just have to remind yourself to appreciate it every day."

Whether because of his respect for the institution,

lessons from his father, bad memories of his own transition (there were rumors that some Clinton staffers had removed the W key from the White House computers on their way out the door), or just basic decency, President Bush would end up doing all he could to make the eleven weeks between my election and his departure go smoothly. Every office in the White House provided my team with detailed "how to" manuals. His staffers made themselves available to meet with their successors, answer questions, and even be shadowed as they carried out their duties. The Bush daughters, Barbara and Jenna, by that time young adults, rearranged their schedules to give Malia and Sasha their own tour of the "fun" parts of the White House. I promised myself that when the time came, I would treat my successor the same way.

The president and I covered a wide range of subjects during that first visit—the economy and Iraq, the press corps and Congress—with him never straying from his jocular, slightly fidgety persona. He provided blunt assessments of a few foreign leaders, warned that people in my own party would end up giving me some of my biggest headaches, and kindly agreed to host a luncheon with all the living presidents sometime before the inauguration.

I was aware that there were necessary limits to a president's candor while talking to his successor—especially one who had run against so much of his record. I was mindful as well that for all President Bush's seeming good humor, my presence in the very office he'd soon be vacating must be stirring up difficult emotions. I followed his lead in not delving too deeply into policy. Mostly, I just listened.

Only once did he say something that surprised me. We were talking about the financial crisis and Secretary Paulson's efforts to structure the rescue program for the banks now that TARP had passed through Congress. "The good news, Barack," he said, "is that by the time you take office, we'll have taken care of the really tough stuff for you. You'll be able to start with a clean slate."

For a moment, I was at a loss for words. I'd been talking to Paulson regularly and knew that cascading bank failures and a worldwide depression were still distinct possibilities. Looking at the president, I imagined all the hopes and convictions he must have carried with him the first time he walked into the Oval Office as president-elect, no less dazzled by its brightness, no less eager than I was to change the world for the better, no less certain that history would judge his presidency a success.

"It took a lot of courage on your part to get TARP passed," I said finally. "To go against public opinion and a lot of people in your own party for the sake of the country."

That much at least was true. I saw no point in saying more.

BACK HOME IN CHICAGO, our lives had shifted sharply. Inside our house, things didn't feel so different, with mornings spent fixing breakfast and getting the girls ready for school, returning phone calls and talking to staffers. But once any of us stepped outside the front door, it was a new world. Camera crews were stationed at the corner, behind recently erected concrete barriers. Secret Service countersniper teams, clad in black, stood watch on rooftops. A visit to Marty and Anita's house, just a few blocks away, became a major endeavor; a trip to my old gym was now out of the question. Riding downtown to our temporary transition office, I realized that the empty roads that Malia had noticed on election night were the new norm. All my entries and exits into buildings happened through loading docks and service elevators, cleared of everyone but a few security guards. It felt as if I now lived in my own portable, perpetual ghost town.

I spent my afternoons forming a government. A new administration brings less turnover than most people imagine: Of the more than three million people, civilian and military, employed by the federal government, only a few thousand are so-called political appointees, serving at the pleasure of the president. Of those, he or she has regular, meaningful contact with fewer than a hundred senior officials and personal aides. As president, I would be able to articulate a vision and set a direction for the country; promote a healthy organizational culture and establish clear lines of responsibility and measures of accountability. I would be the one who made the final decisions on issues that rose to my attention and who explained those decisions to the country at large. But to do all this, I would be dependent on the handful of people serving as my eyes, ears, hands, and feet—those who would become my managers, executors, facilitators, analysts, organizers, team leaders, amplifiers, conciliators, problem solvers, flak catchers, honest brokers, sounding boards, constructive critics, and loyal soldiers.

It was crucial, then, to get these early appointments right—starting with the person who could serve as my chief of staff. Unfortunately the initial response from my number one recruit for the job was less than enthusiastic.

"No fucking way."

That was Rahm Emanuel, the former fundraiser for Richard M. Daley and enfant terrible in the Clinton administration, now a congressman from Chicago's North Side and the mastermind of the 2006 Democratic wave that had taken back the House of Representatives. Short, trim, darkly handsome, hugely ambitious, and manically driven, Rahm was smarter than most of his colleagues in Congress and not known for hiding it. He was also funny, sensitive, anxious, loyal, and famously profane: At a charity roast in his honor a few years earlier, I'd explained how the loss of Rahm's middle finger to a meat slicer when he was a teenager had rendered him practically mute.

"Look, I'm honored you're asking," Rahm told me when I reached out a month before the election. "I'll do anything you need to help. But I'm happy where I am. My wife and kids are happy. And I know too much to believe that shit about a family-friendly White House. Anyway, I'm sure you can find better candidates than me."

I couldn't argue with Rahm about the hardships involved in accepting my offer. In the modern White House, the chief of staff was the day-to-day quarterback, the end of the funnel through which every issue facing the president had to first pass. Few in government (including the president) worked longer hours or under more unrelenting pressure.

But Rahm was wrong about me having a better choice. After two punishing years on the campaign, Plouffe had already told me that he wouldn't initially be joining the administration, in part because his wife, Olivia, had delivered a new baby just three days after the election. Both my Senate chief of staff, Pete Rouse, and former Clinton chief of staff John Podesta, who had agreed to help manage our transition team, had taken themselves out of the running. Although Axe, Gibbs, and Valerie would all accept senior positions in the White House, none had the mix of skills and experience I'd need for the chief of staff job.

Rahm, on the other hand, knew policy, knew politics, knew Congress, knew the White House, and knew financial markets from a stint working on Wall Street. His brashness and impatience rubbed some people the wrong way; as I would learn, his eagerness to "put points on the board" sometimes led him to care less about the substance of a deal than getting a deal done. But with an economic crisis to tackle and what I suspected might be a limited window to get my agenda through a Democratically controlled Congress, I was convinced that his pile-driver style was exactly what I needed.

In the final days before the election, I had worn Rahm down, appealing to his ego but also to the decency and genuine patriotism hidden beneath his wiseass persona. ("The biggest crisis facing the country in our lifetime," I yelled at him, "and you're going to sit on the goddamn sidelines?") Axe and Plouffe, both of whom knew Rahm well and had seen him in action, were thrilled when he accepted the job. But not all of my supporters were as enthusiastic. Hadn't Rahm supported Hillary? a few groused. Didn't he represent the same old triangulating, Davos-attending, Wall Street–coddling, Washington-focused, obsessively centrist version of the

Democratic Party we had been running against? How can you trust him?

These were all variations on a question that would recur in the coming months: What kind of president did I intend to be? I had pulled off a neat trick during the campaign, attracting support from independents and even some moderate Republicans by promising bipartisanship and an end to slash-and-burn politics while maintaining the enthusiasm of those on the left. I had done so not by telling different people what they wanted to hear but by stating what I felt to be the truth: that in order to advance progressive policies like universal healthcare or immigration reform, it was not only possible but necessary to avoid doctrinaire thinking; to place a premium on what worked and listen respectfully to what the other side had to say.

Voters had embraced my message—because it sounded different and they were hungry for different; because our campaign hadn't depended on endorsements from the usual assortment of interest groups and power brokers that might have otherwise forced me into a strict party orthodoxy; because I was new and unexpected, a blank canvas upon which supporters across the ideological spectrum could project their own vision of change.

Once I started making appointments, though, the differing expectations within my coalition began to show. After all, each person I selected for a job in the administration came with his or her own history, paper trail, and set of supporters and detractors. For insiders, at least— the politicians and operatives and reporters whose job it was to read the tea leaves—each appointment signified my true political intentions, evidence of my tilt to the right or to the left, my willingness to break from the past or peddle more of the same. Choices in people reflected choices in policy, and with each choice, the chances of disillusionment grew.

WHEN IT CAME to assembling my economic team, I decided to favor experience over fresh talent. The circumstances, I felt, demanded it. The October jobs report, released three days after the election, was dismal: 240,000 jobs lost (revisions would later reveal that the true number was 481,000). Despite the passage of TARP and continuing emergency measures by Treasury and the Fed, the financial markets remained paralyzed, banks were still on the verge of collapse, and foreclosures showed no signs of slowing down. I loved the various up-and-comers who'd advised me throughout the campaign and felt a kinship with left-leaning economists and activists who saw the current crisis as the result of a bloated and out-of-control financial system in dire need of reform. But with the world economy in free fall, my number one task wasn't remaking the economic order. It was preventing further disaster. For this, I needed people who had managed crises before, people who could calm markets in the grip of panic—people who, by definition, might be tainted by the sins of the past.

For Treasury secretary, it came down to two candidates: Larry Summers, who had held the job under Bill Clinton, and Tim Geithner, Larry's former deputy and then head of the Federal Reserve Bank of New York. Larry was the more obvious choice: An economics major and debate champion at MIT, one of the youngest professors to be tenured at Harvard, and more recently the university's president, he had already served as the World Bank's chief economist, an undersecretary for international affairs, and deputy Treasury secretary before taking the reins from his predecessor and mentor, Bob Rubin. In the mid-1990s, Larry had helped engineer the international response to a series of major financial crises involving Mexico, Asia, and Russia—the closest analogues to the crisis I was now inheriting—and even his fiercest detractors acknowledged his brilliance. As Tim aptly described it, Larry could hear your arguments, restate them better than you could, and then show why you were wrong.

He also had an only partly deserved reputation for arrogance and political incorrectness. As president of Harvard, he'd had a public row with the prominent African American studies professor Cornel West and had later been forced to resign after, among other things, positing that intrinsic differences in high-end aptitude might be one reason women were underrepresented in the math, science, and engineering departments of leading universities.

As I got to know him, I'd come to believe that most of Larry's difficulties in playing well with others had less to do with malice and more to do with obliviousness. For Larry, qualities like tact and restraint just cluttered the mind. He himself seemed impervious to hurt feelings or the usual insecurities, and he would express appreciation (accompanied by mild surprise) when anyone effectively challenged him or thought of something he'd missed. His lack of interest in standard human niceties extended to his appearance, which was routinely disheveled, his ample belly occasionally exposed by a shirt missing a button, his

haphazard approach to shaving often resulting in a distracting patch of stubble under his nose.

Tim was different. The first time I met him, in a New
York hotel a few weeks before the election, the word that
popped into my head was "boyish." He was my age, but
his slight build, unassuming carriage, and elfin face made
him appear considerably younger. During the course of
our hour-long conversation he maintained a soft-spoken,
good-humored equanimity. We had an immediate rapport, partly based on childhood parallels: As a result of
his father's work as a development specialist, he'd spent
much of his youth abroad, instilling in him a reserve
that I recognized in myself.

After getting a master's degree in East Asian studies and
international economics, Tim worked as an Asia specialist
for Henry Kissinger's consulting shop and then joined
Treasury, becoming a junior trade official in Japan. It was
Larry Summers who plucked Tim out of obscurity to serve
as his special assistant, and as Larry rose, so did Tim. Tim
became a central if unheralded player in dealing with
the various financial crises of the 1990s, and it was on the
strength of Larry's recommendation that he would end up
heading the New York Fed. Their relationship spoke not
only to Larry's generosity but also to Tim's quiet confidence and intellectual rigor—qualities that had been
amply tested over the previous year, as Tim had worked
around the clock with Hank Paulson and Ben Bernanke
in an effort to contain the Wall Street meltdown.

Whether out of loyalty to Larry, sheer exhaustion, or
justifiable guilt (like Rahm—and me—Tim still had kids
at home and a wife who longed for a calmer life), Tim
spent much of our first meeting trying to discourage me

from hiring him as Treasury secretary. I came away convinced otherwise. For anyone—even Larry—to match Tim's real-time understanding of the financial crisis or his relationships with the current crop of global financial players would take months, I thought, and that was time that we didn't have. More important, my gut told me that Tim had a basic integrity, a steadiness of temperament, and an ability to problem-solve unsullied by ego or political considerations that would make him invaluable in the task ahead.

In the end, I decided to hire both men—Larry to help figure out what the hell to do (and not do), Tim to organize and steer our response. To make it work, I had to sell Larry on serving not as Treasury secretary but rather as director of the National Economic Council (NEC), which, despite being the White House's top economic job, was considered less prestigious. The director's traditional function was to coordinate the economic policy-making process and act as a diplomatic broker between various agencies, which didn't exactly play to Larry's strengths. But none of that mattered, I told Larry. I needed him, his country needed him, and as far as I was concerned, he'd be an equal to Tim in formulating our economic plan. My earnestness may have had some influence on his thinking—though the promise (at Rahm's suggestion) to make Larry the next chair of the Federal Reserve no doubt helped get him to yes as well.

I had other key posts to fill. To head the Council of Economic Advisers—responsible for providing the president with the best possible data and analysis on all economic matters—I chose Christina Romer, a rosy-cheeked Berkeley professor who had done seminal work on the Great Depression. Peter Orszag, the head of the nonpartisan Congressional Budget Office, accepted the job as director of the Office of Management and Budget, and Melody Barnes, a thoughtful African American lawyer and former chief counsel to Senator Ted Kennedy, was put in charge of the Domestic Policy Council. Jared Bernstein, a left-leaning labor economist, came on board as part of Joe Biden's team, as did Gene Sperling, the bespectacled, hyperarticulate policy wonk who had served four years as Bill Clinton's director of the NEC and who now agreed, along with campaign economists Austan Goolsbee and Jason Furman, to function as roving utility players.

In the months to come, I would spend countless hours with this brain trust and their deputies, asking questions, sifting through recommendations, poring over slide decks and briefing books, formulating policy and then subjecting whatever we had thought up to relentless scrutiny. Arguments were heated, dissent was encouraged, and no idea was rejected because it came from a junior staffer or didn't fit into a particular ideological predisposition.

Still, Tim and Larry were the dominant voices on our economic team. Both men were rooted in the centrist, market-friendly economic philosophy of the Clinton administration, and given the remarkable run of economic prosperity during the 1990s, such a pedigree had long been considered a matter of pride. As the financial crisis worsened, though, that record would come increasingly under fire. Bob Rubin was already seeing his reputation tarnished as a result of his role as senior counselor at Citigroup, one of the financial institutions whose massive exposure in the subprime securities market now fed the contagion. As soon as I announced my economic team, press stories noted that Larry had championed significant deregulation of the financial markets during his time at Treasury; commentators wondered whether, during his tenure at the New York Fed, Tim—along with Paulson and Bernanke—had been too slow to sound the alarm about the risk the subprime market had posed to the financial system.

Some of these criticisms were valid, others grossly unfair. What was certain was that by selecting Tim and Larry, I had yoked myself to their history—and that if we weren't able to right the economic ship quickly, the political price for choosing them would be high.

AROUND THE SAME time that I was finalizing decisions on my economic team, I asked staffers and my Secret Service detail to arrange a clandestine meeting in the fire station at Reagan National Airport. The facility was empty when I arrived, the fire trucks removed to accommodate our motorcade. I stepped into a lounge that had been set up with some refreshments and greeted the compact, silver-haired man in a gray suit seated inside.

"Mr. Secretary," I said, shaking his hand. "Thanks for taking the time."

"Congratulations, Mr. President-Elect," Robert Gates replied, steely-eyed and tight-smiled, before we sat down and got to business.

It's fair to say that President Bush's secretary of defense and I did not hang out in the same circles. In fact, once you got beyond our common Kansas roots (Gates had been born and raised in Wichita), it was hard to imagine two individuals who had traveled such different roads to arrive at the same location. Gates was an Eagle Scout, a former air force intelligence officer, a Russia specialist, and a CIA recruit. At the height of the Cold War, he served in the National Security Council (NSC) under Nixon, Ford, and Carter, and in the CIA under Reagan, before becoming the agency's director under George H. W. Bush. (He'd previously been nominated by Reagan, but questions about his knowledge of the Iran-Contra affair had led him to withdraw.) With Bill Clinton's election, Gates left Washington, D.C., joined corporate boards, and later served as president of Texas A&M University—a post he would hold until 2006, when George W. Bush asked him to replace Donald Rumsfeld at the Pentagon and salvage an Iraq War strategy that was then thoroughly in shambles.

He was a Republican, a Cold War hawk, a card-carrying member of the national security establishment, a prior champion of foreign interventions I had likely protested while in college, and now defense secretary to a president whose war policies I abhorred. And yet I was in the firehouse that day to ask Bob Gates to stay on as my secretary of defense.

As with my economic appointments, my reasons were practical. With 180,000 U.S. troops deployed in Iraq and Afghanistan, any wholesale turnover in the Defense Department seemed fraught with risk. Moreover, whatever differences Gates and I may have had regarding the initial decision to invade Iraq, circumstances had led us to share similar views about the path forward. When President Bush—on Gates's recommendation—had ordered a "surge" of additional U.S. troops in Iraq in early 2007, I had been skeptical, not because I doubted the ability of more U.S. troops to reduce violence there, but because it was framed as an open-ended commitment.

Under Gates's direction, though, the Petraeus-led surge (and a brokered alliance with Sunni tribes in Anbar Province) not only significantly reduced violence but also purchased the Iraqis time and space for politics. With the help of painstaking diplomacy by Secretary of State Condoleezza Rice and, especially, U.S. ambassador to Iraq Ryan Crocker, Iraq was on the path to forming a legitimate government, with elections scheduled for the end of January. Midway through my transition, the Bush administration had even announced a Status of Forces Agreement with the Maliki government that would withdraw U.S. troops from Iraq by the end of 2011— a timetable that effectively mirrored what I'd proposed during the campaign. Meanwhile, Gates publicly emphasized the need for the United States to refocus attention on Afghanistan, one of the central tenets of my foreign policy platform. Tactical questions remained regarding pace, resources, and personnel. But the fundamental strategy of winding down combat operations in Iraq and bolstering our efforts in Afghanistan was now firmly established—and for the moment at least, no one was in a better position to carry out that strategy than the defense secretary currently in place.

I also had sound political reasons for keeping Gates. I had promised to end constant partisan rancor, and Gates's presence in my cabinet would show that I was serious about delivering on that promise. Retaining him would also help generate trust within the U.S. military and the various agencies that made up the intelligence community (known as the IC). Wielding a military budget larger than those of the next thirty-seven countries combined, leaders in the Defense Department and the IC were filled with strong opinions, skilled at bureaucratic infighting, and had a bias for doing things the way they'd always been done. I wasn't intimidated by this; I knew in broad strokes what I wanted to do and expected that habits born of the chain of command—saluting and executing orders from the commander in chief, even those with which one strongly disagreed—were deeply ingrained.

Still, I understood that moving America's national security apparatus in a new direction wasn't easy for any president. If President Eisenhower—the former Supreme Allied Commander and one of the architects of D-Day— had occasionally felt stymied by what he called the "military-industrial complex," there was a high likelihood that pushing reform might be harder for a newly elected African American president who'd never served in uniform, had opposed a mission that many had devoted their lives to achieving, wanted to rein in the military budget, and had surely lost the Pentagon vote by a sizable margin. To get things done now, rather than in a year or two down the line, I needed someone like Gates, who knew how the building worked and where the traps were laid; someone who already had the respect that I— regardless of my title—would in some ways have to earn.

There was a final reason I wanted Gates on my team, and that was to push against my own biases. The image of me that had emerged from the campaign—the starry-eyed idealist who instinctively opposed military action and believed that every problem on the international stage could be solved through high-minded dialogue—had never been entirely accurate. Yes, I believed in diplomacy and thought war should be a last resort. I believed in multilateral cooperation to address problems like climate change, and I believed that the steady promotion of democracy, economic development, and human rights around the world served our long-term national security interests. Those who voted for me or had worked on my campaign tended to share those beliefs, and they were most likely to populate my administration.

But my foreign policy views—and, indeed, my early opposition to the invasion of Iraq—owed at least as much to the "realist" school, an approach that valued restraint, assumed imperfect information and unintended consequences, and tempered a belief in American exceptionalism with a humility about our ability to remake the world in our image. I would often surprise people by citing George H. W. Bush as a recent president whose foreign policy I admired. Bush, along with James Baker, Colin Powell, and Brent Scowcroft, had deftly managed the end of the Cold War and the successful prosecution of the Gulf War.

Gates had come of age working with such men, and in his handling of the Iraq campaign I saw enough overlap between our views to feel confident that we could work together. Having his voice at the table, along with those of people like Jim Jones—the retired four-star general and former head of European Command, whom I had slated as my first national security advisor—guaranteed that I'd hear a broad range of perspectives before making major decisions, and that I would have to continually test even my deepest assumptions against people who had the stature and confidence to tell me when I was wrong.

Of course, all this depended on a basic level of trust between me and Gates. When I had asked a colleague to reach out to him about his possible willingness to stay on, Gates had sent back a list of questions. How long would I expect him to serve? Would I be willing to exercise flexibility in the drawdown of troops from Iraq? How would I approach the Defense Department staffing and budget?

As we sat together in the firehouse, Gates acknowledged that it wasn't typical for a potential cabinet appointee to quiz his or her future boss this way. He hoped I hadn't found it presumptuous. I assured him that I didn't mind, and that his candor and clear thinking were precisely what I was looking for. We went through his list of questions. I had a few of my own. After forty-five minutes, we shook hands and were whisked away in our separate motorcades.

"So?" Axelrod asked upon my return.

"He's in," I said. "I like him." Then I added, "We'll see if he likes me back."

WITHOUT MUCH FUSS, the other pieces of my national security team fell into place: longtime friend and former diplomat Susan Rice as U.S. ambassador to the United Nations; Leon Panetta, a former California congressman and Clinton chief of staff with a well-earned reputation for bipartisanship, as director of the CIA; and retired admiral Dennis Blair as director of national intelligence. Many of my closest advisors from the campaign took on key staff roles, including my debate drill sergeant Tom Donilon as deputy national security advisor, young hotshots Denis McDonough, Mark Lippert, and Ben Rhodes as assistant deputies at the NSC, and Samantha Power in an NSC position newly focused on atrocity prevention and the advancement of human rights.

Just one remaining potential appointee caused any kind of stir. I wanted Hillary Clinton to be my secretary of state.

Observers put forth various theories about my rationale for choosing Hillary: that I needed to unify a still-divided Democratic Party, that I was worried about her second-guessing me from her seat in the Senate, that I had been influenced by Doris Kearns Goodwin's book **Team of Rivals** and was self-consciously mimicking Lincoln by placing a former political opponent in my cabinet.

But really it was simpler than that. I thought Hillary was the best person for the job. Throughout the campaign, I had witnessed her intelligence, preparation, and work ethic. Whatever her feelings toward me, I trusted her patriotism and commitment to duty. Most of all, I was convinced that at a time when diplomatic relations around the world were either strained or suffering from chronic neglect, having a secretary of state with Hillary's star power, relationships, and comfort on the world stage would give us added bandwidth in a way that nobody else could.

With the scars of the campaign still fresh in their minds, not everybody in my camp was convinced. ("You sure you want a secretary of state who ran TV ads saying you weren't ready to be commander in chief?" a friend asked. I had to remind him that my soon-to-be vice president had said the same thing.) Hillary was wary too, and when I first offered her the job, at a meeting in our transition office in Chicago about ten days after the election, I found myself politely rebuffed. She was tired, she said, and looked forward to settling into the more predictable Senate schedule. She still had campaign debt she needed to retire. And then there was Bill to consider. His work in global development and public health at the Clinton Foundation had made a real difference around the world, and both Hillary and I knew that the need to avoid even an appearance of conflicts—particularly with respect to fundraising—would likely place him and the foundation under new constraints.

The concerns she voiced were valid, but I considered them manageable. I asked her to take some time and think it over. Over the course of the next week, I enlisted Podesta, Rahm, Joe Biden, several of our Senate colleagues, and whoever else I could think of to reach out and help make the case to Hillary. Despite the full-court press, when we spoke next, on a late-night phone call, she told me she was still inclined to turn me down. Again I persisted, certain that whatever remaining doubts she might have had less to do with the job and more to do with our potential relationship. I elicited her views on Iraq, North Korea, nuclear proliferation, and human rights. I asked her how she might revitalize the State Department. I assured her that she'd have constant and direct access to me, and the ability to choose her own team. "You're too important for me to take no as an answer," I said at the end of the call.

By the next morning, Hillary had decided to accept

my offer and join the administration. A week and a half later, I introduced her and the rest of my national security team—along with my choice for attorney general, Eric Holder, and my Department of Homeland Security nominee, Governor Janet Napolitano—at a Chicago press conference. Looking at the men and women assembled onstage, I couldn't help noticing that almost all of them were far older than I was, possessed of decades more experience in the highest levels of government, and that at least a couple of them had originally supported someone else for president, unmoved by talk of hope and change. A team of rivals after all, I thought. I'd find out soon enough whether this indicated a well-founded confidence in my ability to lead—or the naïve faith of a novice about to get rolled.

WHEN GEORGE WASHINGTON was elected president in 1789, Washington, D.C., didn't yet exist. The president-elect had to make a seven-day trip by barge and horse-drawn buggy from his home in Mount Vernon, Virginia, to New York City's Federal Hall—the temporary seat of the new national government—for his swearing in. A crowd of ten thousand greeted him. The oath of office was administered, followed by a shout of "Long live George Washington" and a thirteen-gun salute. Washington delivered a muted, fifteen-minute inaugural address, not to the crowd but to the members of Congress within their ill-lit, makeshift chamber. He then headed to a service at a nearby church.

With that, the Father of Our Country was free to get on with the business of making sure America outlasted his tenure.

Over time, presidential inaugurations grew more elaborate. In 1809, Dolley Madison hosted the first inaugural ball in the new capital, with four hundred people shelling out four dollars each for the privilege of attending what to that point was the largest social event ever held in Washington, D.C. Befitting his populist reputation, Andrew Jackson threw open the White House doors to several thousand of his supporters for his inauguration in 1829; the drunken crowd got so rowdy that Jackson was said to have escaped through a window.

For his second inauguration, Teddy Roosevelt wasn't content with military processions and marching bands— he threw in a passel of cowboys and the Apache chief Geronimo. And by the time it was John F. Kennedy's turn in 1961, the inauguration had become a multiday televised spectacle, complete with performances by famous musical artists, a reading by poet laureate Robert Frost, and several fancy balls where Hollywood's leading celebrities could sprinkle stardust on the new president's bankrollers and ward heelers. (Frank Sinatra apparently pulled out all the stops to make the parties Camelot-worthy—although he was forced into what must have been an awkward conversation with his friend and fellow Rat Packer Sammy Davis, Jr., when Joe Kennedy sent word that the presence of Davis and his very white Swedish wife at the inaugural balls might not sit so well with JFK's southern supporters and should therefore be discouraged.)

Given the excitement our campaign had generated, expectations for my inauguration—scheduled for January 20, 2009—were high. As with the Democratic convention, I didn't have much to do with the details of putting it together, confident that the committee we'd set up and my campaign's organizational whiz Alyssa Mastromonaco (then slated to be my Director of Running Stuff) had everything well in hand. Instead, while stages were being erected and bleachers set up along the D.C. parade route, Michelle, the girls, and I went to Hawaii for Christmas, where—in between sorting out my final cabinet appointments, daily consultations with my economic team, and early work on my inaugural address—I tried to catch my breath.

Maya and I spent an afternoon going through Toot's personal effects and then walked the same rocky outcropping near Hanauma Bay where we'd said a final farewell to our mother and scattered her ashes over the ocean below. I pulled together a pickup basketball game with some of my old high school teammates. Our families sang Christmas carols, baked cookies, and debuted what would end up becoming an annual talent show (the dads were fairly judged to be the least talented). I even had a chance to bodysurf at Sandy Beach, one of my favorite haunts as a youth. Shooting down a gently breaking wave, the light curling with the sweep of water and the sky etched with a flight of birds, I could pretend for a moment that I wasn't surrounded by several wet-suited Navy SEALs, that the Coast Guard cutter in the distance had nothing to do with me, that pictures of me shirtless wouldn't later end up on the front pages of newspapers around the world with headlines like FIT FOR OFFICE. When I finally signaled that I was ready to go, the leader of my security team that day—a sardonic agent named Dave Beach who'd been with me from the start and knew me as a friend—tilted his head, shook the water out of his ears, and said matter-of-factly, "I hope you enjoyed that, 'cause it's the last time you'll be able to do it for a long, long while."

I laughed, knowing he was joking . . . or was he? The campaign and its immediate aftermath had offered no time for reflection, so it was only during this brief tropical interlude that all of us—friends, family, staffers, Secret Service—had a chance to wrap our heads around what had happened and try to envision what was yet to come. Everyone seemed happy but slightly tentative, unsure whether it was okay to acknowledge the strangeness of things, trying to figure out what had changed and what had not. And although she didn't show it, no one felt this uncertainty more keenly than the soon-to-be First Lady of the United States.

Over the course of the campaign, I'd watched Michelle adapt to our new circumstances with unerring grace—charming voters, nailing interviews, perfecting a style that showed her to be both chic and accessible. It was less a transformation than an amplification, her essential "Miche-ness" burnished to a high shine. But for all her growing comfort with being in the public eye, behind the scenes Michelle was desperate to carve out some zone of normalcy for our family, a place beyond the distorting reach of politics and fame.

In the weeks after the election, this meant throwing herself into the tasks any couple might go through when having to relocate for a new job. With typical efficiency, she sorted. She packed. She closed accounts, made sure our mail would get forwarded, and helped the University of Chicago Medical Center plan for her replacement.

Her overriding focus, though, was on our daughters. The day after the election she had already arranged for a tour of D.C. schools (both Malia and Sasha crossed the all-girls schools off their list, settling instead on Sidwell Friends, a private school founded by Quakers and the same school Chelsea Clinton had attended) and talked to teachers about managing the girls' transfer into classes midyear. She sought advice from Hillary and from Laura Bush on how to insulate them from the press and grilled the Secret Service on ways to avoid having the girls' security detail disrupt playdates and soccer games. She familiarized herself with the operations of the White House residence and made sure the furniture in the girls' bedrooms wouldn't look like something out of Monticello.

It's not as if I didn't share Michelle's stress. Malia and, especially, Sasha were so young in 2008, all pigtails and braids, missing teeth and round cheeks. How would the White House shape their childhoods? Would it isolate them? Make them moody or entitled? At night, I would listen intently as Michelle gave me the latest intel she'd gathered, then offer my thoughts on this or that issue that was nagging her, providing her with assurances that a sullen remark or small piece of mischief from either of the girls didn't indicate the early effects of their suddenly topsy-turvy world.

But as had been true during so much of the last ten years, the day-to-day burden of parenting rested largely on Michelle. And as she watched how—before I had even assumed office—the vortex of work pulled me in, as she saw her own career sidelined, her tight-knit circle of friends soon to be hundreds of miles away as she made her way in a city where so many people's motives were necessarily suspect, the prospect of loneliness settled on her like a cloud.

All of which helps explain why Michelle asked her mom to come live with us in the White House. That Marian Robinson was even willing to consider it came as something of a surprise to me, for by nature my mother-in-law was cautious, finding satisfaction in steady work, familiar routines, a small circle of family and friends that she'd known for years. She had lived in the same house since the 1960s and rarely ventured out of Chicago; her one extravagance was an annual three-day trip to Vegas with her sister-in-law Yvonne and Mama Kaye to play the slots. And although she adored her grandchildren and had agreed to retire early to help Michelle look after the girls once the campaign heated up, she had always made a point of not hanging around our Chicago home or staying for dinner once her work was done.

"I am **not** going to be one of those old ladies," she'd say with a huff, "who won't leave their kids alone just 'cause they've got nothing better to do."

Still, when Michelle asked her to move to Washington with us, Marian didn't put up much resistance. She knew her daughter wouldn't ask unless it was really important.

There was the practical stuff, of course. For the first few years we were in the White House, it would be Marian who accompanied Malia and Sasha to school every morning and kept them company after school if Michelle was at work. But it was more than that. What really mattered—what wouldn't stop mattering long after the girls had outgrown the need for babysitting—was the way Marian's mere presence kept our family grounded.

My mother-in-law didn't act like she was better than anybody else, so our daughters never even considered that an option. She lived by a doctrine of no fuss and no drama and was unimpressed by any form of opulence or hype. When Michelle came back from a photo shoot or a black-tie dinner, where her every move had been monitored or her hairstyle scrutinized by the press, she could shed her designer dress, throw on a pair of jeans and a T-shirt, and know that her mom was upstairs in her suite on the top floor of the White House, always willing to sit and watch TV with her and talk about the girls or folks back home—or about nothing in particular.

My mother-in-law never complained about anything. Whenever I interacted with her, I'd remember that, no matter what kind of mess I was dealing with, no one had forced me to be the president and that I needed to just suck it up and do my job.

What a gift my mother-in-law was. For us, she became a living, breathing reminder of who we were and where we came from, a keeper of values we'd once thought ordinary but had learned were more rare than we had ever imagined.

WINTER SEMESTER AT Sidwell Friends School started two weeks before Inauguration Day, so after New Year's we flew back to Chicago, scooped up whatever personal effects had not already been shipped ahead, then boarded a government plane for Washington. Blair House, the president's official guesthouse, couldn't accommodate us that early, so we checked into the Hay-Adams hotel, the first of three moves we'd make in the span of three weeks.

Malia and Sasha didn't seem to mind being in a hotel. They especially didn't mind their mom's unusually indulgent attitude toward TV watching, bed jumping, and sampling every dessert on the room-service menu. Michelle accompanied them to their first day of school in a Secret Service vehicle. Later, she would tell me how her heart sank as she watched her precious babies—looking like miniature explorers in their brightly colored coats and backpacks—walking into their new lives surrounded by burly armed men.

At the hotel that night, though, the girls were their usual chattering, irrepressible selves, telling us what a great day they'd had, and how lunch was better than at their old school, and how they had already made a bunch of new friends. As they spoke, I could see the tension on Michelle's face start to lift. When she informed Malia and Sasha that now that school had started, there'd be no more weeknight desserts and TV watching and that it was time to brush their teeth and get ready for bed, I figured things would turn out okay.

Meanwhile, our transition was firing on all cylinders. Initial meetings with my national security and economic teams were productive, with folks sticking to the agenda and grandstanding kept to a minimum. Crammed into nondescript government offices, we set up working groups for every agency and every imaginable topic—job training, airline safety, student loan debt, cancer research, Pentagon procurement—and I spent my days picking the brains of earnest young whiz kids, rumpled academics, business leaders, advocacy groups, and grizzled veterans of previous administrations. Some were auditioning for a job in the administration; others wanted us to adopt proposals that had gone nowhere over the previous eight years. But all seemed eager to help, excited by the prospect of a White House willing to put new ideas to the test.

There were, of course, bumps along the way. Some of my preferred choices for cabinet positions declined or didn't pass vetting. At various points in the day Rahm might pop in to ask me how I wanted to handle some emerging policy or organizational dispute, and behind the scenes there was no shortage of the early jockeying—over titles, turf, access, parking spots—that characterizes any new administration. But overall, the mood was one of focused exhilaration, all of us convinced that with smart, deliberate work we could transform the country in the ways we had promised.

And why not? Polls showed my approval rating close to 70 percent. Each day brought a new round of positive media coverage. Younger staffers like Reggie and Favs were suddenly hot items in the D.C. gossip columns. Despite forecasts for frigid temperatures on Inauguration Day, authorities predicted record crowds, with hotels already booked for miles around. The avalanche of requests for the ticketed events—from elected officials, donors, distant cousins, high school acquaintances, and various important personages we barely knew or hadn't even met—never slowed. Michelle and I did our best to sort through all of them without bruising too many feelings.

"It's like our wedding," I grumbled, "but with a bigger guest list."

Four days before the inauguration, Michelle, the girls, and I flew to Philadelphia, where in homage to Lincoln's whistle-stop train ride from Springfield to Washington for his 1861 inauguration we boarded a vintage railroad car and reprised the last leg of his journey, with one deviation: a stop in Wilmington, where we picked up Joe and Jill Biden. Watching the adoring crowd that had gathered to see them off, hearing Joe joke with all the Amtrak conductors he knew by name after years of commuting, I could only imagine what was going through his mind, rolling down tracks he'd first traveled not in joy but in anguish so very long ago.

I spent much of the time that day chatting with the several dozen guests we'd invited along for the ride, most of them ordinary voters we'd met here and there along the campaign trail. They joined Malia, Sasha, and me in singing "Happy Birthday" as Michelle blew out the candles on her cake (it was her forty-fifth), giving it the feeling of a close family gathering, the kind Michelle so treasured. Occasionally I'd step out onto the train's rear platform, feeling the wind cut against my face, the syncopated rhythm of wheels against tracks somehow slowing down time, and I'd wave to the clusters of people who had gathered along the way. There were thousands of them, mile after mile, their smiles visible from a distance, some standing on flatbed trucks, others pressed up against fences, many holding homemade signs with messages like GRANDMAS 4 OBAMA or WE BELIEVE or YES WE DID or lifting up their kids and urging them to wave.

Such moments continued over the next two days. During a visit to Walter Reed Army Medical Center, I met a young Marine amputee who saluted from his bed and told me he'd voted for me despite being a Republican, and that he would be proud to call me his commander in chief. At a homeless shelter in southeast Washington, a tough-looking teenage boy wordlessly wrapped me in the tightest embrace. My father's step-mother, Mama Sarah, had traveled all the way from her tiny rural village in northwestern Kenya for the inauguration. I smiled as I watched this elderly woman without any formal education, a woman whose home had a tin roof and neither running water nor indoor plumbing, being served dinner in Blair House on china used by prime ministers and kings.

How could my heart not be stirred? How could I resist believing there was something true in all this, something that might last?

Months later, when the magnitude of economic wreckage was fully understood and the public mood had turned dark, my team and I would ask ourselves whether—as a matter of politics and governance—we should have done more to tamp down this collective postelection high and prepare the country for the hardships to come. It's not as if we didn't try. When I go back and read interviews I gave right before taking office, I'm struck by how sober I was—insisting that the economy would get worse before it got better, reminding people that reforming healthcare couldn't happen overnight and that there were no simple solutions in places like Afghanistan. The same goes for my inauguration speech: I tried to paint an honest picture of our circumstances, stripping out some of the loftier rhetoric in favor of calls for responsibility and common effort in the face of daunting challenges.

It's all there, in black and white, a pretty accurate assessment of how the next few years would go. And yet maybe it was for the best that people couldn't hear those cautionary notes. After all, it wasn't hard to find reasons to feel fear and anger in early 2009, to mistrust politicians or the institutions that had failed so many people.

Maybe what was needed was a burst of energy, no matter how fleeting—a happy-seeming story about who we were as Americans and who we might be, the kind of high that could provide just enough momentum to get us through the most treacherous part of the journey.

That feels like what happened. A collective, unspoken decision was made that for a few weeks at least, the country would take a much-needed break from cynicism.

INAUGURATION DAY ARRIVED, bright, windy, and freezing cold. Because I knew that the events had been choreographed with a military precision, and because I tend to live my life about fifteen minutes behind schedule, I set two alarms to make sure I was up on time. A run on the treadmill, breakfast, a shower and shave, repeated tries before the tie knot was up to snuff, and by eight forty-five a.m. Michelle and I were in the car for the two-minute drive from Blair House to St. John's Episcopal Church, where we had invited a friend of ours, Dallas pastor T. D. Jakes, to lead a private service.

For his sermon that morning, Reverend Jakes drew on the Old Testament's Book of Daniel, describing how Shadrach, Meshach, and Abednego, faithful to God despite their service in the royal court, refused to kneel before King Nebuchadnezzar's golden idol; how as a result the three men were thrown into a blazing furnace; and yet how because of their faithfulness, God protected them, helping them to emerge from the furnace unscathed.

In assuming the presidency during such turbulent times, Reverend Jakes explained, I too was being thrown into the flames. The flames of war. The flames of economic collapse. But so long as I stayed true to God and to doing what was right, I too had nothing to fear.

The pastor spoke in a majestic baritone, his broad, dark face smiling down on me from the pulpit. "God is with you," he said, "in the furnace."

Some in the church began to applaud, and I smiled in acknowledgment of his words. But my mind was drifting back to the previous evening, when after dinner I had excused myself from my family, walked upstairs to one of Blair House's many rooms, and received a briefing from the director of the White House Military Office on the "football"— the small leather-jacketed suitcase that accompanies the president at all times and contains the codes needed to launch a nuclear strike. One of the military aides responsible for carrying the football explained the protocols as calmly and methodically as someone might describe how to program a DVR. The subtext was obvious.

I would soon be vested with the authority to blow up the world.

The night before, Michael Chertoff, President Bush's secretary of homeland security, had called to inform us of credible intelligence indicating that four Somali nationals were thought to be planning a terrorist attack at the inauguration ceremony. As a result, the already massive security force around the National Mall would be beefed up. The suspects—young men who were believed to be coming over the border from Canada— were still at large. There was no question that we'd go ahead with the next day's events, but to be safe, we ran through various contingencies with Chertoff and his team, then assigned Axe to draft evacuation instructions that I'd give the crowd if an attack took place while I was onstage.

Reverend Jakes wrapped up his sermon. The choir's final song filled the sanctuary. No one beyond a handful of staffers knew of the terrorist threat. I hadn't even told Michelle, not wanting to add to the day's stress. No one had nuclear war or terrorism on their minds. No one except me. Scanning people in the pews—friends, family members, colleagues, some of whom caught my eye and smiled or waved with excitement—I realized this was now part of my job: maintaining an outward sense of normalcy, upholding for everyone the fiction that we live in a safe and orderly world, even as I stared down the dark hole of chance and prepared as best I could for the possibility that at any given moment on any given day chaos might break through.

At nine fifty-five, we arrived at the North Portico of the White House, where President and Mrs. Bush greeted us and led us inside, to where the Bidens, Vice President Cheney and his family, and congressional leaders and their spouses had gathered for a brief reception. Fifteen minutes ahead of schedule, our staffs suggested that we leave early for the Capitol in order to account for what they described as massive crowds. We loaded into the waiting cars in pairs: leaders of the House and Senate first, then Jill Biden and Mrs. Cheney, Michelle and Mrs. Bush, Joe Biden and Vice President Cheney, with President Bush and me bringing up the rear. It was like the boarding of Noah's Ark.

It was my first time in "the Beast," the oversized black limousine used to transport the president. Reinforced to survive a bomb blast, the thing weighs several tons, with plush black leather seats and the presidential seal stitched on a leather panel above the phone and the armrest. Once closed, the doors of the Beast seal out all sound, and as our convoy slow-rolled down Pennsylvania Avenue, while I made small talk with President Bush, I looked out the bulletproof windows at the throngs of people who were still on their way to the Mall or had already taken seats along the parade route. Most appeared to be in a celebratory mood, cheering and waving as the motorcade passed. But turning the corner onto the final leg of the route, we came upon a group of protesters chanting into bullhorns and holding up signs that read INDICT BUSH and WAR CRIMINAL.

Whether the president saw them I couldn't say—he was deep into an enthusiastic description of what it was like to clear brush at his ranch in Crawford, Texas, where he'd be heading directly after the ceremony. But I felt quietly angry on his behalf. To protest a man in the final hour of his presidency seemed graceless and unnecessary. More generally, I was troubled by what these last-minute protests said about the divisions that were churning across the country—and the weakening of whatever boundaries of decorum had once regulated politics.

There was a trace of self-interest in my feelings, I suppose. In a few hours it would be only me riding in the backseat of the Beast. It wouldn't take long, I figured, before bullhorns and signs were directed my way. This too would be part of the job: finding a way not to take such attacks personally, while avoiding the temptation to shut myself off—as perhaps my predecessor had too often done—from those shouting on the other side of the glass.

We had been wise to leave early; the streets were choked with people, and by the time we arrived at the Capitol we were several minutes behind schedule. Together with the Bushes, we made our way to the Speaker's office for more handshakes, photos, and instructions before participants and guests—including the girls and the rest of our families—began lining up for the procession. Michelle and I were shown the Bible we'd borrowed from the Library of Congress for the administering of my oath, a small, thick volume covered in burgundy velvet with gilt edges, the same Bible Lincoln had used for his own swearing in. Then it was Michelle's turn to go, leaving me, Marvin, and Reggie momentarily alone in a holding room, just like old times.

"Anything in my teeth?" I asked with an exaggerated smile.

"You're good," Marvin said.

"It's cold out there," I said. "Just like Springfield."

"A few more people, though," Reggie said.

A military aide stuck his head into the room and said it was time. I gave Reggie and Marvin fist bumps and followed the congressional committee down the long hallways, through the Capitol Rotunda and National Statuary Hall, past the rows of well-wishers who lined the walls, a gauntlet of honor guards saluting each step, until I finally arrived at the glass doors leading out onto the inaugural platform. The scene beyond was stunning: The crowd blanketed the Mall in an unbroken plane, reaching well past the Washington Monument and out to the Lincoln Memorial, with what must have been hundreds of thousands of handheld flags shimmering under the noonday sun like the surface of an ocean current. For a brief moment, before trumpets sounded and I was announced, I closed my eyes and summoned the prayer that had carried me here, one I would continue to repeat every night I was president.

A prayer of thanks for all I'd been given. A prayer that my sins be forgiven. A prayer that my family and the American people be kept safe from harm.

A prayer for guidance.

TED SORENSEN, JFK's friend, confidant, and chief speechwriter, had been an early supporter of mine. By the time we met, he was almost eighty but still sharp, with a bracing wit. He even traveled on my behalf, a persuasive if also slightly high-maintenance campaign surrogate. (Once, while our motorcade was barreling down the highway in a driving Iowa rainstorm, he leaned forward and yelled at the agent behind the wheel, "Son, I'm half blind but even I can see you're too damn close to that car!") Ted also became a favorite of my young speechwriting team, generously offering advice and occasionally commenting on drafts of their speeches. Since he had co-authored Kennedy's inaugural address ("Ask not what your country can do for you . . ."), they asked him once what had been the secret to writing one of the four or five greatest speeches in American history. Simple, he said: Whenever he and Kennedy sat down to write, they told themselves, "Let's make this good enough to be in a book of the great speeches someday."

I don't know if Ted was trying to inspire my team or just mess with their heads.

I do know that my own address failed to reach JFK's lofty standards. In the days that followed, it received far less attention than did the estimates of the crowd size, the bitterness of the cold, Aretha Franklin's hat, and the slight glitch that occurred between me and Chief Justice John Roberts during the administering of the oath, causing us to meet in the White House's Map Room the following day for an official do-over. Some commentators thought the speech had been unnecessarily dark. Others detected inappropriate criticism of the previous administration.

Still, once I'd finished delivering it, I felt satisfied that I'd spoken honestly and with conviction. I was also relieved that the note to be used in case of a terrorist incident had stayed in my breast pocket.

With the main event behind me, I let myself relax and soak in the spectacle. I was moved by the sight of the Bushes mounting the stairs to their helicopter and turning to wave one final time. I felt pride holding Michelle's hand as we walked a portion of the parade route. I was tickled by the parade participants: Marines, mariachi bands, astronauts, Tuskegee Airmen, and, especially, the high school bands from every state in the Union (including my alma mater Punahou's marching band—Go Buff 'n Blue!).

The day contained just one sad note. During the traditional postinaugural lunch in the Capitol, in between toasts and presentations by our congressional hosts, Teddy Kennedy—who had recently had surgery to remove a cancerous brain tumor—collapsed in a sudden, violent seizure. The room fell silent as emergency medics rushed in. Teddy's wife, Vicki, followed alongside as they wheeled him away, her face stricken with fear, leaving the rest of us to wonder anxiously about his fate, none of us imagining the political consequences that would eventually flow from that moment.

Michelle and I attended a total of ten inaugural balls that evening. Michelle was a chocolate-brown vision in her flowing white gown, and at our first stop I took her in my arms and spun her around and whispered silly things in her ear as we danced to a sublime rendition of "At Last" sung by Beyoncé. At the Commander in Chief's Ball, we split up to dance with two charming and understandably nervous young members of our armed forces.

The other eight balls I'd be hard-pressed to remember.

By the time we got back to the White House, it was well past midnight. A party for our family and closest friends was still going strong in the East Room, with the Wynton Marsalis Quintet showing no signs of letting up. Twelve hours in high heels had taken a toll on Michelle's feet, and since she had to get up an hour earlier than I did to get her hair done for another church service the next morning, I offered to stay and entertain our guests while she headed to bed.

Just a few lights were on by the time I got upstairs. Michelle and the girls were asleep, the sound of night crews clearing dishes and breaking down tables and chairs barely audible from below. I realized I hadn't been alone all day. For a moment I just stood there, looking up and down the enormous central hall, not yet certain of where each of the many doors led, taking in the crystal chandeliers and a baby grand piano, noticing a Monet on one wall, a Cézanne on another, pulling out some of the books on the shelf, examining small busts and artifacts and portraits of people I didn't recognize.

My mind went back to the first time I had seen the

White House, some thirty years ago, when as a young community organizer I had brought a group of students to Washington to lobby their congressman on a bill to increase student aid. The group of us had stood outside the gate along Pennsylvania Avenue, a few students mugging and taking pictures with disposable cameras. I remember staring up at the windows on the second floor, wondering if at that very moment someone might be looking down at us. I had tried to imagine what they might be thinking. Did they miss the rhythms of ordinary life? Were they lonely? Did they sometimes feel a jolt in their heart and wonder how it was that they had ended up where they were?

I'd have my answer soon enough, I thought. Pulling off my tie, I walked slowly down the hall, turning off what lights remained on.

CHAPTER 11

NO MATTER WHAT YOU MIGHT tell yourself, no matter how much you've read or how many briefings you've received or how many veterans of previous administrations you've recruited, nothing entirely prepares you for those first weeks in the White House. Everything is new, unfamiliar, fraught with import. The vast majority of your senior appointees, including cabinet secretaries, are weeks or sometimes months away from being confirmed. Across the White House complex, staffers can be seen securing the requisite IDs, asking where to park, learning how to operate the phones, figuring out where the bathrooms are, and schlepping boxes into the cramped warren of offices in the West Wing or the more capacious rooms in the nearby Eisenhower Executive Office Building (EEOB), all while trying not to look completely overwhelmed. It's like moving-in day on a college campus, except a large percentage of the people involved are middle-aged, in suits, and, along with you, charged with running the most powerful nation on earth.

I didn't have to worry about moving myself in, but my days were a whirlwind. Having witnessed how stumbles out of the gate had hobbled Bill Clinton throughout his first two years in office, Rahm was intent on taking advantage of our postelection honeymoon period to get some things done.

"Trust me," he said. "The presidency is like a new car. It starts depreciating the minute you drive it off the lot."

To build early momentum, he had instructed our transition team to identify campaign promises I could fulfill with the stroke of a pen. I signed an executive order banning torture and launched what was supposed to be a year-long process to close the U.S. military detention center in Guantánamo Bay, Cuba. We instituted some of the toughest ethics rules in White House history, including tightening restrictions on lobbyists. A couple of weeks later, we finalized an agreement with congressional leaders to cover four million more kids under the Children's Health Insurance Program, and shortly after that, we lifted President Bush's moratorium on federally funded embryonic stem-cell research.

I signed my first bill into law on my ninth day in office: the Lilly Ledbetter Fair Pay Act. The legislation was named after an unassuming Alabaman who, deep into a long career at the Goodyear Tire & Rubber Company, had discovered that she'd routinely been paid less than her male counterparts. As discrimination cases go, it should have been a slam dunk, but in 2007, defying all common sense, the Supreme Court had disallowed the lawsuit. According to Justice Samuel Alito, Title VII of the Civil Rights Act required Ledbetter to have filed her claim within 180 days of when the discrimination first occurred—in other words, six months after she received her first paycheck, and many years before she actually discovered the pay disparity. For over a year, Republicans in the Senate had blocked corrective action (with President Bush promising to veto it if it passed). Now, thanks to quick legislative work by our emboldened Democratic majorities, the bill sat on a small ceremonial desk in the East Room.

Lilly and I had become friends during the campaign. I knew her family, knew her struggles. She stood next to me that day as I put my signature on the bill, using a different pen for each letter of my name. (The pens would serve as keepsakes for Lilly and the bill's sponsors—a nice tradition, though it made my signature look like it had been written by a ten-year-old.) I thought not just about Lilly but also about my mother, and Toot, and all the other working women across the country who had ever been passed over for promotions or been paid less than they were worth. The legislation I was signing wouldn't reverse centuries of discrimination. But it was something, a step forward.

This is why I ran, I told myself. This is what the office can do.

We would roll out other comparable initiatives in those first few months, some attracting modest press attention, others noticed only by those directly affected. In normal times, this would have been enough, a series of small wins as our bigger legislative proposals—on healthcare, immigration reform, and climate change—began to work their way through Congress.

But these were not normal times. For the public and the press, for me and my team, only one issue truly mattered: What were we going to do to halt the economy's collapse?

. . .

AS DIRE AS the situation had seemed before the election, it wasn't until a mid-December meeting in Chicago with my new economic team, just over a month before I was sworn in, that I had begun to appreciate the scope of what we were dealing with. Christy Romer, whose cheery demeanor and sensible style brought to mind a 1950s TV-sitcom mom, opened her presentation with a line she'd heard Axelrod use in an earlier meeting.

"Mr. President-Elect," she said, "this is your holy-shit moment."

The chuckles quickly subsided as Christy took us through a series of charts. With over half of America's twenty-five largest financial institutions having either failed, merged, or restructured to avoid bankruptcy during the previous year, what had begun as a crisis on Wall Street had now thoroughly infected the broader economy. The stock market had lost 40 percent of its value. There were foreclosure filings on 2.3 million homes. Household wealth had dropped 16 percent, which, as Tim would later point out, was more than five times the percentage loss that occurred in the aftermath of the 1929 market crash. All this on top of an economy that was already suffering from persistently high levels of poverty, a decline in the share of working-age men who were actually working, a fall in productivity growth, and lagging median wages.

And we had yet to reach the bottom. As people had felt poorer, they'd stopped spending, just as mounting losses had caused banks to stop lending, imperiling more businesses and more jobs. A number of major retailers already had gone belly-up. GM and Chrysler were headed in the same direction. News stations now carried daily reports of mass layoffs at blue-chip companies like Boeing and Pfizer. According to Christy, all arrows pointed in the direction of the deepest recession since the 1930s, with job losses—estimated at 533,000 in November alone—likely to get worse.

"How much worse?" I asked.

"We're not sure," Larry chimed in, "but probably in the millions." He explained that unemployment was typically a "lagging indicator," meaning the full scale of job losses during recessions didn't show up right away, and usually continued well after an economy started growing again. Moreover, economies typically recovered much more slowly from recessions triggered by financial crises than from those caused by fluctuations in the business cycle. In the absence of quick and aggressive intervention by the federal government, Larry calculated, the chances of a second Great Depression were "about one in three."

"Jesus," Joe Biden muttered. I looked out the window of the downtown conference room. A heavy snow swirled soundlessly through a gray sky. Images of tent cities and people lined up at soup kitchens materialized in my head.

"All right, then," I said, turning back to the team. "Since it's too late to ask for a recount, what can we do to lower those odds?"

We spent the next three hours mapping out a strategy. Job one was reversing the cycle of contracting demand. In an ordinary recession, monetary policy would be an option: By lowering interest rates, the Federal Reserve could help make the purchase of everything from homes to cars to appliances significantly cheaper. But while Chairman Ben Bernanke was committed to trying out a range of unorthodox strategies to douse the financial panic, Tim explained, the Fed had used up most of its bullets over the course of the previous year: With interest rates already close to zero, neither businesses nor consumers, already badly overleveraged, showed any inclination to take on more debt.

Our conversation therefore focused on fiscal stimulus, or, in layperson's terms, having the government spend more money. Though I hadn't majored in economics, I was familiar enough with John Maynard Keynes, one of the giants of modern economics and a theoretician of the causes of the Great Depression. Keynes's basic insight had been simple: From the perspective of the individual family or firm, it was prudent to tighten one's belt during a severe recession. The problem was that thrift could be stifling; when everyone tightened their belts at the same time, economic conditions couldn't improve.

Keynes's answer to the dilemma was just as simple: A government needed to step in as the "spender of last resort." The idea was to pump money into the economy until the gears started to turn again, until families grew confident enough to trade in old cars for new ones and innovative companies saw enough demand to start making new products again. Once the economy was kick-started, the government could then turn off the spigot and recoup its money through the resulting boost in tax revenue. In large part, this was the principle behind FDR's New Deal, which took shape after he took office in 1933, at the height of the Great Depression. Whether it was young men in the Civilian Conservation Corps put to work building trails in America's national parks, or farmers receiving government payments for surplus milk, or theater troupes performing as part of the Works Progress Administration, the New Deal's programs helped unemployed Americans get desperately needed paychecks and companies sustain themselves with government orders for steel or lumber, all of which helped bolster private enterprise and stabilize the faltering economy.

As ambitious as it was at the time, New Deal spending actually proved too modest to fully counteract the Great Depression, especially after FDR succumbed to 1936 election-year pressures and pulled back too early on what was then seen by many elite opinion makers as government profligacy. It would take the ultimate stimulus of World War II, when the entire nation mobilized to build an Arsenal of Democracy, to finally break the Depression once and for all. But the New Deal had kept things from getting worse, and Keynesian theory had come to be widely accepted among economists, including politically conservative ones (although Republican-leaning economists typically preferred stimulus in the form of tax cuts rather than government programs).

So we needed a stimulus package. To deliver the necessary impact, how big did it need to be? Before the election, we'd proposed what was then considered an ambitious program of $175 billion. Immediately after the election, examining the worsening data, we had raised the number to $500 billion. The team now recommended something even bigger. Christy mentioned a trillion dollars, causing Rahm to sputter like a cartoon character spitting out a bad meal.

"There's no fucking way," Rahm said. Given the public's anger over the hundreds of billions of dollars already spent on the bank bailout, he said, any number that began "with a **t**" would be a nonstarter with lots of Democrats, not to mention Republicans. I turned to Joe, who nodded in assent.

"What **can** we get passed?" I asked.

"Seven, maybe eight hundred billion, tops," Rahm said. "And that's a stretch."

There was also the question of how stimulus dollars would be used. According to Keynes, it didn't matter much what the government spent the money on, so long as it generated economic activity. But since the levels of spending we were talking about would likely preclude funding for other priorities well into the future, I pushed the team to think about high-profile, high-yield projects— modern versions of the Interstate Highway System or the Tennessee Valley Authority that would not only give the economy an immediate boost but could transform America's longer-term economic landscape. What about a national smart grid that would make the delivery of electricity more secure and efficient? Or a new, highly integrated air traffic control system that would enhance safety and reduce fuel costs and carbon emissions?

Folks around the table were not encouraging. "We've already started asking federal agencies to identify high-impact projects," Larry said, "but I have to be honest, Mr. President-Elect. Those kinds of projects are extremely complicated. They take time to develop . . . and unfortunately time is not on our side." The most important thing was to get the money into people's pockets as quickly as possible, and that aim was best served by providing food stamps and extended unemployment insurance, as well as middle-class tax cuts and aid to states to help them avoid having to lay off teachers, firefighters, and police officers. Studies had shown that spending on infrastructure provided the biggest bang for the buck—but, Larry suggested, even there we should focus on more prosaic undertakings like road repair and patching up aging sewer systems, projects that local governments could use to put people to work right away.

"It's going to be hard to get the public excited about food stamps and repaving roads," Axe said. "Not real sexy."

"Neither's a depression," Tim tartly replied.

Tim was the one person among us who'd already spent a stomach-churning year on the front lines of the crisis. I could hardly blame him for refusing to be swept up in any starry-eyed plans. His biggest concern was that mass unemployment and bankruptcies were further weakening the financial system, creating what he described as "an adverse feedback loop." As Larry took the lead on the stimulus package, Tim and his team would in the meantime try to come up with a plan to unlock the credit markets and stabilize the financial system once and for all. Tim admitted that he wasn't yet sure exactly what would work—or whether the remaining $350 billion in TARP money would be enough to cover it.

And that wasn't the end of our to-do list. A talented team—including Shaun Donovan, the former head of New York City's Department of Housing Preservation and Development and my nominee for housing and urban development secretary, as well as Austan Goolsbee, my longtime economic advisor and a University of Chicago professor, whom I would appoint to the Council of Economic Advisers—had already begun work on plans to shore up the housing market and reduce the flood of foreclosures. We recruited prominent finance whiz Steve Rattner and Ron Bloom, a former investment banker who represented unions in corporate restructurings, to generate strategies to save the auto industry. And my soon-to-be budget director, Peter Orszag, was given the unenviable task of coming up with a plan to pay for the stimulus in the short term while putting the federal budget on a more sustainable path for the long term— this at a time when high levels of emergency spending and lower tax revenues had already driven the federal deficit to more than $1 trillion for the first time in history.

In exchange for Peter's troubles, we wrapped up the meeting by bringing in a cake to celebrate his fortieth birthday. As people gathered around the table to watch him blow out the candles, Goolsbee—whose tweedy name always seemed incongruous with his Jimmy Olsen looks, ebullient humor, and Waco, Texas, twang—appeared beside me.

"That's definitely the worst briefing any incoming president has gotten since FDR in 1932!" he said. He sounded like a boy impressed by the sight of a particularly grisly wound.

"Goolsbee," I said, "that's not even my worst briefing **this week**."

I WAS ONLY half-joking; outside of economic briefings, I was spending much of my transition time in windowless rooms, getting the classified details on Iraq, Afghanistan, and multiple terrorist threats. Still, I remember leaving the meeting on the economy more energized than despondent. Some of my confidence was a matter of postelection adrenaline, I suppose—the untested, maybe delusional belief that I was up for the task at hand. I also felt good about the team I'd assembled; if anyone could come up with the answers we needed, I figured this group could.

Mostly, though, my attitude was a necessary acknowledgment of how life's fortunes balance out. Given all that had gone my way during the campaign, I could hardly complain now about the bad cards we'd been dealt. As I'd remind my team more than once over the course of the next few years, the American people probably wouldn't have taken a chance on electing me if things hadn't been spinning out of control. Our job now was to get the policy right and do what was best for the country, regardless of how tough the politics might be.

That's what I told them, anyway. Privately, I knew that the politics weren't just going to be tough.

They were going to be brutal.

In the days leading up to the inauguration, I had read several books on FDR's first term and the implementation of the New Deal. The contrast was instructive, though not in a good way for us. By the time Roosevelt was elected in 1932, the Great Depression had been wreaking havoc for more than three years. A quarter of the country was unemployed, millions were destitute, and the shantytowns that dotted the American landscape were commonly referred to as "Hoovervilles"—a fair reflection of what people thought of Republican president Herbert Hoover, the man FDR was about to replace.

So widespread was the hardship, so discredited were Republican policies, that when a new bout of bank runs occurred during what was then a four-month transition between presidencies, FDR made a point of rebuffing

Hoover's efforts to enlist his help. He wanted to make sure that in the public's mind, his presidency marked a clean break, untarnished by past blunders. And when, in a stroke of luck, the economy showed signs of life just a month after he took office (before his policies had been even put into effect), FDR was happy not to share the credit with the previous administration.

We, on the other hand, were not going to have the benefit of such clarity. After all, I had already made the decision to help President Bush with his necessary though wildly unpopular response to the banking crisis, placing my hand on the proverbial bloody knife. To further stabilize the financial system, I knew, I'd likely have to do more of the same. (I was already having to twist the arms of some Senate Democrats just to get them to vote for the release of the second, $350 billion tranche of TARP funds.) As voters watched the situation get worse, which Larry and Christy said was all but assured, my popularity—along with that of the Democrats who now controlled Congress—was sure to plummet.

And despite the turmoil of the previous months, despite the horrific headlines of early 2009, nobody—not the public, not Congress, not the press, and (as I'd soon discover) not even the experts—really understood just how much worse things were about to get. Government data at the time was showing a severe recession, but not a cataclysmic one. Blue-chip analysts predicted that the unemployment rate would top out at 8 or 9 percent, not even imagining the 10 percent mark it would eventually reach. When, several weeks after the election, 387 mostly liberal economists had sent a letter to Congress, calling for a robust Keynesian stimulus, they'd put the price tag at $300 to $400 billion—about half of what we were about to propose, and a good indicator of where even the most alarmist experts had the economy pegged. As Axelrod described it, we were about to ask the American public to spend close to a trillion dollars on sandbags for a once-in-a-generation hurricane that only we knew was coming. And once the money was spent, no matter how effective the sandbags proved to be, a whole lot of folks would be flooded out anyway.

"When things are bad," Axe said, walking next to me as we left the December meeting, "no one cares that 'things could have been worse.'"

"You're right," I agreed.

"We've got to level-set people's expectations," he said. "But if we scare them or the markets too much, that will just add to the panic and do more economic damage."

"Right again," I said.

Axe shook his head dolefully. "It's going to be one hell of a midterm election," he said.

This time I said nothing, admiring his occasional, almost endearing ability to state the obvious. As it was, I didn't have the luxury of thinking that far ahead. I had to focus on a second, more immediate political problem.

We had to get the stimulus bill through Congress right away—and Congress didn't work very well.

THERE WAS A pervasive nostalgia in Washington, both before I was elected and during my presidency, for a bygone era of bipartisan cooperation on Capitol Hill. And the truth is that throughout much of the post–World War II era, the lines separating America's political parties really had been more fluid.

By the 1950s, most Republicans had accommodated themselves to New Deal–era health and safety regulations, and the Northeast and the Midwest produced scores of Republicans who were on the liberal end of the spectrum when it came to issues like conservation and civil rights. Southerners, meanwhile, constituted one of the Democratic Party's most powerful blocs, combining a deep-rooted cultural conservatism with an adamant refusal to recognize the rights of African Americans, who made up a big share of their constituency. With America's global economic dominance unchallenged, its foreign policy defined by the unifying threat of communism, and its social policy marked by a bipartisan confidence that women and people of color knew their place, both Democrats and Republicans felt free to cross party lines when required to get a bill passed. They observed customary courtesies when it came time to offer amendments or bring nominations to a vote and kept partisan attacks and hardball tactics within tolerable bounds.

The story of how this postwar consensus broke down—starting with LBJ's signing of the Civil Rights Act of 1964 and his prediction that it would lead to the South's wholesale abandonment of the Democratic Party—has been told many times before. The realignment Johnson foresaw ended up taking longer than he had expected. But steadily, year by year—through Vietnam, riots, feminism, and Nixon's southern strategy; through busing, **Roe v. Wade,** urban crime, and white flight; through affirmative action, the Moral Majority, union busting, and Robert Bork; through assault weapons bans and the rise of Newt Gingrich, gay rights and the Clinton impeachment—America's voters and their representatives became more and more polarized.

Political gerrymandering fortified these trends, as both parties, with the help of voter profiles and computer technology, drew congressional districts with the explicit aim of entrenching incumbency and minimizing the number of competitive districts in any given election. Meanwhile, the splintering of the media and the emergence of conservative outlets meant voters were no longer reliant on Walter Cronkite to tell them what was true; instead, they could hew to sources that reinforced, rather than challenged, their political preferences.

By the time I took office, this "big sort" between red and blue was close to complete. There were still hold-outs in the Senate—a dozen or so moderate-to-liberal Republicans and conservative Democrats who were open to collaboration—but most of them were hanging on to their seats for dear life. In the House, wave elections in 2006 and 2008 had swept a dozen or so conservative Democrats from traditionally GOP districts into office. But on the whole, House Democrats skewed liberal, especially on social issues, with white southern Democrats an endangered species. The shift among House Republicans was even more severe. Purged of just about all of the remaining moderates, their caucus leaned further right than any in modern history, with old-school conservatives jockeying for influence with the newly emboldened breed of Gingrich disciples, Rush Limbaugh bomb throwers, Sarah Palin wannabes, and Ayn Rand acolytes—all of whom brooked no compromise; were skeptical of any government action not involving defense, border security, law enforcement, or the banning of abortion; and appeared sincerely convinced that liberals were bent on destroying America.

On paper, at least, none of this would necessarily stop us from getting a stimulus bill passed. After all, Democrats enjoyed a seventy-seven-seat majority in the House and a seventeen-seat majority in the Senate. But even in the best of circumstances, trying to get the largest emergency spending bill in history through Congress in record time would be a little like getting a python to swallow a cow. I also had to contend with a bit of institutionalized procedural mischief—the Senate filibuster—which in the end would prove to be the most chronic political headache of my presidency.

The filibuster isn't mentioned anywhere in the Constitution. Instead, it came into being by happenstance: In 1805, Vice President Aaron Burr urged the Senate to eliminate the "motion to proceed"—a standard parliamentary provision that allows a simple majority of any legislature to end debate on a piece of business and call for a vote. (Burr, who seems never to have developed the habit of thinking things through, reportedly considered the rule a waste of time.)

It didn't take long for senators to figure out that without a formal way to end debate, any one of them could bring Senate business to a halt—and thereby extract all sorts of concessions from frustrated colleagues—simply by talking endlessly and refusing to surrender the floor. In 1917, the Senate curbed the practice by adopting "cloture," allowing a vote of two-thirds of senators present to end a filibuster. For the next fifty years the filibuster was used only sparingly—most notably by southern Democrats attempting to block anti-lynching and fair-employment bills or other legislation that threatened to shake up Jim Crow. Gradually, though, the filibuster became more routinized and easier to maintain, making it a more potent weapon, a means for the minority party to get its way. The mere threat of a filibuster was often enough to derail a piece of legislation. By the 1990s, as battle lines between Republicans and Democrats hardened, whichever party was in the minority could—and would—block any bill not to their liking, so long as they remained unified and had at least the 41 votes needed to keep a filibuster from being overridden.

Without any constitutional basis, public debate, or even the knowledge of most Americans, passing legislation through Congress had come to effectively require 60 votes in the Senate, or what was often referred to as a "supermajority." By the time I was elected president, the filibuster had become so thoroughly integrated into Senate practice—viewed as an essential and time-honored tradition—that nobody much bothered to discuss the possibility of reforming or doing away with it altogether.

And that is why—having just won an election by an overwhelming electoral margin and with the support of the largest congressional majority in many years—I still couldn't rename a post office, much less pass our stimulus package, without winning a few Republican votes.

How hard could that be?

A MAJOR WHITE HOUSE initiative can take months to prepare. There are scores of meetings involving multiple agencies and perhaps hundreds of staffers. There are extensive consultations with interested stakeholders.

The White House communications team is charged with choreographing a tightly managed campaign to sell the idea to the public, and the machinery of the entire executive branch is marshaled to pull in key committee chairs and ranking members. All of this takes place long before actual legislation is drafted and introduced.

We had no time for any of that. Instead, before I even took office, my still-unofficial and largely unpaid economic team worked nonstop through the holidays to flesh out the key elements of what would become the American Recovery and Reinvestment Act (apparently "stimulus package" wouldn't go over well with the public).

We proposed that nearly $800 billion be divided into three buckets of roughly equal size. In bucket one, emergency payments like supplementary unemployment insurance and direct aid to states to slow further mass layoffs of teachers, police officers, and other public workers. In bucket two, tax cuts targeted at the middle class, as well as various business tax breaks that gave companies a big incentive to invest in new plants or equipment now instead of later. Both the emergency payments and the tax cuts had the advantage of being easy to administer; we could quickly get money out the door and into the pockets of consumers and businesses. Tax cuts also had the added benefit of potentially attracting Republican support.

The third bucket, on the other hand, contained initiatives that were harder to design and would take longer to implement but might have a bigger long-term impact: not just traditional infrastructure spending like road construction and sewer repair but also high-speed rail, solar and wind power installation, broadband lines for underserved rural areas, and incentives for states to reform their education systems—all intended not only to put people to work but to make America more competitive.

Considering how many unmet needs there were in communities all across the country, I was surprised by how much work it took for our team to find worthy projects of sufficient scale for the Recovery Act to fund. Some promising ideas we rejected because they would take too long to stand up or required a huge new bureaucracy to manage. Others missed the cut because they wouldn't boost demand sufficiently. Mindful of accusations that I planned to use the economic crisis as an excuse for an orgy of wasteful liberal boondoggles (and because I in fact wanted to prevent Congress from engaging in wasteful boondoggles, liberal or otherwise), we put in place a series of good-government safeguards: a competitive application process for state and local governments seeking funding; strict audit and reporting requirements; and, in a move we knew would draw howls from Capitol Hill, a firm policy of no "earmarks"—to use the innocuous name for a time-honored practice in which members of Congress insert various pet projects (many dubious) into must-pass legislation.

We had to run a tight ship and maintain high standards, I told my crew. With any luck, the Recovery Act wouldn't just help avert a depression. It could also serve to restore the public's faith in honest, responsible government.

By New Year's Day, most of our initial work was finished. Armed with our proposal and knowing we couldn't afford to work on a conventional timetable, Joe Biden and I traveled to the Capitol on January 5—two weeks before my inauguration—to meet with Senate Majority Leader Harry Reid, Senate Republican leader Mitch McConnell, Speaker of the House Nancy Pelosi, House Republican leader John Boehner, and the other key leaders of the newly installed 111th Congress whose support we'd need to get a bill passed.

Of the four key leaders, I knew Harry best, but I'd had my share of interactions with McConnell during my few years in the Senate. Short, owlish, with a smooth Kentucky accent, McConnell seemed an unlikely Republican leader. He showed no aptitude for schmoozing, backslapping, or rousing oratory. As far as anyone could tell, he had no close friends even in his own caucus; nor did he appear to have any strong convictions beyond an almost religious opposition to any version of campaign finance reform. Joe told me of one run-in he'd had on the Senate floor after the Republican leader blocked a bill Joe was sponsoring; when Joe tried to explain the bill's merits, McConnell raised his hand like a traffic cop and said, "You must be under the mistaken impression that I care." But what McConnell lacked in charisma or interest in policy he more than made up for in discipline, shrewdness, and shamelessness—all of which he employed in the single-minded and dispassionate pursuit of power.

Harry couldn't stand him.

Boehner was a different animal, an affable, gravel-voiced son of a bartender from outside Cincinnati. With his chain-smoking and perpetual tan, his love of golf and a good merlot, he felt familiar to me, cut from the same cloth as many of the Republicans I'd gotten to know as a state legislator in Springfield—regular guys who didn't stray from the party line or the lobbyists who kept them in power but who also didn't consider politics a blood sport and might even work with you if it didn't cost them too much politically. Unfortunately these same human qualities gave Boehner a tenuous grip on his caucus; and having experienced the humiliation of being stripped of a leadership post as a result of insufficient fealty to Newt Gingrich in the late 1990s, he rarely deviated from whatever talking points his staff had prepared for him, at least not in public. Unlike the relationship between Harry and McConnell, however, there was no real enmity between Speaker Nancy Pelosi and Boehner, just mutual frustration—on Nancy's part because of Boehner's unreliability as a negotiating partner and his frequent inability to deliver votes; on Boehner's part because Nancy generally outmaneuvered him.

Boehner wasn't the first to be outflanked by the Speaker. On the surface, Nancy, in her designer suits, matching shoes, and perfectly coiffed hair, looked every bit the wealthy San Francisco liberal she was. Though she could talk a mile a minute, she wasn't particularly good on TV at the time, with a tendency to deliver Democratic nostrums with a practiced earnestness that called to mind an after-dinner speech at a charity gala.

But politicians (usually men) underestimated Nancy at their own peril, for her ascent to power had been no fluke. She'd grown up in the East, the Italian American daughter of Baltimore's mayor, tutored from an early age in the ways of ethnic ward bosses and longshoremen, unafraid to play hardball politics in the name of getting things done. After moving to the West Coast with her husband, Paul, and staying home to raise their five kids while he built a successful business, Nancy eventually put her early political education to good use, rising steadily through the ranks of the California Democratic Party and Congress to become the first female Speaker in American history. She didn't care that Republicans made her their favorite foil; nor was she fazed by the occasional grousing of her Democratic colleagues. The fact was, nobody was tougher or a more skilled legislative strategist, and she kept her caucus in line with a combination of attentiveness, fundraising prowess, and a willingness to cut off at the knees anyone who failed to deliver on commitments they'd made.

Harry, Mitch, Nancy, and John. The Four Tops, we sometimes called them. For most of the next eight years, the dynamics among these individuals would play a key role in shaping my presidency. I became accustomed to the ritualistic quality of our joint meetings, the way they'd file into the room one at a time, each offering a handshake and a muted acknowledgment ("Mr. President . . . Mr. Vice President . . ."); how, once we were all seated, Joe and I and sometimes Nancy would attempt some light-hearted banter, considering ourselves lucky if we got a tepid smile from the other three, while my staff brought in the press pool for the obligatory photo op; how, once the press had been ushered out and we got down to business, the four of them would take care not to show their cards or make firm commitments, their comments often sprinkled with thinly veiled recrimination directed at their counterparts, all of them unified only in their common desire to be somewhere else.

Perhaps because it was our first meeting since the election, perhaps because we were joined by their respective whips and deputies, and perhaps because of the gravity of what lay before us, the Four Tops were all on their best behavior when we gathered that day in early January in the opulent LBJ Room, just off the Senate chamber, along with other congressional leaders. They listened with studied attentiveness as I made the case for the Recovery Act. I mentioned that my team had already reached out to their staffs for input on actual legislation and that we welcomed any suggestions to make the stimulus package more effective. I noted that I also hoped to visit with each of their caucuses immediately after the inauguration to answer further questions. But given the rapidly worsening situation, I said, speed was of the essence: We needed a bill on my desk not in one hundred days but in thirty. I closed by telling those gathered that history would judge all of us by what we did in this moment and that I hoped we could muster the kind of bipartisan cooperation that would restore the confidence of an anxious and vulnerable public.

Considering what I was asking congressional leaders to do—to compress what might normally be a year-long legislative process into one month—the reaction around the room was relatively subdued. My longtime friend Dick Durbin, the Senate whip, asked about increasing the portion of stimulus dollars dedicated to infrastructure. Jim Clyburn, the House majority whip, offered a pointed history lesson on all the ways the New Deal had bypassed Black communities, asking how we were going to prevent the same thing from happening in places like his home state of South Carolina. Virginian Eric Cantor, the second-ranking Republican in the House and one of the conservative Young Turks known to be gunning for Boehner's job, praised some of the tax cut proposals we had included in the package but asked whether a bigger, permanent tax cut wouldn't work better than spending on what he considered failed liberal programs like food stamps.

It was, however, the comments from Harry, Mitch, Nancy, and John, delivered with teeth-clenching civility and requiring a bit of deciphering, that gave me and Joe our best sense of the real state of play.

"Well, Mr. President-Elect," said Nancy, "I think the American people are pretty clear that you inherited a terrible mess. Just terrible. And of course our caucus is prepared to do the responsible thing to clean up this mess that you inherited. But I just hope our friends on the other side of the aisle remember how it was the Democrats, including you, Mr. President-Elect, who stepped up to the plate . . . Despite what we all know was bad politics . . . it was Democrats who were willing to help President Bush with TARP. I hope our Republican friends take the same responsible approach in what, as you said, is a very critical moment."

Translation: Don't think for a minute that we won't be reminding the American people every single chance we get that Republicans caused the financial crisis.

"Our caucus won't like it," Harry said, "but we don't have much choice, so we'll just have to get it done, okay?"

Translation: Don't expect Mitch McConnell to lift a finger to help.

"Well, we're happy to listen, but with all due respect, I don't think the American people are looking for more big spending and bailouts," Boehner said. "They're tightening their belts, and they expect us to do the same."

Translation: My caucus will crucify me if I say anything that sounds cooperative.

"I can't tell you there's much of an appetite for what you're proposing, Mr. President-Elect," McConnell said, "but you're welcome to come to our weekly luncheon to make your case."

Translation: You must be under the mistaken impression that I care.

On our way down the stairs after the meeting was over, I turned to Joe.

"Well, that could have been worse," I said.

"Yeah," Joe said. "No fistfights broke out."

I laughed. "See there? That's progress!"

GIVEN HOW HECTIC everything was in the first few weeks after I took office, I barely had time to dwell on the pervasive, routine weirdness of my new circumstances. But make no mistake, it was weird. There was the way everyone now stood up anytime I walked into a room. "Sit down," I'd growl, telling my team that those kinds of formalities weren't my style. They'd smile and nod—and then do the exact same thing the next time we met.

There was the way my first name all but disappeared, used by nobody but Michelle, our families, and a few close friends, like Marty. Otherwise, it was "Yes, Mr. President" and "No, Mr. President," although over time my staff at least adopted the more colloquial "POTUS" (president of the United States) when talking to or about me inside the White House.

There was the way my daily schedule had suddenly become a behind-the-scenes tug-of-war between various staffers, agencies, and constituencies, each one wanting their causes highlighted or their issues addressed, outcomes spit out through a hidden machinery that I never fully understood. Meanwhile, I discovered that whenever the Secret Service agents whispered into their wrist microphones, they were broadcasting my movements over a staff-monitored radio channel: "Renegade heading to residence" or "Renegade to Situation Room" or "Renegade to Secondary Hold," which was their discreet way of saying I was going to the bathroom.

And there was the ever-present traveling press pool: a herd of reporters and photographers who needed to be alerted anytime I left the White House complex and would follow me in a government-provided van. The arrangement made sense when we traveled on official business, but I soon discovered that it applied in all circumstances, whether Michelle and I were going out to a restaurant or I was heading to a gym to play basketball or planning to watch one of the girls' soccer games at a nearby field. As Gibbs, who was now my press secretary, explained, the rationale was that a president's movements were inherently newsworthy and that the press needed to be on the scene in case something consequential happened. And yet I can't recall the press van ever capturing any image more compelling than me getting out of a car wearing sweatpants. It did have the effect of eliminating whatever scraps of privacy I might still have had when venturing beyond the White House gates. Feeling mildly cranky about it, I asked Gibbs that first week whether we could leave the press behind when I went on personal outings.

"Bad idea," Gibbs said.

"Why? The reporters crammed in that van must know it's a waste of time."

"Yeah, but their bosses don't," Gibbs said. "And remember, you promised to run the most open administration in history. You do this, the press will have a fit."

"I'm not talking about public business," I objected. "I'm talking about taking my wife on a date. Or getting some fresh air." I'd read enough about previous presidents to know that Teddy Roosevelt once spent two weeks camping in Yellowstone, traveling by horse. I knew that during the Great Depression, FDR had passed weeks at a time sailing up the East Coast to an island near Nova Scotia. I reminded Gibbs that Harry Truman had gone for long morning walks through the streets of Washington during his presidency.

"Times have changed, Mr. President," Gibbs said patiently. "Look, it's your decision. But I'm telling you, getting rid of the press pool will create a shitstorm that we don't need right now. It'll also make it harder for me to get cooperation from them when it comes to the girls . . ."

I started to answer, then shut my mouth. Michelle and I had already told Gibbs that our highest priority was making sure the press left our daughters alone when they were out and about. Gibbs knew I wasn't going to do anything to jeopardize that. Having successfully repulsed my rebellion, he was wise enough not to gloat; instead he just patted me on the back and headed to his office, leaving me to mutter under my breath. (To their credit, members of the press would place Malia and Sasha off-limits for the duration of my presidency, an act of basic decency that I deeply appreciated.)

My team did throw me one bone when it came to freedom: I was able to keep my BlackBerry—or, rather, I was given a new, specially modified device, approved only after several weeks of negotiations with various cybersecurity personnel. With it, I could send and receive emails, though only from a vetted list of twenty or so contacts, and the internal microphone and headphone jack had been removed, so that the phone function didn't work. Michelle joked that my BlackBerry was like one of those play phones you give toddlers, where they get to press buttons and it makes noises and things light up but nothing actually happens.

Given these limitations, most of my contact with the outside world depended on three young aides who sat in the Outer Oval: Reggie, who had agreed to stay on as my body man; Brian Mosteller, a fastidious Ohioan who organized all my daily events within the complex; and Katie Johnson, Plouffe's no-nonsense assistant from the campaign who now performed the same function for me. Together they served as my unofficial gatekeepers and personal life-support system, patching through my phone calls, scheduling my haircuts, providing briefing materials, keeping me on time, alerting me to upcoming staff birthdays and purchasing cards for me to sign, telling me when I'd spilled soup on my tie, enduring my rants and bad jokes, and generally keeping me functioning throughout the course of twelve- to sixteen-hour days.

The lone denizen of the Outer Oval past his mid-thirties was Pete Souza, our White House photographer. Middle-aged, compactly built, and with a swarthy complexion that reflected his Portuguese roots, Pete was on his second tour at the White House, having served as an official photographer for the Reagan administration. After various teaching stints and freelance assignments, Pete had landed at the **Chicago Tribune,** where he'd covered the early stages of the Afghan War as well as my start in the U.S. Senate.

I had liked him right away: In addition to having a photojournalist's gift for capturing complex stories in a single image, Pete was smart, unpretentious, a bit curmudgeonly, but never cynical. After we won, he agreed to join the team on the condition that I allow him unfettered access. It was a measure of my confidence in him that I gave the okay, and for the next eight years Pete became a constant presence, skirting the edges of every meeting, witnessing every victory and defeat, occasionally lowering himself onto a creaky knee to get the angle he wanted, never making a sound other than the constant whirr of the camera's shutter.

He also became a good friend.

In this new, curiously sealed habitat of mine, the fondness and trust I felt toward those I worked with and the kindness and support they showed me and my family were a saving grace. This was true for Ray Rogers and Quincy Jackson, the two young navy valets assigned to the Oval Office, who served refreshments to visitors and whipped up a solid lunch for me every day in the tiny kitchenette wedged next to the dining space. Or the White House Communications Agency staffers, among them two brothers named Nate and Luke Emory, who set up lecterns, prompters, and video shoots at a moment's notice. Or Barbara Swann, who brought the mail each day and appeared incapable of anything other than a smile and sweet word for everyone.

And it was true of the residence staff. My family's new living quarters seemed less a home than an extended series of suites in a boutique hotel, complete with a gym, pool, tennis court, movie theater, salon, bowling alley, and medical office. The staff was organized under the direction of chief usher Steve Rochon, a former Coast Guard rear admiral who was hired by the Bushes in 2007, becoming the first African American to hold the post. A cleaning crew came through each day, keeping the place spotless; a rotating team of chefs prepared meals for our family or, as sometimes happened, for a few hundred guests; butlers were on hand to serve those meals or anything else you might want; switchboard operators sat ready to put through calls at all hours and to make sure we woke up in the morning; ushers waited in the small elevator every morning to take me down to work and were there to greet me again upon my evening return; building engineers were on-site to fix what was broken; and in-house florists kept every room filled with magnificent, ever-varying, freshly cut flowers.

(It's worth pointing out here—only because people were often surprised to hear it—that a First Family pays out of pocket for any new furniture, just as it does for everything else it consumes, from groceries to toilet paper to extra staff for a president's private dinner party. The White House budget does set aside funds for a new president to redo the Oval Office, but despite some worn upholstery on the chairs and sofas, I decided that a historic recession wasn't the best time to be going through fabric swatches.)

And for the president, at least, there was a trio of navy valets, first among them a soft-spoken bear of a man named Sam Sutton. On our first full day in the White House, I walked through the hallway closet that connected our bedroom to my bathroom only to find every shirt, suit, and pair of pants I owned perfectly pressed and hung in orderly rows, my shoes shined to a high gloss, every pair of socks or shorts folded and sorted as if in a department store display. When in the evening I returned from the Oval Office and hung my (only lightly mussed!) suit in the closet (a significant improvement over my normal practice of draping it on the nearest doorknob, one of Michelle's pet peeves), Sam came up beside me and gently but firmly explained that it would be better if from now on I just left the care of my clothes up to him—a switch that not only improved my general appearance but no doubt helped my marriage.

None of this was a hardship, of course. Still, it was a little disconcerting. During the campaign, Michelle and I had become accustomed to always having people around, but they hadn't occupied our house, and we definitely weren't used to having butlers and maids. In this new, rarefied air, we worried that the girls would get too coddled and slide into bad habits, and we instituted a rule (enforced with only average success) that they had to clean their rooms and make their beds before school each morning. My mother-in-law, loath to have anyone waiting on her, asked the staff for a lesson on using the washers and dryers so she could do her own laundry. Feeling a little embarrassed myself, I tried to keep the Treaty Room, which served as my personal office in the residence, free of the stacks of books, papers, and assorted junk that had characterized all my previous "Holes."

Gradually, thanks to the steady generosity and

professionalism of the residence staff, we found ourselves settling in. We became especially close to our regular crew of chefs and butlers, with whom we had daily contact. As with my valets, all of them were Black, Latino, or Asian American, and all but one were men (Cristeta Comerford, a Filipina American, had been recently appointed as the White House's executive chef, the first woman to hold the job). And while they were uniformly glad to have well-paying, secure jobs with good benefits, it was hard to miss in their racial makeup the vestiges of an earlier time, when social rank had clear demarcations and those who occupied the office of president felt most comfortable in their privacy when served by those they assumed were not their equals—and, therefore, could not judge them.

The most senior butlers were a pair of big, round-bellied Black men with sly senses of humor and the wisdom that comes from having a front-row seat to history. Buddy Carter had been around since the tail end of the Nixon presidency, first caring for visiting dignitaries at Blair House and then moving to a job in the residence. Von Everett had been around since Reagan. They spoke of previous First Families with appropriate discretion and genuine affection. But without saying much, they didn't hide how they felt about having us in their care. You could see it in how readily Von accepted Sasha's hugs or the pleasure Buddy took in sneaking Malia an extra scoop of ice cream after dinner, in the easy rapport they had talking to Marian and the pride in their eyes when Michelle wore a particularly pretty dress. They were barely distinguishable from Marian's brothers or Michelle's uncles, and in that familiarity they became more, not less, solicitous, objecting if we carried our own plates into the kitchen, alert to even a hint of what they considered substandard service from anyone on the residence staff. It would take us months of coaxing before the butlers were willing to swap their tuxedos for khakis and polo shirts when serving us meals.

"We just want to make sure you're treated like every other president," Von explained.

"That's right," Buddy said. "See, you and the First Lady don't really know what this means to us, Mr. President. Having you here . . ." He shook his head. "You just don't know."

WITH SUPPORT FROM Speaker Pelosi and Democratic House Appropriations Committee chair Dave Obey, as well as heroic efforts from our still-skeletal staff, we were able to get the Recovery Act legislation drafted, introduced in the House, passed out of committee, and scheduled for a full vote of the House—all by the end of my first week in office.

We considered it a minor miracle.

It helped that congressional Democrats were enthusiastic about the core elements of the package—although that didn't stop them from griping about all sorts of particulars. Liberals complained that the business tax cuts were giveaways to the rich. More centrist Dems expressed anxiety about how the big price tag would play with their more conservative constituents. Members across the spectrum complained about how direct aid to states would only help Republican governors balance their budgets and appear fiscally responsible, even as those same governors accused the folks in Congress of spending like drunken sailors.

This kind of low-grade grumbling was par for the course with any major legislative initiative, regardless of who was in the White House. It was especially common among Democrats, who for a variety of reasons (a more diverse makeup, a greater aversion to authority) seemed to take an almost perverse pride in their lack of message discipline. When some of these complaints spilled into the press, with reporters hyping a handful of stray comments as a possible sign of dissension in the ranks, Rahm or I made sure to lob a call at the worst transgressors so we could explain—in plain and sometimes unprintable terms—just why it was that headlines like KEY DEMOCRATS BLAST OBAMA STIMULUS PLAN or DEMOCRATS MAKE CLEAR THEY WILL GUARD TURF were not exactly helpful to the cause.

Our message was received. On the margins, we made some concessions in the drafted legislation, boosting funding for congressional priorities, trimming dollars from some of our own. But when the dust had settled, the legislation contained close to 90 percent of what our economic team had originally proposed, and we'd succeeded in keeping the bill free of earmarks and egregious wastes of money that might discredit it in the eyes of the public.

Just one thing was missing: Republican support.

From the start, none of us had been particularly optimistic about getting a big chunk of Republican votes, especially in the aftermath of billions already spent on financial rescue. Most House Republicans had voted against TARP despite significant pressure from a president of their own party. Those who **had** voted for it continued to face withering criticism from the Right, and there was a growing belief within Republican circles that one of the reasons they had done so badly in successive elections was that they'd allowed President Bush to lead them astray from conservative, small-government principles.

Nevertheless, coming out of our early-January meeting with congressional leaders, I had told my team to ramp up our Republican outreach. Not just for show, I said; make a serious effort.

The decision exasperated some Democrats, especially in the House. Having been in the minority for over a decade, House Democrats had been entirely shut out of the legislative process. Now that they were in control, they were in no mood to see me offer concessions to their former tormentors. They thought I was wasting my time, being naïve. "These Republicans aren't interested in cooperating with you, Mr. President," one member told me bluntly. "They're looking to break you."

I figured they might be right. But for a variety of reasons, I felt it was important to at least test the proposition. Getting the two Republican votes we needed for a filibuster-proof majority in the Senate would be a lot easier, I knew, if we first secured a decent Republican vote count in the House—safety in numbers being a maxim by which almost every politician in Washington lived. Republican votes would also provide useful political cover for Democrats representing conservative-leaning parts of the country, who were already looking ahead to tough reelection races. And truthfully, just the act of negotiating with Republicans served as a handy excuse to deflect some of the less orthodox ideas that occasionally surfaced from our side of the aisle ("I'm sorry, Congressman, but

legalizing marijuana isn't the kind of stimulus we're talking about here . . .").

But for me, reaching out to Republican members
wasn't just tactical. Since my convention speech in
Boston and through the closing days of my campaign, I
had argued that people across the country weren't as
divided as our politics suggested, and that to do big
things we needed to move past partisan bickering. And
what better way to make an honest effort to reach across
the aisle than from a position of strength, at a time when
I didn't necessarily need support from House Republicans
to get my agenda passed? I thought that maybe, with an
open mind and a bit of humility, I might catch GOP
leaders by surprise and ease their suspicions, helping to
build working relationships that could carry over to other
issues. And if, as was more likely, the gambit didn't work
and Republicans rejected my overtures, then at least voters would know who was to blame for Washington's
dysfunction.

To lead our Legislative Affairs office, we had recruited a
savvy former senior House Democratic staffer named Phil
Schiliro. He was tall and balding, with a high-pitched
laugh that masked a quiet intensity, and from Congress's
first day in session Phil set out in search of negotiating
partners, calling in me or Rahm or Joe Biden to help
court individual members where necessary. When some
Republicans expressed interest in more infrastructure,
we told them to give us a list of their priorities. When
others said they couldn't vote for a bill that included
contraception funding dressed up as stimulus, we urged
Democrats to strike the provision. When Eric Cantor

suggested a reasonable modification to one of our tax provisions, despite the fact there was no chance he'd be voting for the bill, I told my staff to make the change, wanting to send a signal that we were serious about giving Republicans a seat at the table.

Yet with each passing day, the prospect of Republican cooperation appeared more and more like a distant mirage. Those who'd initially expressed interest in working with us stopped returning our phone calls. GOP members of the House Appropriations Committee boycotted hearings on the Recovery Act, claiming that they weren't being seriously consulted. Republican attacks on the bill in the press became less restrained. Joe reported that Mitch McConnell had been cracking the whip, preventing members of his caucus from even talking to the White House about the stimulus package, and Democratic House members said they'd heard the same thing from their GOP counterparts.

"We can't play" was how one Republican apparently put it.

Bleak as things looked, I thought I still might have a chance to sway a few members during my visits to the House and Senate Republican caucuses, both of which were scheduled on January 27, the eve of the House vote. I took extra time to prepare my presentation, making sure I had all the facts and figures at my fingertips. The morning before the meetings, Rahm and Phil joined me in the Oval Office to review the arguments we thought Republicans might find most persuasive. We were about to load my motorcade for the drive to Capitol Hill when Gibbs and Axe walked into the Oval Office and showed me an AP wire story that had just come in, right after Boehner's meeting with his caucus. HOUSE REPUBLICANS URGED TO OPPOSE STIMULUS BILL.

"When did this happen?" I asked, scanning the article.

"About five minutes ago," Gibbs said.

"Did Boehner call to give us a heads-up?" I asked.

"No," Rahm said.

"Am I correct to assume, then, that this shit's not on the level?" I said, as the group of us started heading outside toward the Beast.

"That would be correct, Mr. President," Rahm said.

The caucus meetings themselves weren't overtly hostile. Boehner, Cantor, and House Republican Conference chair Mike Pence were already at the lectern when I arrived (deftly avoiding a private conversation about the stunt they'd just pulled), and after Boehner's brief introduction and some polite applause, I stepped up to speak. It was my first time at a House Republicans gathering, and it was hard not to be struck by the room's uniformity: row after row of mostly middle-aged white men, with a dozen or so women and maybe two or three Hispanics and Asians. Most sat stone-faced as I briefly made the case for stimulus—citing the latest data on the economy's meltdown, the need for quick action, the fact that our package contained tax cuts Republicans had long promoted, and our commitment to long-term deficit reduction once the crisis had passed. The audience did perk up when I opened the floor for a series of questions (or, more accurately, talking points pretending to be questions), all of which I cheerfully responded to as if my answers mattered.

"Mr. President, why doesn't this bill do anything

about all those Democratic-sponsored laws that forced banks to give mortgages to unqualified borrowers and were the real cause of the financial crisis?" (Applause.)

"Mr. President, I've got a book here for you that shows the New Deal didn't end the Depression but actually made things worse. Do you agree that the Democrats' so-called stimulus is just repeating those mistakes and will leave a sea of red ink for future generations to clean up?" (Applause.)

"Mr. President, will you get Nancy Pelosi to put her partisan bill aside and start over with the truly open process that the American people are demanding?" (Cheers, applause, a few hoots.)

On the Senate side, the setting felt less stilted. Joe and I were invited to sit around a table with the forty or so senators in attendance, many of them our former colleagues. But the substance of the meeting was not much different, with every Republican who bothered to speak singing from the same hymnal, describing the stimulus package as a pork-filled, budget-busting, "special-interest bailout" that Democrats needed to scrap if they wanted any hope of cooperation.

On the ride back to the White House, Rahm was apoplectic, Phil despondent. I told them it was fine, that I'd actually enjoyed the give-and-take.

"How many Republicans do you think might still be in play?" I asked.

Rahm shrugged. "If we're lucky, maybe a dozen."

That proved optimistic. The next day, the Recovery Act passed the House 244 to 188 with precisely **zero** Republican votes. It was the opening salvo in a battle plan that McConnell, Boehner, Cantor, and the rest would deploy with impressive discipline for the next eight years: a refusal to work with me or members of my administration, regardless of the circumstances, the issue, or the consequences for the country.

YOU MIGHT THINK that for a political party that had just suffered two cycles of resounding defeat, the GOP strategy of pugnacious, all-out obstruction would carry big risks. And during a time of genuine crisis, it sure wasn't responsible.

But if, like McConnell and Boehner, your primary concern was clawing your way back to power, recent history suggested that such a strategy made sense. For all their talk about wanting politicians to get along, American voters rarely reward the opposition for cooperating with the governing party. In the 1980s, Democrats retained their grip on the House (though not the Senate) long after Ronald Reagan's election and the country's shift to the right, in part because of the willingness of "responsible" Republican leaders to help make Congress work; the House flipped only after a Gingrich-led GOP turned Congress into an all-out brawl. Similarly, Democrats made no inroads against a Republican-controlled Congress by helping pass President Bush's tax cuts or his prescription drug plan; they won back the House and Senate when they began challenging the president and Republican leaders on everything from Social Security privatization to the handling of the Iraq War.

Such lessons weren't lost on McConnell and Boehner. They understood that any help they offered my administration in mounting an effective, sustained government response to the crisis would only be to my political benefit—and would tacitly acknowledge the bankruptcy of their own anti-government, anti-regulation rhetoric. If, on the other hand, they fought a rearguard action, if they generated controversy and threw sand in the gears, they at least had a chance to energize their base and slow me and the Democrats down at a time when the country was sure to be impatient.

In executing their strategy, Republican leaders had a couple of things going for them—starting with the nature of modern news coverage. From my time in the Senate and on the campaign trail, I'd gotten to know most of the national political reporters, and on the whole, I found them to be smart, hardworking, ethical, and committed to getting their facts straight. At the same time, conservatives weren't wrong to think that in their personal attitudes the majority of news reporters probably fell at the more liberal end of the political spectrum.

This would seem to make these reporters unlikely accomplices in McConnell's and Boehner's plans. But whether out of fear of appearing biased, or because conflict sells, or because their editors demanded it, or because it was the easiest way to meet the deadlines of a twenty-four-hour, internet-driven news cycle, their collective approach to reporting on Washington followed a depressingly predictable script:

Report what one side says (quick sound bite included).

Report what the other side says (opposing sound bite, the more insulting the better).

Leave it to an opinion poll to sort out who's right.

Over time, my staff and I became so resigned to this style of "he said / he said" coverage that we could joke about it. ("In dueling press conferences today, the debate over the shape of planet Earth heated up, with President

Obama—who claims the Earth is round—coming under withering attack from Republicans who insist that the White House has covered up documents proving the Earth is flat.") In those first few weeks, though, with our White House communications team barely in place, we could still be surprised. Not just by the GOP's willingness to peddle half-truths or outright lies about the contents of the Recovery Act (the claim that we were planning to spend millions on a Mob Museum in Las Vegas, for example, or that Nancy Pelosi had included $30 million to save an endangered mouse), but by the willingness of the press to broadcast or publish these whoppers as straight news.

With enough badgering from us, an outlet might eventually run a story that fact-checked Republican claims. Rarely, though, did the truth catch up to the initial headlines. Most Americans—already trained to believe that the government wasted money—didn't have the time or inclination to keep up with the details of the legislative process or who was or wasn't being reasonable in negotiations. All they heard was what the Washington press corps told them—that Democrats and Republicans were fighting again, politicians were splurging, and the new guy in the White House was doing nothing to change it.

Of course, efforts to discredit the Recovery Act still depended on the ability of GOP leaders to keep their members in line. At a minimum, they needed to make sure the stimulus package didn't get enough support from stray Republicans to be deemed "bipartisan," since (as McConnell would later explain) "when you hang the bipartisan tag on something, the perception is that differences have been worked out." Their task was made easier now that the majority of GOP members hailed from districts or states that were solidly Republican. Their base of voters, fed a steady diet of Fox News, talk radio, and Sarah Palin speeches, was in no mood for compromise; in fact, the biggest threat to these representatives' reelection prospects came from primary challengers who might accuse them of being closet liberals. Rush Limbaugh had already castigated Republicans like McCain for saying that with the election over, they now hoped for my success. "I hope Obama fails!" the talk radio show host had thundered. Back in early 2009, most Republican elected officials didn't consider it wise to be quite that blunt in public (it was a different story in private, as we would later learn). But even those politicians who didn't share Limbaugh's sentiments knew that with that single statement, he was effectively channeling—and shaping—the views of a sizable chunk of their voters.

Big conservative donors weighed in as well. Panicked by the cratering economy and the impact it was already having on their members' bottom lines, traditional business organizations like the Chamber of Commerce eventually came out in favor of the Recovery Act. But their influence over the Republican Party had by then been supplanted by billionaire ideologues like David and Charles Koch, who had spent decades and hundreds of millions of dollars systematically building a network of think tanks, advocacy organizations, media operations, and political operatives, all with the express goal of rolling back every last vestige of the modern welfare state. For them, all taxes were confiscatory, paving the road to socialism; all regulations were a betrayal of free-market principles and the American way of life. They saw my victory as a mortal threat—which is why, shortly after my inauguration, they pulled together a conclave of some of America's wealthiest conservatives in a smartly manicured resort in Indian Wells, California, to map out a strategy to fight back. They didn't want compromise and consensus. They wanted war. And they let it be known that Republican politicians without the stomach to resist my policies at every turn would not only find donations drying up but also might find themselves the target of a well-financed primary challenge.

As for those Republicans who were still tempted to cooperate with me despite lobbying from constituents, donors, and conservative media outlets, good old-fashioned peer pressure usually did the trick. During the transition, I had met with Judd Gregg, a capable, decent GOP senator from New Hampshire, and offered to make him commerce secretary—part of my effort to deliver on my promise of bipartisan governance. He'd readily accepted, and in early February, we announced his nomination. With Republican opposition to the Recovery Act growing more boisterous by the day, though, as McConnell and the rest of leadership worked him over in caucus meetings and on the Senate floor and former First Lady Barbara Bush reportedly stepped in to dissuade him from joining my administration, Judd Gregg lost his nerve. A week after we'd announced his nomination, he called to withdraw.

Not every Republican picked up on the rapidly shifting mood within their own party. On the day the Senate was to vote on the Recovery Act, I found myself in Fort Myers, Florida, at a town hall–style meeting meant to drum up public support for the bill and allow me to answer questions about the economy. Joining me was

Florida governor Charlie Crist, a moderate Republican with a friendly, polished demeanor and the kind of good looks—tanned, silver-haired, sparkling white teeth—that seemed straight out of central casting. Crist was hugely popular at the time, having cultivated an image of someone who could work across party lines, avoiding divisive social issues and instead focusing on promoting business and tourism. He also knew that his state was in big trouble: As one of the hot spots of subprime lending and the housing bubble, Florida had an economy and state budget in free fall and in desperate need of federal help.

It was out of both temperament and necessity, then, that Crist agreed to introduce me at the town hall and publicly endorse the stimulus bill. Despite the fact that home values in Fort Myers had dropped about 67 percent (with a full 12 percent of houses in foreclosure), the crowd was raucous and energized that day, mostly Democratic and still swept up in what Sarah Palin would later call the "hopey, changey stuff." After Crist offered up a reasonable, somewhat cautious explanation of why he supported the Recovery Act, pointing out its benefits for Florida and the need for elected officials to put people before party politics, I gave the governor what was my standard "bro hug"—a handshake, an arm around the back for a pat, an appreciative look in the eye, a thank-you in the ear.

Poor Charlie. How could I know that my two-second gesture would prove to be a political kiss of death for him? Within days of the rally, footage of "the hug"—accompanied by calls for Crist's head—began appearing in right-wing media outlets. In a matter of months, Crist went from a Republican star to a pariah. He was called a poster child for appeasement, the kind of weak-kneed, opportunistic RINO who needed to be made an example of. It would take time for the whole thing to play out: In the 2010 U.S. Senate race, Crist was forced to run as an independent and got clobbered by conservative upstart Marco Rubio; Crist eventually mounted a political comeback only by switching parties and winning one of Florida's congressional seats as a Democrat. Nevertheless, the immediate lesson was not lost on congressional Republicans.

Cooperate with the Obama administration at your own peril.

And if you have to shake his hand, make sure you don't look happy about it.

LOOKING BACK, IT'S hard for me not to fixate on the political dynamics that unfolded in those first weeks of my presidency—how quickly Republican resistance hardened, independent of anything we said or did, and how thoroughly that resistance colored the way the press and ultimately the public viewed the substance of our actions. After all, those dynamics set the course for so much of what happened in the months and years that followed, a cleaving of America's political sensibilities that we are still dealing with a decade later.

But in February 2009, I was obsessed with the economy, not politics. So it's worth pointing out a relevant piece of information that I omitted from the Charlie Crist story: A few minutes before I walked out onstage to give him that hug, I got a call from Rahm letting me know that the Recovery Act had just cleared the Senate, assuring the legislation's eventual passage through Congress.

How we got it done can't be considered a model for

the new brand of politics I'd promised on the campaign trail. It was old-school. Once the House vote made clear that a broadly bipartisan bill wasn't in the cards, our focus narrowed to securing 61 Senate votes—61 because no Republican senator could afford to be tagged as the sole vote that put Obama's bill over the top. In the radio-active atmosphere McConnell had orchestrated, the only Republicans even willing to consider supporting us were three self-identified moderates from states in which I'd won handily: Susan Collins and Olympia Snowe of Maine and Arlen Specter of Pennsylvania. Those three, along with Senator Ben Nelson of Nebraska—the un-official spokesman for the half dozen Democrats from conservative states whose priority on every controversial issue was to position themselves somewhere, anywhere, to the right of Harry Reid and Nancy Pelosi, thereby winning the prized label of "centrist" from Washington pundits—became the gatekeepers through which the Recovery Act had to pass. And none of these four sena-tors were shy about charging a hefty toll.

Specter, who had already battled two bouts of cancer, insisted that $10 billion of the Recovery Act go to the National Institutes of Health. Collins demanded the bill be stripped of dollars for school construction and that it include an "AMT patch"—a tax provision that prevented upper-middle-class Americans from paying a higher tax bill. Nelson wanted extra Medicaid money for rural states. Even as their priorities added billions, the group insisted that the overall bill had to come in under $800 billion, because any figure higher than that just seemed "too much."

As far as we could tell, there was no economic logic to

any of this, just political positioning and a classic squeeze play by politicians who knew they had leverage. But this truth went largely unnoticed; as far as the Washington press corps was concerned, the mere fact that the four senators were working in "bipartisan" fashion signified Solomonic wisdom and reason. Meanwhile, liberal Dems, particularly in the House, were furious with me for letting a "Gang of Four" effectively determine the final contents of the bill. Some went so far as to suggest that I barnstorm against Snowe, Collins, Specter, and Nelson in their home states until they relinquished their "ransom" demands. I told them this wasn't going to happen, having calculated (with concurrence from Joe, Rahm, Phil, Harry, and Nancy) that strong-arming tactics would likely backfire—and also shut the door on getting the quartet's cooperation on any other bill I might try to pass in the future.

Anyway, the clock was ticking; or, as Axe later described it, the house was burning and those four senators had the only fire hose. After a week of negotiations (and plenty of cajoling, pestering, and hand-holding of the senators by me, Rahm, and especially Joe), an agreement was reached. The Gang of Four mostly got what they wanted. In return, we got their votes, while retaining almost 90 percent of the stimulus measures we'd originally proposed. Other than the votes of Collins, Snowe, and Specter, the modified, 1,073-page bill passed both the House and the Senate strictly along party lines. And less than a month after I took office, the American Recovery and Reinvestment Act was ready for me to sign into law.

. . .

THE SIGNING CEREMONY took place before a small crowd at the Denver Museum of Nature and Science. We had asked the CEO of an employee-owned solar energy company to introduce me; and as I listened to him describe what the Recovery Act would mean to his business—the layoffs averted, the new workers he'd hire, the green economy he hoped to promote—I did my best to savor the moment.

By any conventional yardstick, I was about to sign historic legislation: a recovery effort comparable in size to FDR's New Deal. The stimulus package wouldn't just boost aggregate demand. It would help millions weather the economic storm, extending unemployment insurance for the jobless, food assistance for the hungry, and medical care for those whose lives had been upended; supply the broadest onetime tax cut for middle-class and working-poor families since Reagan; and provide the nation's infrastructure and transportation systems the biggest infusion of new spending since the Eisenhower administration.

That's not all. Without losing our focus on short-term stimulus and job creation, the Recovery Act would also put a massive down payment on campaign commitments I'd made to modernize the economy. It promised to transform the energy sector, with an unprecedented investment in clean energy development and efficiency programs. It would finance one of the largest and most ambitious education reform agendas in a generation. It would spur on the transition to electronic medical records, which had the potential to revolutionize America's healthcare system; and it would extend broadband access to classrooms and rural areas that had been previously shut out of the information superhighway.

Any one of these items, if passed as a stand-alone bill, would qualify as a major achievement for a presidential administration. Taken together, they might represent the successful work of an entire first term.

Still, after I toured the solar panels on the museum's rooftop, stepped up to the podium, and thanked the vice president and my team for making it all happen under extreme pressure; after I expressed my appreciation for those in Congress who'd helped get the bill over the finish line; after I used my multiple pens to sign the Recovery Act into law, shook everybody's hand, and gave a few interviews—after all that, as I finally found myself alone in the back of the Beast, the main emotion I felt was not triumph but deep relief.

Or, more accurately, relief with a heavy dose of foreboding.

If it was true that we had gotten a couple of years' worth of work done in a month, we had also spent down a couple of years' worth of political capital just as fast. It was hard to deny, for example, that McConnell and Boehner had clobbered us on the messaging front. Their relentless attacks continued to shape coverage of the Recovery Act, with the press trumpeting every spurious accusation of waste and malfeasance. Some pundits embraced the GOP-driven narratives that I had failed to reach out enough to Republicans in shaping the bill, thereby breaking my promise to govern in a bipartisan fashion. Others suggested that our agreement with Collins, Nelson, Snowe, and Specter represented cynical

Washington horse-trading rather than "change we can believe in."

Public support for the Recovery Act had grown over the weeks it had taken to pass the bill. But soon enough, the noise would have an impact, reversing that trend. Meanwhile, a decent portion of my own Democratic base—still flush with election-night hubris and agitated by Republican unwillingness to roll over and play dead—seemed less content with everything we'd managed to get into the Recovery Act than mad about the much smaller number of things we'd had to give up. Liberal commentators insisted that if I had shown more spine in resisting the Gang of Four's demands, the stimulus would have been bigger. (This despite the fact that it was twice as big as what many of these commentators had been calling for just a few weeks earlier.) Women's groups were unhappy about the contraception provisions that had been removed. Transportation groups complained that the increase in mass transit dollars wasn't all they had sought. Environmentalists seemed to be spending more time objecting to the small fraction of funding that went to clean coal projects than celebrating the Recovery Act's massive investment in renewable energy.

Between Republican attacks and Democratic complaints, I was reminded of the Yeats poem "The Second Coming": My supporters lacked all conviction, while my opponents were full of passionate intensity.

None of this would have worried me if passing the Recovery Act was all we needed to do to get the economy to start working again. I was confident that we could effectively implement the legislation and prove our critics wrong. I knew that Democratic voters would stick with me for the long haul, and my own poll numbers with the general public remained high.

The problem was that we still had at least three or four more big moves to make in order to end the crisis, each one just as urgent, each one just as controversial, each one just as hard to pull off. It was as if, having ascended the face of a big mountain, I now found myself looking out over a series of successively more perilous peaks—while realizing that I had twisted an ankle, bad weather was coming, and I'd used up half my supplies.

I didn't share these feelings with anyone on my team; they were frazzled enough as it was. Suck it up, I told myself. Tighten your laces. Cut your rations.

Keep moving.

CHAPTER 12

Dear President Obama,

Today I was informed that effective June 30, 2009, I will join the rapidly growing number of unemployed in this country . . .

As I tucked my children into bed tonight, fighting the panic that is threatening to consume me, I realized that as a parent, I will not have the opportunity that my parents had. I cannot look at my children and tell them honestly that if you work hard enough and sacrifice enough, then anything is possible. I have learned today that you can make all the right choices, do all the right things, and it still might not be enough, because your government has failed you.

Although my government has been talking quite a bit about protecting and helping middle America, what I have seen has been to the contrary. I see a government that has been catering to lobbyists and special interest groups. I see billions of dollars that are being spent on bailouts for financial institutions . . .

**Thank you for allowing me to voice just a few
of my thoughts on this emotional night.**

> Sincerely,
> Nicole Brandon
> Virginia

IT SEEMED LIKE I READ two or three letters like this every night. I'd slip them back into the folder they had come in, adding it to the high pile of papers on the desk. On that particular night, the face of the Treaty Room's grandfather clock read one in the morning. I rubbed my eyes, decided I needed a better reading lamp, and glanced up at the massive oil painting hanging over the heavy leather couch. It depicted a stern, portly President McKinley standing like a bushy-eyebrowed headmaster while a group of mustached men signed the treaty ending the Spanish-American War in 1898, all of them gathered around the very table where I now sat. It was a fine piece for a museum, but less than ideal for what was now my home office; I made a note to myself to have it replaced with something more contemporary.

Other than the five minutes I'd spent walking across the hall to tuck in the girls and kiss Michelle good night, I'd been planted in my chair since dinnertime, the same way I was just about every night of the week. For me, these were often the quietest and most productive hours of the day, a time when I could catch up on work and prepare myself for whatever was coming next, poring over the stacks of material my staff secretary sent up to the residence for my review. The latest economic data. Decision memos. Informational memos. Intelligence briefings. Legislative proposals. Drafts of speeches. Press conference talking points.

I felt the seriousness of my job most acutely when reading letters from constituents. I received a nightly batch of ten—some written in longhand, others printed-out emails—arranged neatly in a purple folder. They were often the last thing I looked at before going to bed.

It had been my idea, the letters, one that came to me on my second day in office. I figured that taking in a steady dose of constituent mail would be an efficient way for me to reach outside the presidential bubble and hear directly from those I served. The letters were like an IV drip from the real world, an everyday reminder of the covenant I now had with the American people, the trust I carried, and the human impact of each decision I made. I insisted on seeing a representative cross section. ("I don't just want a bunch of happy-talk stuff from supporters," I told Pete Rouse, who was now a senior advisor and the West Wing's resident Yoda.) Other than that, we left it up to our Correspondence Office to choose which of the ten thousand or so letters and emails that flowed into the White House daily went into the folder.

For the first week, what I read was mostly feel-good stuff: notes of congratulations, people telling me how inspired they'd been on Inauguration Day, kids with suggestions for legislation ("You should pass a law to cut down on the amount of homework").

But as weeks went by, the letters became more somber. A man who had worked at the same job for twenty years described the shame he felt when he had to tell his wife and kids he'd been laid off. A woman wrote after the bank foreclosed on her home; she was worried that if she didn't get immediate help, she'd end up on the streets. A student had dropped out of college; his financial aid had run out, and he was moving back into his parents' house. Some letters offered detailed policy recommendations. Others were written in anger ("Why hasn't your Justice Department thrown any of these Wall Street crooks in jail?") or with quiet resignation ("I doubt you'll ever read this, but I thought you should know we are hurting out here").

Most often they were urgent appeals for help, and I would write back on a note card embossed with the presidential seal, explaining the steps we were taking to get the economy moving again, offering whatever encouragement I could. I would then mark the original letter with instructions for my staff. "See if Treasury can check with the bank about a refinancing option," I'd write. Or "Does the VA have a loan program for vets in this situation?" Or simply, "Can we help?"

This would usually be enough to focus the attention of the relevant agency. The letter writer would be contacted. Days or weeks later, I'd receive a follow-up memo explaining the actions taken on their behalf. Sometimes people would get the relief they had sought—their home temporarily saved, a spot in an apprenticeship program.

Still, it was hard to take any satisfaction from individual cases. I knew that each letter represented the desperation of millions across the country, people counting on me to save their jobs or their homes, to restore whatever sense of security they had once felt. No matter how hard my team and I worked, no matter how many initiatives we put into place or how many speeches I gave, there was no getting around the damning, indisputable facts.

Three months into my presidency, more people were suffering than when I began, and no one—including me—could be sure relief was in sight.

ON FEBRUARY 18, the day after I signed the Recovery Act, I flew to Mesa, Arizona, to announce our plan to deal with the collapsing housing market. Other than job loss, no aspect of the economic crisis had a more direct impact on ordinary people. With more than three million homes having gone into some stage of foreclosure in 2008, another eight million were now at risk. Over the final three months of the year, home prices fell almost 20 percent, meaning that even families who could manage their payments suddenly found themselves "underwater"—their house worth less than they owed, their primary investment and nest egg now a millstone of debt around their necks.

The problem was at its worst in states like Nevada and Arizona, two of the epicenters of the subprime-driven housing bubble. There, you could drive through entire subdivisions that looked like ghost towns, with block after block of cookie-cutter houses, many of them newly built but lifeless, properties developed but never sold, or sold and promptly foreclosed upon. Either way, they were empty, some with their windows boarded up. The few homes still occupied stood out like small oases, their postage-stamp lawns green and tended, cars parked in the driveways, lonely outposts against a backdrop of ravaged stillness. I remember talking with a homeowner in one of these developments during a campaign visit to Nevada. He was a sturdy, fortyish man in a white T-shirt who had turned off his lawn mower to shake my hand while a towheaded little boy zipped around behind him on a red tricycle. He was luckier than many of his neighbors, he told me: He'd had enough seniority at the factory where he worked to avoid the first wave of layoffs, and his wife's nursing job seemed relatively secure. Still, the house they'd paid $400,000 to purchase at the height of the bubble was now worth half that amount. They had quietly debated whether their best move was to default on their mortgage and walk away. Toward the end of our conversation, the man looked back at his son.

"I remember my dad talking about the American Dream when I was a kid," he said. "How the most important thing was to work hard. Buy a house. Raise a family. Do things right. What happened to that? When did that become just a load of . . . ?" He trailed off, looking pained before wiping the sweat from his face and restarting his mower.

The question was what my administration could do to help a man like that. He hadn't lost his home, but he'd lost faith in the shared enterprise of our country, its larger ideal.

Affordable-housing advocates and some progressives in Congress were pushing a large-scale government program to not only reduce monthly mortgage payments for people at risk of losing their homes but actually forgive a portion of their outstanding balance. At first blush the idea had obvious appeal: a "bailout for Main Street, not Wall Street," as proponents suggested. But the sheer scale of lost home equity across the country made such a principal-reduction program cost-prohibitive; our team calculated that even something the size of a second TARP—a political impossibility—would have a limited effect when spread out across the $20 trillion U.S. real estate market.

We settled on launching two more modest programs, both of which I detailed that day in Mesa: the Home Affordable Modification Program (HAMP), designed to reduce the monthly mortgage payments of eligible homeowners to no more than 31 percent of their income, and the Home Affordable Refinance Program (HARP), which would help borrowers refinance their mortgage at lower rates even if their homes were underwater. By design, not everyone would be assisted under these programs. They wouldn't help those who, through subprime loans, had bought way more home than their income could support. Nor would they be open to those who had bought real estate as a debt-financed investment, thinking they could flip the property for a profit. Instead, the goal was to target several million families teetering on the edge: those who lived in their homes and had made what had seemed at the time like a responsible purchase, but now needed relief to get them through.

Implementing even these limited programs posed all kinds of logistical hurdles. For example, while it was in the interest of mortgage lenders to keep families in their homes (in an already depressed market, foreclosed homes sold at fire-sale prices, resulting in big losses for the lender), mortgages were no longer held by a discrete set of banks that we could pressure into participating. Instead, they'd been securitized, sold in bits and pieces to various investors around the world. The homeowner never dealt directly with these anonymous lenders, instead sending mortgage payments to a servicing company that operated as little more than a glorified bill collector. Without the legal authority to force these servicing companies to do anything, the best we could do was offer incentives for them to offer homeowners a break. We also had to convince the servicing companies to process millions of applications to determine who was or wasn't eligible for a mortgage modification or refinancing, something they were ill-equipped to do.

And just who, exactly, was deserving of government assistance? This question would insinuate itself into just about every policy debate we had throughout the economic crisis. After all, as bad as things were in 2009, the vast majority of American homeowners were still figuring out a way, by hook or by crook, to stay current on their mortgages. To do so, many had cut back on eating out, canceled their cable TV, or spent down savings intended for their retirement or for their children's college expenses.

Was it fair to devote the hard-earned tax dollars of those Americans to reducing the mortgage payments of a neighbor who'd fallen behind? What if the neighbor had bought a bigger house than they could really afford? What if they had opted for a cheaper but riskier type of mortgage? Did it matter if the neighbor had been duped by a mortgage broker into thinking they were doing the right thing? What if the neighbor had taken their kids to Disneyland the year before rather than putting that money into a rainy-day fund—did that make them less worthy of help? Or what if they had fallen behind on their payments not because they'd put in a new swimming pool or taken a vacation but because they'd lost their job, or because a family member had gotten sick and their employer didn't offer health insurance, or because they just happened to live in the wrong state—how did that change the moral calculus?

For policy makers trying to halt a crisis, none of these questions mattered—at least not in the short term. If your next-door neighbor's house is on fire, you don't want the fire department dispatcher asking whether it was caused by lightning or by someone smoking in bed before agreeing to send a fire truck; you just want the fire put out before it reaches your house. Mass foreclosures were the equivalent of a five-alarm fire that was destroying everyone's home values and taking the economy down with it. And from our perspective, at least, we were the fire department.

Still, questions of fairness were very much on the minds of the public. I wasn't surprised when experts reacted critically to our housing package, suggesting that the $75 billion price tag was too small to address the scale of the problem, or when housing advocates blasted us in the press for not including a means to reduce the overall principal. What my team and I didn't anticipate was the critique that ended up getting the most attention that day in Mesa, maybe because it came from such an unlikely source. The day after the rally, Gibbs mentioned that a CNBC business commentator named Rick Santelli had launched a lengthy on-air rant about our housing plan. Gibbs, whose radar on these things was rarely off, seemed concerned.

"It's getting a lot of play," he said. "And the press pool's asking me about it. You might want to check it out."

That night I watched the video clip on my laptop. I

was familiar with Santelli; he seemed no different from most of the talking heads populating the cable business shows, delivering a mix of market gossip and yesterday's news with the glib conviction of a late-night infomercial host. In this instance, he'd been broadcasting live from the floor of the Chicago Mercantile Exchange, charged up with theatrical outrage and surrounded by traders who were smugly cheering from their desks as he regurgitated a bunch of standard Republican talking points, including the (incorrect) claim that we'd be paying off the mortgages of irresponsible spendthrifts and deadbeats—"losers," Santelli called them—who had gotten in over their heads. "The government is promoting bad behavior!" he shouted. "How many of you people want to pay for your neighbor's mortgage that has an extra bathroom and can't pay their bills?"

Santelli went on to declare that "our Founding Fathers, people like Benjamin Franklin and Jefferson, what we're doing in this country now is making them roll over in their graves." Somewhere in mid-monologue, he suggested "a Chicago tea party in July" to put a stop to big-government giveaways.

It was hard for me not to dismiss the whole thing for what it was: a mildly entertaining shtick intended not to inform but to fill airtime, sell ads, and make the viewers of **Squawk Box** feel like they were real insiders—not one of the "losers." Who, after all, was going to take such half-baked populism seriously? How many Americans considered the traders at the Chicago Merc representative of the country—traders who still had jobs precisely because the government had stepped in to keep the financial system afloat?

In other words, it was bullshit. Santelli knew it. The CNBC anchors bantering with him knew it. And yet it was clear that the traders, at least, fully embraced what Santelli was peddling. They didn't appear chastened by the fact that the game they played had been rigged up and down the line, if not by them then by their employers, the real high rollers in wood-paneled boardrooms. They didn't seem concerned by the fact that for every "loser" who had bought more house than he could afford, there were twenty folks who had lived within their means but were now suffering the fallout from Wall Street's bad bets.

No, these traders were genuinely aggrieved, convinced that they were about to get screwed at the hands of the government. They thought **they** were the victims. One had even leaned into Santelli's mic and declared our housing program a "moral hazard"—deploying an economic term that had entered the popular lexicon, used to explain how policies that shielded banks from their mounting losses might end up encouraging even more financial recklessness in the future. Only now the same term was being wielded to argue against help for families who, through no fault of their own, were about to lose their homes.

I clicked the video feed off, feeling irritated. It was a familiar trick, I thought to myself, the kind of rhetorical sleight of hand that had become a staple of conservative pundits everywhere, whatever the issue: taking language once used by the disadvantaged to highlight a societal ill and turning it on its ear. The problem is no longer discrimination against people of color, the argument goes; it's "reverse racism," with minorities "playing the race card" to get an unfair advantage. The problem isn't sexual harassment in the workplace; it's humorless "feminazis" beating men over the head with their political correctness. The problem is not bankers using the market as their personal casino, or corporations suppressing wages by busting unions and offshoring jobs. It's the lazy and shiftless, along with their liberal Washington allies, intent on mooching off the economy's real "makers and the doers."

Such arguments had nothing to do with facts. They were impervious to analysis. They went deeper, into the realm of myth, redefining what was fair, reassigning victimhood, conferring on people like those traders in Chicago that most precious of gifts: the conviction of innocence, as well as the righteous indignation that comes with it.

I WOULD OFTEN think back to that Santelli clip, which foreshadowed so many of the political battles I'd face during my presidency. For there was at least one sideways truth in what he'd said: Our demands on the government **had** changed over the past two centuries, since the time the Founders had chartered it. Beyond the fundamentals of repelling enemies and conquering territory, enforcing property rights and policing issues that property-holding white men deemed necessary to maintain order, our early democracy had largely left each of us to our own devices. Then a bloody war was fought to decide whether property rights extended to treating Blacks as chattel. Movements were launched by workers, farmers, and women who had experienced firsthand how one man's liberty too often involved their own subjugation. A depression came, and people learned that being left to your own devices could mean penury and shame.

Which is how the United States and other advanced democracies came to create the modern social contract. As our society grew more complex, more and more of the government's function took the form of social insurance, with each of us chipping in through our tax dollars to protect ourselves collectively—for disaster relief if our house was destroyed in a hurricane; unemployment insurance if we lost a job; Social Security and Medicare to lessen the indignities of old age; reliable electricity and phone service for those who lived in rural areas where utility companies wouldn't otherwise make a profit; public schools and universities to make education more egalitarian.

It worked, more or less. In the span of a generation and for a majority of Americans, life got better, safer, more prosperous, and more just. A broad middle class flourished. The rich remained rich, if maybe not quite as rich as they would have liked, and the poor were fewer in number, and not as poor as they'd otherwise have been. And if we sometimes debated whether taxes were too high or certain regulations were discouraging innovation, whether the "nanny state" was sapping individual initiative or this or that program was wasteful, we generally understood the advantages of a society that at least tried to offer a fair shake to everyone and built a floor beneath which nobody could sink.

Maintaining this social compact, though, required trust. It required that we see ourselves as bound together, if not as a family then at least as a community, each member worthy of concern and able to make claims on the whole. It required us to believe that whatever actions the government might take to help those in need were available to you and people like you; that nobody was gaming the system and that the misfortunes or stumbles or circumstances that caused others to suffer were ones to which you at some point in your life might fall prey.

Over the years, that trust proved difficult to sustain. In particular, the fault line of race strained it mightily. Accepting that African Americans and other minority groups might need extra help from the government—that their specific hardships could be traced to a brutal history of discrimination rather than immutable characteristics or individual choices—required a level of empathy, of fellow feeling, that many white voters found difficult to muster. Historically, programs designed to help racial minorities, from "forty acres and a mule" to affirmative action, were met with open hostility. Even universal programs that enjoyed broad support—like public education or public sector employment—had a funny way of becoming controversial once Black and brown people were included as beneficiaries.

And harder economic times strained civic trust. As the U.S. growth rate started to slow in the 1970s— as incomes then stagnated and good jobs declined for those without a college degree, as parents started worrying about their kids doing at least as well as they had done— the scope of people's concerns narrowed. We became more sensitive to the possibility that someone else was getting something we weren't and more receptive to the notion that the government couldn't be trusted to be fair.

Promoting that story—a story that fed not trust but resentment—had come to define the modern Republican Party. With varying degrees of subtlety and varying degrees of success, GOP candidates adopted it as their central theme, whether they were running for president or trying to get elected to the local school board. It became the template for Fox News and conservative radio, the foundational text for every think tank and PAC the Koch Brothers financed: The government was taking money, jobs, college slots, and status away from hardworking, deserving people like **us** and handing it all to people like **them**—those who didn't share our values, who didn't work as hard as we did, the kind of people whose problems were of their own making.

The intensity of these convictions put Democrats on the defensive, making leaders less bold about proposing new initiatives, limiting the boundaries of political debate. A deep and suffocating cynicism took hold. Indeed, it became axiomatic among political consultants of both parties that restoring trust in the government or in any of our major institutions was a lost cause, and that the battle between Democrats and Republicans each election cycle now came down to whether America's squeezed middle class was more likely to identify the wealthy and powerful or the poor and minorities as the reason they weren't doing better.

I didn't want to believe that this was all our politics had to offer. I hadn't run simply to fan anger and allocate blame. I had run to rebuild the American people's trust—not just in the government but in one another. If we trusted one another, democracy worked. If we trusted one another, the social compact held, and we could solve big problems like wage stagnation and declining retirement security. But how could we even begin?

The economic crisis had tipped recent elections in the Democrats' favor. But far from restoring any sense of common purpose or faith in the government's capacity to do good, the crisis had also made people more angry, more fearful, more convinced that the fix was in. What Santelli understood, what McConnell and Boehner understood, was how easily that anger could be channeled, how useful fear could be in advancing their cause.

The forces they represented might have lost the recent battle at the polls—but the larger war, that clash of worldviews, values, and narratives, was the one they would still try to win.

IF ALL THIS seems obvious to me now, it wasn't at the time. My team and I were too busy. Passing the Recovery Act and rolling out our housing plan may have been necessary elements in ending the crisis. They weren't close to being sufficient. In particular, the global financial system was still broken—and the man I was relying on to fix it was not off to a promising start.

Tim Geithner's problems had begun weeks earlier, during the process to get him confirmed as Treasury secretary. Historically, Senate confirmation of cabinet appointments was a relatively routine affair, with senators from both parties operating on the presumption that presidents were entitled to choose their own teams—even if they considered the men and women the president selected to be scoundrels and fools. But in recent years, the Senate's constitutional mandate to "advise and consent" had become one more weapon in the endless cycle of partisan trench warfare. Senate staffers of the opposing party now scoured the records of nominees, looking for any youthful indiscretion or damaging quote that could then be raised in a hearing or used to make news. The nominees' personal lives became the subject of endless and intrusive public questioning. The point of the exercise was not necessarily to torpedo the appointment—eventually most nominees got confirmed—but to distract and politically embarrass the administration. The hazing quality of the proceedings had another consequence: With increasing frequency, highly qualified candidates for top federal jobs would cite the confirmation ordeal—what it might do to their reputations, how it might affect their families—as a reason to decline a high-profile post.

Tim's particular problem had to do with taxes: During the three years he'd spent working for the International Monetary Fund, it turned out, neither he nor his accountants had noticed that the organization did not withhold its U.S. employees' payroll taxes. It was an innocent and apparently common mistake, and when an audit surfaced the problem in 2006, a full two years before he was even considered for the Treasury job, Tim amended his returns and paid what the audit said he owed. Yet given the political climate—and the fact that as Treasury secretary, Tim would be overseeing the IRS—the reaction to his error was unforgiving. Republicans suggested that he had purposely committed tax fraud. Late-night comics made jokes at his expense. Tim grew despondent, telling Axe and Rahm that perhaps I should nominate someone else, which led me to call him late one night to buck him up and insist that he was "my guy."

Although he was confirmed a few days later, Tim was

aware that it was by the smallest margin of any Treasury nominee in U.S. history, and that his credibility both at home and internationally had been damaged. I wasn't as worried about all that; nobody remembered confirmation votes, and I was certain his credibility would quickly rebound. But the confirmation drama reminded me that Tim was still a civilian, a lifelong technocrat who had always operated behind the scenes. It would take him some time—just as it had taken me—to get accustomed to the glare of the spotlight.

The day after Tim's confirmation, he and Larry came to the Oval Office to brief me on the grim state of the financial system. Credit remained frozen. The markets were precarious. Five massive institutions—"five big bombs," Tim called them—were in particular peril: Fannie Mae and Freddie Mac, which had become virtually the only sources of housing finance and were burning through the $200 billion in taxpayer funds Treasury had injected into them the previous year; the insurance giant AIG, which had massive exposure as a result of insuring mortgage-based derivatives and had required $150 billion in TARP over the previous four months just to stay afloat; and two banks, Citigroup and Bank of America, which together constituted about 14 percent of America's bank deposits and had seen their stock drop 82 percent over the previous four months.

A renewed run on any one of these five financial institutions could tip it into insolvency, which in turn could trigger a global financial earthquake even bigger than the one we'd just weathered. And despite the hundreds of billions the government had already devoted to their rescue, there was no way that the remaining $300 billion in TARP funds could cover the current pace of losses. A Federal Reserve analysis predicted that, unless the entire system stabilized soon, the banks might need an additional $300 to $700 billion in government cash infusion—and those numbers didn't include AIG, which would later announce a $62 billion quarterly loss.

Rather than pouring more taxpayer dollars into a leaky bucket, we had to find a way to patch its holes. First and foremost, we needed to restore some semblance of market confidence so that investors who'd fled to safety, pulling trillions of dollars in private capital out of the financial sector, would return from the sidelines and reinvest. When it came to Fannie and Freddie, Tim explained, we had the authority to put more money into them without congressional approval, in part because they'd already been placed in government conservatorship. Right away, we agreed to a new $200 billion capital commitment. This wasn't a comfortable choice, but the alternative was to let the entire U.S. mortgage market effectively vanish.

As for the rest of the financial system, the choices were dicier. A few days later, in another Oval Office meeting, Tim and Larry outlined three basic options. The first, most prominently advocated by FDIC chair and Bush holdover Sheila Bair, involved a reprise of Hank Paulson's original idea for TARP, which was to have the government set up a single "bad bank" that would buy up all the privately held toxic assets, thereby cleansing the banking sector. This would allow investors to feel some form of trust and banks to start lending again.

Not surprisingly, the markets liked this approach, since it effectively dumped future losses in the lap of taxpayers. The problem with the "bad bank" idea, though, as both Tim and Larry pointed out, was that no one knew how to fairly price all the toxic assets currently on the banks' books. If the government paid too much, it would amount to yet another massive taxpayer bailout with few strings attached. If, on the other hand, the government paid too little—and with an estimated $1 trillion in toxic assets still out there, fire-sale prices would be all the government could afford—the banks would have to swallow massive losses right away and would almost certainly go belly-up anyway. In fact, it was precisely because of these pricing complications that Hank Paulson had abandoned the idea back at the start of the crisis.

We had a second possibility, one that on the surface seemed cleaner: to temporarily nationalize those systemically significant financial institutions that—based on the current market price of their assets and liabilities— were insolvent and then force them to go through a restructuring similar to a bankruptcy proceeding, including making shareholders and bondholders take "haircuts" on their holdings and potentially replacing both management and boards. This option fulfilled my desire to "tear the Band-Aid off" and fix the system once and for all, rather than letting the banks limp along in what was sometimes referred to as a "zombie" state—technically still in existence but without enough capital or credibility to function. It also had the benefit of satisfying what Tim liked to refer to as "Old Testament justice"—the public's understandable desire to see those who'd done wrong punished and shamed.

As usual, though, what looked like the simplest

solution wasn't so simple. Once the government nationalized one bank, stakeholders at every other bank would
almost certainly dump their holdings as fast as they
could, fearing that their institution would be next. Such
runs would likely trigger the need to nationalize the
next-weakest bank, and the one after that, and the one
after that, in what would become a cascading government takeover of America's financial sector.

Not only would that cost a whole lot of money; it also
would require the U.S. government to manage these
institutions for as long as it took to eventually sell them
off. And while we were busy contending with a million
inevitable lawsuits (filed not just by Wall Street types but
also by pension funds and small investors angry over the
forced "haircut"), the question would be who would
we put in charge of these banks—especially given that
almost everyone with the requisite experience was likely
to be tainted by some involvement with subprime lending? Who would set their salaries and bonuses? How
would the public feel if these nationalized banks just
kept bleeding money? And to whom could the government ultimately sell these banks, other than to other
banks that might have been similarly complicit in creating the mess in the first place?

In part because there were no good answers to these
questions, Tim had cooked up a third option. His theory
was this: Although nobody doubted that banks were in
bad shape and had a whole bunch of bad assets on their
books, the market panic had so deeply depressed **all** asset
prices that their condition might look worse than it really
was. After all, the overwhelming majority of mortgages
wouldn't end up in default. Not every mortgage-backed

security was worthless, and not every bank was awash in bad bets. And yet as long as the market had trouble discerning genuine insolvency from temporary illiquidity, most investors would simply avoid anything related to the financial sector.

Tim's proposed solution would come to be known as a "stress test." The Federal Reserve would set a benchmark for how much capital each of the nineteen systemically significant banks needed to survive a worst-case scenario. The Fed would then dispatch regulators to pore over each bank's books, rigorously assessing whether or not it had enough of a financial cushion to make it through a depression; if not, the bank would be given six months to raise that amount of capital from private sources. If it still fell short, the government would then step in to provide enough capital to meet the benchmark, with nationalization coming into play only if the government's infusion exceeded 50 percent. Either way, the markets would finally have a clear picture of each bank's condition. Shareholders would see their shares in a bank diluted, but only in proportion to the amount of capital needed for the bank to get well. And taxpayers would be on the hook only as a last resort.

Tim presented this third option more as a framework than a detailed plan, and Larry voiced some skepticism, believing that the banks were irredeemable, that the markets would never believe in the rigors of a government-managed audit, and that the exercise would do little more than delay the inevitable. Tim acknowledged those risks. He added that any stress test would require about three months to complete, during which time the public pressure for us to take more decisive action would only build; in the meantime any number of events could send the markets into an even sharper tailspin.

Larry and Tim stopped talking and waited for my reaction. I sat back in my chair.

"Anything else on the menu?" I asked.

"Not right now, Mr. President."

"Not very appetizing."

"No, Mr. President."

I nodded, pondered the probabilities, and after a few more questions decided that Tim's stress-test approach was our best way forward. Not because it was great—not even because it was good—but because the other approaches were worse. Larry compared it to having a doctor administer a less invasive treatment before opting for radical surgery. If the stress test worked, we could fix the system faster and with less taxpayer money. If it didn't, we'd probably be no worse off and would at least have a better sense of what more radical surgery would entail.

Assuming, of course, that the patient didn't die in the meantime.

A COUPLE OF weeks later, on February 10, Tim addressed the public for the first time as Treasury secretary, speaking in a grand hall inside the Treasury Building called the Cash Room, which for more than a century following the Civil War had operated as a bank, dispensing currency directly from government vaults. The idea was that Tim would unveil the framework for the stress test and outline other measures we were taking to stabilize the floundering banks, sending a signal that despite the uncertainty of the times, we were calm and had a credible plan.

Confidence, of course, is hard to convey if you don't fully feel it. Still bruised by the confirmation hearings, having spent his first few weeks on the job working with only a skeleton staff, and still sorting out the details of how the stress test would work, Tim stepped before a bank of TV cameras and financial journalists that day and promptly tanked.

By every estimation, including his own, the speech was a disaster. He looked nervous, was awkwardly using a teleprompter for the first time, and spoke in only vague terms about the overall plan. The White House communications team had been pressing him to emphasize our intent to get tough on the banks, even as our economic team emphasized the need to reassure the financial markets that there was no need for panic. Meanwhile, the alphabet soup of independent agencies responsible for regulating the financial system had not coalesced around Tim's proposal, and several agency heads, like Sheila Bair, kept pushing their own pet ideas. The result was a classic speech by committee, full of hedged bets and mixed messages, reflecting all the contradictory pressures. And in the rush to get it finished, Tim—who was running on fumes at this point—had devoted almost no time to practicing his delivery.

As he was speaking, the stock market dropped by more than 3 percent. By day's end, it was down almost 5 percent, with financial stocks falling a full 11 percent. Tim's speech was all over the news, being parsed every which way. As Larry had predicted, many analysts viewed the stress test as nothing more than an elaborate whitewash, a new string of bailouts. Commentators across the political spectrum were now openly wondering whether Tim's tenure, my presidency, and the global financial system were headed for the dumpster.

As much as Tim blamed himself during the next morning's postmortem, I recognized it as a systems failure—and a failure on my part to put those who worked under me in a position to succeed. A day earlier, speaking at a press conference of my own, I'd unthinkingly and unfairly put a good deal of advance hype on Tim's speech, telling reporters that he'd be announcing "clear and specific plans" and was set to have "his moment in the sun."

The lessons all around were painful but useful. In the months that followed, I'd drive our team to run a tighter process, with better communications between relevant parts of the administration; to anticipate problems and resolve disputes before we took any plans public, allowing our ideas appropriate time and space to germinate regardless of external pressure; to pay careful attention to how big projects were staffed; and to sweat the details not just of substance but of stagecraft as well.

And one more thing: I told myself not to ever open my big mouth again to set up expectations that, given the circumstances, could not possibly be met.

Still, the damage was done. The world's first impression of my hardworking, all-star economic team was that of a gang that couldn't shoot straight. Republicans crowed. Rahm fielded calls from nervous Democrats. About the only positive thing I could draw from the fiasco was Tim's reaction to it. His spirit could have been crushed, but it wasn't. Instead, he had the resigned air of someone who would take his punishment for the poor speech performance but at the same time was confident that on the bigger stuff, he was right.

I liked that in him. He was still my guy. The best we could do now was hunker down, execute, and hope that our damn plan actually worked.

"MADAM SPEAKER . . . the President of the United States!"

For reasons that still aren't entirely clear to me, a newly elected president's first speech before a joint session of Congress isn't technically considered a State of the Union address. But for all intents and purposes, that's exactly what it is—the first of that annual ritual in which a president has the chance to speak directly to tens of millions of fellow Americans.

My own first address was scheduled for February 24, which meant that even as we were scrambling to get our economic rescue plan in place, I had to steal whatever scraps of time I could to review the drafts Favs worked up. It wasn't an easy assignment for either of us. Other speeches could traffic in broad themes or focus narrowly on a single issue. In the SOTU, as West Wing staffers called it, the president was expected to outline both domestic and foreign policy priorities for the coming year. And no matter how much you dressed up your plans and proposals with anecdotes or catchy phrases, detailed explanations of Medicare expansion or tax credit refundability rarely stirred the heartstrings.

Having been a senator, I was well versed in the politics of standing ovations at the SOTU: the ritualized spectacle in which members of the president's party leapt to their feet and cheered to the rafters at practically every third

My maternal grandparents were from Kansas and eloped just ahead of the bombing of Pearl Harbor. He served in Patton's army, and she worked on a bomber assembly line.

«

When you grow up in Hawaii, hikes through mountain forests and lazy days at the beach are a birthright—as easy as stepping out your front door.

«
I'm clearly proud of my swing.

My mother, Ann Dunham, rebelled against convention, but she was also suspicious of platforms or absolutes. "The world is complicated, Bar," she told me. "That's why it's interesting."

My father, Barack Obama, Sr., grew up in Kenya and studied economics at the University of Hawaii, where he met my mother, and at Harvard. After they divorced, he returned to Africa.

My grandmother and I with my mother the day she got her degree in anthropology from the University of Hawaii.

My mother with my half sisters, Maya Soetoro-Ng (**left**) and Auma Obama.

At our wedding. We missed having Michelle's father and Gramps there, but on that day, I felt like the luckiest man alive.

My joys.

Delivering an old-school soapbox speech in Chillicothe, Illinois, early in my U.S. Senate campaign.

Looking impossibly young while delivering the keynote address at the 2004 Democratic National Convention in Boston. This was probably the last day I was able to walk into a public space unrecognized.

With Michelle after my DNC speech.
»

After the convention, Michelle and I and the girls set out for a weeklong RV trip in downstate Illinois. It was the girls' first real taste of the campaign trail.
≫

Election night, 2004. We won by the biggest margin of any Senate race in Illinois history. The girls were more enthralled by the confetti.
≫

« I was elected to the U.S. Senate on November 2, 2004.

As a rookie senator, I persuaded Pete Rouse to come on as my chief of staff. He was a godsend—vastly experienced, unfailingly decent, and known around town as "the 101st senator." »

» When I arrived in Washington, I was ninety-ninth in seniority, and my temporary office showed it. But with a great team around me, I was able to hit the ground running.

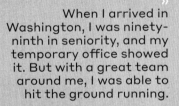

« As a member of the Congressional Black Caucus, I got to work alongside a hero of mine, Representative John Lewis.

On my first official overseas trip as a senator, in August 2005, I toured a conventional weapons destruction facility in Donetsk, Ukraine, with Republican senator Dick Lugar.

During a trip to Kenya in August 2006, Michelle and I wanted to help draw attention to rapid HIV testing by getting tests ourselves. People lined the roads to greet us.

I announced my candidacy for president on February 10, 2007. It was freezing in Springfield, but I barely felt it. I sensed we were tapping into something essential and true about America.

« I missed out on a lot of time with the girls while campaigning. But a day at the Iowa State Fair, with games and snacks and bumper cars? Can't beat that.

Campaigning in Austin, Texas. I had become an outsized symbol of hope, a vessel for a million different dreams, and I worried that a time would come when I would disappoint my supporters.

Storming into Tom Harkin's Annual Steak Fry in 2007 with a bunch of my field organizers. So much of our success in Iowa was due to those unstoppable young staffers and volunteers.

Less than a month before the Iowa caucus, we held a rally in Des Moines. With Oprah there to introduce me, we had a pretty good turnout.

On July 24, 2008, I gave a speech at the Victory Column in Berlin, declaring that, just as an earlier generation had torn down the wall that had once divided Europe, it was our job to tear down other, less visible walls between classes, races, and religions.

With the architect of my campaign, David Plouffe, right before I went onstage to accept the Democratic nomination. Beneath his low-key persona, he was a brilliant strategist.

John McCain and I took a break from campaigning to pay our respects in New York City on September 11, 2008. Within days, the big banks, many of them headquartered only a few blocks away, would begin to collapse.

That same month, as the economy was in free fall, McCain asked President Bush to assemble congressional leaders from both parties at the White House to try to strike a deal on a rescue package.

David Axelrod wasn't just a skilled strategist but a kindred spirit. We started working together in 2002, when I faced long odds in my Senate campaign, and he became one of my most trusted advisors. Meanwhile, Marvin Nicholson (**back right**), my unflappable trip director, had an easy charm and took care of every detail.

Campaigning in the rain in Fredericksburg, Virginia, with less than six weeks to go until the election.

«
Our biggest r[...]
was on Octob[...]
19, when I spo[...]
at the Gatew[...]
Arch in St. Lo[...]
Missouri. Abo[...]
a hundred
thousand peo[...]
showed up.

»
Sitting next to Marian
Robinson, my mother-in-law,
watching the election night
returns. "This is kind of too
much," she said to me.
I knew what she meant.
˅

On election night, more than
two hundred thousand people
came to Chicago's Grant
Park to celebrate. Malia
was worried that nobody
would show up because there
weren't any cars on the road.

My favorite photograph from that night is this one, of people gathered on the steps of the Lincoln Memorial, listening to my acceptance speech on a transistor radio.

IN THIS TEMPLE
AS IN THE HEARTS OF THE PEOPLE
FOR WHOM HE SAVED THE UNION
THE MEMORY OF ABRAHAM LINCOLN
IS ENSHRINED FOREVER

Just before walking
out to take the
oath of office,
I summoned a prayer.

I took the oath on the same
Bible Abraham Lincoln
used for his swearing in
on March 4, 1861.

A sea of Americans. When their flags waved in the sun, it looked like an ocean current. I promised myself I'd give them my best.

≫

Walking the inaugural parade route. As always, Michelle stole the show.

≫

ˆ My first day sitting at the Resolute desk—a gift from Queen Victoria in 1880, carved from the hull of a British ship that a U.S. whaling crew helped salvage from catastrophe.

« The best part of any day was when the girls would stop by.

line, while the opposition party refused to applaud even the most heartwarming story for fear that the cameras might catch them consorting with the enemy. (The sole exception to this rule was any mention of troops overseas.) Not only did this absurd bit of theater highlight the country's divisions at a time when we needed unity; the constant interruptions added at least fifteen minutes to an already long speech. I had considered beginning my address by asking all those in attendance to hold their applause, but unsurprisingly, Gibbs and the comms team had nixed the idea, insisting that a silent chamber would not play well on TV.

But if the process ahead of the SOTU left us feeling harried and uninspired—if at various points I told Favs that after an election night speech, an inauguration speech, and nearly two years of nonstop talking I had absolutely nothing new to say and would be doing the country a favor by emulating Thomas Jefferson and just dropping off my remarks to Congress for the people to read at their leisure—it all vanished the instant I arrived at the threshold of the ornate House chamber and heard the sergeant at arms announce my entrance onto the floor.

"Madam Speaker . . ." Perhaps more than any others, those words and the scene that followed made me conscious of the grandeur of the office I now occupied. There was the thundering applause as I stepped into the chamber; the slow walk down the center aisle through outstretched hands; the members of my cabinet arrayed along the first and second rows; the Joint Chiefs in their crisp uniforms and the Supreme Court justices in their black robes, like members of an ancient guild; the greetings from Speaker Pelosi and Vice President Biden, positioned on either side of me; and my wife beaming down from the upper gallery in her sleeveless dress (that was when the cult of Michelle's arms truly took off), waving and blowing a kiss as the Speaker lowered her gavel and the proceedings commenced.

Although I spoke about my plans to end the war in Iraq, fortify U.S. efforts in Afghanistan, and prosecute the fight against terrorist organizations, the bulk of my address was devoted to the economic crisis. I went over the Recovery Act, our housing plan, the rationale behind the stress test. But there was also a bigger point I wanted to make: that we needed to keep reaching for more. I didn't just want to solve the emergencies of the day; I felt we needed to make a bid for lasting change. Once we'd restored growth to the economy, we couldn't be satisfied with simply returning to business as usual. I made clear that night that I intended to move forward with structural reforms—in education, energy, and climate policy, in healthcare and financial regulation—that would lay the foundation for long-term and broad-based prosperity in America.

The days had long passed since I got nervous on a big stage, and considering how much ground we had to cover, the speech went about as well as I could have hoped. According to Axe and Gibbs, the reviews were fine, the talking heads deeming me suitably "presidential." But apparently they'd been surprised by the boldness of my agenda, my willingness to forge ahead with reforms beyond those that addressed the central business of saving the economy.

It was as if nobody had been listening to the campaign

promises I'd made—or as if they assumed that I hadn't actually meant what I'd said. The response to my speech gave me an early preview of what would become a running criticism during my first two years in office: that I was trying to do too much, that to aspire to anything more than a return to the pre-crisis status quo, to treat change as more than a slogan, was naïve and irresponsible at best, and at worst a threat to America.

AS ALL-CONSUMING AS the economic crisis was, my fledgling administration didn't have the luxury of putting everything else on hold, for the machinery of the federal government stretched across the globe, churning every minute of every day, indifferent to overstuffed in-boxes and human sleep cycles. Many of its functions (generating Social Security checks, keeping weather satellites aloft, processing agricultural loans, issuing passports) required no specific instructions from the White House, operating much like a human body breathes or sweats, outside the brain's conscious control. But this still left countless agencies and buildings full of people in need of our daily attention: looking for policy guidance or help with staffing, seeking advice because some internal breakdown or external event had thrown the system for a loop. After our first weekly Oval Office meeting, I asked Bob Gates, who'd served under seven previous presidents, for any advice he might have in managing the executive branch. He gave me one of his wry, crinkly smiles.

"There's only one thing you can count on, Mr. President," he said. "On any given moment in any given day, somebody somewhere is screwing up."

We went to work trying to minimize screw-ups.

In addition to my regular meetings with the Treasury, state, and defense secretaries and the daily briefings I got from my national security and economic teams, I made a point of sitting down with each member of my cabinet to go over strategic plans for their departments, pushing them to identify roadblocks and set priorities. I visited their respective agencies, often using the occasion to announce a new policy or government practice, and spoke to large gatherings of career government staffers, thanking them for their service and reminding them of the importance of their missions.

There was an endless flow of meetings with various constituency groups—the Business Roundtable, the AFL-CIO, the U.S. Conference of Mayors, veterans' services organizations—to address their concerns and solicit their support. There were big set pieces that absorbed enormous amounts of time (like the presentation of our first federal budget proposal) and innovative public events designed to increase government transparency (like our first-ever live-streamed town hall). Each week I delivered a video address. I sat down for interviews with various print reporters and TV anchors, both national and local. I gave remarks at the National Prayer Breakfast and threw a Super Bowl party for members of Congress. By the first week of March, I'd also held two summits with foreign leaders—one in D.C. with British prime minister Gordon Brown, the other in Ottawa with Canadian prime minister Stephen Harper—each involving its own policy objectives and diplomatic protocols.

For every event, meeting, and policy rollout, a hundred people or more might be frantically working behind the scenes. Every document issued was fact-checked, every person who showed up for a meeting was vetted, every event was planned to the minute, and every policy announcement was carefully scrubbed to make sure it was achievable, affordable, and didn't carry the risk of unforeseen consequences.

This kind of focused industriousness extended to the East Wing, where the First Lady had a small suite of offices and a busy schedule of her own. From the moment we'd arrived at the White House, Michelle had thrown herself into her new job while also making a home for our family. Thanks to her, Malia and Sasha seemed to be taking the transition to our strange new life completely in stride. They tossed balls in the long hallway that ran the length of the residence and made cookies with the White House chefs. Their weekends were filled with playdates and birthday parties with new friends, rec basketball, soccer leagues, tennis lessons for Malia, dance classes and tae kwon do for Sasha. (Much like her mother, Sasha was not to be messed with.) Out in public, Michelle sparkled with charm, her fashion choices attracting favorable notice. Tasked with hosting the annual Governors Ball, Michelle had shaken up tradition by arranging to have Earth, Wind & Fire provide the entertainment, their horn-blasting R&B funk generating moves on the dance floor that I'd never thought I'd see out of a bipartisan gathering of middle-aged public officials.

Look beautiful. Care for your family. Be gracious. Support your man. For most of American history, the First Lady's job had been defined by these tenets, and

Michelle was hitting all the marks. What she hid from the outside world, though, was the way her new role initially chafed, how fraught with uncertainty it felt.

Not all her frustrations were new. For as long as we'd been together, I'd watched my wife struggle the way many women did, trying to reconcile her identity as an independent, ambitious professional with a desire to mother our girls with the same level of care and attentiveness that Marian had given her. I had always tried to encourage Michelle in her career, never presuming that household duties were her province alone; and we'd been lucky that our joint income and a strong network of close-by relatives and friends had given us advantages that many families didn't have. Still, this wasn't enough to insulate Michelle from the wildly unrealistic and often contradictory social pressures that women with children absorbed from the media, their peers, their employers, and, of course, the men in their lives.

My career in politics, with its prolonged absences, had made it even tougher. More than once Michelle had decided not to pursue an opportunity that excited her but would have demanded too much time away from the girls. Even in her last job at the University of Chicago Medical Center, with a supportive boss and the ability to make her own schedule, she'd never fully shaken the sense that she was shortchanging the girls, her work, or both. In Chicago, she had at least been able to avoid being in the public eye and manage the everyday push and pull on her own terms. Now all that had changed. With my election, she'd been forced to give up a job with real impact for a role that—in its original design, at least—was far too small for her gifts. Meanwhile, mothering our kids involved a whole new set of complications—like having to call a parent to explain why Secret Service agents needed to survey their house before Sasha came for a playdate or working with staffers to press a tabloid not to print a picture of Malia hanging out with her friends at the mall.

On top of these things, Michelle suddenly found herself drafted as a symbol in America's ongoing gender wars. Each choice she made, each word she uttered, was feverishly interpreted and judged. When she light-heartedly referred to herself as a "mom in chief," some commentators expressed disappointment that she wasn't using her platform to break down stereotypes about a woman's proper place. At the same time, efforts to stretch the boundaries of what a First Lady should or should not do carried their own peril: Michelle still smarted from the viciousness of some of the attacks leveled at her during the campaign, and one had only to look at Hillary Clinton's experience to know how quickly people could turn on a First Lady who engaged in anything resembling policy making.

Which is why, in those early months, Michelle took her time deciding how she'd use her new office, figuring out how and where she might exert an influence while carefully and strategically setting the tone for her work as First Lady. She consulted with Hillary and with Laura Bush. She recruited a strong team, filling her staff with seasoned professionals whose judgment she trusted. Eventually she decided to take on two causes that were personally meaningful: the alarming jump in America's childhood obesity rates and the embarrassing lack of support for America's military families.

It wasn't lost on me that both issues tapped into frustrations and anxieties that Michelle herself sometimes felt. The obesity epidemic had come to her attention a few years earlier when our pediatrician, noticing that Malia's body mass index had increased somewhat, identified too many highly processed "kid-friendly" foods as the culprit. The news had confirmed Michelle's worries that our harried, overscheduled lives might be adversely impacting the girls. Similarly, her interest in military families had been sparked by emotional roundtable discussions she'd had during the campaign with the spouses of deployed service members. As they'd described feeling a mixture of loneliness and pride, as they'd admitted to occasional resentment at being treated as an afterthought in the larger cause of defending the nation, as they expressed reluctance to ask for help for fear of seeming selfish, Michelle had heard echoes of her own circumstances.

Precisely because of these personal connections, I was sure her impact on both issues would be substantial. Michelle was someone who started from the heart and not the head, from experience rather than abstractions. I also knew this: My wife didn't like to fail. Whatever ambivalence she felt about her new role, she was nonetheless determined to carry it out well.

As a family, we were adapting week by week, each of us finding means to adjust to, cope with, and enjoy our circumstances. Michelle turned to her unflappable mother for counsel anytime she felt anxious, the two of them huddling together on the couch in the solarium on the third floor of the White House. Malia threw herself into her fifth-grade homework and was lobbying us to deliver on our personal campaign promise to get a family dog. Sasha, just seven, still fell asleep at night clutching the frayed chenille blankie she'd had since she was a baby, her body growing so fast you could almost see the difference each day.

Our new housing arrangement brought one especially happy surprise: Now that I lived above the store, so to speak, I was home basically all the time. On most days, the work came to me, not the other way around. Unless I was traveling, I made a point of being at the dinner table by six-thirty each night, even if it meant that later I needed to go back downstairs to the Oval Office.

What a joy that was, listening to Malia and Sasha talk about their days, narrating a world of friend drama, quirky teachers, jerky boys, silly jokes, dawning insights, and endless questions. After the meal was over and they bounded off to do homework and get ready for bed, Michelle and I would sit and catch up for a time, less often about politics and more about news of old friends, movies we wanted to see, and most of all the wondrous process of watching our daughters grow up. Then we'd read the girls bedtime stories, hug them tightly, and tuck them in—Malia and Sasha in their cotton pajamas smelling of warmth and life. In that hour and a half or so each evening, I found myself replenished—my mind cleansed and my heart cured of whatever damage a day spent pondering the world and its intractable problems may have done.

If the girls and my mother-in-law were our anchors in the White House, there were others who helped me and Michelle manage the stress of those early months. Sam Kass, the young man we'd hired to cook for us part-time back in Chicago as the campaign got busy and our worries about the kids' eating habits peaked, had come with us to Washington, joining the White House not just as a chef but also as Michelle's point person on the childhood obesity issue. The son of a math teacher at the girls' old school and a former college baseball player, Sam had an easygoing charm and compact good looks that were enhanced by a shiny, clean-shaven head. He was also a genuine food policy expert, conversant in everything from the effects of monoculture farming on climate change to the links between eating habits and chronic disease. Sam's work with Michelle would prove invaluable; it was brainstorming with him, for example, that gave Michelle the idea to plant a vegetable garden in the South Lawn. But what we got in the bargain was a fun-loving uncle to the girls, a favorite younger brother to Michelle and me, and—along with Reggie Love—someone I could shoot hoops or play a game of pool with anytime I needed to blow off a little steam.

We found similar support from our longtime athletic trainer, Cornell McClellan, a former social worker and martial arts expert who owned his own gym in Chicago. Despite his imposing frame, Cornell was kind and good-humored when he wasn't torturing us with squats, deadlifts, burpees, and lunge walks, and he'd decided that it was his duty to start splitting his time between D.C. and Chicago to make sure the First Family stayed in shape.

Each morning, Monday through Thursday, Michelle and I began our days with both Cornell and Sam, the four of us gathering in the small gym on the third floor of the residence, its wall-mounted television reliably set to

ESPN's **SportsCenter**. There was no disputing that Michelle was Cornell's star pupil, powering through her workouts with unerring focus, while Sam and I were decidedly slower and given to taking longer breaks between sets, distracting Cornell with heated debates—Jordan versus Kobe, Tom Hanks versus Denzel Washington—anytime the regimen got too intense for our liking. For both Michelle and me, that daily hour in the gym became one more zone of normalcy, shared with friends who still called us by our first names and loved us like family, who reminded us of the world we'd once known—and the version of ourselves that we hoped always to inhabit.

THERE WAS A final stress reliever that I didn't like to talk about, one that had been a chronic source of tension throughout my marriage: I was still smoking five (or six, or seven) cigarettes a day.

It was the lone vice that had carried over from the rebel days of my youth. At Michelle's insistence, I had quit several times over the years, and I never smoked in the house or in front of the kids. Once elected to the U.S. Senate, I had stopped smoking in public. But a stubborn piece of me resisted the tyranny of reason, and the strains of campaign life—the interminable car rides through cornfields, the solitude of motel rooms—had conspired to keep me reaching for the pack I kept handy in a suitcase or drawer. After the election, I'd told myself it was as good a time as any to stop—by definition, I was in public just about anytime I was outside the White House residence. But then things got so busy that I found myself delaying my day of reckoning, wandering out to the pool house behind the Oval Office after lunch or up to the third-floor terrace after Michelle and the girls had gone to sleep, taking a deep drag and watching the smoke curl toward the stars, telling myself I'd stop for good as soon as things settled down.

Except things didn't settle down. So much so that by March my daily cigarette intake had crept up to eight (or nine, or ten).

That month, another estimated 663,000 Americans would lose their jobs, with the unemployment rate shooting up to 8.5 percent. Foreclosures showed no signs of abating, and credit remained frozen. The stock market hit what would be its lowest point of the recession, down 57 percent from its peak, with shares of Citigroup and Bank of America approaching penny-stock status. AIG, meanwhile, was like a bottomless maw, its only apparent function being to gobble up as much TARP money as possible.

All this would have been more than enough to keep my blood pressure rising. What made it worse was the clueless attitude of the Wall Street executives whose collective asses we were pulling out of the fire. Just before I took office, for example, the leaders of most of the major banks had gone ahead and authorized more than a billion dollars in year-end bonuses for themselves and their lieutenants, despite having already received TARP funds to prop up their stock prices. Not long after, Citigroup execs somehow decided it was a good idea to order a new corporate jet. (Because this happened on our watch, someone on Tim's team was able to call the company's CEO and browbeat him into canceling the order.)

Meanwhile, bank executives bristled—sometimes privately, but often in the press—at any suggestion that they had in any way screwed up, or should be subject to any constraints when it came to running their business. This last bit of chutzpah was most pronounced in the two savviest operators on Wall Street, Lloyd Blankfein of Goldman Sachs and Jamie Dimon of JPMorgan Chase, both of whom insisted that their institutions had avoided the poor management decisions that plagued other banks and neither needed nor wanted government assistance. These claims were true only if you ignored the fact that the solvency of both outfits depended entirely on the ability of the Treasury and the Fed to keep the rest of the financial system afloat, as well as the fact that Goldman in particular had been one of the biggest peddlers of subprime-based derivatives—and had dumped them onto less sophisticated customers right before the bottom fell out.

Their obliviousness drove me nuts. It wasn't just that Wall Street's attitude toward the crisis confirmed every stereotype of the über-wealthy being completely out of touch with the lives of ordinary people. Each tone-deaf statement or self-serving action also made our job of saving the economy that much harder.

Already, some Democratic constituencies were asking why we weren't being tougher on the banks—why the government wasn't simply taking them over and selling off their assets, for example, or why none of the individuals who had caused such havoc had gone to jail. Republicans in Congress, unburdened by any sense of responsibility for the mess they'd help create, were more than happy to join in on the grilling. In testimony before various congressional committees, Tim (who was now routinely labeled as a "former Goldman Sachs banker" despite having never worked for Goldman and having spent nearly his entire career in public service) would explain the need to wait for the stress-test results. My attorney general, Eric Holder, would later point out that as egregious as the behavior of the banks may have been leading up to the crisis, there were few indications that their executives had committed prosecutable offenses under existing statutes—and we were not in the business of charging people with crimes just to garner good head-lines.

But to a nervous and angry public, such answers—no matter how rational—weren't very satisfying. Concerned that we were losing the political high ground, Axe and Gibbs urged us to sharpen our condemnations of Wall Street. Tim, on the other hand, warned that such populist gestures would be counterproductive, scaring off the investors we needed to recapitalize the banks. Trying to straddle the line between the public's desire for Old Testament justice and the financial markets' need for reassurance, we ended up satisfying no one.

"It's like we've got a hostage situation," Gibbs said to me one morning. "We know the banks have explosives strapped to their chests, but to the public it just looks like we're letting them get away with a robbery."

With tensions growing inside the White House and me wanting to make sure everyone remained on the same page, in mid-March I called together my economic team for a marathon Sunday session in the Roosevelt Room. For several hours that day, we pressed Tim and his deputies for their thoughts on the ongoing stress test—whether it would work, and whether Tim had a Plan B if it didn't. Larry and Christy argued that in light of mounting losses at Citigroup and Bank of America, it was time for us to consider preemptive nationalization—the kind of strategy that Sweden had ultimately pursued when it went through its own financial crisis in the 1990s. This was in contrast, they said, to the "forbearance" strategy that had left Japan in a lost decade of economic stagnation. In response, Tim pointed out that Sweden—with a much smaller financial sector, and at a time when the rest of the world was stable—had nationalized only two of its major banks as a last resort, while providing effective guarantees for its remaining four. An equivalent strategy on our part, he said, might cause the already fragile global financial system to unravel, and would cost a minimum of $200 to $400 billion. ("The chances of getting an additional dime of TARP money from this Congress are somewhere between zero and zero!" Rahm shouted, practically jumping out of his chair.) Some on the team suggested that we at least take a more aggressive posture toward Citigroup and Bank of America—forcing out their CEOs and current boards, for example, before granting more TARP money. But Tim said such steps would be wholly symbolic—and, further, would make us responsible for finding immediate replacements capable of navigating unfamiliar institutions in the midst of the crisis.

It was an exhausting exercise, and as the session ran into the evening hours, I told the team that I was going up to the residence to have dinner and get a haircut and would expect them to have arrived at a consensus by the time I got back. In truth, I'd already gotten what I wanted out of the meeting: confirmation in my own mind that, despite the legitimate issues Larry, Christy, and others had raised about the stress test, it continued to be our best shot under the circumstances. (Or as Tim liked to put it, "Plan beats no plan.")

Just as important, I felt assured that we'd run a good process: that our team had looked at the problem from every conceivable angle; that no potential solution had been discarded out of hand; and that everyone involved—from the highest-ranking cabinet member to the most junior staffer in the room—had been given the chance to weigh in. (For these same reasons, I would later invite two groups of outside economists—one left-leaning, the other conservative—who'd publicly questioned our handling of the crisis to meet me in the Oval, just to see if they had any ideas that we hadn't already considered. They didn't.)

My emphasis on process was born of necessity. What I was quickly discovering about the presidency was that no problem that landed on my desk, foreign or domestic, had a clean, 100 percent solution. If it had, someone else down the chain of command would have solved it already. Instead, I was constantly dealing with probabilities: a 70 percent chance, say, that a decision to do nothing would end in disaster; a 55 percent chance that this approach versus that one **might** solve the problem (with a 0 percent chance that it would work out exactly as intended); a 30 percent chance that whatever we chose wouldn't work at all, along with a 15 percent chance that it would make the problem worse.

In such circumstances, chasing after the perfect solution led to paralysis. On the other hand, going with your gut too often meant letting preconceived notions or the path of least political resistance guide a decision—with cherry-picked facts used to justify it. But with a sound process—one in which I was able to empty out my ego and really listen, following the facts and logic as best I could and considering them alongside my goals and my principles—I realized I could make tough decisions and still sleep easy at night, knowing at a minimum that no one in my position, given the same information, could have made the decision any better. A good process also meant I could allow each member of the team to feel ownership over the decision—which meant better execution and less relitigation of White House decisions through leaks to **The New York Times** or **The Washington Post**.

Returning from my haircut and dinner that night, I sensed that things had played out the way I had hoped. Larry and Christy agreed that it made sense for us to wait and see how the stress test went before taking more drastic action. Tim accepted some useful suggestions about how to better prepare for possibly bad results. Axe and Gibbs offered ideas about improving our communications strategy. All in all, I was feeling pretty good about the day's work.

Until, that is, someone brought up the issue of the AIG bonuses.

It seemed that AIG—which had thus far taken more than $170 billion in TARP funds and still needed more—was paying its employees $165 million in contractually obligated bonuses. Worse yet, a big chunk of the bonuses would go to the division directly responsible for leaving the insurance giant wildly overexposed in the subprime derivative business. AIG's CEO, Edward Liddy (who himself was blameless, having only recently agreed to take the helm at the company as a public service and was paying himself just a dollar a year), recognized that the bonuses were unseemly. But according to Tim, Liddy had been advised by his lawyers that any attempt to withhold the payments would likely result in successful lawsuits by the AIG employees and damage payments potentially coming in at three times the original amount. To cap it off, we didn't appear to have any governmental authority to stop the bonus payments—in part because the Bush administration had lobbied Congress against the inclusion of "claw-back" provisions in the original TARP legislation, fearing that it would discourage financial institutions from participating.

I looked around the room. "This is a joke, right? You guys are just messing with me."

Nobody laughed. Axe started arguing that we had to try to stop the payments, even if our efforts were unsuccessful. Tim and Larry began arguing back, acknowledging the whole thing was terrible but saying that if the government forced a violation of contracts between private parties, we'd do irreparable damage to our market-based system. Gibbs chimed in to suggest that morality and common sense trumped contract law. After a few minutes, I cut everyone off. I instructed Tim to keep looking at ways we might keep AIG from dispensing the bonuses (knowing full well he'd probably come up empty). Then I told Axe to prepare a statement condemning the bonuses that I could deliver the next day (knowing full well that nothing I said would help lessen the damage).

Then I told myself that it was still the weekend and I needed a martini. That was another lesson the presidency was teaching me: Sometimes it didn't matter how good your process was. Sometimes you were just screwed, and the best you could do was have a stiff drink—and light up a cigarette.

THE NEWS OF the AIG bonuses brought the pent-up anger of several months to an uncontrolled boil. Newspaper editorials were scathing. The House quickly passed a bill to tax Wall Street bonuses at 90 percent for people making over $250,000, only to watch it die in the Senate. In the White House briefing room, it seemed like Gibbs fielded questions on no other topic. Code Pink, a quirky antiwar group whose members (mostly women) dressed in pink T-shirts, pink hats, and the occasional pink boa, ramped up protests outside various government buildings and surfaced at hearings where Tim was appearing, hoisting signs with slogans like GIVE US OUR $$$$$ BACK, clearly unimpressed by any argument about the sanctity of contracts.

The following week, I decided to convene a White House meeting with the CEOs of the top banks and financial institutions, hoping to avoid any further surprises. Fifteen of them showed up, all men, all looking dapper and polished, and they all listened with placid expressions as I explained that the public had run out of patience, and that given the pain the financial crisis was causing across the country—not to mention the extraordinary measures the government had taken to support their institutions—the least they could do was show some restraint, maybe even sacrifice.

When it was the executives' turn to respond, each one offered some version of the following: (a) the problems with the financial system really weren't of their making; (b) they **had** made significant sacrifices, including slashing their workforces and reducing their own compensation packages; and (c) they hoped that I would stop fanning the flames of populist anger, which they said was hurting their stock prices and damaging industry morale. As proof of this last point, several mentioned a recent interview in which I'd said that my administration was shoring up the financial system only to prevent a depression, not to help a bunch of "fat cat bankers." When they spoke, it sounded like their feelings were hurt.

"What the American people are looking for in this time of crisis," one banker said, "is for you to remind them that we're all in this together."

I was stunned. "You think it's my **rhetoric** that's made the public angry?" Taking a deep breath, I searched the faces of the men around the table and realized they were being sincere. Much like the traders in the Santelli video, these Wall Street executives genuinely felt picked on. It wasn't just a ploy. I tried then to put myself in their shoes, reminding myself that these were people who had no doubt worked hard to get where they were, who had played the game no differently than their peers and were long accustomed to adulation and deference for having come out on top. They gave large sums to various charities. They loved their families. They couldn't understand why (as one would later tell me) their children were now asking them whether they were "fat cats," or why no one was impressed that they had reduced their annual compensation from $50 or $60 million to $2 million, or why the president of the United States wasn't treating them as true partners and accepting, just to take one example, Jamie Dimon's offer to send over some of

JPMorgan's top people to help the administration design our proposed regulatory reforms.

I tried to understand their perspective, but I couldn't. Instead, I found myself thinking about my grandmother, how in my mind her Kansas prairie character represented what a banker was supposed to be: Honest. Prudent. Exacting. Risk-averse. Someone who refused to cut corners, hated waste and extravagance, lived by the code of delayed gratification, and was perfectly content to be a little bit boring in how she did business. I wondered what Toot would make of the bankers who now sat with me in this room, the same kind of men who'd so often been promoted ahead of her—who in a month made more than she'd made in her entire career, at least in part because they were okay with placing billion-dollar bets with other people's money on what they knew, or should have known, was a pile of bad loans.

Finally I let out something between a laugh and a snort. "Let me explain something, gentlemen," I said, careful not to raise my voice. "People don't need my prompting to be angry. They've got that covered all on their own. The fact is, we're the only ones standing between you and the pitchforks."

I CAN'T SAY my words that day had much impact—other than reinforcing the view on Wall Street that I was anti-business. Ironically, the same meeting would later be cited by critics on the left as an example of how, in my general fecklessness and alleged chumminess with Wall Street, I had failed to hold the banks accountable during the crisis. Both takes were wrong, but this much was true: By committing to the stress test and the roughly two-month wait for its preliminary results, I'd placed on hold whatever leverage I had over the banks. What was also true was that I felt constrained from making any rash moves while I still had so many fronts of the economic crisis to deal with—including the need to keep the U.S. auto industry from driving over a cliff.

Just as the Wall Street implosion was a culmination of long-standing structural problems in the global financial system, what ailed the Big Three automakers—bad management, bad cars, foreign competition, underfunded pensions, soaring healthcare costs, an overreliance on the sale of high-margin, gas-guzzling SUVs—had been decades in the making. The financial crisis and the deepening recession had only hastened the reckoning. By the autumn of 2008, auto sales had plunged 30 percent to their lowest level in more than a decade, and GM and Chrysler were running out of cash. While Ford was in slightly better shape (mainly due to a fortuitous restructuring of its debt just before the crisis hit), analysts questioned whether it could survive the collapse of the other two, given the reliance of all three automakers on a common pool of parts suppliers across North America. Just before Christmas, Hank Paulson had used a creative reading of the TARP authorization to provide GM and Chrysler with more than $17 billion in bridge loans. But without the political capital to force a more permanent solution, the Bush administration had managed only to kick the can down the road until I took office. Now that the cash was about to run out, it was up to me to decide whether to put billions more into the automakers in order to keep them afloat.

Even during the transition, it had been clear to everyone on my team that GM and Chrysler would have to
go through some sort of court-structured bankruptcy.
Without it, there was simply no way that they could cover
the cash they were burning through each month, no matter how optimistic their sales projections. Moreover,
bankruptcy alone wouldn't be enough. To justify further
government support, the automakers would also have to
undergo a painstaking, top-to-bottom business reorganization and find a way to make cars that people wanted to
buy. ("I don't understand why Detroit can't make a damn
Corolla," I muttered more than once to my staff.)

Both tasks were easier said than done. For one
thing, GM's and Chrysler's top management made the
Wall Street crowd look positively visionary. In an early
discussion with our transition economic team, GM CEO
Rick Wagoner's presentation was so slapdash and filled
with happy talk—including projections for a 2 percent
increase in sales every year, despite having seen declining
sales for much of the decade preceding the crisis—that it
rendered even Larry temporarily speechless. As for bankruptcy, the process for both GM and Chrysler would
likely be similar to open-heart surgery: complicated,
bloody, fraught with risk. Just about every stakeholder
(management, workers, suppliers, shareholders, pension-
ers, distributors, creditors, and the communities in which
the manufacturing plants were located) stood to lose
something in the short term, which would be cause for
prolonged, bare-knuckle negotiations when it became
unclear whether the two companies would even survive
another month.

We did have a few things going for us. Unlike the

situation with the banks, forcing GM and Chrysler to reorganize wasn't likely to trigger widespread panic, which gave us more room to demand concessions in exchange for continued government support. It also helped that I had a strong personal relationship with the United Auto Workers, whose leaders recognized that major changes needed to be made in order for its members to hold on to their jobs.

Most important, our White House Auto Task Force—led by Steve Rattner and Ron Bloom and staffed by a brilliant thirty-one-year-old policy specialist named Brian Deese—was turning out to be terrific, combining analytical rigor with an appreciation for the human dimensions of the million-plus jobs at stake in getting this right. They had begun negotiations with the carmakers well before I was even sworn in, giving GM and Chrysler sixty days to come up with formal reorganization plans to demonstrate their viability. To make sure the companies didn't collapse during this period, they'd designed a series of incremental but critical interventions—such as quietly guaranteeing both companies' receivables with suppliers so that they didn't run out of parts.

In mid-March, the Auto Task Force came to the Oval Office to give me their assessment. Neither of the plans that GM and Chrysler had submitted, they said, passed muster; both companies were still living in a fantasy world of unrealistic sales projections and vague strategies for getting costs under control. The team felt that with an aggressive structured bankruptcy, though, GM could get back on track, and recommended that we give the company sixty days to revise its reorganization plan—provided it agreed to replace both Rick Wagoner and the existing board of directors.

When it came to Chrysler, though, our team was split. The smallest of the Big Three, Chrysler was also in the worst financial shape and—outside of its Jeep brand—had what looked to be an unsalvageable product line. Given our limited resources and the perilous state of auto sales more generally, some on the team argued that we'd have a better chance of saving GM if we let Chrysler go. Others insisted that we shouldn't underestimate the potential economic shock of allowing an iconic American company to collapse. Either way, the task force let me know, the situation at Chrysler was deteriorating fast enough that I needed to make my decision right away.

At this point, my assistant Katie poked her head into the Oval Office, telling me I needed to get to the Situation Room for a meeting with my national security team. Figuring I should probably take more than a half hour to decide the fate of the American auto industry, I asked Rahm to reconvene the task force along with my three senior advisors—Valerie, Pete, and Axe—in the Roosevelt Room later that afternoon so I could hear from both sides (more process!). At that meeting, I listened to Gene Sperling make a pitch for saving Chrysler and Christy Romer and Austan Goolsbee explain why continued support of the company likely amounted to throwing good money after bad. Rahm and Axe, ever sensitive to the politics of the situation, pointed out that the country opposed—by a stunning two-to-one margin—any further auto bailouts. Even in Michigan, support barely reached a majority.

Rattner noted that Fiat had recently expressed an interest in buying a significant stake in Chrysler and that its CEO, Sergio Marchionne, had taken over that faltering company in 2004 and, impressively, made it profitable within a year and a half. The discussions with Fiat, however, were still tentative, and nobody could guarantee that any intervention would be enough to get Chrysler back on track. A 51–49 decision, Rattner called it—with a strong likelihood that the odds of success would seem bleaker once the company went into bankruptcy and we had a better look under the hood.

I was thumbing through the charts, scrutinizing numbers, occasionally glancing up at the portraits of Teddy and FDR hanging on the wall, when it came time for Gibbs to speak. He had previously worked on U.S. senator Debbie Stabenow's campaign, in Michigan, and he now pointed to a map in the slide deck that showed every Chrysler plant across the Midwest.

"Mr. President," he said, "I'm not an economist, and I don't know how to run a car company. But I do know we've spent the last three months trying to prevent a second Great Depression. And the thing is, in a lot of these towns that depression has already arrived. We cut Chrysler off now and we might as well be signing a death warrant for every spot you see on the map. Each one has thousands of workers counting on us. The kind of people you met on the campaign trail . . . losing their healthcare, their pensions, too old to start over. I don't know how you walk away from them. I don't think that's why you ran for president."

I stared at the points on the map, more than twenty in all, spread across Michigan, Indiana, and Ohio, my mind wandering back to my earliest days as an organizer in Chicago, when I'd meet with laid-off steelworkers in cold union halls or church basements to discuss their community concerns. I could remember their bodies heavy under winter coats, their hands chapped and callused, their faces—white, Black, brown—betraying the quiet desperation of men who'd lost their purpose. I hadn't been able to help them much then; their plants had already closed by the time I'd arrived, and people like me had no leverage over the distant executives who'd made those decisions. I'd entered politics with the notion that I might someday be able to offer something more meaningful to those workers and their families.

And now here I was. I turned to Rattner and Bloom and told them to get Chrysler on the phone. If, with our help, the company could negotiate a deal with Fiat, I said, and deliver a realistic, hardheaded business plan to emerge from a structured bankruptcy within a reasonable time frame, we owed those workers and their communities that chance.

It was getting close to dinnertime and I still had several calls to make in the Oval. I was about to adjourn the meeting when I noticed Brian Deese tentatively raising his hand. The youngest member of the task force, he'd barely spoken during the discussion, but unbeknownst to me, he'd actually been the one to prepare the map and brief Gibbs on the human costs involved in letting Chrysler go under. (Years later, he'd tell me that he felt the arguments would carry more weight coming from a senior staff member.) Having seen his side prevail and feeling swept up in the moment, though, Deese started pointing out all the potential upsides of the decision I'd just made—including that a Chrysler-Fiat tandem could end up being the first U.S.-based operation to produce cars capable of getting forty miles to the gallon. Except in his nervousness, he said "the first U.S.-produced cars that can go forty miles an **hour**."

The room was quiet for a moment, then broke into laughter. Realizing his mistake, Deese's face, cherubic beneath his mustache and beard, turned bright red. I smiled and rose from my chair.

"You know, it just so happens my first car was a '76 Fiat," I said, gathering up the papers in front of me. "Bought it used, my freshman year of college. Red, five-speed stick. As I remember, it went over forty miles an hour . . . when it wasn't in the shop. Worst car I ever owned." I walked around the table, patted Deese on the arm, and turned back as I was heading out the door. "The people at Chrysler thank you," I said, "for not making **that** particular argument until **after** I made my decision."

IT'S OFTEN SAID that a president gets too much credit when the economy is doing well, and too much blame when it slumps. In normal times, that's true. All kinds of factors—from a decision by the Fed (over which a president by law has no authority) to raise or lower interest rates, to the vicissitudes of the business cycle, to bad weather delaying construction projects or a sudden spike in commodity prices brought on by some conflict on the other side of the world—are likely to have a bigger impact on the day-to-day economy than anything the president does. Even major White House initiatives, like a big tax cut or a regulatory overhaul, don't tend to produce any sort of measurable influence on GDP growth or unemployment rates for months or even years.

As a result, most presidents labor without knowing the economic impact of their actions. Voters can't gauge it either. There's an inherent unfairness to this, I suppose: Depending on accidents of timing, a president can be punished or rewarded at the polls for things entirely beyond his or her control. At the same time, this also offers an administration a certain margin for error, allowing leaders to set policy while feeling secure in the knowledge that not everything depends on them getting things right.

In 2009, however, the situation was different. In the first hundred days of my administration, no margin for error existed. Every move we made counted. Every American was paying attention. Had we restarted the financial system? Had we ended the recession? Put people back to work? Kept people in their homes? Our scorecard was posted daily for everyone to see, with each new fragment of economic data, each news report or anecdote becoming an opportunity for judgment. My team and I carried that knowledge with us the minute we woke up, and it stayed with us until we went to bed.

Sometimes I think it was only the sheer busyness of those months that kept us from succumbing to the overall stress. After the GM and Chrysler decisions, the main pillars of our strategy were basically in place, which meant we could turn our focus to implementation. The Auto Task Force negotiated a change in GM management, brokered Fiat's stake in Chrysler, and helped put together a plausible plan for the structured bankruptcies and reorganization of both car companies. The housing team, meanwhile, hammered together the framework for the HAMP and HARP programs. The Recovery Act's tax cuts and grants to states began to flow, with Joe Biden, together with his able chief of staff Ron Klain, in charge of overseeing the billions of dollars in infrastructure projects with an eye toward minimizing waste or fraud. And Tim and his still-skeletal staff at Treasury, along with the Fed, continued to put out fires across the financial system.

The pace was relentless. When I met with my economic team for our regular morning briefing, the faces of those arrayed in a horseshoe of chairs and couches around the Oval told a tale of exhaustion. Later, I would hear secondhand accounts of how folks had sometimes yelled at one another during staff meetings, the result of legitimate policy disputes, bureaucratic turf battles, anonymous leaks to the press, the absence of weekends, or too many late-night meals of pizza or chili from the Navy Mess on the ground floor of the West Wing. None of this tension spilled into real rancor or kept the work from getting done. Whether due to professionalism, or respect for the presidency, or awareness of what failure might mean for the country, or a solidarity forged from being a collective target for the escalating attacks from all quarters, everyone more or less held it together as we waited for some sign, any sign, that our plans for ending the crisis were in fact going to work.

And finally, in late April, it came. Tim dropped by the Oval one day to tell me that the Federal Reserve, which had remained tight-lipped throughout its review of the banks, had at long last given Treasury a preliminary look at the stress-test results.

"So?" I said, trying to read Tim's expression. "How does it look?"

"Well, the numbers are still subject to some revisions . . ."

I threw up my hands in mock exasperation.

"Better than expected, Mr. President," Tim said.

"Meaning?"

"Meaning we may have turned the corner."

Of the nineteen systemically significant institutions subjected to the stress test, the Fed had given nine a clean bill of health, determining that they wouldn't need to raise more capital. Five other banks required more capital to meet the Fed's benchmark but nonetheless appeared sturdy enough to raise it from private sources. This left five institutions (including Bank of America, Citigroup, and GMAC, the financing arm of General Motors) that were likely to need additional government support. According to the Fed, the collective shortfall looked to be no more than $75 billion—an amount that our remaining TARP funds could comfortably cover if required.

"Never a doubt," I said, deadpan, when Tim was finished briefing me.

It was the first smile I'd seen on his face in weeks.

If Tim felt vindicated by the results of the stress test, he didn't let it show. (He did admit several years later that hearing Larry Summers utter the words "You were right" was pretty satisfying.) As it was, we kept the early information within our tight circle; the last thing we needed was premature celebration. But when the

Fed released its final report two weeks later, its conclusions hadn't changed, and despite some continued skepticism from political commentators, the audience that mattered—the financial markets—found the audit rigorous and credible, inspiring a new rush of confidence. Investors began pumping cash back into financial institutions almost as fast as they'd pulled it out. Corporations found they could borrow again to finance their day-to-day operations. Just as fear had compounded the very real losses the banks had suffered from the subprime lending binge, the stress test—along with massive assurances from the U.S. government—had jolted markets back into rational territory. By June, the ten troubled financial institutions had raised over $66 billion in private capital, leaving only a $9 billion shortfall. The Fed's emergency liquidity fund was able to cut its investment in the financial system by more than two-thirds. And the country's nine largest banks had paid back the U.S. Treasury, returning the $67 billion in TARP funds they'd received—with interest.

Almost nine months after the fall of Lehman Brothers, the panic appeared to be over.

MORE THAN A DECADE has passed since those perilous days at the start of my presidency, and although the details are hazy for most Americans, my administration's handling of the financial crisis still generates fierce debate. Viewed narrowly, it's hard to argue with the results of our actions. Not only did the U.S. banking sector stabilize far sooner than any of its European counterparts; the financial system and the overall economy returned to growth faster than those of just about any other nation in history after such a significant shock. If I had predicted on the day of my swearing in that within a year the U.S. financial system would have stabilized, almost all TARP funds would be fully repaid (having actually **made** rather than cost taxpayers money), and the economy would have begun what would become the longest stretch of continuous growth and job creation in U.S. history, the majority of pundits and experts would have questioned my mental fitness—or assumed I was smoking something stronger than tobacco.

For many thoughtful critics, though, the fact that I had engineered a return to pre-crisis normalcy is precisely the problem—a missed opportunity, if not a flat-out betrayal. According to this view, the financial crisis offered me a once-in-a-generation chance to reset the standards for normalcy, remaking not just the financial system but the American economy overall. If only I had broken up the big banks and sent some white-collar culprits to jail; if only I had put an end to outsized pay packages and Wall Street's heads-I-win, tails-you-lose culture, then maybe today we'd have a more equitable system that served the interests of working families rather than a handful of billionaires.

I understand such frustrations. In many ways, I share them. To this day, I survey reports of America's escalating inequality, its reduced upward mobility and still-stagnant wages, with all the consequent anger and distortions such trends stir in our democracy, and I wonder whether I should have been bolder in those early months, willing to exact more economic pain in the short term in pursuit of a permanently altered and more just economic order.

The thought nags at me. And yet even if it were possible for me to go back in time and get a do-over, I can't say that I would make different choices. In the abstract, all the various alternatives and missed opportunities that the critics offer up sound plausible, simple plot points in a morality tale. But when you dig into the details, each of the options they propose—whether nationalization of the banks, or stretching the definitions of criminal statutes to prosecute banking executives, or simply letting a portion of the banking system collapse so as to avoid moral hazard—would have required a violence to the social order, a wrenching of political and economic norms, that almost certainly would have made things worse. Not worse for the wealthy and powerful, who always have a way of landing on their feet. Worse for the very folks I'd be purporting to save. Best-case scenario, the economy would have taken longer to recover, with more unemployment, more foreclosures, more business closures. Worst-case scenario, we might have tipped into a full-scale depression.

Someone with a more revolutionary soul might respond that all this would have been worth it, that you have to break eggs to make an omelet. But as willing as I had always been to disrupt my own life in pursuit of an idea, I wasn't willing to take those same risks with the well-being of millions of people. In that sense, my first hundred days in office revealed a basic strand of my political character. I was a reformer, conservative in temperament if not in vision. Whether I was demonstrating wisdom or weakness would be for others to judge.

And anyway, such ruminations came later. In the summer of 2009, the race had only just started. Once the economy was stabilized, I knew I'd have more time to push through the structural changes—in taxes, education, energy, healthcare, labor law, and immigration—that I had campaigned on, changes that would make the system fundamentally more fair and expand opportunity for ordinary Americans. Already, Tim and his team were preparing options for a comprehensive Wall Street reform package that I would later present to Congress.

In the meantime, I tried to remind myself that we had steered the nation away from disaster, that our work was already providing some form of relief. Expanded unemployment insurance payments were keeping families across the country afloat. Tax cuts for small businesses were allowing a few more workers to stay on the payroll. Teachers were in classrooms, and cops were on the beat. An auto factory that had threatened to close was still open, while a mortgage refinancing was keeping someone out there from losing a home.

The absence of catastrophe, the preservation of normalcy, wouldn't attract attention. Most of the people impacted wouldn't even know how our policies had touched their lives. But every so often, while reading in the Treaty Room late at night, I'd come across a letter in my purple folder that began with something like this:

Dear President Obama,

I'm sure you'll never read this, but I thought you might want to know that a program you started has been a real lifesaver . . .

I'd set down the letter after reading it and pull out a note card to write the person a brief response. I imagined them getting the official envelope from the White House and opening it up with a look of puzzlement, then a smile. They'd show it to their family, maybe even take it to work. Eventually the letter would fall into a drawer somewhere, forgotten under the accumulation of the new joys and pains that make up a life. That was okay. I couldn't expect people to understand how much their voices actually meant to me—how they had sustained my spirit and beat back whispering doubts on those late, solitary nights.

CHAPTER 13

BEFORE I WAS INAUGURATED, Denis McDonough, my senior campaign foreign policy staffer and soon-to-be head of strategic communications for the National Security Council, insisted that I carve out thirty minutes for what he considered a top-tier priority.

"We need to make sure you can deliver a proper salute."

Denis himself had never served in the military, although there was an order to his movements, a deliberateness and focus, that made some people assume he had. Tall and angular, with a jutting jaw, deep-set eyes, and graying hair that made him appear older than his thirty-nine years, he'd grown up in the small town of Stillwater, Minnesota, one of eleven children in a working-class Irish Catholic family. After graduating from college, he'd traveled through Latin America and taught high school in Belize, gone back to get his master's degree in international affairs, and worked for Tom Daschle, then the Democratic leader in the Senate. In 2007, we'd recruited Denis to serve as a foreign policy staffer in my Senate office, and over the course of the campaign Denis had assumed more and more responsibility—helping me prepare for debates, putting together briefing books, organizing every aspect of my preconvention foreign tour, and endlessly jousting with the traveling press corps.

Even in a team full of type A personalities, Denis stood out. He sweated the details; volunteered for the most difficult, thankless tasks; and could not be outworked: During the Iowa campaign, he spent what little spare time he had canvassing door-to-door, famously shoveling snow for folks after a particularly bad storm, hoping to win their commitment to caucus for me. The same disregard for his own physical well-being that had helped him make his college football team as an undersized strong safety could lead to problems—in the White House, I once had to order him to go home after learning that he'd worked twelve straight hours with a bout of the flu. I came to suspect a religious aspect to this intensity, and though an iconoclastic streak (as well as an adoration of his wife, Kari) led him to steer clear of the collar, he approached his work both as a form of service and as self-abnegation.

Now, as part of his good works here on earth, Denis had taken it upon himself to get me ready for my first day as commander in chief. On the eve of my inauguration, he invited two military guys—including Matt Flavin, a young navy veteran who would serve as my White House veterans affairs staffer—to the transition office to put me through my paces. They started by showing me a bunch of photos of previous presidential salutes that did not make the grade—weak wrists, curled fingers, George W. Bush trying to salute while carrying his dog under his arm. They then evaluated my own form, which was apparently not stellar.

"Elbow a little farther out, sir," said one.

"Fingers tighter, sir," said the other. "The tips should be right at your eyebrow."

After twenty minutes or so, though, my tutors seemed satisfied. Once they'd left, I turned to Denis.

"Anything else you're nervous about?" I teased.

Denis shook his head unconvincingly. "Not nervous, Mr. President-Elect. Just want us to be prepared."

"For what?"

Denis smiled. "For everything."

IT'S A TRUISM that a president's single most important job is to keep the American people safe. Depending on your political predispositions and electoral mandate, you may have a burning desire to fix public education or restore prayer in schools, raise the minimum wage or break the power of public sector unions. But whether Republican or Democrat, the one thing every president must obsess over, the source of chronic, unrelenting tension that burrows deep inside you from the moment you're elected, is the awareness that everybody is depending on you to protect them.

How you approach the task depends on how you define the threats that the country faces. What do we fear most? Is it the possibility of a Russian nuclear attack, or that a bureaucratic miscalculation or glitch in the software launches one of our warheads by mistake? Is it some fanatic blowing himself up on a subway, or the government, under the guise of protecting you from fanatics, tapping into your email account? Is it a gas shortage caused by disruptions to foreign oil supplies, or the oceans rising and the planet frying? Is it an immigrant family sneaking across a river in search of a better life, or a pandemic disease, incubated by poverty and a lack of public services in a poor country overseas, drifting invisibly into our homes?

For most of the twentieth century, for most Americans, the what and why of our national defense seemed pretty straightforward. We lived with the possibility of being attacked by another great power, or being drawn into a conflict between great powers, or having America's vital interests—as defined by the wise men in Washington—threatened by some foreign actor. After World War II, there were the Soviets and the Communist Chinese and their (real or perceived) proxies, ostensibly intent on world domination and threatening our way of life. And then came terrorist attacks emanating from the Middle East, at first on the periphery of our vision, scary but manageable, until just months into a brand-new century, the sight of the Twin Towers crumbling to dust made our worst fears manifest.

I grew up with many of these fears imprinted on me. In Hawaii, I knew families who'd lost loved ones at Pearl Harbor. My grandfather, his brother, and my grandmother's brother had all fought in World War II. I was raised believing that nuclear war was a very real possibility. In grade school, I watched coverage of Olympic athletes being slaughtered by masked men in Munich; in college, I listened to Ted Koppel marking the number of days Americans were being held hostage in Iran. Too young to have known the anguish of Vietnam firsthand, I had witnessed only the honor and restraint of our service members during the Gulf War, and like most Americans I viewed our military operations in Afghanistan after 9/11 as both necessary and just.

But another set of stories had also been etched into me—different though not contradictory—about what America meant to those living in the world beyond it, the symbolic power of a country built upon the ideals of freedom. I remember being seven or eight years old and sitting on the cool floor tiles of our house on the outskirts of Jakarta, proudly showing my friends a picture book of Honolulu with its high-rises and city lights and wide, paved roads. I would never forget the wonder in their faces as I answered their questions about life in America, explaining how everybody got to go to a school with plenty of books, and there were no beggars because most everyone had a job and enough to eat. Later, as a young man, I witnessed my mother's impact as a contractor with organizations like USAID, helping women in remote Asian villages get access to credit, and the lasting gratitude those women felt that Americans an ocean away actually cared about their plight. When I first visited Kenya, I sat with newfound relatives who told me how much they admired American democracy and rule of law—a contrast, they said, to the tribalism and corruption that plagued their country.

Such moments taught me to see my country through the eyes of others. I was reminded of how lucky I was to be an American, to take none of those blessings for granted. I saw firsthand the power our example exerted on the hearts and minds of people around the world. But with that came a corollary lesson: an awareness of what we risked when our actions failed to live up to our image and our ideals, the anger and resentment this could breed, the damage that was done. When I heard Indonesians talk about the hundreds of thousands slaughtered in a coup—widely believed to have CIA backing—that had brought a military dictatorship to power in 1967, or listened to Latin American environmental activists detailing how U.S. companies were befouling their countryside, or commiserated with Indian American or Pakistani American friends as they chronicled the countless times that they'd been pulled aside for "random" searches at airports since 9/11, I felt America's defenses weakening, saw chinks in the armor that I was sure over time made our country less safe.

That dual vision, as much as my skin color, distinguished me from previous presidents. For my supporters, it was a defining foreign policy strength, enabling me to amplify America's influence around the world and anticipate problems that might arise from ill-considered policies. For my detractors, it was evidence of weakness, raising the possibility that I might hesitate to advance American interests because of a lack of conviction, or even divided loyalties. For some of my fellow citizens, it was far worse than that. Having the son of a black African with a Muslim name and socialist ideas ensconced in the White House with the full force of the U.S. government under his command was precisely the thing they wanted to be defended against.

AS FOR THE senior ranks of my national security team, they all considered themselves internationalists to one degree or another: They believed that American leadership was necessary to keep the world moving in a better direction, and that our influence came in many forms. Even the more liberal members of my team, like Denis, had no qualms about the use of "hard power" to go after terrorists and were scornful of leftist critics who made a living blaming the United States for every problem around the globe. Meanwhile, the most hawkish members of my team understood the importance of public diplomacy and considered the exercise of so-called soft power, like foreign aid and student exchange programs, to be essential ingredients in an effective U.S. foreign policy.

The question was one of emphasis. How much concern did we have for the people beyond our borders, and how much should we simply worry about our own citizens? How much was our fate actually tied to the fate of people abroad? To what extent should America bind itself to multilateral institutions like the United Nations, and to what extent should we go it alone in pursuit of our own interests? Should we align ourselves with authoritarian governments that help keep a lid on possible chaos—or was the smarter long-term play to champion the forces of democratic reform?

How members of my administration lined up on these issues wasn't always predictable. But in our internal debates, I could detect a certain generational divide. With the exception of Susan Rice, my youthful U.N. ambassador, all of my national security principals—Secretaries Gates and Clinton, CIA director Leon Panetta, members of the Joint Chiefs of Staff, as well as my national security advisor, Jim Jones, and my director of national intelligence, Denny Blair—had come of age during the height of the Cold War and had spent decades as part of Washington's national security establishment: a dense, interlocking network of current and former White House policy makers, congressional staffers, academics, heads of think tanks, Pentagon brass, newspaper columnists, military contractors, and lobbyists. For them, a responsible foreign policy meant continuity, predictability, and an unwillingness to stray too far from conventional wisdom. It was this impulse that had led most of them to support the U.S. invasion of Iraq; and if the resulting disaster had forced them to reconsider that particular decision, they were still not inclined to ask whether the bipartisan rush into Iraq indicated the need for a fundamental overhaul of America's national security framework.

The younger members of my national security team, including most of the NSC staff, had different ideas. No less patriotic than their bosses, seared by both the horrors of 9/11 and the images of Iraqi prisoners abused by U.S. military personnel at Abu Ghraib, many of them had gravitated to my campaign precisely because I was willing to challenge the assumptions of what we often referred to as "the Washington playbook," whether it was on Middle East policy, our posture on Cuba, our unwillingness to engage adversaries diplomatically, the importance of restoring legal guardrails in the fight against terror, or the elevation of human rights, international development, and climate change from acts of altruism to central aspects of our national security. None of these younger staffers were firebrands, and they respected the institutional knowledge of those with deep foreign policy experience. But they made no apologies for wanting to break from some of the constraints of the past in pursuit of something better.

At times, friction between the new and the old guard inside my foreign policy team would spill into the open. When it did, the media tended to attribute it to a youthful impertinence among my staff and a lack of basic understanding about how Washington worked. That wasn't the case. In fact, it was precisely because staffers like Denis **did** know how Washington worked—because they'd witnessed how the foreign policy bureaucracy could slow-walk, misinterpret, bury, badly execute, or otherwise resist new directions from a president—that they would often end up butting heads with the Pentagon, State Department, and CIA.

And in that sense, the tensions that emerged within our foreign policy team were a product of my own design, a way for me to work through the tensions in my own head. I imagined myself on the bridge of an aircraft carrier, certain that America needed to steer a new course but entirely dependent on a more seasoned and sometimes skeptical crew to execute that change, mindful that there were limits to what the vessel could do and that too sharp a turn could lead to disaster. With the stakes as high as they were, I was coming to realize that leadership, particularly in the national security arena, was about more than executing well-reasoned policy. Awareness of custom and ritual mattered. Symbols and protocol mattered. Body language mattered.

I worked on my salute.

AT THE START of each day of my presidency, I would find a leather binder waiting for me at the breakfast table. Michelle called it "The Death, Destruction, and Horrible Things Book," though officially it was known as the President's Daily Brief, or PDB. Top secret, usually about ten to fifteen pages in length, and prepared overnight by the CIA in concert with the other intelligence agencies, the PDB was intended to provide the president a summary of world events and intelligence analysis, particularly anything that was likely to affect America's national security. On a given day, I might read about terrorist cells in Somalia or unrest in Iraq or the fact that the Chinese or Russians were developing new weapons systems. Nearly always, there was mention of potential terrorist plots, no matter how vague, thinly sourced, or unactionable—a form of due diligence on the part of the intelligence community, meant to avoid the kind of second-guessing that had transpired after 9/11. Much of the time, what I read in the PDB required no immediate response. The goal was to have a continuously up-to-date sense of all that was roiling in the world, the large, small, and sometimes barely perceptible shifts that threatened to upset whatever equilibrium we were trying to maintain.

After reading the PDB, I'd head down to the Oval for a live version of the briefing with members of the NSC and national intelligence staffs, where we'd go over any items considered urgent. The men running those briefings—Jim Jones and Denny Blair—were former four-star officers I'd first met while serving in the Senate (Jones had been Supreme Allied Commander for Europe, while Blair had recently retired from his role as navy admiral in charge of Pacific Command). They looked the part—tall and fit, with close-cropped graying hair and ramrod straight bearings—and although I had originally consulted with them on military matters, both prided themselves on having an expansive view of what constituted national security priorities. Jones, for example, cared deeply about Africa and the Middle East, and following his military retirement he had been involved in security efforts in the West Bank and Gaza. Blair had written extensively on the role of economic and cultural diplomacy in managing a rising China. As a result, the two of them would occasionally arrange for analysts and experts to attend morning PDB sessions and brief me on big-picture, long-term topics: the implications of economic growth in sustaining democratization in sub-Saharan Africa, say, or the possible effects of climate change on future regional conflicts.

More often, though, our morning discussions focused on current or potential mayhem: coups, nuclear weapons, violent protests, border conflicts, and, most of all, war.

The war in Afghanistan, soon to be the longest in American history.

The war in Iraq, where nearly 150,000 American troops were still deployed.

The war against al-Qaeda, which was actively recruiting converts, building a network of affiliates, and plotting attacks inspired by the ideology of Osama bin Laden.

The cumulative costs of what both the Bush administration and the media described as a single, comprehensive "war against terrorism" had been staggering: almost a trillion dollars spent, more than three thousand U.S. troops killed, as many as ten times that number wounded. The toll on Iraqi and Afghan civilians was even higher. The Iraq campaign in particular had divided the country and strained alliances. Meanwhile, the use of extraordinary renditions, black sites, waterboarding, indefinite detention without trial at Guantánamo, and expanded domestic surveillance in the broader fight against terrorism had led people inside and outside the United States to question our nation's commitment to the rule of law.

I'd put forward what I considered to be clear positions on all these issues during the campaign. But that had been from the cheap seats, before I had hundreds of thousands of troops and a sprawling national security infrastructure under my command. Any terrorist attack would now happen on my watch. Any American lives lost or compromised, at home or abroad, would weigh uniquely on my conscience. These were my wars now.

My immediate goal was to review each aspect of our military strategy so that we could take a thoughtful approach to what came next. Thanks to the Status of Forces Agreement (SOFA) that President Bush and Prime Minister Maliki had signed about a month before my inauguration, the broad outlines of a U.S. withdrawal from Iraq had largely been settled. American combat forces needed to be out of Iraqi cities and villages by the end of June 2009, and all U.S. forces would leave the country by the end of 2011. The only question remaining was whether we could or should move faster than that. During the campaign, I had committed to withdrawing U.S. combat forces from Iraq within sixteen months of taking office, but after the election I had told Bob Gates that I'd be willing to show flexibility on the pace of withdrawal so long as we stayed within the SOFA parameters—an acknowledgment that ending a war was an imprecise business, that commanders who were knee-deep in the fighting deserved some deference when it came to tactical decisions, and that new presidents couldn't simply tear up agreements reached by their predecessors.

In February, Gates and our newly installed commander in Iraq, General Ray Odierno, presented me with a plan that withdrew U.S. combat forces from the country in nineteen months—three months later than I had proposed during the campaign but four months sooner than what military commanders were asking for. The plan also called for maintaining a residual force of fifty to fifty-five thousand noncombat U.S. personnel, which would remain in the country till the end of 2011, to train and assist the Iraqi military. Some in the White House questioned the necessity of the extra three months and the large residual force, reminding me that both congressional Democrats and the American people strongly favored an accelerated exit, not a delay.

I approved Odierno's plan anyway, traveling to Camp Lejeune, in North Carolina, to announce the decision before several thousand cheering Marines. As firmly as I had opposed the original decision to invade, I believed America now had both a strategic and a humanitarian interest in Iraq's stability. With combat troops scheduled to leave Iraq's population centers in just five months per the SOFA, our service members' exposure to heavy fighting, snipers, and improvised explosive devices (IEDs) would be greatly diminished as we progressed with the rest of the drawdown. And given the fragility of Iraq's new government, the ragged state of its security forces, the still-active presence of al-Qaeda in Iraq (AQI), and the sky-high levels of sectarian hostility sizzling inside the country, it made sense to use the presence of residual forces as a kind of insurance policy against a return to chaos. "Once we're out," I told Rahm, explaining my decision, "the last thing I want is for us to have to go back in."

IF ARRIVING AT a plan for Iraq was relatively straightforward, finding our way out of Afghanistan was anything but.

Unlike the war in Iraq, the Afghan campaign had always seemed to me a war of necessity. Though the Taliban's ambitions were confined to Afghanistan, their leadership remained loosely allied to al-Qaeda, and their return to power could result in the country once again serving as a launching pad for terrorist attacks against the United States and its allies. Moreover, Pakistan had shown neither the capacity nor the will to dislodge al-Qaeda's leadership from its current sanctuary in a remote, mountainous, and barely governed region straddling the Afghanistan-Pakistan border. This meant that our ability to pin down and ultimately destroy the terrorist network depended on the Afghan government's willingness to let U.S. military and intelligence teams operate in its territory.

Unfortunately the six-year diversion of U.S. attention and resources to Iraq had left the situation in Afghanistan more perilous. Despite the fact that we had more than thirty thousand U.S. troops on the ground and an almost equal number of international coalition troops there, the Taliban controlled large swaths of the country, particularly in the regions along the border with Pakistan.

In places where U.S. or coalition forces weren't present, Taliban fighters overwhelmed a far larger but badly trained Afghan army. Meanwhile, mismanagement and rampant corruption inside the police force, district governorships, and key ministries had eroded the legitimacy of Hamid Karzai's government and siphoned off foreign aid dollars desperately needed to improve living conditions for one of the world's poorest populations.

The lack of a coherent U.S. strategy didn't help matters. Depending on who you talked to, our mission in Afghanistan was either narrow (wiping out al-Qaeda) or broad (transforming the country into a modern, democratic state that would be aligned with the West). Our Marines and soldiers repeatedly cleared the Taliban from an area only to see their efforts squandered for lack of even halfway-capable local governance. Whether because of overambition, corruption, or lack of Afghan buy-in, U.S.-sponsored development programs often failed to deliver as promised, while the issuance of massive U.S. contracts to some of Kabul's shadiest business operators undermined the very anti-corruption efforts designed to win over the Afghan people.

In light of all this, I told Gates that my first priority was to make sure our agencies, both civilian and military, were aligned around a clearly defined mission and a coordinated strategy. He didn't disagree. As a CIA deputy director in the 1980s, Gates had helped oversee the arming of the Afghan mujahideen in their fight against the Soviet occupation of their country. The experience of watching that loosely organized insurgency bleed the mighty Red Army into retreat—only to have elements of that same insurgency later evolve into al-Qaeda—had made Gates mindful of the unintended consequences that could result from rash actions. Unless we established limited and realistic objectives, he told me, "we'll set ourselves up for failure."

The chairman of the Joint Chiefs of Staff, Admiral Mike Mullen, also saw the need for a revamped Afghan strategy. But there was a catch: He and our military commanders first wanted me to authorize the immediate deployment of an additional thirty thousand U.S. troops.

In fairness to Mullen, the request, which had come from the International Security Assistance Force (ISAF) commander in Afghanistan, General Dave McKiernan, had been pending for several months. During the transition, President Bush had put out feelers to see if we wanted him to order the deployment before I took office, but we'd indicated that our preference was to hold off until the incoming team had fully assessed the situation. According to Mullen, McKiernan's request could no longer wait.

At our first full NSC meeting, held in the White House Situation Room (often referred to as "the Sit Room") just two days after my inauguration, Mullen had explained that the Taliban were likely to mount a summer offensive and we'd want additional brigades on the ground in time to try to blunt it. He reported that McKiernan was also worried about providing adequate security for the presidential election, which was originally scheduled for May but would be postponed until August. If we wanted to get troops there in time to achieve those missions, Mullen told me, we needed to put things in motion immediately.

Thanks to the movies, I'd always imagined the Sit

Room as a cavernous, futuristic space, ringed by ceiling-high screens full of high-resolution satellite and radar images and teeming with smartly dressed personnel manning banks of state-of-the-art gizmos and gadgets. The reality was less dazzling: just a small, nondescript conference room, part of a warren of other small rooms wedged into a corner of the West Wing's first floor. Its windows were sealed off with plain wooden shutters; its walls were bare except for digital clocks showing the time in various world capitals and a few flat-screens not much bigger than those found in a neighborhood sports bar. Quarters were close. The principal council members sat around a long conference table, with various deputies and staff crammed into chairs lining the sides of the room.

"Just so I understand," I said to Mullen, trying not to sound too skeptical, "after almost five years where we managed with twenty thousand or fewer U.S. troops, and after adding another ten thousand over the past twenty months or so, it's the Pentagon's assessment that we can't wait another two months before deciding to **double** our troop commitment?" I pointed out that I wasn't averse to sending more troops—during the campaign, I had pledged an additional two brigades for Afghanistan once the Iraq withdrawal was under way. But given that everyone in the room had just agreed that we should bring in a well-regarded former CIA analyst and Middle East expert named Bruce Riedel to lead a sixty-day review meant to shape our Afghan strategy going forward, sending another thirty thousand U.S. troops to Afghanistan before the review was complete felt like a case of putting the cart before the horse. I asked

Mullen ·whether a smaller deployment could serve as a sufficient bridge.

He told me that ultimately it was my decision, adding pointedly that any reduction in the number or further delay would substantially increase risk.

I let others chime in. David Petraeus, who was coming off his success in Iraq and had been elevated to the head of Central Command (which oversaw all military missions in the Middle East and Central Asia, including Iraq and Afghanistan), urged me to approve McKiernan's request. So did Hillary and Panetta, which didn't surprise me: As effective as the two of them would turn out to be in managing their agencies, their hawkish instincts and political backgrounds left them perpetually wary of opposing any recommendation that came from the Pentagon. In private, Gates had expressed to me that he felt some ambivalence about such a significant increase to our Afghan footprint. But given his institutional role, I didn't expect him to directly countermand a recommendation from the chiefs.

Among the principals, only Joe Biden voiced his misgivings. He had traveled to Kabul on my behalf during the transition, and what he saw and heard on the trip—particularly during a contentious meeting with Karzai—had convinced him that we needed to rethink our entire approach to Afghanistan. I knew Joe also still felt burned by having supported the Iraq invasion years earlier. Whatever the mix of reasons, he saw Afghanistan as a dangerous quagmire and urged me to delay a deployment, suggesting it would be easier to put troops in once we had a clear strategy as opposed to trying to pull troops out after we'd made a mess with a bad one.

Rather than deciding on the spot, I assigned Tom Donilon to convene the NSC deputies over the course of the following week to determine more precisely how additional troops would be used and whether deploying them by summer was even possible logistically. We'd revisit the issue, I said, once we had the answer. With the meeting adjourned, I headed out the door and was on my way up the stairs to the Oval when Joe caught up to me and gripped my arm.

"Listen to me, boss," he said. "Maybe I've been around this town for too long, but one thing I know is when these generals are trying to box in a new president." He brought his face a few inches from mine and stage-whispered, "Don't let them jam you."

IN LATER ACCOUNTS of our Afghanistan deliberations, Gates and others would peg Biden as one of the ringleaders who poisoned relations between the White House and the Pentagon. The truth was that I considered Joe to be doing me a service by asking tough questions about the military's plans. Having at least one contrarian in the room made us all think harder about the issues—and I noticed that everyone was a bit freer with their opinions when that contrarian wasn't me.

I never questioned Mullen's motives, or those of the other chiefs and combatant commanders who made up the military's leadership. I found Mullen—a Los Angeles native whose parents had worked in the entertainment business—to be consistently affable, prepared, responsive, and professional. His vice chairman, Marine four-star general James "Hoss" Cartwright, had the sort of self-effacing, pensive manner you wouldn't associate with a former fighter pilot, but when he did speak up, he was full of detailed insights and creative solutions across a whole set of national security problems. Despite differences in temperament, both Mullen and Cartwright shared attributes I found common among the top brass: white men (the military had just one woman and one Black four-star general when I took office) in their late fifties or early sixties who had spent decades working their way up the ranks, amassing stellar service records and, in many cases, advanced academic degrees. Their views of the world were informed and sophisticated, and contrary to the stereotypes, they understood all too well the limits of military action, because of and not despite the fact that they had commanded troops under fire. In fact, during my eight years as president, it was often the generals, rather than civilians, who counseled restraint when it came to the use of force.

Still, men like Mullen were creatures of the system to which they'd devoted their entire adult lives—a U.S. military that prided itself on accomplishing a mission once started, without regard to cost, duration, or whether the mission was the right one to begin with. In Iraq, that had meant an escalating need for more of everything: more troops, more bases, more private contractors, more aircraft, and more intelligence, surveillance, and reconnaissance (ISR). More had not produced victory, but it had at least avoided humiliating defeat and had salvaged the country from total collapse. Now, with Afghanistan looking like it, too, was sliding into a sinkhole, it was perhaps natural that the military leadership wanted more there as well. And because until recently they'd been working with a president who had rarely questioned their plans or denied their requests, it was probably inevitable that the debate over "how much more" would become a recurring source of strife between the Pentagon and my White House.

In mid-February, Donilon reported that the deputies had scrubbed General McKiernan's request and concluded that no more than seventeen thousand troops, along with four thousand military trainers, could be deployed in time to have a meaningful impact on the summer fighting season or Afghan election security. Although we were still a month away from completing our formal review, all the principals except Biden recommended that we deploy that number of troops immediately. I gave the order on February 17, the same day I signed the Recovery Act, having determined that even the most conservative strategy we might come up with would need the additional manpower, and knowing that we still had ten thousand troops in reserve if circumstances required their deployment as well.

A month later, Riedel and his team completed their report. Their assessment offered no surprises, but it did help articulate our principal goal: "to disrupt, dismantle, and defeat al-Qaeda in Pakistan and Afghanistan and to prevent their return to either country in the future."

The report's added emphasis on Pakistan was key: Not only did the Pakistan military (and in particular its intelligence arm, ISI) tolerate the presence of Taliban headquarters and leadership in Quetta, near the Pakistani border, but it was also quietly assisting the Taliban as a means of keeping the Afghan government weak and hedging against Kabul's potential alignment with Pakistan's archrival, India. That the U.S. government had long tolerated such behavior from a purported ally—supporting it with billions of dollars in military and economic aid despite its complicity with violent extremists and its record as a significant and irresponsible proliferator of nuclear weapons technology in the world—said something about the pretzel-like logic of U.S. foreign policy. In the short term, at least, a complete cutoff of military aid to Pakistan wasn't an option, since not only did we rely on overland routes through Pakistan to supply our Afghan operations but the Pakistani government also tacitly facilitated our counterterrorism efforts against al-Qaeda camps within its territory. The Riedel report, though, made one thing clear: Unless Pakistan stopped sheltering the Taliban, our efforts at long-term stability in Afghanistan were bound to fail.

The rest of the report's recommendations centered on building capacity. We needed to drastically improve the Karzai government's ability to govern and provide basic services. We needed to train up the Afghan army and police force so that they would be competent and large enough to maintain security within the country's borders without help from U.S. forces. Exactly how we were going to do all that remained vague. What was clear, though, was that the U.S. commitment the Riedel report was calling for went well beyond a bare-bones counter-terrorism strategy and toward a form of nation-building that probably would have made sense—had we started seven years earlier, the moment we drove the Taliban out of Kabul.

Of course, that's not what we had done. Instead, we had invaded Iraq, broken **that** country, helped spawn an even more virulent branch of al-Qaeda, and been forced to improvise a costly counterinsurgency campaign there. As far as Afghanistan was concerned, those years were lost. Due to the continuing, often valiant efforts of our troops, diplomats, and aid workers on the ground, it was an exaggeration to say that we'd have to start from scratch in Afghanistan. But it nonetheless dawned on me that even in the best-case scenario—even if Karzai cooperated, Pakistan behaved, and our goals were limited to what Gates liked to call "Afghan good enough"—we were still looking at three to five years of intense effort, costing hundreds of billions more dollars and more American lives.

I didn't like the deal. But in what was becoming a pattern, the alternatives were worse. The stakes involved—the risks of a possible collapse of the Afghan government or the Taliban gaining footholds in major cities—were simply too high for us not to act. On March 27, just four weeks after announcing the Iraqi withdrawal plan, I appeared on television with my national security team behind me and laid out our "Af-Pak" strategy based largely on the Riedel recommendations. I knew how the announcement would land. A number of commentators would quickly seize on the irony that having run for the presidency as an antiwar candidate, I had so far sent more troops into combat than I had brought home.

Along with the troop increase, there was one other change in our Afghan posture that Gates asked me to make, one that frankly took me by surprise: In April, during one of our Oval Office meetings, he recommended that we replace our existing commander in Afghanistan, General McKiernan, with Lieutenant General Stanley McChrystal, the former commander of Joint Special Operations Command (JSOC) and current director of the Joint Chiefs.

"Dave's a fine soldier," Gates said, acknowledging that McKiernan had done nothing wrong and that changing a commanding general in the middle of a war was a highly unusual step. "But he's a manager. In an environment this challenging, we need someone with different skills. I couldn't sleep at night, Mr. President, if I didn't make sure our troops had the best possible commander leading them. And I'm convinced Stan McChrystal's that person."

It was easy to see why Gates thought so highly of McChrystal. Within the U.S. military, members of Special Ops were considered a breed apart, an elite warrior class that carried out the most difficult missions under the most dangerous circumstances—the guys in the movies rappelling from helicopters into enemy territory or making amphibious landings under cover of darkness. And within that exalted circle, no one was more admired or elicited more loyalty than McChrystal. A West Point graduate, he'd consistently excelled over the course of a thirty-three-year career. As JSOC commander, he'd help transform Special Ops into a central element in America's defense strategy, personally overseeing dozens of counterterrorism operations that had dismantled much of AQI and killed its founder, Abu Musab al-Zarqawi. Rumor had it that at fifty-four, he still trained with Rangers half his age, and from the looks of him when he stopped by the Oval with Gates for a courtesy visit, I believed it—the man was all muscle, sinew, and bone, with a long, angular face and a piercing, avian gaze. In fact, McChrystal's whole manner was that of someone who's burned away frivolity and distractions from his life. With me, at least, that included small talk: During our conversation, it was mostly "Yes, sir" and "No, sir" and "I'm confident we can get the job done."

I was sold. The change, when announced, was well received, with commentators drawing parallels between McChrystal and David Petraeus—battlefield innovators who could turn a war around. Senate confirmation was swift, and in mid-June, as McChrystal (now a four-star general) prepared to assume command of coalition forces in Afghanistan, Gates asked him to provide us with a fresh, top-to-bottom assessment of conditions there within sixty days, along with recommendations for any changes in strategy, organization, or resourcing of coalition efforts.

Little did I know what this seemingly routine request would bring.

ONE AFTERNOON a couple of months after the Af-Pak announcement, I walked alone across the South Lawn—trailed by a military aide carrying the football and my veterans affairs staffer, Matt Flavin—to board the Marine One helicopter and make the brief flight to Maryland for the first of what would be regular visits to Bethesda Naval Hospital and Walter Reed Army Medical Center. On arrival, I was greeted by commanders of the facility, who gave me a quick overview of the number and condition of wounded warriors on-site before leading me through a maze of stairs, elevators, and corridors to the main patients' ward.

For the next hour, I proceeded from room to room, sanitizing my hands and donning scrubs and surgical gloves where necessary, stopping in the hallway to get some background on the recovering service member from hospital staffers before knocking softly on the door.

Though patients at the hospitals came from every branch of the military, many who were there during my first few years in office were members of the U.S. Army and Marine Corps that patrolled the insurgent-dominated areas of Iraq and Afghanistan and had been injured by gunfire or IEDs. Almost all were male and working-class: whites from small rural towns or fading manufacturing hubs, Blacks and Hispanics from cities like Houston or Trenton, Asian Americans and Pacific Islanders from California. Usually they had family members sitting with them—mostly parents, grandparents, and siblings, though if the service member was older, there would be a wife and kids too—toddlers squirming in laps, five-year-olds with toy cars, teenagers playing video games. As soon as I entered the room, everyone would shift around, smiling shyly, appearing not quite sure what to do. For me, this was one of the vagaries of the job, the fact that my presence reliably caused a disruption and a bout of nervousness among those I was meeting. I tried always to lighten the mood, doing what I could to put people at ease.

Unless fully incapacitated, the service members would usually raise their bed upright, sometimes pulling themselves to a seated position by reaching for the sturdy metal handle on the bedpost. Several insisted on hopping out of bed, often balancing on their good leg to salute and shake my hand. I'd ask them about their hometown and how long they'd been in the service. I'd ask them how they got their injury and how soon they might be starting rehab or be getting fitted for a prosthetic. We often talked sports, and some would ask me to sign a unit flag hung on the wall, and I'd give each service member a commemorative challenge coin. Then we'd all position ourselves around the bed as Pete Souza took pictures with his camera and with their phones, and Matt would give out business cards so they could call him personally at the White House if they needed anything at all.

How those men inspired me! Their courage and determination, their insistence that they'd be back at it in no time, their general lack of fuss. It made so much of what passes for patriotism—the gaudy rituals at football games, the desultory flag waving at parades, the blather of politicians—seem empty and trite. The patients I met had nothing but praise for the hospital teams responsible for their treatment—the doctors, nurses, and orderlies, most of them service members themselves but some of them civilians, a surprising number of them foreign-born, originally from places like Nigeria, El Salvador, or the Philippines. Indeed, it was heartening to see how well these wounded warriors were cared for, beginning with the seamless, fast-moving chain that allowed a Marine injured in a dusty Afghan village to be medevaced to the closest base, stabilized, then transported to Germany and onward to Bethesda or Walter Reed for state-of-the-art surgery, all in a matter of days.

Because of that system—a melding of advanced technology, logistical precision, and highly trained and dedicated people, the kind of thing that the U.S. military does better than any other organization on earth—many soldiers who would have died from similar wounds during the Vietnam era were now able to sit with me at their bedside, debating the merits of the Bears versus the Packers. Still, no level of precision or care could erase the brutal, life-changing nature of the injuries these men had suffered. Those who had lost a single leg, especially if the amputation was below the knee, often described themselves as being lucky. Double or even triple amputees were not uncommon, nor were severe cranial trauma, spinal injuries, disfiguring facial wounds, or the loss of eyesight, hearing, or any number of basic bodily functions. The service members I met were adamant that they had no regrets about sacrificing so much for their country and were understandably offended by anyone who viewed them with even a modicum of pity. Taking their cues from their wounded sons, the parents I met were careful to express only the certainty of their child's recovery, along with their deep wells of pride.

And yet each time I entered a room, each time I shook a hand, I could not ignore how incredibly young most of these service members were, many of them barely out of high school. I couldn't help but notice the rims of anguish around the eyes of the parents, who themselves were often younger than me. I wouldn't forget the barely suppressed anger in the voice of a father I met at one point, as he explained that his handsome son, who lay before us likely paralyzed for life, was celebrating his twenty-first birthday that day, or the vacant expression on the face of a young mother who sat with a baby cheerfully gurgling in her arms, pondering a life with a husband who was probably going to survive but would no longer be capable of conscious thought.

Later, toward the end of my presidency, The New York Times would run an article about my visits to the military hospitals. In it, a national security official from a previous administration opined that the practice, no matter how well intentioned, was not something a commander in chief should do—that visits with the wounded inevitably clouded a president's capacity to make clear-eyed, strategic decisions. I was tempted to call that man and explain that I was never more clear-eyed than on the flights back from Walter Reed and Bethesda. Clear about the true costs of war, and who bore those costs. Clear about war's folly, the sorry tales we humans collectively store in our heads and pass on from generation to generation—abstractions that fan hate and justify cruelty and force even the righteous among us to participate in carnage. Clear that by virtue of my office, I could not avoid responsibility for lives lost or shattered, even if I somehow justified my decisions by what I perceived to be some larger good.

Looking through the helicopter window at the tidy green landscape below, I thought about Lincoln during the Civil War, his habit of wandering through makeshift infirmaries not so far from where we were flying, talking softly to soldiers who lay on flimsy cots, bereft of anti-septics to stanch infections or drugs to manage pain, the stench of gangrene everywhere, the clattering and wheezing of impending death.

I wondered how Lincoln had managed it, what prayers he said afterward. He must have known it was a necessary penance. A penance I, too, had to pay.

AS ALL-CONSUMING AS war and the threat of terrorism were proving to be, other foreign policy issues also required my attention—including the need to manage the international fallout from the financial crisis. That was the major focus of my first extended foreign trip when I traveled to London for the Group of 20 Leaders' Summit in April and then onward to continental Europe, Turkey, and Iraq over the course of eight days.

Before 2008, the G20 had been nothing more than a yearly meeting of finance ministers and central bank governors representing the world's twenty largest economies to exchange information and tend to the routine details of globalization. U.S. presidents reserved their attendance for the more exclusive G8, an annual gathering for leaders of the world's seven largest economies (the United States, Japan, Germany, the United Kingdom, France, Italy, and Canada) plus Russia (which, for geopolitical reasons, Bill Clinton and British prime minister Tony Blair had pushed to include in 1997). This changed when, after Lehman's collapse, President Bush and Hank Paulson wisely invited the leaders of all G20 countries to an emergency meeting in Washington—a recognition that in today's interconnected world, a major financial crisis required the broadest possible coordination.

Beyond a vague pledge to "take whatever further actions are necessary" and an agreement to gather again in 2009, the Washington G20 summit had yielded little in the way of concrete action. But with practically every nation now poised for a recession, and global trade projected to contract by 9 percent, my assignment for the London summit was to unite the diverse set of G20 members around a swift and aggressive joint response. The economic rationale was straightforward: For years, U.S. consumer spending—turbocharged with credit card debt and home equity loans—had been the primary engine of global economic growth. Americans bought cars from Germany, electronics from South Korea, and practically everything else from China; these countries, in turn, bought raw materials from countries further down the global supply chain. Now the party was over. No matter how well the Recovery Act and the stress tests might work, American consumers and businesses were going to be digging themselves out of debt for a while. If other countries wanted to avoid a continued downward spiral, they would have to step up—by implementing stimulus packages of their own; by contributing to a $500 billion International Monetary Fund (IMF) emergency pool that could be tapped as needed by economies in severe distress; and by pledging to avoid a repeat of the protectionist, beggar-thy-neighbor policies that had prolonged the Great Depression.

It all made sense, at least on paper. Before the summit, though, Tim Geithner had warned that getting my foreign counterparts to agree to these steps might require some finesse. "The bad news is, they're all mad at us for blowing up the global economy," he said. "The good news is that they're afraid of what will happen if we do nothing."

Michelle had decided to join me for the first half of the trip, which made me happy. She was less concerned with my performance at the summit—"You'll be fine"— than she was with how to dress for our planned audience with Her Majesty the Queen of England.

"You should wear one of those little hats," I said. "And carry a little handbag."

She gave me a mock scowl. "That's not helpful."

I had flown on Air Force One close to two dozen times by then, but it wasn't until that first transatlantic flight that I truly appreciated the degree to which it served as a symbol of American power. The aircrafts themselves (two customized Boeing 747s share the job) were twenty-two years old, and it showed. The interiors—heavy upholstered leather chairs, walnut tables and paneling, a rust-colored carpet with a pattern of gold stars—called to mind a 1980s corporate boardroom or country club lounge. The communications system for passengers could be spotty; not until well into my second term would we get Wi-Fi on board, and even then it was often slower than what was available on most private jets.

Still, everything on Air Force One projected solidity, competence, and a touch of grandeur—from the conveniences (a bedroom, private office, and shower for the president up front; spacious seating, a conference room, and a bay of computer terminals for my team), to the exemplary service of the air force staff (about thirty on board, willing to cheerfully accommodate the most random requests), to its high-level safety features (the world's best pilots, armored windows, airborne refueling capacity, and an onboard medical unit that included a foldout operating table), to its four-thousand-square-foot interior spread out over three levels, capable of transporting a fourteen-person press pool as well as a number of Secret Service agents.

Unique among world leaders, the American president travels fully equipped so as not to rely on another government's services or security forces. This meant that an armada of Beasts, security vehicles, ambulances, tactical teams, and, when necessary, Marine One helicopters were flown in on air force C-17 transport planes in advance and pre-positioned on the tarmac for my arrival. The heavy footprint—and its contrast with the more modest arrangements required by other heads of state—occasionally prompted consternation from a host country's officials. But the U.S. military and Secret Service offered no room for negotiation, and eventually the host country would relent, partly because its own public and press corps **expected** the arrival of an American president on their soil to look like a big deal.

That it was. Wherever we landed, I'd see people pressing their faces against airport terminal windows or gathering outside the perimeter fencing. Even ground crews paused whatever they were doing to catch a glimpse of Air Force One slowly taxiing down the runway with its elegant blue undercarriage, the words UNITED STATES OF AMERICA appearing crisp and understated on its fuselage, the American flag neatly centered on its tail. Exiting the plane, I'd give the obligatory wave from the top of the stairs, amid the rapid buzz of camera shutters and the eager smiles of the delegation lined up at the base of the steps to greet us, sometimes with a presentation of a bouquet by a woman or child in traditional dress, at other times a full honor guard or military band arrayed on either of side of the red carpet that led me to my vehicle. In all of this, one sensed the faint but indelible residue of ancient rituals—rituals of diplomacy, but also rituals of tribute to an empire.

AMERICA HAD HELD a dominant position on the world stage for the better part of the past seven decades. In the wake of World War II, with the rest of the world either impoverished or reduced to rubble, we had led the way in establishing an interlocking system of initiatives, treaties, and new institutions that effectively remade the international order and created a stable path forward: The Marshall Plan to rebuild Western Europe. The North Atlantic Treaty Organization (NATO) and the Pacific alliances to serve as a bulwark against the Soviet Union and bind former enemies into an alignment with the West. Bretton Woods, the International Monetary Fund, the World Bank, and the General Agreement on Tariffs and Trade (GATT) to regulate global finance and commerce. The United Nations and related multilateral agencies to promote the peaceful resolution of conflicts and cooperation on everything from disease eradication to protection of the oceans.

Our motivations for erecting this architecture had hardly been selfless. Beyond helping to assure our security, it pried open markets to sell our goods, kept sea-lanes available for our ships, and maintained the steady flow of oil for our factories and cars. It ensured that our banks got repaid in dollars, our multinationals' factories weren't seized, our tourists could cash their traveler's checks, and our international calls would go through. At times, we bent global institutions to serve Cold War imperatives or ignored them altogether; we meddled in the affairs of other countries, sometimes with disastrous results; our actions often contradicted the ideals of democracy, self-determination, and human rights we professed to embody.

Still, to a degree unmatched by any superpower in history, America chose to bind itself to a set of international laws, rules, and norms. More often than not, we exercised a degree of restraint in our dealings with smaller, weaker nations, relying less on threats and coercion to maintain a global pact. Over time, that willingness to act on behalf of a common good—even if imperfectly—strengthened rather than diminished our influence, contributing to the system's overall durability, and if America was not always universally loved, we were at least respected and not merely feared.

Whatever resistance there might have been to America's global vision seemed to collapse with the 1991 fall of the Soviet Union. In the dizzying span of little more than a decade, Germany and then Europe were unified; former Eastern bloc countries rushed to join NATO and the European Union; China's capitalism took off; numerous countries across Asia, Africa, and Latin America transitioned from authoritarian rule to democracy; and apartheid in South Africa came to an end. Commentators proclaimed the ultimate triumph of liberal, pluralistic, capitalist, Western-style democracy, insisting that the remaining vestiges of tyranny, ignorance, and inefficiency would soon be swept away by the end of history, the flattening of the world. Even at the time, such exuberance was easy to mock. This much was true, though: At the dawn of the twenty-first century, the United States could legitimately claim that the international order we had forged and the principles we had promoted—a Pax Americana—had helped bring about a world in which billions of people were freer, more secure, and more prosperous than before.

That international order was still in place in the spring of 2009 when I touched down in London. But faith in American leadership had been shaken—not by the 9/11 attacks but by the handling of Iraq, by images of corpses floating down the streets of New Orleans after Hurricane Katrina, and, most of all, by the Wall Street meltdown. A series of smaller financial crises in the 1990s had hinted at structural weaknesses in the global system: the way that trillions of dollars in private capital moving at the speed of light, unchecked by significant international regulation or oversight, could take an economic disturbance in one country and quickly produce a tsunami in markets around the world. Because many of those tremors had started on what was considered capitalism's periphery—places like Thailand, Mexico, and a still-weak Russia—and with the United States and other advanced economies at that point booming, it had been easy to think of these problems as one-offs, attributable to bad decision-making by inexperienced governments. In nearly every instance, the United States had stepped in to save the day, but in exchange for emergency financing and continued access to global capital markets, folks like Bob Rubin and Alan Greenspan (not to mention Rubin's aides at the time, Larry Summers and Tim Geithner) had pushed ailing countries to accept tough medicine, including currency devaluations, deep cuts in public spending, and a number of other austerity measures that shored up their international credit ratings but visited enormous hardship on their people.

Imagine, then, the consternation of these same countries when they learned that even as America lectured them on prudential regulations and responsible fiscal stewardship, our own high priests of finance had been asleep at the switch, tolerating asset bubbles and speculative frenzies on Wall Street that were as reckless as anything happening in Latin America or Asia. The only differences were the amounts of money involved and the potential damage done. After all, having assumed that U.S. regulators knew what they were doing, investors from Shanghai to Dubai had poured massive sums into subprime securities and other U.S. assets. Exporters as big as China and as small as Lesotho had premised their own growth on a stable and expanding U.S. economy. In other words, we had beckoned the world to follow us into a paradisiacal land of free markets, global supply chains, internet connections, easy credit, and democratic governance. And for the moment, at least, it felt to them like they might have followed us over a cliff.

PART FOUR

THE GOOD FIGHT

CHAPTER 14

IT TURNS OUT THAT THERE'S a standard design to every international summit. Leaders pull up one by one in their limos to the entrance of a large convention center and then walk past a phalanx of photographers—a bit like a Hollywood red carpet without the fancy gowns and beautiful people. A protocol officer meets you at the door and leads you into a hall where the host leader is waiting: a smile and a handshake for the cameras, whispered small talk. Then on to the leader's lounge for more handshakes and small talk, until all the presidents, prime ministers, chancellors, and kings head into an impressively large conference room with a massive circular table. At your seat, you find a small nameplate, your national flag, a microphone with operating instructions, a commemorative writing pad and pen of varying quality, a headset for the simultaneous translation, a glass and bottles of water or juice, and maybe a plate of snacks or bowl of mints. Your delegation is seated behind you to take notes and pass along messages.

The host calls the meeting to order. He or she makes opening remarks. And then, for the next day and a half— with scheduled breaks for one-on-one meetings with other leaders (known as "bilaterals" or "bilats"), a "family photo" (all the leaders lined up and smiling awkwardly, not unlike a third-grade class picture), and just enough time in the late afternoon to go back to your suite and change clothes before dinner and sometimes an evening session—you sit there, fighting off jet lag and doing your best to look interested, as everyone around the table, including yourself, takes turns reading a set of carefully scripted, anodyne, and invariably much-longer-than-the-time-allotted remarks about whatever topic happens to be on the agenda.

Later, after I had a few summits under my belt, I would adopt the survival tactics of more experienced attendees—making sure I always carried paperwork to do or something to read, or discreetly pulling other leaders aside to do a bit of secondary business while others commanded the mic. But for that first G20 summit in London, I stayed in my seat and listened intently to every speaker. Like the new kid at school, I was aware that others in the room were taking the measure of me, and I figured a bit of rookie humility might go a long way toward rallying people around the economic measures I was there to propose.

It helped that I already knew a number of leaders in the room, starting with our host, British prime minister Gordon Brown, who had traveled to Washington for a meeting with me just a few weeks earlier. A former chancellor of the exchequer in Tony Blair's Labour government, Brown lacked the sparkly political gifts of his predecessor (it seemed as if every media mention of Brown included the term "dour"), and he'd suffered the misfortune of finally getting his turn at the prime ministership just as

Britain's economy was collapsing and its public was tiring of the Labour Party's decade-long run. But he was thoughtful, responsible, and understood global finance, and although his time in office would prove short-lived, I was fortunate to have him as a partner during those early months of the crisis.

Along with Brown, the most consequential Europeans—not just at the London summit but throughout my first term—were German chancellor Angela Merkel and French president Nicolas Sarkozy. The rivalry between the continent's two most powerful countries had caused nearly two centuries of bloody, on-and-off war. Their reconciliation following World War II became the cornerstone of the European Union (E.U.) and its unprecedented run of peace and prosperity. Accordingly, Europe's ability to move as a bloc—and to serve as America's wingman on the world stage—depended largely on Merkel's and Sarkozy's willingness to work well together.

For the most part they did, despite the fact that temperamentally the two leaders couldn't have been more different. Merkel, the daughter of a Lutheran pastor, had grown up in Communist East Germany, keeping her head down and earning a PhD in quantum chemistry. Only after the Iron Curtain fell did she enter politics, methodically moving up the ranks of the center-right Christian Democratic Union party with a combination of organizational skill, strategic acumen, and unwavering patience. Merkel's eyes were big and bright blue and could be touched by turns with frustration, amusement, or hints of sorrow. Otherwise, her stolid appearance reflected her no-nonsense, analytical sensibility. She was famously suspicious of emotional outbursts or overblown rhetoric, and her team would later confess that she'd been initially skeptical of me precisely because of my oratorical skills. I took no offense, figuring that in a German leader, an aversion to possible demagoguery was probably a healthy thing.

Sarkozy, on the other hand, was **all** emotional outbursts and overblown rhetoric. With his dark, expressive, vaguely Mediterranean features (he was half Hungarian and a quarter Greek Jew) and small stature (he was about five foot five but wore lifts in his shoes to make himself taller), he looked like a figure out of a Toulouse-Lautrec painting. Despite coming from a wealthy family, he readily admitted that his ambitions were fueled in part by a lifelong sense of being an outsider. Like Merkel, Sarkozy had made his name as a leader of the center right, winning the presidency on a platform of laissez-faire economics, looser labor regulations, lower taxes, and a less pervasive welfare state. But unlike Merkel, he lurched all over the map when it came to policy, often driven by headlines or political expedience. By the time we arrived in London for the G20, he was already vocally denouncing the excesses of global capitalism. What Sarkozy lacked in ideological consistency, he made up for in boldness, charm, and manic energy. Indeed, conversations with Sarkozy were by turns amusing and exasperating, his hands in perpetual motion, his chest thrust out like a bantam cock's, his personal translator (unlike Merkel, he spoke limited English) always beside him to frantically mirror his every gesture and intonation as the conversation swooped from flattery to bluster to genuine insight, never straying far from his primary, barely disguised interest, which was to be at the center of the action and take credit for whatever it was that might be worth taking credit for.

As much as I appreciated the fact that Sarkozy had embraced my campaign early on (all but endorsing me in an effusive press conference during my preelection visit to Paris), it wasn't hard to tell which of the two European leaders would prove to be the more reliable partner. I came, though, to see Merkel and Sarkozy as useful complements to each other: Sarkozy respectful of Merkel's innate caution but often pushing her to act, Merkel willing to overlook Sarkozy's idiosyncrasies but deft at reining in his more impulsive proposals. They also reinforced each other's pro-American instincts—instincts that, in 2009, were not always shared by their constituents.

NONE OF THIS meant that they and the other Europeans were pushovers. Guarding the interests of their countries, both Merkel and Sarkozy strongly favored the declaration against protectionism that we were proposing in London—Germany's economy was especially reliant on exports—and recognized the utility of an international emergency fund. But as Tim Geithner had predicted, neither had any enthusiasm for fiscal stimulus: Merkel was worried about deficit spending; Sarkozy preferred a universal tax on stock market transactions and wanted to crack down on tax havens. It took most of the summit for me and Tim to convince the two of them to join us in promoting more immediate ways to address the crisis, calling on each G20 country to implement policies that increased aggregate demand. They would do so, they told me, only if I could convince the rest of the G20 leaders—particularly a group of influential non-Western countries that came to be collectively known as the BRICS—to stop blocking proposals that were important to them.

Economically, the five countries that made up the BRICS—Brazil, Russia, India, China, and South Africa—had little in common, and it wasn't until later that they would actually formalize the group. (South Africa wouldn't formally join until 2010.) But even at the London G20, the animating spirit behind the association was clear. These were big, proud nations that in one way or another had emerged from long slumbers. They were no longer satisfied with being relegated to the margins of history or seeing their status reduced to that of regional powers. They chafed at the West's outsized role in managing the global economy. And with the current crisis, they saw a chance to start flipping the script.

In theory, at least, I could sympathize with their point of view. Together, the BRICS represented just over 40 percent of the world's population but about a quarter of the world's GDP and only a fraction of its wealth. Decisions made in the corporate boardrooms of New York, London, or Paris often had more impact on their economies than the policy choices of their own governments. Their influence within the World Bank and the IMF remained limited, despite the remarkable economic transformations that had taken place in China, India, and Brazil. If the United States wanted to preserve the global system that had long served us, it made sense for us to give these emerging powers a greater say in how it operated—while also insisting that they take more responsibility for the costs of its maintenance.

And yet as I glanced around the table on the summit's second day, I couldn't help but wonder how a larger role for the BRICS in global governance might play out. Brazil's president, Luiz Inácio Lula da Silva, for example, had visited the Oval Office in March, and I'd found him impressive. A grizzled, engaging former labor leader who'd been jailed for protesting the previous military government and then elected in 2002, he had initiated a series of pragmatic reforms that sent Brazil's growth rate soaring, expanded its middle class, and provided housing and education to millions of its poorest citizens. He also reportedly had the scruples of a Tammany Hall boss, and rumors swirled about government cronyism, sweetheart deals, and kickbacks that ran into the billions.

President Dmitry Medvedev, meanwhile, appeared to be a poster child for the new Russia: young, trim, and clothed in hip, European-tailored suits. Except that he wasn't the real power in Russia. That spot was occupied by his patron, Vladimir Putin: a former KGB officer, two-term president and now the country's prime minister, and the leader of what resembled a criminal syndicate as much as it did a traditional government—a syndicate that had its tentacles wrapped around every aspect of the country's economy.

South Africa at the time was in a transition, with interim president Kgalema Motlanthe soon to be replaced by Jacob Zuma, the leader of Nelson Mandela's party, the African National Congress, which controlled the country's parliament. In subsequent meetings, Zuma struck me as amiable enough. He spoke eloquently of the need for fair trade, human development, infrastructure, and more equitable distributions of wealth and opportunity on the African continent. By all accounts, though, much of the goodwill built up through Mandela's heroic struggle was being squandered by corruption and incompetence under ANC leadership, leaving large swaths of the country's black population still mired in poverty and despair.

Manmohan Singh, the prime minister of India, meanwhile, had engineered the modernization of his nation's economy. A gentle, soft-spoken economist in his seventies, with a white beard and a turban that were the marks of his Sikh faith but to the Western eye lent him the air of a holy man, he had been India's finance minister in the 1990s, managing to lift millions of people from poverty. For the duration of his tenure as prime minister, I would find Singh to be wise, thoughtful, and scrupulously honest. Despite its genuine economic progress, though, India remained a chaotic and impoverished place: largely divided by religion and caste, captive to the whims of corrupt local officials and power brokers, hamstrung by a parochial bureaucracy that was resistant to change.

And then there was China. Since the late 1970s, when Deng Xiaoping effectively abandoned Mao Zedong's Marxist-Leninist vision in favor of an export-driven, state-managed form of capitalism, no nation in history had developed faster or moved more people out of abject poverty. Once little more than a hub of low-grade manufacturing and assembly for foreign companies looking to take advantage of its endless supply of low-wage workers, China now boasted topflight engineers and world-class companies working at the cutting edge of advanced technology. Its massive trade surplus made it a major investor on every continent; gleaming cities like Shanghai and Guangzhou had become sophisticated financial centers, home to a burgeoning consumer class. Given its growth rate and sheer size, China's GDP was guaranteed at some point to surpass America's. When you added this to the country's powerful military, increasingly skilled workforce, shrewd and pragmatic government, and cohesive five-thousand-year-old culture, the conclusion felt obvious: If any country was likely to challenge U.S. preeminence on the world stage, it was China.

And yet watching the Chinese delegation operate at the G20, I was convinced that any such challenge was still decades away—and that if and when it came, it would most likely happen as a result of America's strategic mistakes. By all accounts, Chinese president Hu Jintao—a nondescript man in his mid-sixties with a mane of jet-black hair (as far as I could tell, few Chinese leaders turned gray as they aged)—was not seen as a particularly strong leader, sharing authority as he did with other members of the Chinese Communist Party's Central Committee. Sure enough, in our meeting at the margins of the summit, Hu appeared content to rely on pages of prepared talking points, with no apparent agenda beyond encouraging continued consultation and what he referred to as "win-win" cooperation. More impressive to me was China's chief economic policy maker, Premier Wen Jiabao, a small, bespectacled figure who spoke without notes and displayed a sophisticated grasp of the current crisis; his affirmed commitment to a Chinese stimulus package on a scale mirroring that of the Recovery Act was probably the single best piece of news I would hear during my time at the G20. But

even so, the Chinese were in no hurry to seize the reins
of the international world order, viewing it as a headache
they didn't need. Wen had little to say about how to
manage the financial crisis going forward. From his
country's standpoint, the onus was on us to figure it out.

This was the thing that would strike me not just during the London summit but at every international forum
I attended while president: Even those who complained
about America's role in the world still relied on us to keep
the system afloat. To varying degrees, other countries
were willing to pitch in—contributing troops to U.N.
peacekeeping efforts, say, or providing cash and logistical
support for famine relief. Some, like the Scandinavian
countries, consistently punched well above their weight.
But otherwise, few nations felt obliged to act beyond narrow self-interest; and those that shared America's basic
commitment to the principles upon which a liberal,
market-based system depended—individual freedom, the
rule of law, strong enforcement of property rights and
neutral arbitration of disputes, plus baseline levels of
governmental accountability and competence—lacked
the economic and political heft, not to mention the army
of diplomats and policy experts, to promote those principles on a global scale.

China, Russia, and even genuine democracies like
Brazil, India, and South Africa still operated on different
principles. For the BRICS, responsible foreign policy
meant tending to one's own affairs. They abided by the
established rules only insofar as their own interests
were advanced, out of necessity rather than conviction,
and they appeared happy to violate them when they
thought they could get away with it. If they assisted

another country, they preferred to do so on a bilateral basis, expecting some benefit in return. These nations certainly felt no obligation to underwrite the system as a whole. As far as they were concerned, that was a luxury only a fat and happy West could afford.

OF ALL THE BRICS leaders in attendance at the G20, I was most interested in engaging with Medvedev. The U.S. relationship with Russia was at a particularly low point. The previous summer—a few months after Medvedev had been sworn into office—Russia had invaded the neighboring country of Georgia, a former Soviet republic, and illegally occupied two of its provinces, triggering violence between the two countries and tensions with other border nations.

For us, it was a sign of Putin's escalating boldness and general belligerence, a troubling unwillingness to respect another nation's sovereignty and a broader flouting of international law. And in many ways, it appeared he'd gotten away with it: Beyond suspending diplomatic contacts, the Bush administration had done next to nothing to punish Russia for its aggression, and the rest of the world had shrugged its shoulders and moved on, making any belated efforts to isolate Russia almost certain to fail. My administration's hope was to initiate what we were calling a "reset" with Russia, opening a dialogue in order to protect our interests, support our democratic partners in the region, and enlist cooperation on our goals for nuclear nonproliferation and disarmament. To this end, we'd arranged for me to meet privately with Medvedev a day ahead of the summit.

I relied on two Russia experts to prepare me for the

meeting: the State Department's undersecretary for political affairs, Bill Burns, and our NSC senior director for Russian and Eurasian affairs, Michael McFaul. Burns, a career diplomat who'd been the Bush administration's ambassador to Russia, was tall, mustached, and slightly stooped, with a gentle voice and the bookish air of an Oxford don. McFaul, on the other hand, was all energy and enthusiasm, with a wide smile and a blond mop of hair. A native Montanan, he'd advised my campaign while still teaching at Stanford and seemed to end every statement with an exclamation point.

Of the two, McFaul was more bullish about our ability to have an influence on Russia, partly because he'd lived in Moscow in the early 1990s, during the heady days of political transformation, first as a scholar and later as the in-country director of a pro-democracy organization funded in part by the U.S. government. When it came to Medvedev, though, McFaul agreed with Burns that I shouldn't expect too much.

"Medvedev's going to be interested in establishing a good relationship with you, to prove that he belongs on the world stage," he said. "But you have to remember that Putin still calls the shots."

Looking over his biography, I could see why everyone assumed Dmitry Medvedev was on a short leash. In his early forties, raised in relative privilege as the only child of two professors, he'd studied law in the late 1980s, lectured at Leningrad State University, and gotten to know Vladimir Putin when they both worked for the mayor of St. Petersburg in the early 1990s after the dissolution of the Soviet Union. While Putin stayed in politics, eventually becoming prime minister under

President Boris Yeltsin, Medvedev leveraged his political connections to secure an executive position and owner-ship stake in Russia's largest lumber company, at a time when the country's chaotic privatization of state-owned assets offered well-connected shareholders a guaranteed fortune. Quietly he became a wealthy man, called upon to work on various civic projects without having to bear the burden of the spotlight. It wasn't until late 1999 that he got pulled back into government, recruited by Putin for a high-level job in Moscow. Just a month later, Yeltsin abruptly resigned, elevating Putin from prime minister to acting president, with Medvedev rising behind him.

In other words, Medvedev was a technocrat and a behind-the-scenes operator, without much of a public profile or political base of his own. And that's exactly how he came across when he arrived for our meeting at Winfield House, the U.S. ambassador's elegant residence on the outskirts of London. He was a small man, dark-haired and affable, with a slightly formal, almost self-deprecating manner, more international management consultant than politician or party apparatchik. Apparently he understood English, although he preferred speaking with a translator.

I opened our discussion with the subject of his country's military occupation of Georgia. As expected, Medvedev stuck closely to the official talking points. He blamed the Georgian government for precipitating the crisis and insisted that Russia had acted only to protect Russian citizens from violence. He dismissed my argument that the invasion and continued occupation violated Georgia's sovereignty and international law, and he pointedly suggested that, unlike U.S. forces in Iraq, Russian forces had genuinely been greeted as liberators.

Hearing all this, I remembered what the dissident writer Aleksandr Solzhenitsyn once said about politics during the Soviet era, that "the lie has become not just a moral category but a pillar of the State."

But if Medvedev's rebuttal on Georgia reminded me that he was no Boy Scout, I noticed a certain ironic detachment in his delivery, as if he wanted me to know that he didn't really believe everything he was saying. As the conversation shifted to other topics, so did his disposition. On the steps needed to manage the financial crisis, he was well briefed and constructive. He expressed enthusiasm for our proposed "reset" of U.S.-Russian relations, especially when it came to expanding cooperation on nonmilitary issues like education, science, technology, and trade. He surprised us by making an unprompted (and unprecedented) offer to let the U.S. military use Russian airspace to transport troops and equipment to Afghanistan—an alternative that would reduce our exclusive reliance on expensive and not always reliable Pakistani supply routes.

And on my highest-priority issue—U.S.-Russian cooperation to curb nuclear proliferation, including Iran's possible pursuit of nuclear weapons—Medvedev showed a readiness to engage with frankness and flexibility. He accepted my proposal to have our respective experts immediately begin negotiations on cuts to each country's nuclear stockpiles as a follow-up to the existing Strategic Arms Reduction Treaty (START), which was set to expire at the end of 2009. Although he wasn't prepared to commit to an international effort to constrain Iran, he didn't dismiss it out of hand, going so far as to acknowledge that Iran's nuclear and missile programs had advanced much faster than Moscow had expected—a concession that neither McFaul nor Burns could recall a Russian official ever having made, even in private.

Still, Medvedev was far from acquiescent. He made clear during our discussions about nonproliferation that Russia had a priority of its own: wanting us to reconsider the Bush administration's decision to build a missile defense system in Poland and the Czech Republic. He was speaking, I assumed, on behalf of Putin, who correctly understood that the main reason the Poles and the Czechs were eager to host our system was that it would guarantee increased U.S. military capabilities on their soil, providing an additional hedge against Russian intimidation.

The truth is that, unbeknownst to the Russians, we were already reconsidering the idea of a land-based missile defense in Europe. Before I'd left for London, Robert Gates had informed me that the plans developed under Bush had been judged potentially less effective against the most pressing threats (chiefly Iran) than originally envisioned. Gates had suggested that I order a review of other possible configurations before making any decision.

I wasn't willing to grant Medvedev's request to fold missile defense considerations into upcoming START negotiations. I did think, however, that it was in our interest to reduce Russian anxiety. And the fortuitous timing allowed me to make sure Medvedev didn't leave London empty-handed: I presented my intent to review our plans in Europe as a show of willingness to discuss the issue in good faith. I added that progress on halting Iran's nuclear program would almost certainly have a bearing on any decision I might make—a not-so-subtle message, to which Medvedev responded before it was even translated.

"I understand," he said in English, with a slight smile.

Before leaving, Medvedev also extended an invitation for me to visit Moscow during the summer, a meeting I was inclined to accept. After watching his motorcade drive away, I turned to Burns and McFaul and asked what they thought.

"I'll be honest, Mr. President," McFaul said. "I don't know how it could've gone much better. He seemed a lot more open to doing business than I would have expected."

"Mike's right," Burns said, "although I do wonder how much of what Medvedev said was cleared with Putin beforehand."

I nodded. "We'll find out soon enough."

BY THE END of the London summit, the G20 had managed to strike a deal in response to the global financial crisis. The final communiqué, to be issued jointly by the leaders in attendance, included U.S. priorities like additional commitments to stimulus and a rejection of protectionism, along with measures to eliminate tax havens and improve financial oversight that were important to the Europeans. BRICS nations could point to a commitment from the United States and the European Union to examine possible changes in their World Bank and IMF representation. In a rush of enthusiasm, Sarkozy grabbed both me and Tim as we were about to leave the venue.

"This agreement is historic, Barack!" he said. "It has happened because of you . . . No, no, it's true! And Mr. Geithner here . . . he's magnificent!" Sarkozy then started chanting my Treasury secretary's last name like a fan at a football game, loudly enough to turn a few heads in the room. I had to laugh, not only at Tim's evident discomfort but also at the stricken expression on Angela Merkel's face—she had just finished looking over the wording of the communiqué and was now eyeing Sarkozy the way a mother eyes an unruly child.

The international press deemed the summit a success: Not only was the deal more substantive than expected, but our central role in the negotiations had helped to at least partially reverse the view that the financial crisis had permanently damaged U.S. leadership. At the closing press conference, I was careful to credit everyone who'd played a role, praising Gordon Brown in particular for his leadership and arguing that in this interconnected world, no single nation could go it alone. Solving big problems, I said, demanded the kind of international cooperation on display in London.

Two days later, a reporter followed up on this, asking for my views on American exceptionalism. "I believe in American exceptionalism," I said. "Just as I suspect that the Brits believe in British exceptionalism and the Greeks believe in Greek exceptionalism."

Only later would I learn that Republicans and conservative news outlets had seized upon this unremarkable statement, one made in an effort to show modesty and good manners, as evidence of weakness and insufficient patriotism on my part. Pundits began to characterize my interactions with other leaders and citizens of other nations as "Obama's Apology Tour," although they could never point to any actual apologies. Evidently my failure to lecture foreign audiences on American superiority, not to mention my willingness to acknowledge our imperfections and take the views of other countries into account, was somehow undermining. It was another reminder of how splintered our media landscape had become—and how an increasingly poisonous partisanship no longer stopped at the water's edge. In this new world, a foreign policy victory by every traditional standard could be spun as a defeat, at least in the minds of half the country; messages that advanced our interests and built goodwill abroad could lead to a host of political headaches back home.

On a happier note, Michelle was a hit in her international debut, garnering especially glowing press for a visit she made to an all-girls secondary school in central London. As would be true throughout our time in the White House, Michelle reveled in such interactions, able to connect with kids of any age or background, and apparently that magic traveled well. At the school, she talked about her own childhood and the barriers she'd had to overcome, how education had always provided her a path forward. The girls—working-class, many of them of West Indian or South Asian descent—listened in rapt attention as this glamorous woman insisted that she had once been just like them. In the coming years, she'd visit with students from the school several times, including hosting a group of them at the White House. Later, an economist would study the data and conclude that Michelle's engagement with the school had led to a notable spike in the students' standardized test scores, suggesting that her message of aspiration and connection made a true and measurable difference. This "Michelle Effect" was something I was very familiar with—she had the same effect on me. Things like this helped us remember that our work as a First Family wasn't solely a matter of politics and policy.

Michelle did generate her own bit of controversy, though. At a reception for the G20 leaders and their spouses with Queen Elizabeth at Buckingham Palace, she was photographed with her hand resting on Her Majesty's shoulder—an apparent breach of royalty-commoner protocol, although the queen didn't seem to mind, slipping her arm around Michelle in return. Also, Michelle wore a cardigan sweater over her dress during our private meeting with the queen, sending Fleet Street into a horrified tizzy.

"You should have taken my suggestion and worn one of those little hats," I told her the next morning. "And a little matching handbag!"

She smiled and kissed me on the cheek. "And I hope you enjoy sleeping on a couch when you get home," she said brightly. "The White House has so many to choose from!"

THE NEXT FIVE DAYS were a whirlwind—a NATO summit in Baden-Baden, Germany, and Strasbourg, France; meetings and speeches in the Czech Republic and Turkey; and an unannounced visit to Iraq, where—in addition to thanking a raucous assembly of U.S. troops for their courage and sacrifice—I consulted with Prime Minister Maliki about our withdrawal plans and Iraq's continued transition to parliamentary governance.

By the end of the trip I had every reason to feel pretty good. Across the board, we had successfully advanced the U.S. agenda. There had been no major pratfalls on my part. Everyone on my foreign policy team, from cabinet members like Geithner and Gates to the most junior member of the advance staff, had done outstanding work. And far from shying away from association with the United States, the countries we visited seemed hungry for our leadership.

Still, the trip provided sobering evidence of just how much of my first term was going to be spent not on new initiatives but on putting out fires that predated my presidency. At the NATO summit, for instance, we were able to secure alliance support for our Af-Pak strategy— but only after listening to European leaders emphasize how sharply their publics had turned against military cooperation with the United States following the Iraq invasion, and how difficult it was going to be for them to muster political support for additional troops. NATO's central and Eastern European members had also been unnerved by the Bush administration's tepid reaction to Russia's invasion of Georgia and questioned whether the alliance could be counted on to defend them against similar Russian aggression. They had a point: Before the summit, I'd been surprised to learn that NATO lacked the plans or rapid-response capabilities to come to the defense of every ally. It was just one more example of a dirty little secret I was discovering as president, the same thing I'd learned during our Afghanistan review, the same thing the world had learned following the invasion of Iraq: For all their tough talk, Bush administration hawks like Cheney and Rumsfeld had been surprisingly bad at backing up their rhetoric with coherent, effective strategies. Or as Denis McDonough more colorfully put it, "Open any White House drawer and you'll find another turd sandwich."

I did what I could to defuse the central European issue by proposing that NATO develop individualized defense plans for each of its members and by declaring that when it came to our mutual defense obligations, we should make no distinction between junior and senior members of the alliance. This was going to mean more work for our overstretched staff and military, but I tried not to let it raise my blood pressure too much. I reminded myself that every president felt saddled with the previous administration's choices and mistakes, that 90 percent of the job was navigating inherited problems and unanticipated crises. Only if you did that well enough, with discipline and purpose, did you get a real shot at shaping the future.

What did have me worried by the end of the trip was less a particular issue than an overall impression: the sense that for a variety of reasons—some of our own making, some beyond our control—the hopeful tide of democratization, liberalization, and integration that had swept the globe after the end of the Cold War was beginning to recede. Older, darker forces were gathering strength, and the stresses brought about by a prolonged economic downturn were likely to make things worse.

Before the financial crisis, for example, Turkey had appeared to be a nation on the upswing, a case study in globalization's positive effects on emerging economies. Despite a history of political instability and military coups, the majority-Muslim country had been largely aligned with the West since the 1950s, maintaining NATO membership, regular elections, a market-based system, and a secular constitution that enshrined modern principles like equal rights for women. When its current prime minister, Recep Tayyip Erdogan, and his Justice and Development Party had swept into power in 2002–2003, touting populist and often overtly Islamic appeals, it had unsettled Turkey's secular, military-dominated political elite. Erdogan's vocal sympathy for both the Muslim Brotherhood and Hamas in their fight for an independent Palestinian state, in particular, had also made Washington and Tel Aviv nervous. And yet, Erdogan's government thus far had abided by Turkey's constitution, met its NATO obligations, and effectively managed the economy, even initiating a series of modest reforms with the hope of qualifying for E.U. membership. Some observers suggested that Erdogan might offer a model of moderate, modern, and pluralistic political Islam and an alternative to the autocracies, theocracies, and extremist movements that characterized the region.

In a speech before the Turkish parliament and a town hall meeting with Istanbul college students, I tried to echo such optimism. But because of my conversations with Erdogan, I had my doubts. During the NATO summit, Erdogan had instructed his team to block the appointment of highly regarded Danish prime minister Anders Rasmussen as the organization's new secretary-general—not because he thought Rasmussen was unqualified but because Rasmussen's government had declined to act on Turkey's demand that it censor the 2005 publication of cartoons depicting the prophet Muhammad in a Danish newspaper. European appeals about freedom of the press had left Erdogan unmoved, and he had relented only after I'd promised that Rasmussen would have a Turkish deputy and had convinced him that my upcoming visit—and U.S. public opinion of Turkey—would be adversely affected if Rasmussen's appointment didn't go through.

This set a pattern for the next eight years. Mutual self-interest would dictate that Erdogan and I develop a working relationship. Turkey looked to the United States for support of its E.U. bid, as well as military and intelligence assistance in fighting Kurdish separatists who'd been emboldened by the fall of Saddam Hussein. We, meanwhile, needed Turkey's cooperation to combat terrorism and stabilize Iraq. Personally, I found the prime minister to be cordial and generally responsive to my requests. But whenever I listened to him speak, his tall frame slightly stooped, his voice a forceful staccato that rose an octave in response to various grievances or perceived slights, I got the strong impression that his commitment to democracy and the rule of law might last only as long as it preserved his own power.

My questions about the durability of democratic values weren't restricted to Turkey. During my stop in Prague, E.U. officials had expressed alarm about the rise of far-right parties across Europe and how the economic crisis was causing an uptick in nationalism, anti-immigrant sentiment, and skepticism about integration. The sitting Czech president, Václav Klaus, to whom I made a short courtesy visit, embodied some of these trends. A vocal "Eurosceptic" who'd been in office since 2003, he was both ardently pro–free market and an admirer of Vladimir Putin's. And although we tried to keep things light during our conversation, what I knew of his public record—he had supported efforts to censor

Czech television, was dismissive of gay and lesbian rights, and was a notorious climate change denier—didn't leave me particularly hopeful about political trends in central Europe.

It was hard to tell how lasting these trends would be. I told myself it was the nature of democracies—including America's—to swing between periods of progressive change and conservative retrenchment. In fact, what was striking was how easily Klaus would have fit in with the Republican Senate caucus back home, just as I could readily picture Erdogan as a local power broker on the Chicago City Council. Whether this was a source of comfort or concern, I couldn't decide.

I HAD NOT, however, come to Prague to assess the state of democracy. Instead, we had scheduled my one big public speech of the trip to lay out a top foreign policy initiative: the reduction and ultimate elimination of nuclear weapons. I'd worked on the issue since my election to the Senate four years earlier, and while there were risks promoting what many considered a utopian quest, I told my team that in some ways that was the point; even modest progress on the issue required a bold and overarching vision. If I hoped to pass one thing on to Malia and Sasha, it was freedom from the possibility of a human-made apocalypse.

I had a second, more practical reason for focusing on the nuclear issue in a way that would make headlines across Europe: We needed to find a means to prevent Iran and North Korea from advancing their nuclear programs. (The day before the speech, in fact, North Korea had launched a long-range rocket into the Pacific, just to get our attention.) It was time to ramp up international pressure on both countries, including with enforceable economic sanctions; and I knew this would be a whole lot easier to accomplish if I could show that the United States was interested in not just restarting global momentum on disarmament but also actively reducing its own nuclear stockpile.

By the morning of the speech, I was satisfied that we had framed the nuclear issue with enough concrete, achievable proposals to keep me from sounding hopelessly quixotic. The day was clear and the setting spectacular, a town square with the ancient Prague Castle—once home to Bohemian kings and Holy Roman emperors—looming in the background. As the Beast wended its way through the city's narrow and uneven streets, we passed some of the thousands who were gathering to hear the speech. There were people of all ages, but mostly I saw young Czechs, dressed in jeans, sweaters, and scarves, bundled up against a crisp spring wind, their faces flushed and expectant. It was crowds like this, I thought, that had been scattered by Soviet tanks at the end of the 1968 Prague Spring; and it was on these same streets just twenty-one years later, in 1989, that even bigger crowds of peaceful protesters had, against all odds, brought an end to Communist rule.

I had been in law school in 1989. I recalled sitting alone in my basement apartment a few miles from Harvard Square, glued to my secondhand TV set as I watched what would come to be known as the Velvet Revolution unfold. I remember being riveted by those protests and hugely inspired. It was the same feeling I'd had earlier in the year, seeing that solitary figure facing down tanks in Tiananmen Square, the same inspiration I felt whenever I watched grainy footage of Freedom Riders or John Lewis and his fellow civil rights soldiers marching across the Edmund Pettus Bridge in Selma. To see ordinary people sloughing off fear and habit to act on their deepest beliefs, to see young people risking everything just to have a say in their own lives, to try to strip the world of the old cruelties, hierarchies, divisions, falsehoods, and injustices that cramped the human spirit—that, I had realized, was what I believed in and longed to be a part of.

That night, I had been unable to sleep. Rather than reading my casebooks for class the next day, I had written in my journal deep into the night, my brain bursting with urgent, half-formed thoughts, uncertain of what my role might be in this great global struggle but knowing even then that the practice of law would be no more than a way station for me, that my heart would take me elsewhere.

It felt like a long time ago. And yet looking out from the backseat of the presidential limousine, preparing to deliver an address that would be broadcast around the world, I realized there was a direct if wholly improbable line between that moment and this one. I was the product of that young man's dreams; and as we pulled up to the makeshift holding area behind a wide stage, a part of me imagined myself not as the politician I had become but as one of those young people in the crowd, uncompromised by power, unencumbered by the need to accommodate men like Erdogan and Klaus, obliged only to make common cause with those chasing after a new and better world.

After the speech, I had a chance to visit with Václav

Havel, the playwright and former dissident who had been president of the Czech Republic for two terms, finishing in 2003. A participant in the Prague Spring, he'd been blacklisted after the Soviet occupation, had his works banned, and been repeatedly jailed for his political activities. Havel, as much as anyone, had given moral voice to the grassroots democracy movements that had brought the Soviet era to an end. Along with Nelson Mandela and a handful of other living statesmen, he'd also been a distant role model for me. I'd read his essays while in law school. Watching him maintain his moral compass even after his side had won power and he'd assumed the presidency had helped convince me that it was possible to enter politics and come out with your soul intact.

Our meeting was brief, a victim to my schedule. Havel was in his early seventies but looked younger, with an unassuming manner, a warm, craggy face, rusty-blond hair, and a trim mustache. After posing for pictures and addressing the assembled press, we settled into a conference room, where, with the help of his personal translator, we spoke for forty-five minutes or so about the financial crisis, Russia, and the future of Europe. He was concerned that the United States might somehow believe that the problems of Europe were solved when in fact, throughout the former Soviet satellites, the commitment to democracy was still fragile. As memories of the old order faded, and leaders like him who had forged close relationships with America passed from the scene, the dangers of a resurgent illiberalism were real.

"In some ways, the Soviets simplified who the enemy was," Havel said. "Today, autocrats are more sophisticated. They stand for election while slowly undermining the institutions that make democracy possible. They champion free markets while engaging in the same corruption, cronyism, and exploitation as existed in the past." He confirmed that the economic crisis was strengthening the forces of nationalism and populist extremism across the continent, and although he agreed with my strategy to reengage Russia, he cautioned that the annexation of Georgian territory was just the most overt example of Putin's efforts to intimidate and interfere throughout the region. "Without attention from the U.S.," he said, "freedom here and across Europe will wither."

Our time was up. I thanked Havel for his advice and assured him that America would not falter in promoting democratic values. He smiled and told me he hoped he had not added to my burdens.

"You've been cursed with people's high expectations," he said, shaking my hand. "Because it means they are also easily disappointed. It's something I'm familiar with. I fear it can be a trap."

SEVEN DAYS AFTER leaving Washington, my team climbed back onto Air Force One, worn out and ready to return home. I was in the plane's front cabin, about to catch up on some sleep, when Jim Jones and Tom Donilon walked in to brief me on a developing situation involving an issue I'd never been asked about during the campaign.

"Pirates?"

"Pirates, Mr. President," Jones said. "Off the coast of

Somalia. They boarded a cargo ship captained by an American and appear to be holding the crew hostage."

This problem wasn't new. For decades, Somalia had been a failed state, a country on the Horn of Africa carved up and shared uneasily by various warlords, clans, and, more recently, a vicious terrorist organization called al-Shabaab. Without the benefit of a functioning economy, gangs of jobless young men equipped with motorized skiffs, AK-47s, and makeshift ladders had taken to boarding commercial vessels traveling the busy shipping route connecting Asia to the West via the Suez Canal and holding them for ransom. This was the first time an American-flagged ship was involved. We had no indication that the four Somalis had harmed any members of the twenty-person crew, but Secretary Gates had ordered the navy destroyer USS **Bainbridge** and the frigate USS **Halyburton** to the area, and they were expected to have the hijacked vessel within their sights by the time we landed in Washington.

"We'll wake you, sir, if there are further developments," Jones said.

"Got it," I said, feeling the weariness I'd staved off over the past few days starting to settle in my bones. "Also wake me if the locusts come," I said. "Or the plague."

"Sir?" Jones paused.

"Just a joke, Jim. Good night."

CHAPTER 15

OUR ENTIRE NATIONAL SECURITY TEAM spent the next four days absorbed by the drama unfolding on the open seas off Somalia. The quick-thinking crew of the cargo-carrying **Maersk Alabama** had managed to disable the ship's engine before the pirates boarded, and most of its members had hidden in a secure room. Their American captain, a courageous and levelheaded Vermonter named Richard Phillips, meanwhile, had stayed on the bridge. With the 508-foot ship inoperable and their small skiff no longer seaworthy, the Somalis decided to flee on a covered lifeboat, taking Phillips as a hostage and demanding a $2 million ransom. Even as one of the hostage-takers surrendered, negotiations to release the American captain went nowhere. The drama only heightened when Phillips attempted escape by jumping overboard, only to be recaptured.

With the situation growing more tense by the hour, I issued a standing order to fire on the Somali pirates if at any point Phillips appeared to be in imminent danger. Finally, on the fifth day, we got the word: In the middle of the night, as two of the Somalis came out into the open and the other could be seen through a small window holding a gun to the American captain, Navy SEAL snipers took three shots. The pirates were killed. Phillips was safe.

The news elicited high fives all around the White House. **The Washington Post** headline declared it AN EARLY MILITARY VICTORY FOR OBAMA. But as relieved as I was to see Captain Phillips reunited with his family, and as proud as I was of our navy personnel for their handling of the situation, I wasn't inclined to beat my chest over the episode. Partly, it was a simple recognition that the line between success and complete disaster had been a matter of inches—three bullets finding their targets through the darkness rather than being thrown off just a tad by a sudden ocean swell. But I also realized that around the world, in places like Yemen and Afghanistan, Pakistan and Iraq, the lives of millions of young men like those three dead Somalis (some of them boys, really, since the oldest pirate was believed to be nineteen) had been warped and stunted by desperation, ignorance, dreams of religious glory, the violence of their surroundings, or the schemes of older men. They were dangerous, these young men, often deliberately and casually cruel. Still, in the aggregate, at least, I wanted somehow to save them—send them to school, give them a trade, drain them of the hate that had been filling their heads. And yet the world they were a part of, and the machinery I commanded, more often had me killing them instead.

THAT PART OF my job involved ordering people to be killed wasn't a surprise, although it was rarely framed that way. Fighting terrorists—"on their ten-yard line and not ours" as Gates liked to put it—had provided the entire rationale behind the wars in Afghanistan and Iraq.

But as al-Qaeda had scattered and gone underground, metastasizing into a complex web of affiliates, operatives, sleeper cells, and sympathizers connected by the internet and burner phones, our national security agencies had been challenged to construct new forms of more targeted, nontraditional warfare—including operating an arsenal of lethal drones to take out al-Qaeda operatives within the territory of Pakistan. The National Security Agency, or NSA, already the most sophisticated electronic-intelligence-gathering organization in the world, employed new supercomputers and decryption technology worth billions of dollars to comb cyberspace in search of terrorist communications and potential threats. The Pentagon's Joint Special Operations Command, anchored by Navy SEAL teams and Army Special Forces, carried out nighttime raids and hunted down terrorist suspects mostly inside—but sometimes outside—the war zones of Afghanistan and Iraq. And the CIA developed new forms of analysis and intelligence gathering.

The White House, too, had reorganized itself to manage the terrorist threat. Each month, I chaired a meeting in the Situation Room, bringing all the intelligence agencies together to review recent developments and ensure coordination. The Bush administration had developed a ranking of terrorist targets, a kind of "Top 20" list complete with photos, alias information, and vital statistics reminiscent of those on baseball cards; generally, whenever someone on the list was killed, a new target was added, leading Rahm to observe that "al-Qaeda's HR department must have trouble filling that number 21 slot." In fact, my hyperactive chief of staff—who'd spent enough time in Washington to know that his new, liberal president couldn't afford to look soft on terrorism—was obsessed with the list, cornering those responsible for our targeting operations to find out what was taking so long when it came to locating number 10 or 14.

I took no joy in any of this. It didn't make me feel powerful. I'd entered politics to help kids get a better education, to help families get healthcare, to help poor countries grow more food—it was that kind of power that I measured myself against.

But the work was necessary, and it was my responsibility to make sure our operations were as effective as possible. Moreover, unlike some on the left, I'd never engaged in wholesale condemnation of the Bush administration's approach to counterterrorism (CT). I'd seen enough of the intelligence to know that al-Qaeda and its affiliates were continuously plotting horrific crimes against innocent people. Its members weren't amenable to negotiations or bound by the normal rules of engagement; thwarting their plots and rooting them out was a task of extraordinary complexity. In the immediate aftermath of 9/11, President Bush had done some things right, including swiftly and consistently trying to tamp down anti-Islamic sentiment in the United States—no small feat, especially given our country's history with McCarthyism and Japanese internment—and mobilizing international support for the early Afghan campaign. Even controversial Bush administration programs like the Patriot Act, which I myself had criticized, seemed to me potential tools for abuse more than wholesale violations of American civil liberties.

The way the Bush administration had spun the

intelligence to gain public support for invading Iraq (not to mention its use of terrorism as a political cudgel in the 2004 elections) was more damning. And, of course, I considered the invasion itself to be as big a strategic blunder as the slide into Vietnam had been decades earlier. But the actual wars in Afghanistan and Iraq hadn't involved the indiscriminate bombing or deliberate targeting of civilians that had been a routine part of even "good" wars like World War II; and with glaring exceptions like Abu Ghraib, our troops in theater had displayed a remarkable level of discipline and professionalism.

As I saw it, then, my job was to fix those aspects of our CT effort that needed fixing, rather than tearing it out root and branch to start over. One such fix was closing Gitmo, the military prison at Guantánamo Bay—and thus halting the continuing stream of prisoners placed in indefinite detention there. Another was my executive order ending torture; although I'd been assured during my transition briefings that extraordinary renditions and "enhanced interrogations" had ceased during President Bush's second term, the disingenuous, cavalier, and sometimes absurd ways that a few high-ranking holdovers from the previous administration described those practices to me ("A doctor was always present to ensure that the suspect didn't suffer permanent damage or death") had convinced me of the need for bright lines. Beyond that, my highest priority was creating strong systems of transparency, accountability, and oversight—ones that included Congress and the judiciary and would provide a credible legal framework for what I sadly suspected would be a long-term struggle. For that I needed the fresh eyes and critical mindset of the mostly liberal lawyers who worked under me in the White House, Pentagon, CIA, and State Department counsels' offices. But I also needed someone who had operated at the very center of U.S. CT efforts, someone who could help me sort through the various policy trade-offs that were sure to come, and then reach into the bowels of the system to make sure the needed changes actually happened.

John Brennan was that person. In his early fifties, with thinning gray hair, a bad hip (a consequence of his dunking exploits as a high school basketball player), and the face of an Irish boxer, he had taken an interest in Arabic in college, studied at the American University in Cairo, and joined the CIA in 1980 after answering an ad in **The New York Times**. He would spend the next twenty-five years with the agency, as a daily intelligence briefer, a station chief in the Middle East, and, eventually, the deputy executive director under President Bush, charged with putting together the agency's integrated CT unit after 9/11.

Despite the résumé and the tough-guy appearance, what struck me most about Brennan was his thoughtfulness and lack of bluster (along with his incongruously gentle voice). Although unwavering in his commitment to destroy al-Qaeda and its ilk, he possessed enough appreciation of Islamic culture and the complexities of the Middle East to know that guns and bombs alone wouldn't accomplish that task. When he told me he had personally opposed waterboarding and other forms of "enhanced interrogation" sanctioned by his boss, I believed him; and I became convinced that his credibility with the intel community would be invaluable to me.

Still, Brennan had been at the CIA when waterboarding took place, and that association made him a nonstarter as my first agency director. Instead, I offered him the staff position of deputy national security advisor for homeland security and counterterrorism. "Your job," I told him, "will be to help me protect this country in a way that's consistent with our values, and to make sure everyone else is doing the same. Can you do that?" He said he could.

For the next four years, John Brennan would fulfill that promise, helping manage our efforts at reform and serving as my go-between with a sometimes skeptical and resistant CIA bureaucracy. He also shared my burden of knowing that any mistake we made could cost people their lives, which was the reason he could be found stoically working in a windowless West Wing office below the Oval through weekends and holidays, awake while others were sleeping, poring over every scrap of intelligence with a grim, dogged intensity that led folks around the White House to call him "the Sentinel."

IT BECAME CLEAR pretty quickly that putting the fallout from past CT practices behind us and instituting new ones where needed was going to be a slow, painful grind. Closing Gitmo meant we needed to figure out alternative means to house and legally process both existing detainees and any terrorists captured in the future. Prompted by a set of Freedom of Information Act (FOIA) requests that had worked their way through the courts, I had to decide whether documents related to the CIA's Bush-era waterboarding and rendition programs should be declassified (yes to legal memos justifying such practices, since both the memos and the programs themselves were already widely known; no to photos of the practices themselves, which the Pentagon and State Department feared might trigger international outrage and put our troops or diplomats in greater danger). Our legal teams and national security staff wrestled daily with how to set up stronger judicial and congressional oversight for our CT efforts and how to meet our obligations for transparency without tipping off **New York Times**–reading terrorists.

Rather than continue with what looked to the world like a bunch of ad hoc foreign policy decisions, we decided I'd deliver two speeches related to our anti-terrorism efforts. The first, intended mainly for domestic consumption, would insist that America's long-term national security depended on fidelity to our Constitution and the rule of law, acknowledging that in the immediate aftermath of 9/11 we'd sometimes fallen short of those standards and laying out how my administration would approach counterterrorism going forward. The second, scheduled to be given in Cairo, would address a global audience—in particular, the world's Muslims. I had promised to deliver a speech like this during the campaign, and although with everything else going on some of my team suggested canceling it, I told Rahm that backing out wasn't an option. "We may not change public attitudes in these countries overnight," I said, "but if we don't squarely address the sources of tension between the West and the Muslim world, and describe what peaceful coexistence might look like, we'll be fighting wars in the region for the next thirty years."

To help write both speeches I enlisted the immense

talents of Ben Rhodes, my thirty-one-year-old NSC speechwriter and soon-to-be deputy national security advisor for strategic communications. If Brennan represented someone who could act as a conduit between me and the national security apparatus I'd inherited, Ben connected me to my younger, more idealistic self. Raised in Manhattan by a liberal Jewish mother and a Texas lawyer father, both of whom had held government jobs under Lyndon Johnson, he had been pursuing a master's degree in fiction writing at NYU when 9/11 happened. Fueled by patriotic anger, Ben had headed to D.C. in search of a way to serve, eventually finding a job with former Indiana congressman Lee Hamilton and helping to write the influential 2006 Iraq Study Group report.

Short and prematurely balding, with dark brows that seemed perpetually furrowed, Ben had been thrown into the deep end of the pool, immediately asked by our understaffed campaign to crank out position papers, press releases, and major speeches. There'd been some growing pains: In Berlin, for example, he and Favs had landed on a beautiful German phrase—"a community of fate"—to tie together the themes of my one big preelection speech on foreign soil, only to discover a couple of hours before I was to go onstage that the phrase had been used in one of Hitler's first addresses to the Reichstag. ("Probably not the effect you're going for," Reggie Love deadpanned as I burst into laughter and Ben's face turned bright red.) Despite his youth, Ben wasn't shy about weighing in on policy or contradicting my more senior advisors, with a sharp intelligence and a stubborn earnestness that was leavened with a self-deprecating humor and healthy sense of irony. He had a writer's sensibility, one I shared, and it formed the basis for a relationship not unlike the one I'd developed with Favs: I could spend an hour with Ben dictating my arguments on a subject and count on getting a draft a few days later that not only captured my voice but also channeled something more essential: my bedrock view of the world, and sometimes even my heart.

Together, we knocked out the counterterrorism speech fairly quickly, though Ben reported that each time he sent a draft to the Pentagon or CIA for comments, it would come back with edits, red lines drawn through any word, proposal, or characterization deemed even remotely controversial or critical of practices like torture—not-so-subtle acts of resistance from the career folks, many of whom had come to Washington with the Bush administration. I told Ben to ignore most of their suggestions. On May 21, I delivered the speech at the National Archives, standing beside original copies of the Declaration of Independence, the Constitution, and the Bill of Rights—just in case anybody inside or outside the government missed the point.

The "Muslim speech," as we took to calling the second major address, was trickier. Beyond the negative portrayals of terrorists and oil sheikhs found on news broadcasts or in the movies, most Americans knew little about Islam. Meanwhile, surveys showed that Muslims around the world believed the United States was hostile toward their religion, and that our Middle East policy was based not on an interest in improving people's lives but rather on maintaining oil supplies, killing terrorists, and protecting Israel. Given this divide, I told Ben that the focus of our speech had to be less about outlining new policies and more geared toward helping the two sides under-stand each other. That meant recognizing the extraordinary contributions of Islamic civilizations in the advancement of mathematics, science, and art and acknowledging the role colonialism had played in some of the Middle East's ongoing struggles. It meant admitting past U.S. indiffer-ence toward corruption and repression in the region, and our complicity in the overthrow of Iran's democratically elected government during the Cold War, as well as acknowledging the searing humiliations endured by Palestinians living in occupied territory. Hearing such basic history from the mouth of a U.S. president would catch many people off guard, I figured, and perhaps open their minds to other hard truths: that the Islamic funda-mentalism that had come to dominate so much of the Muslim world was incompatible with the openness and tolerance that fueled modern progress; that too often Muslim leaders ginned up grievances against the West in order to distract from their own failures; that a Palestinian state would be delivered only through nego-tiation and compromise rather than incitements to violence and anti-Semitism; and that no society could truly succeed while systematically repressing its women.

WE WERE STILL working on the speech when we landed in Riyadh, Saudi Arabia, where I was scheduled to meet with King Abdullah bin Abdulaziz Al Saud, Custodian of the Two Holy Mosques (in Mecca and Medina) and the most powerful leader in the Arab world. I'd never set foot in the kingdom before, and at the lavish airport welcoming ceremony, the first thing I noticed was the complete absence of women or children on the tarmac or in the terminals—just rows of black-mustached men in military uniforms or the traditional **thawb** and **ghutra**. I had expected as much, of course; that's how things were done in the Gulf. But as I climbed into the Beast, I was still struck by how oppressive and sad such a segregated place felt, as if I'd suddenly entered a world where all the colors had been muted.

The king had arranged for me and my team to stay at his horse ranch outside Riyadh, and as our motorcade and police escort sped down a wide, spotless highway under a blanched sun, the massive, unadorned office buildings, mosques, retail outlets, and luxury car showrooms quickly giving way to scrabbly desert, I thought about how little the Islam of Saudi Arabia resembled the version of the faith I'd witnessed as a child while living in Indonesia. In Jakarta in the 1960s and '70s, Islam had occupied roughly the same place in that nation's culture as Christianity did in the average American city or town, relevant but not dominant. The muezzin's call to prayer punctuated the days, weddings and funerals followed the faith's prescribed rituals, activities slowed down during fasting months, and pork might be hard to find on a restaurant's menu. Otherwise, people lived their lives, with women riding Vespas in short skirts and high heels on their way to office jobs, boys and girls chasing kites, and long-haired youths dancing to the Beatles and the Jackson 5 at the local disco. Muslims were largely indistinguishable from the Christians, Hindus, or college-educated nonbelievers, like my stepfather, as they crammed onto Jakarta's overcrowded buses, filled theater seats at the latest kung-fu movie, smoked outside roadside taverns, or strolled down the cacophonous streets. The overtly pious were scarce in those days, if not the object of derision then at least set apart, like Jehovah's Witnesses handing out pamphlets in a Chicago neighborhood.

Saudi Arabia had always been different. Abdulaziz Ibn Saud, the nation's first monarch and the father of King Abdullah, had begun his reign in 1932 and been deeply wedded to the teachings of the eighteenth-century cleric Muhammad bin Abd al-Wahhab. Abd al-Wahhab's followers claimed to practice an uncorrupted version of Islam, viewing Shiite and Sufi Islam as heretical and observing religious tenets that were considered conservative even by the standards of traditional Arab culture: public segregation of the sexes, avoidance of contact with non-Muslims, and the rejection of secular art, music, and other pastimes that might distract from the faith. Following the post–World War I collapse of the Ottoman Empire, Abdulaziz consolidated control over rival Arab tribes and founded modern Saudi Arabia in accordance with these Wahhabist principles. His conquest of Mecca—birthplace of the prophet Muhammad and the destination for all Muslim pilgrims seeking to fulfill the Five Tenets of Islam—as well as the holy city of Medina provided him with a platform from which to exert an outsized influence over Islamic doctrine around the world.

The discovery of Saudi oil fields and the untold wealth that came from it extended that influence even further. But it also exposed the contradictions of trying to sustain such ultraconservative practices in the midst of a rapidly modernizing world. Abdulaziz needed Western technology, know-how, and distribution channels to fully exploit the kingdom's newfound treasure and formed an alliance with the United States to obtain modern weapons and secure the Saudi oil fields against rival states. Members of the extended royal family retained Western firms to invest their vast holdings and sent their children to Cambridge and Harvard to learn modern business practices. Young princes discovered the attractions of French villas, London nightclubs, and Vegas gaming rooms.

I've wondered sometimes whether there was a point when the Saudi monarchy might have reassessed its religious commitments, acknowledging that Wahhabist fundamentalism—like all forms of religious absolutism—was incompatible with modernity, and used its wealth and authority to steer Islam onto a gentler, more tolerant course. Probably not. The old ways were too deeply embedded, and as tensions with fundamentalists grew in the late 1970s, the royals may have accurately concluded that religious reform would lead inevitably to uncomfortable political and economic reform as well.

Instead, in order to avoid the kind of revolution that had established an Islamic republic in nearby Iran, the Saudi monarchy struck a bargain with its most hard-line clerics. In exchange for legitimizing the House of Saud's absolute control over the nation's economy and government (and for being willing to look the other way when members of the royal family succumbed to certain indiscretions), the clerics and religious police were granted authority to regulate daily social interactions, determine what was taught in schools, and mete out punishments to those who violated religious decrees—from public floggings to the removal of hands to actual crucifixions. Perhaps more important, the royal family steered billions of dollars to these same clerics to build mosques and madrassas across the Sunni world. As a result, from Pakistan to Egypt to Mali to Indonesia, fundamentalism grew stronger, tolerance for different Islamic practices grew weaker, drives to impose Islamic governance grew louder, and calls for a purging of Western influences from Islamic territory—through violence if necessary—grew more frequent. The Saudi monarchy could take satisfaction in having averted an Iranian-style revolution, both within its borders and among its Gulf partners (although maintaining such order still required a repressive internal security service and broad media censorship). But it had done so at the price of accelerating a transnational fundamentalist movement that despised Western influences, remained suspicious of Saudi dalliances with the United States, and served as a petri dish for the radicalization of many young Muslims: men like Osama bin Laden, the son of a prominent Saudi businessman close to the royal family, and the fifteen Saudi nationals who, along with four others, planned and carried out the September 11 attacks.

"RANCH" TURNED OUT to be something of a misnomer. With its massive grounds and multiple villas fitted with gold-plated plumbing, crystal chandeliers, and plush furnishings, King Abdullah's complex looked more like a Four Seasons hotel plopped in the middle of the desert. The king himself—an octogenarian with a jet-black mustache and beard (male vanity seemed to be a common trait among world leaders)—greeted me warmly at the entrance to what appeared to be the main residence. With him was the Saudi ambassador to the United States, Adel al-Jubeir, a clean-shaven, U.S.-educated diplomat whose impeccable English, ingratiating manner, PR savvy, and deep Washington connections had made him the ideal point person for the kingdom's attempts at damage control in the wake of 9/11.

The king was in an expansive mood that day, and with al-Jubeir acting as translator, he fondly recalled the 1945 meeting between his father and FDR aboard the USS **Quincy,** emphasized the great value he placed on the U.S.-Saudi alliance, and described the satisfaction he had felt at seeing me elected president. He approved of the idea of my upcoming speech in Cairo, insisting that Islam was a religion of peace and noting the work he had personally done to strengthen interfaith dialogues. He assured me, too, that the kingdom would coordinate with my economic advisors to make sure oil prices didn't impede the post-crisis recovery.

But when it came to two of my specific requests— that the kingdom and other members of the Arab League consider a gesture to Israel that might help jump-start peace talks with Palestinians and that our teams discuss the possible transfer of some Gitmo prisoners to Saudi rehabilitation centers—the king was noncommittal, clearly wary of potential controversy.

The conversation lightened during the midday banquet the king hosted for our delegation. It was a lavish affair, like something out of a fairy tale, the fifty-foot table laden with whole roasted lambs and heaps of saffron rice and all manner of traditional and Western delicacies. Of the sixty or so people eating, my scheduling director, Alyssa Mastromonaco, and senior advisor Valerie Jarrett were two of the three women present. Alyssa seemed cheery enough as she chatted with Saudi officials across the table, although she appeared to have some trouble keeping the headscarf she was wearing from falling into the soup bowl. The king asked about my family, and I described how Michelle and the girls were adjusting to life in the White House. He explained that he had twelve wives himself—news reports put the number closer to thirty—along with forty children and dozens more grandchildren and great-grandchildren.

"I hope you don't mind me asking, Your Majesty," I said, "but how do you keep up with twelve wives?"

"Very badly," he said, shaking his head wearily. "One of them is always jealous of the others. It's more complicated than Middle East politics."

Later, Ben and Denis came by the villa where I was staying so we could talk about final edits to the Cairo speech. Before settling in to work, we noticed a large travel case on the mantelpiece. I unsnapped the latches and lifted the top. On one side there was a large desert scene on a marble base featuring miniature gold figurines, as well as a glass clock powered by changes in temperature. On the other side, set in a velvet case, was a necklace half the length of a bicycle chain, encrusted with what appeared to be hundreds of thousands of dollars' worth of rubies and diamonds—along with a matching ring and earrings. I looked up at Ben and Denis.

"A little something for the missus," Denis said. He explained that others in the delegation had found cases with expensive watches waiting for them in their rooms. "Apparently, nobody told the Saudis about our prohibition on gifts."

Lifting the heavy jewels, I wondered how many times gifts like this had been discreetly left for other leaders during official visits to the kingdom—leaders whose countries didn't have rules against taking gifts, or at least not ones that were enforced. I thought again about the Somali pirates I had ordered killed, Muslims all, and the many young men like them across the nearby borders of Yemen and Iraq, and in Egypt, Jordan, Afghanistan, and Pakistan, whose earnings in a lifetime would probably never touch the cost of that necklace in my hands. Radicalize just 1 percent of those young men and you had yourself an army of half a million, ready to die for eternal glory—or maybe just a taste of something better.

I set the necklace down and closed the case. "All right," I said. "Let's work."

THE GREATER CAIRO metropolitan area contained more than sixteen million people. We didn't see any of them on the following day's drive from the airport. The famously chaotic streets were empty for miles, save for police officers posted everywhere, a testimony to the extraordinary grip Egyptian president Hosni Mubarak held on his country—and the fact that an American president was a tempting target for local extremist groups.

If Saudi Arabia's tradition-bound monarchy represented one path of modern Arab governance, Egypt's autocratic regime represented the other. In the early 1950s, a charismatic and urbane army colonel named Gamal Abdel Nasser had orchestrated a military overthrow of the Egyptian monarchy and instituted a secular, one-party state. Soon after, he nationalized the Suez Canal, overcoming attempted military interventions by the British and French, which made him a global figure in the fight against colonialism and far and away the most popular leader in the Arab world.

Nasser went on to nationalize other key industries, initiate domestic land reform, and launch huge public works projects, all with the goal of eliminating vestiges of both British rule and Egypt's feudal past. Overseas, he actively promoted a secular, vaguely socialist pan-Arab nationalism, fought a losing war against the Israelis, helped form the Palestinian Liberation Organization (PLO) and the Arab League, and became a charter member of the Non-Aligned Movement, which ostensibly refused to take sides in the Cold War but drew the suspicion and ire of Washington, in part because Nasser was accepting economic and military aid from the Soviets. He also ruthlessly cracked down on dissent and the formation of competing political parties in Egypt, particularly targeting the Muslim Brotherhood, a group that sought to establish an Islamic government through grassroots political mobilization and charitable works, but also included members who occasionally turned to violence.

So dominant was Nasser's authoritarian style of governance that even after his death in 1970, Middle Eastern leaders sought to replicate it. Lacking Nasser's sophistication and ability to connect with the masses, though, men like Syria's Hafez al-Assad, Iraq's Saddam Hussein, and Libya's Muammar Gaddafi would maintain their power largely through corruption, patronage, brutal repression, and a constant if ineffective campaign against Israel.

After Nasser's successor, Anwar Sadat, was assassinated in 1981, Hosni Mubarak took control using roughly the same formula, with one notable difference: Sadat's signing of a peace accord with Israel had made Egypt a U.S. ally, leading successive American administrations to overlook the regime's increasing corruption, shabby human rights record, and occasional anti-Semitism. Flush with aid not just from the United States but from the Saudis and other oil-rich Gulf states, Mubarak never bothered to reform his country's stagnant economy, which now left a generation of disaffected young Egyptians unable to find work.

Our motorcade arrived at Qubba Palace—an elaborate mid-nineteenth-century structure and one of three presidential palaces in Cairo—and after a greeting ceremony, Mubarak invited me to his office for an hour-long discussion. He was eighty-one but still broad-shouldered and sturdy, with a Roman nose, dark hair combed back from his forehead, and heavy-lidded eyes that gave him the air of a man both accustomed to and slightly weary of his own command. After talking with him about the Egyptian economy and soliciting suggestions on how to reinvigorate the Arab-Israeli peace process, I raised the issue of human rights, suggesting steps he might take to release political prisoners and ease restrictions on the press.

Speaking accented but passable English, Mubarak politely deflected my concerns, insisting that his security services targeted only Islamic extremists and that the Egyptian public strongly supported his firm approach. I was left with an impression that would become all too familiar in my dealings with aging autocrats: Shut away in palaces, their every interaction mediated by the hard-faced, obsequious functionaries that surrounded them, they were unable to distinguish between their personal interests and those of their nations, their

actions governed by no broader purpose beyond maintaining the tangled web of patronage and business
interests that kept them in power.

What a contrast it was, then, to walk into Cairo
University's Grand Hall and find a packed house absolutely crackling with energy. We'd pressed the government
to open my address to a wide cross section of Egyptian
society, and it was clear that the mere presence of university
students, journalists, scholars, leaders of women's organizations, community activists, and even some prominent
clerics and Muslim Brotherhood figures among the three
thousand people present would help make this a singular
event, one that would reach a wide global audience via
television. As soon as I stepped onto the stage and delivered the Islamic salutation **"Assalamu alaikum,"** the crowd
roared its approval. I was careful to make clear that no one
speech was going to solve entrenched problems. But as the
cheers and applause continued through my discussions of
democracy, human rights and women's rights, religious
tolerance and the need for a true and lasting peace between
a secure Israel and an autonomous Palestinian state, I
could imagine the beginnings of a new Middle East. In
that moment, it wasn't hard to envision an alternate reality
in which the young people in that auditorium would build
new businesses and schools, lead responsive, functioning
governments, and begin to reimagine their faith in a way
that was at once true to tradition and open to other sources
of wisdom. Perhaps the high-ranking government officials
who sat grim-faced in the third row could imagine it
as well.

I left the stage to a prolonged standing ovation and
made a point of finding Ben, who as a rule got too

nervous to watch any speech he'd helped to write and instead holed up in some back room, tapping into his BlackBerry. He was grinning from ear to ear.

"I guess that worked," I said.

"That was historic," he said, without a trace of irony.

IN LATER YEARS, critics and even some of my supporters would have a field day contrasting the lofty, hopeful tone of the Cairo speech with the grim realities that would play out in the Middle East during my two terms in office. For some, it showed the sin of naïveté, one that undermined key U.S. allies like Mubarak and thus emboldened the forces of chaos. For others, the problem was not the vision set forth in the speech but rather what they considered my failure to deliver on that vision with effective, meaningful action. I was tempted to answer, of course—to point out that I'd be the first to say that no single speech would solve the region's long-standing challenges; that we'd pushed hard on every initiative I mentioned that day, whether large (a deal between the Israelis and the Palestinians) or small (the creation of training programs for would-be entrepreneurs); that the arguments I made in Cairo were ones I'd still make.

But in the end, the facts of what happened are the facts, and I'm left with the same set of questions I first wrestled with as a young organizer. How useful is it to describe the world as it should be when efforts to achieve that world are bound to fall short? Was Václav Havel correct in suggesting that by raising expectations, I was doomed to disappoint them? Was it possible that abstract principles and high-minded ideals were and always would be nothing more than a pretense, a palliative, a way to beat back despair, but no match for the more primal urges that really moved us, so that no matter what we said or did, history was sure to run along its predetermined course, an endless cycle of fear, hunger and conflict, dominance and weakness?

Even at the time, doubts came naturally to me, the sugar high of the speech quickly replaced with thoughts of all the work awaiting me back home and the many forces arrayed against what I hoped to do. The excursion we took immediately after the speech deepened my brooding: a fifteen-minute helicopter ride, high over the sprawling city, until suddenly the jumble of cream-colored, Cubist-looking structures was gone and there was only desert and sun and the wondrous, geometric lines of the Pyramids cutting across the horizon. Upon landing, we were greeted by Cairo's leading Egyptologist, a happily eccentric gentleman with a floppy wide-brimmed hat straight out of an Indiana Jones movie, and for the next several hours my team and I had the place to ourselves. We scaled the ancient, boulder-like stones of each pyramid's face. We stood in the shadow of the Sphinx, staring up at its silent, indifferent gaze. We climbed a narrow, vertical chute to stand within one of the pharaohs' dark inner chambers, the mystery of which was punctuated by Axe's timeless words during our careful descent back down the ladder:

"Goddamn it, Rahm, slow down—your ass is in my face!"

At one point, as I stood watching Gibbs and some of the other staffers trying to mount camels for the obligatory tourist pictures, Reggie and Marvin motioned for me to join them inside the corridor of one of the Pyramids' lesser temples.

"Check it out, boss," Reggie said, pointing at the wall. There, carved in the smooth, porous stone, was the dark image of a man's face. Not the profile typical of hieroglyphics but a straight-on head shot. A long, oval face. Prominent ears sticking straight out like handles. A cartoon of me, somehow forged in antiquity.

"Must be a relative," Marvin said.

We all had a laugh then, and the two of them wandered off to join the camel riders. Our guide couldn't tell me just who it was that the image depicted, or even whether it dated back to the time of the Pyramids. But I stood at the wall for an extra beat, trying to imagine the life behind that etching. Had he been a member of the royal court? A slave? A foreman? Maybe just a bored vandal, camped out at night centuries after the wall had been built, inspired by the stars and his own loneliness to sketch his own likeness. I tried to imagine the worries and strivings that might have consumed him and the nature of the world he'd occupied, likely full of its own struggles and palace intrigues, conquests and catastrophes, events that probably at the time felt no less pressing than those I'd face as soon as I got back to Washington. All of it was forgotten now, none of it mattered, the pharaoh, the slave, and the vandal all long turned to dust.

Just as every speech I'd delivered, every law I passed and decision I made, would soon be forgotten.

Just as I and all those I loved would someday turn to dust.

. . .

BEFORE RETURNING HOME, I retraced a more recent history. President Sarkozy had organized a commemoration of the sixty-fifth anniversary of the Allied landing at Normandy and had asked me to speak. Rather than head directly to France, we stopped first in Dresden, Germany, where Allied bombing toward the end of World War II resulted in a firestorm that engulfed the city, killing an estimated twenty-five thousand people. My visit was a purposeful gesture of respect for a now-stalwart ally. Angela Merkel and I toured a famous eighteenth-century church that had been destroyed by the air raids, only to be rebuilt fifty years later with a golden cross and orb crafted by a British silversmith whose father had been one of the bomber pilots. The silversmith's work served as a reminder that even those on the right side of war must not turn away from their enemy's suffering, or foreclose the possibility of reconciliation.

Merkel and I were later joined by the writer and Nobel laureate Elie Wiesel for a visit to the former Buchenwald concentration camp. This, too, had practical political significance: We'd originally considered a trip to Tel Aviv to follow my speech in Cairo, but in deference to the Israeli government's wishes that I not make the Palestinian question the primary focus of my speech—nor feed the perception that the Arab-Israeli conflict was the root cause of the Middle East's turmoil—we had settled instead on a tour of one of the epicenters of the Holocaust to signal my commitment to the security of Israel and the Jewish people.

I had a more personal reason as well for wanting to

make this pilgrimage. As a young man in college, I'd had a chance to hear Wiesel speak and had been deeply moved by how he chronicled his experiences as a Buchenwald survivor. Reading his books, I'd found an impregnable moral core that both fortified me and challenged me to be better. It had been one of the great pleasures of my time in the Senate that Elie and I became friends. When I told him that one of my great-uncles, Toot's brother Charles Payne, had been a member of the U.S. infantry division that reached one of Buchenwald's subcamps in April 1945 and began the liberation there, Elie had insisted that one day we would go together. Being with him now fulfilled that promise.

"If these trees could talk," Elie said softly, waving toward a row of stately oaks as the two of us and Merkel slowly walked the gravel path toward Buchenwald's main entrance. The sky was low and gray, the press at a respectful distance. We stopped at two memorials to those who died at the camp. One was a set of stone slabs featuring the names of the victims, including Elie's father. The other was a list of the countries they came from, etched on a steel plate that was kept heated to thirty-seven degrees Celsius: the temperature of the human body, meant to be a reminder—in a place premised on hate and intolerance—of the common humanity we share.

For the next hour, we wandered the grounds, passing guard towers and walls lined with barbed wire, staring into the dark ovens of the crematorium and circling the foundations of the prisoners' barracks. There were photographs of the camp as it had once been, mostly taken by U.S. army units at the moment of liberation. One showed Elie at sixteen looking out from one of the bunks, the same handsome face and mournful eyes but jagged with hunger and illness and the enormity of all he had witnessed. Elie described to me and Merkel the daily strategies he and other prisoners had used to survive: how the stronger or luckier ones would sneak food to the weak and the dying; how resistance meetings took place in latrines so foul that no guards ever entered them; how adults organized secret classes to teach children math, poetry, history—not just for learning's sake, but so those children might maintain a belief that they would one day be free to pursue a normal life.

In remarks to the press afterward, Merkel spoke clearly and humbly of the necessity for Germans to remember the past—to wrestle with the agonizing question of how their homeland could have perpetrated such horrors and recognize the special responsibility they now shouldered to stand up against bigotry of all kinds. Then Elie spoke, describing how in 1945—paradoxically—he had emerged from the camp feeling hopeful about the future. Hopeful, he said, because he assumed that the world had surely learned once and for all that hatred was useless and racism stupid and "the will to conquer other people's minds or territories or aspirations . . . is meaningless." He wasn't so sure now that such optimism was justified, he said, not after the killing fields of Cambodia, Rwanda, Darfur, and Bosnia.

But he beseeched us, beseeched me, to leave Buchenwald with resolve, to try to bring about peace, to use the memory of what had happened on the ground where we stood to see past anger and divisions and find strength in solidarity.

I carried his words with me to Normandy, my

second-to-last stop on the trip. On a bright, nearly cloudless day, thousands of people had gathered at the American Cemetery there, set atop a high coastal bluff that overlooked the English Channel's blue, white-capped waters. Coming in by helicopter, I gazed down at the pebbled beaches below, where sixty-five years earlier more than 150,000 Allied troops, half of them Americans, had pitched through high surf to land under relentless enemy fire. They had taken the serrated cliffs of Pointe du Hoc, eventually establishing the beachhead that would prove decisive in winning the war. The thousands of marble headstones, bone-white rows across the deep-green grass, spoke to the price that had been paid.

I was greeted by a group of young Army Rangers who earlier in the day had re-created the parachute jumps that had accompanied D-Day's amphibious landings. They were in dress uniform now, handsome and fit, smiling with a well-earned swagger. I shook hands with each of them, asking where they were from and where they were currently deployed. A sergeant first class named Cory Remsburg explained that most of them had just come back from Iraq; he'd be heading out to Afghanistan in the coming weeks, he said, for his tenth deployment. He quickly added, "That's nothing compared to what the men did here sixty-five years ago, sir. They made our way of life possible."

A survey of the crowd that day reminded me that very few D-Day or World War II vets were still alive and able to make the trip. Many who had made it needed wheelchairs or walkers to get around. Bob Dole, the acerbic Kansan who had overcome devastating injuries during World War II to become one of the most accomplished and respected senators in Washington, was there. So was my Uncle Charlie, Toot's brother, who'd come with his wife, Melanie, as my guest. A retired librarian, he was one of the most gentle and unassuming men I knew. According to Toot, he'd been so shaken by his experiences as a soldier that he barely spoke for six months after returning home.

Whatever wounds they carried, these men exuded a quiet pride as they gathered in their veterans' caps and neat blazers pinned with well-polished service medals. They swapped stories, accepted handshakes and words of thanks from me and other strangers, and were surrounded by children and grandchildren who knew them less for their war heroism than for the lives they had led afterward—as teachers, engineers, factory workers, or store owners, men who had married their sweethearts, worked hard to buy a house, fought off depression and disappointments, coached Little League, volunteered at their churches or synagogues, and seen their sons and daughters marry and have families of their own.

Standing on the stage as the ceremony began, I realized that the lives of these eighty-something-year-old veterans more than answered whatever doubts stirred in me. Maybe nothing would come of my Cairo speech. Maybe the dysfunction of the Middle East would play itself out regardless of what I did. Maybe the best we could hope for was to placate men like Mubarak and kill those who would try to kill us. Maybe, as the Pyramids had whispered, none of it mattered in the long run. But on the only scale that any of us can truly comprehend, the span of centuries, the actions of an American president sixty-five years earlier had set the world on a better course. The sacrifices these men had made, at roughly the same age as the young Army Rangers I'd just met, had made all the difference. Just as the witness of Elie Wiesel, a beneficiary of those sacrifices, made a difference; just as Angela Merkel's willingness to absorb the tragic lessons of her own nation's past made a difference.

It was my turn to speak. I told the stories of a few of the men we had come to honor. "Our history has always been the sum total of the choices made and the actions taken by each individual man and woman," I concluded. "It has always been up to us." Turning back to look at the old men sitting behind me on the stage, I believed this to be true.

CHAPTER 16

OUR FIRST SPRING IN THE WHITE HOUSE arrived early. By mid-March, the air had softened and the days grown longer. As the weather warmed, the South Lawn became almost like a private park to explore. There were acres of lush grass ringed by massive, shady oaks and elms and a tiny pond tucked behind the hedges, with the handprints of presidential children and grandchildren pressed into the paved pathway that led to it. There were nooks and crannies for games of tag and hide-and-go-seek, and there was even a bit of wildlife—not just squirrels and rabbits but a red-tailed hawk that a group of visiting fourth graders had named Lincoln and a slender, long-legged fox that could sometimes be spotted at a distance in the late afternoon and occasionally got bold enough to wander down the colonnade.

Cooped up as we'd been through the winter, we took full advantage of the new backyard. We had a swing set installed for Sasha and Malia, near the swimming pool and directly in front of the Oval Office. Looking up from a late afternoon meeting on this or that crisis, I might glimpse the girls playing outside, their faces set in bliss as they soared high on the swings. We also set up a couple of portable basketball hoops on either end of the tennis courts, so that I could sneak out with Reggie for a quick game of H-O-R-S-E and the staff could play interoffice games of five-on-five.

And with the help of Sam Kass, as well as the White House horticulturalist and a crew of enthusiastic fifth graders from a local elementary school, Michelle planted her garden. What we expected to be a meaningful but modest project to encourage healthy eating ended up becoming a genuine phenomenon, inspiring school and community gardens across the country, attracting worldwide attention, and generating so much produce by the end of that first summer—collards, carrots, peppers, fennel, onions, lettuce, broccoli, strawberries, blueberries, you name it—that the White House kitchen started donating crates of spare vegetables to the local food banks. As an unexpected bonus, a member of the groundskeeping crew turned out to be an amateur beekeeper, and we gave him the okay to set up a small hive. Not only did it end up producing more than a hundred pounds of honey a year, but an enterprising microbrewer in the Navy Mess suggested that we could use the honey in a beer recipe, which led to the purchase of a home brew kit and made me the first presidential brewmaster. (George Washington, I was told, made his own whiskey.)

But of all the pleasures that first year in the White House would deliver, none quite compared to the mid-April arrival of Bo, a huggable, four-legged black bundle of fur, with a snowy-white chest and front paws. Malia and Sasha, who'd been lobbying for a puppy since before the campaign, squealed with delight upon seeing him for the first time, letting him lick their ears and faces as the three of them rolled around on the floor of the residence. It wasn't just the girls who fell in love either. Michelle spent so much time with Bo—teaching him tricks, cradling him in her lap, sneaking him bacon—that Marian confessed to feeling like a bad parent for never having given in to Michelle's girlhood wish for a family dog.

As for me, I got what someone once described as the only reliable friend a politician can have in Washington. Bo also gave me an added excuse to put off my evening paperwork and join my family on meandering after-dinner walks around the South Lawn. It was during those moments—with the light fading into streaks of purple and gold, Michelle smiling and squeezing my hand as the dog bounded in and out of the bushes with the girls giving chase, Malia eventually catching up to us to interrogate me about things like birds' nests or cloud formations while Sasha wrapped herself around one of my legs to see how far I could carry her along—that I felt normal and whole and as lucky as any man has a right to expect.

Bo had come to us as a gift from Ted and Vicki Kennedy, part of a litter that was related to Teddy's own beloved pair of Portuguese water dogs. It was an incredibly thoughtful gesture—not only because the breed was hypoallergenic (a necessity due to Malia's allergies) but also because the Kennedys had made sure that Bo was housebroken before he came to us. When I called to thank them, though, it was only Vicki I could speak with. It had been almost a year since Teddy was diagnosed with a malignant brain tumor, and although he was still

receiving treatment in Boston, it was clear to everyone—
Teddy included—that the prognosis was not good.

I'd seen him in March, when he'd made a surprise
appearance at a White House conference we held to get
the ball rolling on universal-healthcare legislation. Vicki
had worried about the trip, and I'd understood why.
Teddy's walk was unsteady that day; his suit barely fit
after all the weight he'd lost, and despite his cheerful
demeanor, his pinched, cloudy eyes showed the strain it
took just to hold himself upright. And yet he'd insisted
on coming anyway, because thirty-five years earlier the
cause of getting everyone decent, affordable healthcare
had become personal for him. His son Teddy Jr. had been
diagnosed with a bone cancer that led to a leg amputation at the age of twelve. While at the hospital, Teddy
had gotten to know other parents whose children were
just as ill but who had no idea how they'd pay the mounting medical bills. Then and there, he had vowed to do
something to change that.

Through seven presidents, Teddy had fought the good
fight. During the Clinton administration, he helped
secure passage of the Children's Health Insurance Program.
Over the objections of some in his own party, he worked
with President Bush to get drug coverage for seniors. But
for all his power and legislative skill, the dream of establishing universal healthcare—a system that delivered
quality medical care to all people, regardless of their ability to pay—continued to elude him.

Which is why Ted Kennedy had forced himself out of
bed to come to our conference, knowing that while he
could no longer lead the fight, his brief but symbolic

presence might have an effect. Sure enough, when he walked into the East Room, the hundred and fifty people who were present erupted into cheers and lengthy applause. After opening the conference, I called upon him to speak first, and some of his former staffers could be seen tearing up at the sight of their old boss rising to speak. His remarks were short; his baritone didn't boom quite as loudly as it used to when he'd roared on the Senate floor. He looked forward, he said, to being "a foot soldier" in the upcoming effort. By the time we'd moved on to the third or fourth speaker, Vicki had quietly escorted him out the door.

I saw him only once more in person, a couple of weeks later, at a signing ceremony for a bill expanding national service programs, which Republicans and Democrats alike had named in his honor. But I would think of Teddy sometimes when Bo wandered into the Treaty Room, his head down, his tail wagging, before he curled up at my feet. And I'd recall what Teddy had told me that day, just before we walked into the East Room together.

"This is the time, Mr. President," he had said. "Don't let it slip away."

THE QUEST FOR some form of universal healthcare in the United States dates back to 1912, when Theodore Roosevelt, who had previously served nearly eight years as a Republican president, decided to run again—this time on a progressive ticket and with a platform that called for the establishment of a centralized national health service. At the time, few people had or felt the need for private health insurance. Most Americans paid their doctors visit by visit, but the field of medicine was quickly growing more sophisticated, and as more diagnostic tests and surgeries became available, the attendant costs began to rise, tying health more explicitly to wealth. Both the United Kingdom and Germany had addressed similar issues by instituting national health insurance systems, and other European nations would eventually follow suit. While Roosevelt ultimately lost the 1912 election, his party's progressive ideals planted a seed that accessible and affordable medical care might be viewed as a right more than a privilege. It wasn't long, however, before doctors and southern politicians vocally opposed any type of government involvement in healthcare, branding it as a form of bolshevism.

After FDR imposed a nationwide wage freeze meant to stem inflation during World War II, many companies began offering private health insurance and pension benefits as a way to compete for the limited number of workers not deployed overseas. Once the war ended, this employer-based system continued, in no small part because labor unions liked the arrangement, since it enabled them to use the more generous benefit packages negotiated under collective bargaining agreements as a selling point to recruit new members. The downside was that it left those unions unmotivated to push for government-sponsored health programs that might help everybody else. Harry Truman proposed a national healthcare system twice, once in 1945 and again as part of his Fair Deal package in 1949, but his appeal for public support was no match for the well-financed PR efforts of the American Medical Association and other industry lobbyists. Opponents didn't just kill Truman's effort. They convinced a large swath of the public that "socialized medicine" would lead to rationing, the loss of your family doctor, and the freedoms Americans hold so dear.

Rather than challenging private insurance head-on, progressives shifted their energy to help those populations the marketplace had left behind. These efforts bore fruit during LBJ's Great Society campaign, when a universal single-payer program partially funded by payroll tax revenue was introduced for seniors (Medicare) and a not-so-comprehensive program based on a combination of federal and state funding was set up for the poor (Medicaid). During the 1970s and early 1980s, this patchwork system functioned well enough, with roughly 80 percent of Americans covered through either their jobs or one of these two programs. Meanwhile, defenders of the status quo could point to the many innovations brought to market by the for-profit medical industry, from MRIs to lifesaving drugs.

Useful as they were, though, these innovations also further drove up healthcare costs. And with insurers footing the nation's medical bills, patients had little incentive to question whether drug companies were overcharging or if doctors and hospitals were ordering redundant tests and unnecessary treatments in order to pad their bottom lines. Meanwhile, nearly a fifth of the country lived just an illness or accident away from potential financial ruin. Forgoing regular checkups and preventive care because they couldn't afford it, the uninsured often waited until they were very sick before seeking care at hospital emergency rooms, where more advanced illnesses meant more expensive treatment. Hospitals made up for this uncompensated care by increasing prices for insured customers, which in turn further jacked up premiums.

All this explained why the United States spent a lot more money per person on healthcare than any other advanced economy (112 percent more than Canada, 109 percent more than France, 117 percent more than Japan) and for similar or worse results. The difference amounted to hundreds of billions of dollars per year—money that could have been used instead to provide quality childcare for American families, or to reduce college tuition, or to eliminate a good chunk of the federal deficit. Spiraling healthcare costs also burdened American businesses: Japanese and German automakers didn't have to worry about the extra $1,500 in worker and retiree healthcare costs that Detroit had to build into the price of every car rolling off the assembly line.

In fact, it was in response to foreign competition that U.S. companies began off-loading rising insurance costs onto their employees in the late 1980s and '90s, replacing traditional plans that had few, if any, out-of-pocket costs with cheaper versions that included higher deductibles, co-pays, lifetime limits, and other unpleasant surprises hidden in the fine print. Unions often found themselves able to preserve their traditional benefit plans only by agreeing to forgo increases in wages. Small businesses found it tough to provide their workers with health benefits at all. Meanwhile, insurance companies that operated in the individual market perfected the art of rejecting customers who, according to their actuarial data, were most likely to make use of the healthcare system, especially anyone with a "preexisting condition"—which they often defined to include anything from a previous bout of cancer to asthma and chronic allergies.

It's no wonder, then, that by the time I took office there were very few people ready to defend the existing system. More than 43 million Americans were now uninsured, premiums for family coverage had risen 97 percent since 2000, and costs were only continuing to climb. And yet the prospect of trying to get a big healthcare-reform bill through Congress at the height of a historic recession made my team nervous. Even Axe—who'd experienced the challenges of getting specialized care for a daughter with severe epilepsy and had left journalism to become a political consultant in part to pay for her treatment—had his doubts.

"The data's pretty clear," Axe said when we discussed the topic early on. "People may hate the way things work in general, but most of them have insurance. They don't really think about the flaws in the system until somebody in their own family gets sick. They like their doctor. They don't trust Washington to fix anything. And even if they think you're sincere, they worry that any changes you make will cost them money and help somebody else. Plus, when you ask them what changes they'd like to see to the healthcare system, they basically want every possible treatment, regardless of cost or effectiveness, from whatever provider they choose, whenever they want it— for free. Which, of course, we can't deliver. And that's before the insurance companies, the drug companies, the docs start running ads—"

"What Axe is trying to say, Mr. President," Rahm interrupted, his face screwed up in a frown, "is that this can blow up in our faces."

Rahm went on to remind us that he'd had a front-row seat at the last push for universal healthcare, when Hillary Clinton's legislative proposal crashed and burned, creating a backlash that contributed to Democrats losing control of the House in the 1994 midterms. "Republicans will say healthcare is a big new liberal spending binge, and that it's a distraction from solving the economic crisis."

"Unless I'm missing something," I said, "we're doing everything we can do on the economy."

"I know that, Mr. President. But the American people don't know that."

"So what are we saying here?" I asked. "That despite having the biggest Democratic majorities in decades, despite the promises we made during the campaign, we shouldn't try to get healthcare done?"

Rahm looked to Axe for help.

"We all think we should try," Axe said. "You just need to know that if we lose, your presidency will be badly weakened. And nobody understands that better than McConnell and Boehner."

I stood up, signaling that the meeting was over.

"We better not lose, then," I said.

WHEN I THINK back to those early conversations, it's hard to deny my overconfidence. I was convinced that the logic of healthcare reform was so obvious that even in the face of well-organized opposition I could rally the American people's support. Other big initiatives—like immigration reform and climate change legislation—would probably be even harder to get through Congress; I figured that scoring a victory on the item that most affected people's day-to-day lives was our best shot at building momentum for the rest of my legislative agenda. As for the political hazards Axe and Rahm worried about, the recession virtually ensured that my poll numbers were going to take a hit anyway. Being timid wouldn't change that reality. Even if it did, passing up a chance to help millions of people just because it might hurt my reelection prospects . . . well, that was exactly the kind of myopic, self-preserving behavior I'd vowed to reject.

My interest in healthcare went beyond policy or politics; it was personal, just as it was for Teddy. Each time I met a parent struggling to come up with the money to get treatment for a sick child, I thought back to the night Michelle and I had to take a three-month-old Sasha to the emergency room for what turned out to be viral meningitis—the terror and helplessness we felt as the nurses whisked her away for a spinal tap, and the realization that we might never have caught the infection in time had the girls not had a regular pediatrician we felt comfortable calling in the middle of the night. When, on the campaign trail, I met farmworkers or supermarket cashiers suffering from a bum knee or bad back because they couldn't afford a doctor's visit, I thought about one of my best friends, Bobby Titcomb, a commercial fisherman in Hawaii who resorted to professional medical help only for life-threatening injuries (like the time a diving accident resulted in a spear puncturing his lung) because the monthly cost of insurance would have wiped out what he earned from an entire week's catch.

Most of all, I thought about my mom. In mid-June, I headed to Green Bay, Wisconsin, for the first of a series of healthcare town hall meetings we would hold around the country, hoping to solicit citizen input and educate people on the possibilities for reform. Introducing me that day was Laura Klitzka, who was thirty-five years old and had been diagnosed with aggressive breast cancer that had spread to her bones. Even though she was on her husband's insurance plan, repeated rounds of surgery, radiation, and chemo had bumped her up against the policy's lifetime limits, leaving them with $12,000 in unpaid medical bills. Over her husband Peter's objections, she was now pondering whether more treatment was worth it. Sitting in their living room before we headed for the event, she smiled wanly as we watched Peter doing his best to keep track of the two young kids playing on the floor.

"I want as much time with them as I can get," Laura said to me, "but I don't want to leave them with a mountain of debt. It feels selfish." Her eyes started misting, and I held her hand, remembering my mom wasting away in those final months: the times she'd put off checkups that might have caught her disease because she was in between consulting contracts and didn't have coverage; the stress she carried to her hospital bed when her insurer refused to pay her disability claim, arguing that she had failed to disclose a preexisting condition despite the fact that she hadn't even been diagnosed when her policy started. The unspoken regrets.

Passing a healthcare bill wouldn't bring my mom back. It wouldn't douse the guilt I still felt for not having been at her side when she took her last breath. It would probably come too late to help Laura Klitzka and her family.

But it would save **somebody's** mom out there, somewhere down the line. And that was worth fighting for.

. . .

THE QUESTION WAS whether we could get it done. As tough as it had been to pass the Recovery Act, the concept behind the stimulus legislation was pretty simple: enable the government to pump out money as fast as it could in order to keep the economy afloat and people employed. The law didn't take cash out of anyone's pockets, or force a change in how businesses operated, or discontinue old programs in order to pay for new ones. In the immediate term, there were no losers in the deal.

By contrast, any major healthcare bill meant rejiggering one-sixth of the American economy. Legislation of this scope was guaranteed to involve hundreds of pages of endlessly fussed-over amendments and regulations, some of them new, some of them rewrites to previous law, all of them with their own high stakes. A single provision tucked inside the bill could translate to billions of dollars in gains or losses for some sector of the health-care industry. A shift in one number, a zero here or a decimal point there, could mean a million more families getting coverage—or not. Across the country, insurance companies like Aetna and UnitedHealthcare were major employers, and local hospitals served as the economic anchor for many small towns and counties. People had good reasons—life-and-death reasons—to worry about how any change would affect them.

There was also the question of how to pay for the law. To cover more people, I had argued, America didn't need to spend more money on healthcare; we just needed to use that money more wisely. In theory, that was true. But one person's waste and inefficiency was another person's profit or convenience; spending on coverage would show up on the federal books much sooner than the savings from reform; and unlike the insurance companies or Big Pharma, whose shareholders expected them to be on guard against any change that might cost them a dime, most of the potential beneficiaries of reform—the wait-ress, the family farmer, the independent contractor, the cancer survivor—didn't have gaggles of well-paid and experienced lobbyists roaming the halls of Congress on their behalf.

In other words, both the politics and the substance of healthcare were mind-numbingly complicated. I was going to have to explain to the American people, includ-ing those with quality health insurance, why and how reform could work. For this reason, I thought we'd use as open and transparent a process as possible when it came to developing the necessary legislation. "Everyone will have a seat at the table," I'd told voters during the cam-paign. "Not negotiating behind closed doors, but bringing all parties together, and broadcasting those negotiations on C-SPAN, so that the American people can see what the choices are." When I later brought this idea up with Rahm, he looked like he wished I weren't the president, just so he could more vividly explain the stupidity of my plan. If we were going to get a bill passed, he told me, the process would involve dozens of deals and compromises along the way—and it wasn't going to be conducted like a civics seminar.

"Making sausage isn't pretty, Mr. President," he said. "And you're asking for a really big piece of sausage."

ONE THING RAHM and I did agree on was that we had months of work ahead of us, parsing the cost and outcome of each piece of possible legislation, coordinating every effort across different federal agencies and both houses of Congress, and all the while looking for leverage with major players in the healthcare world, from medical providers and hospital administrators to insurers and pharmaceutical companies. To do all this, we needed a top-notch healthcare team to keep us on track.

Luckily we were able to recruit a remarkable trio of women to help run the show. Kathleen Sebelius, the two-term Democratic governor from Republican-leaning Kansas, came on as secretary of health and human services (HHS). A former state insurance commissioner, she knew both the politics and the economics of healthcare and was a gifted enough politician—smart, funny, outgoing, tough, and media savvy—to serve as the public face of health reform, someone we could put on TV or send to town halls around the country to explain what we were doing. Jeanne Lambrew, a professor at the University of Texas and an expert on Medicare and Medicaid, became the director of the HHS Office of Health Reform, basically our chief policy advisor. Tall, earnest, and often oblivious to political constraints, she had every fact and nuance of every healthcare proposal at her fingertips—and could be counted on to keep the room honest if we veered too far in the direction of political expediency.

But it was Nancy-Ann DeParle whom I would come to rely on most as our campaign took shape. A Tennessee lawyer who'd run that state's health programs before serving as the Medicare administrator in the Clinton administration, Nancy-Ann carried herself with the crisp professionalism of someone accustomed to seeing hard work translate into success. How much of that drive could be traced to her experiences growing up Chinese American in a tiny Tennessee town, I couldn't say. Nancy-Ann didn't talk much about herself—at least not with me. I do know that when she was seventeen, her mom died of lung cancer, which might have had something to do with her willingness to give up a lucrative position at a private equity firm to work in a job that required even more time away from a loving husband and two young sons.

It seems I wasn't the only one for whom getting healthcare passed was personal.

Along with Rahm, Phil Schiliro, and deputy chief of staff Jim Messina, who had served as Plouffe's right hand in the campaign and was one of our shrewdest political operators, our healthcare team began to map out what a legislative strategy might look like. Based on our experiences with the Recovery Act, we had no doubt that Mitch McConnell would do everything he could to torpedo our efforts, and that the chances of getting Republican votes in the Senate for something as big and as controversial as a healthcare bill were slim. We could take heart from the fact that instead of the fifty-eight senators who were caucusing with the Democrats when we passed the stimulus bill, we were likely to have sixty by the time any healthcare bill actually came to a vote. Al Franken had finally taken his seat after a contentious election recount in Minnesota, and Arlen Specter had decided to switch parties after being effectively driven out of the GOP—just like Charlie Crist—for supporting the Recovery Act.

Still, our filibuster-proof head count was tenuous, for it included a terminally ill Ted Kennedy and the frail and ailing Robert Byrd of West Virginia, not to mention conservative Dems like Nebraska's Ben Nelson (a former insurance company executive) who could go sideways on us at any minute. Beyond wanting some margin for error, I also knew that passing something as monumental as healthcare reform on a purely party-line vote would make the law politically more vulnerable down the road. Consequently we thought it made sense to shape our legislative proposal in such a way that it at least had a chance of winning over a handful of Republicans.

Fortunately we had a model to work with, one that, ironically, had grown out of a partnership between Ted Kennedy and former Massachusetts governor Mitt Romney, one of John McCain's opponents in the Republican primary for president. Confronting budget shortfalls and the prospect of losing Medicaid funding a few years earlier, Romney had become fixated on finding a way to get more Massachusetts residents properly insured, which would then reduce state spending on emergency care for the uninsured and, ideally, lead to a healthier population in general.

He and his staff came up with a multipronged approach in which every person would be required to purchase health insurance (an "individual mandate"), the same way every car owner was required to carry auto insurance. Middle-income people who couldn't access insurance through their job, didn't qualify for Medicare or Medicaid, and were unable to afford insurance on their own would get a government subsidy to buy coverage. Subsidies would be determined on a sliding scale according to each person's income, and a central online marketplace—an "exchange"—would be set up so that consumers could shop for the best insurance deal. Insurers, meanwhile, would no longer be able to deny people coverage based on preexisting conditions.

These two ideas—the individual mandate and protecting people with preexisting conditions—went hand in hand. With a huge new pool of government-subsidized customers, insurers no longer had an excuse for trying to cherry-pick only the young and healthy for coverage to protect their profits. Meanwhile, the mandate ensured that people couldn't game the system by waiting until they got sick to purchase insurance. Touting the plan to reporters, Romney called the individual mandate "the ultimate conservative idea" because it promoted personal responsibility.

Not surprisingly, Massachusetts's Democratic-controlled state legislature had initially been suspicious of the Romney plan, and not just because a Republican had proposed it; among many progressives, the need to replace private insurance and for-profit healthcare with a single-payer system like Canada's was an article of faith. Had we been starting from scratch, I would have agreed with them; the evidence from other countries showed that a single, national system—basically Medicare for All—was a cost-effective way to deliver quality healthcare. But neither Massachusetts nor the United States was starting from scratch. Teddy, who despite his reputation as a wide-eyed liberal was ever practical, understood that trying to dismantle the existing system and replace it with an entirely new one would be not only a political nonstarter but hugely disruptive economically. Instead, he'd embraced the Romney proposal with enthusiasm and helped the governor line up the Democratic votes in the state legislature required to get it passed into law.

"Romneycare," as it eventually became known, was now two years old and had been a clear success, driving the uninsured rate in Massachusetts down to just under 4 percent, the lowest in the country. Teddy had used it as the basis for draft legislation he'd started preparing many months ahead of the election in his role as chair of the Senate Health and Education Committee. And though Plouffe and Axe had persuaded me to hold off on endorsing the Massachusetts approach during the campaign—the idea of requiring people to buy insurance was extremely unpopular with voters, and I'd instead focused my plan on lowering costs—I was now convinced, as were most healthcare advocates, that Romney's model offered us the best chance of achieving our goal of universal coverage.

People still differed on the details of what a national version of the Massachusetts plan might look like, and as my team and I mapped out our strategy, a number of advocates urged us to settle these issues early by putting out a specific White House proposal for Congress to follow. We decided against that. One of the lessons from the Clintons' failed effort was the need to involve key Democrats in the process, so they'd feel a sense of ownership of the bill. Insufficient coordination, we knew, could result in legislative death by a thousand cuts.

On the House side, this meant working with old-school liberals like Henry Waxman, the wily, pugnacious congressman from California. In the Senate, the landscape was different: With Teddy convalescing, the main player was Max Baucus, a conservative Democrat from Montana who chaired the powerful Finance Committee. When it came to the tax issues that occupied most of the committee's time, Baucus often aligned himself with business lobbies, which I found worrying, and in three decades as a senator he had yet to spearhead the passage of any major legislation. Still, he appeared to be genuinely invested in the issue, having organized a congressional healthcare summit the previous June and having spent months working with Ted Kennedy and his staff on early drafts of a reform bill. Baucus also had a close friendship with Iowa senator Chuck Grassley, the Finance Committee's ranking Republican, and was optimistic that he could win Grassley's support for a bill.

Rahm and Phil Schiliro were skeptical that Grassley was gettable—after all, we'd been down that rabbit hole during the Recovery Act debate. But we decided it was best to let Baucus's process play itself out. He'd already outlined some of his ideas in the press and would soon pull together a healthcare-reform working group that included Grassley and two other Republicans. During an Oval Office meeting, though, I made a point of warning him not to let Grassley string him along.

"Trust me, Mr. President," Baucus said. "Chuck and I have already discussed it. We're going to have this thing done by July."

EVERY JOB HAS its share of surprises. A key piece of equipment breaks down. A traffic accident forces a change in delivery routes. A client calls to say you've won the contract—but they need the order filled three months earlier than planned. If it's the kind of thing that's happened before, the place where you work may have systems and procedures to handle the situation. But even the best organizations can't anticipate everything, in which case you learn to improvise to meet your objectives—or at least to cut your losses.

The presidency was no different. Except that the surprises came daily, often in waves. And over the course of the spring and summer of that first year, as we wrestled with the financial crisis, two wars, and the push for healthcare reform, several unexpected items got added to our already overloaded plate.

The first carried the possibility of a genuine catastrophe. In April, reports surfaced of a worrying flu outbreak in Mexico. The flu virus usually hits vulnerable populations like the elderly, infants, and asthma sufferers hardest, but this strain appeared to strike young, healthy people—and was killing them at a higher-than-usual rate. Within weeks, people in the United States were falling ill with the virus: one in Ohio, two in Kansas, eight in a single high school in New York City. By the end of the month, both our own Centers for Disease Control (CDC) and the World Health Organization (WHO) had confirmed that we were dealing with a variation of the H1N1 virus. In June, the WHO officially declared the first global pandemic in forty years.

I had more than a passing knowledge of H1N1 after working on U.S. pandemic preparedness when I was in the Senate. What I knew scared the hell out of me. In 1918, a strain of H1N1 that came to be known as "the Spanish flu" had infected an estimated half a billion people and killed somewhere between 50 and 100 million—roughly 4 percent of the world's population. In

Philadelphia alone, more than 12,000 died in the span of a few weeks. The effects of the pandemic went beyond the stunning death tolls and shutdown of economic activity; later research would reveal that those who were in utero during the pandemic grew up to have lower incomes, poorer educational outcomes, and higher rates of physical disability.

It was too early to tell how deadly this new virus would be. But I wasn't interested in taking any chances. On the same day that Kathleen Sebelius was confirmed as HHS secretary, we sent a plane to pick her up from Kansas, flew her to the Capitol to be sworn in at a make-shift ceremony, and immediately asked her to spearhead a two-hour conference call with WHO officials and health ministers from Mexico and Canada. A few days later, we pulled together an interagency team to evaluate how ready the United States was for a worst-case scenario.

The answer was, we weren't at all ready. Annual flu shots didn't provide protection against H1N1, it turned out, and because vaccines generally weren't a money-maker for drug companies, the few U.S. vaccine makers that existed had a limited capacity to ramp up produc-tion of a new one. Then we faced questions of how to distribute antiviral medicines, what guidelines hospitals used in treating cases of the flu, and even how we'd handle the possibility of closing schools and imposing quarantines if things got significantly worse. Several veterans of the Ford administration's 1976 swine flu re-sponse team warned us of the difficulties involved in getting out in front of an outbreak without overreacting or triggering a panic: Apparently President Ford, want-ing to act decisively in the middle of a reelection

campaign, had fast-tracked mandatory vaccinations before the severity of the pandemic had been determined,
with the result that more Americans developed a neuro-
logical disorder connected to the vaccine than died from
the flu.

"You need to be involved, Mr. President," one of
Ford's staffers advised, "but you need to let the experts
run the process."

I put my arm around Sebelius's shoulders. "You see
this?" I said, nodding her way. "This . . . is the face of the
virus. Congratulations, Kathleen."

"Happy to serve, Mr. President," she said brightly.
"Happy to serve."

My instructions to Kathleen and the public health
team were simple: Decisions would be made based on
the best available science, and we were going to explain
each step of our response to the public—including
detailing what we did and didn't know. Over the course
of the next six months, we did exactly that. A summer-
time dip in H1N1 cases gave the team time to work with
drugmakers and incentivize new processes for quicker
vaccine production. They pre-positioned medical supplies across regions and gave hospitals increased flexibility
to manage a surge in flu cases. They evaluated—and
ultimately rejected—the idea of closing schools for the
rest of the year, but worked with school districts, businesses, and state and local officials to make sure that
everyone had the resources they needed to respond in the
event of an outbreak.

Although the United States did not escape unscathed—
more than 12,000 Americans lost their lives—we were
fortunate that this particular strain of H1N1 turned out

to be less deadly than the experts had feared, and news that the pandemic had abated by mid-2010 didn't generate headlines. Still, I took great pride in how well our team had performed. Without fanfare or fuss, not only had they helped keep the virus contained, but they'd strengthened our readiness for any future public health emergency—which would make all the difference several years later, when the Ebola outbreak in West Africa would trigger a full-blown panic.

This, I was coming to realize, was the nature of the presidency: Sometimes your most important work involved the stuff nobody noticed.

THE SECOND TURN of events was an opportunity rather than a crisis. At the end of April, Supreme Court justice David Souter called to tell me he was retiring from the bench, giving me my first chance to fill a seat on the highest court in the land.

Getting somebody confirmed to the Supreme Court has never been a slam dunk, in part because the Court's role in American government has always been controversial. After all, the idea of giving nine unelected, tenured-for-life lawyers in black robes the power to strike down laws passed by a majority of the people's representatives doesn't sound very democratic. But since **Marbury v. Madison,** the 1803 Supreme Court case that gave the Court final say on the meaning of the U.S. Constitution and established the principle of judicial review over the actions of the Congress and the president, that's how our system of checks and balances has worked. In theory, Supreme Court justices don't "make law" when exercising these powers; instead, they're supposed to merely "interpret" the Constitution, helping to bridge how its provisions were understood by the framers and how they apply to the world we live in today.

For the bulk of constitutional cases coming before the Court, the theory holds up pretty well. Justices have for the most part felt bound by the text of the Constitution and precedents set by earlier courts, even when doing so results in an outcome they don't personally agree with. Throughout American history, though, the most important cases have involved deciphering the meaning of phrases like "due process," "privileges and immunities," "equal protection," or "establishment of religion"—terms so vague that it's doubtful any two Founding Fathers agreed on exactly what they meant. This ambiguity gives individual justices all kinds of room to "interpret" in ways that reflect their moral judgments, political preferences, biases, and fears. That's why in the 1930s a mostly conservative Court could rule that FDR's New Deal policies violated the Constitution, while forty years later a mostly liberal Court could rule that the Constitution grants Congress almost unlimited power to regulate the economy. It's how one set of justices, in **Plessy v. Ferguson,** could read the Equal Protection Clause to permit "separate but equal," and another set of justices, in **Brown v. Board of Education,** could rely on the exact same language to unanimously arrive at the opposite conclusion.

It turned out that Supreme Court justices made law all the time.

Over the years, the press and the public started paying more attention to Court decisions and, by extension, to the process of confirming justices. In 1955, southern Democrats—in a fit of pique over the **Brown** decision—institutionalized the practice of having Supreme Court nominees appear before the Senate Judiciary Committee to be grilled on their legal views. The 1973 **Roe v. Wade** decision focused further attention on Court appointments, with every nomination from that point on triggering a pitched battle between pro-choice and anti-abortion forces. The high-profile rejection of Robert Bork's nomination in the late 1980s and the Clarence Thomas–Anita Hill hearings in the early 1990s—in which the nominee was accused of sexual harassment—proved to be irresistible TV drama. All of which meant that when it came time for me to replace Justice Souter, identifying a well-qualified candidate was the easy part. The hard part would be getting that person confirmed while avoiding a political circus that could sidetrack our other business.

We already had a team of lawyers in place to manage the process of filling scores of lower court vacancies, and they immediately began compiling an exhaustive list of possible Supreme Court candidates. In less than a week, we'd narrowed it down to a few finalists, who would be asked to submit to an FBI background check and come to the White House for an interview. The short list included former Harvard Law School dean and current solicitor general Elena Kagan and Seventh Circuit appellate judge Diane Wood, both first-rate legal scholars whom I knew from my time teaching constitutional law at the University of Chicago. But as I read through the fat briefing books my team had prepared on each candidate, it was someone I'd never met, Second Circuit appellate judge Sonia Sotomayor, who most piqued my interest. A Puerto Rican from the Bronx, she'd been raised mostly by her mom, a telephone operator who

eventually earned her nurse's license, after her father—
a tradesman with a third-grade education—died when
Sonia was just nine years old. Despite speaking mostly
Spanish at home, Sonia had excelled in parochial school
and won a scholarship to Princeton. There, her experiences echoed what Michelle would encounter at the
university a decade later: an initial sense of uncertainty
and displacement that came with being just one of a
handful of women of color on campus; the need to
sometimes put in extra work to compensate for the gaps
in knowledge that more privileged kids took for granted;
the comfort of finding community among other Black
students and supportive professors; and the realization
over time that she was as smart as any of her peers.

Sotomayor graduated from Yale Law School and went
on to do standout work as a prosecutor in the Manhattan
district attorney's office, which helped catapult her to
the federal bench. Over the course of nearly seventeen
years as a judge, she'd developed a reputation for thoroughness, fairness, and restraint, ultimately leading the
American Bar Association to give her its highest rating.
Still, when word leaked that Sotomayor was among the
finalists I was considering, some in the legal priesthood
suggested that her credentials were inferior to those of
Kagan or Wood, and a number of left-leaning interest
groups questioned whether she had the intellectual heft
to go toe-to-toe with conservative ideologues like Justice
Antonin Scalia.

Maybe because of my own background in legal and
academic circles—where I'd met my share of highly cre-
dentialed, high-IQ morons and had witnessed firsthand
the tendency to move the goalposts when it came to

promoting women and people of color—I was quick to dismiss such concerns. Not only were Judge Sotomayor's academic credentials outstanding, but I understood the kind of intelligence, grit, and adaptability required of someone of her background to get to where she was. A breadth of experience, familiarity with the vagaries of life, the combination of brains and heart—that, I thought, was where wisdom came from. When asked during the campaign what qualities I'd look for in a Supreme Court nominee, I had talked not only about legal qualifications but also about empathy. Conservative commentators had scoffed at my answer, citing it as evidence that I planned to load up the Court with woolly-headed, social-engineering liberals who cared nothing about the "objective" application of the law. But as far as I was concerned, they had it upside down: It was precisely the ability of a judge to understand the context of his or her decisions, to know what life was like for a pregnant teen as well as for a Catholic priest, a self-made tycoon as well as an assembly-line worker, the minority as well as the majority, that was the wellspring of objectivity.

There were other considerations that made Sotomayor a compelling choice. She'd be the first Latina—and only the third woman—to serve on the Supreme Court. And she'd already been confirmed twice by the Senate, once unanimously, making it harder for Republicans to argue that she was an unacceptable choice.

Given my high regard for Kagan and Wood, I was still undecided when Judge Sotomayor came to the Oval Office for a get-to-know-you session. She had a broad, kind face and a ready smile. Her manner was formal and she chose her words carefully, though her years at Ivy

League schools and on the federal bench hadn't sanded away the Bronx accent. I'd been warned by my team not to ask candidates their positions on specific legal controversies like abortion (Republicans on the committee were sure to ask about any conversation between me and a nominee to see if I had applied a "litmus test" in making my choice). Instead, the judge and I talked about her family, her work as a prosecutor, and her broad judicial philosophy. By the end of the interview, I was convinced that Sotomayor had what I was looking for, although I didn't say so on the spot. I did mention that there was one aspect of her résumé that I found troubling.

"What's that, Mr. President?" she asked.

"You're a Yankees fan," I said. "But since you grew up in the Bronx and were brainwashed early in life, I'm inclined to overlook it."

A few days later, I announced my selection of Sonia Sotomayor as a Supreme Court nominee. The news was positively received, and in the run-up to her appearance before the Senate Judiciary Committee, I was happy to see that Republicans had trouble identifying anything in the judge's written opinions or conduct on the bench that might derail her confirmation. Instead, they fastened on two race-related issues to justify their opposition. The first involved a 2008 case in New Haven, Connecticut, in which Sotomayor joined the majority in ruling against a group of primarily white firefighters who'd filed a "reverse discrimination" claim. The second issue concerned a 2001 speech Sotomayor had delivered at the University of California, Berkeley, in which she'd argued that female and minority judges added a much-needed perspective to the federal courts, triggering charges from conservatives that she was incapable of impartiality on the bench.

Despite the temporary dustup, the confirmation hearings proved anticlimactic. Justice Sotomayor was confirmed by a Senate vote of 68–31, with nine Republicans joining all the Democrats except for Teddy Kennedy, who was undergoing treatment for his cancer—about as much support as any nominee was likely to get, given the polarized environment we were operating in.

Michelle and I hosted a reception for Justice Sotomayor and her family at the White House in August, after she was sworn in. The new justice's mother was there, and I was moved to think what must be going through the mind of this elderly woman who'd grown up on a distant island, who'd barely spoken English when she had signed up for the Women's Army Corps during World War II, and who, despite the odds stacked against her, had insisted that somehow her kids would count for something. It made me think of my own mother, and Toot and Gramps, and I felt a flash of sorrow that none of them had ever had a day like this, that they were gone before they'd seen what their dreams for me had come to.

Tamping down my emotions as the justice spoke to the audience, I looked over at a pair of handsome young Korean American boys—Sotomayor's adopted nephews—squirming in their Sunday best. They would take for granted that their aunt was on the U.S. Supreme Court, shaping the life of a nation—as would kids across the country.

Which was fine. That's what progress looks like.

·　·　·

THE SLOW MARCH toward healthcare reform consumed much of the summer. As the legislation lumbered through Congress, we looked for any opportunity to help keep the process on track. Since the White House summit in March, members of my healthcare and legislative teams had participated in countless meetings on the subject up on Capitol Hill, trudging into the Oval at the end of the day like weary field commanders back from the front, offering me reports on the ebb and flow of battle. The good news was that the key Democratic chairs—especially Baucus and Waxman—were working hard to craft bills they could pass out of their respective committees before the traditional August recess. The bad news was that the more everyone dug into the details of reform, the more differences in substance and strategy emerged—not just between Democrats and Republicans but between House and Senate Democrats, between us and congressional Democrats, and even between members of my own team.

Most of the arguments revolved around the issue of how to generate a mix of savings and new revenue to pay for expanding coverage to millions of uninsured Americans. Because of his own inclinations and his interest in producing a bipartisan bill, Baucus hoped to avoid anything that could be characterized as a tax increase. Instead, he and his staff had calculated the windfall profits that a new flood of insured customers would bring to hospitals, drug companies, and insurers and had used those figures as a basis for negotiating billions of dollars in up-front contributions through fees or Medicare payment reductions from each industry. To sweeten the deal,

Baucus was also prepared to make certain policy concessions. For example, he promised the pharmaceutical lobbyists that his bill wouldn't include provisions allowing the reimportation of drugs from Canada—a popular Democratic proposal that highlighted the way Canadian and European government-run healthcare systems used their massive bargaining power to negotiate much cheaper prices than Big Pharma charged inside the United States.

Politically and emotionally, I would've found it a lot more satisfying to just go after the drug and insurance companies and see if we could beat them into submission. They were wildly unpopular with voters—and for good reason. But as a practical matter, it was hard to argue with Baucus's more conciliatory approach. We had no way to get to sixty votes in the Senate for a major healthcare bill without at least the tacit agreement of the big industry players. Drug reimportation was a great political issue, but at the end of the day, we didn't have the votes for it, partly because plenty of Democrats had major pharmaceutical companies headquartered or operating in their states.

With these realities in mind, I signed off on having Rahm, Nancy-Ann, and Jim Messina (who had once been on Baucus's staff) sit in on Baucus's negotiations with healthcare industry representatives. By the end of June, they'd hashed out a deal, securing hundreds of billions of dollars in givebacks and broader drug discounts for seniors using Medicare. Just as important, they'd gotten a commitment from the hospitals, insurers, and drug companies to support—or at least not oppose—the emerging bill.

It was a big hurdle to clear, a case of politics as the art

of the possible. But for some of the more liberal Democrats in the House, where no one had to worry about a fili-buster, and among progressive advocacy groups that were still hoping to lay the groundwork for a single-payer healthcare system, our compromises smacked of ca-pitulation, a deal with the devil. It didn't help that, as Rahm had predicted, none of the negotiations with the industry had been broadcast on C-SPAN. The press started reporting on details of what they called "back-room deals." More than a few constituents wrote in to ask whether I'd gone over to the dark side. And Chairman Waxman made a point of saying he didn't consider his work bound by whatever concessions Baucus or the White House had made to industry lobbyists.

Quick as they were to mount their high horse, House Dems were also more than willing to protect the status quo when it threatened their prerogatives or benefited politically influential constituencies. For example, more or less every healthcare economist agreed that it wasn't enough just to pry money out of insurance and drug company profits and use it to cover more people—in order for reform to work, we also had to do something about the skyrocketing costs charged by doctors and hospitals. Otherwise, any new money put into the system would yield less and less care for fewer and fewer people over time. One of the best ways to "bend the cost curve" was to establish an independent board, shielded from politics and special-interest lobbying, that would set reimbursement rates for Medicare based on the com-parative effectiveness of particular treatments.

House Democrats hated the idea. It would mean giv-ing away their power to determine what Medicare did and didn't cover (along with the potential campaign fundraising opportunities that came with that power). They also worried that they'd get blamed by cranky seniors who found themselves unable to get the latest drug or diagnostic test advertised on TV, even if an expert could prove that it was actually a waste of money.

They were similarly skeptical of the other big proposal to control costs: a cap on the tax deductibility of so-called Cadillac insurance plans—high-cost, employer-provided policies that paid for all sorts of premium services but didn't improve health outcomes. Other than corporate managers and well-paid professionals, the main group covered by such plans were union members, and the unions were adamantly opposed to what would come to be known as "the Cadillac tax." It didn't matter to labor leaders that their members might be willing to trade a deluxe hospital suite or a second, unnecessary MRI for a chance at higher take-home pay. They didn't trust that any savings from reform would accrue to their members, and they were absolutely certain they'd catch flak for any changes to their existing healthcare plans. Unfortunately, so long as the unions were opposed to the Cadillac tax, most House Democrats were going to be too.

The squabbles quickly found their way into the press, making the whole process appear messy and convoluted. By late July, polls showed that more Americans disapproved than approved of the way I was handling healthcare reform, prompting me to complain to Axe about our communications strategy. "We're on the right side of this stuff," I insisted. "We just have to explain it better to voters."

Axe was irritated that his shop was seemingly getting

blamed for the very problem he'd warned me about from the start. "You can explain it till you're blue in the face," he told me. "But people who already have healthcare are skeptical that reform will benefit them, and a whole bunch of facts and figures won't change that."

Unconvinced, I decided I needed to be more public in selling our agenda. Which is how I found myself in a prime-time press conference devoted to healthcare, facing an East Room full of White House reporters, many of whom were already writing the obituary on my number one legislative initiative.

IN GENERAL, I enjoyed the unscripted nature of live press conferences. And unlike the first healthcare forum during the campaign, in which I'd laid an egg as Hillary and John Edwards shined, I now knew my subject cold. In fact, I probably knew it **too** well. During the press conference, I succumbed to an old pattern, giving exhaustive explanations of each facet of the issue under debate. It was as if, having failed to get the various negotiations involving the bill on C-SPAN, I was going to make up for it by offering the public a one-hour, highly detailed crash course on U.S. healthcare policy.

The press corps didn't much appreciate the thoroughness. One news story made a point of noting that at times I adopted a "professorial" tone. Perhaps that was why, when the time came for the last question, Lynn Sweet, a veteran **Chicago Sun-Times** reporter I'd known for years, decided to ask me something entirely off the topic.

"Recently," Lynn said, "Professor Henry Louis Gates, Jr., was arrested at his home in Cambridge. What does that incident say to you, and what does it say about race relations in America?"

Where to start? Henry Louis Gates, Jr., was a professor of English and Afro-American studies at Harvard and one of the country's most prominent Black scholars. He was also a casual friend, someone I'd occasionally run into at social gatherings. Earlier that week, Gates had returned to his home in Cambridge after a trip to China and found his front door jammed shut. A neighbor—having witnessed Gates trying to force the door open—called the police to report a possible break-in. When the responding officer, Sergeant James Crowley, arrived, he asked Gates for identification. Gates refused at first and—according to Crowley—called him racist. Eventually Gates produced his identification but allegedly continued to berate the departing officer from his porch. When a warning failed to quiet Gates down, Crowley and two other officers that he'd called for backup handcuffed him, took him to the police station, and booked him for disorderly conduct. (The charges were quickly dropped.)

Predictably the incident had become a national story. For a big swath of white America, Gates's arrest was entirely deserved, a simple case of someone not showing the proper respect for a routine law enforcement procedure. For Blacks, it was just one more example of the humiliations and inequities, large and small, suffered at the hands of the police specifically and white authority in general.

My own guess as to what had happened was more particular, more human, than the simple black-and-white

morality tale being portrayed. Having lived in
Cambridge, I knew that its police department didn't
have a reputation for harboring a whole bunch of Bull
Connor types. Meanwhile, Skip—as Gates was known
to his friends—was brilliant and loud, one part W.E.B.
Du Bois, one part Mars Blackmon, and cocky enough
that I could easily picture him cussing out a cop to the
point where even a relatively restrained officer might feel
his testosterone kick in.

Still, while no one had been hurt, I found the episode
depressing—a vivid reminder that not even the highest
level of Black achievement and the most accommodating
of white settings could escape the cloud of our racial history. Hearing about what had happened to Gates, I had
found myself almost involuntarily conducting a quick
inventory of my own experiences. The multiple occasions
when I'd been asked for my student ID while walking to
the library on Columbia's campus, something that never
seemed to happen to my white classmates. The unmer-
ited traffic stops while visiting certain "nice" Chicago
neighborhoods. Being followed around by department
store security guards while doing my Christmas shopping. The sound of car locks clicking as I walked across a
street, dressed in a suit and tie, in the middle of the day.

Moments like these were routine among Black friends,
acquaintances, guys in the barbershop. If you were poor,
or working-class, or lived in a rough neighborhood, or
didn't properly signify being a respectable Negro, the
stories were usually worse. For just about every Black
man in the country, and every woman who loved a
Black man, and every parent of a Black boy, it was not
a matter of paranoia or "playing the race card" or

disrespecting law enforcement to conclude that whatever else had happened that day in Cambridge, this much was almost certainly true: A wealthy, famous, five-foot-six, 140-pound, fifty-eight-year-old **white** Harvard professor who walked with a cane because of a childhood leg injury would **not** have been handcuffed and taken down to the station merely for being rude to a cop who'd forced him to produce some form of identification while standing on his own damn property.

Of course, I didn't say all that. Maybe I should have. Instead, I made what I thought were some pretty unremarkable observations, beginning with the acknowledgment that the police had responded appropriately to the 911 call and also that Gates was a friend, which meant I might be biased. "I don't know, not having been there and not seeing all the facts, what role race played in that," I said. "But I think it's fair to say, number one, any of us would be pretty angry; number two, that the Cambridge police acted stupidly in arresting somebody when there was already proof that they were in their own home; and number three, what I think we know separate and apart from this incident is that there is a long history in this country of African Americans and Latinos being stopped by law enforcement disproportionately."

That was it. I left the evening press conference assuming that my four minutes on the Gates affair would be a brief sidebar to the hour I'd spent on healthcare.

Boy, was I wrong. The next morning, my suggestion that the police had acted "stupidly" led every news broadcast. Police union representatives suggested that I had vilified Officer Crowley and law enforcement in general and were demanding an apology. Anonymous sources claimed that strings had been pulled to get Gates's charges dropped without a court appearance. Conservative media outlets barely hid their glee, portraying my comments as a case of an elitist (professorial, uppity) Black president siding with his well-connected (mouthy, race-card-wielding) Harvard friend over a white, working-class cop who was just doing his job. In the daily White House press briefing, Gibbs fielded questions on little else. Afterward, he asked whether I'd consider issuing a clarification.

"What am I clarifying?" I asked. "I thought I was pretty clear the first time."

"The way it's being consumed, people think you called the police stupid."

"I didn't say they were stupid. I said they acted stupidly. There's a difference."

"I get it. But . . ."

"We're not doing a clarification," I said. "It'll blow over."

The next day, though, it hadn't blown over. Instead, the story had completely swamped everything else, including our healthcare message. Fielding nervous calls from Democrats on the Hill, Rahm looked like he was ready to jump off a bridge. You would have thought that in the press conference I had donned a dashiki and cussed out the police myself.

Eventually I agreed to a damage-control plan. I began by calling Sergeant Crowley to let him know I was sorry for having used the word "stupidly." He was gracious and good-humored, and at some point I suggested that he and Gates come visit the White House. The three of us could have a beer, I said, and show the country that good people could get past misunderstandings. Both Crowley and Gates, whom I called immediately afterward, were enthusiastic about the idea. In a press briefing later that day, I told reporters that I continued to believe that the police had overreacted in arresting Gates, just as the professor had overreacted to their arrival at his home. I acknowledged that I could have calibrated my original comments more carefully. Much later I'd learn through David Simas, our in-house polling guru and Axe's deputy, that the Gates affair caused a huge drop in my support among white voters, bigger than would come from any single event during the eight years of my presidency. It was support that I'd never completely get back.

Six days later, Joe Biden and I sat down with Sergeant Crowley and Skip Gates at the White House for what came to be known as the "Beer Summit." It was a low-key, friendly, and slightly stilted affair. As I'd expected based on our phone conversation, Crowley came across as a thoughtful, decent man, while Skip was on his best behavior. For an hour or so, the four of us talked about our upbringings, our work, and ways to improve trust and communication between police officers and the African American community. When our time was up, both Crowley and Gates expressed appreciation for the tours my staff had given their families, though I joked that next time they could probably find easier ways to score an invitation.

After they were gone, I sat alone in the Oval Office, reflecting on it all. Michelle, friends like Valerie and Marty, Black senior officials like Attorney General Eric Holder, ambassador to the U.N. Susan Rice, and U.S. trade representative Ron Kirk—we were all accustomed to running the obstacle course necessary to be effective inside of predominantly white institutions. We'd grown skilled at suppressing our reactions to minor slights, ever ready to give white colleagues the benefit of the doubt, remaining mindful that all but the most careful discussions of race risked triggering in them a mild panic. Still, the reaction to my comments on Gates surprised us all. It was my first indicator of how the issue of Black folks and the police was more polarizing than just about any other subject in American life. It seemed to tap into some of the deepest undercurrents of our nation's psyche, touching on the rawest of nerves, perhaps because it reminded all of us, Black and white alike, that the basis of our nation's social order had never been simply about consent; that it was also about centuries of state-sponsored violence by whites against Black and brown people, and that who controlled legally sanctioned violence, how it was wielded and against whom, still mattered in the recesses of our tribal minds much more than we cared to admit.

My thoughts were interrupted by Valerie, who poked her head in to check on me. She said that the coverage of the "Beer Summit" had been generally positive, although she admitted to having received a bunch of calls from Black supporters who weren't happy. "They don't understand why we'd bend over backward to make Crowley feel welcome," she said.

"What'd you tell them?" I asked.

"I said the whole thing has become a distraction, and you're focused on governing and getting healthcare passed."

I nodded. "And our Black folks on staff . . . how are they doing?"

Valerie shrugged. "The younger ones are a little discouraged. But they get it. With all you've got on your plate, they just don't like seeing you being put in this position."

"Which position?" I said. "Being Black, or being president?"

We both got a good laugh out of that.

CHAPTER 17

BY THE END OF JULY 2009, some version of the healthcare bill had passed out of all the relevant House committees. The Senate Health and Education Committee had completed its work as well. All that remained was getting a bill through Max Baucus's Senate Finance Committee. Once that was done, we could consolidate the different versions into one House and one Senate bill, ideally passing each before the August recess, with the goal of having a final version of the legislation on my desk for signature before the end of the year.

No matter how hard we pressed, though, we couldn't get Baucus to complete his work. I was sympathetic to his reasons for delay: Unlike the other Democratic committee chairs, who'd passed their bills on straight party-line votes without regard for the Republicans, Baucus continued to hope that he could produce a bipartisan bill. But as summer wore on, that optimism began to look delusional. McConnell and Boehner had already announced their vigorous opposition to our legislative efforts, arguing that it represented an attempted "government takeover" of the healthcare system. Frank Luntz, a well-known Republican strategist, had circulated a memo stating that after market-testing no fewer than forty anti-reform messages, he'd concluded that invoking a "government takeover" was the best way to discredit the healthcare legislation. From that point on, conservatives followed the script, repeating the phrase like an incantation.

Senator Jim DeMint, the conservative firebrand from South Carolina, was more transparent about his party's intentions. "If we're able to stop Obama on this," he announced on a nationwide conference call with conservative activists, "it will be his Waterloo. It will break him."

Unsurprisingly, given the atmosphere, the group of three GOP senators who'd been invited to participate in bipartisan talks with Baucus was now down to two: Chuck Grassley and Olympia Snowe, the moderate from Maine. My team and I did everything we could to help Baucus win their support. I had Grassley and Snowe over to the White House repeatedly and called them every few weeks to take their temperature. We signed off on scores of changes they wanted made to Baucus's draft bill. Nancy-Ann became a permanent fixture in their Senate offices and took Snowe out to dinner so often that we joked that her husband was getting jealous.

"Tell Olympia she can write the whole damn bill!" I said to Nancy-Ann as she was leaving for one such meeting. "We'll call it the Snowe plan. Tell her if she votes for the bill, she can have the White House . . . Michelle and I will move to an apartment!"

And still we were getting nowhere. Snowe took pride in her centrist reputation, and she cared deeply about healthcare (she had been orphaned at the age of nine, losing her parents, in rapid succession, to cancer and heart disease). But the Republican Party's sharp rightward tilt had left her increasingly isolated within her own caucus, making her even more cautious than usual, prone to wrapping her indecision in the guise of digging into policy minutiae.

Grassley was a different story. He talked a good game about wanting to help the family farmers back in Iowa who had trouble getting insurance they could count on, and when Hillary Clinton had pushed healthcare reform in the 1990s, he'd actually cosponsored an alternative that in many ways resembled the Massachusetts-style plan we were proposing, complete with an individual mandate. But unlike Snowe, Grassley rarely bucked his party leadership on tough issues. With his long, hangdog face and throaty midwestern drawl, he'd hem and haw about this or that problem he had with the bill without ever telling us what exactly it would take to get him to yes. Phil's conclusion was that Grassley was just stringing Baucus along at McConnell's behest, trying to stall the process and prevent us from moving on to the rest of our agenda. Even I, the resident White House optimist, finally got fed up and asked Baucus to come by for a visit.

"Time's up, Max," I told him in the Oval during a meeting in late July. "You've given it your best shot. Grassley's gone. He just hasn't broken the news to you yet."

Baucus shook his head. "I respectfully disagree, Mr. President," he said. "I know Chuck. I think we're **this** close to getting him." He held his thumb and index finger an inch apart, smiling at me like someone who's discovered a cure for cancer and is forced to deal with foolish skeptics. "Let's just give Chuck a little more time and have the vote when we get back from recess."

A part of me wanted to get up, grab Baucus by the shoulders, and shake him till he came to his senses. I decided that this wouldn't work. Another part of me considered threatening to withhold my political support the next time he ran for reelection, but since he polled higher than I did in his home state of Montana, I figured that wouldn't work either. Instead, I argued and cajoled for another half hour, finally agreeing to his plan to delay an immediate party-line vote and instead call the bill to a vote within the first two weeks of Congress's reconvening in September.

WITH THE HOUSE and the Senate adjourned and both votes still looming, we decided I'd spend the first two weeks of August on the road, holding healthcare town halls in places like Montana, Colorado, and Arizona, where public support for reform was shakiest. As a sweetener, my team suggested that Michelle and the girls join me, and that we visit some national parks along the way.

I was thrilled by the suggestion. It's not as if Malia and Sasha were deprived of fatherly attention or in need of extra summer fun—they'd had plenty of both, with playdates and movies and a whole lot of loafing. Often, I'd come home in the evening and go up to the third floor to find the solarium overtaken by pajama-clad eight- or eleven-year-old girls settling in for a sleepover, bouncing on inflatable mattresses, scattering popcorn and toys everywhere, giggling nonstop at whatever was on Nickelodeon.

But as much as Michelle and I (with the help of infinitely patient Secret Service agents) tried to approximate a normal childhood for my daughters, it was hard if not impossible for me to take them places like an ordinary dad would. We couldn't go to an amusement park together, making an impromptu stop for burgers along the way. I couldn't take them, as I once had, on lazy Sunday afternoon bike rides. A trip to get ice cream or a visit to a bookstore was now a major production, involving road closures, tactical teams, and the omnipresent press pool.

If the girls felt a sense of loss over this, they didn't show it. But I felt it acutely. I especially mourned the fact that I'd probably never get a chance to take Malia and Sasha on the sort of long summer road trip I'd made when I was eleven, after my mother and Toot decided it was time for Maya and me to see the mainland of the United States. It had lasted a month and burned a lasting impression into my mind—and not just because we went to Disneyland (although that was obviously outstanding). We had dug for clams during low tide in Puget Sound, ridden horses through a creek at the base of Canyon de Chelly in Arizona, watched the endless Kansas prairie unfold from a train window, spotted a herd of bison on a dusky plain in Yellowstone, and ended each day with the simple pleasures of a motel ice machine, the occasional swimming pool, or just air-conditioning and clean sheets. That one trip gave me a glimpse of the dizzying freedom of the open road, how vast America was, and how full of wonder.

I couldn't duplicate that experience for my daughters—not when we flew on Air Force One, rode in motorcades, and never bunked down in a place like Howard Johnson's. Getting from Point A to Point B happened too fast and too comfortably, and the days were too stuffed with prescheduled, staff-monitored activity—absent that familiar mix of surprises, misadventures, and boredom— to fully qualify as a road trip. But over the course of an August week, Michelle, the girls, and I had fun all the same. We watched Old Faithful blow and looked out over the ocher expanse of the Grand Canyon. The girls went inner tubing. At night, we played board games and tried to name the constellations. Tucking the girls into bed, I hoped that despite all the fuss that surrounded us, their minds were storing away a vision of life's possibilities and the beauty of the American landscape, just as mine once had; and that they might someday think back on our trips together and be reminded that they were so worthy of love, so fascinating and electric with life, that there was nothing their parents would rather do than share those vistas with them.

OF COURSE, one of the things Malia and Sasha had to put up with on the trip out west was their dad peeling off every other day to appear before large crowds and TV cameras and talk about healthcare. The town halls themselves weren't very different from the ones I'd held earlier in the spring. People shared stories about how the existing healthcare system had failed their families, and asked questions about how the emerging bill might affect their own insurance. Even those who opposed our effort listened attentively to what I had to say.

Outside, though, the atmosphere was very different. We were in the middle of what came to be known as the

"Tea Party summer," an organized effort to marry people's honest fears about a changing America with a right-wing political agenda. Heading to and from every venue, we were greeted by dozens of angry protesters. Some shouted through bullhorns. Others flashed a single-fingered salute. Many held up signs with messages like OBAMACARE SUCKS or the unintentionally ironic KEEP GOVERNMENT OUT OF MY MEDICARE. Some waved doctored pictures of me looking like Heath Ledger's Joker in **The Dark Knight**, with blackened eyes and thickly caked makeup, appearing almost demonic. Still others wore colonial-era patriot costumes and hoisted the DON'T TREAD ON ME flag. All of them seemed most interested in expressing their general contempt for me, a sentiment best summed up by a refashioning of the famous Shepard Fairey poster from our campaign: the same red, white, and blue rendering of my face, but with the word HOPE replaced by NOPE.

This new and suddenly potent force in American politics had started months earlier as a handful of ragtag, small-scale protests against TARP and the Recovery Act. A number of the early participants had apparently migrated from the quixotic, libertarian presidential campaign of Republican congressman Ron Paul, who called for the elimination of the federal income tax and the Federal Reserve, a return to the gold standard, and withdrawal from the U.N. and NATO. Rick Santelli's notorious television rant against our housing proposal back in February had provided a catchy rallying cry for the loose network of conservative activists, and soon websites and email chains had begun spawning bigger rallies, with Tea Party chapters proliferating across the country. In those early months, they hadn't had enough traction to stop the stimulus package from passing, and a national protest on Tax Day in April hadn't amounted to much. But helped by endorsements from conservative media personalities like Rush Limbaugh and Glenn Beck, the movement was picking up steam, with local and then national Republican politicians embracing the Tea Party label.

By summer, the group was focused on stopping the abomination they dubbed "Obamacare," which they insisted would introduce a socialistic, oppressive new order to America. As I was conducting my own relatively sedate healthcare town halls out west, newscasts started broadcasting scenes from parallel congressional events around the country, with House and Senate members suddenly confronted by angry, heckling crowds in their home districts and with Tea Party members deliberately disrupting the proceedings, rattling some of the politicians enough that they were canceling public appearances altogether.

It was hard for me to decide what to make of all this. The Tea Party's anti-tax, anti-regulation, anti-government manifesto was hardly new; its basic story line—that corrupt liberal elites had hijacked the federal government to take money out of the pockets of hardworking Americans in order to finance welfare patronage and reward corporate cronies—was one that Republican politicians and conservative media had been peddling for years. Nor, it turned out, was the Tea Party the spontaneous, grassroots movement it purported to be. From the outset, Koch brother affiliates like Americans for Prosperity, along with other billionaire conservatives who'd been part of the Indian Wells gathering hosted by the Kochs just after I was inaugurated, had carefully nurtured the movement by registering internet domain names and obtaining rally permits; training organizers and sponsoring conferences; and ultimately providing much of the Tea Party's financing, infrastructure, and strategic direction.

Still, there was no denying that the Tea Party represented a genuine populist surge within the Republican Party. It was made up of true believers, possessed with the same grassroots enthusiasm and jagged fury we'd seen in Sarah Palin supporters during the closing days of the campaign. Some of that anger I understood, even if I considered it misdirected. Many of the working- and middle-class whites gravitating to the Tea Party had suffered for decades from sluggish wages, rising costs, and the loss of the steady blue-collar work that provided secure retirements. Bush and establishment Republicans hadn't done anything for them, and the financial crisis had further hollowed out their communities. And so far, at least, the economy had gotten steadily worse with me in charge, despite more than a trillion dollars channeled into stimulus spending and bailouts. For those already predisposed toward conservative ideas, the notion that my policies were designed to help others at their expense—that the game was rigged and I was part of the rigging—must have seemed entirely plausible.

I also had a grudging respect for how rapidly Tea Party leaders had mobilized a strong following and managed to dominate the news coverage, using some of the same social media and grassroots-organizing strategies we'd deployed during my own campaign. I'd spent my entire political career promoting civic participation as a cure for much of what ailed our democracy. I could hardly complain, I told myself, just because it was opposition to my agenda that was now spurring such passionate citizen involvement.

As time went on, though, it became hard to ignore some of the more troubling impulses driving the movement. As had been true at Palin rallies, reporters at Tea Party events caught attendees comparing me to animals or Hitler. Signs turned up showing me dressed like an African witch doctor with a bone through my nose and the caption OBAMACARE COMING SOON TO A CLINIC NEAR YOU. Conspiracy theories abounded: that my healthcare bill would set up "death panels" to evaluate whether people deserved treatment, clearing the way for "government-encouraged euthanasia," or that it would benefit illegal immigrants, in the service of my larger goal of flooding the country with welfare-dependent, reliably Democratic voters. The Tea Party also resurrected and poured gas on an old rumor from the campaign: that not only was I Muslim, but I'd actually been born in Kenya and was therefore constitutionally barred from serving as president. By September, the question of how much nativism and racism explained the Tea Party's rise had become a major topic of debate on the cable shows— especially after former president and lifelong southerner Jimmy Carter offered up the opinion that the extreme vitriol directed toward me was at least in part spawned by racist views.

At the White House, we made a point of not commenting on any of this—and not just because Axe had reams of data telling us that white voters, including many who supported me, reacted poorly to lectures about race.

As a matter of principle, I didn't believe a president should ever publicly whine about criticism from voters— it's what you signed up for in taking the job—and I was quick to remind both reporters and friends that my white predecessors had all endured their share of vicious personal attacks and obstructionism.

More practically, I saw no way to sort out people's motives, especially given that racial attitudes were woven into every aspect of our nation's history. Did that Tea Party member support "states' rights" because he genuinely thought it was the best way to promote liberty, or because he continued to resent how federal intervention had led to an end to Jim Crow, desegregation, and rising Black political power in the South? Did that conservative activist oppose any expansion of the social welfare state because she believed it sapped individual initiative, or because she was convinced that it would benefit only brown people who'd just crossed the border? Whatever my instincts might tell me, whatever truths the history books might suggest, I knew I wasn't going to win over any voters by labeling my opponents racist.

One thing felt certain: A pretty big chunk of the American people, including some of the very folks I was trying to help, didn't trust a word I said. One night around then I watched a news report on a charitable organization called Remote Area Medical that provided medical services in temporary pop-up clinics around the country, operating out of trailers parked outside arenas and fairgrounds. Almost all the patients in the report were white southerners from places like Tennessee, Georgia, and West Virginia—men and women who had jobs but no employer-based insurance or had insurance with deductibles they couldn't afford. Many had driven hundreds of miles—some sleeping in their cars overnight, leaving the engines running to stay warm—to join hundreds of other people lined up before dawn to see one of the volunteer doctors who might pull an infected tooth, diagnose debilitating abdominal pain, or examine a lump in their breast. The demand was so great that patients who arrived after sunup sometimes got turned away.

I found the story both heartbreaking and maddening, an indictment of a wealthy nation that failed too many of its citizens. And yet I knew that almost every one of those people waiting to see a free doctor came from a deep-red Republican district, the sort of place where opposition to our healthcare bill, along with support of the Tea Party, was likely to be strongest. There had been a time—back when I was still a state senator driving around southern Illinois or, later, traveling through rural Iowa during the earliest days of the presidential campaign—when I could reach such voters. I wasn't yet well known enough to be the target of caricature, which meant that whatever preconceptions people may have had about a Black guy from Chicago with a foreign name could be dispelled by a simple conversation, a small gesture of kindness. After sitting down with folks in a diner or hearing their complaints at a county fair, I might not get their vote or even agreement on most issues. But we would at least make a connection, and we'd come away from such encounters understanding that we had hopes, struggles, and values in common.

I wondered if any of that was still possible, now that I lived locked behind gates and guardsmen, my image filtered through Fox News and other media outlets whose

entire business model depended on making their audience angry and fearful. I wanted to believe that the ability
to connect was still there. My wife wasn't so sure. One
night toward the end of our road trip, after we'd tucked
the girls in, Michelle caught a glimpse of a Tea Party rally
on TV—with its enraged flag-waving and inflammatory
slogans. She seized the remote and turned off the set, her
expression hovering somewhere between rage and resignation.

"It's a trip, isn't it?" she said.

"What is?"

"That they're scared of you. Scared of **us**."

She shook her head and headed for bed.

TED KENNEDY DIED on August 25. The morning
of his funeral, the skies over Boston darkened, and by the
time our flight landed the streets were shrouded in thick
sheets of rain. The scene inside the church befitted the
largeness of Teddy's life: the pews packed with former
presidents and heads of state, senators and members of
Congress, hundreds of current and former staffers, the
honor guard, and the flag-draped casket. But it was
the stories told by his family, most of all his children,
that mattered most that day. Patrick Kennedy recalled
his father tending to him during crippling asthma attacks,
pressing a cold towel to his forehead until he fell asleep.
He described how his father would take him out to sail,
even in stormy seas. Teddy Jr. told the story of how, after
he'd lost his leg to cancer, his father had insisted they go
sledding, trudging with him up a snowy hill, picking
him up when he fell, and wiping away his tears when he
wanted to give up, the two of them eventually getting to

the top and racing down the snowy banks. It had been proof, Teddy Jr. said, that his world had not stopped. Collectively, it was a portrait of a man driven by great appetites and ambitions but also by great loss and doubt. A man making up for things.

"My father believed in redemption," Teddy Jr. said. "And he never surrendered, never stopped trying to right wrongs, be they the results of his own failings or of ours."

I carried those words with me back to Washington, where a mood of surrender increasingly prevailed—at least when it came to getting a healthcare bill passed. The Tea Party had accomplished what it had set out to do, generating reams of negative publicity for our efforts, stoking public fear that reform would be too costly, too disruptive, or would help only the poor. A preliminary report by the Congressional Budget Office (CBO), the independent, professionally staffed operation charged with scoring the cost of all federal legislation, priced the initial House version of the healthcare bill at an eye-popping $1 trillion. Although the CBO score would eventually come down as the bill was revised and clarified, the headlines gave opponents a handy stick with which to beat us over the head. Democrats from swing districts were now running scared, convinced that pushing forward with the bill amounted to a suicide mission. Republicans abandoned all pretense of wanting to negotiate, with members of Congress regularly echoing the Tea Party's claim that I wanted to put Grandma to sleep.

The only upside to all this was that it helped me cure Max Baucus of his obsession with trying to placate Chuck Grassley. In a last-stab Oval Office meeting with the two of them in early September, I listened patiently as Grassley ticked off five new reasons why he still had problems with the latest version of the bill.

"Let me ask you a question, Chuck," I said finally. "If Max took every one of your latest suggestions, could you support the bill?"

"Well . . ."

"Are there **any** changes—any at all—that would get us your vote?"

There was an awkward silence before Grassley looked up and met my gaze.

"I guess not, Mr. President."

I guess not.

At the White House, the mood rapidly darkened. Some of my team began asking whether it was time to fold our hand. Rahm was especially dour. Having been to this rodeo before with Bill Clinton, he understood all too well what my declining poll numbers might mean for the reelection prospects of swing-district Democrats, many of whom he'd personally recruited and helped elect, not to mention how it could damage my own prospects in 2012. Discussing our options in a senior-staff meeting, Rahm advised that we try to cut a deal with Republicans for a significantly scaled-back piece of legislation—perhaps allowing people between sixty and sixty-five to buy into Medicare or widening the reach of the Children's Health Insurance Program. "It won't be everything you wanted, Mr. President," he said. "But it'll still help a lot of people, and it'll give us a better chance to make progress on the rest of your agenda."

Some in the room agreed. Others felt it was too early to give up. After reviewing his conversations on Capitol

Hill, Phil Schiliro said he thought there was still a path to passing a comprehensive law with only Democratic votes, but he admitted that it was no sure thing.

"I guess the question for you, Mr. President, is, Do you feel lucky?"

I looked at him and smiled. "Where are we, Phil?"

Phil hesitated, wondering if it was a trick question. "The Oval Office?"

"And what's my name?"

"Barack Obama."

I smiled. "Barack **Hussein** Obama. And I'm here with you in **the Oval Office**. Brother, I **always** feel lucky."

I told the team we were staying the course. But honestly, my decision didn't have much to do with how lucky I felt. Rahm wasn't wrong about the risks, and perhaps in a different political environment, on a different issue, I might have accepted his idea of negotiating with the GOP for half a loaf. On this issue, though, I saw no indication that Republican leaders would throw us a lifeline. We were wounded, their base wanted blood, and no matter how modest the reform we proposed, they were sure to find a whole new set of reasons for not working with us.

More than that, a scaled-down bill wasn't going to help millions of people who were desperate, people like Laura Klitzka in Green Bay. The idea of letting them down—of leaving them to fend for themselves because their president hadn't been sufficiently brave, skilled, or persuasive to cut through the political noise and get what he knew to be the right thing done—was something I couldn't stomach.

. . .

AT THAT POINT, I'd held town halls in eight states, explaining in both broad and intricate terms what healthcare reform could mean. I'd taken phone calls from AARP members on live television, fielding questions about everything from Medicare coverage gaps to living wills. Late at night in the Treaty Room, I pored over the continuing flow of memos and spreadsheets, making sure I understood the finer points of risk corridors and reinsurance caps. If I sometimes grew despondent, even angry, over the amount of misinformation that had flooded the airwaves, I was grateful for my team's willingness to push harder and not give up, even when the battle got ugly and the odds remained long. Such tenacity drove the entire White House staff. Denis McDonough at one point distributed stickers to everyone, emblazoned with the words FIGHT CYNICISM. This became a useful slogan, an article of our faith.

Knowing we had to try something big to reset the healthcare debate, Axe suggested that I deliver a prime-time address before a joint session of Congress. It was a high-stakes gambit, he explained, used only twice in the past sixteen years, but it would give me a chance to speak directly to millions of viewers. I asked what the other two joint addresses had been about.

"The most recent was when Bush announced the War on Terror after 9/11."

"And the other?"

"Bill Clinton talking about his healthcare bill."

I laughed. "Well, that worked out great, didn't it?"

Despite the inauspicious precedent, we decided it was worth a shot. Two days after Labor Day, Michelle and I climbed into the backseat of the Beast, drove up to the Capitol's east entrance, and retraced the steps we'd taken seven months earlier to the doors of the House chamber. The announcement by the sergeant at arms, the lights, television cameras, applause, handshakes along the center aisle—on the surface, at least, everything appeared as it had in February. But the mood in the chamber felt different this time—the smiles a little forced, a murmur of tension and doubt in the air. Or maybe it was just that my mood was different. Whatever giddiness or sense of personal triumph I'd felt shortly after taking office had now been burned away, replaced by something sturdier: a determination to see a job through.

For an hour that evening, I explained as straightforwardly as I could what our reform proposals would mean for the families who were watching: how it would provide affordable insurance to those who needed it but also give critical protections to those who already had insurance; how it would prevent insurance companies from discriminating against people with preexisting conditions and eliminate the kind of lifetime limits that burdened families like Laura Klitzka's. I detailed how the plan would help seniors pay for lifesaving drugs and require insurers to cover routine checkups and preventive care at no extra charge. I explained that the talk about a government takeover and death panels was nonsense, that the legislation wouldn't add a dime to the deficit, and that the time to make this happen was now.

A few days earlier, I'd received a letter from Ted Kennedy. He'd written it back in May but had instructed Vicki to wait until after his death to pass it along. It was a farewell letter, two pages long, in which he'd thanked me for taking up the cause of healthcare reform, referring to it as "that great unfinished business of our society" and the cause of his life. He added that he would die with some comfort, believing that what he'd spent years working toward would now, under my watch, finally happen.

So I ended my speech that night by quoting from Teddy's letter, hoping that his words would bolster the nation just as they had bolstered me. "What we face," he'd written, "is above all a moral issue; at stake are not just the details of policy, but fundamental principles of social justice and the character of our country."

According to poll data, my address to Congress boosted public support for the healthcare bill, at least temporarily. Even more important for our purposes, it seemed to stiffen the spine of wavering congressional Democrats. It did not, however, change the mind of a single Republican in the chamber. This was clear less than thirty minutes into the speech, when—as I debunked the phony claim that the bill would insure undocumented immigrants—a relatively obscure five-term Republican congressman from South Carolina named Joe Wilson leaned forward in his seat, pointed in my direction, and shouted, his face flushed with fury, "You lie!"

For the briefest second, a stunned silence fell over the chamber. I turned to look for the heckler (as did Speaker Pelosi and Joe Biden, Nancy aghast and Joe shaking his head). I was tempted to exit my perch, make my way down the aisle, and smack the guy in the head. Instead, I simply responded by saying "It's not true" and then carried on with my speech as Democrats hurled boos in Wilson's direction.

As far as anyone could remember, nothing like that

had ever happened before a joint session address—at least not in modern times. Congressional criticism was swift and bipartisan, and by the next morning Wilson had apologized publicly for the breach of decorum, calling Rahm and asking that his regrets get passed on to me as well. I downplayed the matter, telling a reporter that I appreciated the apology and was a big believer that we all make mistakes.

And yet I couldn't help noticing the news reports saying that online contributions to Wilson's reelection campaign spiked sharply in the week following his outburst. Apparently, for a lot of Republican voters out there, he was a hero, speaking truth to power. It was an indication that the Tea Party and its media allies had accomplished more than just their goal of demonizing the healthcare bill. They had demonized me and, in doing so, had delivered a message to all Republican officeholders: When it came to opposing my administration, the old rules no longer applied.

DESPITE HAVING GROWN UP in Hawaii, I have never learned to sail a boat; it wasn't a pastime my family could afford. And yet for the next three and a half months, I felt the way I imagine sailors feel on the open seas after a brutal storm has passed. The work remained arduous and sometimes monotonous, made tougher by the need to patch leaks and bail water. Maintaining speed and course in the constantly shifting winds and currents required patience, skill, and attention. But for a span of time, we had in us the thankfulness of survivors, propelled in our daily tasks by a renewed belief that we might make it to port after all.

For starters, after months of delay, Baucus finally opened debate on a healthcare bill in the Senate Finance Committee. His version, which tracked the Massachusetts model we'd all been using, was stingier with its subsidies to the uninsured than we would have preferred, and we insisted that he replace a tax on all employer-based insurance plans with increased taxes on the wealthy. But to everyone's credit, the deliberations were generally substantive and free of grandstanding. After three weeks of exhaustive work, the bill passed out of committee by a 14-to-9 margin. Olympia Snowe even decided to vote yes, giving us a lone Republican vote.

Speaker Pelosi then engineered the quick passage of a consolidated House bill over uniform and boisterous GOP opposition, with a vote held on November 7, 2009. (The bill had actually been ready for some time, but Nancy had been unwilling to bring it to the House floor—and force her members to cast tough political votes—until she had confidence that the Senate effort wasn't going to fizzle.) If we could get the full Senate to pass a similarly consolidated version of its bill before the Christmas recess, we figured, we could then use January to negotiate the differences between the Senate and House versions, send a merged bill to both chambers for approval, and with any luck have the final legislation on my desk for signature by February.

It was a big if—and one largely dependent on my old friend Harry Reid. True to his generally dim view of human nature, the Senate majority leader assumed that Olympia Snowe couldn't be counted on once a final version of the healthcare bill hit the floor. ("When McConnell really puts the screws to her," he told me matter-of-factly, "she'll fold like a cheap suit.") To overcome the possibility of a filibuster, Harry couldn't afford to lose a single member of his sixty-person caucus. And as had been true with the Recovery Act, this fact gave each one of those members enormous leverage to demand changes to the bill, regardless of how parochial or ill-considered their requests might be.

This wouldn't be a situation conducive to high-minded policy considerations, which was just fine with Harry, who could maneuver, cut deals, and apply pressure like nobody else. For the next six weeks, as the consolidated bill was introduced on the Senate floor and lengthy debates commenced on procedural matters, the only action that really mattered took place behind closed doors in Harry's office, where he met with the holdouts one by one to find out what it would take to get them to yes. Some wanted funding for well-intentioned but marginally useful pet projects. Several of the Senate's most liberal members, who liked to rail against the outsized profits of Big Pharma and private insurers, suddenly had no problem at all with the outsized profits of medical device manufacturers with facilities in their home states and were pushing Harry to scale back a proposed tax on the industry. Senators Mary Landrieu and Ben Nelson made their votes contingent on billions of additional Medicaid dollars specifically for Louisiana and Nebraska, concessions that the Republicans cleverly labeled "the Louisiana Purchase" and "the Cornhusker Kickback."

Whatever it took, Harry was game. Sometimes **too** game. He was good about staying in touch with my team, giving Phil or Nancy-Ann the chance to head off legislative changes that could adversely affect the core parts of our reforms, but occasionally he'd dig his heels in on some deal he wanted to cut, and I'd have to intervene with a call. Listening to my objections, he'd usually relent, but not without some grumbling, wondering how on earth he would get the bill passed if he did things my way.

"Mr. President, you know a lot more than I do about healthcare policy," he said at one point. "But I know the Senate, okay?"

Compared to the egregious pork-barreling, logrolling, and patronage-dispensing tactics Senate leaders had traditionally used to get big, controversial bills like the Civil Rights Act or Ronald Reagan's 1986 Tax Reform Act, or a package like the New Deal, passed, Harry's methods were fairly benign. But those bills had passed during a time when most Washington horse-trading stayed out of the papers, before the advent of the twenty-four-hour news cycle. For us, the slog through the Senate was a PR nightmare. Each time Harry's bill was altered to mollify another senator, reporters cranked out a new round of stories about "backroom deals." Whatever bump in public opinion my joint address had provided to the reform effort soon vanished—and things got markedly worse when Harry decided, with my blessing, to strip the bill of something called "the public option."

From the very start of the healthcare debate, policy wonks on the left had pushed us to modify the Massachusetts model by giving consumers the choice to buy coverage on the online "exchange," not just from the likes of Aetna and Blue Cross Blue Shield but also from a newly formed insurer owned and operated by the government. Unsurprisingly, insurance companies had balked at the idea of a public option, arguing that they would not be able to compete against a government insurance plan that could operate without the pressures of making a profit. Of course, for public-option proponents, that was exactly the point: By highlighting the cost-effectiveness of government insurance and exposing the bloated waste and immorality of the private insurance market, they hoped the public option would pave the way for a single-payer system.

It was a clever idea, and one with enough traction that Nancy Pelosi had included it in the House bill. But on the Senate side, we were nowhere close to having sixty votes for a public option. There was a watered-down version in the Senate Health and Education Committee bill, requiring any government-run insurer to charge the same rates as private insurers, but of course that would have defeated the whole purpose of a public option. My team and I thought a possible compromise might involve offering a public option only in those parts of the country where there were too few insurers to provide real competition and a public entity could help drive down premium prices overall. But even that was too much for the more conservative members of the Democratic caucus to swallow, including Joe Lieberman of Connecticut, who announced shortly before Thanksgiving that under no circumstances would he vote for a package that contained a public option.

When word got out that the public option had been removed from the Senate bill, activists on the left went ballistic. Howard Dean, the former Vermont governor and onetime presidential candidate, declared it "essentially the collapse of health reform in the United States Senate." They were especially outraged that Harry and I

appeared to be catering to the whims of Joe Lieberman—
an object of liberal scorn who'd been defeated in the
2006 Democratic primary for his consistently hawkish
support for the Iraq War and had then been forced to
run for reelection as an independent. It wasn't the first
time I'd chosen practicality over pique when it came to
Lieberman: Despite the fact he'd endorsed his buddy
John McCain in the last presidential campaign, Harry
and I had quashed calls to strip him of various committee assignments, figuring we couldn't afford to have him
bolt the caucus and cost us a reliable vote. We'd been
right about that—Lieberman had consistently supported
my domestic agenda. But his apparent power to dictate
the terms of healthcare reform reinforced the view among
some Democrats that I treated enemies better than allies
and was turning my back on the progressives who'd put
me in office.

I found the whole brouhaha exasperating. "What is it
about sixty votes these folks don't understand?" I groused
to my staff. "Should I tell the thirty million people who
can't get covered that they're going to have to wait another
ten years because we can't get them a public option?"

It wasn't just that criticism from friends always stung
the most. The carping carried immediate political consequences for Democrats. It confused our base (which,
generally speaking, had no idea what the hell a public
option was) and divided our caucus, making it tougher
for us to line up the votes we'd need to get the healthcare
bill across the finish line. It also ignored the fact that all
the great social welfare advances in American history,
including Social Security and Medicare, had started off
incomplete and had been built upon gradually, over

time. By preemptively spinning what could be a monumental, if imperfect, victory into a bitter defeat, the criticism contributed to a potential long-term demoralization of Democratic voters—otherwise known as the "What's the point of voting if nothing ever changes?" syndrome—making it even harder for us to win elections and move progressive legislation forward in the future.

There was a reason, I told Valerie, why Republicans tended to do the opposite—why Ronald Reagan could preside over huge increases in the federal budget, federal deficit, and federal workforce and still be lionized by the GOP faithful as the guy who successfully shrank the federal government. They understood that in politics, the stories told were often as important as the substance achieved.

We made none of these arguments publicly, though for the rest of my presidency the phrase "public option" became a useful shorthand inside the White House anytime Democratic interest groups complained about us failing to defy political gravity and securing less than 100 percent of whatever they were asking for. Instead, we did our best to calm folks down, reminding disgruntled supporters that we'd have plenty of time to fine-tune the legislation when we merged the House and Senate bills. Harry kept doing Harry stuff, including keeping the Senate in session weeks past the scheduled adjournment for the holidays. As he'd predicted, Olympia Snowe braved a blizzard to stop by the Oval and tell us in person that she'd be voting no. (She claimed it was because Harry was rushing the bill through, though word was that McConnell had threatened to strip her of her ranking post on the Small Business Committee if she voted for it.) But none of this mattered. On Christmas Eve, after twenty-four days of debate, with Washington blanketed in snow and the streets all but empty, the Senate passed its healthcare bill, titled the Patient Protection and Affordable Care Act—the ACA—with exactly sixty votes. It was the first Christmas Eve vote in the Senate since 1895.

A few hours later, I settled back in my seat on Air Force One, listening to Michelle and the girls discuss how well Bo was adjusting to his first plane ride as we headed to Hawaii for the holiday break. I felt myself starting to relax just a little. We were going to make it, I thought to myself. We weren't docked yet, but thanks to my team, thanks to Nancy, Harry, and a whole bunch of congressional Democrats who'd taken tough votes, we finally had land within our sights.

Little did I know that our ship was about to crash into rocks.

OUR MAGIC, FILIBUSTER-PROOF hold on the Senate existed for only one reason. After Ted Kennedy died in August, the Massachusetts legislature had changed state law to allow the governor, Democrat Deval Patrick, to appoint a replacement rather than leaving the seat vacant until a special election could be held. But that was just a stopgap measure, and now, with the election scheduled for January 19, we needed a Democrat to win the seat. Fortunately for us, Massachusetts happened to be one of the most Democratic states in the nation, with no Republican senators elected in the previous thirty-seven years. The Democratic nominee for the Senate, attorney general Martha Coakley, had maintained a steady, double-digit lead over her Republican opponent, a little-known state senator named Scott Brown.

With the race seemingly well in hand, my team and I spent the first two weeks of January preoccupied by the challenge of brokering a healthcare bill acceptable to both House and Senate Democrats. It was not pleasant. Disdain between the two chambers of Congress is a time-honored tradition in Washington, one that even transcends party; senators generally consider House members to be impulsive, parochial, and ill-informed, while House members tend to view senators as long-winded, pompous, and ineffectual. By the start of 2010, that disdain had curdled into outright hostility. House Democrats—tired of seeing their huge majority squandered and their aggressively liberal agenda stymied by a Senate Democratic caucus held captive by its more conservative members—insisted that the Senate version of the healthcare bill had no chance in the House. Senate Democrats—fed up with what they considered House grandstanding at their expense—were no less recalcitrant. Rahm and Nancy-Ann's efforts to broker a deal appeared to be going nowhere, with arguments erupting over even the most obscure provisions, members cursing at one another and threatening to walk out.

After a week of this, I'd had enough. I called Pelosi, Reid, and negotiators from both sides down to the White House, and for three straight days in mid-January we sat around the Cabinet Room table, methodically going through every dispute, sorting out areas where House members had to take Senate constraints into account and where the Senate had to give, with me reminding everyone all the while that failure was not an option and that we'd do this every night for the next month if that's what it took to reach an agreement.

Though progress was slow, I felt pretty good about our prospects. That is, until the afternoon I stopped by Axelrod's small office and found him and Messina leaning over a computer like a pair of doctors examining the X-rays of a terminal patient.

"What's the matter?" I asked.

"We've got problems in Massachusetts," Axe said, shaking his head.

"How bad?"

"Bad," Axe and Messina said in unison.

They explained that our Senate candidate, Martha Coakley, had taken the race for granted, spending her time schmoozing elected officials, donors, and labor bigwigs rather than talking to voters. To make matters worse, she'd taken a vacation just three weeks before the election, a move the press had roundly panned. Meanwhile, Republican Scott Brown's campaign had caught fire. With his everyman demeanor and good looks, not to mention the pickup truck he drove to every corner of the state, Brown had effectively tapped into the fears and frustrations of working-class voters who were getting clobbered by the recession and—because they lived in a state that already provided health insurance to all its residents—saw my obsession with passing a federal healthcare law as a big waste of time.

Apparently neither the tightening poll numbers nor nervous calls from my team and Harry had shaken Coakley out of her torpor. The previous day, when asked by a reporter about her light campaign schedule, she had brushed the question off, saying, "As opposed to standing outside Fenway Park? In the cold? Shaking hands?"—a sarcastic reference to Scott Brown's New Year's Day campaign stop at Boston's storied ballpark, where the city's hockey team, the Boston Bruins, were hosting the annual NHL Winter Classic against the Philadelphia Flyers. In a town that worshipped its sports teams, it would be hard to come up with a line more likely to turn off large segments of the electorate.

"She didn't say that," I said, dumbfounded.

Messina nodded toward his computer. "It's right here on the **Globe** website."

"Nooooo!" I moaned, grabbing Axe by the lapels and shaking him theatrically, then stomping my feet like a toddler in the throes of a tantrum. "No, no, no!" My shoulders slumped as my mind ran through the implications. "She's going to lose, isn't she?" I said finally.

Axe and Messina didn't have to answer. The weekend before the election, I tried to salvage the situation by flying to Boston to attend a Coakley rally. But it was too late. Brown won comfortably. Headlines around the country spoke of a STUNNING UPSET and HISTORIC DEFEAT. The verdict in Washington was swift and unforgiving.

Obama's healthcare bill was dead.

EVEN NOW, it's hard for me to have a clear perspective on the Massachusetts loss. Maybe the conventional wisdom is right. Maybe if I hadn't pushed so hard on healthcare during that first year, if instead I'd focused all my public events and pronouncements on jobs and the financial crisis, we might have saved that Senate seat. Certainly, if we'd had fewer items on our plate, my team and I might have noticed the warning signs earlier and coached Coakley harder, and I might have done more campaigning in Massachusetts. It's equally possible, though, that given the grim state of the economy, there was nothing we could have done—that the wheels of history would have remained impervious to our puny interventions.

I know that at the time all of us felt we'd committed a colossal blunder. Commentators shared in that assessment. Op-ed pieces called for me to replace my team, starting with Rahm and Axe. I didn't pay much attention. I figured any mistakes were mine to own, and I took pride in having built a culture—both during the campaign and inside the White House—where we didn't go looking for scapegoats when things went south.

But it was harder for Rahm to ignore the chatter. Having spent most of his career in Washington, the daily news cycle was how he kept score—not just on the administration's performance but on his own place in the world. He constantly courted the city's opinion makers, aware of how quickly winners became losers and how mercilessly White House staffers were picked apart in the wake of any failure. In this case, he saw himself as unfairly maligned: It was he, after all, who more than anyone had warned me about the political peril in pressing ahead with the healthcare bill. And as we're all prone to do when hurt or aggrieved, he couldn't help venting to friends around town. Unfortunately that circle of friends turned out to be too wide. About a month after the Massachusetts election, **Washington Post** columnist Dana Milbank wrote a piece in which he mounted a vigorous defense of Rahm, arguing that "Obama's greatest mistake was failing to listen to Emanuel on health care" and outlining why a scaled-back healthcare package would have been the smarter strategy.

Having your chief of staff appear to distance himself from you after you've been knocked down in a fight is less than ideal. Though I wasn't happy with the column, I didn't think Rahm had deliberately prompted it. I chalked it up to carelessness under stress. Not everyone, though, was so quick to forgive. Valerie, ever protective of me, was furious. Reactions among other senior staffers, already shaken by the Coakley loss, ranged from anger to disappointment. That afternoon, Rahm entered the Oval appropriately contrite. He hadn't meant to do it, he said, but he'd let me down and was prepared to tender his resignation.

"You're not resigning," I said. I acknowledged that he'd messed up and would need to square things with the rest of the team. But I also told him he'd been a great chief of staff, that I was confident that the error would not be repeated, and that I needed him right where he was.

"Mr. President, I'm not sure—"

I cut him off. "You know what your real punishment is?" I said, clapping him on the back as I ushered him toward the door.

"What's that?"

"You have to go pass the goddamn healthcare bill!"

That I still considered this possible wasn't as crazy as it seemed. Our original plan—to negotiate a compromise bill between House and Senate Democrats and then pass that legislation through both chambers—was now out of the question; with only fifty-nine votes, we'd never avoid a filibuster. But as Phil had reminded me the night we'd received the Massachusetts results, we had one remaining path, and it didn't involve going back to the Senate. **If the House could just pass the Senate bill without changes,** they could send it straight to my desk for signature and it would become law. Phil believed that it might be possible to then invoke a Senate procedure called budget reconciliation—in which legislation that involved strictly financial matters could be put up for a vote with the agreement of a simple majority of senators rather than the usual sixty. This would allow us to engineer a limited number of improvements to the Senate bill via separate legislation. Still, there was no getting around the fact that we'd be asking House Democrats to swallow a version of healthcare reform they'd previously rejected out of hand—one with no public option, a Cadillac tax the unions opposed, and a cumbersome patchwork of fifty state exchanges instead of a single national marketplace through which people could buy their insurance.

"You still feeling lucky?" Phil asked me with a grin.

Actually, I wasn't.

But I was feeling confident in the Speaker of the House.

The previous year had only reinforced my appreciation for Nancy Pelosi's legislative skills. She was tough, pragmatic, and a master at herding members of her contentious caucus, often publicly defending some of her fellow House Democrats' politically untenable positions while softening them up behind the scenes for the inevitable compromises required to get things done.

I called Nancy the next day, explaining that my team had drafted a drastically scaled-back healthcare proposal as a fallback but that I wanted to push ahead with passing the Senate bill through the House and needed her support to do it. For the next fifteen minutes, I was subjected to one of Nancy's patented stream-of-consciousness rants—on why the Senate bill was flawed, why her caucus members were so angry, and why the Senate Democrats were cowardly, shortsighted, and generally incompetent.

"So does that mean you're with me?" I said when she finally paused to catch her breath.

"Well, that's not even a question, Mr. President," Nancy said impatiently. "We've come too far to give up now." She thought for a moment. Then, as if testing out an argument she'd later use with her caucus, she added, "If we let this go, it would be rewarding the Republicans for acting so terribly, wouldn't it? We're not going to give them the satisfaction."

After I hung up the phone, I looked up at Phil and Nancy-Ann, who'd been milling around the Resolute desk, listening to my (mostly wordless) side of the conversation, trying to read my face for a sign of what was happening.

"I love that woman," I said.

EVEN WITH THE SPEAKER fully on board, the task of rounding up the necessary votes in the House was daunting. Aside from having to drag progressives kicking and screaming to support a bill tailored to the sensibilities of Max Baucus and Joe Lieberman, the election of Scott Brown less than a year before the midterms had spooked every moderate Democrat who would be in a competitive race. We needed something to help shift the doom-and-gloom narrative and give Nancy time to work her members.

As it turned out, our opposition gave us exactly what we needed. Months earlier, the House Republican caucus had invited me to participate in a question-and-answer session at their annual retreat, scheduled for January 29. Anticipating that the topic of healthcare might come up, we suggested at the last minute that they open the event to the press. Whether because he didn't want the hassle of dealing with pushback from excluded reporters or because he was feeling emboldened by the Scott Brown victory, John Boehner agreed.

He shouldn't have. In a nondescript Baltimore hotel conference room, with caucus chair Mike Pence presiding and the cable networks capturing every exchange, I stood on the stage for an hour and twenty-two minutes fielding questions from Republican House members, mostly about healthcare. For anyone watching, the session confirmed what those of us who'd been working on the issue already knew: The overwhelming majority of them had little idea of what was actually in the bill they so vehemently opposed, weren't entirely sure about the details of their proposed alternatives (to the extent that they had any), and weren't equipped to discuss the topic outside the hermetically sealed bubble of conservative media outlets.

Returning to the White House, I suggested that we press our advantage by inviting the Four Tops and a bipartisan group of key congressional leaders to come to Blair House for an all-day meeting on healthcare. Once again, we arranged to have the proceedings broadcast live, this time through C-SPAN, and again the format allowed Republicans to make whatever points or ask whatever questions they wanted. Having been caught off guard once, they came prepared with a script this time. House GOP whip Eric Cantor brought a copy of the House bill, all 2,700 pages of it, and plopped it on the table in front of him as a symbol of an out-of-control government takeover of healthcare. Boehner insisted that our proposal was "a dangerous experiment" and that we should start over. John McCain launched into a lengthy harangue about backroom deals, prompting me at one point to remind him that the campaign was over. But when it came to actual policy—when I asked GOP leaders what exactly they proposed to help drive down medical costs, protect people with preexisting conditions, and cover thirty million Americans who couldn't otherwise get insurance—their answers were as threadbare as Chuck Grassley's had been during his visit to the Oval months before.

I'm sure that more people watched bowling that week than caught even five minutes of these conversations on TV, and it was clear throughout both sessions that nothing I said was going to have the slightest impact on Republican behavior (other than motivating them to bar TV cameras from my future appearances before their caucuses). What mattered was how the two events served to reinvigorate House Democrats, reminding them that we were on the right side of the healthcare issue, and that rather than focusing on the Senate bill's shortcomings, they could take heart in how the bill promised to help millions of people.

BY THE BEGINNING of March, we had confirmed that Senate rules would allow us to clean up parts of the Senate bill through reconciliation. We enhanced the subsidies to help more people. We trimmed the Cadillac tax to placate the unions and got rid of the twin embarrassments of the "Cornhusker Kickback" and "Louisiana Purchase." Valerie's public engagement team did great work lining up endorsements from groups like the American Academy of Family Physicians, the American Medical Association, the American Nurses Association, and the American Heart Association, while a grassroots network of advocacy groups and volunteers worked overtime to educate the public and keep the pressure on Congress. Anthem, one of America's largest insurers, announced a 39 percent rate hike, conveniently reminding people of what they didn't like about the current system. And when the United States Conference of Catholic Bishops announced that it couldn't support the bill (convinced that the bill's language prohibiting the use of federal subsidies for abortion services wasn't explicit enough), an unlikely ally arrived in the form of Sister Carol Keehan, a soft-spoken, perpetually cheerful nun who headed up the nation's Catholic hospitals. Not only did the sixty-six-year-old Daughter of Charity break with the bishops by insisting that passage of the bill was vital to fulfilling her organization's mission of caring for the sick; she inspired the leaders of Catholic women's orders and organizations representing more than fifty thousand American nuns to sign a public letter endorsing the bill.

"I love nuns," I told Phil and Nancy-Ann.

Despite all this work, our tally still showed us at least ten votes shy of what we needed for passage. Public opinion remained sharply divided. The press had run out of fresh stories to write. There were no more dramatic gestures or policy tweaks that might make the politics easier. Success or failure now depended entirely on the choices of the thirty or so House Democrats who represented swing districts, all of whom were being told that a vote in favor of the ACA could cost them their seat.

I spent much of each day talking one-on-one to these members, sometimes in the Oval Office, more often by phone. Some cared only about the politics, closely monitoring polls in their district and letters and phone calls from constituents. I tried to give them my honest assessment: that support for the healthcare reform bill would improve once it passed, though maybe not until after the midterms; that a "no" vote was more likely to turn off Democrats than it was to win over Republicans and independents; and that whatever they did, their fates in six months would most likely hinge on the state of the economy and my own political standing.

A few were looking for White House support on some unrelated project or bill they were working on. I sent them to Rahm or Pete Rouse to see what we could do.

But most of the conversations weren't transactional. In a roundabout way, what representatives were looking for was clarity—about who they were and what their consciences demanded. Sometimes I just listened as they ran through the pros and cons. Often, we compared notes about what had inspired us to get into politics, talking about the nervous excitement of that first race and all the things we'd hoped to accomplish, the sacrifices we and our families had made to get where we were and the people who'd helped us along the way.

This is it, I'd say to them finally. The point of it all. To have that rare chance, reserved for very few, to bend history in a better direction.

And what was striking was how, more often than not, that was enough. Veteran politicians decided to step up despite active opposition in their conservative districts— folks like Baron Hill of southern Indiana, Earl Pomeroy of North Dakota, and Bart Stupak, a devout Catholic from Michigan's Upper Peninsula who worked with me on getting the abortion funding language to a point where he could vote for it. So did political neophytes like Betsy Markey of Colorado, or John Boccieri of Ohio and Patrick Murphy of Pennsylvania, both young Iraq War vets, all of them seen as rising stars in the party. In fact, it was often those with the most to lose who needed the least convincing. Tom Perriello, a thirty-five-year-old human rights lawyer turned congressman who'd eked out a victory in a majority-Republican district that covered a wide swath of Virginia, spoke for a lot of them when he explained his decision to vote for the bill.

"There are things more important," he told me, "than getting reelected."

It's not hard to find people who hate Congress, voters who are convinced that the Capitol is filled with poseurs and cowards, that most of their elected officials are in the pocket of lobbyists and big donors and motivated by a hunger for power. When I hear such criticism, I usually nod and acknowledge that there are some who live up to these stereotypes. I admit that watching the daily scrum that takes place on the House or Senate floor can sap even the hardiest spirit. But I also tell people about Tom Perriello's words to me before the healthcare vote. I describe what he and many others did so soon after they'd first been elected. How many of us are tested in that way, asked to risk careers we've long dreamed of in the service of some greater good?

Those people can be found in Washington. That, too, is politics.

THE FINAL VOTE on healthcare came on March 21, 2010—more than a year after we held that first White House summit and Ted Kennedy made his surprise appearance. Everyone in the West Wing was on edge. Both Phil and the Speaker had done informal head counts that showed us getting over the hump, but just barely. We knew it was always possible that a House member or two could have a sudden change of heart, and we had few, if any, votes to spare.

I had another source of worry, one I hadn't allowed myself to dwell on but that had been in the back of my mind from the start. We'd now marshaled, defended, fretted over, and compromised on a 906-page piece of legislation that would affect the lives of tens of millions of Americans. The Affordable Care Act was dense, thorough, popular with only one side politically, impactful, and surely imperfect. And now it would need to be implemented. Late in the afternoon, after Nancy-Ann and I had worked through a round of last-minute calls to members heading off to vote, I stood up and looked out the window, across the South Lawn.

"This law better work," I told her. "Because starting tomorrow, we own the American healthcare system."

I decided not to watch the preliminary hours of speechmaking that went on in the House chamber, instead waiting to join the vice president and the rest of the team in the Roosevelt Room once the actual voting began, around seven-thirty p.m. One by one, the votes accumulated as House members pressed either "yea" or "nay" buttons on electronic voting panels, the running tally projected on the TV screen. As the "yeas" slowly ticked up, I could hear Messina and a few others muttering under their breath, "Come on . . . come on." Finally the vote hit 216, one more than we needed. Our bill would go on to pass by a margin of seven votes.

The room erupted in cheers, with people hugging and high-fiving as if they'd just witnessed their ball club winning with a walk-off home run. Joe grabbed me by the shoulders, his famous grin even wider than usual. "You did it, man!" he said. Rahm and I embraced. He'd brought his thirteen-year-old son, Zach, to the White House that evening to watch the vote. I leaned down and told Zach that because of his dad, millions of people would finally have healthcare if they got sick. The kid beamed. Back in the Oval, I made congratulatory calls to Nancy Pelosi and Harry Reid, and when I was done, I found Axelrod standing by the door. His eyes were a little red. He told me he'd needed some time alone in his office following the vote, as it had brought back a flood of memories of what he and his wife, Susan, had gone through when their daughter Lauren had been first stricken with epileptic seizures.

"Thanks for sticking with this," Axe said, his voice choked up. I put my arm around him, feeling my own emotions swell.

"This is why we do the work," I said. "This. Right here."

I had invited everyone who worked on the bill up to the residence for a private celebration, about a hundred people in all. It was Sasha and Malia's spring break, and Michelle had taken them to New York for a few days, so I was on my own. The evening was warm enough that we could mingle outside on the Truman Balcony, with the Washington Monument and Jefferson Memorial lit up in the distance, and I made an exception to my rule of weekday sobriety. Martini in hand, I made the rounds, hugging and thanking Phil, Nancy-Ann, Jeanne, and Kathleen for all the work they'd done. I shook hands with scores of junior staffers, many of whom I'd never met and who no doubt felt a little overwhelmed to be standing where they were. I knew they had toiled in the background, crunching numbers, preparing drafts, sending out press releases, and answering congressional inquiries, and I wanted them to know how critical their work had been.

For me, this was a celebration that mattered. The night we'd had in Grant Park after winning the election had been extraordinary, but it had been just a promise, not yet realized. This night meant more to me, a promise fulfilled.

After everyone had left, well past midnight, I walked down the hallway to the Treaty Room. Bo was curled up on the floor. He'd passed much of the evening on the balcony with my guests, threading through the crowd, looking for a pat on the head or maybe a dropped canapé to snack on. Now he looked pleasantly fatigued, ready to sleep. I leaned down to give him a scratch behind the ears. I thought about Ted Kennedy, and I thought about my mom.

It was a good day.

PART FIVE

THE WORLD AS IT IS

CHAPTER 18

JUST AS DELIVERING A SALUTE became second nature to me, repeated anytime I boarded Marine One or Air Force One or interacted with our troops, I slowly grew more comfortable—and efficient— in my role as commander in chief. The morning PDB became more concise as my team and I got better acquainted with a recurring cast of foreign policy characters, scenarios, conflicts, and threats. Connections that had once been opaque were now obvious to me. I could tell you off the top of my head which allied troops were where in Afghanistan and how reliable they were in a fight, which Iraqi ministers were ardent nationalists and which carried water for the Iranians. The stakes were too high, the problems too knotty, for any of this to ever feel entirely routine. Instead, I came to experience my responsibilities the way I imagine a bomb-disposal expert feels about clipping a wire or a tightrope walker feels as she steps off the platform, having learned to shed excess fear for the sake of focus—while trying not to get so relaxed that I made sloppy mistakes.

There was one task that I never allowed myself to get even remotely comfortable with. Every week or so, my assistant Katie Johnson set on my desk a folder containing condolence letters to the families of fallen service members for me to sign. I'd close the door to my office, open the folder, and pause over each letter, reading the name aloud like an incantation, trying to summon an image of the young man (female casualties were rare) and what his life had been like—where he'd grown up and gone to school, the birthday parties and summer swims that had made up his childhood, the sports teams he'd played on, the sweethearts he'd pined for. I'd think about his parents, and his wife and kids if he had them. I signed each letter slowly, careful not to smudge the heavy beige paper with my left-handed, sideways grip of the pen. If the signature didn't look the way I wanted, I'd have the letter reprinted, knowing full well that nothing I did would ever be enough.

I wasn't the only person to send such letters. Bob Gates also corresponded with the families of those killed in Iraq and Afghanistan, though we rarely if ever talked about it.

Gates and I had developed a strong working relationship. We met regularly in the Oval Office, and I found him to be practical, even-keeled, and refreshingly blunt, with the quiet confidence to both argue his case and occasionally change his mind. His skillful management of the Pentagon made me willing to overlook those times he tried to manage me as well, and he wasn't afraid to take on Defense Department sacred cows, including efforts to rein in the defense budget. He could be prickly, especially with my younger White House staffers, and our differences in age, upbringing, experience, and political orientation made us something short of friends. But we recognized in each other a common work ethic and sense of duty—not only to the nation that had trusted us to keep it safe but to the troops whose courage we witnessed every day, and to the families they had left behind.

It helped that on most national security issues our judgments aligned. Entering the summer of 2009, for example, Gates and I shared a guarded optimism about developments in Iraq. Not that the conditions there were rosy. The Iraqi economy was in shambles—the war had destroyed much of the country's basic infrastructure, while plunging world oil prices had sapped the national budget—and due to parliamentary gridlock, Iraq's government had difficulty carrying out even the most basic tasks. During my brief visit there in April, I'd offered Prime Minister Maliki suggestions for how he might embrace needed administrative reforms and more effectively reach out to Iraq's Sunni and Kurdish factions. He'd been polite but defensive (apparently he wasn't a student of Madison's "Federalist No. 10"): As far as he was concerned, Shiites in Iraq were the majority, his party's coalition had won the most votes, Sunnis and Kurds were hindering progress with their unreasonable demands, and any notions of accommodating the interests or protecting the rights of Iraq's minority populations were an inconvenience he assumed only as a result of U.S. pressure.

The conversation had been a useful reminder to me that elections alone don't produce a functioning democracy; until Iraq found a way to strengthen its civic institutions and its leaders developed habits of compromise, the country would continue to struggle. Still, the fact that Maliki and his rivals were expressing hostility and mistrust through politics rather than through the barrel of a gun counted as progress. Even with U.S. forces withdrawing from Iraqi population centers, AQI-sponsored terrorist attacks had continued to decline, and our commanders reported a steady improvement in the performance of Iraqi security forces. Gates and I agreed that the United States would need to play a critical role in Iraq for years to come—advising key ministries, training its security forces, breaking deadlocks between factions, and helping finance the country's reconstruction. But barring significant reversals, the end of America's war in Iraq was finally in sight.

The same couldn't be said about Afghanistan.

The additional troops I'd authorized in February had helped check Taliban gains in some areas and were working to secure the upcoming presidential election. But our forces had not reversed the country's deepening cycle of violence and instability, and as a result of increased fighting over a wider swath of territory, U.S. casualties had spiked.

Afghan casualties were also on the rise, with more civilians caught in the cross fire, falling prey to suicide attacks and sophisticated roadside bombs planted by insurgents. Afghans increasingly complained about certain U.S. tactics—nighttime raids on homes suspected of harboring Taliban fighters, for example—that they viewed as dangerous or disruptive but that our commanders deemed necessary to carry out their missions. On the political front, President Karzai's reelection strategy mainly consisted of buying off local power brokers, intimidating opponents, and shrewdly playing various ethnic factions against one another. Diplomatically, our high-level outreach to Pakistani officials appeared to have had no effect on their continued tolerance of Taliban safe havens inside their country. And all the while, a reconstituted al-Qaeda operating in the border areas with Pakistan still posed a major threat.

Given the lack of meaningful progress, we were all eager to see what our new ISAF commander, General Stanley McChrystal, had to say about the situation. At the end of August, having spent weeks in Afghanistan with a team of military and civilian advisors, McChrystal turned in the top-to-bottom assessment that Gates had asked for. A few days later, the Pentagon sent it to the White House.

Rather than provide clear answers, it set off a whole new round of troublesome questions.

MOST OF MCCHRYSTAL'S assessment detailed what we already knew: The situation in Afghanistan was bad and getting worse, with the Taliban emboldened, the Afghan army weak and demoralized, and Karzai, who prevailed in an election tainted by violence and fraud, still in charge of a government that was viewed by the Afghan people as corrupt and inept. What got everyone's attention, though, was the report's conclusion. To turn the situation around, McChrystal proposed a full-blown counterinsurgency (COIN) campaign: a military strategy meant to contain and marginalize insurgents not just by fighting them but by simultaneously working to increase stability for the country's wider population—ideally quelling some of the fury that had driven insurgents to take up arms in the first place.

Not only was McChrystal proposing a more ambitious approach than what I'd envisioned when I'd adopted the Riedel report recommendations in the spring, he was also requesting at least forty thousand troops on top of those I'd already deployed—which would bring the total number of U.S. troops in Afghanistan close to one hundred thousand for the foreseeable future.

"So much for being the antiwar president," Axe said.

It was tough not to feel as if I'd been subjected to a bait and switch—that the Pentagon's acquiescence to my more modest initial increase of seventeen thousand troops and four thousand military trainers had been merely a temporary, tactical retreat on the path to getting more. Among members of my team, divisions over Afghanistan that had been evident back in February began to harden. Mike Mullen, the Joint Chiefs, and David Petraeus all endorsed McChrystal's COIN strategy in its entirety; anything less, they argued, was likely to fail and would signal a dangerous lack of American resolve to friends and foes alike. Hillary and Panetta quickly followed suit. Gates, who'd previously expressed concern over the wisdom of expanding our military footprint in a country famously resistant to foreign occupation, was more circumspect but told me he'd been persuaded by McChrystal that a smaller U.S. force wouldn't work, and that if we coordinated closely with the Afghan security forces to protect local populations and better trained our soldiers to respect Afghan culture, we could avoid the problems that had plagued the Soviets in the 1980s. Meanwhile, Joe and a sizable number of NSC staffers viewed McChrystal's proposal as just the latest attempt by an unrestrained military to drag the country deeper into a futile, wildly expensive nation-building exercise, when we could and should be narrowly focused on counterterrorism (CT) efforts against al-Qaeda.

After reading McChrystal's sixty-six-page assessment, I shared Joe's skepticism. As far as I could tell, there was no clear exit strategy; under McChrystal's plan, it would take five to six years just to get U.S. troop numbers back down to what they were now. The costs were staggering—at least $1 billion for every thousand additional troops deployed. Our men and women in uniform, some on their fourth or fifth tours after close to a decade of war, would face an even greater toll. And given the resilience of the Taliban and the dysfunction of Karzai's government, there was no guarantee of success. In their written endorsement of the plan, Gates and the generals acknowledged that no amount of U.S. military power could stabilize Afghanistan "as long as pervasive corruption and preying upon the people continue to characterize governance" inside the country. I saw no possibility of **that** condition being met anytime soon.

Still, some hard truths prevented me from rejecting McChrystal's plan out of hand. The status quo was untenable. We couldn't afford to let the Taliban return to power, and we needed more time to train more capable Afghan security forces and to root out al-Qaeda and its leadership. As confident as I felt in my own judgment, I couldn't ignore the unanimous recommendation of experienced generals who'd managed to salvage some measure of stability in Iraq and were already in the thick of the fight in Afghanistan. I therefore asked Jim Jones and Tom Donilon to organize a series of NSC meetings where—away from congressional politics and media grousing—we could methodically work through the details of McChrystal's proposal, see how they matched up with our previously articulated objectives, and settle on the best way forward.

As it turned out, the generals had other ideas. Just two days after I received the report, **The Washington Post** published an interview with David Petraeus in which he declared that any hope for success in Afghanistan would require substantially more troops and a "fully resourced, comprehensive" COIN strategy. About ten days later, fresh off our first discussion of McChrystal's proposal in the Situation Room, Mike Mullen appeared before the Senate Armed Services Committee for a previously scheduled hearing and made the same argument, dismissing any narrower strategy as insufficient to the goal of defeating al-Qaeda and keeping Afghanistan from becoming a future base for attacks against the homeland. A few days after that, on September 21, the **Post** published a synopsis of McChrystal's report that had leaked to Bob Woodward, under the headline MCCHRYSTAL: MORE FORCES OR "MISSION FAILURE." This was followed in short order by McChrystal giving an interview to **60 Minutes** and delivering a speech in London, in both instances promoting the merits of his COIN strategy over other alternatives.

The reaction was predictable. Republican hawks like John McCain and Lindsey Graham seized on the generals' media blitz, offering the familiar refrain that I should "listen to my commanders on the ground" and fulfill McChrystal's request. News stories appeared daily, hyping the ever-growing rift between the White House and the Pentagon. Columnists accused me of "dithering" and questioned whether I had the intestinal fortitude to lead a nation during wartime. Rahm remarked that in all his years in Washington, he'd never seen such an orchestrated, public campaign by the Pentagon to box in a president. Biden was more succinct:

"It's fucking outrageous."

I agreed. It was hardly the first time that disagreements inside my team had spilled into the press. But it was the first instance during my presidency when I felt as if an entire agency under my charge was working its own agenda. I decided it was also going to be the last. Shortly after Mullen's congressional testimony, I asked him and Gates to see me in the Oval Office.

"So," I said after we'd taken our seats and I'd offered them coffee. "Did I not make myself clear about how I wanted time to evaluate McChrystal's assessment? Or does your building just have a basic lack of respect for me?"

The two men shifted uncomfortably on the couch. As is usually the case when I'm angry, I didn't raise my voice.

"From the day I was sworn in," I continued, "I've gone out of my way to create an environment where everyone's views are heard. And I think I've shown myself willing to make unpopular decisions when I thought it was necessary for our national security. Would you agree with that, Bob?"

"I would, Mr. President," Gates said.

"So, when I set up a process that's going to decide whether I send tens of thousands more troops into a deadly war zone at the cost of hundreds of billions of dollars, and I see my top military leaders short-circuiting that process to argue their position in public, I have to wonder. Is it because they figure they know better and don't want to be bothered answering my questions? Is it because I'm young and didn't serve in the military? Is it because they don't like my politics . . . ?"

I paused, letting the question linger. Mullen cleared his throat.

"I think I speak for all your flag officers, Mr. President," he said, "when I say we have the highest respect for you and the office."

I nodded. "Well, Mike, I'll take your word on that. And I give you **my** word that I'll make my decision about Stan's proposal based on the Pentagon's advice and what I believe best serves the interests of this country. But until I do," I said, leaning in for emphasis, "I'd sure like to stop having my military advisors telling me what I **have** to do on the front page of the morning paper. Is that fair?"

He agreed that it was. We moved on to other matters.

LOOKING BACK, I'm inclined to believe Gates when he said there was no coordinated plan by Mullen, Petraeus, or McChrystal to force my hand (although he'd later admit to hearing from a reliable source that some-one on McChrystal's staff had leaked the general's report to Woodward). I know that all three men were motivated by a sincere conviction in the rightness of their position, and that they considered it to be part of their code as military officers to provide their honest assessment in public testimony or press statements without regard to political consequences. Gates was quick to remind me that Mullen's outspokenness had aggravated President Bush as well, and he was right to point out that senior officials in the White House were often just as guilty of trying to work the press behind the scenes.

But I also think that the episode illustrated just how accustomed the military had become to getting whatever it wanted during the Bush years, and the degree to which basic policy decisions—about war and peace, but also about America's budget priorities, diplomatic goals, and the possible trade-offs between security and other values—had been steadily farmed out to the Pentagon and the CIA. It was easy to see the factors behind this: the impulse after 9/11 to do whatever it took to stop the terrorists and the reluctance of the White House to ask any tough questions that might get in the way; a military forced to clean up the mess that resulted from the decision to invade Iraq; a public that rightly saw the military as more competent and trustworthy than the civilians who were supposed to make policy; a Congress that was chiefly interested in avoiding responsibility for hard foreign policy problems; and a press corps that could be overly deferential to anyone with stars on their shoulders.

Men like Mullen, Petraeus, McChrystal, and Gates— all of them proven leaders with a singular focus on the hugely difficult tasks before them—had simply filled a vacuum. America had been lucky to have those men in the positions they were in, and when it came to the later phases of the Iraq War, they'd mostly made the right calls. But as I'd told Petraeus that first time we met in Iraq, right before I was elected, it was the job of the president to think broadly, not narrowly, and to weigh the costs and benefits of military action against everything else that went into making the country strong.

As much as any specific differences over strategy or tactics, such fundamental issues—the civilian control of policy making, the respective roles of the president and his military advisors in our constitutional system, and the considerations each brought to bear in deciding about war—became the subtext of the Afghan debate. And it was on these issues that the differences between me and Gates became more obvious. As one of Washington's savviest operators, Gates understood as well as anybody congressional pressure, public opinion, and budgetary constraints. But for him, these were obstacles to navigate around, not legitimate factors that should inform our decisions. Throughout the Afghan debate, he was quick to ascribe any objections Rahm or Biden might raise—about the difficulty in rounding up the votes in Congress for the $30 to $40 billion a year in additional spending that McChrystal's plan might require, or the weariness that the nation might feel after close to a decade of war—as mere "politics."

To other people, though never directly to me, Gates would sometimes question my commitment to the war and the strategy I'd adopted back in March, no doubt attributing it to "politics" as well. It was hard for him to see that what he dismissed as politics was democracy as it was supposed to work—that our mission had to be defined not only by the need to defeat an enemy but by the need to make sure the country wasn't bled dry in the process; that questions about spending hundreds of billions on missiles and forward operating bases rather than schools or healthcare for kids weren't tangential to national security but central to it; that the sense of duty he felt so keenly toward the troops already deployed, his genuine, admirable desire that they be given every chance to succeed, might be matched by the passion and patriotism of those interested in limiting the number of young Americans placed in harm's way.

MAYBE IT WASN'T Gates's job to think about those things, but it was mine. And so, from mid-September till mid-November, I presided over a series of nine two-to-three-hour meetings in the Sit Room to evaluate McChrystal's plan. The sheer length of the deliberations became a story in Washington, and though my talk with Gates and Mullen had put a stop to on-the-record editorializing from the top generals, leaks, anonymous quotes, and speculation continued to appear regularly in the press. I did my best to block out the noise, aided by the knowledge that many of my loudest critics were the same commentators and so-called experts who had actively promoted or been swept up in the rush to invade Iraq.

Indeed, one of the chief arguments for adopting McChrystal's plan was its similarities to the COIN strategy Petraeus had used during the U.S. surge in Iraq. As a general matter, Petraeus's emphasis on training local forces, improving local governance, and protecting local populations—rather than seizing territory and piling up insurgent body counts—made sense. But Afghanistan in 2009 wasn't Iraq in 2006. The two countries represented different circumstances demanding different solutions. With each Sit Room session, it became clearer that the expansive view of COIN that McChrystal imagined for Afghanistan not only went beyond what was needed to destroy al-Qaeda—it went beyond what was likely achievable within my term of office, if it was achievable at all.

John Brennan reemphasized that unlike al-Qaeda in Iraq, the Taliban was too deeply woven into the fabric of Afghan society to be eradicated—and that despite their sympathies toward al-Qaeda, they showed no signs of plotting attacks outside Afghanistan against the United States or its allies. Our ambassador in Kabul, former general Karl Eikenberry, doubted that the Karzai government could be reformed and feared that a large troop infusion and further "Americanization" of the war would take all pressure off Karzai to get his act together. McChrystal's lengthy timetable for both installing troops and pulling them out looked less like an Iraq-style surge than a long-term occupation, leading Biden to ask why—with al-Qaeda in Pakistan and almost entirely targeted with drone strikes—we should commit one hundred thousand troops to rebuilding the country next door.

In front of me, at least, McChrystal and the other generals dutifully responded to each of these concerns—in some cases persuasively, in others not so much. Despite their patience and good manners, they had trouble hiding their frustration at having their professional judgments challenged, especially by those who'd never put on a uniform. (McChrystal's eyes narrowed when, on more than one occasion, Biden started explaining to him what was necessary to carry out successful counterterrorism operations.) Tensions between White House staffers and the Pentagon got worse, with NSC staff feeling stonewalled when it came to getting information in a timely fashion and Gates quietly fuming over what he considered to be the NSC's constant micromanagement. The bad blood even spilled over into relationships **within** departments. Joint Chiefs vice chairman James "Hoss" Cartwright and Lieutenant General Douglas Lute—an NSC deputy and "war czar" during the final two years of the Bush administration whom I'd asked to stay on— would both see their stock drop inside the Pentagon the minute they agreed to help Biden flesh out a less troop-intensive, more CT-oriented alternative to McChrystal's plan. Hillary, meanwhile, considered Eikenberry's end runs around official State Department channels as verging on insubordination and wanted him replaced.

It's fair to say, then, that by the third or fourth go-round of PowerPoint slides, battlefield maps, and balky video feeds, along with the ever-present fluorescent lighting, bad coffee, and stale air, everyone was sick of Afghanistan, sick of meetings, and sick of one another. As for me—well, I felt the weight of the office more than at any other time since I'd been sworn in. I tried not to let it show, keeping my expressions neutral as I asked questions, took notes, and occasionally doodled on the margins of the pad the staff had set out before me (abstract patterns, mostly, sometimes people's faces or beach scenes— a seagull flying over a palm tree and ocean waves). But every so often my frustrations would flare, especially whenever I heard anyone respond to a tough question by falling back on the argument that we needed to send more troops in order to show "resolve."

What does that mean exactly? I'd ask, sometimes too sharply. That we keep doubling down on bad decisions we've already made? Does anyone think that spinning our wheels in Afghanistan for another ten years will impress our allies and strike fear in our enemies? It reminded me, I'd later tell Denis, of the nursery rhyme about an old lady who swallowed a spider to catch a fly.

"She ends up swallowing a horse," I said.

"And she's dead, of course," Denis said.

Sometimes, after one of these marathon sessions, I'd wander back to the small pool house near the Oval to have a cigarette and soak in the silence, feeling the knots in my back, shoulders, neck—signs of sitting too much, but also of my state of mind. If only the decision on Afghanistan **was** a matter of resolve, I thought—just will and steel and fire. That had been true for Lincoln as he tried to save the Union, and for FDR after Pearl Harbor, with America and the world facing a mortal threat from expansionist powers. In such circumstances, you harnessed all you had to mount a total war. But in the here and now, the threats we faced—deadly but stateless terrorist networks; otherwise feeble rogue nations out to get weapons of mass destruction—were real but not existential, and so resolve without foresight was worse than useless. It led us to fight the wrong wars and career down rabbit holes. It made us administrators of inhospitable terrain and bred more enemies than we killed. Because of our unmatched power, America had choices about what and when and how to fight. To claim otherwise, to insist that our safety and our standing in the world required us to do all that we could for as long as we could in every single instance, was an abdication of moral responsibility, the certainty it offered a comforting lie.

AROUND SIX in the morning on October 9, 2009, the White House operator jolted me from sleep to say that Robert Gibbs was on the line. Calls that early from my staff were rare, and my heart froze. Was it a terrorist attack? A natural disaster?

"You were awarded the Nobel Peace Prize," Gibbs said.

"What do you mean?"

"They just announced it a few minutes ago."

"For what?"

Gibbs tactfully ignored the question. Favs would be waiting outside the Oval to work with me on whatever statement I wanted to make, he said. After I hung up, Michelle asked what the call was about.

"I'm getting the Nobel Peace Prize."

"That's wonderful, honey," she said, then rolled over to get a little more shut-eye.

An hour and a half later, Malia and Sasha stopped by the dining room as I was having breakfast. "Great news, Daddy," Malia said, hitching her backpack over her shoulders. "You won the Nobel Prize . . . and it's Bo's birthday!"

"Plus, it's gonna be a three-day weekend!" Sasha added, doing a little fist pump. They both kissed me on the cheek before heading out the door for school.

In the Rose Garden, I told the assembled press corps that less than a year into my presidency, I didn't feel that I deserved to be in the company of those transformative figures who'd been honored in the past. Instead, I saw the prize as a call to action, a means for the Nobel committee to give momentum to causes for which American leadership was vital: reducing the threats of nuclear weapons and climate change; shrinking economic inequality; upholding human rights; and bridging the racial, ethnic, and religious divides that so often fed conflict. I said I thought the award should be shared with others around the world who labored, often without recognition, for justice, peace, and human dignity.

Walking back into the Oval, I asked Katie to hold the congratulatory calls that were starting to come in and took a few minutes to consider the widening gap between the expectations and the realities of my presidency. Six days earlier, three hundred Afghan militants had overrun a small U.S. military outpost in the Hindu Kush, killing eight of our soldiers and wounding twenty-seven more. October would become the deadliest month for U.S. troops in Afghanistan since the start of the war eight years earlier. And rather than ushering in a new era of peace, I was facing the prospect of committing more soldiers to war.

LATE THAT MONTH, Attorney General Eric Holder and I took a midnight flight to Dover Air Force Base, in Delaware, to witness the return to U.S. soil of the remains of fifteen U.S. soldiers and three drug enforcement agents who'd been killed in back-to-back incidents in Afghanistan—a deadly helicopter crash and two roadside bombings in Kandahar Province. A president's attendance at these "dignified transfers," as they were called, was rare, but I thought it important, now more than ever, to be present. Since the Gulf War, the Defense Department had barred media coverage of the homecomings of service members' caskets, but with the help of Bob Gates, I'd reversed this policy earlier in the year—leaving the decision to individual families. Having at least some of these transfers publicly documented, I felt, gave our country a clearer means to reckon with the costs of war, the pain of each loss. And on this night, at the end of a devastating month in Afghanistan, with the future of the war under debate, one of the families had elected to have the moment recorded.

There was a constant hush throughout the four or five hours I was on the base. In the small, plain chapel, where Holder and I joined the families who had gathered. Inside the cargo bay of the C-17 aircraft that held the eighteen flag-draped transfer cases, where an army chaplain's solemn prayer echoed against the metallic walls. On the tarmac, where we stood at attention and watched six pallbearers dressed in army fatigues, white gloves, and black berets carry the heavy cases one by one to the rows of waiting vehicles, the world silent except for the howl of wind and the cadence of steps.

On the flight back, with sunrise still a few hours away, the only words I could remember from the entire visit were those of one soldier's mother: "Don't leave those boys who are still over there hanging." She looked exhausted, her face hollowed by grief. I promised I wouldn't, not knowing whether that meant sending more soldiers to finish the mission for which her son had made the ultimate sacrifice, or winding down a muddled and lengthy conflict that would cut short the lives of other people's children. It was left for me to decide.

A week later, another disaster struck our military, this time closer to home. On November 5, a U.S. Army major and psychiatrist named Nidal Hasan walked into a building at the Fort Hood army base in Killeen, Texas, pulled out a semiautomatic pistol he'd purchased at a local gun store, and opened fire, killing thirteen people and wounding scores of others before being shot and apprehended by base police officers. Once again, I flew to comfort grieving families, then spoke at an outdoor memorial service. As a trumpet played taps, its plaintive melody punctuated by muffled sobs in the audience, my eyes traveled the memorials to the fallen soldiers: a framed photograph, a pair of empty combat boots, a helmet set atop a rifle.

I thought about what John Brennan and FBI director Robert Mueller had told me in briefings on the shooting: Hasan, a U.S.-born Muslim with a troubling record of erratic behavior, appeared to have been radicalized over the internet. In particular, he'd been inspired by—and repeatedly sent emails to—a charismatic Yemeni American cleric named Anwar al-Awlaki, who had a broad international following and was believed to be the leading figure in al-Qaeda's increasingly active branch in Yemen. According to Mueller and Brennan, there were early indications that the Defense Department, the FBI, and the Joint Terrorism Task Force had all been alerted in one way or another to Hasan's possible drift toward radicalism, but that interagency information-sharing systems had failed to connect the dots in a way that might have headed off the tragedy.

The eulogies ended. Taps began again. Across Fort Hood, I imagined soldiers busily preparing for deployments to Afghanistan and the fight against the Taliban. And I couldn't help but wonder whether the greater threat might now actually lie elsewhere—not just in Yemen or Somalia but also in the specter of homegrown terrorism; in the febrile minds of men like Hasan and a borderless cyberworld, the power and reach of which we didn't yet fully comprehend.

. . .

IN LATE NOVEMBER 2009, we held our ninth and final Afghan review session. For all the drama, the substantive differences between members of my team had by this point shrunk considerably. The generals conceded that eradicating the Taliban from Afghanistan was unrealistic. Joe and my NSC staff acknowledged that CT operations against al-Qaeda couldn't work if the Taliban overran the country or inhibited our intelligence collection. We landed on a set of achievable objectives: reducing the level of Taliban activity so they didn't threaten major population centers; pushing Karzai to reform a handful of key departments, like the Ministries of Defense and Finance, rather than trying to get him to revamp the entire government; accelerating the training of local forces that would eventually allow the Afghan people to secure their own country.

The team also agreed that meeting even these more modest objectives was going to require additional U.S. troops.

The only remaining dispute was how many and for how long. The generals continued to hold out for McChrystal's original request of forty thousand, without providing a good explanation for why the more limited set of objectives we'd agreed to didn't reduce by a single soldier the number of troops needed. The "CT Plus" option that Biden had worked up with Hoss Cartwright and Douglas Lute called for another twenty thousand troops to be devoted solely to CT operations and training—but it wasn't clear why either of those functions needed anything close to that many extra U.S. personnel. In both cases, I worried that the numbers were

still being driven by ideological and institutional concerns rather than by the objectives we'd set.

Ultimately it was Gates who came up with a workable
resolution. In a private memo to me, he explained that
McChrystal's request anticipated the United States replacing the ten thousand Dutch and Canadian troops their
governments had pledged to bring home. If I authorized
three brigades, for a total of thirty thousand U.S. troops,
it might be possible to use that commitment to leverage
the other ten thousand from our allies. Gates also
agreed that we treat any infusion of new troops more as a
surge than an open-ended commitment, both by accelerating the pace of their arrival and by setting a timetable of
eighteen months for them to start coming home.

For me, Gates's acceptance of a timetable was particularly significant. In the past, he'd joined the Joint Chiefs
and Petraeus in resisting the idea, claiming that timetables
signaled to the enemy that they could wait us out. He
was now persuaded that Karzai might never make hard
decisions about his own government's responsibilities
absent the knowledge that we'd be bringing troops home
sooner rather than later.

After talking it over with Joe, Rahm, and the NSC
staff, I decided to adopt Gates's proposal. There was a
logic to it that went beyond simply splitting the difference between McChrystal's plan and the option Biden
had worked up. In the short term, it gave McChrystal
the firepower he needed to reverse the Taliban's momentum, protect population centers, and train up Afghan
forces. But it set clear limits to COIN and put us firmly
on the path of a narrower CT approach two years
out. Haggling remained over how firm to make the

thirty-thousand-troop cap (the Pentagon had a habit of deploying the approved number and then coming back with requests for thousands of "enablers"—medics, intelligence officers, and the like—which, it insisted, shouldn't count toward the total), and it took some time for Gates to sell the approach in his building. But a few days after Thanksgiving, I called an evening meeting in the Oval with Gates, Mullen, and Petraeus, as well as Rahm, Jim Jones, and Joe, where, in essence, I had everyone sign on the dotted line. NSC staffers had prepared a detailed memo outlining my order, and along with Rahm and Joe they'd persuaded me that having the Pentagon brass look me in the eye and commit to an agreement laid out on paper was the only way to avoid their publicly second-guessing my decision if the war went south.

It was an unusual and somewhat heavy-handed gesture, one that no doubt grated on Gates and the generals and that I regretted almost immediately. A fitting end, I thought, to a messy, difficult stretch for my administration. I could take some satisfaction, though, in the fact that the review had served its purpose. Gates acknowledged that without producing a perfect plan, the hours of debate had made for a better plan. It forced us to refine America's strategic objectives in Afghanistan in a way that prevented mission creep. It established the utility of timetables for troop deployments in certain circumstances, something that had been long contested by the Washington national security establishment. Beyond putting an end to Pentagon freelancing for the duration of my presidency, it helped reaffirm the larger principle of civilian control over America's national security policy making.

Still, the bottom line was that I'd be sending more young people to war.

We announced the planned troop deployment on December 1 at West Point, the oldest and most storied of America's service academies. A Continental Army post during the Revolutionary War, a little over an hour north of New York City, it's a beautiful place—a series of black-and-gray granite structures arranged like a small city high among green rolling hills, with a view over the broad and winding Hudson River. Before my speech, I visited with the West Point superintendent and glimpsed some of the buildings and grounds that had produced a who's who of America's most decorated military leaders: Grant and Lee, Patton and Eisenhower, MacArthur and Bradley, Westmoreland and Schwarzkopf.

It was impossible not to be humbled and moved by the tradition those men represented, the service and sacrifice that had helped forge a nation, defeat fascism, and halt the march of totalitarianism. Just as it was necessary to recall that Lee had led a Confederate Army intent on preserving slavery and Grant had overseen the slaughter of Indian tribes; that MacArthur had defied Truman's orders in Korea to disastrous effect and Westmoreland had helped orchestrate an escalation in Vietnam that would scar a generation. Glory and tragedy, courage and stupidity—one set of truths didn't negate the other. For war was contradiction, as was the history of America.

The large auditorium near the center of West Point's campus was full by the time I arrived, and aside from VIPs like Gates, Hillary, and the Joint Chiefs, the audience was made up almost entirely of cadets. They were in uniform: gray tunics with black trim over white collars.

The sizable number of Blacks, Latinos, Asian Americans, and women in their ranks offered vivid testimony to the changes that had taken place since the school graduated its first class in 1805. As I entered the stage to a band playing the ceremonial ruffles and flourishes, the cadets stood in unison and applauded; and looking out at their faces—so earnest and full of the glow of youth, so certain of their destiny and eager to defend their country—I felt my heart swell with an almost paternal pride. I just prayed that I and the others who commanded them were worthy of their trust.

NINE DAYS LATER, I flew to Oslo to receive the Nobel Peace Prize. The image of those young cadets weighed on me. Rather than ignore the tension between getting a peace prize and expanding a war, I decided to make it the centerpiece of my acceptance address. With the help of Ben Rhodes and Samantha Power, I wrote a first draft, drawing on the writings of thinkers like Reinhold Niebuhr and Gandhi to organize my argument: that war is both terrible and sometimes necessary; that reconciling these seemingly contradictory ideas requires the community of nations to evolve higher standards for both the justification and the conduct of war; and that avoidance of war requires a just peace, founded on a common commitment to political freedom, a respect for human rights, and concrete strategies to expand economic opportunity around the world. I finished writing the speech in the dead of night aboard Air Force One as Michelle slept in our cabin, my weary eyes drawn away from the page every so often by the sight of a spectral moon over the Atlantic.

Like everything in Norway, the Nobel ceremony—held in a brightly lit auditorium seating a few hundred people—was sensibly austere: There was a lovely performance by the young jazz artist Esperanza Spalding, an introduction by the head of the Nobel committee, and then my address, all finished in around ninety minutes. The speech itself was well received, even by some conservative commentators who remarked on my willingness to remind European audiences of the sacrifices made by U.S. troops in underwriting decades of peace. That evening, the Nobel committee hosted a black-tie dinner in my honor, where I was seated next to the king of Norway, a gracious, elderly man who told me about sailing through his country's fjords. My sister Maya, along with friends like Marty and Anita, had flown in to join us, and everyone looked very sophisticated as they sipped champagne and chewed on grilled elk and later danced to a surprisingly good swing orchestra.

What I remember most, though, was a scene that took place before dinner, at the hotel. Michelle and I had just finished getting dressed when Marvin knocked on the door and told us to look out our fourth-story window. Pulling back the shades, we saw that several thousand people had gathered in the early dusk, filling the narrow street below. Each person held aloft a single lit candle—the city's traditional way to express its appreciation for that year's peace prize winner. It was a magical sight, as if a pool of stars had descended from the sky; and as Michelle and I leaned out to wave, the night air brisk on our cheeks, the crowd cheering wildly, I couldn't help but think about the daily fighting that continued to consume Iraq and Afghanistan and all the cruelty and suffering and injustice that my administration had barely even begun to deal with. The idea that I, or any one person, could bring order to such chaos seemed laughable; on some level, the crowds below were cheering an illusion. And yet, in the flickering of those candles, I saw something else. I saw an expression of the spirit of millions of people around the world: the U.S. soldier manning a post in Kandahar, the mother in Iran teaching her daughter to read, the Russian pro-democracy activist mustering his courage for an upcoming demonstration—all those who refused to give up on the idea that life could be better, and that whatever the risks and hardships, they had a role to play.

Whatever you do won't be enough, I heard their voices say.

Try anyway.

CHAPTER 19

RUNNING FOR THE PRESIDENCY, I'd promised Americans a different kind of foreign policy than the sort we'd been practicing since 9/11. Iraq and Afghanistan offered stark lessons in how quickly a president's options narrowed once a war had begun. I was determined to shift a certain mindset that had gripped not just the Bush administration but much of Washington—one that saw threats around every corner, took a perverse pride in acting unilaterally, and considered military action as an almost routine means of addressing foreign policy challenges. In our interactions with other nations, we had become obdurate and short-sighted, resistant to the hard, slow work of building coalitions and consensus. We'd closed ourselves off from other points of view. I believed that America's security depended on strengthening our alliances and international institutions. I saw military action as a tool of last, not first, resort.

We had to manage the wars we were in. But I also wanted to put this broader faith in diplomacy to the test.

It began with a change in tone. From the start of my administration, we made sure that every foreign policy statement coming out of the White House emphasized the importance of international cooperation and America's intention to engage other nations, big and small, on the basis of mutual interest and respect. We looked for small but symbolic ways to shift policy—like boosting the international affairs budget at the State Department or bringing the United States out of arrears on its U.N. dues after several years in which the Bush administration and the Republican-controlled Congress had withheld certain payments.

Consistent with the adage that 80 percent of success is a matter of showing up, we also made a point of visiting parts of the world that had been neglected by the Bush administration, with its all-consuming focus on terrorism and the Middle East. Hillary, in particular, was a whirlwind that first year, hopping from continent to continent as doggedly as she'd once campaigned for the presidency. Seeing the excitement her visits generated in foreign capitals, I felt vindicated in my decision to appoint her as America's top diplomat. It wasn't just that she was treated as a peer by world leaders. Wherever she went, the public saw her presence in their country as a sign that they really mattered to us.

"If we want other countries to support our priorities," I told my NSC team, "we can't just bully them into it. We've got to show them we're taking their perspectives into account—or at least can find them on a map."

To be known. To be heard. To have one's unique identity recognized and seen as worthy. It was a universal human desire, I thought, as true for nations and peoples as it was for individuals. If I understood that basic truth more than some of my predecessors, perhaps it was because I'd spent a big chunk of my childhood abroad and had family in places long considered "backward" and "under-developed." Or maybe it was because as an African American, I'd experienced what it was like not to be fully seen inside my own country.

Whatever the reason, I made a point of showing an interest in the history, culture, and people of the places we visited. Ben joked that my overseas speeches could be reduced to a simple algorithm: "[Greeting in foreign language—often badly pronounced.] It's wonderful to be in this beautiful country that's made lasting contri-butions to world civilization. [List of stuff.] There's a long history of friendship between our two nations. [Inspiring anecdote.] And it's in part due to the contri-butions of the millions of proud [hyphenated Americans] whose ancestors immigrated to our shores that the United States is the nation it is today." It might have been corny, but the smiles and nods of foreign audiences showed the extent to which simple acts of acknowledg-ment mattered.

For the same reason, we tried to include some high-profile sightseeing on all my foreign trips, something to get me out of hotels and beyond the palace gates. My interest in touring Istanbul's Blue Mosque or visiting a local eatery in Ho Chi Minh City, I knew, would make a far more lasting impression on the average Turkish or Vietnamese citizen than any bilateral meeting or press conference talking point. Just as important, these stops gave me a chance to interact at least a little with ordinary people rather than just government officials and wealthy elites, who in many countries were viewed as out of touch.

But our most effective public diplomacy tool came

straight out of my campaign playbook: During my international trips, I made a point of hosting town hall meetings with young people. The first time we tried it, with a crowd of more than three thousand European students during the NATO summit in Strasbourg, we weren't sure what to expect. Would I get heckled? Would I bore them with long, convoluted answers? But after an unscripted hour in which members of the audience enthusiastically questioned me on everything from climate change to fighting terrorism and offered their own good-humored observations (including the fact that "Barack" means "peach" in Hungarian), we decided to make it a regular feature of my foreign travel.

The town halls usually were broadcast live on the country's national stations, and whether they emanated from Buenos Aires, Mumbai, or Johannesburg, they attracted a large viewership. For folks in many parts of the world, the sight of a head of state making him- or herself accessible for direct questioning from citizens was a novelty—and a more meaningful argument for democracy than any lecture I might give. In consultation with our local embassies, we often invited young activists from the host country's marginalized groups—religious or ethnic minorities, refugees, LGBTQ students—to participate. By handing them a microphone and letting them tell their own stories, I could expose a nation of viewers to the justness of their claims.

The young people I met in those town halls were a steady source of personal inspiration. They made me laugh and sometimes made me tear up. In their idealism, they reminded me of the youthful organizers and volunteers who had propelled me into the presidency, and of the bonds we share across racial, ethnic, and national boundaries when we learn to set aside our fear. No matter how frustrated or discouraged I might have felt going in, I always came out of those town halls feeling recharged, as if I'd been dipped in a cool forest spring. So long as young men and women like that exist in every corner of this earth, I told myself, there is reason enough to hope.

AROUND THE WORLD, public attitudes toward the United States had steadily improved since I'd taken office, demonstrating that our early diplomatic work was paying off. This heightened popularity made it easier for our allies to sustain or even boost their troop contributions in Afghanistan, knowing that their citizens trusted our leadership. It gave me and Tim Geithner more leverage when coordinating the international response to the financial crisis. After North Korea started testing ballistic missiles, Susan Rice was able to get the Security Council to pass robust international sanctions, in part because of her skill and tenacity but also, she told me, because "a lot of countries want to be seen as being aligned with you."

Still, there were limits to what a diplomatic charm offensive could accomplish. At the end of the day, each nation's foreign policy remained driven by its own economic interests, geography, ethnic and religious schisms, territorial disputes, founding myths, lasting traumas, ancient animosities—and, most of all, the imperatives of those who had and sought to maintain power. It was the rare foreign leader who was susceptible to moral suasion alone. Those who sat atop repressive governments could for the most part safely ignore public opinion. To make progress on the thorniest foreign policy issues, I needed a second kind of diplomacy, one of concrete rewards and punishments designed to alter the calculations of hard, ruthless leaders. And, throughout my first year, interactions with the leaders of three countries in particular—Iran, Russia, and China—gave me an early indication of how difficult that would be.

Of the three, Iran posed the least serious challenge to America's long-term interests but won the prize for "Most Actively Hostile." Heir to the great Persian empires of antiquity, once an epicenter of science and art during Islam's medieval golden age, Iran had for many years barely registered in the minds of U.S. policy makers. With Turkey and Iraq on its western border and Afghanistan and Pakistan to the east, it was generally viewed as just another poor Middle Eastern country, its territory shrunk by civil conflict and ascendant European powers. In 1951, though, Iran's secular, left-leaning parliament moved to nationalize the country's oil fields, seizing control of profits that had once gone to the British government, which owned a majority stake in Iran's biggest oil production and export company. Unhappy to be boxed out, the Brits imposed a naval blockade to prevent Iran from shipping oil to would-be buyers. They also convinced the Eisenhower administration that the new Iranian government was tilting toward the Soviets, leading Eisenhower to greenlight Operation Ajax, a CIA-MI6-engineered coup that deposed Iran's democratically elected prime minister and consolidated power in the hands of the country's young monarch, Shah Mohammad Reza Pahlavi.

Operation Ajax set a pattern for U.S. miscalculation in dealing with developing countries that lasted throughout the Cold War: mistaking nationalist aspirations for

Communist plots; equating commercial interests with national security; subverting democratically elected governments and aligning ourselves with autocrats when we determined it was to our benefit. Still, for the first twenty-seven years, U.S. policy makers must have figured their gambit in Iran had worked out just fine. The shah became a stalwart ally who extended contracts to U.S. oil companies and bought plenty of expensive U.S. weaponry. He maintained friendly relations with Israel, gave women the right to vote, used the country's growing wealth to modernize the economy and the education system, and mingled easily with Western businesspeople and European royalty.

Less obvious to outsiders was a simmering discontent with the shah's extravagant spending, ruthless repression (his secret police were notorious for torturing and killing dissidents), and promotion of Western social mores that, in the eyes of conservative clerics and their many followers, violated the core tenets of Islam. Nor did CIA analysts pay much attention to the growing influence of an exiled messianic Shiite cleric, Ayatollah Khomeini, whose writings and speeches denounced the shah as a Western puppet and called on the faithful to replace the existing order with an Islamic state governed by sharia law. So U.S. officials were caught by surprise when a series of demonstrations inside Iran at the start of 1978 blossomed into a full-blown populist revolution. In successive waves, followers of Khomeini's were joined in the streets by disaffected workers, unemployed youths, and pro-democracy forces seeking a return to constitutional rule. By the beginning of 1979, with the number of demonstrators swelling into the millions, the shah quietly fled the country and was briefly admitted into the United States for medical treatment. America's nightly newscasts were filled with images of the ayatollah—white-bearded, with the smoldering eyes of a prophet—stepping off a plane in triumphant return from exile before a sea of adoring supporters.

Most Americans knew little about this history as the revolution unfolded—or why people in a faraway country were suddenly burning Uncle Sam in effigy and chanting "Death to America." I sure didn't. I was seventeen at the time, still in high school and just on the cusp of political awareness. I only vaguely understood the details of all that happened next: how Khomeini installed himself as supreme leader and sidelined former secular and reformist allies; how he formed the paramilitary Islamic Revolutionary Guard Corps (IRGC) to crush anybody who challenged the new regime; and how he used the drama that unfolded when radicalized students stormed the U.S. embassy and took American hostages to help solidify the revolution and humiliate the world's most powerful nation.

But it's hard to overstate just how much, thirty years later, the fallout from these events still shaped the geopolitical landscape of my presidency. Iran's revolution inspired a slew of other radical Islamic movements intent on duplicating its success. Khomeini's call to overthrow Sunni Arab monarchies turned Iran and the House of Saud into bitter enemies and sharpened sectarian conflict across the Middle East. Iraq's attempted 1980 invasion of Iran and the bloody eight-year war that followed— a war in which the Gulf states provided Saddam Hussein with financing while the Soviets supplied Khomeini's

military with arms, including chemical weapons—
accelerated Iran's sponsorship of terrorism as a way to
offset its enemies' military advantages. (The United
States, under Reagan, cynically tried to have it both ways,
publicly backing Iraq while secretly selling arms to Iran.)
Khomeini's vow to wipe Israel off the map—manifest in
the IRGC's support for armed proxies like the Lebanon-
based Shiite militia Hezbollah and the military wing of
the Palestinian resistance group Hamas—made the
Iranian regime Israel's single greatest security threat and
contributed to the general hardening of Israeli attitudes
toward possible peace with its neighbors. More broadly,
Khomeini's rendering of the world as a Manichaean
clash between the forces of Allah and those of "the Great
Satan" (America) seeped like a toxin into the minds not
just of future jihadists but of those in the West already
inclined to view Muslims as objects of suspicion and fear.

Khomeini died in 1989. His successor, Ayatollah Ali
Khamenei, a cleric who'd barely traveled outside his own
country and never would again, apparently matched
Khomeini in his hatred of America. Despite his title as
supreme leader, Khamenei's authority wasn't absolute—
he had to confer with a powerful council of clerics, while
day-to-day responsibility for the running of the government fell to a popularly elected president. There'd been a
period toward the end of the Clinton administration
and the start of the Bush administration when more
moderate forces inside Iran had gained a little traction,
offering the prospect of a thaw in U.S.-Iranian relations.
After 9/11, Iran's then president, Mohammad Khatami,
had even reached out to the Bush administration with
offers to help with America's response in neighboring

Afghanistan. But U.S. officials had ignored the gesture, and once President Bush named Iran, along with Iraq and North Korea, as part of an "axis of evil" in his 2002 State of the Union speech, whatever diplomatic window existed effectively slammed shut.

BY THE TIME I took office, conservative hard-liners were firmly back in charge in Tehran, led by a new president, Mahmoud Ahmadinejad, whose manic anti-Western outbursts, Holocaust denial, and persecution of gays and others he considered a threat made him a perfect distillation of the regime's most hateful aspects. Iranian weapons were still being sent to militants intent on killing American soldiers in Iraq and Afghanistan. The U.S. invasion of Iraq had greatly strengthened Iran's strategic position in the region by replacing its sworn enemy, Saddam Hussein, with a Shiite-led government subject to Iranian influence. Hezbollah, Iran's proxy, had emerged as the most powerful faction in Lebanon, with Iranian-supplied missiles that could now reach Tel Aviv. The Saudis and Israelis spoke in alarming tones of an expanding "Shiite Crescent" of Iranian influence and made no secret of their interest in the possibility of a U.S.-initiated regime change.

Under any circumstances, then, Iran would have been a grade A headache for my administration. But it was the country's accelerating nuclear program that threatened to turn a bad situation into a full-blown crisis.

The regime had inherited nuclear facilities built during the time of the shah, and under the U.N.'s Nuclear Non-Proliferation Treaty—to which Iran had been a signatory since its ratification in 1970—it had the right to use nuclear energy for peaceful means. Unfortunately the same centrifuge technology used to spin and enrich the low-enriched uranium (LEU) that fueled nuclear power plants could be modified to produce weapons-grade, highly enriched uranium (HEU). As one of our experts put it, "With enough HEU, a smart high school physics student with access to the internet can produce a bomb." Between 2003 and 2009, Iran boosted its total number of uranium-enriching centrifuges from a hundred to as many as five thousand, far more than any peaceful program could justify. The U.S. intelligence community was reasonably confident that Iran didn't have a nuclear weapon yet. But it was also convinced that the regime had narrowed its "breakout capacity"—the window of time needed to produce enough uranium to build a viable nuclear weapon—to a potentially dangerous point.

An Iranian nuclear arsenal wouldn't need to threaten the U.S. homeland; just the possibility of a nuclear strike or nuclear terrorism in the Middle East would severely limit a future U.S. president's options to check Iranian aggression toward its neighbors. The Saudis would likely react by pursuing their own rival "Sunni bomb," triggering a nuclear arms race in the world's most volatile region. Meanwhile, Israel—reportedly holding a trove of undeclared nuclear weapons itself—viewed a nuclear-armed Iran as an existential threat and was allegedly drawing up plans for a preemptive strike against Iran's facilities. Any action, reaction, or miscalculation by any of these parties could plunge the Middle East—and the United States—into yet another conflict at a time when we still had 180,000 highly exposed troops along Iran's borders, and when any big spike in oil prices could send the world economy deeper into a tailspin. At times during my administration we gamed out the scenarios for what a conflict with Iran would look like; I left those conversations weighed down by the knowledge that if war became necessary, nearly everything else I was trying to achieve would likely be upended.

For all these reasons, my team and I had spent much of the transition discussing how to prevent Iran from getting a nuclear weapon—ideally through diplomacy rather than by starting another war. We settled on a two-step strategy. Because there had been almost no high-level contact between the United States and Iran since 1980, step one involved direct outreach. As I'd said in my inaugural address, we were ready to extend a hand to those willing to unclench their fists. Within weeks of taking office, I'd sent a secret letter to Ayatollah Khamenei through a channel we had with Iranian diplomats at the United Nations, suggesting that we open a dialogue between our two countries on a range of issues, including Iran's nuclear program. Khamenei's answer was blunt: Iran had no interest in direct talks. He did, however, take the opportunity to suggest ways the United States could stop being an imperialist bully.

"Guess he's not unclenching his fist anytime soon," Rahm said after reading a copy of Khamenei's letter, which had been translated from Farsi.

"Only enough to give me the middle finger," I said.

The truth was, none of us in the White House had expected a positive response. I'd sent the letter anyway because I wanted to establish that the impediment to diplomacy was not America's intransigence—it was Iran's.

I reinforced a message of openness to the broader Iranian public through a traditional Persian New Year's (Nowruz) greeting that we put online in March.

As it was, any prospects of an early breakthrough were extinguished in June 2009, when Iranian opposition candidate Mir-Hossein Mousavi credibly accused government officials of vote rigging to help reelect Ahmadinejad to a second term as president. Millions of protesters inside Iran took to the streets to challenge the election results, launching a self-described "Green Movement" that posed one of the most significant internal challenges to the Islamic state since the 1979 Revolution.

The ensuing crackdown was merciless and swift. Mousavi and other opposition leaders were placed under house arrest. Peaceful marchers were beaten, and a significant number were killed. One night, from the comfort of my residence, I scanned the reports of the protests online and saw video of a young woman shot in the streets, a web of blood spreading across her face as she began to die, her eyes gazing upward in reproach.

It was a haunting reminder of the price so many people around the world paid for wanting some say in how they were governed, and my first impulse was to express strong support for the demonstrators. But when I gathered my national security team, our Iran experts advised against such a move. According to them, any statement from me would likely backfire. Already, regime hard-liners were pushing the fiction that foreign agents were behind the demonstrations, and activists inside Iran feared that any supportive statements from the U.S. government would be seized upon to discredit their movement. I felt obliged to heed these warnings, and

signed off on a series of bland, bureaucratic statements—
"We continue to monitor the entire situation closely";
"The universal rights to assembly and free speech must
be respected"—urging a peaceful resolution that reflected
the will of the Iranian people.

As the violence escalated, so did my condemnation.
Still, such a passive approach didn't sit well with me—
and not just because I had to listen to Republicans howl
that I was coddling a murderous regime. I was learning
yet another difficult lesson about the presidency: that my
heart was now chained to strategic considerations and
tactical analysis, my convictions subject to counterintui-
tive arguments; that in the most powerful office on earth,
I had less freedom to say what I meant and act on what I
felt than I'd had as a senator—or as an ordinary citizen
disgusted by the sight of a young woman gunned down
by her own government.

Having been rebuffed in our attempts to open a dialogue with Iran, and with the country spiraling into
chaos and further repression, we shifted to step two of
our nonproliferation strategy: mobilizing the international community to apply tough, multilateral economic
sanctions that might force Iran to the negotiating table.
The U.N. Security Council had already passed multiple
resolutions calling on Iran to halt its enrichment activities. It had also authorized limited sanctions against Iran
and formed a group called the P5+1—representing the
five permanent Security Council members (the United
States, the United Kingdom, France, Russia, and China)
plus Germany—to meet with Iranian officials in the
hope of pushing the regime back into Nuclear Non-
Proliferation Treaty compliance.

The problem was that the existing sanctions were too weak to have much of an impact. Even U.S. allies like Germany continued to do a healthy amount of business with Iran, and just about everyone bought its oil. The Bush administration had unilaterally imposed additional U.S. sanctions, but those were largely symbolic, since U.S. companies had been blocked from doing business with Iran since 1995. With oil prices high and its economy growing, Iran had been more than happy to string along the P5+1 with regular negotiating sessions that produced nothing other than a commitment to more talking.

To get Iran's attention, we'd have to persuade other countries to tighten the vise. And that meant getting buy-in from a pair of powerful, historic adversaries that didn't like sanctions as a matter of principle, had friendly diplomatic and commercial relations with Iran—and mistrusted U.S. intentions almost as much as Tehran did.

HAVING COME OF AGE in the 1960s and '70s, I was old enough to recall the Cold War as the defining reality of international affairs, the force that chopped Europe in two, fueled a nuclear arms race, and generated proxy wars around the globe. It shaped my childhood imagination: In schoolbooks, newspapers, spy novels, and movies, the Soviet Union was the fearsome adversary in a contest between freedom and tyranny.

I was also part of a post-Vietnam generation that had learned to question its own government and saw how—from the rise of McCarthyism to support for South Africa's apartheid regime—Cold War thinking had often led America to betray its ideals. This awareness didn't stop me from believing we should contain the spread of Marxist totalitarianism. But it made me wary of the notion that good resided only on our side and bad on theirs, or that a people who'd produced Tolstoy and Tchaikovsky were inherently different from us. Instead, the evils of the Soviet system struck me as a variation on a broader human tragedy: The way abstract theories and rigid orthodoxy can curdle into repression. How readily we justify moral compromise and relinquish our freedoms. How power can corrupt and fear can compound and language can be debased. None of that was unique to Soviets or Communists, I thought; it was true for all of us. The brave struggle of dissidents behind the Iron Curtain felt of a piece with, rather than distinct from, the larger struggle for human dignity taking place elsewhere in the world—including America.

When, in the mid-1980s, Mikhail Gorbachev took over as the general secretary of the Communist Party and ushered in the cautious liberalization known as perestroika and glasnost, I studied what happened closely, wondering if it signaled the dawning of a new age. And when, just a few years later, the Berlin Wall fell and democratic activists inside Russia lifted Boris Yeltsin to power, sweeping aside the old Communist order and dissolving the Soviet Union, I considered it not just a victory for the West but a testimony to the power of a mobilized citizenry and a warning for despots everywhere. If the tumult that engulfed Russia in the 1990s—economic collapse, unfettered corruption, right-wing populism, shadowy oligarchs—gave me pause, nevertheless I held out hope that a more just, prosperous, and free Russia would emerge from the inevitably difficult transition to free markets and representative government.

I'd mostly been cured of that optimism by the time I became president. It was true that Yeltsin's successor, Vladimir Putin, who had come to power in 1999, claimed no interest in a return to Marxism-Leninism ("a mistake," he once called it). And he had successfully stabilized the nation's economy, in large part thanks to a huge increase in revenues brought about by rising oil prices. Elections were now held in accordance with the Russian constitution, capitalists were everywhere, ordinary Russians could travel abroad, and pro-democracy activists like the chess master Garry Kasparov could get away with criticizing the government without an immediate trip to the Gulag.

And yet, with each year that Putin remained in power, the new Russia looked more like the old. It became clear that a market economy and periodic elections could go hand in hand with a "soft authoritarianism" that steadily concentrated power in Putin's hands and shrank the space for meaningful dissent. Oligarchs who cooperated with Putin became some of the world's wealthiest men. Those who broke from Putin found themselves subject to various criminal prosecutions and stripped of their assets—and Kasparov ultimately did spend a few days in jail for leading an anti-Putin march. Putin's cronies were handed control of the country's major media outlets, and the rest were pressured into ensuring him coverage every bit as friendly as the state-owned media had once provided Communist rulers. Independent journalists and civic leaders found themselves monitored by the FSB (the modern incarnation of the KGB)—or, in some cases, turned up dead.

What's more, Putin's power didn't rest on simple coercion. He was genuinely popular (his approval ratings at home rarely dipped below 60 percent). It was a popularity rooted in old-fashioned nationalism—the promise to restore Mother Russia to its former glory, to relieve the sense of disruption and humiliation so many Russians had felt over the previous two decades.

Putin could sell that vision because he'd experienced those disruptions himself. Born into a family without connections or privilege, he'd methodically climbed the Soviet ladder—reservist training with the Red Army, law studies at Leningrad State University, a career in the KGB. After years of loyal and effective service to the state, he'd secured a position of modest stature and respectability, only to see the system he'd devoted his life to capsize overnight when the Berlin Wall fell in 1989. (He was at that time stationed with the KGB in Dresden, East Germany, and he reportedly spent the next few days scrambling to destroy files and standing guard against possible looters.) He'd made a quick pivot to the emerging post-Soviet reality, allying himself to democratic reformer Anatoly Sobchak, a mentor from law school who became mayor of St. Petersburg. Moving into national politics, Putin rose through the ranks of the Yeltsin administration with breathtaking speed, using his power in a variety of posts—including director of the FSB—to pick up allies, dole out favors, gather secrets, and outmaneuver rivals. Yeltsin appointed Putin prime minister in August 1999 and then four months later—hobbled by corruption scandals, bad health, a legendary drinking problem, and a record of catastrophic economic mismanagement—surprised everyone by vacating his office. That made Putin, then forty-seven, the acting president of Russia and provided him with the head start he needed to get elected to a full presidential term three months later. (One of Putin's first acts was to grant Yeltsin a blanket pardon for any wrongdoing.)

In the hands of the shrewd and the ruthless, chaos had proven a gift. But whether out of instinct or calculation, Putin also understood the Russian public's longing for order. While few people had an interest in returning to the days of collective farming and empty store shelves, they were tired and scared and resented those—both at home and abroad—who appeared to have taken advantage of Yeltsin's weakness. They preferred a strong hand, which Putin was only too happy to provide.

He reasserted Russian control over the predominantly Muslim province of Chechnya, making no apologies for matching the brutal terrorist tactics of separatist rebels there with unrelenting military violence. He revived Soviet-style surveillance powers in the name of keeping the people safe. When democratic activists challenged Putin's autocratic tendencies, he dismissed them as tools of the West. He resurrected pre-Communist and even Communist symbols and embraced the long-suppressed Russian Orthodox Church. Fond of showy public works projects, he pursued wildly expensive spectacles, including a bid to host the Winter Olympics in the summer resort town of Sochi. With the fastidiousness of a teenager on Instagram, he curated a constant stream of photo ops, projecting an almost satirical image of masculine vigor (Putin riding a horse with his shirt off, Putin playing hockey), all the while practicing a casual chauvinism and homophobia, and insisting that Russian values were being infected by foreign elements. Everything Putin did fed the narrative that under his firm, paternal guidance, Russia had regained its mojo.

There was just one problem for Putin: Russia wasn't a superpower anymore. Despite having a nuclear arsenal second only to our own, Russia lacked the vast network of alliances and bases that allowed the United States to project its military power across the globe. Russia's economy remained smaller than those of Italy, Canada, and Brazil, dependent almost entirely on oil, gas, mineral, and arms exports. Moscow's high-end shopping districts testified to the country's transformation from a creaky state-run economy to one with a growing number of billionaires, but the pinched lives of ordinary Russians spoke to how little of this new wealth trickled down. According to various international indicators, the levels of Russian corruption and inequality rivaled those in parts of the developing world, and its male life expectancy in 2009 was lower than that of Bangladesh. Few, if any, young Africans, Asians, or Latin Americans looked to Russia for inspiration in the fight to reform their societies, or felt their imaginations stirred by Russian movies or music, or dreamed of studying there, much less immigrating. Shorn of its ideological underpinnings, the once-shiny promise of workers uniting to throw off their chains, Putin's Russia came off as insular and suspicious of outsiders—to be feared, perhaps, but not emulated.

It was this gap between the truth of modern-day Russia and Putin's insistence on its superpower status, I thought, that helped account for the country's increasingly combative foreign relations. Much of the ire was directed at us: In public remarks, Putin became sharply critical of American policy. When U.S.-backed initiatives came before the U.N. Security Council, he made sure Russia blocked them or watered them down—particularly anything touching on human rights. More consequential were Putin's escalating efforts to prevent former Soviet bloc countries, now independent, from breaking free of Russia's orbit. Our diplomats routinely received complaints from Russia's neighbors about instances of intimidation, economic pressure, misinformation campaigns, covert electioneering, contributions to pro-Russian political candidates, or outright bribery. In the case of Ukraine, there'd been the mysterious poisoning of Viktor Yushchenko, a reformist activist turned president whom Moscow opposed. And then, of course, there had been the invasion of Georgia during the summer of 2008.

It was hard to know how far down this dangerous path Russia planned to go. Putin was no longer Russia's president: Despite dominating the polls, he'd chosen to abide by Russia's constitutional prohibition against three consecutive terms, swapping places with Dmitry Medvedev, his former deputy, who upon being elected president in 2008 had promptly installed Putin as his prime minister. The consensus among analysts was that Medvedev was merely keeping the presidential seat warm until 2012, when Putin would be eligible to run again. Still, Putin's decision not just to step down but to promote a younger man with a reputation for relatively liberal, pro-Western views suggested he at least cared about appearances. It even offered the possibility that Putin would eventually leave elective office and settle into the role of power broker and elder statesman, allowing a new generation of leadership to put Russia back on the path toward a modern, lawful democracy.

All that was possible—but not likely. Since the time of the czars, historians had noted Russia's tendency to adopt with much fanfare the latest European ideas—whether representative government or modern bureaucracy, free markets or state socialism—only to subordinate or abandon such imported notions in favor of older, harsher ways of maintaining the social order. In the battle for Russia's identity, fear and fatalism usually beat out hope and change. It was an understandable response to a thousand-year history of Mongol invasions, byzantine intrigues, great famines, pervasive serfdom, unbridled tyranny, countless insurrections, bloody revolutions, crippling wars, years-long sieges, and millions upon millions slaughtered—all on a frigid landscape that forgave nothing.

IN JULY, I flew to Moscow for my first official visit to Russia as president, accepting the invitation Medvedev had extended at the G20 meeting in April. My thought was that we could continue with our proposed "reset"—focusing on areas of common interest while acknowledging and managing our significant differences. School was out for the summer, which meant that Michelle, Malia, and Sasha could join me. And under the pretext of needing help with the girls (and with the promise of a tour of the Vatican and an audience with the pope when we continued on to Italy for a G8 summit), Michelle convinced my mother-in-law and our close friend Mama Kaye to come along as well.

Our daughters had always been great travelers,

cheerfully enduring our annual nine-hour round-trip commercial flights between Chicago and Hawaii, never whining or throwing tantrums or kicking the seats in front of them, instead engrossing themselves in the games, puzzles, and books that Michelle doled out with military precision at regular intervals. Flying on Air Force One was a definite upgrade for them, with a choice of in-flight movies, actual beds to sleep in, and a flight crew plying them with all kinds of snacks. But still, traveling overseas with the president of the United States presented a new set of challenges. They got woken up just a few hours after falling asleep to put on new dresses and fancy shoes and have their hair combed tight so that they'd be presentable once we landed. They had to smile for photographers as we walked down the stairs, then introduce themselves to a row of gray-haired dignitaries who stood waiting on the tarmac—careful to maintain eye contact and not mumble, as their mother had taught them, and trying not to look bored as their dad engaged in meaningless chitchat before everyone climbed into the awaiting Beast. Rolling down a Moscow freeway, I asked Malia how she was holding up. She looked catatonic, her big brown eyes staring blankly at a spot over my shoulder.

"I think," she said, "this is the most tired I've ever been **in my entire life.**"

A midmorning nap seemed to cure the girls' jet lag, and there are moments of us together in Moscow that I recall as if they happened yesterday. Sasha striding beside me through the grand, red-carpeted halls of the Kremlin, followed by a set of towering uniformed Russian officers, her hands in the pockets of a tan trench coat as if she were a pint-sized secret agent. Or Malia trying to suppress a grimace after she gamely agreed to taste caviar in a rooftop restaurant overlooking Red Square. (True to form, Sasha refused the heap of slimy black stuff on my spoon, even at the risk of not getting a crack at the ice cream station later.)

But traveling as the First Family wasn't the same as traveling during the campaign, when we'd ride an RV from town to town and Miche and the girls would stay at my side through parades and county fairs. I now had my itinerary and they had theirs—along with their own support staff, briefings, and official photographer. At the end of our first night in Moscow, when we reunited at the Ritz-Carlton, the four of us lay on the bed and Malia asked why I hadn't gone with them to see the Russian dancers and dollmakers. Michelle leaned over and whispered conspiratorially, "Your father's not allowed to have fun. He has to sit in boring meetings all day."

"Poor Daddy," Sasha said, patting me on the head.

The setting for my official meeting with Medvedev was suitably impressive: one of the palaces within the Kremlin complex, its high, gilded ceilings and elaborate appointments restored to their former czarist glory. Our discussion was cordial and professional. At a joint press conference, we artfully finessed the continuing friction around Georgia and missile defense, and we had plenty of "deliverables" to announce, including an agreed-upon framework for the negotiation of the new strategic arms treaty, which would reduce each side's allowable nuclear warheads and delivery systems by up to one-third. Gibbs was more excited by Russia's agreement to lift restrictions on certain U.S. livestock exports, a change worth more than $1 billion to American farmers and ranchers.

"Something folks back home actually care about," he said with a grin.

That evening, Michelle and I were invited to Medvedev's dacha, a few miles outside the city center, for a private dinner. From reading Russian novels, I'd imagined a larger but still-rustic version of the traditional country home. Instead, we found ourselves on an enormous estate cloistered in a bank of tall trees. Medvedev and his wife, Svetlana—a cheerful, matronly blonde with whom Michelle and the girls had spent much of the day—greeted us at the front door, and after a brief tour, we walked out through a garden to dine in a large, wood-beamed gazebo.

Our conversation barely touched on politics. Medvedev was fascinated by the internet and quizzed me about Silicon Valley, expressing his desire to boost Russia's tech sector. He took a keen interest in my workout routine, describing how he swam for thirty minutes each day. We shared stories about our experiences teaching law, and he confessed his affection for hard rock bands like Deep Purple. Svetlana expressed concerns about how their thirteen-year-old son, Ilya, would manage adolescence with the added attention of being the president's son—a challenge Michelle and I understood all too well. Medvedev speculated that the boy would eventually prefer attending university abroad.

We bid the Medvedevs farewell shortly after dessert, taking care that the members of our team were fully loaded into the travel van before our motorcade snaked out of the compound. Gibbs and Marvin had been entertained by members of Medvedev's team elsewhere on the property, plied with vodka shots and schnapps, putting them in a jovial mood that wouldn't survive the next morning's wake-up call. As Michelle fell asleep beside me in the darkness of the car, I was struck by just how ordinary the night had been—how, with the exception of the translators who'd sat discreetly behind us while we ate, we could have been attending a dinner party in any well-to-do American suburb. Medvedev and I had more than a few things in common: Both of us had studied and taught law, gone on to marry and start families a few years later, dabbled in politics, and been helped along by older, cagier politicians. It made me wonder how much the differences between us could be explained by our respective characters and dispositions, and how much was merely the result of our different circumstances. Unlike him, I had the good fortune of having been born in a nation where political success hadn't required me to ignore billion-dollar kickbacks or the blackmailing of political opponents.

I MET VLADIMIR PUTIN for the first time the following morning when I traveled to his dacha, located in a suburb outside Moscow. Our Russia experts, Mike McFaul and Bill Burns, as well as Jim Jones, joined me for the ride. Having had some past interactions with Putin, Burns suggested that I keep my initial presentation short. "Putin's sensitive to any perceived slights," Burns said, "and in his mind, he's the more senior leader. You might want to open the meeting by asking him his opinion about the state of U.S.-Russian relations and let him get a few things off his chest."

After turning through an imposing gate and continuing down a long driveway, we pulled up in front of a mansion, where Putin welcomed us for the obligatory photo op. Physically, he was unremarkable: short and compact—a wrestler's build—with thin, sandy hair, a prominent nose, and pale, watchful eyes. As we exchanged pleasantries with our respective delegations, I noticed a casualness to his movements, a practiced disinterest in his voice that indicated someone accustomed to being surrounded by subordinates and supplicants. Someone who'd grown used to power.

Accompanied by Sergey Lavrov, Russia's urbane foreign minister and former U.N. representative, Putin led us to a broad outdoor patio, where an elaborate spread had been arranged for our benefit, with eggs and caviar, breads and teas, served by male waiters in traditional peasant dress and high leather boots. I thanked Putin for his hospitality, noted the progress our countries had made with the previous day's agreements, and asked for his assessment of the U.S.-Russia relationship during his time in office.

Burns hadn't been kidding when he said the man had a few things to get off his chest. I'd barely finished the question before Putin launched into an animated and seemingly endless monologue chronicling every perceived injustice, betrayal, and slight that he and the Russian people had suffered at the hands of the Americans. He'd liked President Bush personally, he said, and had reached out after 9/11, pledging solidarity and offering to share intelligence in the fight against a common enemy. He'd helped the United States secure airbases in Kyrgyzstan and Uzbekistan for the Afghan campaign. He'd even offered Russia's help in handling Saddam Hussein.

And where had it gotten him? Rather than heed his warnings, he said, Bush had gone ahead and invaded Iraq, destabilizing the entire Middle East. The U.S. decision seven years earlier to pull out of the Anti-Ballistic Missile Treaty and its plans to house missile defense systems on Russia's borders continued to be a source of strategic instability. The admission of former Warsaw Pact countries into NATO during both the Clinton and Bush administrations had steadily encroached on Russia's "sphere of influence," while U.S. support for the "color revolutions" in Georgia, Ukraine, and Kyrgyzstan—under the specious guise of "democracy promotion"—had turned Russia's once-friendly neighbors into governments hostile to Moscow. As far as Putin was concerned, the Americans had been arrogant, dismissive, unwilling to treat Russia as an equal partner, and constantly trying to dictate terms to the rest of the world—all of which, he said, made it hard to be optimistic about future relations.

About thirty minutes into what was supposed to have been an hour-long meeting, my staffers started sneaking glances at their watches. But I decided not to interrupt. It seemed clear that Putin had rehearsed the whole thing, but his sense of grievance was real. I also knew that my continued progress with Medvedev depended on the forbearance of Putin. After about forty-five minutes, Putin finally ran out of material, and rather than trying to stick to our schedule, I began answering him point by point. I reminded him that I'd personally opposed the invasion of Iraq, but I also rejected Russia's actions in Georgia, believing that each nation had the right to determine its own alliances and economic relationships without interference. I disputed the idea that a limited

defense system designed to guard against an Iranian missile launch would have any impact on Russia's mighty
nuclear arsenal, but mentioned my plan to conduct a
review before taking further steps on missile defense in
Europe. As for our proposed "reset," the goal wasn't to
eliminate all differences between our two countries, I
explained; it was to get past Cold War habits and establish a realistic, mature relationship that could manage
those differences and build on shared interests.

At times, the conversation got contentious, especially
on Iran. Putin dismissed my concerns about Iran's nuclear
program and bristled at my suggestion that he suspend a
pending sale of the powerful Russian-designed S-300
surface-to-air missile system to the regime. The system
was purely defensive, he said, adding that reneging on a
contract worth $800 million would risk both the bottom
line and the reputation of Russian arms manufacturers.
But for the most part he listened attentively, and by the
end of what had turned into a two-hour marathon, he
expressed openness, if not enthusiasm, for the reset effort.

"Of course, on all these issues, you will have to work
with Dmitry," Putin told me as he walked me to my
waiting motorcade. "These are now his decisions." Our
eyes met as we shook hands, both of us knowing that the
statement he'd just made was dubious, but for now, at
least, it was the closest thing I was going to get to an
endorsement.

The meeting with Putin wreaked havoc on the rest of
the day's schedule. We raced back to Moscow, where
I was slated to deliver the commencement address
to bright-eyed young Russians studying international

business and finance. Beforehand, in a holding room off the stage, I had a brief pull-aside with former Soviet leader Mikhail Gorbachev. Seventy-eight years old and still robust, with the signature red birthmark splashed across his head, he struck me as a strangely tragic figure. Here was a man who'd once been one of the most powerful people on earth, whose instincts for reform and efforts at denuclearization—no matter how tentative—had led to an epic global transformation and earned him the Nobel Peace Prize. He now found himself largely disdained within his own country, both by those who felt he'd surrendered to the West and by those who considered him a Communist throwback whose time was long past. Gorbachev told me he was enthusiastic about a reset and my proposals for a nuclear-free world, but after fifteen minutes I had to cut the conversation short to deliver my speech. Although he said he understood, I could tell he was disappointed—a reminder for both of us of the fleeting, fickle nature of public life.

Then it was off to an abbreviated Kremlin lunch with Medvedev and a ballroom of important personages, followed by a roundtable discussion with U.S. and Russian business leaders, where boilerplate appeals for greater economic cooperation were exchanged. By the time I arrived at the summit of U.S. and Russian civil society leaders that McFaul had organized, I could feel jet lag kicking in. I was content to take a seat, catch my breath, and listen to the remarks of those speaking before me.

It was my kind of crowd: democracy activists, heads of nonprofits, and community organizers working at a grassroots level on issues like housing, public health, and political access. They mostly toiled in obscurity, jostled for money to keep their operations afloat, and rarely had a chance to travel outside their home cities, much less do so at the invitation of a U.S. president. One of the Americans was even someone I'd worked with during my organizing days back in Chicago.

Maybe it was the juxtaposition of my past and my present that kept me thinking about my conversation with Putin. When Axe asked for my impressions of the Russian leader, I'd said that I found him strangely familiar, "like a ward boss, except with nukes and a U.N. Security Council veto." This prompted a laugh, but I hadn't meant it as a joke. Putin did, in fact, remind me of the sorts of men who had once run the Chicago machine or Tammany Hall—tough, street smart, unsentimental characters who knew what they knew, who never moved outside their narrow experiences, and who viewed patronage, bribery, shakedowns, fraud, and occasional violence as legitimate tools of the trade. For them, as for Putin, life was a zero-sum game; you might do business with those outside your tribe, but in the end, you couldn't trust them. You looked out for yourself first and then for your own. In such a world, a lack of scruples, a contempt for any high-minded aspirations beyond accumulating power, were not flaws. They were an advantage.

In America, it had taken generations of protest, progressive lawmaking, muckraking journalism, and dogged advocacy to check, if not fully eliminate, such raw exercises of power. That reform tradition was in large part what had inspired me to enter politics. And yet, in order to reduce the risk of nuclear catastrophe or another Middle East war, I'd just spent the morning courting an autocrat who no doubt kept dossiers on every Russian activist in the room and could have any one of them harassed, jailed, or worse whenever he pleased. If Putin did go after one of these activists, how far would I go in taking him to task—especially knowing that it probably wouldn't change his behavior? Would I risk the completion of START negotiations? Russian cooperation on Iran? And how did one measure such trade-offs anyway? I could tell myself that compromises existed everywhere, that in order to get things done back home, I'd cut deals with politicians whose attitudes weren't so different from Putin's and whose ethical standards didn't always bear scrutiny. But this felt different. The stakes were higher—on both sides of the ledger.

Standing up finally to speak, I praised the people in the room for their courage and dedication and urged them to focus not just on democracy and civil rights but also on concrete strategies to provide jobs, education, healthcare, and decent housing. Addressing the Russians in the audience, I said that America couldn't and shouldn't fight their battles for them, that Russia's future was for them to determine; but I added that I would be rooting for them, firm in my conviction that all people aspire to the principles of human rights, the rule of law, and self-governance.

The room burst into applause. McFaul beamed. I felt glad about being able to lift, however briefly, the spirits of good people doing hard and sometimes dangerous work. I believed that, even in Russia, it would pay off in the long run. Still, I couldn't shake the fear that Putin's way of doing business had more force and momentum than I cared to admit, that in the world as it was, many of these hopeful activists might soon be marginalized or crushed by their own government—and there'd be very little I could do to protect them.

CHAPTER 20

T HE NEXT TIME I MET with Medvedev in person was in late September, when heads of state and government from around the world converged on Manhattan for the annual opening session of the U.N. General Assembly. "UNGA Week," we called it, and for me and my foreign policy team it represented a seventy-two-hour, sleep-depriving obstacle course. With roads blocked and security tightened, New York traffic was more hellish than usual, even for the presidential motorcade. Practically every foreign leader wanted a meeting, or at least a photo for the folks back home. There were consultations with the U.N. secretary-general, meetings for me to chair, luncheons to attend, receptions to be hosted, causes to be championed, deals to be brokered, and multiple speeches to be written—including a major address before the General Assembly, a sort of global State of the Union that, in the eight years we worked together, Ben and I somehow never managed to finish writing until fifteen minutes before I was due to speak.

Despite the crazy schedule involved, the sight of the U.N. headquarters—its main building a soaring white monolith overlooking the East River—always put me in a hopeful, expectant mood. I attributed this to my mother. I remember as a boy, maybe nine or ten, asking her about the U.N., and having her explain how, after World War II, global leaders decided that they needed a place where people from a diversity of countries could meet to resolve their differences peacefully.

"Humans aren't that different from animals, Bar," she told me. "We fear what we don't know. When we're afraid of people and feel threatened, it's easier to fight wars and do other stupid things. The United Nations is a way for countries to meet and learn about each other and not be so afraid."

As always, my mother possessed a reassuring certainty that despite humanity's primal impulses, reason, logic, and progress would eventually prevail. After our conversation, I imagined the goings-on at the U.N. to be like an episode of **Star Trek,** with Americans, Russians, Scots, Africans, and Vulcans exploring the stars together. Or the "It's a Small World" display at Disneyland, where moon-faced children with different skin tones and colorful costumes would all sing a cheerful tune. Later, for a homework assignment, I read the U.N.'s 1945 founding charter and was struck by how its mission matched my mother's optimism: "to save succeeding generations from the scourge of war," "reaffirm faith in fundamental human rights," "establish conditions under which justice and respect for the obligations arising from treaties and other sources of international law can be maintained," and "promote social progress and better standards of life in larger freedom."

Needless to say, the U.N. hadn't always lived up to these lofty intentions. Like its ill-fated predecessor, the League of Nations, the organization was only as strong as

its most powerful members allowed it to be. Any significant action required consensus among the five permanent
members of the Security Council—the United States,
the Soviet Union (later Russia), the United Kingdom,
France, and China—each possessing an absolute veto. In
the middle of the Cold War, the chances of reaching any
consensus had been slim, which is why the U.N. had
stood idle as Soviet tanks rolled into Hungary or U.S.
planes dropped napalm on the Vietnamese countryside.

Even after the Cold War, divisions within the Security
Council continued to hamstring the U.N.'s ability to
tackle problems. Its member states lacked either the
means or the collective will to reconstruct failing states
like Somalia, or prevent ethnic slaughter in places like
Sri Lanka. Its peacekeeping missions, dependent on vol-
untary troop contributions from member states, were
consistently understaffed and ill-equipped. At times, the
General Assembly devolved into a forum for posturing,
hypocrisy, and one-sided condemnations of Israel; more
than one U.N. agency became embroiled in corruption
scandals, while vicious autocracies like Khamenei's Iran
and Assad's Syria would maneuver to get seats on the
U.N. Human Rights Council. Within the Republican
Party, the U.N. became a symbol of nefarious one-world
globalism. Progressives bemoaned its impotence in the
face of injustice.

And yet I remained convinced that, for all its shortcomings, the U.N. served a vital function. U.N. reports
and findings could sometimes shame countries into
better behavior and strengthen international norms.
Because of the U.N.'s work in mediation and peacekeeping, cease-fires had been brokered, conflicts had been

averted, and lives had been saved. The U.N. played a role in more than eighty former colonies becoming sovereign nations. Its agencies helped lift tens of millions of people out of poverty, eradicated smallpox, and very nearly wiped out polio and Guinea worm. Whenever I walked through the U.N. complex—my Secret Service detail brushing back the crowds of diplomats and staffers who typically milled along the wide, carpeted corridors for a handshake or a wave, their faces reflecting every shape and hue of the human family—I was reminded that inside were scores of men and women who pushed against boulders every day, trying to convince governments to fund vaccination programs and schools for poor children, rallying the world to stop a minority group from being slaughtered or young women from being trafficked. Men and women who anchored their lives to the same idea that had anchored my mother, an idea captured in a verse woven into a tapestry that hung in the great-domed General Assembly hall:

Human beings are members of a whole
In creation of one essence and soul.

Ben informed me that those lines were written by the thirteenth-century Persian poet Sa'adi, one of the most beloved figures in Iranian culture. We found this ironic, given how much of my time at UNGA was devoted to trying to curb Iran's development of nuclear weapons. Apparently, Khamenei and Ahmadinejad didn't share the poet's gentle sensibilities.

Since rejecting my offer of bilateral talks, Iran had shown no signs of scaling back its nuclear program. Its negotiators continued to stall and bluster in sessions with P5+1 members, insisting that Iran's centrifuges and enriched uranium stockpiles had entirely civilian purposes. These claims of innocence were spurious, but they provided Russia and China with enough of an excuse to keep blocking the Security Council from considering tougher sanctions against the regime.

We continued to press our case, and a pair of new developments helped bring about a shift in Russian attitudes. First, our arms control team, ably headed by nonproliferation expert Gary Samore, had worked with the International Atomic Energy Agency (IAEA) on a creative new proposal meant to test Iran's true intentions. Under the proposal, Iran would ship its existing stockpile of LEU to Russia, which would process it into HEU; Russia would then transport the HEU to France, where it would be converted into a form of fuel that met Iran's legitimate civilian needs but had no possible military application. The proposal was a stopgap measure: It left Iran's nuclear architecture in place and wouldn't prevent Iran from enriching more LEU in the future. But depleting its current stockpiles would delay "breakout capacity" by up to a year, thus buying us time to negotiate a more permanent solution. Just as important, the proposal made Russia a key implementation partner and showed Moscow our willingness to exhaust all reasonable approaches when it came to Iran. During the course of UNGA, Russia signed off on the idea; we even referred to it as "the Russia proposal." Which meant that when the Iranians ultimately rejected the proposal at a P5+1 meeting held later that year in Geneva, they weren't just thumbing their noses at the

Americans. They were snubbing Russia, one of their few remaining defenders.

Cracks in the Russia-Iran relationship deepened after I handed Medvedev and Lavrov an intelligence bombshell during a private meeting on the margins of UNGA: We'd discovered that Iran was on the verge of completing construction of a secret enrichment facility buried deep inside a mountain near the ancient city of Qom. Everything about the facility—its size, configuration, and location on a military installation—indicated Iran's interest in shielding its activities from both detection and attack, features inconsistent with a civilian program. I told Medvedev we were showing him the evidence first, before we made it public, because the time for half measures was over. Without Russian agreement on a forceful international response, the chance for a diplomatic resolution with Iran would likely slip away.

Our presentation seemed to rattle the Russians. Rather than try to defend Iran's actions, Medvedev expressed his disappointment with the regime and acknowledged the need for a recalibration of the P5+1's approach. He went even further in public remarks afterward, telling the press that "sanctions rarely lead to productive results . . . but in some cases sanctions are inevitable." For our side, the statement was a welcome surprise, confirming our growing sense of Medvedev's reliability as a partner.

We decided against revealing the existence of the Qom facility during a U.N. Security Council meeting on nuclear security issues that I was scheduled to chair; although the iconic setting would have made for good theater, we needed time to thoroughly brief the IAEA and the other P5+1 members. We also wanted to avoid drawing comparisons to the dramatic—and ultimately discredited—Security Council presentation regarding Iraqi WMDs made by Colin Powell in the run-up to the Iraq War. Instead, we gave the story to **The New York Times** just before G20 leaders were scheduled to meet in Pittsburgh.

The effect was galvanizing. Reporters speculated about possible Israeli missile strikes on Qom. Members of Congress called for immediate action. At a joint press conference with French president Sarkozy and British prime minister Brown, I emphasized the need for a strong international response but refrained from getting specific on sanctions so as to avoid boxing in Medvedev before he'd had a chance to work through the issue with Putin. Assuming we could keep Medvedev engaged, we had just one more major diplomatic hurdle to clear: convincing a skeptical Chinese government to cast a vote for sanctions against one of its main oil suppliers.

"How likely is that?" McFaul asked me.

"Don't know yet," I said. "Turns out avoiding a war is harder than getting into one."

SEVEN WEEKS LATER, Air Force One touched down in Beijing for my first official visit to China. We were instructed to leave any non-governmental electronic devices on the plane and to operate under the assumption that our communications were being monitored.

Even across oceans, Chinese surveillance capabilities were impressive. During the campaign, they'd hacked into our headquarters' computer system. (I took it as a positive sign for my election prospects.) Their ability to remotely convert any mobile phone into a recording device was widely known. To make calls involving national security matters from our hotel, I had to go to a suite down the hall fitted with a sensitive compartmented information facility (SCIF)—a big blue tent plopped down in the middle of the room that hummed with an eerie, psychedelic buzz designed to block any nearby listening devices. Some members of our team dressed and even showered in the dark to avoid the hidden cameras we could assume had been strategically placed in every room. (Marvin, on the other hand, said he made a point of walking around his room naked and with the lights on—whether out of pride or in protest wasn't entirely clear.)

Occasionally, the brazenness of Chinese intelligence verged on comedy. At one point, my commerce secretary, Gary Locke, was on his way to a prep session when he realized he'd forgotten something in his suite. Upon opening the door, he discovered a pair of housekeepers making up his bed while two gentlemen in suits carefully thumbed through the papers on his desk. When Gary asked what they were doing, the men walked wordlessly past him and disappeared. The housekeepers never looked up, just moved on to changing out the towels in the bathroom as if Gary were invisible. Gary's story generated plenty of head shakes and chuckles from our team, and I'm sure that someone down the diplomatic food chain eventually filed a formal complaint. But no one brought up the incident when we sat down later for our official meeting with President Hu Jintao and the rest of the Chinese delegation. We had too much business to do with the Chinese—and did enough of our own spying on them—to want to make a stink.

This about summed up the state of U.S.-China affairs at the time. On the surface, the relationship we'd inherited looked relatively stable, without the high-profile diplomatic ruptures we'd seen with the Russians. Out of the gate, Tim Geithner and Hillary had met repeatedly with their Chinese counterparts and formalized a working group to address various bilateral concerns. In my meetings with President Hu during the London G20, we'd talked of pursuing win-win policies that could benefit our two countries. But beneath the diplomatic niceties lurked long-simmering tensions and mistrust—not only around specific issues like trade or espionage but also around the fundamental question of what China's resurgence meant for the international order and America's position in the world.

That China and the United States had managed to avoid open conflict for more than three decades was not just luck. From the start of China's economic reforms and decisive opening to the West back in the 1970s, the Chinese government had faithfully followed Deng Xiaoping's counsel to "hide your strength and bide your time." It prioritized industrialization over a massive military buildup. It invited U.S. companies searching for low-wage labor to move their operations to China and cultivated successive U.S. administrations to help it obtain World Trade Organization (WTO) membership in 2001, which in turn gave China greater access to U.S. markets. Although the Chinese Communist Party maintained tight control over the country's politics, it made no effort to export its ideology; China transacted business with all comers, whether democracies or dictatorships, claiming virtue in not judging the way other countries managed their internal affairs. China could throw its elbows around when it felt its territorial claims being challenged, and it bristled at Western criticism of its human rights record. But even on flashpoints like U.S. arms sales to Taiwan, Chinese officials did their best to ritualize disputes—registering displeasure through strongly worded letters or the cancellation of bilateral meetings but never letting things escalate to the point where they might impede the flow of shipping containers full of Chinese-made sneakers, electronics, and auto parts into U.S. ports and a Walmart near you.

This strategic patience had helped China husband its resources and avoid costly foreign adventures. It had also helped obscure how systematically China kept evading, bending, or breaking just about every agreed-upon rule of international commerce during its "peaceful rise." For years, it had used state subsidies, as well as currency manipulation and trade dumping, to artificially depress the price of its exports and undercut manufacturing operations in the United States. Its disregard for labor and environmental standards accomplished the same thing. Meanwhile, China used nontariff barriers like quotas and embargoes; it also engaged in the theft of U.S. intellectual property and placed constant pressure on U.S. companies doing business in China to surrender key technologies to help speed China's ascent up the global supply chain.

None of this made China unique. Just about every rich country, from the United States to Japan, had used mercantilist strategies at various stages of their development to boost their economies. And from China's perspective, you couldn't argue with the results: Only a generation after millions died of mass starvation, China had transformed itself into the world's third-largest economy, accounting for nearly half of the world's steel production, 20 percent of its manufacturing, and 40 percent of the clothing Americans bought.

What **was** surprising was Washington's mild response. Back in the early 1990s, leaders of organized labor had sounded the alarm about China's increasingly unfair trading practices, and they'd found plenty of congressional Democrats, particularly from rust-belt states, to champion the cause. The Republican Party had its share of China critics as well, a mix of Pat Buchanan–style populists enraged by what they saw as America's slow surrender to a foreign power and aging Cold War hawks still worried about communism's godless advance.

But as globalization shifted into overdrive during the Clinton and Bush years, these voices found themselves in the minority. There was too much money to be made. U.S. corporations and their shareholders liked the reduced labor costs and soaring profits that resulted from shifting production to China. U.S. farmers liked all the new Chinese customers buying their soybeans and pork. Wall Street firms liked the scores of Chinese billionaires looking to invest their newfound wealth, as did the slew of lawyers, consultants, and lobbyists brought on to service the expanding U.S.-China commerce. Even as most congressional Democrats remained unhappy with China's trading practices, and the Bush administration filed a handful of complaints against China with the WTO, by the time I took office, a rough consensus had emerged among U.S. foreign-policy-making elites and big party donors: Instead of engaging in protectionism,

America needed to take a page from the Chinese play-book. If we wanted to stay number one, we needed to work harder, save more money, and teach our kids more math, science, engineering—and Mandarin.

My own views on China didn't fit neatly in any camp. I didn't share my union supporters' instinctive opposition to free trade, and I didn't believe we could fully reverse globalization, any more than it was possible to shut down the internet. I thought that Clinton and Bush had made the right call in encouraging China's integration into the global economy—history told me that a chaotic and impoverished China posed a bigger threat to the United States than a prosperous one. I considered China's success at lifting hundreds of millions of people out of extreme poverty to be a towering human achievement.

Still, the fact remained that China's gaming of the international trading system had too often come at America's expense. Automation and advanced robotics may have been the bigger culprit in the decline of U.S. manufacturing jobs, but Chinese practices—with the help of corporate outsourcing—had accelerated those losses. The flood of Chinese goods into the United States had made flat-screen TVs cheaper and helped keep infla-tion low, but only at the price of depressing the wages of U.S. workers. I'd promised to fight on those workers' behalf for a better deal on trade, and I intended to keep that promise.

With the world's economy hanging by a thread, though, I had to consider when and how best to do that. China held more than $700 billion in U.S. debt and had massive foreign currency reserves, making it a necessary partner in managing the financial crisis. To pull ourselves and the rest of the world out of the recession, we needed China's economy growing, not contracting. China wasn't going to change its trading practices without firm pressure from my administration; I just had to make sure we didn't start a trade war that tipped the world into a depression and harmed the very workers I'd vowed to help.

In the run-up to our China trip, my team and I settled on a strategy to thread the needle between too tough and not tough enough. We'd start by presenting President Hu with a list of problem areas we wanted to see fixed over a realistic time frame, while avoiding a public confrontation that might further spook the jittery financial markets. If the Chinese failed to act, we'd steadily ratchet up the public pressure and take retaliatory actions—ideally in an economic environment that was no longer so fragile.

To nudge China toward better behavior, we also hoped to enlist the help of its neighbors. That was going to take some work. The Bush administration's total absorption with problems in the Middle East, as well as the Wall Street fiasco, had led some Asian leaders to question America's relevance in the region. Meanwhile, China's booming economy made even close U.S. allies like Japan and South Korea increasingly dependent on its markets and wary of getting on its bad side. The one thing we had going for us was that in recent years China had started overplaying its hand, demanding one-sided concessions from weaker trading partners and threatening the Philippines and Vietnam over control of a handful of small but strategic islands in the South China Sea. U.S. diplomats reported a growing resentment toward such heavy-handed tactics—and a desire for a more sustained American presence as a counterweight to Chinese power.

To take advantage of this opening, we scheduled stops for me in Japan and South Korea, as well as a meeting in Singapore with the ten countries that made up the Association of Southeast Asian Nations (ASEAN). Along the way, I'd announce my intention to pick up the baton on an ambitious new U.S.-Asia trade agreement the Bush administration had started to negotiate—with an emphasis on locking in the types of enforceable labor and environmental provisions that Democrats and unions complained had been missing in previous deals, like the North American Free Trade Agreement (NAFTA). We explained to reporters that the overall goal of what we later called a "pivot to Asia" wasn't to contain China or stifle its growth. Rather, it was to reaffirm U.S. ties to the region, and to strengthen the very framework of international law that had allowed countries throughout the Asia-Pacific region—including China—to make so much progress in such a short time.

I doubted the Chinese would see it that way.

IT HAD BEEN more than twenty years since I'd traveled to Asia. Our seven-day tour started in Tokyo, where I delivered a speech on the future of the U.S.-Japan alliance and met with Prime Minister Yukio Hatoyama to discuss the economic crisis, North Korea, and the proposed relocation of the U.S. Marine base in Okinawa. A pleasant if awkward fellow, Hatoyama was Japan's fourth prime minister in less than three years and the second since I'd taken office—a symptom of the sclerotic, aimless politics that had plagued Japan for much of the decade. He'd be gone seven months later.

A brief visit with Emperor Akihito and Empress Michiko at the Imperial Palace left a more lasting impression. Diminutive and well into their seventies, they greeted me in impeccable English, with him dressed in a Western suit and her in a brocaded silk kimono, and I bowed as a gesture of respect. They led me into a receiving room, cream-colored and sparsely decorated in the traditional Japanese style, and over tea they inquired about Michelle, the girls, and my impression of U.S.-Japan relations. Their manners were at once formal and self-effacing, their voices soft as the patter of rain, and I found myself trying to imagine the emperor's life. What must it have been like, I wondered, to be born to a father who'd been considered a god, and then forced to assume a largely symbolic throne decades after the Japanese Empire had suffered its fiery defeat? The empress's story interested me even more: The daughter of a wealthy industrialist, she'd been educated in Catholic schools and graduated from college with a degree in English literature; she was also the first commoner in the twenty-six-hundred-year history of the Chrysanthemum Throne to marry into the imperial family—a fact that endeared her to the Japanese public but reputedly caused strains with her in-laws. As a departing gift, the empress gave me a composition she'd written for the piano, explaining with surprising frankness how her love of music and poetry had helped her survive bouts of loneliness.

Later, I learned that my simple bow to my elderly Japanese hosts had sent conservative commentators into a fit back home. When one obscure blogger called it "treasonous," his words got picked up and amplified in the mainstream press. Hearing all this, I pictured the emperor entombed in his ceremonial duties and the empress, with her finely worn, graying beauty and smile brushed with melancholy, and I wondered when exactly such a sizable portion of the American Right had become so frightened and insecure that they'd completely lost their minds.

From Tokyo, I traveled to Singapore to meet with the leaders of the ten ASEAN countries. My attendance wasn't without potential controversy: Myanmar, one of ASEAN's members, had been ruled for more than forty years by a brutal, repressive military junta, and both Presidents Clinton and Bush had declined invitations to meet with the group so long as Myanmar was included. To me, though, alienating nine Southeast Asian countries to signal disapproval toward one didn't make much sense, especially since the United States maintained friendly relations with a number of the ASEAN countries that were hardly paragons of democratic virtue, including Vietnam and Brunei. With Myanmar, the United States had comprehensive sanctions in place. Our best chance of influencing its government beyond that, we decided, would come from showing a willingness to talk.

Myanmar's prime minister was a mild-mannered, elf-ish general named Thein Sein, and as it turned out my interaction with him went no further than a brief handshake and didn't cause much of a stir. The ASEAN leaders expressed enthusiasm for our message of U.S. reengagement, while the Asian press emphasized my childhood ties to the region—a first for an American president and evident, they said, in my fondness for local street food and my ability to greet the Indonesian president in Bahasa.

The truth is that I'd forgotten most of my Indonesian beyond simple greetings and ordering off a menu. But despite my long absence, I was struck by how familiar Southeast Asia felt to me, with its languorous, humid air, the whiffs of fruit and spice, the subtle restraint in the way people interacted. Singapore, though, with its wide boulevards, public gardens, and high-rise office buildings, was hardly the tidy former British colony I remembered from childhood. Even in the 1960s, it had been one of the region's success stories—a city-state populated by Malays, Indians, and Chinese that, thanks to a combination of free-market policies, bureaucratic competence, minimal corruption, and notoriously stringent political and social control, had become a center for foreign investment. But globalization and broader growth trends in Asia had sent the country's economy soaring even higher. With its fine restaurants and designer stores packed with businessmen in suits and young people in the latest hip-hop fashion, the wealth on display now rivaled that of New York or Los Angeles.

In a sense, Singapore remained exceptional: Most of the other ASEAN countries still struggled with varying levels of entrenched poverty, just as their commitment to democracy and the rule of law remained wildly uneven. One thing they seemed to have in common, though, was a shift in how they imagined themselves. The people I talked to—whether heads of state, businesspeople, or human rights activists—remained respectful of American power. But they no longer viewed the West as the center of the world, with their own countries inalterably cast as bit players. Instead, they considered themselves at least equal to their former colonizers, their dreams for their people no longer capped by geography or race.

As far as I was concerned, that was a good thing, an extension of America's faith in the dignity of all people and a fulfillment of the promise we'd long made to the world: Follow our lead, liberalize your economies, and hopefully your governments and you, too, can share in our prosperity. Like Japan and South Korea, more and more ASEAN countries had taken us at our word. It was part of my job as U.S. president to make sure that they played fair—that their markets were as open to us as our markets were to them, that their continued development didn't depend on exploiting their workers or destroying the environment. So long as they competed with us on a level playing field, I considered Southeast Asia's progress something for America to welcome, not fear. I wonder now whether that's what conservative critics found so objectionable about my foreign policy, why something as minor as a bow to the Japanese emperor could trigger such rage: I didn't seem threatened, as they were, by the idea that the rest of the world was catching up to us.

SHANGHAI—OUR FIRST stop in China—seemed like Singapore on steroids. Visually, it lived up to the hype, a sprawling, modern metropolis of twenty million cacophonous souls, every inch of it bustling with commerce, traffic, construction cranes. Huge ships and barges loaded with goods bound for the world's markets glided up and down the Huangpu. Throngs of people strolled along the expansive river walk, stopping every so often to admire the futuristic skyscrapers that stretched in all directions and at night were as bright as the Las Vegas

Strip. At an ornate banquet hall, the mayor of the city—an up-and-comer in the Communist Party who, with his tailored suit and jaunty sophistication, somehow reminded me of Dean Martin—pulled out all the stops for a luncheon between our delegation and Chinese and American business leaders, with rare delicacies and wine pairings that would suit a high-end wedding at the Ritz. Reggie Love, my ever-constant body man, was most impressed with a waitstaff made up entirely of stunning young women in flowing white gowns, as slender and tall as runway models.

"Who knew Communists looked like that," he said, shaking his head.

The contradiction between China's official ideology and such conspicuous displays of wealth didn't come up when I met with several hundred college students at a town hall that same day. The Chinese authorities, wary of my usual unscripted format, had handpicked the participants from some of Shanghai's most elite universities—and although they were courteous and enthusiastic, their questions had little of the probing, irreverent quality that I was used to hearing from youth in other countries. ("So what measures will you take to deepen this close relationship between cities of the United States and China?" was about as tough as it got.) I couldn't decide whether party officials had prescreened all the questions or the students just knew better than to say anything that could land them in hot water.

After shaking hands and chatting with some of the students at the end of the program, I concluded that at least some of their earnest patriotism wasn't simply for show. They were too young to have experienced the horrors of the Cultural Revolution or witnessed the crackdown in Tiananmen Square; that history wasn't taught in school, and I doubted their parents talked about it. If some of the students chafed against the way the government blocked their access to websites, they likely experienced the full weight of China's repressive apparatus mainly as an abstraction, as remote from their personal experience as the U.S. criminal justice system might be to middle-class, suburban white kids back home. For the entirety of their lives, China's system had lifted them and their families along an upward trajectory, while from a distance, at least, Western democracies seemed stuck in neutral, full of civic discord and economic inefficiency.

It was tempting to think that the attitudes of these students would change over time, either because a slowdown in China's growth rate would thwart their material expectations or because, having reached a certain measure of economic security, they would start wanting those things the GDP couldn't measure. But that was hardly guaranteed. In fact, China's economic success had made its brand of authoritarian capitalism a plausible alternative to Western-style liberalism in the minds of young people not just in Shanghai but across the developing world. Which of those visions they ultimately embraced would help determine the geopolitics of the next century; and I left the town hall acutely aware that winning over this new generation depended on my ability to show that America's democratic, rights-based, pluralistic system could still deliver on the promise of a better life.

Beijing wasn't as flashy as Shanghai, though driving from the airport we passed what seemed like twenty straight miles of newly built high-rises, as if ten Manhattans had been erected overnight. Business districts and residential areas gave way to government buildings and imposing monuments once we reached the city's core. As usual, my meeting with President Hu Jintao was a sleepy affair: Whatever the topic, he liked to read from thick stacks of prepared remarks, pausing every so often for translations to English that seemed to have been prepared in advance and, somehow, always lasted longer than his original statement. When it was my turn to speak, he'd shuffle through his papers, looking for whatever response his aides had prepared for him. Efforts to break the monotony with personal anecdotes or the occasional joke ("Give me the name of your contractor," I told him after learning that the massive, columned Great Hall of the People had been built in less than a year) usually resulted in a blank stare, and I was tempted more than once to suggest that we could save each other time by just exchanging papers and reading them at our leisure.

Still, my time with Hu gave me the chance to put down a set of clear markers on U.S. priorities: managing the economic crisis and North Korea's nuclear program; the need to peacefully resolve maritime disputes in the South China Sea; the treatment of Chinese dissidents; and our push for new sanctions against Iran. On the last item, I appealed to Chinese self-interest, warning that without meaningful diplomatic action, either we or the Israelis might be forced to strike Iran's nuclear facilities, with far worse consequences for Chinese oil supplies. As expected, Hu was noncommittal on sanctions, but judging by his shift in body language and the furious notetaking by his ministers, the seriousness of our message on Iran got his attention.

I took a similarly blunt approach on trade issues when I met the next day with Premier Wen Jiabao, who, despite the lesser title, served as China's key economic decision maker. Unlike President Hu, Wen seemed comfortable exchanging views extemporaneously—and was straightforward in his defense of China's trade policies. "You must understand, Mr. President, that despite what you see in Shanghai and Beijing, we're still a developing country," he said. "One-third of our population still lives in severe poverty . . . more people than in the entire United States. You can't expect us to adopt the same policies that apply to a highly advanced economy like your own."

He had a point: For all of his country's remarkable progress, the average Chinese family—especially outside the major cities—still had a lower income than all but the very poorest of Americans. I tried to put myself in Wen's shoes, having to integrate an economy that straddled the information age and feudalism while generating enough jobs to meet the demands of a population the size of North and South America combined. I would have sympathized more had I not known that high-ranking Communist Party officials—including Wen—had a habit of steering state contracts and licenses to family members and siphoning billions into offshore accounts.

As it was, I told Wen that given the massive trade imbalances between our two countries, the United States could no longer overlook China's currency manipulation and other unfair practices; either China started changing course or we'd have to take retaliatory measures. Hearing this, Wen tried a different tack, suggesting that I just give him a list of U.S. products we wanted China to buy more of and he'd see what he could do. (He was especially keen on including military and high-tech items that America barred from export to China for national security reasons.) I explained that we needed a structural solution, not piecemeal concessions, and in the back-and-forth between us, I felt like I was haggling over the price of chickens at a market stall rather than negotiating trade policy between the world's two largest economies. I was reminded once again that for Wen and the rest of China's leaders, foreign policy remained purely transactional. How much they gave and how much they got would depend not on abstract principles of international law but on their assessment of the other side's power and leverage. Where they met no resistance, they'd keep on taking.

Our first day in Beijing ended with the obligatory state dinner, complete with a cultural program that included classic Chinese opera; a medley of performances by Tibetan, Uighur, and Mongolian dance troupes (the emcee helpfully noted that all minority groups were respected in China, which would have been news to thousands of Tibetan and Uighur political prisoners); and a rendition of Stevie Wonder's "I Just Called to Say I Love You" by the People's Liberation Army Orchestra in my honor. ("We know he's your favorite," President Hu leaned over to tell me.) After five days on the road with our clocks turned upside down, our entire crew was running on fumes; at the table next to ours, Larry Summers was fast asleep, his mouth open and his head lolling back, causing Favs to shoot out an email to the group: "It looks like SOMEONE's in need of a second stimulus."

Groggy but determined, everyone (including Larry) fought through their jet lag the next day to visit a nearby section of the Great Wall. The day was cold, the wind cutting, the sun a dim watermark on the gray sky, and no one said much as we trudged up the steep stone ramparts that snaked along the mountain's spine. Sections of the Great Wall had been maintained since 200 B.C., our guide explained, although the portion where we were standing dated to the fifteenth century, an effort by the Ming dynasty to keep out Mongol and Manchu invaders. For hundreds of years, the wall had held. This prompted Reggie to ask me how the Ming dynasty finally ended.

"Internal strife," I said. "Power struggles, corruption, peasants starving 'cause the rich got greedy or just didn't care . . ."

"So, the usual," Reggie said.

I nodded. "The usual."

THE PRESIDENCY CHANGES your time horizons. Rarely do your efforts bear fruit right away; the scale of most problems coming across your desk is too big for that, the factors at play too varied. You learn to measure progress in smaller steps—each of which may take months to accomplish, none of which merit much public notice—and to reconcile yourself to the knowledge that your ultimate goal, if ever achieved, may take a year or two or even a full term to realize.

Nowhere is this truer than in the conduct of foreign

policy. So when, in the spring of 2010, we began to see results from some of our major diplomatic initiatives, I felt pretty encouraged. Tim Geithner reported that the Chinese had quietly started letting their currency appreciate. In April, I flew back to Prague, where Russian president Medvedev and I held a signing ceremony for the New START, which would cut the number of deployed nuclear warheads by a third on each side, with rigorous inspection mechanisms to ensure compliance.

And in June, with key votes from both Russia and China, the U.N. Security Council passed Resolution 1929, imposing unprecedented new sanctions on Iran, including a ban on weapons sales, a suspension of new international financial activities by Iranian banks, and a broad mandate to bar any commerce that could help Iran expand its nuclear weapons program. It would take a couple of years for Iran to feel the full effects, but in combination with a new set of U.S. sanctions, we now had the tools we needed to bring Iran's economy to a halt unless and until it agreed to negotiate. It also gave me a powerful rationale for counseling patience in conversations with Israelis and others who saw the nuclear issue as a handy excuse for a U.S.-Iran military confrontation.

Getting Russia and China on board had been a team effort. Hillary and Susan Rice spent countless hours cajoling, charming, and occasionally threatening their Russian and Chinese counterparts. McFaul, Burns, and Samore all provided critical strategic and technical support, helping us knock down or work around whatever objections the Russian and Chinese negotiators might present. And my relationship with Medvedev proved decisive in getting the sanctions finally in place. On the margins of each international summit I attended, he and I carved out time to work through logjams in the negotiations; as we got closer to the Security Council vote, it seemed as if we talked by phone once a week ("Our ears are getting sore," he joked toward the end of one marathon session). Time and again, Medvedev ended up going further than either Burns or McFaul had thought possible, given Moscow's long-standing ties to Iran and the millions that well-connected Russian arms manufacturers stood to lose once the new sanctions went into effect. On June 9, the day of the Security Council vote, Medvedev surprised us once again by announcing the cancellation of S-300 missiles sales to Iran, a reversal not only of his previous position but also of Putin's. To offset some of Russia's losses, we agreed to lift existing sanctions on several Russian firms that had previously sold arms to Iran; I also committed to speed up negotiations on Russia's belated entry into the WTO. Still, by aligning with us on Iran, Medvedev showed himself willing to stake his presidency on a closer relationship with the United States—a promising sign for future collaboration on our other international priorities, I told Rahm, "so long as Putin doesn't cut him off at the knees."

The passage of sanctions, the signing of the New START, some movement by China on improving its trade practices: These didn't qualify as world-changing victories. Certainly none of them merited a Nobel Prize—although had they happened eight or nine months earlier, I might have felt a little less sheepish about receiving the award. At most, these were building blocks, steps on a long and uncharted road. Could we create a nuclear-free future? Would we prevent another war in the Middle East? Was there a way to coexist peacefully with our most formidable rivals? None of us knew the answers—but for the moment, at least, it felt like we were on the path forward.

CHAPTER 21

AT DINNER ONE NIGHT, Malia asked me what I was going to do about tigers.

"What do you mean, sweetie?"

"Well, you know they're my favorite animal, right?"

Years earlier, during our annual Christmas visit to Hawaii, my sister Maya had taken a then-four-year-old Malia to the Honolulu Zoo. It was a small but charming place, tucked into the corner of Kapiʻolani Park near Diamond Head. As a kid I'd spent hours there, climbing the banyan trees, feeding the pigeons that waddled through the grass, howling at the long-limbed gibbons high up in the bamboo rafters. Malia had been captivated by one of the tigers during the visit, and her auntie had bought her a small, stuffed version of the great cat at the gift shop. "Tiger" had fat paws, a round belly, and an inscrutable Mona Lisa smile, and he and Malia became inseparable—though by the time we got to the White House, his fur was a little worse for wear, having survived food spills, several near losses during sleepovers, multiple washings, and a brief kidnapping at the hands of a mischievous cousin.

I had a soft spot for Tiger.

"Well," Malia continued, "I did a report about tigers

for school, and they're losing their habitat because people are cutting down the forests. And it's getting worse, 'cause the planet's getting warmer from pollution. Plus, people kill them and sell their fur and bones and stuff. So tigers are going extinct, which would be terrible. And since you're the president, you should try to save them."

Sasha chimed in, "You should do something, Daddy."

I looked at Michelle, who shrugged. "You **are** the president," she said.

THE TRUTH IS, I was grateful that my young daughters weren't shy about pointing out the responsibility of the adults around them to help preserve a healthy planet. Although I've lived all my life in cities, many of my best memories involve the outdoors. Some of this is just the product of my Hawaiian upbringing, where hikes through lush mountain forests or afternoons slicing through turquoise waves are a birthright, as easy as stepping out your front door—pleasures that cost nothing, belonged to no one, and were accessible to all. My time in Indonesia, running along terraced paddy fields as water buffalo glanced up with mud-covered snouts, had reinforced a love of open space; so did my travels in my twenties, a time when—thanks to a lack of attachments and a tolerance for cheap lodgings—I'd had the chance to trek through Appalachian trails, paddle a canoe down the Mississippi, and watch the sun rise over the Serengeti.

My mother reinforced this affinity for the natural world. In the grandeur of its design—the skeleton of a leaf, the labors of an ant colony, the glow of a bleach-white moon—she experienced the wonder and humility that others reserved for religious worship, and in our youth, she'd lectured Maya and me about the damage humans could inflict when they were careless in building cities or drilling oil or throwing away garbage. ("Pick up that candy wrapper, Bar!") She'd pointed out, as well, how the burdens of such damage most often fell on the poor, who had no choice about where to live and couldn't shield themselves from poisoned air and contaminated water.

But if my mother was an environmentalist at heart, I don't remember her ever applying the label to herself. I think it's because she'd spent most of her career working in Indonesia, where the dangers of pollution paled in comparison to more immediate risks—like hunger. For millions of struggling villagers who lived in developing countries, the addition of a coal-fired electrical generator or a new, smoke-belching factory often represented their best chance for more income and relief from backbreaking toil. To them, worrying about maintaining pristine landscapes and exotic wildlife was a luxury only Westerners could afford.

"You can't save trees by ignoring people," my mother would say.

This notion—that for most of humankind, concern about the environment came only after their basic material needs were met—stuck with me. Years later, as a community organizer, I helped mobilize public housing residents to press for the cleanup of asbestos in their neighborhood; in the state legislature, I was a reliable enough "green" vote that the League of Conservation Voters endorsed me when I ran for the U.S. Senate. Once on Capitol Hill, I criticized the Bush administration's efforts to weaken various anti-pollution laws and championed efforts to preserve the Great Lakes. But at no stage in my political career had I made environmental issues my calling card. Not because I didn't consider them important but because for my constituents, many of whom were working-class, poor air quality or industrial runoff took a backseat to the need for better housing, education, healthcare, and jobs. I figured somebody else could worry about the trees.

The ominous realities of climate change forced a shift in my perspective.

Each year, it seemed, the prognosis worsened, as an ever-increasing cloud of carbon dioxide and other greenhouse gases—from power plants, factories, cars, trucks, planes, industrial-scale livestock operations, deforestation, and all the other hallmarks of growth and modernization—contributed to record temperatures. By the time I was running for president, the clear consensus among scientists was that in the absence of bold, coordinated international action to reduce emissions, global temperatures were destined to climb another two degrees Celsius within a few decades. Past that point, the planet could experience an acceleration of melting ice caps, rising oceans, and extreme weather from which there was no return.

The human toll of a rapid climate shift was hard to predict. But the best estimates involved a hellish combination of severe coastal flooding, drought, wildfires, and hurricanes that stood to displace millions of people and overwhelm the capacities of most governments. This in turn would increase the risk of global conflict and insect-borne disease. Reading the literature, I pictured caravans of lost souls wandering a cracked earth in search of arable land, regular Katrina-sized catastrophes across every continent, island nations swallowed up by the sea. I wondered what would happen to Hawaii, or the great glaciers of Alaska, or the city of New Orleans. I imagined Malia, Sasha, and my grandchildren living in a harsher, more dangerous world, stripped of many of the wondrous sights I'd taken for granted growing up.

If I aspired to lead the free world, I decided, I'd have to make climate change a priority of my campaign and my presidency.

But how? Climate change is one of those issues governments are notoriously bad at dealing with, requiring politicians to put in place disruptive, expensive, and unpopular policies **now** in order to prevent a slow-rolling crisis in the future. Thanks to the work of a few farsighted leaders, like former vice president Al Gore, whose efforts to educate the public on global warming had garnered a Nobel Peace Prize and who remained active in the fight to mitigate climate change, awareness was slowly growing. Younger, more progressive voters were especially receptive to calls for action. Still, key Democratic interest groups—especially the big industrial unions—resisted any environmental measures that might threaten jobs for their members; and in polls we conducted at the start of my campaign, the average Democratic voter ranked climate change near the bottom of their list of concerns.

Republican voters were even more skeptical. There'd been a time when the federal government's role in protecting the environment enjoyed the support of both parties. Richard Nixon had worked with a Democratic Congress to create the Environmental Protection Agency (EPA) in 1970. George H. W. Bush championed a strengthening of the Clean Air Act in 1990. But those times had passed. As the GOP's electoral base had shifted to the South and the West, where conservation efforts had long rankled oil drillers, mining interests, developers, and ranchers, the party had turned environmental protection into another front in the partisan culture war. Conservative media outlets portrayed climate change as a job-killing hoax hatched by tree-hugging extremists. Big Oil funneled millions of dollars into a web of think tanks and public relations firms committed to obscuring the facts about climate change.

In contrast to his father, George W. Bush and members of his administration actively downplayed evidence of a warming planet and refused to engage in international efforts to curb greenhouse gases, despite the fact that for the first half of his presidency the United States ranked as the world's largest emitter of carbon dioxide. As for congressional Republicans, just acknowledging the reality of human-made climate change invited suspicion from party activists; suggesting shifts in policy to deal with it might get you a primary opponent.

"We're like pro-life Democrats," a former Republican Senate colleague with a nominally pro-environmental voting record told me ruefully one day. "We'll soon be extinct."

Faced with these realities, my team and I had done our best to highlight climate change during the campaign without costing ourselves too many votes. I came out early in favor of an ambitious "cap-and-trade" system to reduce greenhouse gases but avoided getting into details that might give future opponents a juicy target for attack. In speeches, I minimized the conflict between action on climate change and economic growth and made a point of emphasizing the nonenvironmental benefits of improving energy efficiency, including its potential to reduce our dependence on foreign oil. And in a nod to the political center, I promised an "all of the above" energy policy that would allow for continued development of domestic oil and gas production as America transitioned to clean energy, as well as funding for ethanol, clean coal technologies, and nuclear power—positions that were unpopular with environmentalists but mattered deeply to swing-state constituencies.

My happy talk about a painless shift to a carbon-free future prompted grumbling from some climate change activists. They hoped to hear me issue a call for bigger sacrifice and harder choices—including a moratorium or outright ban on oil and gas drilling—in order to confront an existential threat. In a perfectly rational world, that might have made sense. In the actual and highly irrational world of American politics, my staff and I were pretty sure that having me paint doomsday scenarios was a bad electoral strategy.

"We won't be doing anything to protect the environment," Plouffe had barked when questioned by a group of advocates, "if we lose Ohio and Pennsylvania!"

WITH THE ECONOMY in a tailspin, the politics around climate change actually worsened after the election ("Nobody gives a shit about solar panels when their home's in foreclosure," Axe said bluntly), and there was speculation in the press that we might quietly put the issue on the back burner. I suppose it's a measure of both my cockiness at the time and the importance of the issue that the thought never crossed my mind. Instead, I told Rahm to put climate change on the same priority footing as healthcare, and to start assembling a team capable of moving our agenda forward.

We got off to a good start when we convinced Carol Browner—who'd headed the EPA during the Clinton administration—to serve in the newly created position of White House "climate czar," coordinating our efforts across key agencies. Tall and willowy, with an endearing mix of nervous energy and can-do enthusiasm, Carol possessed intimate knowledge of the issue, contacts across Capitol Hill, and credibility with all the major environmental groups. To lead the EPA, I appointed Lisa Jackson, an African American chemical engineer who'd spent fifteen years at the agency and later became New Jersey's commissioner of environmental protection. She was a savvy political operator, with the charm and easy humor of her native New Orleans. To fully understand the scientific frontiers involved in transforming America's energy sector, we relied on my secretary of energy, Steven Chu—a Nobel Prize–winning physicist from Stanford and the previous director of California's renowned Lawrence Berkeley National Laboratory. Steve looked the part of an academic, with wire-rimmed glasses and an earnest but slightly distracted air, and more than once staffers would have to search the White House grounds because he'd lost track of his schedule and wandered off just as we were about to start a meeting. But he was as smart as his résumé indicated, with a gift for explaining highly technical issues in terms that smaller-brained humans like me could actually understand.

With Carol playing point, our climate change brain trust proposed a comprehensive policy agenda that included, among other measures, setting a hard cap on carbon emissions, which—if successful—could cut U.S. greenhouse gas emissions by 80 percent by 2050. It wouldn't be enough to keep the planet's temperature from rising more than two degrees Celsius, but it would at least get the ball rolling and provide a framework for more aggressive cuts down the road. Just as important, establishing an ambitious but realistic target would give America the standing to push the world's other major emitters—especially China—to follow our example. The goal was to negotiate and sign a major international climate agreement before the end of my presidency. We began with the Recovery Act, understanding that we had an opportunity to use stimulus dollars to transform the energy sector, making investments in clean energy research and development that would lead to steep declines in the cost of wind and solar power. Our calculus was simple: To hit our greenhouse gas reduction targets, we would have to wean the U.S. economy off fossil fuels—and we couldn't do that without effective alternatives.

Keep in mind that in 2009, electric cars were still a novelty. Solar panel manufacturers catered only to a niche market. And solar- and wind-generated power accounted for only a small fraction of America's total electricity output—both because it still cost more than power from coal- and gas-fueled generators and because there were legitimate questions about its reliability when the sun didn't shine or the wind didn't blow. Experts were confident that costs would keep dropping as more clean power generators came online, and that the development of more efficient battery storage technologies could solve the reliability problem. But building new power plants took lots of money, as did energy R&D, and neither private sector investors nor major utility companies had shown much of an appetite for making what felt like risky bets. Certainly not now, when even the most successful clean power companies were scrambling to keep their doors open.

In fact, just about every renewable energy company, from advanced vehicle manufacturers to biofuel producers, faced the same dilemma: No matter how good their technology was, they still had to operate in an economy that for more than a century had been constructed almost entirely around oil, gas, and coal. This structural disadvantage wasn't simply the result of free-market forces. Federal, state, and local governments had invested trillions of dollars—whether through direct subsidies and tax breaks or through the construction of infrastructure like pipelines, highways, and port terminals—to help maintain both the steady supply of and the constant demand for cheap fossil fuels. U.S. oil companies were among the world's most profitable corporations and yet still received millions in federal tax breaks each year. To have a fair chance to compete, the clean energy sector needed a serious boost.

That's what we hoped the Recovery Act could deliver.

Of the roughly $800 billion in available stimulus, we directed more than $90 billion toward clean energy initiatives across the country. Within a year, an Iowa Maytag plant I'd visited during the campaign that had been shuttered because of the recession was humming again, with workers producing state-of-the-art wind turbines. We funded construction of one of the world's largest wind farms. We underwrote the development of new battery storage systems and primed the market for electric and hybrid trucks, buses, and cars. We financed programs to make buildings and businesses more energy efficient, and collaborated with Treasury to temporarily convert the existing federal clean energy tax credit into a direct-payments program. Within the Department of Energy, we used Recovery Act money to launch the Advanced Research Projects Agency–Energy (ARPA-E), a high-risk, high-reward research program modeled after DARPA, the famous Defense Department effort launched after **Sputnik** that helped develop not only advanced weapons systems like stealth technology but also an early iteration of the internet, automated voice activation, and GPS.

It was exciting stuff—although our pursuit of game-changing energy breakthroughs almost guaranteed that some Recovery Act investments wouldn't pan out. The most conspicuous flop involved a decision to expand an Energy Department loan program started during the Bush administration that offered long-term working capital to promising clean energy companies. On the whole, the Energy Department's Loan Guarantee Program would yield an impressive track record, helping innovative companies like the carmaker Tesla take their businesses to the next level. The default rate on its loans was a measly 3 percent, and the idea was that the fund's successes would more than make up for its handful of failures.

Unfortunately one of the larger defaults would occur on my watch: a whopping $535 million loan to a solar panel company named Solyndra. The company had patented what was then considered revolutionary technology, but of course the investment carried risk. As the Chinese flooded the markets with cheap, heavily subsidized solar panels of their own, Solyndra began to teeter and in 2011 would go belly-up. Given the size of the default—not to mention the fact that my team had arranged for me to visit the company's California facility just as the first financial warning bells were beginning to ring—Solyndra became a PR nightmare. The press would spend weeks highlighting the story. Republicans reveled.

I tried to take it in stride. I reminded myself that it was part and parcel of the presidency for nothing to ever work exactly as planned. Even successful initiatives—well executed and with the purest of intentions—usually harbored some hidden flaw or unanticipated consequence. Getting things done meant subjecting yourself to criticism, and the alternative—playing it safe, avoiding controversy, following the polls—was not only a recipe for mediocrity but a betrayal of the hopes of those citizens who'd put you in office.

Still, as time went by, I couldn't help but fume (sometimes I'd actually picture myself with steam puffing out of my ears, as in a cartoon) at how Solyndra's failure stood to overshadow the Recovery Act's remarkable success in galvanizing the renewable energy sector. Even in its first year, our "clean energy moonshot" had begun to invigorate the economy, generate jobs, trigger a surge in solar- and wind-power generation, as well as a leap in energy efficiency, and mobilize an arsenal of new technologies to help combat climate change. I delivered speeches across the country, explaining the significance of all this. "It's working!" I wanted to shout. But environmental activists and clean energy companies aside, no one seemed to care. It was nice to know, as one executive assured us, that without the Recovery Act "the entire solar and wind industry in the U.S. would've probably been wiped out." That didn't stop me from wondering how long we could keep championing policies that paid long-term dividends but still somehow resulted in us getting clobbered over the head.

OUR INVESTMENT IN clean energy was only the first step in meeting our greenhouse gas emissions targets. We also had to change America's day-to-day energy habits, whether that meant companies rethinking how they heated and cooled their buildings or families deciding to go green on the next car they bought. We hoped to bring about some of this through a climate change bill designed to tilt incentives toward clean energy across the economy. But according to Lisa and Carol, we didn't need to wait for congressional action to alter at least some business and consumer behavior. We just had to take full advantage of our regulatory powers under existing law.

The most important of those laws was the Clean Air Act, the 1963 landmark legislation that authorized the federal government to monitor air pollution, leading to the establishment of enforceable clean air standards in the 1970s. The law, which had been reaffirmed with support from both parties in Congress as recently as 1990, stated that the EPA "shall by regulation" set standards to curb auto emissions that "in [its] judgment cause, or contribute to, air pollution which may reasonably be anticipated to endanger public health or welfare."

If you believed in climate science, then the carbon

dioxide pouring out of automobile tailpipes clearly qualified as air pollution. Apparently, President Bush's EPA
administrator didn't (believe in science, that is). In 2003,
he determined that the Clean Air Act wasn't meant to
give the agency authority to regulate greenhouse gases—
and that even if it did, he **still** wouldn't use it to change
emission standards. Several states and environmental
organizations sued, and in the 2007 ruling **Massachusetts
v. EPA,** a narrow majority of the U.S. Supreme Court
held that President Bush's EPA had failed to apply
"reasoned judgment" based on science in making its
determination and ordered the agency to go back and
redo its homework.

For the next two years the Bush administration did
nothing, but we were now in a position to take the
Supreme Court's decision out for a spin. Lisa and Carol
recommended that we gather up the scientific evidence,
issue a finding that greenhouse gases were subject to EPA
regulation, and immediately use that authority to raise
fuel-efficiency standards for all cars and trucks built or
sold in the United States. Circumstances couldn't have
been more favorable for that sort of rulemaking: Although
U.S. carmakers and the United Auto Workers (UAW)
generally opposed higher fuel-efficiency standards, my
decision to continue devoting billions in TARP money
to keep their industry afloat had made them "more open-
minded," as Carol so delicately put it. If we acted fast
enough, Lisa thought, we could have regulations in place
before the automakers' next model year. The resulting
drop in U.S. gasoline consumption could save roughly
1.8 billion barrels of oil and reduce our annual greenhouse gas emissions by 20 percent; we'd also establish a

useful precedent for having the EPA regulate other greenhouse gas sources in future years.

To me, the plan was a no-brainer, though Rahm and I agreed that even with the automakers on board, having the EPA issue new mileage standards would generate plenty of political static. After all, GOP leaders considered the rollback of federal regulations a tier-one priority, right up there with lowering taxes on the rich. Business groups and big conservative donors like the Koch brothers had invested heavily in a decades-long campaign to make "regulation" a dirty word; you couldn't open the editorial pages of **The Wall Street Journal** without finding some attack on an out-of-control "regulatory state." To the anti-regulation crowd, the pros and cons of higher mileage standards mattered less than what a new rule symbolized: yet another example of unelected Washington bureaucrats trying to micromanage people's lives, sap America's economic vitality, violate private property rights, and undermine the Founding Fathers' vision of representative government.

I didn't put a lot of stock in such arguments. As far back as the Progressive Era, oil trusts and railroad monopolies had used similar language to attack government efforts to loosen their stranglehold on the U.S. economy. So had opponents of FDR's New Deal. And yet throughout the twentieth century, in law after law and in cooperation with presidents of both parties, Congress had kept delegating regulatory and enforcement authority to a host of specialized agencies, from the U.S. Securities and Exchange Commission (SEC) to the Occupational Safety and Health Administration (OSHA) to the Federal Aviation Administration (FAA).

The reason was simple: As society grew more complex, corporations grew more powerful, and citizens demanded more from the government, elected officials simply did not have time to regulate so many diverse industries. Nor did they have the specialized knowledge required to set rules for fair dealing across financial markets, evaluate the safety of the latest medical device, make sense of new pollution data, or anticipate all the ways employers might discriminate against their employees on account of race or gender.

In other words, if you wanted good government, then expertise mattered. You needed public institutions stocked with people whose job it was to pay attention to important stuff so the rest of us citizens didn't have to. And it was thanks to those experts that Americans could worry less about the quality of the air we breathed or the water we drank, that we had recourse when employers failed to pay us the overtime we were due, that we could count on over-the-counter drugs not killing us, and that driving a car or flying on a commercial airplane was exponentially safer today than it had been just twenty or thirty or fifty years ago. The "regulatory state" conservatives complained so bitterly about had made American life a hell of a lot better.

That's not to say that every criticism of federal regulation was bogus. There were times when bureaucratic red tape burdened businesses unnecessarily or delayed innovative products from getting to market. Some regulations really did cost more than they were worth. Environmental groups, in particular, hated a 1980 law that required an obscure executive branch subagency called the Office of Information and Regulatory Affairs (OIRA) to perform a cost-benefit analysis on every new federal regulation. They were convinced that the process favored corporate interests, and they had a point: It was a lot easier to measure a business's profits and losses than it was to put a price on preserving an endangered bird or reducing the probability that a kid got asthma.

Still, for both policy and political reasons, I felt that progressives couldn't afford to ignore economics. Those of us who believed in the government's ability to solve big problems had an obligation to pay attention to the real-world impact of our decisions and not just trust in the goodness of our intentions. If a proposed agency rule to preserve wetlands was going to lop acreage off a family farm, that agency should have to take the farmer's losses into account before moving forward.

It was precisely because I cared about getting this stuff right that I appointed Cass Sunstein, a former colleague at the University of Chicago Law School, to head up OIRA and serve as our resident cost-benefit expert. An eminent constitutional scholar who'd written a dozen books and was often mentioned as a future Supreme Court justice, Cass actually lobbied me for the OIRA post, an indication of his passion for service, his indifference to prestige, and a high nerd quotient that made him ideally suited for the job. (He was also sweet as can be, a world-class squash player, and the individual with the single most slovenly desk I ever set eyes on.) Over the next three years, Cass and his small team would grind away in the nondescript OIRA office across the street from the White House, ensuring that the regulations we proposed actually helped enough people to justify their costs. I also asked him to lead a thorough review of all existing federal regulations so that we could get rid of those that were unnecessary or obsolete.

Cass unearthed some doozies: old requirements that forced hospitals, doctors, and nurses to spend more than $1 billion annually on paperwork requirements and administrative burdens; a bizarre environmental regulation that classified milk as "oil," subjecting dairy farmers to annual costs in excess of $100 million; and a pointless mandate imposed on truckers to spend $1.7 billion in wasted time filling out forms after each run. But the vast majority of regulations Cass reviewed stood up to scrutiny—and by the end of my presidency, even Republican analysts would find that the benefits of our regulations outweighed their costs by a six-to-one margin.

Lisa and Carol's proposal to raise mileage standards ended up being one of those regulations. As soon as I gave them the go-ahead, they got to work. They had a good partner in my secretary of transportation, Ray LaHood, a former congressman from Peoria and a gentlemanly old-school Republican whose gregarious nature and earnest commitment to bipartisanship made him popular on both sides of the aisle. On a sunny day in May, I found myself standing in the Rose Garden, flanked by a group of auto-industry leaders, as well as the president of the UAW, to announce an agreement that would boost fuel efficiency on all new cars and light trucks from 27.5 miles per gallon to 35.5 by 2016. The plan stood to cut greenhouse gas emissions by more than 900 million metric tons over the lifetime of the new vehicles, the equivalent of taking 177 million cars off the road or shutting down 194 coal-fired power plants.

In their remarks that day, the automakers stayed on message, expressing confidence in their ability to meet the new targets and the benefits to their business of having a single national standard rather than a patchwork of different state laws. The speed and lack of contentiousness with which we'd arrived at a deal took reporters by surprise, and several of them asked Carol what role the auto bailout might have played in sparking this newfound kumbaya spirit. "Not once did we ever mention bailouts during negotiations," she insisted. Later, in the Oval, I asked her if what she'd said was true.

"Absolutely," she answered. "Of course, I can't say the bailouts never crossed their minds . . ."

Meanwhile, I set Steve Chu on a mission to update every efficiency standard he could find, using the power of a little-enforced 1987 law that gave the Department of Energy authority to set energy-efficiency standards on everything from lightbulbs to commercial air conditioners. The man was like a kid in a candy store, regaling me with detailed explanations of his latest standard-setting exploits. ("You'd be amazed at the environmental impact of just a five percent improvement on refrigerator efficiency!") And although it was hard to match his excitement over washers and dryers, the results really were pretty amazing: By the time I left office, those new appliance standards were on track to remove another 210 million metric tons of greenhouse gases from the atmosphere annually.

Over the next several years, carmakers and appliance manufacturers hit the higher efficiency goals we'd set without much fuss and ahead of schedule, confirming Steve's assertion that when done properly, ambitious regulatory standards actually spurred businesses to innovate. If consumers noticed that the energy-efficient models of cars or appliances were sometimes more expensive, they didn't complain; they were likely to make up the difference in lower electricity bills or fuel costs, and prices typically settled back down once the new technologies became the norm.

To our surprise, even McConnell and Boehner didn't get particularly worked up about our energy regulations—perhaps because they didn't think it was a winning issue for them and didn't want to divert attention from their efforts to defeat Obamacare. Not all Republicans showed such restraint. One day, Pete Rouse wandered into the Oval to show me media clips containing various remarks from Congresswoman Michele Bachmann of Minnesota, founder of the House Tea Party Caucus and an eventual Republican candidate for president. Bachmann had been decrying newfangled energy-efficient lightbulbs as an un-American "Big Brother intrusion" and a threat to public health; they also signaled what she declared to be a larger plot by Democrats to impose a radical "sustainability" agenda, in which all U.S. citizens would eventually be forced to "move to the urban core, live in tenements, [and] take light rail to their government jobs."

"Looks like our secret is out, Mr. President," Pete said.

I nodded gravely. "Better hide the recycling bins."

WHILE ENERGY-SAVING cars and dishwashers were a step forward, the ultimate pathway to lasting change, we knew, lay in getting comprehensive climate legislation through Congress. A bill had the potential to reach every sector of the economy that contributed to greenhouse gas emissions, not just vehicles and appliances. On top of that, the news stories and public dialogue sparked by the legislative process would help drive home the perils of rising global temperatures, and—if all went well—Congress would feel a sense of ownership of the final product. Perhaps most important, federal legislation would have genuine staying power, unlike regulations, which could be reversed unilaterally by a future Republican administration.

Of course, legislation depended on our ability to overcome a Senate filibuster. And unlike the situation with the Recovery Act, where when push came to shove we'd been able to marshal every Democratic vote we needed, Harry Reid warned me that we were certain to lose at least a couple of Senate Dems from oil- and coal-producing states who were looking at tough reelections. To get sixty votes, we were going to need to convince at least two or three Republicans to support a bill that a majority of their voters firmly opposed, and that Mitch McConnell had sworn to defeat.

Initially, at least, we thought our best bet was the guy I'd beat in the race for president.

John McCain had downplayed his support for climate change legislation during his campaign, especially after he selected a running mate whose energy policy—"Drill, baby, drill!"—proved to be a Republican crowd favorite. But to his credit, McCain had never fully abandoned the position he'd staked out earlier in his Senate career, and in the (very) brief halo of good feeling right after the election, he and I had discussed working together to get a climate bill passed. Around the time I was sworn into office, McCain had reportedly joined forces with his best buddy in the Senate, Joe Lieberman, to put together a bipartisan alternative to more liberal legislation being proposed by Barbara Boxer, the California Democrat who chaired the Environment and Public Works Committee.

Unfortunately, inside GOP circles, McCain's brand of bipartisan compromise was badly out of fashion. Right-wingers despised him more than ever, blaming his lack of conservative conviction for Republican losses in the House and Senate. In late January 2009, a former congressman and right-wing radio host named J. D. Hayworth floated the possibility of running against McCain in the Arizona primary the next year—the first serious challenge McCain had faced since joining the Senate twenty-two years earlier. I imagine the sheer indignity of the situation must have made McCain's blood boil, but the politician in him dictated that he quickly shore up his right flank—and joining forces with me on major environmental legislation certainly wasn't going to do that. We soon got word through Lieberman's office that McCain was off the bill.

At the same time, not a single House Republican would even consider cosponsoring climate legislation. That left the two senior Democrats on the relevant committee, Henry Waxman of California and Ed Markey of Massachusetts, content to draft a bill on their own and pass it solely with Democratic votes. In the short term, this made our lives easier: Waxman and Markey broadly aligned with us on policy, their staffs knew what they were doing, and they welcomed our suggestions. But it also meant that the two congressmen felt little need to consider views less liberal than existed inside their own caucus, raising the prospect that the bill they produced could end up reading like an environmental group's wish list and send a number of fence-sitting Senate Democrats into cardiac arrest.

Hoping to head off a House/Senate impasse, Rahm gave Phil Schiliro the unenviable task of urging Waxman to start a dialogue with the likely sponsors of a Senate bill, including Lieberman, so that we could get a jump on narrowing the differences between the two sides. A week or so later, I called Phil into the Oval and asked how the conversation with Waxman had gone. Phil dropped his gangly frame onto the couch, grabbed an apple from the bowl I kept on the coffee table, and shrugged.

"Not great," he said, his voice landing somewhere between a chuckle and a sigh. Before joining my team, Phil had spent years working in Waxman's office, most recently as chief of staff, so the two knew each other well. Waxman had given him an earful, he said, channeling the frustration that House Dems already felt toward the Senate Dems (and us) for what they considered to be a litany of previous sins: scaling back the Recovery Act, failing to even bring various House bills up for a vote for fear of putting moderate or conservative senators in a bind, and generally being spineless tools.

"He said the Senate is 'the place where good ideas go to die,'" Phil said.

"Can't argue with him there," I said.

"We'll just have to sort it all out in a conference committee, after each chamber's passed its own bill," Phil said, trying his best to project an upbeat tone.

In our effort to keep the House and Senate bills at least within shouting distance of each other, we did have one thing working in our favor: Lieberman and Boxer, as well as the House Dems and most environmental groups, had embraced a cap-and-trade system similar to what I'd endorsed during the campaign as the preferred mechanism to achieve big cuts in greenhouse gases. Here's how it worked: The federal government would cap the amount of greenhouse gas companies could emit, leaving it up to each company to figure out how to hit those targets. Companies exceeding their limit would pay a penalty. Companies that stayed below their limit could sell their unused pollution "credits" to less-efficient businesses. By setting a price on pollution and creating a market for environmentally friendly behavior, a cap-and-trade approach gave corporations an incentive to develop and adopt the latest green technologies; and with each technological advance, the government could lower the caps even further, encouraging a steady and virtuous cycle of innovation.

There were other ways to put a price on greenhouse gas pollution. Some economists thought it was simpler, for example, to impose a "carbon tax" on all fossil fuels, discouraging their use by making them more expensive. But one of the reasons everyone had converged on a cap-and-trade proposal was that it had already been successfully tried—and **by a Republican president,** no less. Back in 1990, George H. W. Bush's administration had put a cap-and-trade system in place to curb the sulfur dioxide coming out of factory smokestacks and contributing to acid rain, which was destroying lakes and forests across the East Coast. Despite dire predictions that the measure would lead to factory closures and mass layoffs, the offending companies had quickly figured out

cost-efficient ways to retrofit their factories, and within a
few years, the problem of acid rain had all but disappeared.

Setting up a cap-and-trade system for greenhouse gas
emissions involved a whole new level of scale and complexity. The fights over each detail promised to be fierce,
with lobbyists swarming and every member of Congress
whose vote we needed angling for this or that concession.
And as the struggle to pass healthcare legislation was also
teaching me, the mere fact that Republicans had once
supported a policy idea championed by one of their own
did not mean they'd support **the exact same idea** coming
from a Democratic president.

Still, I had to believe that having a successful precedent gave us a real shot at getting a deal done. Carol,
Phil, and the rest of the White House legislative staff
spent much of spring 2009 shuttling back and forth
between chambers, prodding the action along, smooth-
ing over problems, and providing the main players and
their staffs with whatever technical support or policy
guidance they needed. All this was happening while we
were still trying to mend the economy, pull the healthcare bill into shape, put an immigration package
together, get judicial nominees confirmed, and move a
dozen other smaller initiatives through Congress—
a testament to how hard the team drove itself. It also
lent Rahm's office—sparsely decorated, the big conference table at its center usually littered with coffee cups,
cans of Diet Coke, and the occasional half-eaten snack—
the overcaffeinated atmosphere of an air traffic control
center.

Then, on a muggy day in late June, our labors started

to pay off. The White House Social Office had arranged for a staff picnic on the South Lawn, and I had just begun circulating through the crowd, holding babies and posing for pictures with the proud parents of staff members, when Rahm came bounding across the grass, a sheet of paper rolled up in his hand.

"The House just passed a climate bill, Mr. President," he said.

"That's great!" I said, giving him a high five. "How close was the vote?"

Rahm showed me his tally: 219–212. "We actually got eight moderate Republicans. We lost a couple of Dems we were counting on, but I'll deal with them. In the meantime, you should call Nancy, Waxman, and Markey to thank them. They had to work the members pretty hard."

Rahm lived for days like this, when we scored a clear win. But as we walked back to the Oval, stopping to greet others along the way, I noticed that my usually irrepressible chief of staff seemed a little subdued. Rahm went on to explain what was nagging at him: So far, the Senate had failed to even release its version of a climate bill, much less start moving it through the relevant committees. McConnell, meanwhile, was displaying a singular talent for grinding Senate votes to a halt. Given the already slow process, the window for us getting a climate bill done before Congress adjourned in December was rapidly closing. And after that, we'd likely have even more trouble making it to the finish line, since Democrats in both the House and the Senate would be reluctant to vote on yet another big, controversial bill just as they started campaigning for the midterms.

"Gotta have faith, brother," I said, clapping him on the back.

Rahm nodded, but his eyes, even darker than usual, betrayed doubt.

"I just don't know if we've got enough runway to land all these planes," he said.

The implication being that one or more might crash.

THE SKITTISH MOOD in Congress was not the only reason I hoped to have cap-and-trade legislation in hand by December: There was a U.N. global summit on climate change due to happen in Copenhagen that same month. After eight years of the United States absenting itself from international climate negotiations under George W. Bush, expectations abroad were soaring. And I could hardly urge other governments to act aggressively on climate change if the United States didn't lead by example. I knew that having a domestic bill would improve our bargaining position with other nations and help spur the kind of collective action needed to protect the planet. Greenhouse gases, after all, don't respect borders. A law reducing emissions in one country might make its citizens feel morally superior, but if other nations didn't follow suit, temperatures would just keep rising. So as Rahm and my legislative team were busy in the halls of Congress, my foreign policy team and I looked for a way to restore America's stature as a leader in international climate efforts.

Our leadership on this front had once been all but presumed. In 1992, when the world convened in Rio de Janeiro for what became known as the "Earth Summit," President George H. W. Bush joined representatives from 153 other nations in signing the U.N. Framework Convention on Climate Change—the first global agreement to try to stabilize greenhouse gas concentrations before they reached catastrophic levels. The Clinton administration soon took up the baton, working with other nations to translate the broad goals announced at Rio into a binding treaty. The final result, called the Kyoto Protocol, laid out detailed plans for coordinated international action, including specific greenhouse gas reduction targets, a global carbon-trading system similar to cap-and-trade, and financing mechanisms to help poor countries adopt clean energy and preserve carbon-neutralizing forests like the Amazon.

Environmentalists hailed Kyoto as a turning point in the fight against global warming. Around the world, participating countries got their governments to ratify the treaty. But in the United States, where treaty ratification requires an affirmative vote from two-thirds of the Senate, Kyoto hit a brick wall. It was 1997, Republicans controlled the Senate, and few considered climate change to be a real problem. Indeed, the then chair of the Senate Foreign Relations Committee, archconservative Jesse Helms, proudly despised environmentalists, the U.N., and multilateral treaties in equal measure. Powerful Democrats like West Virginia senator Robert Byrd were also quick to oppose any measures that might hurt fossil fuel industries vital to their state.

Seeing the writing on the wall, President Clinton decided not to send Kyoto to the Senate for a vote, preferring delay to defeat. Though Clinton's political fortunes would recover after he'd survived impeachment, Kyoto remained mothballed for the remainder of his presidency. Any glimmer of hope for the treaty's eventual ratification was snuffed out entirely once George W. Bush beat Al Gore in the 2000 election. Which is how it came to pass that in 2009, a year after the Kyoto Protocol finally went into full effect, the United States was one of only five nations not party to the agreement. The other four, in no particular order: Andorra and Vatican City (both of which were so tiny, with a combined population of about eighty thousand, that they were granted "observer" status rather than asked to join); Taiwan (which would have been happy to participate but couldn't because its status as an independent nation was still contested by the Chinese); and Afghanistan (which had the reasonable excuse of having been shattered by thirty years of occupation and a bloody civil war).

"You know things have hit a low point when our closest allies think we're worse on an issue than North Korea," Ben said, shaking his head.

Reviewing this history, I sometimes imagined a parallel universe in which the United States, without rival immediately following the end of the Cold War, had put its immense power and authority behind the climate change fight. I imagined the transformation of the world's energy grid and the reduction in greenhouse gases that might have been achieved; the geopolitical benefits that would have flowed from weakening the grip of petrodollars and the autocracies supported by those dollars; the culture of sustainability that could have taken root in developed and developing countries alike. But as I huddled with my team to chart a strategy for this universe, I had to acknowledge a glaring truth: Even with the Democrats now in charge of the Senate, there was still no way for me to secure sixty-seven votes to ratify the existing Kyoto framework.

We were having enough trouble getting the Senate to come up with a workable domestic climate bill. Barbara Boxer and Massachusetts Democrat John Kerry had spent months drafting potential legislation, but they'd been unable to find a Republican colleague willing to cosponsor it, signaling that the bill was unlikely to pass and that a new, more centrist approach might be in order.

Having lost John McCain as a Republican ally, our hopes shifted to one of his closest friends in the Senate, Lindsey Graham of South Carolina. Short in stature, with a puggish face and a gentle southern drawl that in an instant could flip from warm to menacing, Graham was known primarily as an ardent national security hawk—a member, along with McCain and Lieberman, of the so-called Three Amigos, who'd served as the biggest boosters of the Iraq War. Graham was also smart, charming, sarcastic, unscrupulous, media savvy, and—thanks partly to his genuine adoration of McCain—occasionally willing to stray from conservative orthodoxy, most notably in his support for immigration reform. Having been reelected to another six-year term, Graham was in a position to take some risks, and although he'd never shown much interest in climate change in the past, he seemed intrigued by the possibility of filling McCain's shoes and brokering a meaningful bipartisan deal. Early in October, he offered to help deliver the handful of Republicans needed to get climate legislation through the Senate—but only if Lieberman helped steer the process and Kerry could convince environmentalists to offer up concessions on subsidies for the nuclear power industry and the opening up of additional U.S. coastlines to offshore oil drilling.

I wasn't wild about having to depend on Graham. I knew him from my time in the Senate as someone who liked to play the role of the sophisticated, self-aware conservative, disarming Democrats and reporters with blunt assessments of his party's blind spots, extolling the need for politicians to break out of their ideological straitjackets. More often than not, though, when it came time to actually cast a vote or take a position that might cost him politically, Graham seemed to find a reason to wriggle out of it. ("You know how in the spy thriller or the heist movie, you're introduced to the crew at the beginning?" I told Rahm. "Lindsey's the guy who double-crosses everyone to save his own skin.") Realistically, though, our options were limited ("Unless Lincoln and Teddy Roosevelt are walking through that door, buddy," Rahm replied, "he's all we got"); and mindful that any close association with the White House might spook him, we decided to give Graham and his fellow cosponsors a wide berth as they crafted their version of the bill, figuring we could fix any troublesome provisions later in the process.

Meanwhile, we prepared for what lay ahead in Copenhagen. With the Kyoto Protocol set to expire in 2012, U.N.-sponsored negotiations for a follow-up treaty had been under way for over a year already, with the goal of finalizing an agreement in time for the December summit. We weren't, however, inclined to sign a new treaty modeled too closely on the original. My advisors and I had concerns about Kyoto's policy design—in particular, its use of a concept called "common but differentiated responsibilities," which placed the burden of cutting greenhouse gas emissions almost exclusively on advanced, energy-intensive economies like those of the United States, the European Union, and Japan. As a matter of fairness, asking rich countries to do more about climate change than poor countries made complete sense: Not only was the existing buildup of greenhouse gases largely the result of a hundred years of Western industrialization, but rich countries also had a much higher per capita carbon footprint than other places. And there were limits to how much you could expect poor countries like Mali, Haiti, or Cambodia—places where lots of people still lacked even basic electricity—to cut their already negligible emissions (and possibly slow their short-term growth). After all, Americans or Europeans could achieve far greater effects simply by adjusting their thermostats up or down a few degrees.

The trouble was, the Kyoto Protocol had interpreted "differentiated responsibilities" to mean that emerging powers like China, India, and Brazil had **no** binding obligations to curb their emissions. This might have made sense when the protocol was drawn up, twelve years earlier, before globalization had fully transformed the world economy. But in the middle of a brutal recession, with Americans already seething over the steady outsourcing of U.S. jobs, a treaty that placed environmental constraints on domestic factories without asking for parallel action from those operating in Shanghai or Bangalore just wasn't going to fly. As it was, China had surpassed the United States in annual carbon dioxide emissions in 2005, with India's numbers also on the rise.

And while it remained true that the average Chinese or Indian citizen consumed a fraction of the energy used by the average American, experts projected a doubling of those countries' carbon footprints in the coming decades, as more and more of their two billion–plus people aspired to the same modern conveniences that folks in rich countries enjoyed. If that happened, then the planet was going to be underwater regardless of what anybody else did—an argument that Republicans (at least those who didn't deny climate change altogether) liked to use as an excuse for having the United States do nothing at all.

We needed a fresh approach. With critical guidance from Hillary Clinton and the State Department's special envoy for climate change, Todd Stern, my team came up with a proposal for a scaled-back interim agreement, anchored around three shared commitments. First, the agreement would require **every** nation—including emerging powers like China and India—to put forward a self-determined plan for greenhouse gas reduction. Each country's plan would differ based on its wealth, energy profile, and stage of development and would be revised at regular intervals as that country's economic and technological capacities increased. Second, while these national plans wouldn't be enforceable under international law the way treaty obligations were, each country would agree to measures allowing the other parties to independently verify that it was following through on its pledged reductions. Third, wealthy countries would provide poor countries with billions of dollars in aid for climate mitigation and adaptation, so long as those poor countries met their (far more modest) commitments.

Designed right, this new approach would force China and other emerging powers to start putting skin in the game, while also retaining the Kyoto concept of "common but differentiated responsibilities." By establishing a credible system to validate other countries' efforts to reduce emissions, we'd also strengthen our case with Congress for the need to pass our own domestic climate change legislation—and, we hoped, lay the groundwork for a more robust treaty in the near future. But Todd, an intense, detail-oriented lawyer who'd served as the Clinton administration's senior negotiator at Kyoto, warned that our proposal would be a tough sell internationally. The E.U. countries, all of which had ratified Kyoto and taken steps to reduce emissions, were anxious to come up with a pact that included legally binding reduction commitments from the United States and China. China, India, and South Africa, on the other hand, liked the status quo just fine and were fiercely resisting any changes to Kyoto. Activists and environmental groups from around the globe were scheduled to attend the summit. Many of them saw Copenhagen as a make-or-break moment and would consider anything short of a binding treaty with tough new limits as a failure.

More specifically, **my** failure.

"It's not fair," Carol said, "but they think that if you're serious about climate change, you should be able to get Congress and other countries to do whatever's necessary."

I couldn't blame environmentalists for setting a high bar. The science demanded it. But I also knew it was pointless to make promises I could not yet keep. I'd need more time and a better economy before I could persuade the American public to support an ambitious climate treaty. I was also going to need to convince China to work with us—and I was probably going to need a bigger majority in the Senate. If the world was expecting the United States to sign a binding treaty at Copenhagen, then I needed to lower expectations—starting with those of the secretary-general of the United Nations, Ban Ki-moon.

Two years into his term as the world's most prominent diplomat, Ban Ki-moon had yet to make much of an impression on the global stage. Some of this was just the nature of the job: Although the U.N. secretary-general presides over a budget of many billions of dollars, a sprawling bureaucracy, and a host of international agencies, his or her power is largely derivative, dependent on an ability to herd 193 countries toward something resembling a common direction. Ban's relatively low profile was also the result of his understated, methodical style—a paint-by-numbers approach to diplomacy that had undoubtedly served him well during his thirty-seven-year career in his native South Korea's foreign service and diplomatic corps but that stood in sharp contrast to the urbane charisma of his predecessor at the U.N., Kofi Annan. You didn't go into a meeting with Ban expecting to hear captivating stories, witty asides, or dazzling insights. He didn't ask how your family was doing or share details of his own life outside the job. Instead, after a vigorous handshake and repeated thank-yous for seeing him, Ban would dive headlong into a stream of talking points and factoids, delivered in fluent but heavily accented English and the earnest, formulaic jargon of a U.N. communiqué.

Despite his lack of pizzazz, I would come to like and respect Ban. He was honest, straightforward, and irrepressibly positive, someone who on several occasions stood up to pressure from member states in pursuit of much-needed U.N. reforms and who instinctively came down on the right side of issues even if he didn't always have the capacity to move others to do the same. Ban was also persistent—especially on the topic of climate change, which he had designated as one of his top priorities. The first time we met in the Oval Office, less than two months after I'd taken office, he'd started pressing me for a commitment to attend the Copenhagen summit.

"Your presence, Mr. President," Ban said, "will send a very powerful signal about the urgent need for international cooperation on climate change. Very powerful."

I had explained all that we planned to do domestically to cut U.S. emissions, as well as the challenges of getting any Kyoto-style treaty through the Senate anytime soon. I described our idea of an interim agreement, and how we were forming a "major emitters group," separate from U.N.-sponsored negotiations, to see if we could find common ground with China on the issue. As I spoke, Ban nodded politely, occasionally jotting down notes or adjusting his glasses. But nothing I said appeared to knock him off his principal mission.

"With your critical engagement, Mr. President," he said, "I'm sure we can drive these negotiations to a successful agreement."

And so it went for months to come. No matter how many times I repeated my concerns about the course the U.N.-sponsored negotiations were taking, no matter how blunt I was about the U.S. position on a binding,

Kyoto-style treaty, Ban would return to underscoring the need for my presence at Copenhagen in December. He brought it up at G20 meetings. He raised it at G8 meetings. Finally, at the U.N. General Assembly plenary in New York in September, I relented, promising the secretary-general I'd do my best to attend so long as the conference appeared likely to produce an agreement we could live with. Afterward, I turned to Susan Rice and said I felt like a high schooler who'd been pressured to go to the prom with the nerdy kid who's too nice to reject.

By the time the Copenhagen conference kicked off in December, it seemed that my worst fears were coming to pass. Domestically, we were still waiting for the Senate to schedule a vote on cap-and-trade legislation, and in Europe, the treaty dialogue had hit an early deadlock. We'd sent Hillary and Todd ahead of me to try to drum up support for our proposed interim agreement, and over the phone, they described a chaotic scene, with the Chinese and other BRICS leaders dug in on their position, the Europeans frustrated with both us and the Chinese, the poorer countries clamoring for more financial assistance, Danish and U.N. organizers feeling overwhelmed, and the environmental groups in attendance despairing over what increasingly looked like a dumpster fire. Given the strong odor of imminent failure, not to mention the fact that I was still busy trying to get other critical legislation through Congress before the Christmas recess, Rahm and Axe questioned whether I should even make the trip.

Despite my misgivings, I decided that even a slight possibility of corralling other leaders into an international agreement overrode the fallout from a likely failure. To make the trip more palatable, Alyssa Mastromonaco came up with a skinnied-down schedule that had me flying to Copenhagen after a full day in the Oval and spending about ten hours on the ground—just enough time to deliver a speech and conduct a few bilateral meetings with heads of state—before turning around and heading home. Still, it's fair to say that as I boarded Air Force One for the red-eye across the Atlantic, I was less than enthusiastic. Settling into one of the plane's fat leather conference-room chairs, I ordered a tumbler of vodka in the hope that it would help me get a few hours' sleep and watched Marvin fiddle with the controls of the big-screen TV in search of a basketball game.

"Has anyone ever considered," I said, "the amount of carbon dioxide I'm releasing into the atmosphere as a result of these trips to Europe? I'm pretty sure that between the planes, the helicopters, and the motorcades, I've got the biggest carbon footprint of any single person on the whole goddamn planet."

"Huh," Marvin said. "That's probably right." He found the game we were looking for, turned up the sound, then added, "You might not want to mention that in your speech tomorrow."

IT WAS A GLOOMY, arctic morning when we arrived in Copenhagen, the roads into the city shrouded in mist. The conference site itself looked like a converted mall. We found ourselves wandering through a maze of elevators and corridors, one of them inexplicably lined with mannequins, before meeting up with Hillary and Todd to get the current state of play. As part of the proposed interim agreement, I'd authorized Hillary to commit the United States to making a 17 percent reduction in greenhouse gas emissions by 2020, as well as a $10 billion pledge toward the $100 billion international Green Climate Fund to help poor countries with climate change mitigation and adaptation efforts. According to Hillary, delegates from a number of nations had expressed interest in our alternative—but so far the Europeans were holding out for a fully binding treaty, while China, India, and South Africa appeared content to let the conference crash and burn and blame it on the Americans.

"If you can persuade the Europeans and the Chinese to support an interim agreement," Hillary said, "then it's possible, maybe even likely, that the rest of the world falls in line."

Clear on my assignment, we paid a courtesy visit to the Danish prime minister, Lars Løkke Rasmussen, who was presiding over the final days of negotiating sessions. Like all the Nordic countries, Denmark outperformed in international affairs, and Rasmussen himself reflected many of the qualities that I'd come to associate with the Danes—he was thoughtful, well-informed, pragmatic, and humane. But the task he'd been given—trying to cobble together a global consensus on a complicated, contentious issue over which the world's biggest powers were at odds—would have been tough for anyone. For the forty-five-year-old leader of a small country who'd been in office for only eight months, it had proven downright impossible. The press had had a field day with stories of how Rasmussen had lost control of the conference, with delegates repeatedly objecting to his proposals, questioning his rulings, and challenging his authority, like unruly teenagers with a substitute teacher. By the time we met, the poor man looked shell-shocked, his bright blue eyes strained with exhaustion, his blond hair matted against his head as if he'd just finished a wrestling match. He listened intently as I explained our strategy and asked a few technical questions about how an interim agreement might work. Mostly, though, he seemed relieved to watch me try my hand at salvaging a deal.

From there, we moved to a large makeshift auditorium, where I described to the plenary the three components of our proposed interim agreement, as well as the alternative: inaction and acrimony while the planet slowly burned. The crowd was muted but respectful, and Ban was there to congratulate me offstage, grabbing my hand in both of his, behaving as if it was entirely normal for him to now expect me to try to salvage the stalled negotiations and ad-lib my way to a last-minute agreement with other world leaders.

The rest of the day was unlike any other summit I attended as president. Apart from the pandemonium of the plenary session, we had a series of sideline meetings, moving from one to the next through corridors stuffed with people who craned their necks and took photos. Other than me, the most important player in attendance that day was the Chinese premier, Wen Jiabao. He'd brought a giant delegation with him, and the group of them had thus far been inflexible and imperious in meetings, refusing to agree that China should submit to any form of international review of their emissions, confident in the knowledge that through their alliance with Brazil, India, and South Africa, they had enough votes to kill any deal. Meeting one-on-one with Wen for a bilat, I pushed back, warning that even if China saw avoiding any obligation toward transparency as a short-term win, it would prove to be a long-term disaster for the planet. We agreed to keep talking through the day.

It was progress, but just barely. The afternoon evaporated as negotiating sessions continued. We managed to extract a draft agreement endorsed by E.U. members and a number of other delegates, but we got nowhere in follow-up sessions with the Chinese, as Wen declined to attend and instead dispatched junior members of his delegation who were predictably inflexible. Late in the day, I was led to yet another room, this one crowded with unhappy Europeans.

Most of the key leaders were there, including Merkel, Sarkozy, and Gordon Brown, all wearing the same bleary-eyed look of frustration. Now that Bush was gone and Democrats were in charge, they wanted to know, why couldn't the United States ratify a Kyoto-style treaty? In Europe, they said, even the far-right parties accept the reality of climate change—what is wrong with Americans? We know the Chinese are a problem, but why not wait until a future agreement to force their hand?

For what felt like an hour, I let them vent, answering questions, sympathizing with their concerns. Eventually the reality of the situation settled over the room, and it was left to Merkel to say it out loud.

"I think what Barack describes is not the option we had hoped for," she said calmly, "but it may be our only option today. So . . . we wait to see what the Chinese and the others say, and then we decide." She turned to me. "You'll go meet them now?"

"Yep."

"Good luck, then," Merkel said. She shrugged with a tilt of the head, a downward pull of the mouth, a slight raising of the eyebrows—the gesture of someone experienced with getting on with unpleasant necessities.

Whatever momentum we felt coming out of the meeting with the Europeans quickly dissipated once Hillary and I got back to our holding room. Marvin reported that a ferocious snowstorm was rolling through the East Coast, so to get us back to D.C. safely, Air Force One needed to be wheels-up in two and a half hours.

I looked at my watch. "What time's my follow-up meeting with Wen?"

"Well, boss, that's the other problem," Marvin said. "We can't find him." He explained that when staffers had reached out to their Chinese counterparts, they'd been told that Wen was already on his way to the airport. There were rumors that he was actually still in the building, in a meeting with the other leaders who'd been pushing back against having their emissions monitored, but we weren't able to confirm it.

"So you're saying he's ducking me."

"We got folks out looking."

A few minutes later, Marvin came back in to tell us that Wen and the leaders of Brazil, India, and South Africa had been spotted in a conference room a few levels up.

"All right, then," I said. I turned to Hillary. "When's the last time you crashed a party?"

She laughed. "It's been a while," she said, looking like the straitlaced kid who's decided to throw caution to the wind.

With a gaggle of staffers and Secret Service agents hustling behind us, we made our way upstairs. At the end of a long corridor, we found what we were looking for: a room with glass walls, just large enough to hold a conference table, around which sat Premier Wen, Prime Minister Singh, and Presidents Lula and Zuma, along with a few of their ministers. The Chinese security team began moving forward to intercept us, hands held up as if ordering us to stop, but realizing who we were, they hesitated. With a smile and a nod, Hillary and I strolled past and entered the room, leaving a fairly noisy tussle between security details and the staffers in our wake.

"You ready for me, Wen?" I called out, watching the Chinese leader's face drop in surprise. I then walked around the table to shake each of their hands. "Gentlemen! I've been looking everywhere for you. How about we see if we can do a deal?"

Before anybody could object, I grabbed an empty chair and sat down. Across the table, Wen and Singh remained impassive, while Lula and Zuma looked sheepishly down at the papers in front of them. I explained that I had just met with the Europeans and that they were prepared to accept our proposed interim agreement if the group present would support language ensuring a credible mechanism to independently verify that countries were meeting their greenhouse gas reduction commitments. One by one, the other leaders explained why our proposal was unacceptable: Kyoto was working just fine; the West was responsible for global warming and now expected poorer countries to impede their development to solve the problem; our plan would violate the principle of "common but differentiated responsibilities"; the verification mechanism we were suggesting would violate their national sovereignty. After about a half hour of this, I leaned back in my chair and looked directly at Premier Wen.

"Mr. Premier, we're running out of time," I said, "so

let me cut to the chase. Before I walked into this room, I assume, the plan was for all of you to leave here and announce that the U.S. was responsible for the failure to arrive at a new agreement. You think that if you hold out long enough, the Europeans will get desperate and sign another Kyoto-style treaty. The thing is, I've been very clear to them that I can't get our Congress to ratify the treaty you want. And there is no guarantee Europe's voters, or Canada's voters, or Japan's voters, are going to be willing to keep putting their industries at a competitive disadvantage and paying money to help poor countries deal with climate change when the world's biggest emitters are sitting on the sidelines.

"Of course, I may be wrong," I said. "Maybe you can convince everyone that we're to blame. But that won't stop the planet from getting warmer. And remember, I've got my own megaphone, and it's pretty big. If I leave this room without an agreement, then my first stop is the hall downstairs where all the international press is waiting for news. And I'm going to tell them that I was prepared to commit to a big reduction in our greenhouse gases, and billions of dollars in new assistance, and that each of you decided it was better to do nothing. I'm going to say the same thing to all the poor countries that stood to benefit from that new money. And to all the people in your own countries that stand to suffer the most from climate change. And we'll see who they believe."

Once the translators in the room caught up to me, the Chinese environmental minister, a burly, round-faced man in glasses, suddenly stood up and started speaking in Mandarin, his voice rising, his hands waving in my direction, his face reddening in agitation. He went on like this for a minute or two, the entire room not quite sure what was happening. Eventually, Premier Wen lifted a slender, vein-lined hand and the minister abruptly sat back down. I suppressed the urge to laugh and turned to the young Chinese woman who was translating for Wen.

"What did my friend there just say?" I asked. Before she could answer, Wen shook his head and whispered something. The translator nodded and turned back to me.

"Premier Wen says that what the environmental minister said is not important," she explained. "Premier Wen asks if you have the agreement you're proposing with you, so that everyone can look at the specific language again."

IT TOOK ANOTHER half hour of haggling, with the other leaders and their ministers hovering over me and Hillary as I used a ballpoint pen to mark up some of the language in the creased document I'd been carrying in my pocket, but by the time I left the room, the group had agreed to our proposal. Rushing back downstairs, I spent another thirty minutes getting the Europeans to sign off on the modest changes the developing-country leaders had requested. The language was quickly printed out and circulated. Hillary and Todd worked the delegates from other key countries to help broaden the consensus. I made a brief statement to the press announcing the interim agreement, after which we loaded up our motorcade and raced to the airport.

We made our window for takeoff with ten minutes to spare.

There was a cheerful buzz on the flight back as staffers recounted the day's adventures for the benefit of those who hadn't been present. Reggie, who'd been with me long enough not to be impressed by much of anything anymore, flashed a wide grin as he poked his head into my quarters, where I was reading through a stack of briefing memos.

"I gotta say, boss," he told me, "that was some real gangster shit back there."

I did feel pretty good. On the biggest of stages, on an issue that mattered and with the clock ticking, I'd pulled a rabbit out of a hat. Granted, the press gave the interim agreement mixed reviews, but given the chaos of the conference and the obstinacy of the Chinese, I still saw it as a win—a stepping-stone that could help us get our climate change bill through the Senate. Most important, we'd succeeded in getting China and India to accept—no matter how grudgingly or tentatively—the notion that every country, and not just those in the West, had a responsibility to do its part to slow climate change. Seven years later, that basic principle would prove essential to achieving the breakthrough Paris Agreement.

Still, as I sat at my desk and looked out the window, the darkness interrupted every few seconds by a flashing light at the tip of the plane's right wing, I was overtaken by more sobering thoughts. I thought about how much work we'd had to put in to land the deal—the countless hours of labor by a gifted and dedicated staff; the behind-the-scenes negotiations and calling in of chits; the promises of aid; and finally an eleventh-hour intervention that had relied as much on my seat-of-the-pants bluster as on any set of rational arguments. All that for an interim agreement that—even if it worked entirely as planned—would be at best a preliminary, halting step·

toward solving a possible planetary tragedy, a pail of water thrown on a raging fire. I realized that for all the power inherent in the seat I now occupied, there would always be a chasm between what I knew should be done to achieve a better world and what in a day, week, or year I found myself actually able to accomplish.

The forecasted storm had hit Washington by the time we landed, the low clouds sending down a steady mix of snow and freezing rain. In northern cities like Chicago, the trucks would already be out, plowing the streets and scattering salt, but even a hint of snow tended to paralyze the notoriously ill-equipped D.C. area, closing schools and snarling traffic. With Marine One unable to transport us because of the weather, the drive back to the White House took extra time as our motorcade navigated the icy roads.

It was late when I walked into the residence. Michelle was in bed, reading. I told her about my trip and asked how the girls were doing.

"They're very excited about the snow," she said, "even if I'm not." She looked at me with a sympathetic grin. "Malia's probably going to ask you at breakfast whether you saved the tigers."

I nodded, pulling off my tie.

"I'm working on it," I said.

PART SIX

IN THE BARREL

CHAPTER 22

I T'S IN THE NATURE OF politics, and certainly the presidency, to go through rough patches—times when, because of a boneheaded mistake, an unforeseen circumstance, a sound but unpopular decision, or a failure to communicate, the headlines turn sour and the public finds you wanting. Usually this lasts for a couple of weeks, maybe a month, before the press loses interest in smacking you around, either because you fixed the problem, or you expressed contrition, or you chalked up a win, or something deemed more important pushes you off the front page.

If the rough patch lasts long enough, though, you may find yourself in a dreaded situation in which problems compound, then congeal into a broader narrative about you and your presidency. The negative stories don't let up, which leads to a drop in your popularity. Your political adversaries, smelling blood in the water, go after you harder, and allies aren't as quick to defend you. The press starts digging for additional problems inside your administration, to confirm the impression that you're in political trouble. Until—like the daredevils and fools of old at Niagara Falls—you find yourself trapped in the proverbial barrel, tumbling through the crashing waters, bruised and disoriented, no longer sure which way is up, powerless to arrest your descent, waiting to hit bottom and hoping, without evidence, that you'll survive the impact.

For most of my second year in office, we were in the barrel.

We'd seen it coming, of course, especially after the Tea Party summer and the ruckus surrounding the Affordable Care Act. My approval ratings, which had held fairly steady during my first six months in office, ticked down throughout the fall. Press coverage became more critical, on matters both significant (like my decision to send more troops into Afghanistan) and strange (like the case of the Salahis, a pair of Washington social climbers who found a way to crash a state dinner and have their photo taken with me).

Nor had our troubles let up over the holidays. On Christmas Day, a young Nigerian named Umar Farouk Abdulmutallab had boarded a Northwest Airlines flight from Amsterdam to Detroit and tried to detonate explosive materials sewn into his underwear. Tragedy had been averted only because the contraption hadn't worked; seeing smoke and flames coming from under the would-be terrorist's blanket, a passenger restrained him and flight attendants extinguished the flames, allowing the plane to land safely. Having just arrived in Hawaii with Michelle and the girls for a much-needed ten-day break, I spent most of the next several days on the phone with my national security team and the FBI, trying to determine who exactly Abdulmutallab was, whom he'd been working with, and why both airport security and our terrorist watch list hadn't kept him from boarding a U.S.-bound plane.

What I failed to do in those first seventy-two hours, though, was follow my initial instincts, which were to get on television, explain to the American people what had happened, and assure them that it was safe to travel. My team had made a sensible argument for waiting: It was important, they said, for the president to have all the facts before making a statement to the public. And yet my job involved more than just managing the government or getting the facts right. The public also looked to the president to explain a difficult and often scary world. Rather than coming off as prudent, my absence from the airwaves made me seem unengaged, and soon we were taking incoming fire from across the political spectrum, with less charitable commentators suggesting that I cared more about my tropical vacation than I did about threats against the homeland. It didn't help that my usually unflappable secretary of homeland security, Janet Napolitano, briefly stumbled in one of her TV interviews, responding to a question about where security had broken down by saying that "the system worked."

Our mishandling of the so-called Underwear Bomber played into Republican accusations that Democrats were soft on terrorism, weakening my hand on issues like closing the detention center at Guantánamo Bay. And like the other gaffes and unforced errors that occurred during my first year, this one no doubt contributed to my slide in the polls. But according to Axe, who spent his days poring over political data, cross-tabbed by political party, age, race, gender, geography, and Lord knows what else, my sinking political fortunes heading into 2010 could be traced to one overriding factor.

The economy still stank.

On paper, our emergency measures—along with the Federal Reserve's interventions—appeared to be working. The financial system was up and running, and banks were on the way to solvency. Housing prices, while still way down from their peak, had at least temporarily stabilized, and U.S. auto sales had started to climb. Thanks to the Recovery Act, consumer and business spending had rebounded slightly, and states and cities had slowed (though not stopped) their layoffs of teachers, cops, and other public workers. Across the country, major building projects were under way, picking up some of the slack that had resulted from the collapse of housing construction. Joe Biden and his chief of staff, my former debate coach Ron Klain, had done an excellent job of overseeing the flow of stimulus dollars, with Joe often devoting chunks of his day to picking up the phone and barking at state or local officials whose projects were behind schedule or who weren't providing us with adequate documentation. An audit found that as a result of their efforts, just 0.2 percent of Recovery Act dollars had been improperly spent—a statistic that even the best-run private sector companies might envy, given the amounts of money and the number of projects involved.

Still, to the millions of Americans dealing with the aftermath of the crisis, things felt worse, not better. They were still at risk of losing their homes to foreclosure. Their savings were depleted, if not entirely wiped out. Most troubling of all, they still couldn't find work.

Larry Summers had warned that unemployment was a

"lagging indicator": Companies typically didn't start laying off employees until several months into a recession and didn't resume hiring until well after a recession ended. Sure enough, while the pace of job loss gradually slowed over the course of 2009, the number of unemployed people continued to grow. The unemployment rate didn't peak until October, hitting 10 percent—the highest since the early 1980s. The news was so consistently bad that I found myself developing a knot in my stomach on the first Thursday of every month, when the Labor Department sent the White House an advance copy of its monthly jobs report. Katie claimed that she could usually gauge the contents of the report by my economic team's body language: If they averted their gaze, she told me, or spoke in hushed tones, or just dropped off a manila envelope for her to give me, rather than waiting around to hand it to me in person, she knew we were in for another rough month.

If Americans were understandably frustrated with the recovery's glacial pace, the bank bailout sent them over the edge. Man, did folks hate TARP! They didn't care that the emergency program had worked better than expected, or that more than half of the money given to the banks had already been repaid with interest, or that the broader economy couldn't have started healing until the capital markets were working again. Across the political spectrum, voters considered the bank bailouts a scam that had allowed the barons of finance to emerge from the crisis relatively unscathed.

Tim Geithner liked to point out that this wasn't strictly true. He would list all the ways Wall Street had paid for its sins: investment banks gone belly-up, bank

CEOs ousted, shares diluted, billions of dollars in losses. Likewise, Attorney General Holder's lawyers at the Justice Department would soon start racking up record settlements from financial institutions that were shown to have violated the law. Still, there was no getting around the fact that many of the people most culpable for the nation's economic woes remained fabulously wealthy and had avoided prosecution mainly because the laws as written deemed epic recklessness and dishonesty in the boardroom or on the trading floor less blameworthy than the actions of a teenage shoplifter. Whatever the economic merits of TARP or the legal rationale behind the Justice Department's decisions not to press criminal charges, the whole thing reeked of unfairness.

"Where's **my** bailout?" continued to be a popular refrain. My barber asked me why no bank executives had gone to jail; so did my mother-in-law. Housing advocates asked why banks had received hundreds of billions in TARP funds while only a fraction of that amount was going toward directly helping homeowners at risk of foreclosure pay down their mortgages. Our answer—that given the sheer size of the U.S. housing market, even a program as big as TARP would have only a nominal effect on the rate of foreclosures, and any additional money we got out of Congress was more effectively used to boost employment—sounded heartless and unpersuasive, especially when the programs we **had** set up to help homeowners refinance or modify their mortgages fell woefully short of expectations.

Eager to get out ahead of the public outrage, or at least the line of fire, Congress set up multiple oversight committees, with Democrats and Republicans taking turns denouncing the banks, questioning regulators' decisions, and casting as much blame as possible on the other party. In 2008 the Senate had appointed a special inspector general to monitor TARP, a former prosecutor named Neil Barofsky who knew little about finance but had a gift for generating sensational headlines and attacked our decision-making with zeal. The further the possibility of a financial meltdown receded from view, the more everyone questioned whether TARP had even been necessary in the first place. And because we were now in charge, it was often Tim and other members of my administration occupying the hot seat, defending the seemingly indefensible.

Republicans weren't shy about taking advantage, suggesting that TARP had always been a Democratic idea. On a daily basis, they launched broadsides at the Recovery Act and the rest of our economic policies, insisting that "stimulus" was just another name for out-of-control, liberal pork-barrel spending and more bailouts for special interests. They blamed the Recovery Act for the exploding federal deficit we'd inherited from the Bush administration, and—to the extent that they even bothered to offer alternative policies—argued that the best way to fix the economy was for the government to slash its budget and get its fiscal house in order, the same way hard-pressed families across the country were "tightening their belts."

Add it all up, and by early 2010, polls showed that significantly more Americans disapproved of my economic stewardship than approved—a flashing red light that helped explain not only the loss of Ted Kennedy's seat in Massachusetts but also Democratic losses in off-year gubernatorial races in New Jersey and Virginia, states I'd won handily just twelve months earlier. According to Axe, voters in focus groups couldn't distinguish between TARP, which I'd inherited, and the stimulus; they just knew that the well-connected were getting theirs while they were getting screwed. They also thought that Republican calls for budget cuts in response to the crisis—"austerity," as economists liked to call it—made more intuitive sense than our Keynesian push for increased government spending. Congressional Democrats from swing districts, already nervous about their reelection prospects, began distancing themselves from the Recovery Act and shunning the word "stimulus" altogether. Those further to the left, freshly angered by the lack of a public option in the healthcare bill, renewed their complaints that the stimulus hadn't been big enough and that Tim and Larry were too cozy with Wall Street. Even Nancy Pelosi and Harry Reid started questioning our White House communications strategy—especially our penchant for denouncing "excessive partisanship" and "special interests" in Washington rather than going harder at the Republicans.

"Mr. President," Nancy said to me on one call, "I tell my members that what you've managed to do in such a short time is historic. I'm just so very proud, really. But right now, the public doesn't know what you've accomplished. They don't know how awful the Republicans are behaving, just trying to block you on everything. And voters aren't going to know if you aren't willing to tell them."

Axe, who oversaw our communications shop, was

exasperated when I mentioned my conversation with the Speaker. "Maybe Nancy can tell us how to spin ten percent unemployment," he harrumphed. He reminded me that I'd run on the promise to change Washington, not to engage in the usual partisan food fight. "We can bash Republicans all we want," he said, "but at the end of the day, we're going to keep taking on water so long as the best we can tell voters is 'Sure, things are terrible—but it could've been worse.'"

He had a point; given the state of the economy, there were limits to what any messaging strategy could accomplish. We had known from the start that the politics of the recession were going to be rough. But Nancy was also right to be critical. I was the one, after all, who'd taken such great pride in not letting short-term politics intrude on our response to the economic crisis, as if the rules of political gravity didn't apply to me. When Tim had expressed concern that overly harsh rhetoric directed at Wall Street might dissuade private investors from recapitalizing the banks and therefore prolong the financial crisis, I'd agreed to tone it down, despite objections from Axe and Gibbs. Now a sizable part of the country thought I cared more about the banks than I cared about them. When Larry had suggested that we pay out the Recovery Act's middle-class tax cuts in biweekly increments rather than in one lump sum because research showed that people were more likely to spend the money that way, giving the economy a quicker boost, I'd said great, let's do it—even though Rahm had warned that it meant no one would notice the slight bump in each paycheck. Now surveys showed that the majority of Americans believed that I'd **raised** rather than lowered their taxes—all to pay for bank bailouts, the stimulus package, and healthcare.

FDR would never have made such mistakes, I thought. He had understood that digging America out of the Depression was less a matter of getting every New Deal policy exactly right than of projecting confidence in the overall endeavor, impressing upon the public that the government had a handle on the situation. Just as he'd known that in a crisis people needed a story that made sense of their hardships and spoke to their emotions— a morality tale with clear good guys and bad guys and a plot they could easily follow.

In other words, FDR understood that to be effective, governance couldn't be so antiseptic that it set aside the basic stuff of politics: You had to sell your program, reward supporters, punch back against opponents, and amplify the facts that helped your cause while fudging the details that didn't. I found myself wondering whether we'd somehow turned a virtue into a vice; whether, trapped in my own high-mindedness, I'd failed to tell the American people a story they could believe in; and whether, having ceded the political narrative to my critics, I was going to be able to wrest it back.

AFTER MORE THAN a year of unrelentingly bad economic numbers, we finally received a glimmer of hope: The March 2010 jobs report showed the economy gaining 162,000 new jobs—the first month of solid growth since 2007. When Larry and Christy Romer came into the Oval to deliver the news, I gave them both fist bumps and declared them "Employees of the Month."

"Do we each get a plaque for that, Mr. President?" Christy asked.

"We can't afford plaques," I said. "But you get to lord it over the rest of the team."

The April and May reports were positive as well, offering the tantalizing possibility that the recovery might finally be picking up steam. None of us inside the White House thought a jobless rate over 9 percent called for a victory lap. We agreed, though, that it made both economic and political sense to start more emphatically projecting a sense of forward momentum in my speeches. We even began planning for a nationwide tour in the early summer, where I'd highlight communities on the rebound and companies that were hiring again. "Recovery Summer," we would call it.

Except Greece imploded.

Although the financial crisis had originated on Wall Street, its impact across Europe had been just as severe. Months after we'd gotten the U.S. economy growing again, the European Union remained mired in recession, with its banks fragile, its major industries yet to recover from the huge drop in global trade, and unemployment in some countries running as high as 20 percent. The Europeans didn't have to contend with the sudden collapse of their housing industry the way we did, and their more generous safety nets helped cushion the recession's impact on vulnerable populations. On the other hand, the combination of greater demands on public services, reduced tax revenues, and ongoing bank bailouts had placed severe pressure on government budgets. And unlike the United States—which could cheaply finance rising deficits even in a crisis, as risk-averse investors rushed to buy our Treasury bills—countries like Ireland, Portugal, Greece, Italy, and Spain found it increasingly difficult to borrow. Their efforts to placate financial markets by cutting government spending only lowered already weak aggregate demand and deepened their recessions. This, in turn, produced even bigger budget shortfalls, necessitated additional borrowing at ever higher interest rates, and rattled financial markets even more.

We couldn't afford to be passive observers to all this. Problems in Europe acted as a significant drag on the U.S. recovery: The European Union was our largest trading partner, after all, and U.S. and European financial markets were practically joined at the hip. Through much of 2009, Tim and I had urged European leaders to take more decisive action to mend their economies. We advised them to clear up the issues with their banks once and for all (the "stress test" E.U. regulators had applied to their financial institutions was so slipshod that a pair of Irish banks needed government rescues just a few months after regulators had certified them as sound). We pushed any E.U. countries with stronger balance sheets to initiate stimulus policies comparable to our own, in order to jump-start business investment and increase consumer demand across the continent.

We got exactly nowhere. Although liberal by American standards, Europe's biggest economies were almost all led by center-right governments, elected on the promise of balanced budgets and free-market reforms rather than more government spending. Germany, in particular—the European Union's one true economic powerhouse and its most influential member—continued to see fiscal rectitude as the answer to all economic woes. The more I'd gotten to know Angela Merkel, the more I'd come to like her; I found her steady, honest, intellectually rigorous, and instinctually kind. But she was also conservative by temperament, not to mention a savvy politician who knew her constituency, and whenever I suggested to her that Germany needed to set an example by spending more on infrastructure or tax cuts, she politely but firmly pushed back. "Ya, Barack, I think maybe that's not the best approach for us," she would say, her face pulling into a slight frown, as if I'd suggested something a little tawdry.

Sarkozy didn't serve as much of a counterweight. Privately, he voiced sympathy for the idea of economic stimulus, given France's high unemployment rate ("Don't worry, Barack . . . I'm working on Angela, you'll see"). But he had trouble pivoting away from the fiscally conservative positions that he himself had taken in the past, and as far as I could tell, he wasn't organized enough to come up with a clear plan for his own country, much less for all of Europe.

And while the United Kingdom's prime minister, Gordon Brown, agreed with us on the need for European governments to boost short-term spending, his Labour Party would lose its majority in Parliament in May 2010, and Brown would find himself replaced by Conservative leader David Cameron. In his early forties, with a youthful appearance and a studied informality (at every international summit, the first thing he'd do was take off his jacket and loosen his tie), the Eton-educated Cameron possessed an impressive command of the issues, a facility with language, and the easy confidence of someone who'd never been pressed too hard by life. I liked him personally, even when we butted heads, and for the next six years he'd prove to be a willing partner on a host of international issues, from climate change (he believed in the science) to human rights (he supported marriage equality) to aid for developing countries (throughout his tenure, he'd managed to allocate 1.5 percent of the U.K.'s budget to foreign aid, a significantly higher percentage than I'd ever convince the U.S. Congress to approve). On economic policy, though, Cameron hewed closely to free-market orthodoxy, having promised voters that his platform of deficit reduction and cuts to government services—along with regulatory reform and expanded trade—would usher in a new era of British competitiveness.

Instead, predictably, the British economy would fall deeper into a recession.

The stubborn embrace of austerity by key European leaders, despite all of the contrary evidence, was more than a little frustrating. But given everything else on my plate, the situation in Europe hadn't been keeping me up at night. That all began to change in February 2010, though, when a Greek sovereign debt crisis threatened to unravel the European Union—and sent me and my economic team scrambling to avert yet another round of global financial panic.

Greece's economic problems weren't new. For decades, the country had been plagued by low productivity, a bloated and inefficient public sector, massive tax avoidance, and unsustainable pension obligations. Despite that, throughout the 2000s, international capital markets had been happy to finance Greece's steadily escalating deficits, much the same way that they'd been happy to finance a heap of subprime mortgages across the United States. In the wake of the Wall Street crisis, the mood grew less generous. When a new Greek government announced that its latest budget deficit far exceeded previous estimates, European bank stocks plunged and international lenders balked at lending Greece more money. The country suddenly teetered on the brink of default.

Normally the prospect of a small country not paying its bills on time would have a limited effect outside its borders. Greece's GDP was roughly the size of Maryland's, and other countries faced with similar problems were typically able to hammer out an agreement with creditors and the IMF, allowing them to restructure their debt, maintain their international creditworthiness, and eventually get back on their feet.

But in 2010, economic conditions weren't normal. Greece's attachment to an already shaky Europe made its sovereign debt problems the equivalent of a lit stick of dynamite being tossed into a munitions factory. Because it was a member of the European Union's common market, where companies and people worked, traveled, and traded under a unified set of regulations and without regard to national borders, Greece's economic troubles easily migrated. Banks in other E.U. countries were some of Greece's biggest lenders. Greece was also one of sixteen countries that had adopted the euro, meaning it had no currency of its own to devalue or independent monetary remedies that it could pursue. Without an immediate, large-scale rescue package from its fellow eurozone members, Greece might have no alternative but to pull out of the currency compact, an unprecedented move with uncertain economic ramifications. Already, market fears about Greece had caused big spikes in the rates banks were charging Ireland, Portugal, Italy, and Spain to cover their sovereign debt. Tim worried that an actual Greek default and/or exit from the eurozone might lead skittish capital markets to effectively cut off credit to those bigger countries altogether, administering a shock to the financial system as bad or even worse than the one we'd just been through.

"Is it just me," I asked after Tim had finished laying out various hair-raising scenarios, "or are we having trouble catching a break?"

And so, out of nowhere, stabilizing Greece suddenly became one of our top economic and foreign policy priorities. In face-to-face meetings and over the phone that spring, Tim and I put on a full-court press to get the European Central Bank and the IMF to produce a rescue package robust enough to calm the markets and allow Greece to cover its debt payments, while helping the new government set up a realistic plan to reduce the country's structural deficits and restore growth. To guard against possible contagion effects on the rest of Europe, we also recommended that the Europeans construct a credible "firewall"—basically, a joint loan fund with enough heft to give capital markets confidence that in an emergency the eurozone stood behind its members' debts.

Once again, our European counterparts had other ideas. As far as the Germans, the Dutch, and many of the other eurozone members were concerned, the Greeks had brought their troubles on themselves with their shoddy governance and spendthrift ways. Although Merkel assured me that "we won't do a Lehman" by letting Greece default, both she and her austerity-minded finance minister, Wolfgang Schäuble, appeared determined to condition any assistance on an adequate penance, despite our warnings that squeezing an already battered Greek economy too hard would be counterproductive. The desire to apply some of that Old Testament justice and discourage moral hazard was reflected in Europe's initial offer: a loan of up to €25 billion, barely enough to cover a couple of months of Greek debt, contingent on the new government enacting deep cuts in worker pensions, steep tax increases, and freezes on public sector wages. Not wanting to commit political suicide, the Greek government said thanks but no thanks, especially after the country's voters responded to news reports of the European proposal with widespread riots and strikes.

Europe's early design for an emergency firewall wasn't much better. The initial figure proposed by eurozone authorities to capitalize the loan fund—€50 billion—was woefully inadequate. On a call with his fellow finance ministers, Tim had to explain that to be effective, the fund would have to be at least ten times that size. Eurozone officials also insisted that to access the fund, a member country's bondholders would have to undergo a mandatory "haircut"—in other words, accept a certain percentage of losses on what they were owed. This sentiment was perfectly understandable; after all, the interest lenders charged on a loan was supposed to factor in the risk that the borrower might default. But as a practical matter, any haircut requirement would make private capital far less willing to lend debt-ridden countries like Ireland and Italy any more money, thus defeating the firewall's entire purpose.

For me, the whole thing felt like a dubbed TV rerun of the debates we'd had back home in the aftermath of the Wall Street crisis. And while I was crystal clear about what European leaders like Merkel and Sarkozy needed to do, I had sympathy for the political bind they were in. After all, I'd had a hell of a time trying to convince American voters that it made sense to spend billions of taxpayer dollars bailing out banks and helping strangers avoid foreclosure or job loss inside our own country. Merkel and Sarkozy, on the other hand, were being asked to persuade their voters that it made sense to bail out a bunch of foreigners.

I realized then that the Greek debt crisis was as much a geopolitical problem as it was a problem of global finance, one that exposed the unresolved contradictions at the heart of Europe's decades-long march toward greater integration. In those heady days after the fall of the Berlin Wall, in the years of methodical restructuring that followed, that project's grand architecture—the common market, the euro, the European Parliament, and a Brussels-based bureaucracy empowered to set policy on a wide range of regulatory issues—expressed an optimism in the possibilities of a truly unified continent, purged of the toxic nationalism that had spurred centuries of bloody conflict. To a remarkable degree, the experiment had worked: In exchange for giving up some elements of their sovereignty, the European Union's member states had enjoyed a measure of peace and widespread prosperity perhaps unmatched by any collection of people in human history.

But national identities—the distinctions of language, culture, history, and levels of economic development—were stubborn things. And as the economic crisis worsened, all those differences the good times had papered over started coming to the fore. How prepared were citizens in Europe's wealthier, more efficient nations to take on a neighboring country's obligations or to see their tax dollars redistributed to those outside their borders? Would citizens of countries in economic distress accept sacrifices imposed on them by distant officials with whom they felt no affinity and over whom they had little or no power? As the debate about Greece heated up, public discussions inside some of the original E.U. countries, like Germany, France, and the Netherlands, would sometimes veer beyond disapproval of the Greek government's policies and venture into a broader indictment of the Greek people— how they were more casual about work or how they tolerated corruption and considered basic responsibilities like paying one's taxes to be merely optional. Or, as I'd overhear one E.U. official of undetermined origin tell another while I was washing my hands in a G8 summit lavatory:

"They don't think like us."

Leaders like Merkel and Sarkozy were too invested in European unity to traffic in such stereotypes, but their politics dictated that they proceed cautiously in agreeing to any rescue plan. I noticed that they rarely mentioned that German and French banks were some of Greece's biggest lenders, or that much of the Greeks' accumulated debt had been racked up buying German and French exports—facts that might have made clear to voters why saving the Greeks from default amounted to saving their own banks and industries. Maybe they worried that such an admission would turn voter attention away from the failures of successive Greek governments and toward the failures of those German and French officials charged with supervising bank lending practices. Or maybe they feared that if their voters fully understood the underlying implications of European integration—the extent to which their economic fates, for good and for ill, had become bound up with those of people who were "not like us"—they might not find it entirely to their liking.

In any event, by early May, the financial markets got scary enough that European leaders faced reality. They agreed to a joint E.U.-IMF loan package that would allow Greece to make its payments for the next three years. The package still included austerity measures that everyone involved knew would be too onerous for the Greek government to implement, but at least it gave other E.U. governments the political cover they needed to approve the deal. Later in the year, the eurozone countries also tentatively agreed to a firewall on the scale that Tim had suggested, and without a mandatory "haircut" requirement. European financial markets would remain a roller-coaster ride throughout 2010, and the situation in not just Greece but also Ireland, Portugal, Spain, and Italy remained perilous. Without the leverage to force a permanent fix for Europe's underlying problems, Tim and I had to content ourselves with having temporarily helped to defuse another bomb.

As for the crisis's effect on the U.S. economy, whatever momentum the recovery had gathered at the beginning of the year came to a screeching halt. The news out of Greece sent the U.S. stock market sharply downward. Business confidence, as measured by monthly surveys, dropped as well, with the new uncertainties causing managers to put off planned investments. The jobs report for June returned to negative territory—and would stay that way into the fall.

"Recovery Summer" turned out to be a bust.

THE MOOD IN the White House changed that second year. It wasn't that anyone started taking the place for granted; each day, after all, brought new reminders of how privileged we were to be playing a part in writing history. And there sure wasn't any drop in effort. To an outsider, staff meetings might have looked more relaxed as people got to know one another and grew familiar with their roles and responsibilities. But beneath the easy banter, everyone understood the stakes involved, the need for us to execute even routine tasks to the most exacting of standards. I never had to tell anyone in the White House to work hard or go the extra mile. Their own fear of dropping the ball—of disappointing me, colleagues, constituencies that were counting on us— drove people far more than any exhortation I might deliver.

Everybody was sleep-deprived, perpetually. Rarely did senior staffers put in less than a twelve-hour day, and almost all of them came in for at least part of each weekend. They didn't have a one-minute commute like I did or a bevy of chefs, valets, butlers, and assistants to shop, cook, pick up dry cleaning, or take the kids to school. Single staffers stayed single longer than they might have liked. Those staffers lucky enough to have partners often relied on an overburdened and lonely spouse, creating the kinds of chronic domestic tensions that Michelle and

I were more than familiar with. People missed their children's soccer games and dance recitals. People got home too late to tuck toddlers into bed. Those like Rahm, Axe, and others, who'd decided against putting their families through the disruption of moving to Washington, barely saw their spouses and kids at all.

If anyone complained about this, they did so privately. Folks knew what they signed up for when joining an administration. "Work-life balance" wasn't part of the deal—and given the perilous state of the economy and the world, the volume of incoming work wouldn't slow down anytime soon. Just as athletes in a locker room don't talk about nagging injuries, the members of our White House team learned to suck it up.

Still, the cumulative effects of exhaustion—along with an increasingly angry public, an unsympathetic press, disenchanted allies, and an opposition party with both the means and the intent to turn everything we did into an interminable slog—had a way of fraying nerves and shortening tempers. I began hearing more consternation over Rahm's occasional outbursts during early-morning staff meetings, accusations that Larry cut people out of certain economic policy discussions, whispers that people felt shortchanged when Valerie took advantage of her personal relationship with me and Michelle to do end runs around White House processes. Tensions flared between younger foreign policy staffers like Denis and Ben, who were accustomed to running ideas by me informally before putting them through a formal process, and my national security advisor, Jim Jones, who'd come out of a military culture in which chains of command were inviolate and subordinates were expected to stay in their lanes.

Members of my cabinet had their own frustrations. While Hillary, Tim, Robert Gates, and Eric Holder got most of my attention by virtue of their posts, other cabinet members were performing yeomen's work without a lot of hand-holding. Secretary of Agriculture Tom Vilsack, the hard-charging former governor of Iowa, would leverage Recovery Act dollars to spark a host of new economic development strategies for struggling rural communities. Labor secretary Hilda Solis and her team were working to make it easier for low-wage workers to get overtime pay. My old friend Arne Duncan, the former Chicago school superintendent, now secretary of education, was leading the effort to raise standards in low-performing schools across the country, even when it drew the wrath of the teachers' unions (who were understandably wary of anything that might involve more standardized tests) and conservative activists (who thought that the effort to institute a common core curriculum was a plot by liberals to indoctrinate their children).

Despite such achievements, the daily grind of running a federal agency didn't always match the more glamorous role (advisor and confidant to the president, frequent visitor to the White House) that some in the cabinet had imagined for themselves. There was a time when presidents like Lincoln relied almost exclusively on their cabinets to formulate policy; a bare-bones White House staff handled little more than the president's personal needs and correspondence. But as the federal government had expanded in the modern era, successive presidents looked to centralize more and more decision-making under one roof, swelling the number and influence of White House personnel. Meanwhile, cabinet members became more specialized, consumed with the task of managing massive, far-flung principalities rather than bending the president's ear.

The shift in power showed up in my calendar. Whereas folks like Rahm or Jim Jones saw me almost every day, only Hillary, Tim, and Gates had standing meetings in the Oval. Other secretaries had to fight to get on my schedule, unless an issue involving their agency became a top White House priority. Full cabinet meetings, which we tried to hold once a quarter, gave people a chance to share information, but they were too big and unwieldy to allow for much actual business; just getting everybody seated in the Cabinet Room was something of an ordeal, with folks having to take turns sidling awkwardly between the heavy leather chairs. In a town where proximity and access to the president were taken as a measure of clout (the reason why senior staffers coveted the West Wing's cramped, ill-lit, and notoriously rodent-infested offices rather than the spacious suites in the EEOB across the street), it didn't take long for some cabinet members to start feeling underutilized and underappreciated, relegated to the periphery of the action and subject to the whims of often younger, less experienced White House staffers.

None of these issues were unique to my presidency, and it's a credit to both my cabinet and my staff that they maintained their focus even as the work environment got tougher. With few exceptions, we avoided the open hostilities and constant leaks that had characterized some previous administrations. Without exception, we avoided scandal. I'd made clear at the start of my administration that I'd have zero tolerance for ethical lapses, and people who had a problem with that didn't join us in the first place. Even so, I appointed a former Harvard Law School classmate of mine, Norm Eisen, as special counsel to the president for ethics and government reform, just to help keep everybody—including me—on track. Cheerful and punctilious, with sharp features and the wide, unblinking eyes of a zealot, Norm was perfect for the job—the kind of guy who relished the well-earned nickname "Dr. No." When asked once what sorts of out-of-town conferences were okay for administration officials to attend, his response was short and to the point:

"If it sounds fun, you can't go."

Keeping up morale, on the other hand, wasn't something I could delegate. I tried to be generous in my praise, measured in my criticism. In meetings, I made a point of eliciting everyone's views, including those of more junior staffers. Small stuff mattered—making sure it was me who brought out the cake for somebody's birthday, for example, or taking the time to call someone's parents for an anniversary. Sometimes, when I had a few unscheduled minutes, I'd just wander through the West Wing's narrow halls, poking my head into offices to ask people about their families, what they were working on, and whether there was anything they thought we could be doing better.

Ironically, one aspect of management that took me longer to learn than it should have was the need to pay closer attention to the experiences of women and people of color on the staff. I'd long believed that the

more perspectives around a table, the better an organization performed, and I took pride in the fact that
we'd recruited the most diverse cabinet in history. Our
White House operation was similarly loaded with talented, experienced African Americans, Latinos, Asian
Americans, and women, a group that included domestic
policy advisor Melody Barnes, deputy chief of staff Mona
Sutphen, political director Patrick Gaspard, director of
intergovernmental affairs Cecilia Muñoz, White House
cabinet secretary Chris Lu, staff secretary Lisa Brown,
and the head of the Council on Environmental Quality,
Nancy Sutley. All of them were exemplary at their jobs
and played key roles in shaping policy. Many became not
just valued advisors but good friends.

My non-white and non-male cabinet members
didn't have to worry, though, about fitting into their
workplace; within their buildings, they were at the top of
the food chain and everyone else adjusted to them.
Women and people of color in the White House, on the
other hand, had to wrestle—at various times and to
varying degrees—with the same nagging questions, frustrations, and doubts that faced their counterparts in
other professional settings, from corporate suites to university departments. **Did Larry dismiss my proposal in
front of the president because he thought it wasn't
fully fleshed out, or was it because I wasn't assertive
enough? Or was it because he doesn't take women as
seriously as men? Did Rahm consult with Axe and
not me on that issue because he happened to need a
political perspective, or because the two of them have
a long-standing relationship? Or is it that he's not as
comfortable with Black people?**

Should I say something? Am I being overly sensitive?

As the first African American president, I felt a particular obligation to model an inclusive workplace. Still,
I tended to discount the role that race and gender—as
opposed to the friction that typically arises when you get
a group of stressed-out, type A high achievers confined
in close quarters—actually played in office dynamics.
Maybe it was because everyone was on their best behavior in front of me; when I did hear about problems
popping up among staffers, it was usually through Pete
or Valerie, in whom, by virtue of age and temperament,
others seemed most comfortable confiding. I knew that
the brash styles of Rahm, Axe, Gibbs, and Larry—not to
mention their politically conditioned nervousness about
taking a strong stand on wedge issues like immigration,
abortion, and relations between police and minority
communities—were sometimes received differently by
the women and people of color on the team. On the
other hand, those guys were combative with **everybody,**
including one another. Knowing them as well as I did,
I felt that as much as any of us growing up in America
can be free of bias, they passed the test. So long as I
didn't hear about anything egregious, I figured that it
was enough for me to set a good example for the team
by treating people with courtesy and respect. Day-
to-day cases of bruised egos, turf battles, or perceived
slights, they could handle among themselves.

But late in our first year, Valerie asked to see me and
reported deepening dissatisfaction among the senior
women in the White House—and it was only then that
I started to examine some of my own blind spots. I
learned that at least one woman on the team had been

driven to tears after being upbraided in a meeting. Tired of having their views repeatedly dismissed, several other senior women had effectively stopped talking in meetings altogether. "I don't think the men even realize how they're coming across," Valerie said, "and as far as the women are concerned, that's part of the problem."

I was troubled enough that I suggested that a dozen women on the staff join me for dinner so that they'd have a chance to air things out. We held it in the Old Family Dining Room, on the first floor of the residence, and perhaps because of the fancy setting, with the high ceilings, black-tied butlers, and fine White House china, it took a little time before the women opened up. Feelings around the table weren't uniform, and no one said they'd been on the receiving end of overtly sexist remarks. But as I listened to these accomplished women talk for well over two hours, it became clear the degree to which patterns of behavior that were second nature for many of the senior men on the team—shouting or cursing during a policy debate; dominating a conversation by constantly interrupting other people (especially women) in midsentence; restating a point that somebody else (often a female staffer) had made half an hour earlier as if it were your own—had left them feeling diminished, ignored, and increasingly reluctant to voice their opinions. And while many of the women expressed appreciation for the degree to which I actively solicited their views during meetings, and said they didn't doubt my respect for their work, their stories forced me to look in the mirror and ask myself how much my own inclination toward machismo—my tolerance for a certain towel-snapping atmosphere in meetings, the enjoyment I took in a good verbal jousting—may have contributed to their discomfort.

I can't say that we resolved all of the concerns raised that night ("It's hard to unravel patriarchy in a single dinner," I said to Valerie afterward), any more than I could guarantee that my periodic check-ins with the Black, Latino, Asian, and Native American members of the team ensured that they always felt included. I do know that when I spoke to Rahm and the other senior men about how their female colleagues were feeling, they were surprised and chastened and vowed to do better. The women, meanwhile, seemed to take to heart my suggestion that they assert themselves more in discussions ("If somebody tries to talk over you, tell them you're not finished!")—not only for their own mental health but because they were knowledgeable and insightful and I needed to hear what they had to say if I was going to do my job well. A few months later, as we walked together from the West Wing to the EEOB, Valerie told me that she'd noticed some improvement in how the staffers were interacting.

"And how are you holding up?" she asked me.

I stopped at the top of the EEOB's stairs to search my jacket pockets for some notes I needed for the meeting we were about to attend. "I'm good," I said.

"You sure?" Her eyes narrowed as she searched my face like a doctor examining a patient for symptoms. I found what I was looking for and started walking again.

"Yeah, I'm sure," I said. "Why? Do I seem different to you?"

Valerie shook her head. "No," she said. "You seem exactly the same. That's what I don't understand."

· · ·

IT WASN'T THE first time Valerie had commented on how little the presidency had changed me. I understood that she meant it as a compliment—her way of expressing relief that I hadn't gotten too full of myself, lost my sense of humor, or turned into a bitter, angry jerk. But as war and the economic crisis dragged on and our political problems began to mount, she started worrying that maybe I was acting a little **too** calm, that I was just bottling up all the stress.

She wasn't the only one. Friends started sending notes of encouragement, somber and heartfelt, as if they'd just learned that I had a serious illness. Marty Nesbitt and Eric Whitaker discussed flying in to hang out and watch a ball game—a "boys' night," they said, just to take my mind off things. Mama Kaye, arriving for a visit, expressed genuine surprise at how well I looked in person.

"What'd you expect?" I teased, reaching down to give her a big hug. "You thought I was going to have a rash on my face? That my hair'd be falling out?"

"Oh, stop it," she said, playfully hitting me on the arm. She leaned back and looked at me the same way Valerie had, searching for signs. "I guess I just thought you'd look more tired. Are you getting enough to eat?"

Puzzled by all this solicitude, I happened to mention it to Gibbs one day. He chuckled. "Let me tell you, boss," he said, "if you watched cable news, **you'd** be worried about you too." I knew what Gibbs was driving at: Once you became president, people's perceptions of you—even the perceptions of those who knew you best—were inevitably shaped by the media. What I hadn't fully appreciated, though, at least not until I scanned a few news broadcasts, was how the images producers used in stories about my administration had shifted of late. Back when we were riding high, toward the end of the campaign and the start of my presidency, most news footage showed me active and smiling, shaking hands or speaking in front of dramatic backdrops, my gestures and facial expressions exuding energy and command. Now that most of the stories were negative, a different version of me appeared: older-looking, walking alone along the colonnade or across the South Lawn to Marine One, my shoulders slumped, my eyes downcast, my face weary and creased with the burdens of the office.

Being in the barrel put the sadder version of me on permanent display.

In fact, life as I was experiencing it didn't feel nearly so dire. Like my staff, I could have used more sleep. Each day had its share of aggravations, worries, and disappointments. I'd stew over mistakes I'd made and question strategies that hadn't panned out. There were meetings I dreaded, ceremonies I found foolish, conversations I would have rather avoided. While I continued to refrain from yelling at people, I cursed and complained plenty, and felt unfairly maligned at least once a day.

But as I'd discovered about myself during the campaign, obstacles and struggles rarely shook me to the core. Instead, depression was more likely to creep up on me when I felt useless, without purpose—when I was wasting my time or squandering opportunities. Even during my worst days as president, I never felt **that** way. The job didn't allow for boredom or existential paralysis, and when I sat down with my team to figure out the answer to a knotty problem, I usually came away energized rather than drained. Every trip I took—touring a manufacturing plant to see how something got made or visiting a lab where scientists explained a recent breakthrough—fed my imagination. Comforting a rural family displaced by a storm or meeting with inner-city teachers who were striving to reach kids others had written off, and allowing myself to feel, if just for a moment, what they were going through, made my heart bigger.

The fuss of being president, the pomp, the press, the physical constraints—all that I could have done without. The actual work, though?

The work, I loved. Even when it didn't love me back.

Outside of the job, I had tried to make peace with living in the bubble. I maintained my rituals: the morning workout, the dinner with my family, an evening walk on the South Lawn. In the early months of my presidency, that routine included reading a chapter from **Life of Pi** to Sasha each night before tucking her and Malia into bed. When it came time to choose our next book, though, Sasha decided that she, like her sister, had gotten too old to be read to. I hid my dismay and took to playing a nightly game of pool with Sam Kass instead.

We'd meet on the third floor of the residence after dinner, once Michelle and I had talked through our days and Sam had had a chance to clean up the kitchen. I'd put on some Marvin Gaye or OutKast or Nina Simone from my iPod, and the loser from the previous night's game would rack, and for the next half hour or so we'd play eight-ball. Sam would dish up White House gossip or ask for advice about his love life. I'd relay something funny one of the girls had said or go off on a brief political rant. Mostly, though, we just trash-talked and tried improbable shots, the crack of the break or the soft click of a ball rolling into a corner pocket clearing my mind before I headed to the Treaty Room to do my evening work.

Initially, the pool game had also given me an excuse to duck out and have a cigarette on the third-floor landing. Those detours stopped when I quit smoking, right after I signed the Affordable Care Act into law. I'd chosen that day because I liked the symbolism, but I'd made the decision a few weeks earlier, when Malia, smelling a cigarette on my breath, frowned and asked if I'd been smoking. Faced with the prospect of lying to my daughter or setting a bad example, I called the White House doctor and asked him to send me a box of nicotine gum. It did the trick, for I haven't had a cigarette since. But I did end up replacing one addiction with another: Through the remainder of my time in office, I would chomp on gum ceaselessly, the empty packets constantly spilling out of my pockets and leaving a trail of shiny square bread crumbs for others to find on the floor, under my desk, or wedged between sofa cushions.

Basketball offered another reliable refuge. When my schedule allowed, Reggie Love would organize a game on the weekend, rounding up some of his buddies and reserving time for us on an indoor court at the Fort McNair army base, the FBI headquarters, or the Department of the Interior. The runs were intense—with a couple of exceptions, most of the regular participants were former Division I college players in their late twenties or early thirties—and while I hated to admit it, I was usually one of the weaker players on the floor. Still, as long as I didn't try to do too much, I found I could hold my own, setting picks, feeding whoever on our team was hot and hitting a jumper when I was open, running the break and losing myself in the flow and camaraderie of competition.

Those pickup games represented continuity for me, a tether to my old self, and when my team beat Reggie's, I'd make sure he heard about it all week. But the enjoyment I got from playing basketball was nothing compared to the thrill—and stress—of rooting for Sasha's fourth-grade rec league team.

They called themselves the Vipers (props to whoever thought of the name), and each Saturday morning during the season, Michelle and I would travel to a small public park field house in Maryland and sit in the bleachers with the other families, cheering wildly whenever one of the girls came remotely close to making a basket, shouting reminders to Sasha to box out or get back on defense, and doing our best not to be "those parents," the kind who yell at the refs. Maisy Biden, Joe's granddaughter and one of Sasha's best friends, was the star of the team, but for most of the girls it was their first experience with organized basketball. Apparently the same was true for their coaches, a friendly young couple who taught at Sidwell and who, by their own admission, didn't consider basketball their primary sport. After observing an adorable but chaotic first couple of games, Reggie and I took it upon ourselves to draw up some plays and volunteered to conduct a few informal Sunday afternoon practice sessions with the team. We worked on the basics (dribbling, passing, making sure your shoelaces were tied before you ran onto the court), and although Reggie could get a little too intense when we ran drills ("Paige, don't let Isabel punk you like that!"), the girls seemed to have as much fun as we did. When the Vipers won the league championship in an 18–16 nail-biter, Reggie and I celebrated like it was the NCAA finals.

Every parent savors such moments, I suppose, when the world slows down, your strivings get pushed to the back of your mind, and all that matters is that you are present, fully, to witness the miracle of your child growing up. Given all the time I'd missed with the girls over years of campaigning and legislative sessions, I cherished the normal "dad stuff" that much more. But, of course, nothing about our lives was completely normal any longer, as I was reminded the following year when, in true Washington fashion, a few of the parents from a rival Sidwell team started complaining to the Vipers coaches, and presumably the school, that Reggie and I weren't offering training sessions to their kids too. We explained that there was nothing special about our practices—that it was just an excuse for me to spend extra time with Sasha—and offered to help other parents organize practices of their own. But when it became clear that the complaints had nothing to do with basketball ("They must think being coached by you is something they can put on a Harvard application," Reggie scoffed) and that the Vipers coaches were feeling squeezed, I decided it would be simpler for all concerned if I went back to just being a fan.

Despite a few exasperating incidents like that, there was no denying that our status as the First Family conferred plenty of benefits. Museums around town let us visit after hours, allowing us to avoid the crowds (Marvin and I still laugh over the time he decided to strategically plant himself in front of a large and very detailed portrait of a naked man at the Corcoran Gallery for fear that the girls might see it). Because the Motion Picture Association of America sent us DVDs of new releases, the White House movie theater got plenty of use, although Michelle's tastes and mine often diverged: She preferred rom-coms, while according to her, my favorite movies usually involved "terrible things happening to people, and then they die."

The incredible White House staff also made it easy for us to entertain guests. No longer did we have to worry, as most working parents with young kids do, about muster-ing the energy after a long week at the office to shop, cook, or straighten up a house that looks like it's been hit by a tornado. Along with weekend get-togethers with our regular circle of friends, we began hosting small din-ner parties in the residence every few months, inviting artists, writers, scholars, business leaders, and others whose paths we'd crossed and wanted to know better. Usually the dinners would last until well past midnight, full of wine-fueled conversations that inspired us (Toni Morrison, at once regal and mischievous, describing her friendship with James Baldwin); instructed us (the co-chair of my Council of Advisors on Science and Technology, Dr. Eric Lander, describing the latest break-throughs in genetic medicine); enchanted us (Meryl Streep leaning over to softly recite in Mandarin the lyrics to a song about clouds that she'd learned for a part years ago); and generally made me feel better about humanity's prospects.

But maybe the best White House perk involved music. One of Michelle's goals as First Lady was to make the White House more welcoming—a "People's House" in which all visitors would feel represented, rather than a remote, exclusive fortress of power. Working with the White House Social Office, she organized more tours for local school groups and started a mentorship program that paired disadvantaged kids with White House staffers. She opened up the South Lawn for trick-or-treating on Halloween, and held movie nights for military families.

As part of that effort, her office arranged for us to host a regular American music series in tandem with public television, in which some of the country's leading artists—household names like Stevie Wonder, Jennifer Lopez, and Justin Timberlake but also up-and-comers like Leon Bridges and living legends like B. B. King—spent part of a day conducting music workshops with area youths before performing in front of a couple hundred guests on an East Room stage, or sometimes on the South Lawn. Along with the Gershwin Prize concert, which the White House traditionally put on each year to honor a leading composer or performer, the series gave my family front-row seats three or four times a year at a live, star-studded musical extravaganza.

Every genre was represented: Motown and Broadway show tunes; classic blues and a Fiesta Latina; gospel and hip-hop; country, jazz, and classical. The musicians typically rehearsed the day before they were scheduled to appear, and if I happened to be upstairs in the residence as they were running through their set, I could hear the sounds of drums and bass and electric guitar reverberating through the Treaty Room floor. Sometimes I'd sneak down the back stairs of the residence and slip into the East Room, standing in the rear so as not to attract attention, and just watch the artists at work: a duet figuring

out their harmonies, a headliner tweaking an arrangement with the house band. I'd marvel at everyone's
mastery of their instruments, the generosity they showed
toward one another as they blended mind, body, and
spirit, and I'd feel a pang of envy at the pure, unambigu-
ous joy of their endeavors, such a contrast to the political
path I had chosen.

As for the actual concerts, they were absolutely electric. I can still picture Bob Dylan, with just a bassist, a
piano player, and his guitar, tenderly reworking "The
Times They Are a-Changin'." When finished, he stepped
off the stage, shook my hand, gave a little grin and bow
in front of me and Michelle, and vanished without a
word. I remember a young playwright of Puerto Rican
descent named Lin-Manuel Miranda, who told us in the
photo line before an evening of poetry, music, and
the spoken word that he planned to debut the first song
of what he hoped would be a hip-hop musical on the
life of America's first Treasury secretary, Alexander
Hamilton. We were politely encouraging but secretly
skeptical, until he got up onstage and started dropping
beats and the audience went absolutely nuts.

And there was the time Paul McCartney serenaded my
wife with "Michelle." She laughed, a little embarrassed, as
the rest of the audience applauded, and I wondered what
Michelle's parents would have said back in 1965, the year
the song came out, if someone had knocked on the door
of their South Side home and told them that someday the
Beatle who wrote it would be singing it to their daughter
from a White House stage.

Michelle loved those concerts as much as I did. But I
suspect she would have preferred to have attended them

as a guest rather than a host. On the surface, she had every reason to feel good about her own adjustment to our new life: Our daughters seemed happy; she'd quickly made a new circle of friends, many of them the mothers of Malia's and Sasha's classmates; and she had a little more flexibility than I did to leave the White House complex unnoticed. Her initiative to reduce childhood obesity—called Let's Move!—had been well received and was already showing meaningful results, and in collaboration with Jill Biden she would soon launch a new initiative, called Joining Forces, that would provide support to military families. Whenever she appeared in public, whether it was visiting a public school classroom or trading good-natured barbs with late-night television hosts, people seemed irresistibly drawn to her genuineness and warmth, her smile and quick wit. In fact, it was fair to say that, unlike me, she had not missed a step or hit a false note from the moment we'd arrived in Washington.

And yet, despite Michelle's success and popularity, I continued to sense an undercurrent of tension in her, subtle but constant, like the faint thrum of a hidden machine. It was as if, confined as we were within the walls of the White House, all of her previous sources of frustration became more concentrated, more vivid, whether it was my round-the-clock absorption with work, or the way politics exposed our family to constant scrutiny and attacks, or the tendency of even friends and family members to treat her role as secondary in importance.

More than anything, the White House reminded her daily that fundamental aspects of her life were no longer entirely within her control. Who we spent time with, where we went on vacation, where we'd be living after the 2012 election, even the safety of her family—all of it was at some level subject to how well I performed at my job, or what the West Wing staff did or didn't do, or the whims of voters, or the press corps, or Mitch McConnell, or the jobs numbers, or some completely unanticipated event occurring on the other side of the planet. Nothing was fixed anymore. Not even close. And so, consciously or not, a part of her stayed on alert, no matter what small triumphs and joys a day or week or month might bring, waiting and watching for the next turn of the wheel, bracing herself for calamity.

Michelle rarely shared such feelings directly with me. She knew the load I was carrying and saw no point in adding to it; for the foreseeable future, at least, there wasn't much I could do to change our circumstances. And maybe she stopped talking because she knew I'd try to reason away her fears, or try to placate her in some inconsequential way, or imply that all she needed was a change in attitude.

If I was fine, she should be too.

There remained stretches when it really did feel fine, evenings when the two of us snuggled under a blanket to watch a show on TV, Sunday afternoons when we got down on the carpet with the girls and Bo and the entire second floor of the residence filled up with laughter. More often, though, Michelle retired to her study once dinner was done, while I headed down the long hall to the Treaty Room. By the time I was finished with work, she'd already be asleep. I'd undress, brush my teeth, and slip under the covers, careful not to wake her. And although I rarely had trouble falling asleep during my time in the White House—I'd be so tired that within five minutes of my head hitting the pillow I'd usually be out cold—there were nights when, lying next to Michelle in the dark, I'd think about those days when everything between us felt lighter, when her smile was more constant and our love less encumbered, and my heart would suddenly tighten at the thought that those days might not return.

It makes me wonder now, with the benefit of hindsight, whether Michelle's was the more honest response to all the changes we were going through; whether in my seeming calm as crises piled up, my insistence that everything would work out in the end, I was really just protecting myself—and contributing to her loneliness.

I know that it was around this time that I started having a recurring dream. In it, I find myself on the streets of some unnamed city, a neighborhood with trees, storefronts, light traffic. The day is pleasant and warm, with a soft breeze, and people are out shopping or walking their dogs or coming home from work. In one version I'm riding a bike, but most often I'm on foot, and I'm strolling along, without any thoughts in particular, when suddenly I realize that no one recognizes me. My security detail is gone. There's nowhere I have to be. My choices have no consequence. I wander into a corner store and buy a bottle of water or iced tea, making small talk with the person behind the counter. I settle down on a nearby bench, pop open the cap on my drink, take a sip, and just watch the world passing by.

I feel like I've won the lottery.

. . .

RAHM THOUGHT HE had the answer for regaining political momentum. The Wall Street crisis had
exposed a breakdown in the system for regulating financial markets, and during the transition, I'd asked our
economic team to develop legislative reforms that would
make a future crisis less likely. As far as Rahm was concerned, the sooner we got such a "Wall Street reform" bill
drafted and up for a vote, the better.

"It puts us back on the side of the angels," he said.
"And if the Republicans try to block it, we'll shove it up
their ass."

There was every reason to expect that Mitch
McConnell would fight us on new financial regulations.
After all, he'd made a career of opposing any and all
forms of government regulation (environmental laws,
labor laws, workplace safety laws, campaign finance
laws, consumer protection laws) that might constrain
corporate America's ability to do whatever it damn well
pleased. But McConnell also understood the political
hazards of the moment—voters still associated the
Republican Party with big business and yacht-owning
billionaires—and he didn't plan on letting his party's
standard anti-regulation position get in the way of his
quest for the Senate majority. And so, while he made no
secret of his intention to filibuster my agenda at every
turn, a task made easier after Scott Brown's victory in the
Massachusetts Senate race deprived Democrats of their
sixtieth vote, he let Tim know in a meeting in his office
on Capitol Hill that he'd make an exception for Wall
Street reform. "He's going to vote against whatever we
propose," Tim told us after returning from the meeting,

"and so will most of his caucus. But he said we should be able to find five or so Republicans who'll work with us and he won't do anything to stop them."

"Anything else?" I asked.

"Only that obstruction is working for them," Tim said. "He seemed pretty pleased with himself."

McConnell's concession to the public mood was significant, but it didn't mean we'd have an easy time getting Wall Street reform through Congress. Banking industry executives continued to show no remorse for the economic havoc they'd caused. Nor did bankers show gratitude for all we'd done to yank them out of the fire (accusations that I was "anti-business" had become a regular feature in the financial press). On the contrary, they viewed our efforts to tighten regulations on their operations as unacceptably burdensome, if not downright offensive. They also retained one of the most powerful lobbying operations in Washington, with influential constituencies in every state and the deep pockets to spread campaign donations across both parties.

Beyond all-out opposition from the banks, we had to confront the sheer complexity of trying to regulate the modern financial system. Gone were the days when most of America's money ran in a simple, circular loop, with banks taking in customers' deposits and using that money to make plain vanilla loans to families and businesses. Trillions of dollars now moved across multiple borders in the blink of an eye. The holdings of nontraditional financial operations like hedge funds and private equity firms rivaled those of many banks, while computer-driven trading and exotic products like derivatives had the power to make or break markets. Within the United

States, oversight of this diffuse system was split among an assortment of federal agencies (the Fed, Treasury, FDIC, SEC, CFTC, OCC), most of which operated independently and fiercely protected their turf. Effective reform meant corralling these different players under a common regulatory framework; it also meant syncing up U.S. efforts with those made by regulators in other countries so that firms couldn't simply run their transactions through overseas accounts to avoid more stringent rules.

Finally we had to contend with sharp differences within the Democratic Party about both the shape and scope of reform. For those who leaned closer to the political center (and that included Tim and Larry as well as the majority of Democrats in Congress), the recent crisis had revealed serious but fixable flaws in an otherwise solid financial system. Wall Street's status as the world's preeminent financial center depended on growth and innovation, the argument went, and cycles of boom and bust—with corresponding swings between irrational exuberance and irrational panic—were built-in features not only of modern capitalism but of the human psyche. Since it was neither possible nor even desirable to eliminate all risk to investors and firms, the goals of reform were defined narrowly: Put guardrails around the system to reduce the most excessive forms of risk-taking, ensure transparency in the operations of major institutions, and "make the system safe for failure," as Larry put it, so that those individuals or financial institutions that made bad bets didn't drag everyone else down with them.

To many on the left, this sort of targeted approach to reform fell woefully short of what was needed and would merely put off a long-overdue reckoning with a system that failed to serve the interests of ordinary Americans. They blamed some of the economy's most troubling trends on a bloated, morally suspect financial sector— whether it was the corporate world's preference for cost cutting and layoffs over long-term investments as a way of boosting short-term earnings, or the use of debt-financed acquisitions by certain private equity firms to strip down existing businesses and resell their spare parts for undeserved profit, or the steady rise in income inequality and the shrinking share of taxes paid by the über-rich. To reduce these distorting effects and stop the speculative frenzies that so often triggered financial crises, they urged, we should consider a more radical overhaul of Wall Street. The reforms they favored included capping the size of U.S. banks and reinstating Glass-Steagall, a Depression-era law that had prohibited FDIC-insured banks from engaging in investment banking, which had been mostly repealed during the Clinton administration.

In a lot of ways, these intraparty divisions on financial regulation reminded me of the healthcare debate, when advocates of a single-payer system had dismissed any accommodations to the existing private insurance system as selling out. And just as had been true in the healthcare debate, I had some sympathy for the Left's indictment of the status quo. Rather than efficiently allocate capital to productive uses, Wall Street really **did** increasingly function like a trillion-dollar casino, its outsized profits and compensation packages overly dependent on ever-greater leverage and speculation. Its obsession with quarterly earnings **had** warped corporate decision-making and encouraged short-term thinking.

Untethered to place, indifferent to the impact of globalization on particular workers and communities, the financial markets **had** helped accelerate the offshoring of jobs and the concentration of wealth in a handful of cities and economic sectors, leaving huge swaths of the country drained of money, talent, and hope.

Big, bold policies could make a dent in these problems, most of which had to do with rewriting the tax code, strengthening labor laws, and changing the rules of corporate governance. All three items were high on my to-do list.

But when it came to regulating the nation's **financial** markets to make the system more stable, the Left's prescription missed its mark. The evidence didn't show that limiting the size of U.S. banks would have prevented the recent crisis or the need for federal intervention once the system began to unravel. JPMorgan's assets dwarfed those of Bear Stearns and Lehman Brothers, but it was those smaller firms' highly leveraged bets on securitized subprime mortgages that had set off a panic. The last major U.S. financial crisis, back in the 1980s, hadn't involved big banks at all; instead, the system had been rocked by a deluge of high-risk loans by thousands of small, poorly capitalized regional savings and loan associations (S&Ls) in cities and small towns across the country. Given the scope of their operations, we thought it made sense for regulators to give mega-banks like Citi or Bank of America extra scrutiny—but cutting their assets in half wouldn't change that. And since the banking sectors of most European and Asian countries were actually more concentrated than they were here, limiting the size of U.S. banks would put them at a big disadvantage in the international marketplace, all without eliminating the overall risk to the system.

For similar reasons, the growth of the non-bank financial sector made Glass-Steagall's distinction between investment banks and FDIC-insured commercial banks largely obsolete. The largest bettors on subprime mortgage securities—AIG, Lehman, Bear, Merrill, as well as Fannie and Freddie—weren't commercial banks backed by federal guarantees. Investors hadn't cared about the absence of guarantees and poured so much money into them anyway that the entire financial system was threatened when they started to fail. Conversely, traditional FDIC-insured banks like Washington Mutual and IndyMac got into trouble not by behaving like investment banks and underwriting high-flying securities but by making tons of subprime loans to unqualified buyers in order to drive up their earnings. Given how easily capital now flowed between various financial entities in search of higher returns, stabilizing the system required that we focus on the risky practices we were trying to curb rather than the type of institution involved.

And then there were the politics. We didn't have anything close to the votes in the Senate for either reviving Glass-Steagall or passing legislation to shrink U.S. banks, any more than we'd had the votes for a single-payer healthcare system. Even in the House, Dems were anxious about any perception of overreaching, especially if it caused the financial markets to pull in their horns again and made the economy worse. "My constituents hate Wall Street right now, Mr. President," one suburban Democrat told me, "but they didn't sign up for a complete teardown." FDR may have once had a mandate from voters to try anything, including a restructuring of American capitalism, after three wrenching years of the Depression, but partly because we'd stopped the situation from ever getting that bad, our mandate for change was a whole lot narrower. Our best chance for broadening that mandate, I figured, was to notch a few wins while we could.

IN JUNE 2009, after months of fine-tuning, our draft legislation for financial reform was ready to take to Congress. And while it didn't contain all the provisions the Left had been looking for, it remained a massively ambitious effort to revamp twentieth-century regulations for the twenty-first-century economy.

At the core of the package was a proposal to increase the percentage of capital that all financial institutions of "systemic" importance—whether banks or non-banks— were required to hold. More capital meant less borrowing to finance risky bets. Greater liquidity meant these institutions could better weather sudden runs during a market downturn. Forcing Wall Street's main players to maintain a bigger capital cushion against losses would fortify the system as a whole; and to make sure these institutions hit their marks, they'd have to regularly undergo the same kind of stress test we'd applied at the height of the crisis.

Next we needed a formal mechanism to allow any single firm, no matter how big, to fail in an orderly way, so that it wouldn't contaminate the entire system. The FDIC already had the power to put any federally insured bank through what amounted to a structured bankruptcy proceeding, with rules governing how assets were liquidated and how claimants divvied up whatever remained.

Our draft legislation gave the Fed a comparable "resolution authority" over all systemically important institutions, whether they were banks or not.

To improve consistency of enforcement, we proposed streamlining the functions and responsibilities of various federal agencies. To facilitate quicker responses in the event of a major market disruption, we formalized authority for many of the emergency actions—"foam on the runway," our economic team called it—that the Fed and Treasury had deployed during the recent crisis. And to catch potential problems before they got out of hand, our draft legislation tightened up rules governing the specialized markets that constituted much of the financial system's plumbing. We paid particular attention to the buying and selling of derivatives, those often impenetrable forms of securities that had helped intensify losses across the system once the subprime mortgage market collapsed. Derivatives had legitimate uses—all sorts of companies used them to hedge their risk against big swings in currency or commodity prices. But they also offered irresponsible traders some of the biggest opportunities for the kinds of high-stakes gambling that put the entire system at risk. Our reforms would push most of these transactions into a public exchange, allowing for clearer rules and greater supervision.

The bulk of these proposals were highly technical, involving aspects of the financial system that were hidden from public view. But there was a final element of our draft legislation that had less to do with high finance and more to do with people's everyday lives. The crisis on Wall Street couldn't have happened without the explosion of subprime mortgage lending. And although plenty of those loans went to sophisticated borrowers—those who understood the risks involved with adjustable rate mortgages and balloon payments as they flipped Florida condos or purchased Arizona vacation homes—a larger percentage had been marketed and sold to working-class families, many of them Black and Hispanic, people who believed they were finally gaining access to the American Dream only to see their homes and their savings snatched away in foreclosure proceedings.

The failure to protect consumers from unfair or misleading lending practices wasn't restricted to mortgages. Perpetually short on cash no matter how hard they worked, millions of Americans regularly found themselves subject to exorbitant interest rates, hidden fees, and just plain bad deals at the hands of credit card issuers, payday lenders (many of them quietly owned or financed by blue-chip banks), used-car dealers, cut-rate insurers, retailers selling furniture on installment plans, and purveyors of reverse mortgages. Often they found themselves in a downward spiral of compounding debt, missed payments, shot credit, and repossessions that left them in a deeper hole than where they'd started. Across the country, sketchy financial-industry practices contributed to rising inequality, reduced upward mobility, and the kinds of hidden debt bubbles that made the economy more vulnerable to major disruptions.

Having already signed legislation reforming the credit card industry, I agreed with my team that the aftermath of the crisis offered us a unique chance to make more progress on the consumer protection front. As it happened, Harvard law professor and bankruptcy expert Elizabeth Warren had come up with an idea that might deliver the kind of impact we were looking for: a new consumer finance protection agency meant to bolster the patchwork of spottily enforced state and federal regulations already in place and to shield consumers from questionable financial products the same way the Consumer Product Safety Commission kept shoddy or dangerous consumer goods off the shelves.

I was a longtime admirer of Warren's work, dating back to the 2003 publication of her book **The Two-Income Trap,** in which Warren and her coauthor, Amelia Tyagi, provided an incisive and passionate description of the growing pressures facing working families with children. Unlike most academics, Warren showed a gift for translating financial analysis into stories that ordinary folks could understand. In the intervening years, she had emerged as one of the financial industry's most effective critics, prompting Harry Reid to appoint her as chair of the congressional panel overseeing TARP.

Tim and Larry were apparently less enamored with Warren than I was, each of them having been called to make repeated appearances before her committee. Although they appreciated her intelligence and embraced her idea of a consumer finance protection agency, they saw her as something of a grandstander.

"She's really good at taking potshots at us," Tim said in one of our meetings, "even when she knows there aren't any serious alternatives to what we're already doing."

I looked up in mock surprise. "Well, that's shocking," I said. "A member of an oversight committee playing to the crowd? Rahm, you ever heard of such a thing?"

"No, Mr. President," Rahm said. "It's an outrage."

Even Tim had to crack a smile.

. . .

THE PROCESS OF getting Wall Street reform through Congress was no less laborious than our adventures with the Affordable Care Act, but it didn't receive nearly as much attention. Partly this had to do with the subject matter. Even members and lobbyists intent on killing the legislation kept a relatively low profile, not wanting to be seen as defenders of Wall Street so soon after the crisis, and many of the bill's finer points were too arcane to generate interest in the popular press.

One issue that did capture headlines involved a proposal by former Federal Reserve chairman Paul Volcker to prohibit FDIC-insured banks from trading on their own accounts or operating their own hedge funds and private equity shops. According to Volcker, this sort of provision offered a simple way to restore some of the prudential boundaries that Glass-Steagall had placed around commercial banks. Before we knew it, our willingness to include the "Volcker Rule" in our legislation became a litmus test among many on the left for how serious we were about Wall Street reform. Volcker, a gruff, cigar-smoking, six-foot-seven economist by training, was an unlikely hero for progressives. In 1980, as Fed chairman, he'd hiked U.S. interest rates to an unprecedented 20 percent in order to break the back of America's then-raging inflation, resulting in a brutal recession and 10 percent unemployment. The Fed's painful medicine had angered unions and many Democrats at the time; on the other hand, it had not only tamed inflation but helped lay the groundwork for stable economic growth in the 1980s and '90s, making Volcker a revered figure in both New York and Washington.

In recent years, Volcker had grown bluntly critical of Wall Street's worst excesses, gaining some liberal admirers. He'd endorsed my campaign early, and I'd come to value his counsel enough that I appointed him to chair an advisory group on the economic crisis. With his no-nonsense demeanor, and his belief in free-market efficiency as well as in public institutions and the common good, he was something of a throwback (my grandmother would have liked him), and after hearing him out in a private meeting in the Oval, I was persuaded that his proposal to curb proprietary trading made sense. When I discussed the idea with Tim and Larry, though, they were skeptical, arguing that it would be difficult to administer and might impinge on legitimate services that banks provided their customers. To me, their position sounded flimsy—one of the few times during our work together when I felt they harbored more sympathy for the financial industry's perspective than the facts warranted—and for weeks I continued to press them on the matter. At the start of 2010, as Tim grew concerned that momentum for Wall Street reform was beginning to lag, he finally recommended we make a version of the Volcker Rule part of our legislative package.

"If it helps us get the bill passed," Tim said, "we can find a way to make it work."

For Tim, it was a rare concession to political optics. Axe and Gibbs, who'd been filling my in-box with polls showing that 60 percent of voters thought my administration was too friendly toward the banks, were thrilled with the news; they suggested that we announce the proposal at the White House with Volcker on hand. I asked if the general public would understand such an obscure rule change.

"They don't need to understand it," Gibbs said. "If the banks hate it, they'll figure it must be a good thing."

With the basic parameters of our legislation set, it fell to House Financial Services Committee chairman Barney Frank and Senate Banking Committee chairman Chris Dodd, both twenty-nine-year veterans of Congress, to help get it passed. They were an unlikely pair. Barney had made his name as a liberal firebrand and the first member of Congress to come out as gay. His thick glasses, disheveled suits, and strong Jersey accent lent him a workingman's vibe, and he was as tough, smart, and knowledgeable as anyone in Congress, with a withering, rapid-fire wit that made him a favorite of reporters and a headache for political opponents. (Barney once spoke to one of my classes while I was a student at Harvard Law, during which he dressed me down for asking what he apparently considered a dumb question. I didn't think it was that dumb. Thankfully, he didn't remember our first encounter.)

Chris Dodd, on the other hand, came off as the consummate Washington insider. Immaculately dressed, his silver hair as shiny and crisp as a TV news anchor's, always ready to roll out a bit of Capitol Hill gossip or an Irish tall tale, he'd grown up in politics—the son of a former U.S. senator, one of Ted Kennedy's best friends, pals with any number of industry lobbyists despite his liberal voting record. We'd developed a warm relationship while I was in the Senate, based in part on Chris's good-natured acknowledgment of the absurdity of the place ("You didn't think this was actually on the level, did you?" he'd say with a wink after some colleague made an impassioned plea on behalf of a bill while actively trying to undermine said bill behind the scenes). But he took pride in his effectiveness as a legislator, and had been one of the driving forces behind such impactful laws as the Family and Medical Leave Act.

Together, they made a formidable team, each perfectly suited for the politics of their chamber. In the House, a dominant Democratic majority meant that passing a financial-reform bill was never in question. Instead, our main task was keeping our own members on track. Not only did Barney have a firm command of the legislative details; he had the credibility inside the Democratic caucus to temper impractical demands from fellow progressives, as well as the clout to ward off efforts by more transactional Democrats to water down the legislation on behalf of special interests. In the Senate, where we needed every vote we could find, Chris's patient bedside manner and willingness to reach out to even the most recalcitrant Republicans helped soothe the nerves of conservative Democrats; he also gave us a useful conduit to industry lobbyists who opposed the bill but didn't find Chris scary.

Despite these advantages, moving what came to be known as "Dodd-Frank" involved the same kind of sausage-making that had been required to pass the healthcare bill, with a flurry of compromises that often left me privately steaming. Over our strong objections, the car dealers won an exemption from our new consumer protection agency's oversight: With prominent dealerships in every congressional district, many of them considered pillars of the community for their sponsorship of Little League teams or donations to the local hospital, even the most regulation-happy Democrat ran scared of potential blowback. Our effort to streamline the number of regulatory agencies overseeing the financial system died an inglorious death; with each agency subject to the jurisdiction of a different congressional committee (the Commodity Futures Trading Commission, for example, reported to the House and Senate Agriculture Committees), Democratic committee chairs fiercely resisted the idea of giving up their leverage over some part of the financial industry. As Barney explained to Tim, we could conceivably consolidate the SEC and the CFTC: "Just not in the United States."

In the Senate, where the need to get to the sixty-vote threshold in order to overcome a filibuster gave every senator leverage, we were left to contend with all sorts of individual requests. Republican Scott Brown, fresh off a victorious campaign in which he'd railed against Harry Reid's various "backroom deals" to get the healthcare bill passed, indicated a willingness to vote for Wall Street reform—but not without a deal of his own, asking if we could exempt a pair of favored Massachusetts banks from the new regulations. He saw no irony in this. A group of left-leaning Democrats introduced with much fanfare an amendment that they claimed would make the Volcker Rule's restrictions on proprietary trading even tougher. Except that when you read the fine print, their amendment carved out loopholes for a smorgasbord of interests—the insurance industry, real estate investments, trusts, and on and on—that did big business in these senators' individual states.

"Another day in the world's greatest deliberative body," Chris said.

At times, I felt like the fisherman in Hemingway's

The Old Man and the Sea, sharks gnawing at my catch as I tried to tow it to shore. But as the weeks passed, the core of our reforms survived the amendment process remarkably intact. A number of provisions introduced by congressional members—including improved disclosure of executive compensation in public companies, increased transparency in credit-rating agencies, and new claw-back mechanisms to prevent Wall Street executives from walking away with millions in bonuses as a result of questionable practices—actually made the bill better. Thanks to strong cooperation between our two lead sponsors, the conference to reconcile differences between the House and Senate versions of the bill saw none of the intraparty squabbling that had played out during the negotiations over healthcare. And in mid-July 2010, after a vote of 237–192 in the House and 60–39 in the Senate (with three Republicans voting "aye" in each chamber), we held a White House ceremony where I signed into law the Dodd-Frank Wall Street Reform and Consumer Protection Act.

It was a significant triumph: the most sweeping change to the rules governing America's financial sector since the New Deal. The law had its warts and unwanted compromises, and it certainly wouldn't put an end to every instance of foolishness, greed, shortsightedness, or dishonesty on Wall Street. But by establishing the equivalent of "better building codes, smoke detectors, and sprinkler systems," as Tim liked to describe it, Dodd-Frank would check a number of reckless practices, give regulators the tools to put out financial fires before they got out of hand, and make crises on the scale we'd just seen far less likely. And in the new Consumer Financial Protection Bureau

(CFPB), American families now had a powerful advocate in their corner. Through its work, they could expect a fairer, more transparent credit market, and real savings as they tried to buy a house, finance a car, deal with a family emergency, send their kids to college, or plan for retirement.

But if my team and I could take pride in the substance of what we'd achieved, we also had to acknowledge what had become obvious even before the bill was signed: Dodd-Frank's historic reforms weren't going to give us much of a political lift. Despite valiant efforts by Favs and the rest of my speechwriters, it was hard to make "derivative clearinghouses" and "proprietary trading bans" sound transformational. Most of the law's improvements to the system would remain invisible to the public—more a matter of bad outcomes prevented than tangible benefits gained. The idea of a consumer agency for financial products was popular with voters, but the CFPB would take time to set up, and people were looking for help right away. With conservatives denouncing the legislation as a guarantee of future bailouts and another step toward socialism, and with progressives unhappy that we hadn't done more to remake the banks, it was easy for voters to conclude that the sound and fury around Dodd-Frank signified nothing more than the usual Washington scrum—especially since, by the time it passed, all anybody wanted to talk about was a gaping, gushing hole at the bottom of the ocean.

» Rahm letting me know that the House had just passed a landmark climate bill. My chief of staff lived for days like this, when we scored a clear win.

⌃ A marathon Sunday session with my economic team, including (**from left**) Larry Summers, Tim Geithner, and Christy Romer.

« Senate Majority Leader Harry Reid and I hit it off early on. Despite our differences in age and experience, we both had the sense that we had overcome long odds.

Even as we navigated the pressures of those first months in the White House, Michelle and I could always make each other laugh. And having our friend and senior advisor Valerie Jarrett close by made everything easier.

Bo showed up at the White House ready to explore. He was a gift from Ted and Vicki Kennedy and instantly made the place more of a home.

» Touring the Pyramids of Giza offered a humbling reminder that this world endures long after we're gone.

« Palestinians in Gaza watching me speak in Cairo on June 4, 2009. During the campaign, I'd pledged to deliver an address to the world's Muslims, believing that acknowledging the sources of tension between the West and the Muslim world would be a first step toward peaceful coexistence.

» Congratulating Sonia Sotomayor just before she officially became a Supreme Court justice. I believed that her life experiences gave her a fuller understanding of the real-world context of the Court's decisions.

Denis McDonough was one of my closest advisors on foreign policy and a good friend. He sweated the details; volunteered for the most difficult, thankless tasks; and could not be outworked.

«

»
French president Nicolas Sarkozy and German chancellor Angela Merkel—two leaders who couldn't be more temperamentally different—at the G8 Summit in July 2009.

«
Ben Rhodes started out as my National Security Counc speechwriter and proved vital. I could count on him tc turn in a draft speech that no only captured my voice but channeled my worldview.

A visit to Vladimir Putin's dacha included a long monologue by our host, chronicling every perceived injustice, betrayal, and slight that he and the Russian people had suffered at the hands of the arrogant Americans.

The girls made every trip they joined better. Here's eight-year-old Sasha strolling through the Kremlin like a pint-sized secret agent in a trench coat.

My "body man" Reggie Love and I took it upon ourselves to help coach Sasha's fourth-grade basketball team. When the Vipers won the championship in an 18–16 nail-biter, we celebrated like it was the NCAA finals.

»

«

With press secretary Robert Gibbs (**center**), whose smart-aleck humor and keen instincts often saved the day, and Reggie Love, who never took it easy on me on the basketball court.

»

Stealing a moment to read. The quiet never lasted long.

Part of the argument I made to Michelle before running for president was that if I pulled it off, kids all over the world would see themselves and their possibilities differently. And that alone would be worth it.

I can still hear Bob Dylan reworking a stirring version of "The Times They Are a-Changin'" before shaking my hand and vanishing without a word.

At Dover Air Force Base with Attorney General Eric Holder (**far right**) for the dignified transfer of eighteen Americans who had died in Afghanistan. It was rare for presidents to attend transfers, but I thought it was important that a commander in chief reckon with the true cost of war.

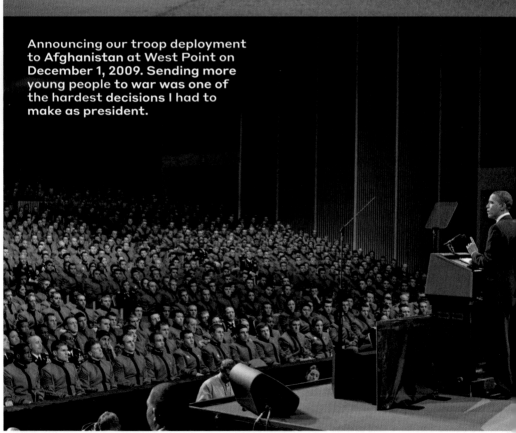

Announcing our troop deployment to Afghanistan at West Point on December 1, 2009. Sending more young people to war was one of the hardest decisions I had to make as president.

I first met Sergeant First Class Cory Remsburg in Normandy, several weeks before he headed to his tenth deployment in Afghanistan. By coincidence, I encountered him again at the Bethesda Naval Hospital, after he'd been severely injured by an IED. Over the years, we visited and stayed in touch.

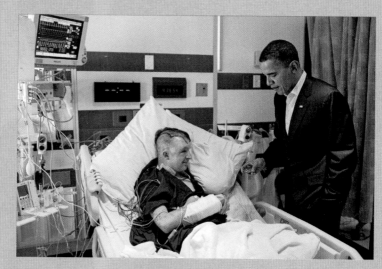

Meeting some of our brave young men and women in Afghanistan in March 2010. They inspired me so much.

Members of my national security team at West Point. The hours we spent debating the deployment plan forced us to refine America's strategic objectives in Afghanistan in a way that prevented mission creep.

Queen Elizabeth II embodied the special relationship between the United States and the United Kingdom, and Michelle and I always loved spending time with her.

With President Hu Jintao at the Great Hall of the People in Beijing.

» Going over my address to a joint session of Congress on healthcare reform with speechwriter Jon Favreau. I could be a demanding editor.

« Standing in the Roosevelt Room with Joe Biden and my staff on March 21, 2010, as the Affordable Care Act secured the votes to pass. I thought about my mom, who'd died of cancer, and all the Americans like her who'd needed this for so long.

Celebrating the passage of the Affordable Care Act with Secretary of Health and Human Services Kathleen Sebelius and Speaker Nancy Pelosi, the toughest, most skilled legislative strategist I've met. »

Getting a briefing on the **Deepwater Horizon** disaster during a trip to the Gulf Coast. U.S. Coast Guard commandant Admiral Thad Allen (**seated, left**) and EPA administrator Lisa Jackson (**far right**) were essential members of the team managing our response to the oil spill.

»

A swing-set summit with eleven-year-old Malia, who was always full of questions. Here, she's asking me about the oil spill.

»

Serving on the National Security Council, with a focus on atrocity prevention and human rights, Samantha Power was a close friend—and a temperature check on my conscience.

...didn't feel that I deserved to be in the company of the transformative figures who'd been given the Nobel Peace Prize. Instead, I saw the prize as a call to action.

With Joe on my way to sign Dodd-Frank, our Wall Street reform bill, into law. I kept my word and made sure he was always the last voice in the room. In return I received wise counsel—and found another brother.

August 31, 2010: Abou[t] to announce the end o[f] combat operations in Ira[q] from the same desk wher[e] President Bush announce[d] their beg[inn]ing. A lon[g] time [com]ing, but [a] pr[om]ise kep[t]

May 1, 2011: With my national security team, watching as Navy SEALs raided Osama bin Laden's compound. It was the first and only time as president that I watched a military operation unfold in real time.

Dining at the presidential palace in New Delhi with Prime Minister Manmohan Singh, a thoughtful and uncommonly decent man.

»

«

President Mahmoud Abbas, President Hosni Mubarak, and Prime Minister Benjamin Netanyahu checking their watches to see if the sun had officially set. It was the Muslim month of Ramadan, and we had to be sure the fast had been lifted before sitting down to dinner.

«

Preparing to face the press corps the day after the Democrats were routed in the 2010 midterms.

I treasured any time I got with my family. A visit to the **Christ the Redeemer** statue in Rio de Janeiro turned out to be magical.

For eight years the walk down the West Colonnade framed my day—a minute-long, open-air commute from home to office and back again.

CHAPTER 23

THE FIRST OFFSHORE OIL DRILLING operations in the Gulf of Mexico were simple affairs, wooden platforms constructed in shallow waters beginning in the late 1930s. As technology advanced and America's thirst for oil grew unabated, companies ventured farther and farther from land, and by 2010 more than three thousand rigs and production platforms sat off the coasts of Texas, Louisiana, Mississippi, and Alabama, dotting the horizon like castles on stilts. They became a potent symbol of oil's central role in the regional economy: the billions in annual revenue it generated and the tens of thousands of people whose livelihoods depended, directly or indirectly, on siphoning up the remains of the ancient plants and animals converted by nature into the viscous black gold pooled beneath the ocean floor.

And when it came to rigs, few were more impressive than the **Deepwater Horizon**. Roughly thirty stories tall and longer than a football field, this mobile, half-billion-dollar semisubmersible could function in water as deep as ten thousand feet and drill exploratory wells several miles deeper than that. Operating a rig this size cost around $1 million a day, but major oil companies considered the expense well worth it. Their continued growth and profits depended on tapping potentially vast reservoirs buried at what were previously unreachable depths.

The **Deepwater Horizon** was owned by the Switzerland-based contractor Transocean and since 2001 had been leased by BP, one of the largest oil companies in the world. BP had used the rig to explore the U.S. section of the Gulf, discovering at least two enormous and potentially lucrative reservoirs beneath the seafloor. Just one of those fields, the Tiber, contained what was estimated to be a mind-boggling three billion barrels of oil. To access it, **Deepwater** crews had in 2009 drilled one of the deepest wells on record—35,055 feet under 4,130 feet of water, or farther beneath the ocean's surface than the height of Mount Everest.

Hoping to repeat that success, BP dispatched the **Deepwater Horizon** to drill an exploratory well in another prospective oil field, called the Macondo, in early 2010. Located about fifty miles off the coast of Louisiana, the Macondo wasn't quite as far down as the Tiber—a "mere" twenty thousand feet or so. But in ultradeep underwater drilling, there was no such thing as a routine job. Accessing each reservoir raised unique challenges, often involving weeks of tinkering, complex calculations, and ad hoc decisions. And Macondo proved to be an especially difficult field, mainly due to fragile formation and uneven levels of fluid pressure.

The project quickly fell weeks behind schedule, costing BP millions of dollars. Engineers, designers, and contractors disputed aspects of the well's design. Nevertheless, by April 20, the well reached three and a half miles below the ocean's surface and appeared almost complete. A team from Halliburton, a contractor on the project, injected cement down the well bore to seal the edges of the pipe. Once the cement had set, BP engineers began to conduct a series of safety tests before moving the **Deepwater** on to its next assignment.

Shortly after five p.m., one of those tests revealed possible gas leakage through the cement casing, signaling a potentially dangerous situation. Despite the warning signs, BP engineers decided to continue their process, pumping out the muddy lubricant used to offset pressure imbalances during drilling. By nine-thirty p.m., a powerful surge of gas had entered the drill pipe. A four-hundred-ton set of emergency valves called the blowout preventer—designed to seal off the well in the event of a sudden pressure increase—malfunctioned, allowing the highly pressurized and combustible gas to erupt through the platform and shoot a black geyser of mud lubricant up into the sky. Clouds of gas collected inside the rig's engine control room and quickly ignited, rocking the entire structure with a pair of violent explosions. A tower of flames torched the night sky, as crew members scrambled into lifeboats or jumped into the debris-filled waters. Of the 126 persons aboard the rig, 98 managed to escape without physical harm, 17 were injured, and 11 platform workers remained unaccounted for. The **Deepwater Horizon** would continue to burn for the next thirty-six hours, its massive ball of fire and smoke visible for miles.

I WAS IN the residence when I got word of what was happening in the Gulf, having just returned from a West

Coast fundraising trip for Democratic congressional candidates. My first thought was "Not again." Just fifteen days earlier, a coal dust explosion at Massey Energy's Upper Big Branch Mine, in West Virginia, had killed twenty-nine miners, the worst mining disaster in nearly forty years. Although the investigation of that disaster was still in its early stages, we already knew that Massey had a long history of safety violations. In contrast, the **Deepwater** rig hadn't had a serious accident in seven years. Still, I couldn't help but connect the two events and consider the human costs of the world's dependence on fossil fuels: the number of people who each day were forced to risk lungs, limbs, and sometimes their lives to fill our gas tanks and keep the lights on—and generate otherworldly profits for distant executives and shareholders.

I knew also that the explosion would have serious implications for our energy agenda. A few weeks earlier, I'd authorized the Department of the Interior to allow the sale of certain offshore leases, which would open oil exploration (though not yet actual production) in the eastern Gulf and some waters off the Atlantic states and Alaska. I was following through on a campaign promise: In the midst of surging gas prices and with the McCain-Palin proposal to open America's coastline to wholesale drilling gaining traction in public polls, I'd pledged to consider a more limited expansion of drilling as part of an "all of the above" energy strategy. As a matter of policy, any transition to a clean energy future would take decades to complete; in the meantime, I had no problem with increasing U.S. oil and gas production to reduce our reliance on imports from petrostates like Russia and Saudi Arabia.

Above all, my decision to allow new exploratory drilling was a last-ditch effort to salvage our climate change legislation, which was by then on life support. The previous fall, when GOP senator Lindsey Graham had agreed to help put together a bipartisan climate bill, he had warned that we'd have to give something up in order to win enough Republican support to overcome a filibuster, and more offshore drilling had been at the top of his list. Taking Graham at his word, Joe Lieberman and John Kerry spent months working in tandem with Carol Browner, trying to persuade environmental groups that the trade was worth it, pointing out that the environmental risks of offshore drilling had been reduced by improvements in technology and that any final agreement would preclude oil companies from operating in sensitive areas like the Arctic National Wildlife Refuge.

At least some environmental groups were prepared to play ball. Unfortunately, as the months passed, it became increasingly obvious that Graham couldn't deliver on his end of the bargain. It's not that he didn't try. He worked to line up the oil companies behind a deal and courted moderate Republicans like Susan Collins and Olympia Snowe, as well as oil-state senators like Alaska's Lisa Murkowski, hoping they'd cosponsor the bill. But no matter how many concessions Kerry and Lieberman were prepared to make, Graham couldn't get any takers within the GOP caucus. The political price for cooperating with my administration remained too high.

Graham himself had started taking heat for his work

on the climate bill, from both constituents and conservative media. His demands for staying with the bill
escalated, making it harder for Kerry to keep environmental groups on board. Even our announcement that
we were laying the groundwork to open up new areas to
drilling drew Graham's ire; rather than viewing it as a
show of good faith on our part, he complained that we'd
undercut him by taking away a key bargaining chip.
Rumors began circulating that he was looking for an
opportune time to abandon the effort altogether.

All this came before the **Deepwater** accident. With
newscasts suddenly flashing hellish images of a burning
rig, we knew that environmental groups were sure to
back off any bill that expanded offshore drilling. That, in
turn, would give Graham the excuse he needed to jump
ship. No matter how I sliced it, I could draw only one
conclusion: My already slim chances of passing climate
legislation before the midterm elections had just gone up
in smoke.

THE MORNING AFTER the **Deepwater** blowout,
I took some solace in reports that much of the oil released
by the explosion was burning off at the ocean's surface, at
least slightly reducing the prospects of severe environmental damage. Carol confirmed that BP's emergency
vessels and the U.S. Coast Guard had made it to the
scene quickly, that search-and-rescue operations for
the missing rig workers were ongoing, and that we were
in close contact with state and local authorities. Under a
federal law passed in the wake of the 1989 **Exxon Valdez**
tanker accident in Alaska, BP bore full responsibility for
cleaning up the spill. Nevertheless, I mobilized the Coast

Guard, as well as the EPA and the Department of the Interior, to assess the damage and provide any support the company might need.

Figuring we had a reasonable handle on the situation, I kept to my schedule, traveling to New York the following day to give a speech on Wall Street reform. By the time I arrived, though, the disaster had intensified. Weakened by the ongoing inferno, the entire **Deepwater** structure had collapsed and sunk into the ocean, spewing black smoke as all thirty-three thousand tons of it disappeared from view, almost certainly damaging the undersea apparatus beneath it. With the unknowns rapidly multiplying, I asked Rahm to set up a briefing upon my return, gathering U.S. Coast Guard commandant Admiral Thad Allen, Janet Napolitano of Homeland Security, and Secretary of the Interior Ken Salazar, whose department was responsible for overseeing offshore drilling. As it turned out, the only time we could fit in a meeting was six p.m.—right after I finished addressing the couple hundred people we'd invited to a previously arranged Rose Garden reception celebrating the fortieth anniversary of Earth Day.

It was a bit of cosmic irony that I was in no mood to appreciate.

"Hell of a farewell tour we're giving you, Thad," I said, shaking hands with Admiral Allen as he and the rest of the group filed into the Oval Office. Stout and ruddy-faced, with a whisk-broom mustache, Allen was just a month away from retiring after thirty-nine years of service in the Coast Guard.

"Well, hopefully we can get this mess under control for you before I go, Mr. President," Allen replied.

I signaled for everyone to have a seat. The tone grew

somber as Allen explained that the Coast Guard had diminished hopes when it came to the search-and-rescue operations—too much time had passed for any of the **Deepwater**'s eleven missing crew members to have survived in open seas. As for the cleanup, he reported that BP and the Coast Guard response teams had deployed specially equipped boats to skim oil left from the explosion off the water's surface. Fixed-wing aircraft were scheduled to begin dropping chemical dispersants to break up the oil into smaller droplets. And the Coast Guard was working with BP and the impacted states to pre-position booms—floating barriers of sponge and plastic—to help prevent the possibility of oil spreading to the shore.

"What's BP saying about liability?" I asked, turning to Salazar. Balding and bespectacled, with a sunny disposition and a fondness for cowboy hats and bolo ties, Ken had been elected to the Senate in 2004, the same year I was. He'd become a trusted colleague and was an ideal choice for interior secretary, having led the Department of Natural Resources in Colorado before becoming the state's first Hispanic attorney general. He'd grown up in the stunningly beautiful ranchlands of south-central Colorado's San Luis Valley, where branches of his family had lived continuously since the 1850s, and was intimately familiar with the dueling impulses to exploit and to conserve the federal lands that had shaped so much of that region's history.

"I heard from them today, Mr. President," Salazar said. "BP has confirmed that they'll pay any damages that aren't covered by the Oil Spill Liability Trust Fund." This was good news, I thought. While individual oil companies were responsible for the entire cost of cleaning up their spills, Congress had put a paltry $75 million cap on their obligation to compensate third parties like fishermen or coastal businesses for damages. Instead, oil companies were required to pay into a joint trust fund that would cover any excess damages up to $1 billion. But Carol had already alerted us that if the oil slick wasn't sufficiently contained, that might not be enough. By securing an early pledge from BP to make up any shortfall, we could at least provide affected states with some assurance that their residents would have their losses covered.

At the end of the meeting, I asked the team to keep me informed of new developments and reminded them to use whatever federal resources we had at our disposal to mitigate the economic and environmental impacts. Walking everyone out of the Oval, I noticed Carol looking pensive. I asked her to hang back for a minute so I could speak to her alone.

"Is there something we didn't cover?" I asked.

"Not really," Carol said. "I just think we need to prepare for the worst."

"Meaning?" I asked.

Carol shrugged. "BP's claiming that oil isn't leaking out of the well. If we're lucky, they'll turn out to be right. But we're talking about a pipe that travels a mile down to a well on the bottom of the ocean floor. So I doubt anyone knows for sure."

"What if they're wrong?" I asked. "What if there is a leak beneath the surface?"

"If they can't seal it quickly," she said, "then we've got a nightmare on our hands."

．　．　．

IT TOOK LESS than two days to confirm Carol's fears. The Macondo well **was** discharging oil below the surface—and not just a trickle. At first, BP engineers identified the leak as coming from a break in the pipe that had occurred when the rig sank, discharging an estimated one thousand barrels of oil into the Gulf each day. By April 28, underwater cameras had discovered two more leaks, and those estimates had risen to five thousand barrels a day. At the surface, the oil slick had grown to roughly six hundred square miles and was close to reaching the Louisiana coast, poisoning fish, dolphins, and sea turtles and threatening long-term damage to the marshes, estuaries, and inlets that were home to birds and other wildlife.

Even more alarming was the fact that BP didn't seem to know how long it would take to successfully plug the well. The company insisted that there were several viable options, including the use of remotely operated vehicles to unjam the blowout preventer, stuffing the hole with rubber or other materials, placing a containment dome above the well to funnel oil up to the surface so it could be collected, or drilling intersecting relief wells so that cement could be pumped in to block the flow of oil. According to our experts, however, the first three of those options weren't guaranteed to work, while the fourth might "take several months." At the rate we believed oil was gushing out, that could add up to a nineteen-million-gallon spill—about 70 percent more than had been released during **Exxon Valdez.**

Suddenly we faced the prospect of the worst environmental disaster in U.S. history.

We assigned Thad Allen the job of national incident commander; imposed a thirty-day moratorium on new offshore drilling, as well as a fishing ban in the contaminated area; and declared the Macondo disaster a "spill of national significance." The federal government coordinated a response across many entities, including engaging with citizen volunteers. Soon more than two thousand people were working around the clock to contain the spill, operating an armada that comprised seventy-five vessels, including tugboats, barges, and skimmers, plus dozens of aircraft and 275,000 feet of flotation booms. I sent Napolitano, Salazar, and Lisa Jackson of the EPA to the Gulf to monitor the work, and I told Valerie I wanted her talking to the governors of Louisiana, Alabama, Mississippi, Texas, and Florida (all five of whom happened to be Republican) every single day to find out what more we could do to help.

"Tell them if they've got a problem, I want to hear from them directly," I said to Valerie. "I want us to be so goddamn responsive that they get sick of hearing from us."

It's fair to say, then, that by May 2, when I visited a Coast Guard station in Venice, Louisiana, to get a first-hand look at the cleanup operations, we were throwing everything we had at the disaster. As with most presidential trips, the point was not so much to gather new information but to communicate concern and resolve. After delivering a press statement in the driving rain outside the station, I spoke with a group of fishermen, who told me they'd recently been hired by BP to lay down booms across the path of the spill and were understandably worried about the spill's long-term impact on their livelihoods.

I also spent a good deal of time that day with Bobby Jindal, the former congressman and health policy expert in the Bush administration who had leveraged his sharp-edged conservatism to become the nation's first Indian American governor. Smart, ambitious, and in his late thirties, Jindal was viewed as an up-and-comer within his party and had been selected to deliver the televised GOP response to my first joint session address. But the **Deepwater** incident, which threatened to shut down vital Louisiana industries like commercial seafood and tourism, put him in an awkward spot: Like most GOP politicians, he was a champion of Big Oil and an equally fervent opponent of strengthening environmental regulations.

Scrambling to get ahead of any shift in public sentiment, Jindal spent most of his time pitching me a plan to rapidly erect a barrier island—a berm—along a portion of the Louisiana coast. This, he insisted, would help keep the impending oil slick at bay.

"We've already got the contractors lined up to do the job," he said. His tone was confident, verging on cocky, though his dark eyes betrayed a wariness, almost pain, even when he smiled. "We just need your help to get the Army Corps of Engineers to approve it and BP to pay for it."

In fact, I'd already heard about the "berm" idea; preliminary assessments from our experts suggested that it was impractical, expensive, and potentially counterproductive. I suspected that Jindal knew as much. The proposal was mainly a political play, a way for him to look proactive while avoiding the broader questions the spill raised about the risks of deepwater drilling.

Regardless, given the scope of the crisis I didn't want to be seen as dismissing any idea out of hand, and I assured the governor that the Army Corps of Engineers would give his berm plan a quick and thorough evaluation.

With the weather too foul to fly Marine One, we spent much of the day driving. Sitting in the backseat of the SUV, I surveyed the patchy membrane of vegetation, mud, silt, and marsh that spread unevenly on either side of the Mississippi River and into the Gulf. For centuries, humans had fought to bend this primordial landscape to their will, just as Jindal was now proposing to do with his berm—building dikes, dams, levees, channels, sluices, ports, bridges, roads, and highways in the service of commerce and expansion, and rebuilding time and again after hurricanes and floods, undaunted by the implacable tides. There was a certain nobility in such stubbornness, I thought, part of the can-do spirit that had built America.

Yet when it came to the ocean and the mighty river that emptied into it, the victories of engineering turned out to be fleeting, the prospect of control illusory. Louisiana was losing more than ten thousand acres of land every year, as climate change raised sea levels and made hurricanes in the Gulf more fierce. The constant dredging, banking, and rerouting of the Mississippi to ease passage for ships and cargo meant that less sediment washed down from upriver to restore the land that was lost. The very activity that had made the region a commercial hub and allowed the oil industry to thrive was now hastening the sea's steady advance. Looking out the rain-streaked window, I wondered how long the road I was traveling would last, with its gas stations and convenience stores, before it too was swallowed by the waves.

. . .

A PRESIDENT HAS no choice but to continually multitask. ("You're like the guy in the circus," Michelle told me once, "just spinning plates at the end of a stick.") Al-Qaeda didn't suspend its operations because of a financial crisis; a devastating earthquake in Haiti didn't time itself to avoid relief efforts overlapping with a long-planned, forty-seven-nation nuclear security summit I was chairing. And so, as stressed as I was about the **Deepwater** disaster, I tried not to let it consume me. In the weeks following my Louisiana visit, I carefully tracked our response, relying on detailed daily briefings while also attending to the ten or twelve other pressing matters that demanded my attention.

I visited a manufacturing plant in Buffalo to discuss the economic recovery and continued to work with a bipartisan fiscal commission that was looking for ways to stabilize the long-term U.S. deficit. There were calls to Merkel on Greece and Medvedev on the ratification of START, a formal state visit from President Felipe Calderón of Mexico focused on border cooperation, and a working lunch with President Karzai of Afghanistan. Along with the usual terrorist threat briefings, strategy sessions with my economic team, and a slew of ceremonial duties, I interviewed candidates for a Supreme Court seat that had opened up after Justice John Paul Stevens announced his retirement in early April. I settled on the brilliant young solicitor general and former Harvard Law School dean Elena Kagan, who, like Justice Sotomayor, would emerge from the Senate hearings relatively unscathed and be confirmed a few months later.

But no matter how many other plates I had spinning in the air, at the end of each day my mind would be pulled back to the **Deepwater** spill. If I squinted hard, I could tell myself there'd been **some** progress. BP had successfully shut off the smallest of the three underwater leaks, using robots to fit a valve on the ruptured pipe. Admiral Allen had brought a semblance of order to the cleanup efforts on the ocean surface, which by mid-May had grown to nearly a thousand vessels and an army of close to twenty thousand BP workers, members of the Coast Guard and National Guard, shrimpers, fishermen, and volunteers. Valerie did such an outstanding job of staying close to the five governors whose states were threatened by the spill that, despite their party affiliations, most had only good things to say about the federal response. ("Me and Bob Riley have become best buddies," she said with a smile, referring to the Republican governor of Alabama.) The lone exception was Governor Jindal; Valerie reported that on several occasions, he'd make a request for White House help on some issue, only to put out a press release ten minutes later blasting us for ignoring Louisiana.

Still, the oil kept coming. BP's robots couldn't close the jammed blowout preventer, leaving the two main leaks unsealed. The company's first effort to place a containment dome over the leaks also failed, due to issues caused by frigid temperatures so far down. It became increasingly obvious that BP's team didn't know exactly how to proceed—and that none of the federal agencies that typically handled spills did either. "We're used to dealing with an oil slick from a tanker accident or a busted pipe," Admiral Allen explained to me. "Trying to seal a live oil well a mile under the surface . . . this is more like a space mission."

It was an apt analogy—and the reason I decided to turn to Steve Chu for help. Despite the title, the secretary of energy doesn't normally have jurisdiction over oil drilling. But we figured it couldn't hurt to have a Nobel Prize–winning physicist involved in our response, and after discovering the underwater leaks, we asked Chu to brief the team on the science involved in shutting them down. Despite Carol's warning to be succinct, his Situation Room presentation ran about twice as long as he'd been allotted and involved thirty slides. Most of the room was lost after the fifth one. Rather than waste all that brainpower on us, I instructed him to head down to Houston, where BP's response team was headquartered, to work with the engineers there on a possible fix.

Meanwhile, public attitudes about the disaster began to shift. Throughout the first few weeks of the spill, BP bore the brunt of the blame. Not only did Americans tend to be skeptical of oil companies, but BP's CEO, Tony Hayward, was a walking PR disaster—stating in the media that the spill involved a "relatively tiny" amount of oil in "a very big ocean"; arguing in another interview that no one wanted to see the hole plugged more than him because "I'd like my life back"; and generally living up to every stereotype of the arrogant, out-of-touch multinational executive. (His obtuseness reminded me that BP—previously known as British Petroleum—had started off as the Anglo-Persian Oil Company: the same company whose unwillingness to split royalties with Iran's government in the 1950s had led to the coup that ultimately resulted in that country's Islamic Revolution.)

As the crisis passed the thirty-day mark, though, attention increasingly turned to my administration's possible culpability for the mess. In particular, news stories and congressional hearings fastened on a series of exemptions from standard safety and environmental guidelines that BP had received from the Minerals Management Service (MMS), the subagency within the Interior Department responsible for granting leases, collecting royalties, and overseeing offshore drilling operations in federal waters. There hadn't been anything unusual about the exemptions MMS had granted to BP on the Macondo well; when it came to managing the risks of deepwater drilling, the agency's officials routinely ignored their staff scientists and engineers and deferred to industry experts they believed to be better versed in the latest processes and technologies.

Of course, that was exactly the problem. Before I had taken office, we'd heard about MMS's coziness with the oil companies and its regulatory shortcomings—including a well-publicized scandal toward the end of the Bush administration involving kickbacks, drugs, and sexual favors—and we'd promised to reform the place. And, in fact, as soon as he'd taken over the Interior Department, Ken Salazar **had** cleaned up some of the more egregious problems. What he hadn't had the time or resources to do was to fundamentally reorganize MMS so that it had the capacity to tightly regulate such a well-heeled and technologically complex industry.

I couldn't really fault Salazar for this. Changing practices and culture inside government agencies was hard, and rarely completed in a matter of months. We were confronting similar issues at agencies charged with regulating the financial system, where overstretched and underpaid regulators could barely keep up with the sophisticated, constantly evolving operations of massive international financial institutions. But that didn't excuse the fact that no one on my team had warned me that MMS still had such serious problems before recommending that I endorse Interior's plan to open up additional areas to exploratory drilling. And anyway, in the middle of a crisis, no one wanted to hear about the need to put more money into federal agencies. Nor did they want to hear about how raising civil servants' salaries would help those agencies improve management and compete with the private sector to attract topflight technical talent. Folks just wanted to know who had let BP drill a hole three and a half miles below the ocean's surface without knowing how to plug it—and the bottom line was, it had happened on our watch.

While questions about MMS kept reporters busy, what really turned public attitudes was BP's late-May decision—which I supported in the interest of transparency—to start releasing live, real-time video feeds of the leaks coming from the company's underwater cameras. The early images of the burning **Deepwater Horizon** rig had received wide coverage. But footage of the spill itself—consisting mostly of overhead shots, faint streaks of crimson against the blue-green ocean—hadn't fully captured the potential devastation. Even when oil-sheened waves and blobs of oil known as tar balls started reaching the outer shores of Louisiana and Alabama, camera crews didn't have a lot of arresting visuals to work

with—particularly since, after decades of offshore drilling, the waters of the Gulf weren't all that pristine to
begin with.

The underwater video feed changed all this. Suddenly
people around the world could see the oil pulsing in thick
columns from the surrounding wreckage. Sometimes
it appeared sulfurous yellow, sometimes brown or black,
depending on the lighting from the camera. The roiling
plumes looked forceful, menacing, like emanations from
hell. Cable news networks began broadcasting the footage
in a corner of the screen around the clock, along with a
digital timer reminding viewers of the number of days,
minutes, and seconds since the spill had begun.

The videos seemed to confirm calculations that our
own analysts had made, independent of BP: The leaks
were likely pumping out anywhere between four and ten
times the original estimate of five thousand barrels of oil
daily. But more so than the frightening numbers, the
images of the underwater gushers—along with a sudden
increase in B-roll footage of pelicans coated in oil—made
the crisis real in people's minds. Folks who hadn't been
paying much attention to the spill suddenly wanted to
know why we weren't doing something to stop it. In the
dentist's office, Salazar found himself staring at the video
feed on a ceiling-mounted TV as he underwent an emergency root canal. Republicans called the spill "Obama's
Katrina," and soon we were under fire from Democrats
as well—most notably former Clinton aide and longtime
Louisianan James Carville, who, appearing on **Good
Morning America,** issued a blistering, high-volume attack
on our response, directing his criticism specifically at me:
"Man, you got to get down here and take control of this!

Put somebody in charge of this thing and get this moving!" A nine-year-old boy in a wheelchair who was visiting the Oval Office through the Make-a-Wish Foundation warned me that if I didn't get the leak filled soon, I was "going to have a lot of political problems." Even Sasha came into my bathroom one morning while I was shaving to ask, "Did you plug the hole yet, Daddy?"

In my own mind, those dark cyclones of oil came to symbolize the string of constant crises we were going through. More than that, they felt alive somehow— a malevolent presence, actively taunting me. To that point in my presidency, I'd maintained a fundamental confidence that no matter how bad things got, whether with the banks, the auto companies, Greece, or Afghanistan, I could always come up with a solution through sound process and smart choices. But these leaks seemed to defy a timely solution, no matter how hard I pushed BP or my team, and no matter how many meetings I held in the Sit Room, poring over data and diagrams as intently as I did in any war-planning session. With that feeling of temporary helplessness, a certain bitterness began creeping into my voice—a bitterness I recognized as a companion to self-doubt.

"What does he think I'm supposed to do?" I growled at Rahm after hearing of Carville's broadside. "Put on my fucking Aquaman gear and swim down there myself with a wrench?"

The chorus of criticism culminated in a May 27 White House press conference that had me fielding tough questions on the oil spill for about an hour. I methodically listed everything we'd done since the **Deepwater** had exploded, and I described the technical intricacies of the various strategies being employed to cap the well. I acknowledged problems with MMS, as well as my own excessive confidence in the ability of companies like BP to safeguard against risk. I announced the formation of a national commission to review the disaster and figure out how such accidents could be prevented in the future, and I reemphasized the need for a long-term response that would make America less reliant on dirty fossil fuels.

Reading the transcript now, a decade later, I'm struck by how calm and cogent I sound. Maybe I'm surprised because the transcript doesn't register what I remember feeling at the time or come close to capturing what I **really** wanted to say before the assembled White House press corps:

That MMS wasn't fully equipped to do its job, in large part because for the past thirty years a big chunk of American voters had bought into the Republican idea that government was the problem and that business always knew better, and had elected leaders who made it their mission to gut environmental regulations, starve agency budgets, denigrate civil servants, and allow industrial polluters do whatever the hell they wanted to do.

That the government didn't have better technology than BP did to quickly plug the hole because it would be expensive to have such technology on hand, and we Americans didn't like paying higher taxes—especially when it was to prepare for problems that hadn't happened yet.

That it was hard to take seriously **any** criticism from a character like Bobby Jindal, who'd done Big Oil's bidding throughout his career and would go on to support an oil industry lawsuit trying to get a federal court to lift our temporary drilling moratorium; and that if he and other Gulf-elected officials were truly concerned about the well-being of their constituents, they'd be urging their party to stop denying the effects of climate change, since it was precisely the people of the Gulf who were the most likely to lose homes or jobs as a result of rising global temperatures.

And that the only way to truly guarantee that we didn't have another catastrophic oil spill in the future was to stop drilling entirely; but that wasn't going to happen because at the end of the day we Americans loved our cheap gas and big cars more than we cared about the environment, except when a complete disaster was staring us in the face; and in the absence of such a disaster, the media rarely covered efforts to shift America off fossil fuels or pass climate legislation, since actually **educating** the public on long-term energy policy would be boring and bad for ratings; and the one thing I **could** be certain of was that for all the outrage being expressed at the moment about wetlands and sea turtles and pelicans, what the majority of us were really interested in was having the problem go away, for me to clean up yet one more mess decades in the making with some quick and easy fix, so that we could all go back to our carbon-spewing, energy-wasting ways without having to feel guilty about it.

I didn't say any of that. Instead I somberly took responsibility and said it was my job to "get this fixed." Afterward, I scolded my press team, suggesting that if they'd done better work telling the story of everything we were doing to clean up the spill, I wouldn't have had to tap-dance for an hour while getting the crap kicked out of me. My press folks looked wounded. Sitting alone in the Treaty Room later that night, I felt bad about what I had said, knowing I'd misdirected my anger and frustration.

It was those damned plumes of oil that I really wanted to curse out.

FOR THE NEXT six weeks, the spill continued to dominate the news. As efforts to kill the well kept coming up short, we compensated by making more of a show of my personal involvement. I made two more trips to Louisiana, as well as visits to Mississippi, Alabama, and Florida. Working with Admiral Allen, who'd agreed to delay his retirement until the crisis was over, we found ways to meet every governor's request, including a scaled-down plan for Jindal's berm. Salazar had signed an order that effectively dissolved MMS, dividing responsibilities for energy development, safety regulation, and revenue collection between three new independent agencies. I announced the formation of a bipartisan commission tasked with recommending ways to prevent future off-shore drilling disasters. I held a full cabinet meeting on the crisis and had a heart-wrenching visit with the families of the eleven **Deepwater** workers killed in the explosion. I even delivered an Oval Office address on the spill—the first such address of my presidency. The format, with me sitting behind the Resolute desk, felt stilted, of another era, and by all accounts I wasn't very good.

The flood of appearances and announcements had the intended effect of muting, if not fully eliminating, the bad stories in the press. But it was the results of two earlier decisions I'd made that ultimately got us through the crisis.

The first involved making sure that BP followed through on its earlier promise to compensate third parties harmed by the spill. Typically the process for filing claims required victims to jump through a bunch of bureaucratic hoops or even hire a lawyer. Resolving those claims could take years, by which time a small tour-boat operator or restaurant owner might have already lost his or her business. We thought the victims in this case deserved more immediate relief. We also figured now was the time for maximum leverage: BP's stock was tanking, its global image was being pummeled, the Justice Department was investigating the company for possible criminal negligence, and the federal drilling moratorium we'd imposed was creating huge uncertainty for shareholders.

"Can I squeeze the hell out of them?" Rahm asked.

"Please do," I said.

Rahm went to work, badgering, cajoling, and threatening as only he could, and by the time I sat across the table from Tony Hayward and BP's chairman, Carl-Henric Svanberg, for a June 16 meeting in the Roosevelt Room, they were ready to wave the white flag. (Hayward, who said little in the meeting, would announce his departure from the company a few weeks later.) Not only did BP agree to put $20 billion into a response fund to compensate victims of the spill, but we arranged for the money to be placed in escrow and administered independently by Ken Feinberg, the same lawyer who'd managed the fund for 9/11 victims and reviewed executive-compensation plans for banks receiving TARP money.

The fund didn't solve the environmental disaster. But it fulfilled my promise that all the fishermen, shrimpers, charter companies, and others who were racking up losses due to the crisis would get their due.

The second good decision I'd made was putting Steve Chu on the job. My energy secretary had been underwhelmed by his initial interactions with BP engineers ("They don't know what they're dealing with," Chu said), and he was soon splitting his time between Houston and D.C., telling Thad Allen that BP "shouldn't do anything unless they clear it with me." In no time, he had recruited a team of independent geophysicists and hydrologists to work with him on the problem. He convinced BP to use gamma-ray imaging to help diagnose what had gone wrong with the blowout preventer and to install pressure gauges to get real data on what was happening at the base of the well. Chu and his team also hammered home the point that any effort to cap it should be preceded by a thorough consideration of how that work risked triggering a cascade of uncontrollable underground leaks—and an even worse catastrophe.

Chu and the BP engineers eventually agreed that the best solution was to fit a second, smaller blowout preventer—called a capping stack—on top of the one that had failed, using a series of sequential valves to shut down the leak. But after looking over BP's initial design— and getting government scientists and engineers at Los Alamos National Laboratory and elsewhere to run a series of simulations on their supercomputers—Chu determined that it was inadequate, and the group quickly went to work on crafting a modified version. Axe stopped into the Oval one day and told me he'd just run into Chu at a nearby deli, sitting with his food barely touched, drawing various models of capping stacks on his napkin.

"He started trying to explain how the contraption worked," Axe said, "and I told him I was having enough trouble figuring out what I should order for lunch."

The final capping stack weighed seventy-five tons, stood thirty feet tall, and, because of Chu's insistence, included multiple pressure gauges that would give us crucial data revealing its efficacy. Within weeks, the stack was in place above the well and ready to be tested. On July 15, BP engineers shut down the stack's valves. The cap held. For the first time in eighty-seven days, oil wasn't leaking from the Macondo well.

Consistent with the luck we'd been having, a tropical storm threatened to pass through the Macondo site the following week. Chu, Thad Allen, and BP's managing director, Bob Dudley, had to quickly decide whether or not to reopen the valves before the vessels involved in the containment efforts and the BP staff members monitoring the integrity of the capping stack had to clear out of the storm path. If their calculations on subsurface pressure proved wrong, there was a risk that the stack wouldn't hold and, worse, could cause the ocean floor to fracture, triggering even more problematic leaks. Loosening the valves, of course, meant we'd restart the flow of oil into the Gulf, which was something nobody wanted. After running a final set of numbers, Chu agreed that it was worth the gamble and we should keep the valves closed as the storm ripped through.

Once again, the cap held.

There were no celebrations in the White House when we heard the news—just enormous relief. It would take a couple more months and a series of additional procedures before BP declared the Macondo well permanently sealed, and cleanup efforts would continue through the end of the summer. The fishing ban was gradually lifted, and seafood from the Gulf was certified as safe. Beaches were reopened, and in August I took the family to Panama City Beach, Florida, for a two-day "holiday," to boost the region's tourism industry. A picture from that trip, taken by Pete Souza and later released by the White House, shows me and Sasha splashing in the water, a signal to Americans that it was safe to swim in the Gulf. Malia's missing from the photo because she was away at summer camp. Michelle is missing because, as she had explained to me shortly after I was elected, "one of my main goals as First Lady is to never be photographed in a bathing suit."

In many ways, we had dodged the worst-case scenario, and in the months that followed even critics like James Carville would acknowledge that our response had been more effective than we'd been given credit for. The Gulf's shorelines and beaches suffered less visible damage than expected, and just a year after the accident, the region would enjoy its biggest tourism season ever. We formed a Gulf coastline restoration project, funded by additional penalties levied against BP, allowing federal, state, and local authorities to start reversing some of the environmental degradation that had been taking place long before the explosion. With some nudging from federal courts, BP ultimately paid settlements in excess of what was in the $20 billion response fund. And although the preliminary report of the oil spill commission I had set up would rightly criticize MMS oversight of BP's activities at the Macondo field, as well as our failure to accurately assess the enormity of the leaks immediately after the explosion, by the fall, both the press and the public had largely moved on.

Still, I continued to be haunted by the images of those plumes of oil rushing out of a cracked earth and into the sea's ghostly depths. Experts inside the administration told me that it would take years to understand the true extent of the environmental damage resulting from the **Deepwater** spill. The best estimates concluded that the Macondo well had released at least four million barrels of oil into open waters, with at least two-thirds of that amount having been captured, burned off, or otherwise dispersed. Where the rest of the oil ended up, what gruesome toll it took on wildlife, how much oil would eventually settle back onto the ocean floor, and what long-term effect that might have on the entire Gulf ecosystem—it would be years before we'd have the full picture.

What wasn't a mystery was the spill's political impact. With the crisis behind us and the midterm elections now on the horizon, we felt ready to project a cautious optimism to the public—to argue that the country was finally turning a corner and to highlight all the work my administration had done in the previous sixteen months to make a concrete difference in people's lives. But the only impression registering with voters was of yet one more calamity the government seemed powerless to solve. I asked Axe to give me his best assessment of the chances that Democrats would retain control of the House of Representatives. He looked at me like I was joking.

"We're screwed," he said.

· · ·

FROM THE DAY I took office, we'd known that the midterms were going to be tough. Historically, the party controlling the White House almost always lost congressional seats after its first two years in power, as at least some voters found reason for disappointment. Voter turnout also dropped substantially in the midterm elections, and—thanks in part to America's long history of voter discrimination, as well as many states' continued use of complicated procedures that made casting a ballot more difficult than it needed to be—the falloff was most pronounced among younger, lower-income, and minority voters, demographic groups that tended to vote Democratic.

All this would have made the midterms challenging for us, even in a time of relative peace and prosperity. Which, of course, we weren't in. Although companies had started hiring again, the unemployment rate remained stuck around 9.5 percent through June and July, mainly because cash-strapped state and local governments were still shedding employees. At least once a week, I'd huddle with my economic team in the Roosevelt Room, trying to come up with some variation on additional stimulus plans that we might shame at least a few Senate Republicans into supporting. But beyond a grudging extension of emergency unemployment insurance benefits before Congress adjourned for the August recess, McConnell generally managed to keep his caucus in line.

"I hate to say it," a Republican senator told me when he came by the White House for another matter, "but the worse people feel right now, the better it is for us."

The economy wasn't the only headwind we faced.

Public opinion polls typically gave Republicans an edge over Democrats when it came to national security, and from the day I'd taken office, the GOP had looked to press that advantage, seizing every opportunity to paint my administration as weak on defense and soft on terrorism. For the most part, the attacks had failed: As disenchanted as voters were with my economic steward-ship, they'd continued to give me solid marks on keeping them safe. Those numbers had held steady after the attack at Fort Hood and the thwarted Christmas Day bombing; they even remained largely unchanged when, in May 2010, a man named Faisal Shahzad—a natural-ized American citizen raised in Pakistan and trained by the Pakistani Taliban—tried unsuccessfully to detonate a car bomb in the middle of Times Square.

Still, the fact that 180,000 U.S. troops remained deployed in wars overseas cast a pall over the midterms. And while we were entering the final phase of withdrawal from Iraq, with the last combat brigades due home in August, the summer fighting season in Afghanistan was likely to once again bring about a distressing rise in U.S. casualties. I'd been impressed with Stan McChrystal's leadership of coalition forces there: The additional troops I'd authorized had helped regain territory from the Taliban; the training of the Afghan army had ramped up; McChrystal had even convinced President Karzai to venture out beyond his palace and start engaging the population he claimed to represent.

And yet each time I met with wounded soldiers at Walter Reed and Bethesda, I was reminded of the awful costs of such incremental progress. Whereas my earlier visits had taken roughly an hour, I was more often spending at least twice that time, as the hospital appeared to be filled almost to capacity. On one visit, I entered a room to find the bedridden victim of an IED blast being tended to by his mother. Thick stitches ran along the side of the young man's partially shaved head; his right eye appeared blinded and his body partly paralyzed, with one badly injured arm encased in a soft cast. According to the doctor who briefed me before I went in, the patient had spent three months in a coma before regaining consciousness. He'd suffered permanent brain damage and had just undergone surgery to rebuild his skull.

"Cory, the president's here to see you," the soldier's mother said encouragingly. The young man couldn't speak but registered a faint smile and nod.

"It's great to meet you, Cory," I said, gently shaking his free hand.

"Actually, you two have met before," the mother said. "See?" She pointed to a photograph that had been taped to the wall, and I stepped closer to examine a picture of me with a group of smiling Army Rangers. It dawned on me then that the wounded soldier lying in the bed was Sergeant First Class Cory Remsburg, the spirited young paratrooper I'd spoken with less than a year earlier, during the commemoration of the Allied landing at Normandy. The one who'd told me he was on his way to Afghanistan for his tenth deployment.

"Of course . . . Cory," I said, glancing over at the mother. Her eyes forgave me for not having recognized her son. "How are you feeling, man?"

"Show him how you're feeling, Cory," the mother said.

Slowly and with great effort, he raised his arm and offered me a thumbs-up. Taking pictures of the two of us, Pete looked visibly shaken.

Maybe what had happened to Cory and so many like him didn't sit at the forefront of voters' minds the same way it did mine. Since the shift to an all-volunteer military in the 1970s, fewer Americans had family members, friends, or neighbors who served in combat. But at the very least, the mounting casualties left a weary nation as uncertain as ever about the direction of what increasingly seemed like an endless war. That uncertainty was only compounded in June when a lengthy **Rolling Stone** profile of Stan McChrystal hit the newsstands.

The article, titled "The Runaway General," was largely critical of the U.S. war effort, suggesting that I'd been rolled by the Pentagon into doubling down on a hopeless cause. But that wasn't new. Instead, what grabbed Washington's attention was the access McChrystal had granted to the reporter and the slew of caustic remarks the general and his team had leveled at allies, elected officials, and members of the administration. In one scene, the reporter describes McChrystal and an aide joking about possible responses to questions about Vice President Biden. ("Are you asking about Vice President Biden?" McChrystal is quoted as saying. "Who's that?" To which the aide chimes in, "Did you say: Bite Me?") In another, McChrystal complains about having to have dinner with a French minister in Paris ("I'd rather have my ass kicked") and groans over an email from Hillary's special advisor, longtime diplomat Richard Holbrooke ("I don't even want to open it"). And while I'm largely spared the worst of the mockery, a member of McChrystal's team notes his boss's disappointment in our meeting right before I appointed him coalition commander, suggesting that I should have given the general more personal attention.

Beyond the hard feelings the article was bound to generate—reopening divisions within the Afghan team that I'd hoped were behind us—it made McChrystal and his crew sound like a bunch of cocky frat boys. I could only imagine how Cory Remsburg's parents would feel if they read the article.

"I don't know what the hell he was thinking," Gates said to me, making an effort at damage control.

"He wasn't," I said curtly. "He got played."

My team asked me how I wanted to handle it. I told them I hadn't decided but that while I made up my mind, I wanted McChrystal on the next flight back to Washington. At first, I was inclined to let the general off with a stern reprimand—and not just because Bob Gates insisted that he remained the best man to lead the war effort. I knew that if anyone ever recorded some of the private conversations that took place between me and my senior staff, we might sound pretty obnoxious ourselves. And although McChrystal and his inner circle had shown atrocious judgment in speaking like that in front of any reporter, whether out of carelessness or vanity, every one of us in the White House had said something on tape that we shouldn't have at one time or another. If I wouldn't fire Hillary, Rahm, Valerie, or Ben for telling tales out of school, why should I treat McChrystal any differently?

Over the course of twenty-four hours, I decided that this **was** different. As every military commander liked to remind me, America's armed forces depended entirely on rigid discipline, clear codes of conduct, unit cohesion, and strict chains of command. Because the stakes were always higher. Because any failure to act as part of a team, any individual mistakes, didn't just result in embarrassment or lost profits. People could die. Any corporal or captain who publicly disparaged a bunch of superior officers in such vivid terms would pay a grave price. I saw no way to apply a different set of rules to a four-star general, no matter how gifted, courageous, or decorated he was.

That need for accountability and discipline extended to matters of civilian control over the military—a point I'd emphasized in the Oval Office with Gates and Mullen, apparently to insufficient effect. I actually admired McChrystal's rebel spirit, his apparent disdain for pretense and authority that, in his view, hadn't been earned. It no doubt had made him a better leader—and accounted for the fierce loyalty he elicited from the troops under his command. But in that **Rolling Stone** article, I'd heard in him and his aides the same air of impunity that seemed to have taken hold among some in the military's top ranks during the Bush years: a sense that once war began, those who fought it shouldn't be questioned, that politicians should just give them what they ask for and get out of the way. It was a seductive view, especially coming from a man of McChrystal's caliber. It also threatened to erode a bedrock principle of our representative democracy, and I was determined to put an end to it.

The morning was hot and muggy when McChrystal and I finally sat down alone in the Oval Office. He seemed chastened but composed. To his credit, he made no excuses for his remarks. He didn't suggest that he'd been misquoted or taken out of context. He simply apologized for his mistake and offered his letter of resignation. I explained why, despite my admiration of him and my gratitude for his service, I had decided to accept it.

After McChrystal left, I held a press conference in the Rose Garden to outline the reasons for my decision and to announce that General Dave Petraeus would be assuming command of coalition forces in Afghanistan. It was Tom Donilon who'd come up with the idea of moving Petraeus into the job. Not only was he the country's most widely known and respected military leader, but as the head of Central Command he was already intimately familiar with our Afghan strategy. The news went over about as well as we could have hoped for under the circumstances. Still, I walked out of the press conference feeling livid about the whole situation. I told Jim Jones to gather everyone on the national security team right away. The meeting didn't last long.

"I'm putting everybody on notice that I am fed up," I said, my voice steadily rising. "I don't want to hear any commentary about McChrystal in the press. I don't want any more spin or rumors or backbiting. What I want is for people to do their damn jobs. And if there are people here who can't act like they're on a team, then they'll be gone too. I mean it."

The room fell silent. I turned around and left, with Ben trailing behind me; apparently we were scheduled to work on a speech.

"I liked Stan," I said quietly as we walked.

"You didn't really have a choice," Ben said.

"Yeah," I said, shaking my head. "I know. It doesn't make it go down better."

ALTHOUGH THE FIRING of McChrystal made headlines (and reinforced the conviction among the GOP faithful that I was unfit to serve as commander in chief), it wasn't the kind of story that necessarily moved swing voters in an election. As the midterms approached, the Republicans instead focused on a national security issue that struck closer to home. It turned out that a solid majority of Americans really didn't like the idea of trying terrorist suspects in civilian criminal courts on U.S. soil. In fact, most weren't particularly concerned about giving them full or fair trials at all.

We'd gotten an early inkling of this as we'd tried to move forward with my pledge to close the detention center at Guantánamo. In the abstract, most congressional Democrats bought my argument that holding foreign prisoners there indefinitely without trial was a bad idea. The practice violated our constitutional traditions and flouted the Geneva Conventions; it complicated our foreign policy and discouraged even some of our closest allies from cooperating with us on anti-terrorism efforts; and, perversely, it boosted al-Qaeda's recruitment and generally made us less safe. A few Republicans—most notably John McCain—agreed.

But to actually close the facility, we had to figure out what to do with the 242 detainees being held at Guantánamo when I took office. Many were ill-trained, low-level fighters who'd been randomly scooped up on the battlefield and posed little or no threat to the United

States. (The Bush administration itself had previously released more than five hundred such detainees to their home countries or to a third country.) But a small number of Gitmo prisoners were sophisticated al-Qaeda operatives, known as high-value detainees (HVDs)—like Khalid Sheikh Mohammed, one of the self-professed masterminds behind the 9/11 attacks. The men in this category were accused of being directly responsible for the murder of innocent people, and as far as I was concerned, releasing them would be both dangerous and immoral.

The solution had seemed clear: We could repatriate the remaining low-level detainees to their home countries, where they would be monitored by their governments and slowly reintegrated into their societies, and put the HVDs on trial in U.S. criminal courts. Except the more we'd looked into it, the more roadblocks we'd encountered. When it came to repatriation, for instance, many low-level detainees came from countries that didn't have the capacity to safely handle their return. In fact, the largest contingent—ninety-nine men—was from Yemen, a dirt-poor country with a barely functioning government, deep tribal conflicts, and the single most active al-Qaeda chapter outside Pakistan's Federally Administered Tribal Areas (FATA).

International law also prohibited us from repatriating detainees who we had grounds to believe might be abused, tortured, or killed by their own government. Such was the case with a group of Uighurs being held at Gitmo: members of a Muslim ethnic minority who had fled to Afghanistan because of brutal, long-standing repression in their native China. The Uighurs had no real beef with the United States. Beijing, however, considered them terrorists—and we had little doubt that they risked a rough reception if we sent them to China.

The prospect of bringing HVDs to trial in U.S. courts was perhaps even more complicated. For one thing, the Bush administration hadn't placed a high priority on preserving chains of evidence or maintaining clear records regarding the circumstances in which detainees had been captured, so many prisoners' files were a mess. Also, a number of HVDs, including Khalid Sheikh Mohammed, had been tortured during their interrogations, rendering not only their confessions but also any evidence linked to those interrogations inadmissible under the rules of ordinary criminal proceedings.

Bush administration officials hadn't considered any of this to be a problem since, in their view, all Gitmo detainees qualified as "unlawful enemy combatants," exempt from the protections of the Geneva Conventions and unentitled to civilian trials. Instead, to adjudicate cases, the administration had created an alternative system of "military commissions" in which U.S. military judges determined guilt or innocence and lower standards of evidence and weaker procedural safeguards prevailed. Few legal observers found the administration's approach to adequately meet the minimum requirements of due process; and as a result of constant legal challenges, delays, and procedural snags, the commissions had managed to decide only three cases in two years. Meanwhile, a month before I was elected, lawyers representing seventeen Uighurs held at Gitmo had successfully petitioned a U.S. federal judge to review their detention, leading him to order their release from military custody and setting the stage for a lengthy legal battle over jurisdiction. Similar appeals on behalf of other prisoners were also pending.

"This isn't just a turd sandwich," Denis observed after one of our sessions on Gitmo. "It's a turd smorgasbord."

Despite these difficulties, we started chipping away at the problem. I ordered the suspension of any new cases being brought before military commissions—although in a nod to the Pentagon, I agreed to have an interagency team review whether the commissions could be reformed and used as a backup in the event that we couldn't try certain detainees in civilian court. We set up a formal process to evaluate which detainees could be safely released, whether to their home countries or to other nations willing to take them. Working with lawyers at the Pentagon and the CIA, Attorney General Eric Holder and a team of Justice Department prosecutors began reviewing prisoner files to see what further evidence was required to bring to trial and convict each HVD at Gitmo. We began looking for a U.S. facility—whether on a military installation or within the existing federal prison system—that could immediately house transferred Gitmo detainees while we determined their ultimate dispositions.

That's when Congress began to freak out. Republicans got wind of rumors that we were considering the possible resettlement of Uighurs in Virginia (most were ultimately sent to third countries, including Bermuda and the island nation of Palau) and took to the airwaves, warning voters that my administration planned to move terrorists into their neighborhoods—maybe even next door. This made congressional Democrats understandably nervous, and they ultimately agreed to a provision added to a defense spending bill that prohibited the use of any taxpayer funds for the transfer of detainees to the United States for anything but a trial; it also required Bob Gates to submit a formal plan to Congress before a new facility could be chosen and Guantánamo shut down. Dick Durbin approached us in the spring of 2010 with the possibility of using a largely vacant state prison in Thomson, Illinois, to house up to ninety Gitmo detainees. Despite the jobs it was likely to bring for residents of a rural town hard-hit by the economic crisis, Congress refused to fund the $350 million needed to buy and renovate the facility, with even some liberal Democrats echoing Republican arguments that any detention center located on U.S. soil would become a prime target for future terrorist attacks.

None of this made sense to me. Terrorist plotters weren't Navy SEALs; if al-Qaeda were to plan another attack in the United States, detonating a crude explosive in a New York subway or crowded Los Angeles mall would be far more devastating—and a lot easier—than trying to mount an assault on a hardened correctional facility in the middle of nowhere staffed by heavily armed U.S. military personnel. In fact, well over a hundred convicted terrorists were already serving time without incident in federal prisons scattered across the country. "We're acting like these guys are a bunch of supervillains straight out of a James Bond movie," I said to Denis in exasperation. "The average inmate at a supermax prison would eat these detainees for lunch."

Nonetheless, I could understand that people had very real fears—fears born of the lingering trauma of 9/11 and continually stoked by the previous administration and much of the media (not to mention countless movies and TV shows) for almost a decade. Indeed, several Bush administration alumni—in particular, former vice president Dick Cheney—made it their mission to keep fanning those fears, viewing my decisions to revamp the handling of terrorist suspects as an attack on their legacy. In a series of speeches and television appearances, Cheney insisted that the use of tactics like waterboarding and indefinite detention had prevented "something much bigger and far worse" than the 9/11 attacks. He accused me of reverting to a pre-2001 "law enforcement mode" in dealing with terrorists rather than understanding the "concept of military threat," and he claimed that in doing this, I was increasing the risk of another attack.

Cheney's assertion that my administration wasn't treating al-Qaeda as a military threat was hard to square with the additional battalions I'd deployed to Afghanistan or the scores of al-Qaeda operatives we were targeting with drone strikes. And Cheney probably wasn't the best messenger for **any** argument, given how personally unpopular he was with the American public—thanks in large part to his catastrophic judgment on Iraq. Still, the idea that we shouldn't treat terrorists like "ordinary criminals" did resonate with a lot of voters. And it had gotten even more traction in the aftermath of "Underwear Bomber" Umar Farouk Abdulmutallab's attempt to bring down a jet the previous Christmas.

In handling that case, both the Justice Department and the FBI had followed procedure. At Eric Holder's direction, and with the concurrence of the Pentagon and the CIA, federal officials had arrested the Nigerian-born Abdulmutallab as a criminal suspect as soon as the Northwest Airlines plane landed in Detroit and had transported him to receive medical care. Because the top priority was ascertaining that there were no further immediate threats to public safety—other bombers on other planes, for example—the first team of FBI agents questioning Abdulmutallab did so without reading him the Miranda warnings, using a well-established legal precedent that allowed law enforcement an exception when neutralizing an active threat. Speaking to agents for nearly an hour, the suspect provided valuable intelligence about his al-Qaeda connections, his training in Yemen, the source of his explosive device, and what he knew of other plots. He was later read his rights and given access to counsel.

According to our critics, we had practically set the man free. "Why in God's name would you stop questioning a terrorist?!" former New York mayor Rudy Giuliani declared on TV. Joe Lieberman insisted that Abdulmutallab qualified as an enemy combatant and, as such, should have been turned over to military authorities for interrogation and detention. And in the heated Massachusetts Senate race that was going on at the time, Republican Scott Brown used our handling of the case to put Democrat Martha Coakley on the defensive.

The irony, as Eric Holder liked to point out, was that the Bush administration had handled almost every case involving terrorist suspects apprehended on U.S. soil (including Zacarias Moussaoui, one of the planners behind 9/11) **in exactly the same way.** They'd done so because the U.S. Constitution demanded it: In the two instances where the Bush administration had declared terrorist suspects arrested in the United States "enemy combatants" subject to indefinite detention, the federal courts had stepped in and forced their return to the criminal system. Moreover, following the law actually worked. Bush's Justice Department had successfully convicted more than a hundred terrorist suspects, with sentences at least as tough as the few that had been handed down through military commissions. Moussaoui, for example, was serving multiple life sentences in federal prison. These lawful criminal prosecutions had in the past drawn lavish praise from conservatives, including Mr. Giuliani.

"It wouldn't be so aggravating," Eric told me one day, "if Giuliani and some of these other critics actually believed the stuff they're saying. But he's a former prosecutor. He **knows** better. It's just shameless."

As the point person in our effort to bring America's counterterrorism practices into alignment with its constitutional principles, Eric would bear the brunt of this manufactured outrage. He didn't seem to mind, knowing it came with the job—although he didn't consider it entirely a coincidence that he was the favorite target in my administration for much of the Republican vitriol and Fox News conspiracy theorizing.

"When they're yelling at **me,** brother," Eric would say, patting my back with a wry smile, "I know they're thinking of you."

I could see why those who opposed my presidency might have considered Eric a handy stand-in. Tall and even-tempered, he'd grown up in Queens, New York, the son of middle-class parents of Barbadian descent. ("They gave you that island vibe," I told him.) He'd attended my alma mater, Columbia University, a decade before I got there, where he'd played basketball and participated in campus sit-ins; while at law school, he'd become interested in civil rights, interning one summer at the NAACP Legal Defense Fund. And, like me, he'd chosen public service rather than a job in a corporate law firm, working as a prosecutor in the Justice Department's Public Integrity Section and later as a federal judge on the D.C. Superior Court. Bill Clinton eventually nominated him to be the U.S. attorney for the District of Columbia and, later, the deputy attorney general of the United States—the first African American to serve in either position.

Eric and I both had an abiding faith in the law, a belief—tempered by personal experience and our knowledge of history—that through reasoned argument and fidelity to the ideals and institutions of our democracy, America could be made better. It was on the basis of those shared assumptions, more than our friendship or any particular agreement on issues, that I'd wanted him as my attorney general. It was also why I would end up being so scrupulous about shielding his office from White House interference in pending cases and investigations.

There was no law expressly prohibiting such interference. At the end of the day, the AG and his or her deputies were part of the executive branch and thus served at the pleasure of the president. But the AG was first and foremost the people's lawyer, not the president's consigliere. Keeping politics out of the Justice Department's investigative and prosecutorial decisions was a crucial democratic imperative, made glaringly apparent when the Watergate hearings revealed that Richard Nixon's AG, John Mitchell, had actively participated in the cover-up of White House misdeeds and initiated criminal investigations into the president's enemies. The Bush administration had been accused of violating that norm in 2006 when it fired nine U.S. attorneys whom it apparently considered insufficiently committed to its ideological agenda; and the one blemish on Eric Holder's otherwise spotless record was the suggestion that he'd succumbed to political pressure when, as deputy AG, he'd supported Bill Clinton's criminal pardon of a major donor in the waning days of the administration. Eric later said he regretted the decision, and it was precisely the kind of situation I was intent on avoiding. So, while he and I regularly discussed broad Justice Department policy, we were careful to steer clear of any topic that would even appear to compromise his independence as America's top law enforcement officer.

Still, there was no getting around the fact that any attorney general's decisions had political ramifications—as my White House team liked to remind me and as Eric sometimes forgot. He was surprised and offended, for example, when, a month into my presidency, Axe took him to task for failing to clear a Black History Month speech in which he referred to America as "a nation of cowards" when it came to its unwillingness to discuss race issues—a true enough observation but not necessarily the headline we were looking for at the end of my first few weeks in office. The heat we took at the White House for the Justice Department's legally sound but politically toxic decision not to indict any of the bank executives for their role in the financial crisis also seemed to catch him off guard. And maybe it was this guilelessness, his confidence that logic and reason would ultimately prevail, that led Eric to miss how quickly the political ground was shifting when he announced late in 2009 that Khalid Sheikh Mohammed and four other 9/11 co-conspirators would finally go on trial in a lower Manhattan courtroom.

On paper, we all thought the idea made sense. Why not use the prosecution of Guantánamo's most notorious prisoners to showcase the U.S. criminal justice system's ability to handle terrorist cases in a fair, aboveboard manner? And what better venue to deliver justice than one in the city that had suffered the most from that horrific crime, in a courtroom just a few blocks from Ground Zero? After months of painstaking work, Eric and his team felt sure that the case against the 9/11 plotters could be made without relying on information obtained through "enhanced interrogations"—in part because we now had more cooperation from other countries that had previously been reluctant to get involved. New York mayor Michael Bloomberg had endorsed Eric's plan. So had New York's senior senator, Democrat Chuck Schumer.

Then, in the weeks surrounding the attempted Christmas Day bombing, the prevailing opinion in New York spun a dizzying 180 degrees. A group of families of 9/11 victims organized a series of demonstrations to protest Eric's decision. We found out later that its leader, the sister of one of the pilots killed in the Pentagon attack, had formed an organization dedicated to opposing any and all efforts to reverse Bush-era national security policies—and funded by conservative donors and supported by prominent Republicans (including Liz Cheney, the former vice president's daughter). Next, Mayor Bloomberg—who was reportedly getting pressure from real estate interests concerned about what a trial might do to their redevelopment plans—abruptly withdrew his support, claiming a trial would be too expensive and disruptive. Chuck Schumer quickly followed suit, as did Senate Intelligence Committee chair Dianne Feinstein. With New York officials, a vocal contingent of 9/11 families, and influential members of our own party all lined up against us, Eric felt he had no choice but to beat a tactical retreat, confirming that while he remained determined to try the 9/11 co-conspirators in civilian rather than military courts, the Justice Department would explore venues outside of New York.

It was a significant setback for our overall strategy to close Gitmo, and civil liberties groups and progressive columnists faulted me and the rest of the White House for not having anticipated political pushback to the trials, and for not mounting a more vigorous defense once the plan ran into trouble. They may have been right. Maybe if we had focused all of our attention on it for a month or so, to the exclusion of our efforts on healthcare or financial reform or climate change or the economy, we might have rallied the public to our side and forced New York City officials to back down. I would have enjoyed that fight. No doubt, it was a fight worth having.

But at the time, at least, it was a fight that none of us in the White House thought we could win. Certainly, Rahm was happy to see Eric's plan tabled, since he was the one who had to field calls all day from terrified congressional Democrats, begging us to stop trying to push so many boulders up the hill. For the truth was, after an ambitious first year in office, I didn't have a lot of political capital left—and what little remained we were husbanding to try to get as many initiatives as we could through Congress before the 2010 midterms brought about a possible shift in party control.

In fact, Rahm would get frustrated with me for wading into a related controversy at the end of that summer, when the same group of 9/11 families that opposed the trial of Khalid Sheikh Mohammed in Manhattan launched a campaign to block the construction of an Islamic community center and mosque near Ground Zero, saying it was offensive to them and the memory of those who'd died in the World Trade Center attacks. To his credit, Mayor Bloomberg forcefully defended the project on the grounds of religious freedom, as did other city officials and even some 9/11 families. Nevertheless, right-wing commentators quickly seized on the issue, often in nakedly anti-Islamic terms; national polls showed that a majority of Americans were opposed to the mosque's location; and GOP political operatives spotted an opportunity to make life uncomfortable for Democrats running in the midterms.

As it so happened, the controversy reached a boiling point the same week we had a scheduled White House **iftar** dinner with an assortment of Muslim American leaders to mark the month of Ramadan. The gathering was meant to be a low-key affair, a way to extend the same recognition to Muslims that we did to members of other faiths during their key religious holidays—but the next time Rahm and I talked, I told him that I intended to use the occasion to publicly come down on the side of those building the mosque.

"Last I checked, this is America," I said, stuffing files in my briefcase before I headed up to the residence for dinner. "And in **America,** you can't single out one religious group and tell them they can't build a house of worship on their own property."

"I get it, Mr. President," Rahm said. "But you need to know that if you say something, it's going to be hung around the necks of our candidates in every swing district around the country."

"I'm sure you're right," I answered as I walked to the door. "But if we can't speak out on something this basic, then I don't know what the point is of us being here."

Rahm sighed. "At the rate we're going," he said, "we may not be."

IN AUGUST, MY FAMILY and I flew up to Martha's Vineyard for a ten-day vacation. We'd first visited the island off the coast of Cape Cod fifteen or so years earlier, at the invitation of one of my law firm's partners, Allison Davis, and with the encouragement of Valerie, who'd spent summers there with her family when she was growing up. With its broad beaches and windswept dunes, the fishing boats coming into dock, the small farms and green meadows framed by oak forests and old stone walls, the place had a quiet beauty and unhurried vibe that suited us. We appreciated, as well, the Vineyard's history: Freed slaves had been part of its earliest settlements, and Black families had rented summer homes there for generations, making it that rare resort community where Blacks and whites seemed equally at home. We had taken the girls there for a week or two every other summer, usually renting a small place in Oak Bluffs, close enough to town that you could bike there and with a porch where you could sit and watch the sun go down. Together with Valerie and other friends, we'd spend lazy days with our feet in the sand and a book in hand, swimming in water that the girls loved but was a little too cold for my

Hawaiian tastes, sometimes spotting a pod of seals close to shore. Later, we'd walk to Nancy's to eat the best fried shrimp on earth, and then Malia and Sasha would run off with their friends to get ice cream or ride the small carousel or play games at the local arcade.

We couldn't do things quite the same way now that we were the First Family. Instead of taking the ferry into Oak Bluffs, we now arrived on the Marine One helicopter. The house we now rented was a twenty-eight-acre estate on a tonier part of the island, large enough to accommodate staff and Secret Service and isolated enough to maintain a secure perimeter. Arrangements were made for us to go to a private beach, empty for a mile in either direction; our bike rides now followed a tightly prescribed loop, which the girls rode exactly once to indulge me before declaring it "kind of lame." Even on vacation, I started my day with the PDB and a briefing from Denis or John Brennan concerning the assorted mayhem transpiring around the world, and crowds of people and TV crews were always waiting for us when we went to a restaurant for dinner.

Still, the smell of the ocean and sparkle of sunlight against the late summer leaves, the walks along the beach with Michelle, and the sight of Malia and Sasha toasting marshmallows around a bonfire, their faces set in Zen-like concentration—those things remained. And with each day of extra sleep, laughter, and uninterrupted time with those I loved, I could feel my energy returning, my confidence restored. So much so that by the time we returned to Washington, on August 29, 2010, I'd managed to convince myself that we still had a chance to win the midterms and keep Democrats in charge of both the

House and the Senate, the polls and conventional wisdom be damned.

And why not? The truth was that we **had** saved the economy from a likely depression. We **had** stabilized the global financial system and yanked the U.S. auto industry back from the brink of collapse. We **had** put guardrails on Wall Street and made historic investments in clean energy and the nation's infrastructure; protected public lands and reduced air pollution; connected rural schools to the internet and reformed student loan programs so that tens of billions of dollars that had once gone into bank coffers would instead be used to provide direct grants to thousands of young people who otherwise might not be able to afford college.

Taken together, our administration and the Democrat-controlled Congress could rightly claim to have gotten more done, to have delivered more significant legislation that made a real impact on the lives of the American people, than any single session of Congress in the past forty years. And if we had much work yet to do—if too many people were still out of work and at risk of losing their homes; if we hadn't yet passed climate change legislation or fixed a broken immigration system—then it was directly attributable to the size of the mess we'd inherited, along with Republican obstruction and filibusters, all of which American voters could change by casting their ballots in November.

"The problem is I've been cooped up in this building," I said to Favs as we sat together in the Oval working up my stump speech. "Voters just hear these sound bites coming out of Washington—Pelosi said this, McConnell

said that—and they have no way to sort out what's
true and what's not. This is our chance to get back out
there and find a way to cut through that. Tell a clear
story about what's really happened to the economy—
how the last time Republicans were behind the wheel,
they drove the car into the ditch, and how we've spent
the last two years pushing it out . . . and now that we've
just about got the car running again, the last thing the
American people can afford to do is to give them back
the keys!" I paused to look at Favs, who'd been busy typ-
ing on his computer. "What do you think? I think that
works."

"It might," Favs said, although not as enthusiastically
as I would have hoped.

In the six weeks leading up to the election, I barn-
stormed the country, trying to rally support for Democratic
candidates, from Portland, Oregon, to Richmond,
Virginia, from Las Vegas, Nevada, to Coral Gables,
Florida. The crowds were energized, filling up basketball
auditoriums and public parks, chanting, "Yes we can!" and
"Fired up! Ready to go!" as loudly as they had when I ran
for president, hoisting signs, cheering wildly when I introduced the Democratic congresswoman or governor who
needed their vote, having a hoot as I told them we couldn't
afford to give the keys to the car back to Republicans. On
the surface, at least, it was just like old times.

But even without looking at the polls, I could sense a
change in the atmosphere on the campaign trail: an air of
doubt hovering over each rally, a forced, almost desperate
quality to the cheers and laughter, as if the crowds and I
were a couple at the end of a whirlwind romance, trying
to muster up feelings that had started to fade. How could

I blame them? They had expected my election to transform our country, to make government work for ordinary people, to restore some sense of civility in Washington. Instead, many of their lives had grown harder, and Washington seemed just as broken, distant, and bitterly partisan as ever.

During the presidential campaign, I'd grown accustomed to the occasional heckler or two turning up at our rallies, usually anti-abortion protesters who'd shout at me before being drowned out by a chorus of boos and gently escorted out by security. But more often now the hecklers would turn out to be those whose causes I supported—activists let down by what they considered to be a lack of progress on their issues. I was greeted at several stops by protesters holding up signs calling for an end to "Obama's wars." Young Hispanics asked why my administration was still deporting undocumented workers and separating families at the border. LGBTQ activists demanded to know why I hadn't ended the "Don't Ask, Don't Tell" policy, which forced non-straight members of the military to hide their sexual orientation. A group of particularly loud and persistent college students shouted about AIDS funding for Africa.

"Didn't we increase AIDS funding?" I asked Gibbs as we left a rally where I'd been interrupted three or four times.

"We did," he said. "They're saying you didn't increase it **enough**."

I soldiered on through the end of October, coming off the trail only to spend a day or two in meetings at the White House before hitting the road again, my voice increasingly hoarse as I made my last-minute appeals.

Whatever irrational optimism I'd carried with me from vacation had been long extinguished, and by Election Day—November 2, 2010—the question was no longer whether we'd lose the House, but only how badly. Moving between a terrorism threat briefing in the Situation Room and a session in the Oval with Bob Gates, I stopped by Axe's office, where he and Jim Messina had been tracking early turnout data coming in from swing districts across the country.

"What's it looking like?" I asked.

Axe shook his head. "We'll lose at least thirty seats. Maybe more."

Rather than stick around for the wake, I headed up to the residence at my usual time, telling Axe I'd check in once most of the polls had closed and asking my assistant Katie to send up a list of likely calls I'd have to make that night—first to the four congressional leaders, and later to any Democratic incumbents who'd lost. Not until I'd had dinner and tucked in the girls at bedtime did I call Axe from the Treaty Room to receive the news: Turnout had been low, with only four out of every ten eligible voters casting ballots, and a profound drop in the numbers of young people voting. The Democrats had been routed, tracking toward a loss of sixty-three House seats, the worst beating the party had taken since sacrificing seventy-two seats at the midpoint of FDR's second term. Worse yet, many of our most promising young House members had gone down, folks like Tom Perriello of Virginia and John Boccieri of Ohio, Patrick Murphy of Pennsylvania and Betsy Markey of Colorado—the ones who had taken the tough votes on healthcare and the Recovery Act; the ones who, despite being from swing districts, had consistently stood up to lobbyists' pressure and the polls and even the advice of their political staffs to do what they thought was right.

"They all deserved better," I said to Axe.

"Yes," he said. "They did."

Axe signed off, promising to give me a more detailed readout in the morning. I sat alone with the phone receiver in my hand, one finger depressing the switch hook, my head congested with thoughts. After a minute, I dialed the White House operator.

"I've got some calls I need to make," I said.

"Yes, Mr. President," she said. "Katie sent us the list. Who would you like to start with?"

CHAPTER 24

"WHOSE BID IS IT?"

Pete Souza and I sat opposite Marvin and Reggie at the Air Force One conference room table, all of us a bit bleary-eyed as we sorted through our cards. We were on our way to Mumbai—the first leg of a nine-day trip to Asia that would include not only my first visit to India but also a stop in Jakarta, a G20 meeting in Seoul, and an Asia-Pacific Economic Cooperation (APEC) meeting in Yokohama, Japan. The plane had been humming with activity earlier in the flight, with staffers working on laptops and policy advisors huddling over the schedule. After ten hours in the air, with a refueling stop at Ramstein Air Base in Germany, almost everybody on board (including Michelle, in the forward cabin; Valerie, on the couch outside the conference room; and several senior staffers stretched out at odd angles on the floor) had gone to sleep. Unable to wind down, I'd enlisted our regular foursome for a game of Spades, and I was trying to read through my briefing book and signing a stack of correspondence between plays. My divided attention—along with Reggie's second gin and tonic—may have accounted for the fact that Marvin and Pete were up six games to two on us, at ten dollars a pop.

"It's your bid, sir," Marvin said.

"What you got, Reg?" I asked.

"Maybe one," Reggie said.

"We'll go board," I said.

"We're going eight," Pete said.

Reggie shook his head in disgust. "We're switching decks after the next hand," he muttered, taking another sip of his drink. "These cards are cursed."

ONLY THREE DAYS had passed since the midterm elections, and I was grateful for the chance to get out of Washington. The results had left Democrats shell-shocked and Republicans exuberant, and I'd woken up the next morning with a mix of weariness, hurt, anger, and shame, the way a boxer must feel after coming out on the wrong end of a heavyweight bout. The dominant story line in the postelection coverage suggested that the conventional wisdom had been right all along: that I'd attempted to do too much and hadn't stayed focused on the economy; that Obamacare was a fatal error; that I'd tried to resurrect the kind of big-spending, big-government liberalism that even Bill Clinton had pronounced dead years ago. The fact that in my press conference the day after the election I refused to admit as much, that I seemed to cling to the idea that my administration had pursued the right policies—even if we clearly hadn't managed to sell them effectively—struck pundits as arrogant and delusional, the sign of a sinner who wasn't contrite.

The truth was, I **didn't** regret paving the way for twenty million people to get health insurance. Nor did I regret the Recovery Act—the hard evidence showed that austerity in response to a recession would have been disastrous. I didn't regret how we'd handled the financial crisis, given the choices we'd faced (although I did regret not having come up with a better plan to help stem the tide of foreclosures). And I sure as hell wasn't sorry I'd proposed a climate change bill and pushed for immigration reform. I was just mad that I hadn't yet gotten either item through Congress—mainly because, on my very first day in office, I hadn't had the foresight to tell Harry Reid and the rest of the Senate Democrats to revise the chamber rules and get rid of the filibuster once and for all.

As far as I was concerned, the election didn't prove that our agenda had been wrong. It just proved that—whether for lack of talent, cunning, charm, or good fortune—I'd failed to rally the nation, as FDR had once done, behind what I knew to be right.

Which to me was just as damning.

Much to the relief of Gibbs and my press shop, I'd ended the press conference before baring my stubborn, tortured soul. I realized that justifying the past mattered less than planning what to do next.

I was going to have to find a way to reconnect with the American people—not just to strengthen my hand in negotiations with Republicans but to get reelected. A better economy would help, but even that was hardly assured. I needed to get out of the White House bubble, to engage more frequently with voters. Meanwhile, Axe offered his own assessment of what had gone wrong, saying that in the rush to get things done, we'd neglected our promise to change Washington—by sidelining special interests, and increasing transparency and fiscal responsibility across the federal government. If we wanted to win back the voters who'd left us, he argued, we had to reclaim those themes.

But was that right? I wasn't so sure. Yes, we'd been hurt by the sausage-making around the ACA, and fairly or not, we'd been tarnished by the bank bailouts. On the other hand, I could point to scores of "good government" initiatives we'd introduced, whether it was placing limits on the hiring of former lobbyists, or giving the public access to data from federal agencies, or scouring agency budgets to eliminate waste. All these actions were worthy on their merits, and I was glad we'd taken them; it was one of the reasons we hadn't had a whiff of scandal around my administration.

Politically, though, no one seemed to care about our work to clean up the government—any more than they credited us for having bent over backward to solicit Republican ideas on every single one of our legislative initiatives. One of our biggest promises had been to end partisan bickering and focus on practical efforts to address citizen demands. Our problem, as Mitch McConnell had calculated from the start, was that so long as Republicans uniformly resisted our overtures and raised hell over even the most moderate of proposals, anything we did could be portrayed as partisan, controversial, radical— even illegitimate. In fact, many of our progressive allies believed that we hadn't been partisan **enough**. In their view, we'd compromised too much, and by continually chasing the false promise of bipartisanship, we'd not only empowered McConnell and squandered big Democratic majorities; we'd thrown a giant wet blanket over our base—as evidenced by the decision of so many Democrats to not bother to vote in the midterms.

Along with having to figure out a message and policy reboot, I was now facing significant turnover in White House personnel. On the foreign policy team, Jim Jones—who, despite his many strengths, had never felt fully comfortable in a staff role after years of command—had resigned in October. Luckily, Tom Donilon was proving to be a real workhorse and had ably assumed the national security advisor role, with Denis McDonough moving up to deputy national security advisor and Ben Rhodes assuming many of Denis's old duties. On economic policy, Peter Orszag and Christy Romer had returned to the private sector, replaced by Jack Lew, a seasoned budget expert who'd managed OMB under Bill Clinton, and Austan Goolsbee, who'd been working with us on the recovery. Then there was Larry Summers, who had stopped by the Oval one day in September to tell me that with the financial crisis behind us, it was time for him to exit. He'd be leaving at year's end.

"What am I going to do without you around to explain why I'm wrong?" I asked, only half-joking. Larry smiled.

"Mr. President," he said, "you were actually less wrong than most."

I'd grown genuinely fond of those who were leaving. Not only had they served me well, but despite their various idiosyncrasies, they'd each brought a seriousness of purpose—a commitment to policy making based on reason and evidence—that was born of a desire to do right by the American people. It was, however, the impending loss of my two closest political advisors, as well as the need to find a new chief of staff, that unsettled me most.

Axe had always planned to leave after the midterms. Having lived apart from his family for two years, he badly needed a break before joining my reelection campaign. Gibbs, who'd been in the foxhole with me continuously since I'd won my Senate primary race, was just as worn down. Although he remained as well prepared and fearless a press secretary as ever, the strain of standing at a podium day after day, taking all the hits that had been coming our way, had made his relationship with the White House press corps combative enough that the rest of the team worried that it was negatively affecting our coverage.

I was still getting used to the prospect of fighting the political battles ahead without Axe and Gibbs at my side, though I took heart in the continuity provided by our young and skillful communications director, Dan Pfeiffer, who had worked closely with them on messaging since the start of our 2007 campaign. As for Rahm, I considered it a minor miracle that he'd lasted as long as he had without either killing somebody or dropping dead from a stroke. We'd made a habit of conducting our end-of-day meetings outside when the weather allowed, strolling two or three times around the driveway that encircled the South Lawn as we tried to figure out what to do about the latest crisis or controversy. More than once we'd asked ourselves why we'd chosen such stressful lives.

"After we're finished, we should try something simpler," I said to him one day. "We could move our families to Hawaii and open a smoothie stand on the beach."

"Smoothies are too complicated," Rahm said. "We'll sell T-shirts. But just white T-shirts. In medium. That's it—no other colors or patterns or sizes. We don't want to have to make any decisions. If customers want something different, they can go someplace else."

I had recognized the signs that Rahm was close to burnout, but I'd assumed he'd wait for the new year to leave. Instead, he'd used one of our evening walks in early September to tell me that longtime Chicago mayor Richard M. Daley had just announced that he wouldn't be seeking a seventh consecutive term. Rahm wanted to run—it was a job he'd dreamed of since entering politics—and with the election happening in February, he needed to leave the White House by the first of October if he hoped to have a go at it.

He looked genuinely distraught. "I know I'm putting you in a bind," he said, "but with only five and a half months to run a race—"

I stopped him before he could finish and said he'd have my full support.

A week or so later, at a private farewell ceremony in the residence, I presented him with a framed copy of a to-do list that I'd handwritten on a legal pad and passed to him during my first week in office. Almost every item had been checked off, I told the assembled staff, a measure of how effective he'd been. Rahm teared up— a blemish on his tough-guy image for which he later cursed me.

None of this turnover was unusual for an administration, and I saw the potential benefits to shaking things up. More than once we'd been accused of being too insular and tightly controlled, in need of fresh perspectives. Rahm's skill set would be less relevant without a Democratic House to help advance legislation. With

Pete Rouse serving as interim chief of staff, I was leaning toward hiring Bill Daley, who'd been commerce secretary in the Clinton administration and was the brother of Chicago's outgoing mayor, to replace Rahm. Balding and about a decade older than me, with a distinctive South Side accent that evoked his Irish working-class roots, Bill had a reputation as an effective, pragmatic dealmaker with strong relationships with both labor and the business community; and while I didn't know him the way I knew Rahm, I thought his affable, nonideological style might be well suited for what I expected to be a less frantic phase of my administration. And along with some new faces, I was thrilled that I'd be getting one back starting in January when David Plouffe, fresh from a two-year sabbatical with his family, would return as a senior advisor and provide our White House operation with the same strategic thinking, intense focus, and lack of ego that had benefited us so much during the campaign.

Still, I couldn't help feeling a little melancholy over the changes the new year would bring: I'd be surrounded by even fewer people who'd known me before I was president, and by fewer colleagues who were also friends, who'd seen me tired, confused, angry, or defeated and yet had never stopped having my back. It was a lonely thought at a lonely time. Which probably explains why I was still playing cards with Marvin, Reggie, and Pete when I had a full day of meetings and appearances scheduled to start in less than seven hours.

"Did you guys just win again?" I asked Pete after we finished the hand.

Pete nodded, prompting Reggie to gather up all the cards, rise from his chair, and toss them into the trash bin.

"Hey, Reg, that's still a good deck!" Pete said, not bothering to disguise his pleasure at the beatdown he and Marvin had just administered. "Everybody loses sometimes."

Reggie flashed a hard look at Pete. "Show me someone who's okay with losing," he said, "and I'll show you a loser."

I'D NEVER BEEN to India before, but the country had always held a special place in my imagination. Maybe it was its sheer size, with one-sixth of the world's population, an estimated two thousand distinct ethnic groups, and more than seven hundred languages spoken. Maybe it was because I'd spent a part of my childhood in Indonesia listening to the epic Hindu tales of the Ramayana and the Mahābhārata, or because of my interest in Eastern religions, or because of a group of Pakistani and Indian college friends who'd taught to me to cook **dahl** and **keema** and turned me on to Bollywood movies.

More than anything, though, my fascination with India had to do with Mahatma Gandhi. Along with Lincoln, King, and Mandela, Gandhi had profoundly influenced my thinking. As a young man, I'd studied his writings and found him giving voice to some of my deepest instincts. His notion of **satyagraha,** or devotion to truth, and the power of nonviolent resistance to stir the conscience; his insistence on our common humanity and the essential oneness of all religions; and his belief in every society's obligation, through its political, economic, and social arrangements, to recognize the equal worth and dignity of all people—each of these ideas resonated with me. Gandhi's actions had stirred me even more than his words;

he'd put his beliefs to the test by risking his life, going to prison, and throwing himself fully into the struggles of his people. His nonviolent campaign for Indian independence from Britain, which began in 1915 and continued for more than thirty years, hadn't just helped overcome an empire and liberate much of the subcontinent, it had set off a moral charge that pulsed around the globe. It became a beacon for other dispossessed, marginalized groups— including Black Americans in the Jim Crow South—intent on securing their freedom.

Michelle and I had a chance early in the trip to visit Mani Bhavan, the modest two-story building tucked into a quiet Mumbai neighborhood that had been Gandhi's home base for many years. Before the start of our tour, our guide, a gracious woman in a blue sari, showed us the guestbook Dr. King had signed in 1959, when he'd traveled to India to draw international attention to the struggle for racial justice in the United States and pay homage to the man whose teachings had inspired him.

The guide then invited us upstairs to see Gandhi's private quarters. Taking off our shoes, we entered a simple room with a floor of smooth, patterned tile, its terrace doors open to admit a slight breeze and a pale, hazy light. I stared at the spartan floor bed and pillow, the collection of spinning wheels, the old-fashioned phone and low wooden writing desk, trying to imagine Gandhi present in the room, a slight, brown-skinned man in a plain cotton dhoti, his legs folded under him, composing a letter to the British viceroy or charting the next phase of the Salt March. And in that moment, I had the strongest wish to sit beside him and talk. To ask him where he'd found the strength and imagination to do so much with so very little. To ask how he'd recovered from disappointment.

He'd had more than his share. For all his extraordinary gifts, Gandhi hadn't been able to heal the subcontinent's deep religious schisms or prevent its partitioning into a predominantly Hindu India and an overwhelmingly Muslim Pakistan, a seismic event in which untold numbers died in sectarian violence and millions of families were forced to pack up what they could carry and migrate across newly established borders. Despite his labors, he hadn't undone India's stifling caste system. Somehow, though, he'd marched, fasted, and preached well into his seventies—until that final day in 1948, when on his way to prayer, he was shot at point-blank range by a young Hindu extremist who viewed his ecumenism as a betrayal of the faith.

IN MANY RESPECTS, modern-day India counted as a success story, having survived repeated changeovers in government, bitter feuds within political parties, various armed separatist movements, and all manner of corruption scandals. The transition to a more market-based economy in the 1990s had unleashed the extraordinary entrepreneurial talents of the Indian people—leading to soaring growth rates, a thriving high-tech sector, and a steadily expanding middle class. As a chief architect of India's economic transformation, Prime Minister Manmohan Singh seemed like a fitting emblem of this progress: a member of the tiny, often persecuted Sikh religious minority who'd risen to the highest office in the land, and a self-effacing technocrat who'd won people's trust not by appealing to their passions but by bringing about higher living standards and maintaining a well-earned reputation for not being corrupt.

Singh and I had developed a warm and productive relationship. While he could be cautious in foreign policy, unwilling to get out too far ahead of an Indian bureaucracy that was historically suspicious of U.S. intentions, our time together confirmed my initial impression of him as a man of uncommon wisdom and decency; and during my visit to the capital city of New Delhi, we reached agreements to strengthen U.S. cooperation on counterterrorism, global health, nuclear security, and trade.

What I couldn't tell was whether Singh's rise to power represented the future of India's democracy or merely an aberration. Our first evening in Delhi, he and his wife, Gursharan Kaur, hosted a dinner party for me and Michelle at their residence, and before joining the other guests in a candlelit courtyard, Singh and I had a few minutes to chat alone. Without the usual flock of minders and notetakers hovering over our shoulders, the prime minister spoke more openly about the clouds he saw on the horizon. The economy worried him, he said. Although India had fared better than many other countries in the wake of the financial crisis, the global slowdown would inevitably make it harder to generate jobs for India's young and rapidly growing population. Then there was the problem of Pakistan: Its continuing failure to work with India to investigate the 2008 terrorist attacks on hotels and other sites in Mumbai had significantly increased tensions between the two countries, in part because Lashkar-e-Tayyiba, the terrorist organization responsible, was believed to have links to Pakistan's intelligence service. Singh had resisted calls to retaliate against Pakistan after the attacks, but his restraint had cost him politically. He feared that rising anti-Muslim sentiment had strengthened the influence of India's main opposition party, the Hindu nationalist Bharatiya Janata Party (BJP).

"In uncertain times, Mr. President," the prime minister said, "the call of religious and ethnic solidarity can be intoxicating. And it's not so hard for politicians to exploit that, in India or anywhere else."

I nodded, recalling the conversation I'd had with Václav Havel during my visit to Prague and his warning about the rising tide of illiberalism in Europe. If globalization and a historic economic crisis were fueling these trends in relatively wealthy nations—if I was seeing it even in the United States with the Tea Party—how could India be immune? For the truth was that despite the resilience of its democracy and its impressive recent economic performance, India still bore little resemblance to the egalitarian, peaceful, and sustainable society Gandhi had envisioned. Across the country, millions continued to live in squalor, trapped in sunbaked villages or labyrinthine slums, even as the titans of Indian industry enjoyed lifestyles that the rajas and moguls of old would have envied. Violence, both public and private, remained an all-too-pervasive part of Indian life. Expressing hostility toward Pakistan was still the quickest route to national unity, with many Indians taking great pride in the knowledge that their country had developed a nuclear weapons program to match Pakistan's, untroubled by the fact that a single miscalculation by either side could risk regional annihilation.

Most of all, India's politics still revolved around religion, clan, and caste. In that sense, Singh's elevation as prime minister, sometimes heralded as a hallmark of the country's progress in overcoming sectarian divides, was somewhat deceiving. He hadn't originally become prime minister as a result of his own popularity. In fact, he owed his position to Sonia Gandhi—the Italian-born widow of former prime minister Rajiv Gandhi and the head of the Congress Party, who'd declined to take the job herself after leading her party coalition to victory and had instead anointed Singh. More than one political observer believed that she'd chosen Singh precisely because as an elderly Sikh with no national political base, he posed no threat to her forty-year-old son, Rahul, whom she was grooming to take over the Congress Party.

Both Sonia and Rahul Gandhi sat at our dinner table that night. She was a striking woman in her sixties, dressed in a traditional sari, with dark, probing eyes and a quiet, regal presence. That she—a former stay-at-home mother of European descent—had emerged from her grief after her husband was killed by a Sri Lankan separatist's suicide bomb in 1991 to become a leading national politician testified to the enduring power of the family dynasty. Rajiv was the grandson of Jawaharlal Nehru, India's first prime minister and an icon in the independence movement. His mother, Nehru's daughter, Indira Gandhi, had spent a total of sixteen years as prime minister herself, relying on a more ruthless brand of politics than her father had practiced, until 1984 when she, too, was assassinated.

At dinner that night, Sonia Gandhi listened more than she spoke, careful to defer to Singh when policy matters came up, and often steered the conversation toward her son. It became clear to me, though, that her power was attributable to a shrewd and forceful intelligence. As for Rahul, he seemed smart and earnest, his good looks resembling his mother's. He offered up his thoughts on the future of progressive politics, occasionally pausing to probe me on the details of my 2008 campaign. But there was a nervous, unformed quality about him, as if he were a student who'd done the coursework and was eager to impress the teacher but deep down lacked either the aptitude or the passion to master the subject.

As it was getting late, I noticed Singh fighting off sleep, lifting his glass every so often to wake himself up with a sip of water. I signaled to Michelle that it was time to say our goodbyes. The prime minister and his wife walked us to our car. In the dim light, he looked frail, older than his seventy-eight years, and as we drove off I wondered what would happen when he left office. Would the baton be successfully passed to Rahul, fulfilling the destiny laid out by his mother and preserving the Congress Party's dominance over the divisive nationalism touted by the BJP?

Somehow, I was doubtful. It wasn't Singh's fault. He had done his part, following the playbook of liberal democracies across the post–Cold War world: upholding the constitutional order; attending to the quotidian, often technical work of boosting the GDP; and expanding the social safety net. Like me, he had come to believe that this was all any of us could expect from democracy, especially in big, multiethnic, multireligious societies like India and the United States. Not revolutionary leaps or major cultural overhauls; not a fix for every social pathology or lasting answers for those in search of purpose and meaning in their lives. Just the observance of rules that allowed us to sort out or at least tolerate our differences, and government policies that raised living standards and improved education enough to temper humanity's baser impulses.

Except now I found myself asking whether those impulses—of violence, greed, corruption, nationalism, racism, and religious intolerance, the all-too-human desire to beat back our own uncertainty and mortality and sense of insignificance by subordinating others—were too strong for any democracy to permanently contain. For they seemed to lie in wait everywhere, ready to resurface whenever growth rates stalled or demographics changed or a charismatic leader chose to ride the wave of people's fears and resentments. And as much as I might have wished otherwise, there was no Mahatma Gandhi around to tell me what I might do to hold such impulses back.

HISTORICALLY, CONGRESSIONAL ambitions tend to be low during the six- or seven-week stretch between Election Day and the Christmas recess, especially with a shift in party control about to happen. The dispirited losers just want to go home; the winners want to run out the clock until the new Congress gets sworn in. On January 5, 2011, we'd be seating the most Republican House of Representatives since 1947, which meant I'd be unable to get any legislation called for a vote, much less passed, without the assent of the incoming Speaker of the House, John Boehner. And if there was any question about his agenda, Boehner had already announced that the first bill he'd be calling to a vote was a total repeal of the ACA.

We did, however, have a window of opportunity during the coming lame-duck session. Having returned from my visit to Asia, I was intent on getting several key initiatives across the finish line before Congress adjourned for the holidays: ratification of the New START on nuclear nonproliferation that we'd negotiated with the Russians; repeal of "Don't Ask, Don't Tell," the law that barred gays, lesbians, and bisexuals from openly serving in the military; and passage of the DREAM Act, which would establish a path to citizenship for a large swath of children of undocumented immigrants. Pete Rouse and Phil Schiliro, who between them had nearly seventy years of Capitol Hill experience, looked dubious when I ran through my lame-duck to-do list. Axe actually chortled.

"Is that it?" he asked sarcastically.

Actually, it wasn't. I'd forgotten to mention that we needed to pass a child nutrition bill that Michelle had made a central plank in her fight against childhood obesity. "It's good policy," I said, "and Michelle's team's done a great job lining up support from children's health advocates. Plus, if we don't get it passed, I won't be able to go home."

I understood some of my staff's skepticism about trying to move such an ambitious agenda. Even if we could muster the sixty votes needed for each of those controversial bills, it wasn't clear that Harry Reid could get enough cooperation from Mitch McConnell to schedule so many votes in such a short time. Still, I didn't think I was being entirely delusional. Almost every item on my list already had some legislative traction and had either cleared or seemed likely to clear the House. And while we hadn't had much luck overcoming GOP-led Senate filibusters previously, I knew that McConnell had a big-ticket item of his own that he desperately wanted to get done: passing a law to extend the so-called Bush tax cuts, which would otherwise automatically expire at the end of the year.

This gave us leverage.

I'd long opposed my predecessor's signature domestic legislation, laws passed in 2001 and 2003 that changed the U.S. tax code in ways that disproportionately bene-fited high-net-worth individuals while accelerating the trend of wealth and income inequality. Warren Buffett liked to point out that the law enabled him to pay taxes at a significantly lower rate—proportionate to his income, which came almost entirely from capital gains and dividends—than his secretary did on her salary. The laws' changes to the estate tax alone had reduced the tax burden for the top 2 percent of America's richest families by more than $130 billion. Not only that, but by taking roughly $1.3 trillion in projected revenue out of the U.S. Treasury, the laws had helped turn a federal budget sur-plus under Bill Clinton into a burgeoning deficit—a deficit that many Republicans were now using to justify their calls for cuts to Social Security, Medicare, Medicaid, and the rest of America's social safety net.

The Bush tax cuts might have been bad policy, but they had also modestly lowered the tax bill of most Americans, which made rolling them back politically tricky. Polls consistently showed a strong majority of Americans favoring higher taxes on the rich. But even well-to-do lawyers and doctors didn't consider themselves rich, especially if they lived in high-cost areas; and after a decade in which the bottom 90 percent of earners had seen stagnant wages, very few people thought their own taxes should go up. During the campaign, my team and I had settled on what we considered a policy sweet spot, proposing that the Bush tax cuts be repealed selectively, affecting only those families with income greater than $250,000 a year (or individuals earning more than $200,000). This approach had almost universal support from congressional Democrats, would affect only the richest 2 percent of Americans, and would still yield roughly $680 billion over the next decade, funds we could use to expand childcare, healthcare, job training, and education programs for the less well-off.

I hadn't changed my mind on any of this—getting the rich to pay more in taxes was not only a matter of fairness but also the only way to fund new initiatives. But as had been true with so many of my campaign proposals, the financial crisis had forced me to rethink **when** we should try to do it. Early in my term, when it looked like the country might career into a depression, my economic team had persuasively argued that any increase in taxes—even those targeting rich people and Fortune 500 companies—would be counterproductive, since it would take money out of the economy precisely at a time when we wanted individuals and businesses to get out there and spend. With the economy barely on the mend, the prospect of tax hikes still made the team nervous.

And as it was, Mitch McConnell had threatened to block anything less than a full extension of the Bush tax cuts. Which meant that our only option for getting rid of them right away—an option many progressive commentators urged us to take—involved doing nothing and simply letting everybody's tax rates automatically revert to higher, Clinton-era levels on the first of January. Democrats could then return in the new year and propose replacement legislation that would reduce tax rates for Americans making less than $250,000 a year, essentially daring Republicans to vote no.

It was a strategy we strongly considered. But Joe Biden and our legislative team worried that given how badly we'd lost in the midterms, centrist Democrats might break ranks on the issue and then Republicans would use those defections to marshal a vote that made the tax cuts permanent. Politics aside, the problem with playing chicken with the GOP, I decided, was the immediate impact it would have on a still-fragile economy. Even if we could hold our Democrats in line and Republicans ultimately buckled under the pressure, it still could take months to get any tax legislation through a divided Congress. In the meantime, middle- and working-class Americans would have smaller paychecks, businesses would rein in their investments even further, the stock market would tank again, and the economy would almost certainly end up back in a recession.

After gaming out various scenarios, I sent Joe up to Capitol Hill to negotiate with McConnell. We would support a two-year extension of all the Bush tax cuts— but only if Republicans agreed to extend emergency unemployment benefits, the Recovery Act's lower- to middle-class tax credit (Making Work Pay), and another package of refundable tax credits benefiting the working poor for an equivalent period. McConnell immediately balked. Having previously declared that "the single most important thing we want to achieve is for President Obama to be a one-term president," he was apparently loath to let me claim that I'd cut taxes for the majority of Americans without Republicans having forced me to do it. I couldn't say I was surprised; one of the reasons I'd chosen Joe to act as an intermediary—in addition to his Senate experience and legislative acumen—was my awareness that in McConnell's mind, negotiations with the vice president didn't inflame the Republican base in quite the same way that any appearance of cooperating with (Black, Muslim socialist) Obama was bound to do.

After a lot of back-and-forth, and after we'd agreed to swap the Making Work Pay tax credit for a payroll tax cut, McConnell finally relented and, on December 6, 2010, I was able to announce that a comprehensive agreement had been reached.

From a policy perspective, we were pleased with the outcome. While it was painful to keep the tax cuts for the wealthy in place for another two years, we'd managed to extend tax relief for middle-class families while leveraging an additional $212 billion worth of economic stimulus specifically targeted at those Americans most in need—the kind of package we'd have no chance of passing through a Republican-controlled House as a stand-alone bill. As for the politics behind the deal, I explained to Valerie that the two-year time frame represented a high-stakes wager between the Republicans and me. I was betting that in November 2012, I'd be coming off a successful reelection campaign, allowing me to end the tax cuts for the wealthy from a position of strength.

They were betting that they'd beat me—and that a new Republican president would help them make the Bush tax cuts permanent.

The fact that the deal left so much riding on the next presidential election might explain why it immediately provoked outrage from left-leaning commentators. They accused me of caving to McConnell and Boehner and of being compromised by my buddies on Wall Street and advisors like Larry and Tim. They warned that the payroll tax cut would weaken the Social Security Trust Funds; that the refundable tax credits benefiting the working poor would prove ephemeral; and that in two years' time, the Bush tax cuts for the wealthy would be made permanent, just like the Republicans had always wanted.

In other words, they, too, expected me to lose.

As it so happened, the same mid-December week we announced the deal with McConnell, Bill Clinton joined me in the Oval Office dining room for a visit. Whatever tensions had existed between us during the campaign had largely dissipated by then, and I found it useful to hear the lessons he'd learned after suffering a similar midterm shellacking at the hands of Newt Gingrich in 1994. At some point, we got into the nitty-gritty of the tax agreement I'd just made, and Clinton couldn't have been more enthusiastic.

"You need to tell that to some of our friends," I said, noting the blowback we were getting from certain Democratic circles.

"If I have the chance, I will," Clinton said.

That gave me an idea. "How about you get the chance right now?" Before he could answer, I walked over to Katie's desk and asked her to have the press team rustle up any correspondents who were in the building. Fifteen minutes later, Bill Clinton and I stepped into the White House briefing room.

Explaining to the startled reporters that they might like to get some perspective on our tax deal from the person who'd overseen just about the best U.S. economy we'd experienced in recent history, I turned the podium over to Clinton. It didn't take long for the former president to own the room, mustering all of his raspy-voiced, lip-biting Arkansas charm to make the case for our deal with McConnell. In fact, shortly after the impromptu press conference began, I realized I had another commitment to get to, but Clinton was clearly enjoying himself so much that I didn't want to cut him off. Instead, I leaned into the microphone to say that I had to leave but that President Clinton could stick around. Later, I asked Gibbs how the whole thing had played.

"The coverage was great," Gibbs said. "Though a few of the talking heads said that you diminished yourself by giving Clinton the platform."

I wasn't too worried about that. I knew that Clinton's poll numbers were a whole lot higher than mine at the time, partly because the conservative press that had once vilified him now found it useful to offer him up as a contrast to me, the kind of reasonable, centrist Democrat, they said, that Republicans could work with. His endorsement would help us sell the deal to the broader public and tamp down any potential rebellion among congressional Democrats. It was an irony that I—like many modern leaders—eventually learned to live with: You never looked as smart as the ex-president did on the sidelines.

Our temporary détente with McConnell on taxes allowed us to focus on the rest of my lame-duck to-do list. Michelle's child nutrition bill had already received enough Republican support to pass in early December with relatively little fuss, despite accusations from Sarah Palin (now a Fox News commentator) that Michelle was intent on taking away the freedom of American parents to feed their children as they saw fit. Meanwhile, the House was working through the details of a food safety bill that would pass later in the month.

Ratifying New START in the Senate proved more challenging—not only because, as a treaty, it required 67 rather than 60 votes but because domestically there was no strong constituency clamoring to get it done. I had to nag Harry Reid to prioritize the issue during the lame-duck sessions, explaining that U.S. credibility—not to mention my own standing with other world leaders—was at stake, and that a failure to ratify the treaty would undermine our efforts to enforce sanctions against Iran and get other countries to tighten up their own nuclear security. Once I got Harry's grudging commitment to bring the treaty up for a vote ("I don't know how I'll find the floor time, Mr. President," he grumbled over the phone, "but if you tell me it's important I'll do my best, okay?"), we went to work lining up Republican votes. The Joint Chiefs' endorsement of the treaty helped; so did strong support from my old friend Dick Lugar, who remained the ranking Republican on the Senate Foreign Relations Committee and rightly viewed New START as an extension of his earlier work on nuclear nonprolif-eration.

Even so, closing the deal required me to commit to a

multiyear, multibillion-dollar modernization of the infra-structure around the United States' nuclear stockpile, at the insistence of conservative Arizona senator Jon Kyl. Given my long-term goal of eliminating nuclear weapons, not to mention all the better ways I could think of to use billions of federal dollars, this concession felt like a devil's bargain, though our in-house experts, many of whom were dedicated to nuclear disarmament, assured me that our aging nuclear weapons systems did need upgrades in order to reduce the risk of a catastrophic miscalculation or accident. And when New START finally cleared the Senate by a 71–26 vote, I breathed a big sigh of relief.

THE WHITE HOUSE never looked more beautiful than during the holiday season. Huge pine wreaths with red velvet bows lined the walls along the colonnade and the main corridor of the East Wing, and the oaks and magnolias in the Rose Garden were strewn with lights. The official White House Christmas tree, a majestic fir delivered by horse-drawn carriage, occupied most of the Blue Room, but trees almost as spectacular filled nearly every public space in the residence. Over the course of three days, an army of volunteers organized by the Social Office decorated the trees, halls, and Grand Foyer with a dazzling array of ornaments, while the White House pastry chefs prepared an elaborate ginger-bread replica of the residence, complete with furniture, curtains, and—during my presidency—a miniature version of Bo.

The holiday season also meant we hosted parties practically every afternoon and evening for three and a half

weeks straight. These were big, festive affairs, with three
to four hundred guests at a time, laughing and chomping
on lamb chops and crab cakes and drinking eggnog and
wine while members of the United States Marine Band,
spiffy in their red coats, played all the holiday standards.
For me and Michelle, the afternoon parties were easy—
we just dropped by for a few minutes to wish everyone
well from behind a rope line. But the evening events
called for us to position ourselves in the Diplomatic
Reception Room for two hours or more, posing for photos with nearly every guest. Michelle didn't mind doing
this at the parties we hosted for the families of Secret
Service personnel and the residence staff, despite what
standing in heels for that long did to her feet. Her holiday
spirits dimmed, however, when it came to feting members of Congress and the political media. Maybe it was
because they demanded more attention ("Stop making
so much small talk!" she'd whisper to me during momen-
tary breaks in the action); or because some of the same
people who regularly appeared on TV calling for her
husband's head on a spike somehow had the nerve to put
their arms around her and smile for the camera as if they
were her best high school chums.

Back in the West Wing, much of my team's energy
in the weeks before Christmas went toward pushing
through the two most controversial bills left on my
docket: "Don't Ask, Don't Tell" (DADT) and the
DREAM Act. Alongside abortion, guns, and just about
anything to do with race, the issues of LGBTQ rights
and immigration had occupied center stage in America's
culture wars for decades, in part because they raised the
most basic question in our democracy—namely, who do

we consider a true member of the American family, deserving of the same rights, respect, and concern that we expect for ourselves? I believed in defining that family broadly—it included gay people as well as straight, and it included immigrant families that had put down roots and raised kids here, even if they hadn't come through the front door. How could I believe otherwise, when some of the same arguments for their exclusion had so often been used to exclude those who looked like me?

That's not to say that I dismissed those with different views on LGBTQ and immigration rights as heartless bigots. For one thing, I had enough self-awareness—or at least a good enough memory—to know that my own attitudes toward gays, lesbians, and transgender people hadn't always been particularly enlightened. I grew up in the 1970s, a time when LGBTQ life was far less visible to those outside the community, so that Toot's sister (and one of my favorite relatives), Aunt Arlene, felt obliged to introduce her partner of twenty years as "my close friend Marge" whenever she visited us in Hawaii.

And like many teenage boys in those years, my friends and I sometimes threw around words like "fag" or "gay" at each other as casual put-downs—callow attempts to fortify our masculinity and hide our insecurities. Once I got to college and became friends with fellow students and professors who were openly gay, though, I realized the overt discrimination and hate they were subject to, as well as the loneliness and self-doubt that the dominant culture imposed on them. I felt ashamed of my past behavior—and learned to do better.

As for immigration, during my youth I'd given the issue little thought beyond the vague mythology of Ellis

Island and the Statue of Liberty transmitted through popular culture. The progression of my thinking came later, when my organizing work in Chicago introduced me to the predominantly Mexican communities of Pilsen and Little Village—neighborhoods where the usual categories of native-born Americans, naturalized citizens, green-card holders, and undocumented immigrants all but dissolved, since many, if not most, families included all four. Over time, people shared with me what it was like to have to hide your background, always afraid that the life you'd worked so hard to build might be upended in an instant. They talked about the sheer exhaustion and expense of dealing with an often heartless or arbitrary immigration system, the sense of helplessness that came with having to work for employers who took advantage of your immigration status to pay you subminimum wages. The friendships I made and the stories I heard in those Chicago neighborhoods, and from LGBTQ people during college and my early career, had opened my heart to the human dimensions of issues that I'd once thought of in mainly abstract terms.

For me, the "Don't Ask, Don't Tell" situation was straightforward: I considered a policy that prevented LGBTQ persons from openly serving in our military to be both offensive to American ideals and corrosive to the armed forces. DADT was the result of a flawed compromise between Bill Clinton—who'd campaigned on the idea of ending the outright ban on LGBTQ people serving in the military—and his Joint Chiefs, who'd insisted that such a change would damage morale and retention. Since going into effect in 1994, DADT had done little to protect or dignify anyone and, in fact, had led to the discharge of more than thirteen thousand service members solely due to their sexual orientation. Those who remained had to hide who they were and who they loved, unable to safely put up family pictures in their work spaces or attend social functions on base with their partners. As the first African American commander in chief, I felt a special responsibility to end the policy, mindful that Blacks in the military had traditionally faced institutional prejudice and been barred from leadership roles and for decades had been forced to serve in segregated units—a policy Harry Truman had finally ended with an executive order in 1948.

The question was how best to accomplish the change. From the outset, LGBTQ advocates urged me to follow Truman's example and simply issue an order to reverse the policy—particularly since I'd already used executive orders and memoranda to address other regulations adversely affecting LGBTQ people, including the grant- ing of hospital visitation rights and the extension of benefits to domestic partners of federal employees. But in short-circuiting the consensus building involved in passing legislation, an executive order increased the like- lihood of resistance to the new policy inside the military, and foot-dragging in its implementation. And, of course, a future president could always reverse an executive order with the mere stroke of a pen.

I'd concluded that the optimal solution was to get Congress to act. To do that, I needed the military's top leaders as active and willing partners—which, in the middle of two wars, I knew wouldn't be easy. Previous Joint Chiefs had opposed repealing DADT, reasoning that the integration of openly gay service members might adversely impact unit cohesion and discipline.

(Congressional opponents of repeal, including John McCain, claimed that introducing such a disruptive new policy during wartime amounted to a betrayal of our troops.) To their credit, though, Bob Gates and Mike Mullen didn't flinch when I told them, early in my term, that I intended to reverse DADT. Gates said that he'd already asked his staff to quietly begin internal planning on the issue, less out of any personal enthusiasm for the policy change than out of a practical concern that federal courts might ultimately find DADT unconstitutional and force a change on the military overnight. Rather than try to talk me out of my position, he and Mullen asked that I let them set up a task force to evaluate the implications of the proposed change on military operations—which would ultimately conduct a comprehensive survey of troops' attitudes toward having openly gay members in their ranks. The objective, Gates said, was to minimize disruption and division.

"If you're going to do this, Mr. President," Gates added, "we should at least be able to tell you how to do it right."

I warned Gates and Mullen that I didn't consider discrimination against LGBTQ people to be an issue subject to plebiscite. Nevertheless, I agreed to their request, partly because I trusted them to set up an honest evaluation process but mainly because I suspected that the survey would show our troops—most of whom were decades younger than the high-ranking generals—to be more open-minded toward gays and lesbians than people expected. Appearing before the Senate Armed Services Committee on February 2, 2010, Gates further validated my trust when he said, "I fully support the president's decision" to reexamine DADT. But it was Mike Mullen's testimony before the committee that same day that really made news, as he became the first sitting senior U.S. military leader in history to publicly argue that LGBTQ persons should be allowed to openly serve: "Mr. Chairman, speaking for myself and myself only, it is my personal belief that allowing gays and lesbians to serve openly would be the right thing to do. No matter how I look at this issue, I cannot escape being troubled by the fact that we have in place a policy which forces young men and women to lie about who they are in order to defend their fellow citizens. For me personally, it comes down to integrity, theirs as individuals and ours as an institution."

Nobody in the White House had coordinated with Mullen on the statement; I'm not even sure that Gates had known ahead of time what Mullen planned to say. But his unequivocal statement immediately shifted the public debate and created important political cover for fence-sitting senators, who could then feel justified in embracing the repeal.

Mullen's testimony came months before the evaluation process he and Gates had requested was completed, which caused some political headaches. Proponents of repeal started coming hard at us, both privately and in the press, unable to understand why I wouldn't simply issue an executive order when the chairman of the Joint Chiefs supported a policy change—especially because, while we took our sweet time with a survey, LGBTQ service members were still being discharged. Valerie and her team bore the brunt of the friendly fire, particularly Brian Bond, a highly regarded gay activist who served as our principal liaison to the community. For months,

Brian had to defend my decision-making, as skeptical friends, former colleagues, and members of the press suggested that he'd been co-opted, questioning his commitment to the cause. I can only imagine the toll this took on him personally.

The criticism grew louder in September 2010 when, as Gates had predicted, a federal district court in California ruled that DADT was unconstitutional. I asked Gates to formally suspend all discharges while the case was appealed. But no matter how hard I pressed, he repeatedly refused my request, arguing that as long as DADT was in place, he was obligated to enforce it; and I knew that ordering him to do something he considered inappropriate might force me to have to find a new defense secretary. It was perhaps the only time I came close to yelling at Gates, and not just because I considered his legal analysis faulty. He seemed to consider the frustrations we were hearing from LGBTQ advocates—not to mention the anguished stories of gay and lesbian service members who were under his charge—as one more bit of "politics" from which I should shield him and the Pentagon, rather than a central consideration in his own decision-making. (Ultimately he did at least modify DADT's administrative procedures in such a way that nearly all actual discharges were halted while we awaited resolution on the issue.)

Mercifully, toward the end of that same month, the results from the troop study finally came in. They confirmed what I'd suspected: Two-thirds of those surveyed thought that allowing those gay, lesbian, and bisexual colleagues to serve openly would have little or no impact on—or might actually improve—the military's ability to execute its missions. In fact, most troops believed that they were either already working or had worked with LGBTQ service members and had experienced no difference in their ability to perform their duties.

Get exposed to other people's truths, I thought, and attitudes change.

With the survey in hand, Gates and Mullen officially endorsed the repeal of DADT. Meeting with me in the Oval Office, the other Joint Chiefs pledged to implement the policy without undue delay. In fact, General James Amos, the Marine commandant and a firm opponent of repeal, drew smiles when he said, "I can promise you, Mr. President, that none of these other branches are going to do it faster or better than the U.S. Marine Corps." And on December 18, the Senate passed the bill 65–31, with eight Republican votes.

A few days later, former and current LGBTQ service members filled an auditorium at the Department of the Interior as I signed the bill. Many were in dress uniform, their faces expressing a medley of joy, pride, relief, and tears. As I addressed the crowd, I saw a number of the advocates who'd been some of our fiercest critics just a few weeks earlier now smiling in appreciation. Spotting Brian Bond, I gave him a nod. But the biggest applause that day was reserved for Mike Mullen—a long, heartfelt standing ovation. As I watched the admiral standing on the stage, visibly moved despite the awkward grin on his face, I couldn't have been happier for him. It wasn't often, I thought, that a true act of conscience is recognized that way.

WHEN IT CAME to immigration, everyone agreed that the system was broken. The process of immigrating legally to the United States could take a decade or longer, often depending on what country you were coming from and how much money you had. Meanwhile, the economic gulf between us and our southern neighbors drove hundreds of thousands of people to illegally cross the 1,933-mile U.S.-Mexico border each year, searching for work and a better life. Congress had spent billions to harden the border, with fencing, cameras, drones, and an expanded and increasingly militarized border patrol. But rather than stop the flow of immigrants, these steps had spurred an industry of smugglers—**coyotes**—who made big money transporting human cargo in barbaric and sometimes deadly fashion. And although border crossings by poor Mexican and Central American migrants received most of the attention from politicians and the press, about 40 percent of America's unauthorized immigrants arrived through airports or other legal ports of entry and then overstayed their visas.

By 2010, an estimated eleven million undocumented persons were living in the United States, in large part thoroughly woven into the fabric of American life. Many were longtime residents, with children who either were U.S. citizens by virtue of having been born on American soil or had been brought to the United States at such an early age that they were American in every respect except for a piece of paper. Entire sectors of the U.S. economy relied on their labor, as undocumented immigrants were often willing to do the toughest, dirtiest work for meager pay—picking the fruits and vegetables that stocked our grocery stores, mopping the floors of offices, washing dishes at restaurants, and providing care to the elderly. But although American consumers benefited from this invisible workforce, many feared that immigrants were taking jobs from citizens, burdening social services programs, and changing the nation's racial and cultural makeup, which led to demands for the government to crack down on illegal immigration. This sentiment was strongest among Republican constituencies, egged on by an increasingly nativist right-wing press. However, the politics didn't fall neatly along partisan lines: The traditionally Democratic trade union rank and file, for example, saw the growing presence of undocumented workers on construction sites as threatening their livelihoods, while Republican-leaning business groups interested in maintaining a steady supply of cheap labor (or, in the case of Silicon Valley, foreign-born computer programmers and engineers) often took pro-immigration positions.

Back in 2007, the maverick version of John McCain, along with his sidekick Lindsey Graham, had actually joined Ted Kennedy to put together a comprehensive reform bill that offered citizenship to millions of undocumented immigrants while more tightly securing our borders. Despite strong support from President Bush, it had failed to clear the Senate. The bill did, however, receive twelve Republican votes, indicating the real possibility of a future bipartisan accord. I'd pledged during the campaign to resurrect similar legislation once elected, and I'd appointed former Arizona governor Janet Napolitano as head of the Department of Homeland Security—the agency that oversaw U.S. Immigration and Customs Enforcement (ICE) and U.S. Customs and Border Protection—partly because of her knowledge of border issues and her reputation for having previously managed immigration in a way that was both compassionate and tough.

My hopes for a bill had thus far been dashed. With the economy in crisis and Americans losing jobs, few in Congress had any appetite to take on a hot-button issue like immigration. Kennedy was gone. McCain, having been criticized by the right flank for his relatively moderate immigration stance, showed little interest in taking up the banner again. Worse yet, my administration was deporting undocumented workers at an accelerating rate. This wasn't a result of any directive from me, but rather it stemmed from a 2008 congressional mandate that both expanded ICE's budget and increased collaboration between ICE and local law enforcement departments in an effort to deport more undocumented immigrants with criminal records. My team and I had made a strategic choice not to immediately try to reverse the policies we'd inherited in large part because we didn't want to provide ammunition to critics who claimed that Democrats weren't willing to enforce existing immigration laws—a perception that we thought could torpedo our chances of passing a future reform bill. But by 2010, immigrant-rights and Latino advocacy groups were criticizing our lack of progress, much the same way LGBTQ activists had gone after us on DADT. And although I continued to urge Congress to pass immigration reform, I had no realistic path for delivering a new comprehensive law before the midterms.

Enter the DREAM Act. The idea that young, undocumented immigrants who'd been brought to the United States as children could be given some sort of relief had been floating around for years, and at least ten versions of the DREAM Act had been introduced in Congress since 2001, each time failing to garner the needed votes. Advocates often presented it as a partial but meaningful step on the road to wider reform. The act would grant "Dreamers"—as these young people had come to be called—temporary legal residence and a pathway to citizenship, so long as they met certain criteria. According to the most recent bill, they had to have entered the United States before the age of sixteen, lived here for five continuous years, graduated from high school or obtained a GED, and attended college for two years or joined the military—and they could have no serious criminal record. Individual states could make Dreamers legally eligible for reduced tuition rates at public colleges and universities—the only realistic way many of them could afford higher education.

Dreamers had grown up going to American schools, playing American sports, watching American TV, and hanging out at American malls. In some cases, their parents had never even told them they weren't citizens; they learned of their undocumented status only when they tried to get a driver's license or submitted an application for college financial aid. I'd had a chance to meet many Dreamers, both before and after I entered the White House. They were smart, poised, and resilient—as full of potential as my own daughters. If anything, I found the Dreamers to be less cynical about America than many of their native-born contemporaries—precisely because their circumstances had taught them not to take life in this country for granted.

The case for allowing such young people to stay in the

United States, the only country many of them had ever known, was so morally compelling that Kennedy and McCain had incorporated the DREAM Act into their 2007 immigration bill. And without the prospect of passing a more comprehensive rewrite of U.S. immigration laws in the immediate future, Harry Reid—who, in the months leading up to the midterms, had been locked in a tight reelection contest in his home state of Nevada and needed a strong Hispanic turnout to put him over the top—had promised to call the DREAM Act for a vote during the lame-duck session.

Unfortunately, Harry made this last-minute announcement on the campaign trail without giving us, his Senate colleagues, or immigration reform groups any notice. Though not thrilled with Harry's lack of coordination with her ("You'd think he could have picked up the phone"), Nancy Pelosi did her part, quickly pushing the legislation through the House. But in the Senate, McCain and Graham denounced Harry's decision as a campaign stunt and said they wouldn't vote for the DREAM Act as a stand-alone bill since it was no longer linked to increased enforcement. The five Republican senators who'd voted for the 2007 McCain-Kennedy bill and were still in office were less declarative about their intentions, but all sounded wobbly. And since we couldn't count on every Democrat to support the bill—especially after the disastrous midterms—all of us in the White House found ourselves scrambling to drum up the sixty votes needed to overcome a filibuster during the waning days before the Senate wrapped up business for the year.

Cecilia Muñoz, the White House director of intergovernmental affairs, was our point person on the effort.

When I was a senator, she'd been the senior vice president of policy and legislative affairs at the National Council of La Raza, the nation's largest Latino advocacy organization, and ever since she'd advised me on immigration and other issues. Born and raised in Michigan and the daughter of Bolivian immigrants, Cecilia was measured, modest, and—as I used to joke with her—"just plain nice," bringing to mind everyone's favorite young elementary or middle school teacher. She was also tough and tenacious (and a fanatical Michigan football fan). Within a matter of weeks, she and her team had launched an all-out media blitz in support of the DREAM Act, pitching stories, marshaling statistics, and enlisting practically every cabinet member and agency (including the Defense Department) to host some kind of event. Most important, Cecilia helped bring together a crew of young Dreamers who were willing to disclose their undocumented status in order to share their personal stories with undecided senators and media outlets. Several times, Cecilia and I talked about the courage of these young people, agreeing that at their age we could never have managed such pressure.

"I just want to win so bad for them," she told me.

And yet, despite the countless hours we spent in meetings and on the phone, the likelihood of getting sixty votes for the DREAM Act began to look increasingly bleak. One of our best prospects was Claire McCaskill, the Democratic senator from Missouri. Claire was one of my early supporters and best friends in the Senate, a gifted politician with a razor-sharp wit, a big heart, and not an ounce of hypocrisy or pretension. But she also came from a conservative, Republican-leaning state and was a juicy target for the GOP in its effort to wrest back control of the Senate.

"You know I want to help those kids, Mr. President," Claire said when I reached her by phone, "but the polling in Missouri is just terrible on anything related to immigration. If I vote for this, there's a good chance I lose my seat."

I knew she wasn't wrong. And if she lost, we might lose the Senate, along with any possibility of ever getting the DREAM Act or comprehensive immigration reform or anything else passed. How was I to weigh that risk against the urgent fates of the young people I'd met—the uncertainty and fear they were forced to live with every single day, the possibility that with no notice any one of them might be rounded up in an ICE raid, detained in a cell, and shipped off to a land that was as foreign to them as it would be to me?

Before hanging up, Claire and I made a deal to help square the circle. "If your vote's the one that gets us to sixty," I said, "then those kids are going to need you, Claire. But if we're way short, there's no point in you falling on your sword."

The Senate voted on the DREAM Act on a cloudy Saturday a week before Christmas, the same day it voted to repeal DADT. I watched on the small TV in the Oval Office with Pete Souza, Reggie, and Katie as the roll call appeared, tallying the votes in favor: 40, 50, 52, 55. There was a pause, the chamber in a state of suspension, a last chance for a senator to change their mind, until the gavel finally fell.

We'd come up five votes short.

I took the stairs up to the second floor of the West

Wing and headed to Cecilia's office, where she and her young team had been watching the vote. Most of the room was in tears, and I gave everybody hugs. I reminded them that because of their work we'd come closer to passing the DREAM Act than any previous effort; and that it would be our job to keep pushing as long as we were here, until we finally met our goal. Everyone nodded quietly, and I went back downstairs. On my desk, Katie had left a printout of the roll call. Running my fingers down the page, I noticed that Claire McCaskill had voted "yea." I asked Katie to get Claire on the phone.

"I thought you were a 'no' unless the bill was close," I said when she picked up.

"Damn it, Mr. President, I thought so too," Claire said. "But when it came time to record my vote, and I started thinking about those kids who'd come by my office . . ." Her voice caught in her throat, thick with emotion. "I just couldn't do it to them. I couldn't let them think I didn't care. Anyway," she went on, composing herself, "looks like you're going to have to help me raise a whole lot of money so I can beat back those Republican ads calling me soft on immigration."

I promised Claire I would. Even though there'd be no bill-signing ceremony for her to attend and no audience to give her a standing ovation, I believed that my friend's quiet exercise of conscience, no less than Mike Mullen's, was one more step toward a better country.

Our failure to pass the DREAM Act was a bitter pill to swallow. Still, all of us in the White House took heart in the fact that we'd managed to pull off the most significant lame-duck session in modern history. In six weeks, the House and Senate had together clocked a remarkable forty-eight days in session and enacted ninety-nine laws—more than a quarter of the 111th Congress's total legislation over two years. What's more, the public seemed to notice the burst of congressional productivity. Axe reported a rise in both consumer confidence and my approval ratings—not because my message or policies had changed but because Washington had gotten a bunch of stuff done. It was as if, for the span of a month and a half, democracy was normal again, with the usual give-and-take between parties, the push and pull of interest groups, the mixed blessing of compromise. What more might we have accomplished, I wondered, and how much further along would the economic recovery be, had this sort of atmosphere prevailed from the start of my term?

PART SEVEN

ON THE HIGH WIRE

CHAPTER 25

IF AT THE END OF 2010, anyone had asked me where the next major Middle East crisis would most likely occur, I could have offered them a rich menu of possibilities. There was Iraq, of course, where despite progress, it often felt as if a return to chaos was just a market bombing or militia attack away. The international sanctions we'd imposed on Iran in response to its nuclear program had started to cause some pain, and any defiance or desperation from the regime could lead to a confrontation that spun out of control. Yemen—one of the world's true hard-luck cases—had become headquarters to al-Qaeda in the Arabian Peninsula, which was now the deadliest and most active chapter of the terrorist network.

And then there were the few hundred miles of winding, contested border that separated Israel from the Palestinian territories of the West Bank and the Gaza Strip.

Mine was hardly the first U.S. administration to lose sleep over those relatively thin pieces of real estate. The conflict between Arabs and Jews had been an open sore on the region for almost a century, dating back to the 1917 Balfour Declaration, in which the British, who were then occupying Palestine, committed to create a "national home for the Jewish people" in a region overwhelmingly populated by Arabs. Over the next twenty or so years, Zionist leaders mobilized a surge of Jewish migration to Palestine and organized highly trained armed forces to defend their settlements. In 1947, in the wake of World War II and in the shadow of the Holocaust's unspeakable crimes, the United Nations approved a partition plan to establish two sovereign states, one Jewish, the other Arab, with Jerusalem— a city considered holy by Muslims, Christians, and Jews alike—to be governed by an international body. Zionist leaders embraced the plan, but Arab Palestinians, as well as surrounding Arab nations that were also just emerging from colonial rule, strenuously objected. As Britain withdrew, the two sides quickly fell into war. And with Jewish militias claiming victory in 1948, the State of Israel was officially born.

For the Jewish people, it was a dream fulfilled, a state of their own in their historic homeland after centuries of exile, religious persecution, and the more recent horrors of the Holocaust. But for the roughly seven hundred thousand Arab Palestinians who found themselves stateless and driven from their lands, the same events would be a part of what became known as the Nakba, or "Catastrophe." For the next three decades, Israel would engage in a succession of conflicts with its Arab neighbors—most significantly the Six-Day War of 1967, in which a greatly outnumbered Israeli military routed the combined armies of Egypt, Jordan, and Syria. In the process, Israel seized control of the West Bank and East Jerusalem from Jordan, the Gaza Strip and the Sinai Peninsula from Egypt, and the Golan Heights from Syria. The memory of those losses, and the humiliation that came with it, became a defining aspect of Arab nationalism, and support for the Palestinian cause a central tenet of Arab foreign policy.

Meanwhile, Palestinians living within the occupied territories, mostly in refugee camps, found themselves governed by the Israel Defense Forces (IDF), with their movements and economic activity severely restricted, prompting calls for armed resistance and resulting in the rise of the Palestine Liberation Organization (PLO). Arab politicians routinely denounced Israel, often in explicitly anti-Semitic terms, and most governments in the region embraced the PLO's chairman, Yasser Arafat, as a freedom fighter—even as his organization and its affiliates engaged in escalating and bloody terrorist attacks against unarmed civilians.

The United States was no bystander in all this. Jewish Americans had suffered generations of discrimination in their own country, but they and other Jews emigrating from the West to Israel still shared language, customs, and appearance with their white Christian brethren, and in comparison to Arabs, they still enjoyed far more sympathy from the American public. Harry Truman had been the first foreign leader to formally recognize Israel as a sovereign state, and the American Jewish community pressed U.S. officials to assist the fledgling nation. With the world's two Cold War superpowers vying for influence in the Middle East, the United States became Israel's primary patron—and with that, Israel's problems with its neighbors became America's problems as well.

Practically every U.S. president since then had tried

to resolve the Arab-Israeli conflict, with varying degrees of success. The historic Camp David Accords, brokered in 1978 by Jimmy Carter, achieved a lasting peace between Israel and Egypt and returned Sinai to Egyptian control. The agreement, which yielded a Nobel Peace Prize for the Israeli prime minister, Menachem Begin, and the Egyptian president, Anwar Sadat, also moved Egypt further out of the Soviet orbit and made the two countries critical U.S. security partners (as well as the largest recipients of U.S. economic and military aid in the world, by a wide margin). But it left the Palestinian issue unresolved. Fifteen years later, with the Cold War over and U.S. influence at its zenith, Bill Clinton brought Israeli prime minister Yitzhak Rabin and Arafat together for the signing of the first Oslo Accord. In it, the PLO finally recognized Israel's right to exist, while Israel recognized the PLO as the rightful representative of the Palestinian people and agreed to the creation of the Palestinian Authority, which would have limited but meaningful governance over the West Bank and the Gaza Strip.

Along with giving Jordan license to follow Egypt's example and conclude its own peace deal with Israel, Oslo provided a framework for the eventual creation of an autonomous Palestinian state, one that, ideally, would coexist with a secure Israel that was at peace with its neighbors. But old wounds, and the lure of violence over compromise among factions on both sides, proved too much to overcome. Rabin was assassinated by a far-right Israeli extremist in 1995. His liberal successor, Shimon Peres, served for seven months before losing a snap election to Benjamin "Bibi" Netanyahu, leader of the right-wing Likud party, whose platform had once included total annexation of the Palestinian territories. Unhappy about the Oslo Accords, harder-line organizations like Hamas and the Palestinian Islamic Jihad set about undermining the credibility of Arafat and his Fatah party with Palestinians, calling for armed struggle to take back Arab lands and push Israel into the sea.

After Netanyahu was defeated in the 1999 election, his more liberal successor, Ehud Barak, made efforts to establish a broader peace in the Middle East, including outlining a two-state solution that went further than any previous Israeli proposal. Arafat demanded more concessions, however, and talks collapsed in recrimination. Meanwhile, one day in September 2000, Likud party leader Ariel Sharon led a group of Israeli legislators on a deliberately provocative and highly publicized visit to one of Islam's holiest sites, Jerusalem's Temple Mount. It was a stunt designed to assert Israel's claim over the wider territory, one that challenged the leadership of Ehud Barak and enraged Arabs near and far. Four months later, Sharon became Israel's next prime minister, governing throughout what became known as the Second Intifada: four years of violence between the two sides, marked by tear gas and rubber bullets directed at stone-throwing protesters; Palestinian suicide bombs detonated outside an Israeli nightclub and in buses carrying senior citizens and schoolchildren; deadly IDF retaliatory raids and the indiscriminate arrest of thousands of Palestinians; and Hamas rockets launched from Gaza into Israeli border towns, answered by U.S.-supplied Israeli Apache helicopters leveling entire neighborhoods.

Approximately a thousand Israelis and three thousand

Palestinians died during this period—including scores of children—and by the time the violence subsided, in 2005, the prospects for resolving the underlying conflict had fundamentally changed. The Bush administration's focus on Iraq, Afghanistan, and the War on Terror left it little bandwidth to worry about Middle East peace, and while Bush remained officially supportive of a two-state solution, he was reluctant to press Sharon on the issue. Publicly, Saudi Arabia and other Gulf states continued to offer support to the Palestinian cause, but they were increasingly more concerned with limiting Iranian influence and rooting out extremist threats to their own regimes. The Palestinians themselves had splintered after Arafat's death in 2004: Gaza came under the control of Hamas and soon found itself under a tightly enforced Israeli blockade, while the Fatah-run Palestinian Authority, which continued to govern the West Bank, came to be viewed by even some of its supporters as feckless and corrupt.

Most important, Israeli attitudes toward peace talks had hardened, in part because peace no longer seemed so crucial to ensuring the country's safety and prosperity. The Israel of the 1960s that remained lodged in the popular imagination, with its communal kibbutz living and periodic rationing of basic supplies, had been transformed into a modern economic powerhouse. It was no longer the plucky David surrounded by hostile Goliaths; thanks to tens of billions of dollars in U.S. military aid, the Israeli armed forces were now matchless in the region. Terrorist bombings and attacks within Israel had all but ceased, due in some measure to the fact that Israel had erected a wall more than four hundred miles long between itself and the Palestinian population centers in the West Bank, punctuated with strategically placed checkpoints to control the flow of Palestinian workers in and out of Israel. Every so often, rocket fire from Gaza still endangered those living in Israeli border towns, and the presence of Jewish Israeli settlers in the West Bank sometimes triggered deadly skirmishes. For most residents of Jerusalem or Tel Aviv, however, the Palestinians lived largely out of sight, their struggles and resentments troubling but remote.

Given everything that was already on my plate when I became president, it would have been tempting to just do my best to manage the status quo, quash any outbreaks of renewed violence between Israeli and Palestinian factions, and otherwise leave the whole mess alone. But taking into account the broader foreign policy concerns, I decided I couldn't go that route. Israel remained a key U.S. ally, and even with the threats reduced, it still endured terrorist attacks that jeopardized not only its citizens but also the thousands of Americans who lived or traveled there. At the same time, just about every country in the world considered Israel's continued occupation of the Palestinian territories to be a violation of international law. As a result, our diplomats found themselves in the awkward position of having to defend Israel for actions that we ourselves opposed. U.S. officials also had to explain why it wasn't hypocritical for us to press countries like China or Iran on their human rights records while showing little concern for the rights of Palestinians. Meanwhile, the Israeli occupation continued to inflame the Arab community and feed anti-American sentiment across the Muslim world.

In other words, the absence of peace between Israel and the Palestinians made America less safe. Negotiating a workable solution between the two sides, on the other hand, stood to strengthen our security posture, weaken our enemies, and make us more credible in championing human rights around the world—all in one fell swoop.

In truth, the Israeli-Palestinian conflict also weighed on me personally. Some of the earliest moral instruction I got from my mother revolved around the Holocaust, an unconscionable catastrophe that, like slavery, she explained, was rooted in the inability or unwillingness to recognize the humanity of others. Like many American kids of my generation, I'd had the story of Exodus etched in my brain. In sixth grade, I'd idealized the Israel described to me by a Jewish camp counselor who'd lived on a kibbutz—a place where everyone was equal, he said, everyone pitched in, and everyone was welcome to share in the joys and struggles of repairing the world. In high school, I'd devoured the works of Philip Roth, Saul Bellow, and Norman Mailer, moved by stories of men trying to find their place in an America that didn't welcome them. Later, studying the early civil rights movement in college, I'd been intrigued by the influence of Jewish philosophers like Martin Buber on Dr. King's sermons and writings. I'd admired how, across issues, Jewish voters tended to be more progressive than just about any other ethnic group, and in Chicago, some of my most stalwart friends and supporters had come from the city's Jewish community.

I believed there was an essential bond between the Black and the Jewish experiences—a common story of exile and suffering that might ultimately be redeemed by a shared thirst for justice, a deeper compassion for others, a heightened sense of community. It made me fiercely protective of the right of the Jewish people to have a state of their own, though, ironically, those same shared values also made it impossible for me to ignore the conditions under which Palestinians in the occupied territories were forced to live.

Yes, many of Arafat's tactics had been abhorrent. Yes, Palestinian leaders had too often missed opportunities for peace; there'd been no Havel or Gandhi to mobilize a nonviolent movement with the moral force to sway Israeli public opinion. And yet none of that negated the fact that millions of Palestinians lacked self-determination and many of the basic rights that even citizens of non-democratic countries enjoyed. Generations were growing up in a starved and shrunken world from which they literally couldn't escape, their daily lives subject to the whims of a distant, often hostile authority and the suspicions of every blank-faced, rifle-carrying soldier demanding to see their papers at each checkpoint they passed.

By the time I took office, though, most congressional Republicans had abandoned any pretense of caring about what happened to the Palestinians. Indeed, a strong majority of white evangelicals—the GOP's most reliable voting bloc—believed that the creation and gradual expansion of Israel fulfilled God's promise to Abraham and heralded Christ's eventual return. On the Democratic side, even stalwart progressives were loath to look less pro-Israel than Republicans, especially since many of them were Jewish themselves or represented sizable Jewish constituencies.

Also, members of both parties worried about crossing the American Israel Public Affairs Committee (AIPAC), a powerful bipartisan lobbying organization dedicated to ensuring unwavering U.S. support for Israel. AIPAC's clout could be brought to bear on virtually every congressional district in the country, and just about every politician in Washington—including me—counted AIPAC members among their key supporters and donors. In the past, the organization had accommodated a spectrum of views on Middle East peace, insisting mainly that those seeking its endorsement support a continuation of U.S. aid to Israel and oppose efforts to isolate or condemn Israel via the U.N. and other international bodies. But as Israeli politics had moved to the right, so had AIPAC's policy positions. Its staff and leaders increasingly argued that there should be "no daylight" between the U.S. and Israeli governments, even when Israel took actions that were contrary to U.S. policy. Those who criticized Israeli policy too loudly risked being tagged as "anti-Israel" (and possibly anti-Semitic) and confronted with a well-funded opponent in the next election.

I'd been on the receiving end of some of this during my presidential campaign, as Jewish supporters reported having to beat back assertions in their synagogues and on email chains that I was insufficiently supportive of—or even hostile toward—Israel. They attributed these whisper campaigns not to any particular position I'd taken (my backing of a two-state solution and opposition to Israeli settlements were identical to the positions of the other candidates) but rather to my expressions of concern for ordinary Palestinians; my friendships with certain critics of Israeli policy, including an activist and Middle

East scholar named Rashid Khalidi; and the fact that, as Ben bluntly put it, "You're a Black man with a Muslim name who lived in the same neighborhood as Louis Farrakhan and went to Jeremiah Wright's church." On Election Day, I'd end up getting more than 70 percent of the Jewish vote, but as far as many AIPAC board members were concerned, I remained suspect, a man of divided loyalties: someone whose support for Israel, as one of Axe's friends colorfully put it, wasn't "felt in his **kishkes**"—"guts," in Yiddish.

"YOU DON'T GET progress on peace," Rahm had warned me in 2009, "when the American president and the Israeli prime minister come from different political backgrounds." We had been discussing the recent return of Bibi Netanyahu as Israel's prime minister, after the Likud party had managed to cobble together a right-leaning coalition government despite winning one less seat than its main opponent, the more centrist Kadima party. Rahm, who'd briefly been a civilian volunteer in the Israeli army and had sat in the front row at Bill Clinton's Oslo negotiations, had agreed that we should try to restart Israeli-Palestinian peace talks, if for no other reason than that it might keep the situation from getting worse. But he wasn't optimistic—and the more time I spent with Netanyahu and his Palestinian counterpart, Mahmoud Abbas, the more I understood why.

Built like a linebacker, with a square jaw, broad features, and a gray comb-over, Netanyahu was smart, canny, tough, and a gifted communicator in both Hebrew and English. (He'd been born in Israel but spent most of his formative years in Philadelphia, and traces of that city's accent lingered in his polished baritone.) His family had deep roots in the Zionist movement: His grandfather, a rabbi, emigrated from Poland to British-governed Palestine in 1920, while his father—a professor of history best known for his writings on the persecution of Jews during the Spanish Inquisition—became a leader in the movement's more militant wing before Israel's founding. Although raised in a secular household, Netanyahu inherited his father's devotion to the defense of Israel: He'd been a member of a special forces unit in the IDF and had fought in the 1973 Yom Kippur War, and his older brother had died a hero in the legendary Entebbe raid of 1976, in which Israeli commandos rescued 102 passengers from Palestinian terrorists who had hijacked an Air France flight.

Whether Netanyahu also inherited his father's unabashed hostility toward Arabs ("The tendency towards conflict is in the essence of the Arab. He is an enemy by essence. His personality won't allow him any compromise or agreement") was harder to say. What was certain was that he had built his entire political persona around an image of strength and the message that Jews couldn't afford phony pieties—that they lived in a tough neighborhood and so had to be tough. This philosophy neatly aligned him with the most hawkish members of AIPAC, as well as Republican officials and wealthy American right-wingers. Netanyahu could be charming, or at least solicitous, when it served his purposes; he'd gone out of his way, for example, to meet me in a Chicago airport lounge shortly after I'd been elected to the U.S. Senate, lavishing praise on me for an inconsequential pro-Israel bill I'd supported in the Illinois state legislature. But his vision of himself as the chief defender of the Jewish people against calamity allowed him to justify almost anything that would keep him in power—and his familiarity with American politics and media gave him confidence that he could resist whatever pressure a Democratic administration like mine might try to apply.

My early discussions with Netanyahu—both over the phone and during his visits to Washington—had gone well enough, despite our very different worldviews. He was most interested in talking about Iran, which he rightly viewed as Israel's largest security threat, and we agreed to coordinate efforts to prevent Tehran from obtaining a nuclear weapon. But when I raised the possibility of restarting peace talks with the Palestinians, he was decidedly noncommittal.

"I want to assure you, Israel wants peace," Netanyahu said. "But a true peace has to meet Israel's security needs." He made it clear to me that he thought Abbas was likely unwilling or unable to do so, a point he would also stress in public.

I understood his point. If Netanyahu's reluctance to enter into peace talks was born of Israel's growing strength, then the reluctance of Palestinian president Abbas was born of political weakness. White-haired and mustached, mild-mannered and deliberate in his movements, Abbas had helped Arafat found the Fatah party, which later became the dominant party of the PLO, spending most of his career managing diplomatic and administrative efforts in the shadow of the more charismatic chairman. He'd been the preferred choice of both the United States and Israel to lead the Palestinians after Arafat's death, in large part due to his unequivocal recognition of Israel and his long-standing renunciation of violence. But his innate caution and willingness to cooperate with the Israeli security apparatus (not to mention reports of corruption inside his administration) had damaged his reputation with his own people. Having already lost control of Gaza to Hamas in the 2006 legislative elections, he viewed peace talks with Israel as a risk not worth taking—at least not without some tangible concessions that would provide him political cover.

The immediate question was how to coax Netanyahu and Abbas to the negotiating table. To come up with answers, I relied on a talented group of diplomats, starting with Hillary, who was well versed on the issues and already had relationships with many of the region's major players. To underscore the high priority I'd placed on the issue, I appointed former Senate majority leader George Mitchell as my special envoy for Middle East peace. Mitchell was a throwback—a hard-driving, pragmatic politician with a thick Maine accent who had demonstrated his peacemaking skills by negotiating the 1998 Good Friday Agreement, which brought an end to the decades-long conflict between Catholics and Protestants in Northern Ireland.

We began by calling for a temporary freeze on Israel's construction of new settlements in the West Bank, a significant sticking point between the two parties, so that negotiations might proceed in earnest. Settlement construction, once limited to small outposts of religious believers, had over time become de facto government policy, and in 2009, there were about three hundred thousand Israeli settlers living outside the country's recognized borders. Developers, meanwhile, continued to build tidy subdivisions in and around the West Bank and East Jerusalem, the disputed, predominantly Arab section of the city that Palestinians hoped to one day make their capital. All this was done with the blessing of politicians who either shared the religious convictions of the settler movement, saw the political benefit of catering to settlers, or were simply interested in alleviating Israel's housing crunch. For Palestinians, the explosion in settlements amounted to a slow-motion annexation of their land and stood as a symbol of the Palestinian Authority's impotence.

We knew that Netanyahu would probably resist the idea of a freeze. The settlers had become a meaningful political force, their movement well represented within Netanyahu's coalition government. Moreover, he would complain that the good-faith gesture we'd be asking from the Palestinians in return—that Abbas and the Palestinian Authority take concrete steps to end incitements to violence inside the West Bank—was a great deal harder to measure. But given the asymmetry in power between Israel and the Palestinians—there wasn't much, after all, that Abbas could give the Israelis that the Israelis couldn't already take on their own—I thought it was reasonable to ask the stronger party to take a bigger first step in the direction of peace.

As expected, Netanyahu's initial response to our proposed settlement freeze was sharply negative, and his allies in Washington were soon publicly accusing us of weakening the U.S.-Israeli alliance. The White House phones started ringing off the hook, as members of my national security team fielded calls from reporters, leaders of American Jewish organizations, prominent supporters, and members of Congress, all wondering why we were picking on Israel and focusing on settlements when everyone knew that Palestinian violence was the main impediment to peace. One afternoon, Ben hurried in late for a meeting, looking particularly harried after having spent the better part of an hour on the phone with a highly agitated liberal Democratic congressman.

"I thought he opposes settlements," I said.

"He does," Ben said. "He also opposes us doing anything to actually stop settlements."

This sort of pressure continued for much of 2009, along with questions about my **kishkes**. Periodically, we'd invite the leaders of Jewish organizations or members of Congress to the White House for meetings with me and my team, so that we could assure them of our ironclad commitment to Israel's security and the U.S.-Israel relationship. It wasn't a hard argument to make; despite my difference with Netanyahu on a settlement freeze, I'd delivered on my promise to enhance U.S.-Israel cooperation across the board, working to counteract the Iranian threat and to help fund the eventual development of an "Iron Dome" defense system, which would allow Israel to shoot down Syrian-made rockets coming from Gaza or from Hezbollah positions inside Lebanon. Nevertheless, the noise orchestrated by Netanyahu had the intended effect of gobbling up our time, putting us on the defensive, and reminding me that normal policy differences with an Israeli prime minister—even one who presided over a fragile coalition government—exacted a domestic political cost that simply didn't exist when I dealt with the United Kingdom, Germany, France, Japan, Canada, or any of our other closest allies.

But shortly after I delivered my Cairo speech, in early June 2009, Netanyahu cracked open the door to progress by responding with an address of his own in which he declared, for the first time, his conditional support for a two-state solution. And after months of wrangling, he and Abbas finally agreed to join me for a face-to-face discussion while they were both in town for the annual leaders' gathering at the U.N. General Assembly at the end of September. The two men were courteous to each other (Netanyahu garrulous and physically at ease, Abbas largely expressionless, save for the occasional nod) but appeared unmoved when I urged them to take some risks for peace. Two months later, Netanyahu agreed to institute a ten-month freeze on the issuance of new settlement permits in the West Bank. Pointedly he refused to extend the freeze to construction in East Jerusalem.

Any optimism I felt about Bibi's concession was short-lived. No sooner had Netanyahu announced the temporary freeze than Abbas dismissed it as meaningless, complaining about the exclusion of East Jerusalem and the fact that construction of already-approved projects was continuing apace. He insisted that in the absence of a total freeze, he would not join any talks. Other Arab leaders quickly echoed these sentiments, spurred in part by editorializing from Al Jazeera, the Qatari-controlled media outlet that had become the dominant news source in the region, having built its popularity by fanning the flames of anger and resentment among Arabs with the same algorithmic precision that Fox News deployed so skillfully with conservative white voters in the States.

The situation only got messier in March 2010, when, just as Joe Biden was visiting Israel on a goodwill mission, the Israeli Interior Ministry announced permits for the construction of sixteen hundred new housing units in East Jerusalem. Although Netanyahu insisted that his office had nothing to do with the timing of the permits, the move reinforced perceptions among Palestinians that the freeze was a sham and the United States was in on it. I instructed Hillary to call Netanyahu and let him know I wasn't happy, and we reiterated our suggestion that his government show more restraint on expanding settlements. His response, delivered at AIPAC's annual conference in Washington later that month, was to declare to thunderous applause that "Jerusalem is not a settlement—it is our capital."

The following day, Netanyahu and I sat down for a meeting at the White House. Downplaying the growing tension, I accepted the fiction that the permit announcement had been just a misunderstanding, and our discussions ran well over the allotted time. Because I had another commitment and Netanyahu still had a few items he wanted to cover, I suggested we pause and resume the conversation in an hour, arranging in the meantime for his delegation to regroup in the Roosevelt Room. He said he was happy to wait, and after that second session, we ended the evening on cordial terms, having met for more than two hours total. The next day, however, Rahm stormed into the office, saying there were media reports that I'd deliberately snubbed Netanyahu by keeping him waiting, leading to accusations that I had allowed a case of personal pique to damage the vital U.S.-Israel relationship.

That was a rare instance when I outcursed Rahm.

Looking back, I sometimes ponder the age-old question of how much difference the particular characteristics of individual leaders make in the sweep of history—whether those of us who rise to power are mere conduits for the deep, relentless currents of the times or whether we're at least partly the authors of what's to come. I wonder whether our insecurities and our hopes, our childhood traumas or memories of unexpected kindness carry as much force as any technological shift or socioeconomic trend. I wonder whether a President Hillary Clinton or President John McCain might have elicited more trust from the two sides; whether things might have played out differently if someone other than Netanyahu had occupied the prime minister's seat or if Abbas had been a younger man, more intent on making his mark than protecting himself from criticism.

What I do know is that despite the hours Hillary and George Mitchell spent doing shuttle diplomacy, our plans for peace talks went nowhere until late in August 2010, just one month before the settlement freeze was set to expire, when Abbas finally agreed to direct talks, thanks largely to the intervention of Egyptian president Hosni Mubarak and King Abdullah of Jordan. Abbas conditioned his participation, however, on Israel's willingness to keep the settlement freeze in place—the same freeze he'd spent the previous nine months decrying as useless.

With no time to lose, we arranged to have Netanyahu, Abbas, Mubarak, and Abdullah join me at meetings and an intimate White House dinner on September 1 to launch the talks. The day was largely ceremonial—the hard work of hammering out a deal would shift to Hillary, Mitchell, and the negotiating teams. Still, we dressed up the whole affair with photo ops and press availabilities and as much fanfare as we could muster, and the atmosphere among the four leaders was warm and collegial throughout. I still have a photograph of the five of us looking at President Mubarak's watch to check that the sun had officially set, since it was the Muslim month of Ramadan, and we had to confirm that the religiously prescribed fast had been lifted before seating everyone for dinner.

In the soft light of the Old Family Dining Room, each of us took turns describing our visions for the future. We talked of predecessors like Begin and Sadat, Rabin and Jordan's King Hussein, who'd had the courage and wisdom to bridge old divides. We spoke of the costs of endless conflict, the fathers who never came home, the mothers who had buried their children.

To an outsider, it would have seemed a hopeful moment, the start of something new.

And yet later that night, when the dinner was over and the leaders had gone back to their hotels and I sat in the Treaty Room going over my briefs for the next day, I couldn't help feeling a vague sense of disquiet. The speeches, the small talk, the easy familiarity—it all felt **too** comfortable, almost ritualized, a performance that each of the four leaders had probably participated in dozens of times before, designed to placate the latest U.S. president who thought things could change. I imagined them shaking hands afterward, like actors taking off their costumes and makeup backstage, before returning to the world that they knew—a world in which Netanyahu could blame the absence of peace on Abbas's weakness while doing everything he could to keep him weak, and

Abbas could publicly accuse Israel of war crimes while quietly negotiating business contracts with the Israelis, and Arab leaders could bemoan the injustices endured by Palestinians under occupation while their own internal security forces ruthlessly ferreted out dissenters and malcontents who might threaten their grip on power. And I thought of all the children, whether in Gaza or in Israeli settlements or on the street corners of Cairo and Amman, who would continue to grow up knowing mainly violence, coercion, fear, and the nursing of hatred because, deep down, none of the leaders I'd met with believed anything else was possible.

A world without illusions—that's what they'd call it.

The Israelis and Palestinians would end up meeting only twice in direct peace talks—once in Washington, the day after our White House dinner, and then again twelve days later for a two-part conversation, with Mubarak hosting negotiators in the Egyptian resort town of Sharm el Sheikh before the group moved to Netanyahu's Jerusalem residence. Hillary and Mitchell reported that the discussions were substantive, with the United States dangling incentives to both sides, including plumped-up aid packages, and even considering a possible early release of Jonathan Pollard, an American convicted of spying for Israel who'd become a hero to many right-leaning Israelis.

But it was all to no avail. The Israelis refused to extend the settlement freeze. The Palestinians withdrew from negotiations. By December 2010, Abbas was threatening to go to the U.N., seeking recognition of a Palestinian state—and to the International Criminal Court, seeking Israel's prosecution for alleged war crimes in Gaza. Netanyahu was threatening to make life harder for the

Palestinian Authority. George Mitchell tried to put things in perspective, reminding me that during negotiations to end the Northern Ireland conflict, "We had seven hundred bad days—and one good one." Still, it felt as if in the near term, at least, the window for any peace deal had closed.

In the months to come, I'd think back often to my dinner with Abbas and Netanyahu, Mubarak and King Abdullah, the pantomime of it, their lack of resolve. To insist that the old order in the Middle East would indefinitely hold, to believe that the children of despair wouldn't revolt, at some point, against those who maintained it— that, it turned out, was the greatest illusion of all.

INSIDE THE WHITE HOUSE, we had frequently discussed the long-term challenges facing North Africa and the Middle East. As petrostates failed to diversify their economies, we asked ourselves what would happen when their oil revenues dried up. We bemoaned the restrictions placed on women and girls—hindering their ability to go to school, work, or, in some cases, even drive a car. We noted the stalled growth and its disproportionate impact on the younger generations in Arabic-speaking nations: People under the age of thirty made up about 60 percent of the population and were suffering unemployment rates double that of the rest of the world.

Most of all, we worried about the autocratic, repressive nature of nearly every Arab government—not just the lack of true democracy but also the fact that those who held power seemed entirely unaccountable to the people they ruled. Even as conditions varied from country to country, most of these leaders maintained their grip through an old formula: restricted political participation and expression, pervasive intimidation and surveillance at the hands of police or internal security services, dysfunctional judicial systems and insufficient due process protections, rigged (or nonexistent) elections, an entrenched military, heavy press censorship, and rampant corruption. Many of these regimes had been in place for decades, held together by nationalist appeals, shared religious beliefs, tribal bonds, familial ties, and webs of patronage. It was possible that the stifling of dissent combined with plain inertia would be enough to keep them going for a while. But although our intelligence agencies mainly focused on tracking the actions of terrorist networks, and our diplomats were not always attuned to what was happening on "the Arab street," we could see indications of a growing discontent among ordinary Arabs—which, given the lack of legitimate outlets to express such frustration, could spell trouble. Or, as I told Denis after returning from my first visit to the region as president, "Sometime, somewhere, things are going to blow."

What to do with that knowledge? There was the rub. For at least half a century, U.S. policy in the Middle East had focused narrowly on maintaining stability, preventing disruptions to our oil supplies, and keeping adversarial powers (first the Soviets, then the Iranians) from expanding their influence. After 9/11, counterterrorism took center stage. In pursuing each of these goals, we'd made autocrats our allies. They were predictable, after all, and committed to keeping a lid on things. They hosted our military bases and cooperated with us on counterterrorism efforts. And, of course, they did lots of business with U.S. companies. Much of our national security apparatus in the region depended on their cooperation and in many instances had become thoroughly entangled with theirs. Every so often, a report would surface from the Pentagon or Langley, recommending that U.S. policy pay more attention to human rights and governance issues when dealing with our Middle East partners. But then the Saudis would deliver a vital tip that kept an explosive device from being loaded onto U.S.-bound cargo planes or our naval base in Bahrain would prove critical in managing a flare-up with Iran in the Strait of Hormuz, and those reports would be relegated to the bottom of a drawer. Across the U.S. government, the possibility that some sort of populist uprising might bring down one of our allies had historically been met with resignation: Sure, it was likely to happen, the same way a bad hurricane will hit the Gulf Coast or the Big One will hit California; but since we couldn't say exactly when or where, and since we didn't have the means to stop it anyway, the best thing to do was prepare contingency plans and get ready to manage the aftershocks.

I liked to think that my administration resisted such fatalism. Building upon my Cairo speech, I had used interviews and public remarks to urge the governments of the Middle East to heed the voices of citizens calling for reform. In meetings with Arab leaders, my team often put human rights issues on the agenda. The State Department worked diligently behind the scenes to protect journalists, free political dissidents, and widen the space for civic engagement.

And yet only rarely did the United States scold allies like Egypt or Saudi Arabia publicly for their human rights violations. Given our concerns over Iraq, al-Qaeda, and Iran, not to mention Israel's security needs, the stakes felt too high to risk rupturing our relationships. Accepting this type of realism, I told myself, was part of the job. Except that every so often, the story of a women's rights activist being arrested in Riyadh would reach my desk, or I'd read about a local employee of an international human rights organization languishing in a Cairo jail, and I'd feel haunted. I knew that my administration would never be able to transform the Middle East into an oasis of democracy, but I believed we could and should be doing a hell of a lot more to encourage progress toward it.

It was during one of those moods that I set aside time for lunch with Samantha Power.

I'd met Samantha while I was in the Senate, after I read her Pulitzer Prize–winning book, **"A Problem from Hell": America and the Age of Genocide**—a moving, tightly reasoned discussion of America's lackluster response to genocide and the need for stronger global leadership in preventing mass atrocities. She was teaching at Harvard at the time, and when I reached out, she jumped at my suggestion that we share ideas over dinner the next time she was in D.C. She turned out to be younger than I'd expected, in her mid-thirties, tall and gangly, with red hair, freckles, and big, thickly lashed, almost sorrowful eyes that crinkled at the corners when she laughed. She was also intense. She and her Irish mother had immigrated to the States when she was nine; she'd played basketball in high school, graduated from Yale, and worked as a freelance journalist covering the Bosnian war. Her experiences there—bearing witness to slaughter and ethnic cleansing—had inspired her to get a law degree, hoping it would give her the tools to cure some part of the world's madness. That evening, after she'd run me through an exhaustive list of U.S. foreign policy errors that she insisted needed correcting, I suggested she might want to get out of the ivory tower and work with me for a spell.

The conversation that started over dinner that night continued on and off for the next several years. Samantha joined my Senate staff as a foreign policy fellow, advising on issues like the genocide then taking place in Darfur. She worked on my presidential campaign, where she met her future husband, my friend and eventual regulatory czar Cass Sunstein, and became one of our top foreign policy surrogates. (I did have to put her in the penalty box, removing her from the campaign, when, during what she thought was an off-the-record moment with a reporter, she called Hillary "a monster.") Following the election, I hired her for a senior position at the NSC, where she did excellent work, mainly out of the limelight, including designing a broad global initiative to increase government transparency and reduce corruption in countries around the world.

Samantha was one of my closest friends in the White House. Much like Ben, she evoked my own youthful idealism, the part of me still untouched by cynicism, cold calculation, or caution dressed up as wisdom. And I suspect it was precisely because she knew that side of me, and understood which heartstrings to pull, that at times she drove me nuts. I didn't actually see her much from day to day, and that was part of the problem; whenever Samantha got time on my calendar, she felt obliged to remind me of every wrong I hadn't yet righted. ("So, what ideals have we betrayed lately?" I'd ask.) She was shattered, for example, when on Armenian Remembrance Day I failed to explicitly acknowledge the early-twentieth-century genocide of Armenians at the hands of the Turks (the need to name genocide unequivocally was a central thesis of her book). I had good reason for not making a statement at the time—the Turks were deeply touchy about the issue, and I was in delicate negotiations with President Erdogan on managing America's withdrawal from Iraq—but still, she made me feel like a heel. But as exasperating as Samantha's insistence could be, every so often I needed a dose of her passion and integrity, both as a temperature check on my conscience and because she often had specific, creative suggestions for how to deal with messy problems that no one in the administration was spending enough time thinking about.

Our lunch in May 2010 was a case in point. Samantha showed up that day ready to talk about the Middle East—in particular, the fact that the United States hadn't lodged an official protest of the Egyptian government's recent two-year extension of a state of "emergency law" that had been in place continuously since Mubarak's election in 1981. The extension codified his dictatorial power by suspending the constitutional rights of Egyptians. "I understand there are strategic considerations when it comes to Egypt," Samantha said, "but does anybody stop to ask whether it's good strategy?"

I told her that, actually, I had. I wasn't a big fan of Mubarak, but I'd concluded that a one-off statement criticizing a law that had been in place for almost thirty years wouldn't be all that useful. "The U.S. government's an ocean liner," I said. "Not a speedboat. If we want to change our approach to the region, then we need a strategy that builds over time. We'd have to get buy-in from the Pentagon and the intel folks. We'd have to calibrate the strategy to give allies in the region time to adjust."

"Is anybody doing that?" Samantha said. "Coming up with that strategy, I mean?"

I smiled, seeing the wheels turning in her head.

Not long afterward, Samantha and three NSC colleagues—Dennis Ross, Gayle Smith, and Jeremy Weinstein—presented me with the blueprint for a Presidential Study Directive stating that U.S. interests in stability across the Middle East and North Africa were adversely affected by the United States' uncritical support of authoritarian regimes. In August I used that directive to instruct the State Department, Pentagon, CIA, and other government agencies to examine ways the United States could encourage meaningful political and economic reforms in the region to nudge those nations closer to the principles of open government, so that they might avoid the destabilizing uprisings, violence, chaos, and unpredictable outcomes that so often accompanied sudden change. The NSC team set about conducting biweekly meetings with Middle East experts from across government to develop specific ideas for reorienting U.S. policy.

Many of the veteran diplomats and experts they talked to were predictably skeptical of the need for any change to U.S. policy, arguing that as unsavory as some of our Arab allies might be, the status quo served America's core interests—something that wasn't guaranteed if more populist governments took their place.

Over time, though, the team was able to arrive at a coherent set of principles to guide a shift in strategy. Under the emerging plan, U.S. officials across agencies would be expected to deliver a consistent and coordinated message on the need for reform; they would develop specific recommendations for liberalizing political and civic life in various countries and offer a range of new incentives to encourage their adoption. By mid-December, the documents laying out the strategy were just about ready for my approval, and although I realized that it wouldn't change the Middle East overnight, I was heartened by the fact that we were starting to steer America's foreign policy machinery in the right direction.

If only our timing had been a bit better.

THE SAME MONTH, in the North African nation of Tunisia, an impoverished fruit vendor set himself on fire outside a local government building. It was an act of protest, born of desperation: one citizen's furious response to a government he knew to be corrupt and indifferent to his needs. By all accounts, the man, twenty-six-year-old Mohamed Bouazizi, was not an activist, nor was he especially concerned with politics. He belonged to a generation of Tunisians raised in a stagnant economy and under the thumb of a repressive dictator named Zine el-Abidine Ben Ali. And after being repeatedly harassed by municipal inspectors and denied a hearing in front of a judge, he was simply fed up. According to a bystander, at the moment of his self-immolation, Bouazizi shouted—to nobody in particular and to everyone at once—"How do you expect me to make a living?"

The fruit vendor's anguish set off weeks of nationwide

demonstrations against the Tunisian government, and on January 14, 2011, Ben Ali and his family fled to Saudi Arabia. Meanwhile, similar protests, made up mostly of young people, were beginning to happen in Algeria, Yemen, Jordan, and Oman, the first flickers of what became known as the Arab Spring.

As I prepared to give my State of the Union address on January 25, my team debated the extent to which I should comment on the events happening almost at warp speed in the Middle East and North Africa. With public protest having effectively driven a sitting autocrat from power in Tunisia, people across the region seemed galvanized and hopeful about the possibilities for wider change. Still, the complexities were daunting and good outcomes far from guaranteed. In the end, we added a single, straightforward line to my speech:

"Tonight, let us be clear: The United States of America stands with the people of Tunisia, and supports the democratic aspirations of all people."

From the U.S. perspective, the most significant developments were in Egypt, where a coalition of Egyptian youth organizations, activists, left-wing opposition parties, and prominent writers and artists had issued a nationwide call for mass protests against President Mubarak's regime. On the same day as my State of the Union, close to fifty thousand Egyptians poured into Tahrir Square, in downtown Cairo, demanding an end to emergency law, police brutality, and restrictions on political freedom. Thousands of others participated in similar protests across the country. The police were attempting to disperse the crowds using batons, water cannons, rubber bullets, and tear gas, and Mubarak's government would not only issue an official ban on protesting but also block Facebook, YouTube, and Twitter in an effort to hamper the demonstrators' ability to organize or connect with the outside world. For days and nights to come, Tahrir Square would resemble a permanent encampment, with legions of Egyptians standing in defiance of their president, calling for "bread, freedom, and dignity."

This was precisely the scenario my Presidential Study Directive had sought to avoid: the U.S. government suddenly caught between a repressive but reliable ally and a population insistent on change, voicing the democratic aspirations we claimed to stand for. Alarmingly, Mubarak himself seemed oblivious about the uprising taking place around him. I'd spoken to him by phone just a week earlier, and he'd been both helpful and responsive as we'd discussed ways to coax the Israelis and Palestinians back to the negotiating table, as well as his government's call for unity in response to the bombing of a Coptic Christian church in Alexandria, carried out by Muslim extremists. But when I'd brought up the possibility that the protests that had begun in Tunisia might spread to his own country, Mubarak had dismissed it, explaining that "Egypt is not Tunisia." He'd assured me that any protest against his government would quickly die down. Listening to his voice, I'd imagined him sitting in one of the cavernous, ornately decorated rooms inside the presidential palace where we'd first met—the curtains drawn, him looking imperious in a high-backed chair as a few aides took notes or just watched, coiled in readiness to attend to his needs. Insulated as he was, he would see what he wanted to see, I thought, and hear what he wanted to hear—and none of it boded well.

Meanwhile, the news footage from Tahrir Square brought back different memories. The crowds in those first few days appeared to be disproportionately young and secular—not unlike the students and activists who'd been in the audience of my Cairo speech. In interviews, they came off as thoughtful and informed, insisting on their commitment to nonviolence and their desire for democratic pluralism, rule of law, and a modern, innovative economy that could deliver jobs and a better standard of living. In their idealism and courage in challenging an oppressive social order, they appeared no different from the young people who had once helped tear down the Berlin Wall or stood in front of tanks in Tiananmen Square. They weren't so different, either, from the young people who'd helped elect me president.

"If I were an Egyptian in my twenties," I told Ben, "I'd probably be out there with them."

Of course, I wasn't an Egyptian in my twenties. I was president of the United States. And as compelling as these young people were, I had to remind myself that they—along with the university professors, human rights activists, secular opposition party members, and trade unionists also on the front lines of the protests—represented only a fraction of the Egyptian population. If Mubarak stepped down, creating a sudden power vacuum, they weren't the ones most likely to fill it. One of the tragedies of Mubarak's dictatorial reign was that it had stunted the development of the institutions and traditions that might help Egypt effectively manage a transition to democracy: strong political parties, an independent judiciary and media, impartial election monitors, broad-based civic associations, an effective civil service,

ON THE HIGH WIRE

and respect for minority rights. Outside the military, which was deeply entrenched throughout Egyptian society and reportedly had a significant stake in large swaths of the economy, the most powerful and cohesive force in the country was the Muslim Brotherhood, the Sunni-based Islamist organization whose central objective was to see Egypt—and the entire Arab world—governed by sharia law. Thanks to its grassroots organizing and charitable work on behalf of the poor (and despite the fact that Mubarak had officially banned it), the Brotherhood boasted a substantial membership. It also embraced political participation rather than violence as a way of advancing its goals, and in any fair and free election, the candidates it backed would be odds-on favorites to win. Still, many governments in the region viewed the Brotherhood as a subversive, dangerous threat, and the organization's fundamentalist philosophy made it both unreliable as a custodian for democratic pluralism and potentially problematic for U.S.-Egyptian relations.

In Tahrir Square, the demonstrations continued to swell, as did violent clashes between protesters and police. Apparently awakened from his slumber, Mubarak went on Egyptian television on January 28 to announce that he was replacing his cabinet, but he offered no signs that he intended to respond to the demands for broader reform. Convinced that the problem wasn't going away, I consulted my national security team to try to come up with an effective response. The group was divided, almost entirely along generational lines. The older and more senior members of my team—Joe, Hillary, Gates, and Panetta—counseled caution, all of them having known and worked with Mubarak for years. They emphasized the role his government had long played in keeping peace with Israel, fighting terrorism, and partnering with the United States on a host of other regional issues. While they acknowledged the need to press the Egyptian leader on reform, they warned that there was no way of knowing who or what might replace him. Meanwhile, Samantha, Ben, Denis, Susan Rice, and Joe's national security advisor, Tony Blinken, were convinced that Mubarak had fully and irretrievably lost his legitimacy with the Egyptian people. Rather than keep our wagon hitched to a corrupt authoritarian order on the verge of collapse (and appear to be sanctioning the escalating use of force against protesters), they considered it both strategically prudent and morally right for the U.S. government to align itself with the forces of change.

I shared both the hopes of my younger advisors and the fears of my older ones. Our best bet for a positive outcome, I decided, was to see if we could persuade Mubarak to embrace a series of substantive reforms, including ending the emergency law, restoring political and press freedoms, and setting a date for free and fair national elections. Such an "orderly transition," as Hillary described it, would give opposition political parties and potential candidates time to build followings and develop serious plans to govern. It would also allow Mubarak to retire as an elder statesman, which might help mitigate perceptions in the region that we were willing to dump longtime allies at the slightest hint of trouble.

It went without saying that trying to convince an aging, embattled despot to ride off into the sunset, even if it was in his own interests, would be a delicate operation. After the Situation Room discussion, I phoned

Mubarak again, raising the idea of him putting forward a bolder set of reforms. He instantly grew combative, characterizing the protesters as members of the Muslim Brotherhood and insisting once again that the situation would soon return to normal. He did agree, though, to my request to send an envoy—Frank Wisner, who'd been a U.S. ambassador to Egypt in the late 1980s—to Cairo for more extensive private consultations.

Using Wisner to make a direct, face-to-face appeal to the Egyptian president had been Hillary's idea, and I thought it made sense: Wisner was literally a scion of the American foreign policy establishment, his father having been an iconic leader during the foundational years of the CIA, and he was someone Mubarak knew well and trusted. At the same time, I understood that Wisner's history with Mubarak and his old-school approach to U.S. diplomacy might make him conservative in evaluating the prospects for change. Before he left, I called him with clear instructions to "be bold": I wanted him to push Mubarak to announce that he would step down after new elections were held—a gesture I hoped would be dramatic and specific enough to give protesters confidence that change really was coming.

While we awaited the outcome of Wisner's mission, the media became more focused on my administration's reaction to the crisis—and, more specifically, whose side we were on. So far, we'd issued little more than generic public statements in an effort to buy ourselves time. But Washington reporters—many of whom clearly found the cause of the young protesters compelling—began pressing Gibbs on why we weren't unambiguously standing with the forces of democracy. Foreign leaders in the region, meanwhile, wanted to know why we weren't supporting Mubarak more forcefully. Bibi Netanyahu insisted that maintaining order and stability in Egypt mattered above all else, telling me that otherwise "you will see Iran in there in two seconds." King Abdullah of Saudi Arabia was even more alarmed; the spread of protests in the region was an existential threat to a family monarchy that had long squelched any form of internal dissent. He also believed that the Egyptian protesters weren't in fact speaking for themselves. He ticked off the "four factions" he believed were behind the protests: the Muslim Brotherhood, Hezbollah, al-Qaeda, and Hamas.

Neither of these leaders' analyses stood up to scrutiny. The Sunnis, who made up the vast majority of Egyptians (and all of the Muslim Brotherhood), were hardly susceptible to the influence of Shiite Iran and Hezbollah, and there was absolutely no evidence that al-Qaeda or Hamas was behind the demonstrations in any way. Still, even younger, more reform-minded leaders in the region, including King Abdullah of Jordan, feared the possibility of protests engulfing their countries, and while they used more sophisticated language, they clearly expected the United States to choose, as Bibi had put it, "stability" over "chaos."

By January 31, Egyptian army tanks were stationed throughout Cairo, the government had shut down internet service across the city, and protesters were planning a nationwide general strike for the next day. Wisner's readout on his meeting with Mubarak arrived: The Egyptian president would publicly commit not to run for another term but had stopped short of suspending emergency law or agreeing to support a peaceful transfer of power. The report only widened the split within my national security team: The more senior members saw Mubarak's concession as enough justification to stick with him, while the younger staffers considered the move— much like Mubarak's sudden decision to appoint his chief of intelligence, Omar Suleiman, as vice president—as no more than a stalling tactic that would fail to placate the demonstrators. Tom Donilon and Denis let me know that staff debates had turned acrimonious and that report- ers were picking up on the discrepancy between Joe's and Hillary's cautiously anodyne statements and the more strident criticism of Mubarak coming from Gibbs and others in the administration.

Partly to make sure that everyone was singing from the same hymnal while we determined our next steps, I paid an unscheduled visit to a meeting of the NSC Principals Committee in the Situation Room late in the afternoon on February 1. The discussion had barely begun when an aide informed us that Mubarak was addressing the Egyptian people on a nationwide broadcast. We turned on the room's TV monitor so we could watch it in real time. Dressed in a dark suit and reading from a prepared text, Mubarak appeared to be following through on his pledge to Wisner, saying that he had never intended to nominate himself for another term as president and announcing that he would call on the Egyptian parliament—a parlia- ment he entirely controlled—to discuss speeding up a timeline for new elections. But the terms of an actual transfer of power were so vague that any Egyptian watch- ing would likely conclude that whatever promises Mubarak was now making could and would be reversed the moment the protests died down. In fact, the Egyptian president devoted the bulk of the speech to accusing provocateurs and unnamed political forces of hijacking the protests to undermine the nation's security and stability. He insisted that he would continue to fulfill his responsibility, as someone who had "never, ever been seeking power," to protect Egypt from agents of chaos and violence. When he finished the address, someone turned off the monitor, and I leaned back in my chair, stretching my arms behind my head.

"That," I said, "is not going to cut it."

I wanted to take one last shot at convincing Mubarak to initiate a real transition. Returning to the Oval Office, I placed a call to him, and I put the phone on speaker mode so that my assembled advisors could hear. I began by complimenting him on his decision not to run again. I could only imagine how difficult it might be for Mubarak, someone who'd first assumed power when I was in college and had outlasted four of my predecessors, to hear what I was about to say.

"Now that you've made this historic decision for a transition of power," I said, "I want to discuss with you how it will work. I say this with the utmost respect . . . I want to share my honest assessment about what I think will accomplish your goals." I then cut to the bottom line: If he stayed in office and dragged out the transition process, I believed, the protests would continue and possibly spin out of control. If he wanted to ensure the election of a responsible government that wasn't dominated by the Muslim Brotherhood, then now was the time for him to step down and use his stature behind the scenes to help usher in a new Egyptian government.

Although Mubarak and I normally spoke to each

other in English, he chose this time to address me in Arabic. I didn't need the translator to catch the agitation in his voice. "You don't understand the culture of the Egyptian people," he declared, his voice rising. "President Obama, if I go into the transition this way, it will be the most dangerous thing for Egypt."

I acknowledged that I didn't know Egyptian culture the way he did, and that he'd been in politics far longer than I had. "But there are moments in history where just because things have been the same way in the past doesn't mean they will be the same way in the future. You've served your country well for over thirty years. I want to make sure you seize this historic moment in a way that leaves a great legacy for you."

We went back and forth like this for several more minutes, with Mubarak insisting on the need for him to remain where he was and repeating that the protests would soon be over. "I know my people," he said toward the end of the call. "They are emotional people. I will talk to you after a while, Mr. President, and I will tell you that I was right."

I hung up the phone. For a moment, the room was silent, everyone's eyes glued on me. I had given Mubarak my best advice. I had offered him a plan for a graceful exit. Any leader who replaced him, I knew, might end up being a worse partner for the United States—and potentially worse for the Egyptian people. And the truth was, I could have lived with any genuine transition plan he might have presented, even if it left much of the regime's existing network intact. I was enough of a realist to assume that had it not been for the stubborn persistence of those young people in Tahrir Square, I'd have worked with Mubarak for the rest of my presidency, despite what he stood for—just as I would continue to work with the rest of the "corrupt, rotting authoritarian order," as Ben liked to call it, that controlled life in the Middle East and North Africa.

Except those kids were in Tahrir Square. Because of their brash insistence on a better life, others had joined them—mothers and laborers and shoemakers and taxi drivers. Those hundreds of thousands of people had, for a brief moment at least, lost their fear, and they wouldn't stop demonstrating unless Mubarak restored that fear the only way he knew how: through beatings and gunfire, detentions and torture. Earlier in my presidency, I hadn't managed to influence the Iranian regime's vicious crackdown on Green Movement protesters. I might not be able to stop a China or Russia from crushing its own dissidents. But the Mubarak regime had received billions of U.S. taxpayer dollars; we supplied them with weapons, shared information, and helped train their military officers; and for me to allow the recipient of that aid, someone we called an ally, to perpetrate wanton violence on peaceful demonstrators, with all the world watching— that was a line I was unwilling to cross. It would do too much damage, I thought, to the idea of America. It would do too much damage to me.

"Let's prepare a statement," I said to my team. "We're calling on Mubarak to step down now."

CONTRARY TO THE BELIEFS of many in the Arab world (and more than a few American reporters), the United States is not a grand puppet master whimsically pulling the strings of the countries with which it does business. Even governments that rely on our military and economic assistance think first and foremost of their own survival, and the Mubarak regime was no exception. After I publicly announced my conviction that it was time for Egypt to start a quick transition to a new government, Mubarak remained defiant, testing how far he could go in intimidating the protesters. The next day, while the Egyptian army stood idly by, gangs of pro-Mubarak supporters descended on Tahrir Square—some on camels and horses, brandishing whips and clubs, others hurling firebombs and rocks from surrounding rooftops—and began assaulting the demonstrators. Three protesters were killed and six hundred were injured; over the course of several days, authorities detained more than fifty journalists and human rights activists. The violence continued into the next day, along with large-scale counterdemonstrations organized by the government. Pro-Mubarak forces even began roughing up foreign reporters, accusing them of actively inciting the opposition.

My biggest challenge during those tense several days was keeping everybody in my administration on the same page. The message coming out of the White House was clear. When Gibbs was asked what I meant when I said that the transition in Egypt had to begin "now," he said simply, "Now means yesterday." We were also successful in getting our European allies to issue a joint statement that mirrored my own. Around the same time, though, Hillary was interviewed at a security conference in Munich and seemed to go out of her way to warn of the dangers in any rapid transition in Egypt. At the same conference, Frank Wisner—who no longer had an official role in the administration and claimed to be speaking only as a private citizen—voiced the opinion that Mubarak should stay in power during any transition period. Hearing this, I told Katie to track down my secretary of state. When I got her on the phone, I didn't mask my displeasure.

"I understand full well the potential problems with any move away from Mubarak," I said, "but I've made a decision, and I can't have a bunch of mixed messages out there right now." Before Hillary could respond, I added, "And tell Wisner I don't give a damn about what capacity he's speaking in—he needs to be quiet."

Despite the occasional frustrations I experienced in dealing with a national security establishment that remained uncomfortable with the prospect of an Egypt without Mubarak, that same establishment—particularly the Pentagon and the intelligence community—probably had more impact on the final outcome in Egypt than any high-minded statements coming from the White House. Once or twice a day, we had Gates, Mullen, Panetta, Brennan, and others quietly reach out to high-ranking officers in the Egyptian military and intelligence services, making clear that a military-sanctioned crackdown on the protesters would have severe consequences on any future U.S.-Egyptian relationship. The implication of this military-to-military outreach was plain: U.S.-Egyptian cooperation, and the aid that came with it, wasn't dependent on Mubarak's staying in power, so Egypt's generals and intelligence chiefs might want to carefully consider which actions best preserved their institutional interests.

Our messaging appeared successful, for by the evening of February 3, Egyptian army troops had positioned themselves to keep the pro-Mubarak forces separate from the protesters. The arrests of Egyptian journalists and human rights activists began to slow. Encouraged by the change in the army's posture, more demonstrators flowed peacefully into the square. Mubarak would hang on for another week, vowing not to bow to "foreign pressure." But on February 11, just two and a half weeks after the first major protest in Tahrir Square, a weary-looking Vice President Suleiman appeared on Egyptian television to announce that Mubarak had left office and a caretaker government led by the Supreme Council of the Armed Forces would initiate the process for new elections.

In the White House, we watched CNN broadcast footage of the crowd in Tahrir Square erupting in celebration. Many staffers were jubilant. Samantha sent me a message saying how proud she was to be a part of the administration. Walking down the colonnade on our way to my press statement to reporters, Ben couldn't wipe the smile off his face. "It's pretty amazing," he said, "being a part of history like that." Katie printed out a wire photo and left it on my desk; it showed a group of young protesters in the Egyptian square hoisting a sign that read, YES WE CAN.

I was relieved—and cautiously hopeful. Still, I did find myself occasionally thinking about Mubarak, who just a few months earlier had been my guest in the Old Family Dining Room. Rather than flee the country, the elderly leader had apparently taken up residence in his private compound in Sharm el Sheikh. I pictured him there, sitting in lavish surroundings, a dim light casting shadows across his face, alone with his thoughts.

I knew that for all the celebration and optimism in the air, the transition in Egypt was only the beginning of a struggle for the soul of the Arab world—a struggle whose outcome remained far from certain. I remembered the conversation I'd had with Mohammed bin Zayed, the crown prince of Abu Dhabi and the de facto ruler of the United Arab Emirates, immediately after I called for Mubarak to step down. Young, sophisticated, close to the Saudis, and perhaps the savviest leader in the Gulf, MBZ, as we called him, hadn't minced words in describing how the news was being received in the region.

MBZ told me that U.S. statements on Egypt were being watched closely in the Gulf, with increasing alarm. What would happen if protesters in Bahrain called for King Hamad to step down? Would the United States put out that same kind of statement that we had on Egypt?

I had told him I hoped to work with him and others to avoid having to choose between the Muslim Brotherhood and potentially violent clashes between governments and their people.

"The public message does not affect Mubarak, you see, but it affects the region," MBZ told me. He suggested that if Egypt collapsed and the Muslim Brotherhood took over, there would be eight other Arab leaders who would fall, which is why he was critical of my statement. "It shows," he said, "that the United States is not a partner we can rely on in the long term."

His voice was calm and cold. It was less a plea for help, I realized, than a warning. Whatever happened to Mubarak, the old order had no intention of conceding power without a fight.

IF ANYTHING, ANTI-GOVERNMENT demonstrations in other countries only grew in scope and intensity following Mubarak's resignation, as more and more people came to believe that change was possible. A handful of regimes successfully managed to make at least symbolic reform in response to protesters' demands while avoiding significant bloodshed or upheaval: Algeria lifted its nineteen-year-old emergency law, the king of Morocco engineered constitutional reforms that modestly increased the power of the country's elected parliament, and Jordan's monarch would soon do the same. But for many Arab rulers, the main lesson out of Egypt was the need to systematically, ruthlessly crush the protests—no matter how much violence that might require and no matter how much international criticism such crackdowns might generate.

Two of the countries that saw the worst violence were Syria and Bahrain, where sectarian divisions ran high and privileged minorities governed large and resentful majorities. In Syria, the March 2011 arrest and torture of fifteen schoolboys who had sprayed anti-government graffiti on city walls set off major protests against the Alawite Shiite–dominated regime of President Bashar al-Assad in many of the country's predominantly Sunni communities. After tear gas, water cannons, beatings, and mass arrests failed to quell the demonstrations, Assad's security forces went on to launch full-scale military operations across several cities, complete with live fire, tanks, and house-to-house searches. Meanwhile, just as MBZ had predicted, in the small island nation of Bahrain, huge, mostly Shiite demonstrations against the government of King Hamad bin Isa bin Salman al-Khalifa were taking place in the capital city of Manama, and the Bahraini government responded with force, killing scores of protesters and injuring hundreds more. As outrage over police brutality fueled even bigger demonstrations, the beleaguered Hamad went further, taking the unprecedented step of inviting armed divisions of the Saudi and Emirati armies to help suppress his own citizens.

My team and I spent hours wrestling with how the United States could influence events inside Syria and Bahrain. Our options were painfully limited. Syria was a longtime adversary of the United States, historically allied with Russia and Iran, as well as a supporter of Hezbollah. Without the economic, military, or diplomatic leverage we'd had in Egypt, the official condemnations of the Assad regime we made (and our later imposition of a U.S. embargo) had no real effect, and Assad could count on Russia to veto any efforts we might make to impose international sanctions through the U.N. Security Council. With Bahrain, we had the opposite problem: The country was a longtime U.S. ally and hosted the U.S. Navy's Fifth Fleet. That relationship allowed us to privately pressure Hamad and his ministers to partially answer the protesters' demands and to rein in the police violence. Still, Bahrain's ruling establishment viewed the protesters as Iranian-influenced enemies who had to be contained. In concert with the Saudis and the Emiratis, the Bahraini regime was going to force us to make a choice, and all were aware that when push came to shove, we couldn't afford to risk our strategic position in the Middle East by severing relations with three Gulf countries.

In 2011, no one questioned our limited influence in Syria—that would come later. But despite multiple statements from my administration condemning the violence in Bahrain and efforts to broker a dialogue between the government and more moderate Shiite opposition leaders, our failure to break with Hamad—especially in the wake of our posture toward Mubarak—was roundly criticized. I had no elegant way to explain the apparent inconsistency, other than to acknowledge that the world was messy; that in the conduct of foreign policy, I had to constantly balance competing interests, interests shaped by the choices of previous administrations and the contingencies of the moment; and that just because I couldn't in every instance elevate our human rights agenda over other considerations didn't mean that I shouldn't try to do what I could, when I could, to advance what I considered to be America's highest values. But what if a government starts massacring not hundreds of its citizens but thousands and the United States has the power to stop it? Then what?

FOR FORTY-TWO YEARS, Muammar Gaddafi had ruled Libya with a viciousness that, even by the standards of his fellow dictators, spilled into madness. Prone to flamboyant gestures, incoherent rants, and odd behavior (in advance of the 2009 UNGA meetings in New York, he'd tried to get approval to erect a massive Bedouin tent in the middle of Central Park for himself and his entourage), he had nevertheless been ruthlessly efficient in stamping out dissent in his country, using a combination of secret police, security forces, and state-sponsored militias to jail, torture, and murder anyone who dared to oppose him. Throughout the 1980s, his government had also been one of the leading state sponsors of terrorism around the world, facilitating such horrific attacks as the 1988 bombing of Pan Am Flight 103, which killed citizens of twenty-one countries, including 189 Americans. Gaddafi had more recently tried to wrap himself in the cloak of respectability by ending his support for international terrorism and dismantling his nascent nuclear program (which led Western countries, including the United States, to resume diplomatic relations). But inside Libya itself, nothing had changed.

Less than a week after Mubarak left power in Egypt, Gaddafi's security forces fired into a large group of civilians who'd gathered to protest the arrest of a human rights lawyer. Within days, the protests had spread, and more than a hundred had been killed. A week later, much of the country was in open rebellion, with anti-Gaddafi forces taking control of Benghazi, Libya's second-largest city. Libyan diplomats and former loyalists, including the country's ambassador to the U.N., began to defect, appealing to the international community to come to the aid of the Libyan people. Accusing the protesters of being fronts for al-Qaeda, Gaddafi unleashed a campaign of terror, declaring, "Everything will burn." By the beginning of March, the death count had risen to a thousand.

Appalled by the escalating carnage, we quickly did everything we could short of using military force to stop Gaddafi. I called for him to relinquish power, arguing that he had lost the legitimacy to govern. We imposed economic sanctions, froze billions of dollars in assets that belonged to him and his family, and, at the U.N. Security Council, passed an arms embargo and referred the case of Libya to the International Criminal Court, where Gaddafi and others could be tried for committing crimes against humanity. But the Libyan leader was undeterred.

Analysts forecasted that once Gaddafi's forces reached Benghazi, tens of thousands of lives could be lost.

It was around this time that a chorus grew, first among human rights organizations and a handful of columnists, and then members of Congress and much of the media, demanding that the United States take military action to stop Gaddafi. In many ways, I considered this a sign of moral progress. For most of America's history, the thought of using our combat forces to stop a government from killing its own people would have been a nonstarter—because such state-sponsored violence happened all the time; because U.S. policy makers didn't consider the death of innocent Cambodians, Argentinians, or Ugandans relevant to our interests; and because many of the perpetrators were our allies in the fight against communism. (This included the reportedly CIA-backed military coup that toppled a Communist government in Indonesia in 1965, two years before my mother and I arrived there, with a bloody aftermath that resulted in between five hundred thousand and a million deaths.) In the 1990s, though, more timely international reporting of such crimes, combined with America's ascendance as the world's lone superpower after the Cold War, had led to a reexamination of U.S. inaction and prompted the successful American-led NATO intervention in the Bosnian conflict. Indeed, the obligation of the United States to prioritize the prevention of atrocities in its foreign policy was what Samantha's book had been all about—one of the reasons I'd brought her into the White House.

And yet, as much as I shared the impulse to save innocent people from tyrants, I was profoundly wary of ordering any kind of military action against Libya, for the same reason that I'd declined Samantha's suggestion that my Nobel Prize address include an explicit argument for a global "responsibility to protect" civilians against their own governments. Where would the obligation to intervene end? And what were the parameters? How many people would need to have been killed, and how many more would have to be at risk, to trigger a U.S. military response? Why Libya and not the Congo, for example, where a series of civil conflicts had resulted in millions of civilian deaths? Would we intervene only when there was no chance of U.S. casualties? Bill Clinton had thought the risks were low back in 1993, when he sent special operations forces into Somalia to capture members of a warlord's organization in support of U.S. peacekeeping efforts there. In the incident known as "Black Hawk Down," eighteen service members were killed and seventy-three more wounded.

The truth is that war is never tidy and always results in unintended consequences, even when launched against seemingly powerless countries on behalf of a righteous cause. When it came to Libya, advocates for U.S. intervention had tried to obfuscate that reality by latching on to the idea of imposing a no-fly zone to ground Gaddafi's military planes and prevent bombing, which they presented as an antiseptic, risk-free way of saving the Libyan people. (Typical question from a White House reporter at the time: "How many more people have to die before we take this one step?") What they were missing was the fact that establishing a no-fly zone in Libyan airspace would require us to first fire missiles into Tripoli to destroy Libya's air defenses—a clear act of war against a country that posed no threat to us. Not only that, but it wasn't even clear that a no-fly zone would have any effect, since Gaddafi was using ground forces and not air bombardment to attack opposition strongholds.

America was also still knee-deep in the wars in Iraq and Afghanistan. I had just ordered U.S. forces in the Pacific to help the Japanese handle the worst nuclear accident since Chernobyl, brought on by a tsunami that had leveled the city of Fukushima; we were seriously concerned about the potential of radioactive fallout reaching the West Coast. Add in the fact that I was still dealing with a U.S. economy that was barely above water and a Republican Congress that had pledged to undo everything my administration had accomplished in our first two years, and it's fair to say that I found the idea of waging a new war in a distant country with no strategic importance to the United States to be less than prudent. I wasn't the only one. Bill Daley, who'd become my chief of staff in January, seemed bewildered that anyone was even entertaining the notion.

"Maybe I'm missing something, Mr. President," he said during one of our evening wrap-ups, "but I don't think we got clobbered in the midterms because voters don't think you're doing enough in the Middle East. Ask ten people on the street and nine of them don't even know where the heck Libya is."

And yet, as reports of hospitals filling up with gruesome injuries and young people being unceremoniously executed on the streets continued to trickle out of Libya, support around the world for intervention gathered steam. To the surprise of many, the Arab League voted in support of an international intervention against Gaddafi—a sign not only of how extreme the levels of violence in Libya had become but also of the extent to which the Libyan strongman's erratic behavior and meddling in the affairs of other countries had isolated him from his fellow Arab leaders. (The vote may also have been a handy way for countries in the region to deflect attention from their own human rights abuses, given that nations like Syria and Bahrain remained members in good standing.) Meanwhile, Nicolas Sarkozy, who'd been criticized mercilessly in France for supporting the Ben Ali regime in Tunisia till the bitter end, suddenly decided to make saving the Libyan people his personal cause. Together with David Cameron, he announced his intention to immediately introduce a resolution in the U.N. Security Council on behalf of France and the United Kingdom, authorizing an international coalition to initiate a no-fly zone over Libya—a resolution on which we'd have to take a position.

On March 15, I convened a meeting of my national security team to discuss the pending Security Council resolution. We began with a briefing on Gaddafi's progress: Libyan troops with heavy armaments were poised to overtake a town on the outskirts of Benghazi, which could allow them to cut off water, food, and power to the city's six hundred thousand residents. With his forces massed, Gaddafi was pledging to go "house by house, home by home, alley by alley, person by person, until the country is cleansed of dirt and scum." I asked Mike Mullen what difference a no-fly zone would make. Essentially none, he told me, confirming that since Gaddafi was using ground forces almost exclusively, the only way to stop an assault on Benghazi was to target those forces directly with air strikes.

"In other words," I said, "we are being asked to participate in a no-fly zone that will make everyone look like they're doing something but that won't actually save Benghazi."

I then asked for people's recommendations. Gates and Mullen were strongly opposed to any U.S. military action, emphasizing the stress that missions in Iraq and Afghanistan were already placing on our troops. They were also convinced—correctly, I thought—that despite the rhetoric from Sarkozy and Cameron, the U.S. military would end up having to carry most of the load for any operation in Libya. Joe considered it foolish to get involved in yet another war abroad, while Bill remained astonished that we were even having the debate.

As I worked my way around the room, though, the voices for intervention weighed in. Hillary had been conferenced in from Paris, where she was attending a G8 meeting, and said she'd been impressed by the Libyan opposition leader she'd met there. Despite—or perhaps because of—her realpolitik on Egypt, she now favored us joining an international mission. Speaking from our U.N. offices in New York, Susan Rice said the situation reminded her of the international community's failure to intervene in the 1994 genocide in Rwanda. She'd been a member of Bill Clinton's National Security Council at the time and remained haunted by the lack of action. If a relatively modest action could save lives, she argued, we should take it—though she suggested that rather than sign on to the proposal for a no-fly zone, we should present our own resolution seeking a broader mandate to take whatever actions were necessary to protect Libyan civilians from Gaddafi's forces.

A few of the younger staffers expressed concern that a military action against Libya might have the unintended consequence of convincing countries like Iran that they needed nuclear weapons as a hedge against a future U.S. attack. But as had been true with Egypt, Ben and Tony Blinken felt we had a responsibility to support those forces protesting for democratic change in the Middle East—particularly if the Arab states and our closest allies were prepared to act with us. And while Samantha remained uncharacteristically clinical when describing the potential death toll in Benghazi should we decide not to act, I knew that she was in daily, direct contact with Libyans pleading for help. I almost didn't need to ask what her position was.

I checked my watch, knowing I was soon due to host an annual dinner with the U.S. military's combatant commanders and their spouses in the Blue Room of the residence. "All right," I said. "I'm not ready to make a decision yet. But based on what I'm hearing, here's the one thing we're **not** going to do—we're not going to participate in some half-assed no-fly zone that won't achieve our objective."

I told the team we'd reconvene in a couple of hours, by which time I expected to hear real options for what an effective intervention would look like, including an analysis of the costs, human resources, and risks involved. "Either we do this right," I said, "or we stop pretending that we're serious about saving Benghazi just to make ourselves feel better."

By the time I arrived in the Blue Room, Michelle and our guests had already assembled. We took photos with each commander and spouse, making small talk about our kids and trading jokes about our golf games. During dinner I sat next to a young Marine and his wife; he had stepped on an IED while working as a bomb technician in Afghanistan and lost both his legs. He was still getting accustomed to his prosthetics, he told me, but he looked to be in good spirits and was handsome in his uniform. I could see on his wife's face the mixture of pride, determination, and suppressed anguish that had become so familiar to me during my visits with military families over the previous two years.

All the while, my brain was churning with calculations, thinking about the decision I'd have to make as soon as Buddy and Von and the other butlers cleared away the dessert plates. The arguments Mullen and Gates had made against military action in Libya were compelling. I'd already sent thousands of young men like the Marine sitting next to me into battle, and there was no guarantee, whatever those on the sidelines might think, that a new war wouldn't lead others to suffer such injuries, or worse. I was irritated that Sarkozy and Cameron had jammed me on the issue, in part to solve their domestic political problems, and I felt scornful of the Arab League's hypocrisy. I knew that Bill was right: that outside of Washington, there wasn't a lot of support for what America was being asked to do, and that the minute anything about a U.S. military operation in Libya went south, my political problems would only worsen.

I also knew that unless we took the lead, the European plan would likely go nowhere. Gaddafi's troops would lay siege to Benghazi. At best, a protracted conflict would ensue, perhaps even a full-blown civil war. At worst, tens of thousands or more would be starved, tortured, or shot in the head. And at the moment, at least, I was perhaps the one person in the world who could keep that from happening.

The dinner ended. I told Michelle I'd be home in an hour and made my way back to the Situation Room, where the team had been reviewing options and sat awaiting further instructions.

"I think I've got a plan that might work," I said.

CHAPTER 26

WE MET FOR ANOTHER TWO hours that night in the Situation Room, going point by point through the plan I'd sketched out in my mind during dinner, knowing we had to try to prevent a massacre in Libya while minimizing the risks and burdens on an already overstretched U.S. military. I was ready to take a meaningful stance against Gaddafi and to give the Libyan people an opportunity to engineer a new government. But we would do it swiftly, with the support of allies, and with the parameters of our mission clearly spelled out.

I told the team I wanted to start as Susan Rice had suggested—by persuading the French and British to back off their proposal for a no-fly zone so that we could put an amended resolution before the Security Council, asking for a broader mandate to halt attacks by Gaddafi's forces in order to protect Libyan civilians. Meanwhile, the Pentagon would develop a military campaign that involved a clear division of labor among allies. In the campaign's first phase, the United States would help stop Gaddafi's advance on Benghazi and take out his air-defense systems—a task for which we were uniquely suited, given our superior capabilities. After that we'd hand off the bulk of the operation to the Europeans and the participating Arab states. European fighter jets would be principally responsible for carrying out any targeted air strikes needed to keep Gaddafi's forces from advancing against civilian populations (in essence, establishing a no-fly **and** no-drive zone), with Arab allies mainly providing logistical support. Because North Africa was in Europe's backyard and not ours, we would also ask the Europeans to pay for much of the post-conflict aid that would be required to rebuild Libya and help the country transition to democracy once Gaddafi was no longer in power.

I asked Gates and Mullen what they thought. Although they were still reluctant to engage in what was essentially a humanitarian mission while in the middle of two other wars, they acknowledged that the plan was viable, limited the cost and risk to U.S. personnel, and could probably reverse Gaddafi's momentum in a matter of days.

Susan and her team worked with Samantha through the night, and the next day we circulated a revised draft resolution among U.N. Security Council members. The main drama ahead of the vote was whether Russia would veto the new measure, so while Susan sought to persuade her counterparts on the floor of the U.N., we hoped that our efforts over the past two years with Dmitry Medvedev would help gain his support, stressing to Russia that beyond the moral imperatives of preventing a mass atrocity, it was in both Russia's and America's interests to make sure that we didn't see a prolonged civil war in Libya, as the country could then become a breeding ground for terrorism. It was clear that Medvedev had serious reservations about any Western-led military action that could lead to regime change, but he also wasn't inclined to run interference for Gaddafi. In the end, the Security Council approved our resolution on March 17 by a vote of ten to zero, with five abstentions (Russia among them). I called the two key European leaders, Sarkozy and Cameron, both of whom showed barely disguised relief that we had handed them a ladder with which to get down from the limb they'd climbed out on. Within days, all elements of the operation were in place, with the Europeans agreeing that their forces would operate under a NATO command structure, and with enough Arab participation—from the Jordanians, Qataris, and Emiratis—to insulate us from accusations that the Libya mission was yet another case of Western powers waging war against Islam.

With the Pentagon prepared and awaiting my order to begin air strikes, I publicly offered Gaddafi one last chance, urging him to pull his forces back and respect the rights of Libyans to engage in peaceful protest. I hoped that, with the world lined up against him, his survival instincts might kick in and he'd try to negotiate a safe exit to a willing third country, where he could live out his days with the millions in oil money that over the years he'd siphoned into various Swiss bank accounts. But it seemed that whatever attachment Gaddafi might have once had to reality had been severed.

As it happened, I had to depart that evening for Brazil for the start of a four-day, three-nation tour designed to boost the United States' image in Latin America. (The Iraq War, as well as the Bush administration's drug interdiction and Cuba policies, hadn't played well there.) The best part was that we'd deliberately scheduled the trip to take place during Malia and Sasha's spring break, allowing us to travel as a family.

What we hadn't factored in was an imminent military conflict. As Air Force One touched down in the capital city of Brasília, Tom Donilon informed me that Gaddafi's troops showed no signs of pulling back—and had in fact started breaching the perimeter of Benghazi.

"You're probably going to have to issue an order sometime today," he said.

Under any circumstances, launching a military action while visiting another country posed a problem. The fact that Brazil generally tried to avoid taking sides in international disputes—and had abstained in the Security Council vote on the Libya intervention—only made matters worse. This was my first visit to South America as president and my first time meeting Brazil's newly elected president, Dilma Rousseff. She was an economist and a former chief of staff to her charismatic predecessor, Lula da Silva, and was interested in, among other things, improving trade relations with the United States. She and her ministers greeted our delegation warmly as we arrived at the presidential palace, an airy, modernist structure with winged buttresses and high glass walls. Over the next several hours, we discussed ways to deepen U.S.-Brazilian cooperation on energy, trade, and climate change. But with global speculation swirling over when and how strikes against Libya would start, the tension became hard to ignore. I apologized to Rousseff for any awkwardness the situation was causing. She shrugged, her dark eyes fixed on me with a mix of skepticism and concern.

"We'll manage," she said in Portuguese. "I hope this will be the least of your problems."

As my meeting with Rousseff ended, Tom and Bill Daley hurried me to a nearby holding room, explaining that Gaddafi's forces were still on the move and that now was our best window for making a call. To formally commence military operations, I needed to reach Mike Mullen. Except the state-of-the-art, secure mobile communications system—the system that was supposed to let me function as commander in chief from any place on the planet—apparently wasn't working.

"Sorry, Mr. President . . . we're still having trouble connecting."

As our communications technicians rushed about checking for loose cords and faulty portals, I sat down in a chair and scooped a handful of almonds from a bowl on a side table. I had long stopped sweating the logistical details of the presidency, knowing that I was surrounded at all times by a highly competent crew. Still, I could see the beads of sweat breaking across foreheads around the room. Bill, on his first foreign trip as chief of staff and no doubt feeling the pressure, was apoplectic.

"This is unbelievable!" he said, his voice rising in pitch.

I checked my watch. Ten minutes had passed, and our next meeting with the Brazilians was pending. I looked at Bill and Tom, who both appeared on the verge of strangling someone.

"Why don't we just use your cell phone?" I said to Bill.

"What?"

"It won't be a long conversation. Just check to make sure you've got enough bars."

After some consultations among the team members regarding the advisability of me using a nonsecure line, Bill dialed the number and handed me his phone.

"Mike?" I said. "Can you hear me?"

"I can, Mr. President."

"You have my authorization."

And with those four words, spoken into a device that had probably also been used to order pizza, I initiated the first new military intervention of my presidency.

FOR THE NEXT two days, even as U.S. and British warships began firing Tomahawk missiles and destroying Libya's air defenses, we kept my schedule largely unchanged. I met with a group of U.S. and Brazilian CEOs to discuss ways to expand commercial ties. I attended a cocktail reception with government officials and took pictures with U.S. embassy staffers and their families. In Rio de Janeiro, I gave an address to a couple thousand of Brazil's most prominent political, civic, and business leaders about the challenges and opportunities our countries shared as the hemisphere's two largest democracies. All the while, though, I was checking in with Tom for news about Libya, imagining the scenes unfolding more than five thousand miles away: the rush of missiles piercing the air; the cascade of explosions, the rubble and smoke; the faces of Gaddafi loyalists as they looked to the sky and calculated their chances of survival.

I was distracted, but I also understood that my presence in Brazil mattered, especially to Afro-Brazilians, who made up just over half of the country's population and experienced the same sort of deeply entrenched— though frequently denied—racism and poverty as Black folks did back home. Michelle, the girls, and I visited a sprawling favela on the western end of Rio, where we dropped in at a youth center to watch a capoeira troupe perform and I kicked a soccer ball around with a handful of local kids. By the time we were leaving, hundreds of people had massed outside the center, and although my Secret Service detail nixed the idea of me taking a stroll through the neighborhood, I persuaded them to let me step through the gate and greet the crowd. Standing in the middle of the narrow street, I waved at the Black and brown and copper-toned faces; residents, many of them children, clustered on rooftops and small balconies and pressed against the police barricades. Valerie, who was traveling with us and witnessed the whole scene, smiled as I walked back inside, saying, "I'll bet that wave changed the lives of some of those kids forever."

I wondered if that was true. It's what I had told myself at the start of my political journey, part of my justification to Michelle for running for president—that the election and leadership of a Black president stood to change the way children and young people everywhere saw themselves and their world. And yet I knew that whatever impact my fleeting presence might have had on those children of the favelas and however much it might cause some to stand straighter and dream bigger, it couldn't compensate for the grinding poverty they encountered every day: the bad schools, polluted air, poisoned water, and sheer disorder that many of them had to wade through just to survive. By my own estimation, my impact on the lives of poor children and their families so far had been negligible—even in my own country. My time had been absorbed by just trying to keep the circumstances of the poor, both at home and abroad, from worsening: making sure a global recession didn't drastically drive up their ranks or eliminate whatever slippery foothold they might have in the labor market; trying to head off a change in climate that might lead to a deadly flood or storm; or, in the case of Libya, trying to prevent a madman's army from gunning people down in the streets. That wasn't nothing, I thought—as long as I didn't start fooling myself into thinking it was anywhere close to enough.

On the short Marine One flight back to the hotel, the helicopter tracked along the magnificent chain of forested mountains that line the coast, with Rio's iconic ninety-eight-foot-high **Christ the Redeemer** statue suddenly coming into view, perched atop the conical peak known as Corcovado. We had made plans to visit the site that evening. Leaning in close to Sasha and Malia, I pointed out the landmark: a distant, cloaked figure with outstretched arms, white against blue sky.

"Look . . . that's where we're going tonight."

The two girls were listening to their iPods while thumbing through some of Michelle's magazines, their eyes scanning glossy images of dewy-faced celebrities I didn't recognize. After I waved my hands to get their attention, they took out their earbuds, swiveled their heads in unison toward the window, and nodded wordlessly, pausing for a beat as if to humor me before putting the buds back in their ears. Michelle, who appeared to be dozing to music from her own iPod, offered no comment.

Later, as we sat having dinner at our hotel's outdoor

restaurant, we were informed that a heavy fog had settled over Corcovado and we might have to cancel the trip to see **Christ the Redeemer**. Malia and Sasha didn't look all that disappointed. I watched as they questioned the waiter about the dessert menu and felt a little bruised by their lack of enthusiasm. With more of my time spent monitoring developments in Libya, I was seeing the family even less on this trip than I did at home, and it compounded my sense—already too frequent of late— that my daughters were growing up faster than I'd expected. Malia was about to be a teenager—her teeth glinting with braces, her hair in a ropy ponytail, her body stretched as if on some invisible rack, so that somehow overnight she'd become long and lean and almost as tall as her mother. At nine, Sasha at least still looked like a kid, with her sweet grin and dimpled cheeks, but I'd noticed a shift in her attitude toward me: She was less inclined to let me tickle her these days; she seemed impatient and a touch embarrassed when I tried to hold her hand in public.

I continued to marvel at how steady the two of them were, how well they'd adapted to the odd and extraordinary circumstances in which they were growing up, gliding seamlessly between audiences with the pope and trips to the mall. Mostly, they were allergic to any special treatment or undue attention, just wanting to be like the other kids at school. (When, on the first day of fourth grade, a classmate had tried to get a photo of Sasha, she had taken it upon herself to snatch the camera, warning that he'd better not try that again.) In fact, both girls vastly preferred hanging out at friends' houses, partly because those households seemed to be less strict about the snacks they ate and the amount of TV they watched, but mainly because it was easier in those places to pretend their lives were normal, even with a Secret Service detail parked on the street outside. And all of this was fine, except for the fact that their lives were never less normal than when they were with me. I couldn't help fearing that I might lose whatever precious time I had with them before they flew the nest. . . .

"We're good," Marvin said, walking up to our table. "Fog's lifted."

The four of us then piled into the back of the SUV, and soon we were heading up a winding, tree-lined road in the dark, until our convoy halted abruptly in front of a wide, spotlit plaza. A massive, shining figure seemed to beckon us through the mist. As we made our way up a series of steps, our necks craning back to take in the sight, I felt Sasha grab my hand. Malia slipped an arm around my waist.

"Are we supposed to pray or something?" Sasha asked.

"Why not?" I said. We huddled together then, our heads bowed in silence, with me knowing that at least one of my prayers that night had been answered.

WHETHER OUR BRIEF pilgrimage to that mountaintop helped fulfill my other prayer, I can't say for certain. I do know that the first few days of the Libya campaign went as well as possible. Gaddafi's air defenses were quickly dismantled. European jets had moved into place as promised (with Sarkozy making certain it was a French plane that first crossed into Libyan airspace), executing a series of air strikes against the forces advancing on Benghazi. Within days, Gaddafi's forces had retreated and our no-fly/no-drive zone had been effectively established across much of the eastern part of the country.

Still, as our Latin American tour continued, I remained on pins and needles. Each morning, I consulted with my national security team via secure videoconference and got updates from General Carter Ham, the commander overseeing the operation, as well as from military leadership at the Pentagon, before reviewing a detailed list of next steps. Beyond maintaining a clear sense of how well we were meeting our military objectives, I wanted to make sure our allies held up their end of the bargain and that the U.S. role didn't stray beyond the narrow parameters I'd set. I was well aware that the American public's support for what we were doing was exceedingly thin, and that any setbacks could prove devastating.

We did have one bad scare. On our first night in Santiago, Chile, Michelle and I attended a state dinner hosted by Sebastián Piñera, the gregarious, center-right billionaire who'd been elected president just a year earlier. I was sitting at the head table, listening to Piñera talk about the growing market in China for Chilean wine, when I felt a tap on my shoulder and turned to find Tom Donilon, looking even more stressed than usual.

"What is it?" I asked.

He leaned in to whisper in my ear: "We just received a report that a U.S. fighter jet crashed over Libya."

"Shot down?"

"Technical failure," he said. "Two servicemen ejected before the crash, and we've picked up one, the pilot. He's fine . . . but the weapons officer is still missing. We've got search-and-rescue teams near the site of the crash, and I'm in direct contact with the Pentagon, so as soon as there's news, I'll let you know."

As Tom walked away, Piñera gave me a searching look.

"Everything all right?" he asked.

"Yeah, sorry about that," I replied, my mind quickly running through scenarios—most of them bad.

For the next ninety minutes or so, I smiled and nodded as Piñera and his wife, Cecilia Morel Montes, told us about their children and how they first met and the best season to visit Patagonia. At some point, a Chilean folk-rock band called Los Jaivas started to perform what sounded like a Spanish version of **Hair**. The entire time, I waited for another tap on the shoulder. All I could think about was the young officer I had sent into war, who was now possibly injured or captured or worse. I felt as if I might burst. Not until Michelle and I were about to climb into the Beast after dinner did I finally see Tom heading toward us. He was slightly out of breath.

"We have him," he said. "It seems he was picked up by some friendly Libyans, and he's going to be fine."

I wanted to kiss Tom at that moment, but I kissed Michelle instead.

When someone asks me to describe what it feels like to be the president of the United States, I often think about that stretch of time spent sitting helplessly at the state dinner in Chile, contemplating the knife's edge between perceived success and potential catastrophe—in this case, the drift of a soldier's parachute over a faraway desert in the middle of the night. It wasn't simply that each decision I made was essentially a high-stakes wager; it was the fact that unlike in poker, where a player expects and can afford to lose a few big hands even on the way to a winning night, a single mishap could cost a life, and overwhelm—both in the political press and in my own heart—whatever broader objective I might have achieved.

As it was, the jet crash ended up becoming a relative blip. By the time I returned to Washington, the overwhelming superiority of the international coalition's air forces had left Gaddafi's loyalists with few places to hide, and opposition militias—including many high-ranking defectors from the Libyan army—began advancing westward. Twelve days into the operation, NATO took command of the mission, with several European countries assuming responsibility for repelling Gaddafi's forces. By the time I addressed the nation on March 28, the U.S. military had begun to move into a supporting role, primarily helping with logistics, refueling aircraft, and identifying targets.

Given that a number of Republicans had been vocal advocates for intervention, we might have expected some grudging praise for the swift precision of our operation in Libya. But a funny thing had happened while I was traveling. Some of the same Republicans who had demanded that I intervene in Libya had decided that they were now against it. They criticized the mission as being too broad, or coming too late. They complained that I hadn't consulted with Congress enough, despite the fact that I'd met with senior congressional leaders on the eve of the campaign. They cast doubt on the legal basis for my decision, suggesting that I should have sought congressional authorization under the War Powers Act, a legitimate, long-standing question about presidential power, were it not coming from a party that had repeatedly given previous administrations carte blanche on the foreign policy front, particularly when it came to waging war. The Republicans seemed unembarrassed by the inconsistency. Effectively, they were putting me on notice that even issues of war and peace, life and death, were now part of a grim, unrelenting partisan game.

They weren't the only ones playing games. Vladimir Putin had been publicly criticizing the U.N. resolution—and, by implication, Medvedev—for allowing a wide mandate for military action in Libya. It was inconceivable that Putin hadn't signed off on Medvedev's decision to have Russia abstain rather than veto our resolution, or that he'd failed to understand its scope at the time; and as Medvedev himself pointed out in response to Putin's comments, coalition fighter jets were continuing to bomb Gaddafi's forces only because the Libyan strongman showed no signs of calling them into retreat or muzzling the vicious mercenary fighters he sponsored. But clearly that was beside the point. In openly second-guessing Medvedev, Putin seemed to have decided to deliberately make his handpicked successor look bad—a sign, I had to assume, that Putin planned to formally retake the reins in Russia.

Still, March ended without a single U.S. casualty in Libya, and for an approximate cost of $550 million—not much more than what we spent per day on military operations in Iraq and Afghanistan—we had accomplished our objective of saving Benghazi and its neighboring cities and perhaps tens of thousands of lives. According to Samantha, it was the quickest international military intervention to prevent a mass atrocity in modern history. What would happen with regard to Libya's government remained unclear. With Gaddafi ordering further attacks even in the face of NATO bombing operations, and with the opposition fueled by a loose coalition of rebel militias, my team and I worried about the prospect of prolonged civil war. According to the U.S. diplomat Hillary had sent to Benghazi to act as a liaison to the emerging governing council there, the opposition was at least saying all the right things about what a post-Gaddafi Libya would look like, emphasizing the importance of free and fair elections, human rights, and rule of law. But with no democratic traditions or institutions to draw on, the councillors had their work cut out for them—and with Gaddafi's police force no longer in place, the security situation in Benghazi and other rebel areas now had a Wild West aspect.

"Who is it that we sent to Benghazi?" I asked, after hearing one of these dispatches.

"A guy named Chris Stevens," Denis told me. "Used to be chargé d'affaires at the U.S. embassy in Tripoli, a bunch of Middle East posts before that. Apparently, he and a small team slipped into Benghazi on a Greek cargo ship. Supposed to be excellent."

"Brave guy," I said.

ONE QUIET SUNDAY in April, I found myself alone in the residence—the girls were off somewhere with their buddies, Michelle was having lunch with friends—and so I decided to head downstairs to do some work. It was a cool day, in the sixties with a mix of sun and clouds, and walking along the colonnade I took time to appreciate the plush beds of tulips—yellow, red, pink—the groundskeepers had planted in the Rose Garden. I rarely worked at the Resolute desk on weekends, since there were always at least a few West Wing tours passing through, and visitors could catch a glimpse of the Oval Office from behind a red velvet rope only if I wasn't there. Instead, I usually set up shop in the Oval's adjoining dining room and study, a comfortable, private area filled with mementos I'd gathered over the years: a framed **Life** magazine cover of the Selma march, signed by John Lewis; a brick from Abraham Lincoln's law office in Springfield; a pair of boxing gloves from Muhammad Ali; Ted Kennedy's painting of the Cape Cod coastline, which he'd sent to me as a gift after I'd admired it in his office. But as the clouds broke and sunlight splashed across the window, I moved myself to the terraced patio just outside the dining room—a lovely, secluded space with hedges and plantings on one side and a small fountain on the other.

I'd carried down a stack of memos to read, but my mind kept drifting. I had just announced that I'd be running for reelection. It was a formality, really, a matter of filing the papers and filming a short video announcement—a stark contrast to that heady, frigid day in Springfield four years earlier when I'd declared my candidacy before a crowd of thousands, promising to deliver hope and change. It seemed like an eternity ago, a time of optimism and youthful energy and undeniable innocence. My reelection campaign would be an entirely different endeavor. Certain of my vulnerability, Republicans were already lining up for the chance to run against me. I'd noticed that my political team had begun to layer a series of early fundraisers into my schedule, anticipating an expensive, bare-knuckle contest. Part of me resented the idea of gearing up for the election so soon—for if my first campaign seemed a distant memory, my actual work as president felt as if it had only just begun. But there was no point arguing about it. I could read the polls myself.

The irony was that our labors of the previous two years were finally bearing some fruit. When I hadn't been dealing with foreign policy issues, I'd been traveling the country, highlighting the shuttered auto factories that had just reopened, the small businesses that had been saved, the wind farms and energy-efficient vehicles that pointed the way to a clean energy future. A number of infrastructure projects funded by the Recovery Act—roads, community centers, light-rail lines—were already completed. A host of ACA provisions had already come into force. In so many different ways, we'd made the federal government better, more efficient and more responsive. But until the economy really started picking up, none of it would matter much politically. So far, we'd managed to ward off a "double-dip" second recession, in large part thanks to the billions of stimulus dollars we'd attached to the Bush tax cut extension during the lame-duck session. But just barely. And by the looks of it, the new House majority seemed intent on shifting the economy into reverse.

From the moment he'd been elected Speaker in January, John Boehner had insisted that House Republicans had every intention of following through on their campaign pledge to end what he called my "job-crushing spending binge of the last two years." Speaking after my 2011 State of the Union address, Paul Ryan, the House Budget Committee chair, had predicted that as a result of such out-of-control spending, the federal debt would "soon eclipse our entire economy and grow to catastrophic levels in the years ahead." The new crop of GOP members, many of whom had run on a Tea Party platform, were pressing Boehner hard for an immediate, drastic, and permanent reduction in the size of the federal government—a reduction that they believed would finally restore America's constitutional order and take their country back from corrupt political and economic elites.

Purely as a matter of economics, all of us in the White House thought that enacting the House GOP's agenda of deep federal spending cuts would result in absolute disaster. Unemployment remained at about 9 percent. The housing market had yet to recover. Americans were still trying to work off the $1.1 trillion in credit card debt and other loans they'd accumulated over the previous decade; millions of people owed more on their mortgages than their homes were worth. Businesses and banks faced a similar debt hangover and remained cautious about investing in expansion or making new loans. It was true that the federal deficit had risen sharply since I'd taken office—mainly as a result of lower tax revenues and increased spending on social programs in the aftermath of what was now commonly known as the Great Recession. At my request, Tim Geithner was already mapping out plans to bring the deficit back to pre-crisis levels once the economy had fully rebounded. I'd also formed a commission, headed by former Clinton chief of staff Erskine Bowles and former Wyoming senator Alan Simpson, to come up with a sensible plan for long-term deficit and debt reduction. But for now, the best thing we could do to lower the deficit was to boost economic growth—and with aggregate demand as weak as it was, this meant more federal spending, not less.

The problem was that I'd lost the argument in the midterms, at least among those who'd bothered to go to the polls. Not only could Republicans claim they were following the will of the voters in seeking to cut spending, but the election results seemed to have turned all of Washington into deficit hawks. The media was suddenly sounding the alarm about America living beyond its means. Commentators decried the legacy of debt we were foisting on future generations. Even CEOs and Wall Street types, many of whom had benefited, directly or indirectly, from the bailout of the financial system, had the temerity to jump on the anti-deficit bandwagon, insisting that it was high time politicians in Washington did the "courageous" thing by cutting "entitlement spending"—using the misleading catchall term for Social Security, Medicare, Medicaid, and other social safety net programs. (Few of them expressed interest in sacrificing their own tax breaks to address this supposed crisis.)

In our first skirmish with Boehner, over funding levels for the rest of the 2011 fiscal year, we'd conceded just $38 billion in spending cuts, an amount large enough for Boehner to take back to his conservative caucus members (they had originally sought nearly twice as much) but small enough inside a $3.6 trillion budget to avoid any real economic harm—especially since a big chunk of those cuts amounted to accounting tricks and wouldn't reduce vital services or programs. Boehner had already signaled, though, that the Republicans would soon be coming back for more, even suggesting that his caucus might withhold the votes necessary to increase the statutory debt limit if we didn't meet future demands. None of us believed that the GOP would actually act that irresponsibly. After all, raising the debt ceiling was a routine legislative duty observed by both parties, a matter of paying for spending that Congress had already approved, and the failure to do so would result in the United States defaulting on its debt for the first time in history. Still, the fact that Boehner had even broached such a radical idea—and the fact that it had quickly gained traction among Tea Party members and conservative media outlets—offered a hint of what was in store.

Is that, I wondered, what my presidency was now reduced to? Fighting rearguard actions to keep the Republicans from sabotaging the American economy and undoing whatever I'd done? Could I really hope to find common ground with a party that increasingly seemed to consider opposition to me to be its unifying principle, the objective that superseded all others? There was a reason why in selling our recent budget deal to his caucus, Boehner had apparently emphasized how "angry" I was during our discussions—a useful fiction that I'd told my team not to dispute in the interest of keeping the deal on track. For his members, there was no greater selling point. In fact, more and more, I'd noticed how the mood we'd first witnessed in the fading days of Sarah Palin's campaign rallies and on through the Tea Party summer had migrated from the fringe of GOP politics to the center—an emotional, almost visceral, reaction to my presidency, distinct from any differences in policy or ideology. It was as if my very presence in the White House had triggered a deep-seated panic, a sense that the natural order had been disrupted.

Which is exactly what Donald Trump understood when he started peddling assertions that I had not been born in the United States and was thus an illegitimate president. For millions of Americans spooked by a Black man in the White House, he promised an elixir for their racial anxiety.

The suggestion that I hadn't been born in the United States wasn't new. At least one conservative crank had pushed the theory as far back as my Senate race in Illinois. During the primary campaign for president, some disgruntled Hillary supporters had recirculated the claim, and while her campaign strongly disavowed it, conservative bloggers and talk radio personalities had picked it up, setting off feverish email chains among right-wing activists. By the time the Tea Party seized on it during my first year in office, the tale had blossomed into a full-blown conspiracy theory: I hadn't just been born in Kenya, the story went, but I was also a secret Muslim socialist, a Manchurian candidate who'd been groomed from childhood—and planted in the United States using falsified documents—to infiltrate the highest reaches of the American government.

Still, it wasn't until February 10, 2011, the day before Hosni Mubarak stepped down in Egypt, that this absurd theory really got traction. During a speech at the Conservative Political Action Conference in Washington, Trump hinted that he might run for president, asserting that "our current president came out of nowhere. . . . The people that went to school with him, they never saw him, they don't know who he is. It's crazy."

At first, I paid no attention. My biography had been exhaustively documented. My birth certificate was on file in Hawaii, and we'd posted it on my website back in 2008 to deal with the first wave of what came to be called "birtherism." My grandparents had saved a clipping from the August 13, 1961, edition of the **Honolulu Advertiser** that announced my birth. As a kid, I'd walked past Kapiʻolani Medical Center, where my mother had delivered me, on my way to school every day.

As for Trump, I'd never met the man, although I'd become vaguely aware of him over the years—first as an attention-seeking real estate developer; later and more ominously as someone who'd thrust himself into the Central Park Five case, when, in response to the story about five Black and Latino teens who'd been imprisoned for (and were ultimately exonerated of) brutally raping a white jogger, he'd taken out full-page ads in four major newspapers demanding the return of the death penalty; and finally as a TV personality who marketed himself and his brand as the pinnacle of capitalist success and gaudy consumption.

For most of my first two years in office, Trump was apparently complimentary of my presidency, telling **Bloomberg** that "overall I believe he's done a very good job"; but maybe because I didn't watch much television, I found it hard to take him too seriously. The New York developers and business leaders I knew uniformly described him as all hype, someone who'd left a trail of bankruptcy filings, breached contracts, stiffed employees, and sketchy financing arrangements in his wake, and whose business now in large part consisted of licensing his name to properties he neither owned nor managed. In fact, my closest contact with Trump had come midway through 2010, during the **Deepwater Horizon** crisis, when he'd called Axe out of the blue to suggest that I put him in charge of plugging the well. When informed that the well was almost sealed, Trump had shifted gears, noting that we'd recently held a state dinner under a tent on the South Lawn and telling Axe that he'd be willing to build "a beautiful ballroom" on White House grounds—an offer that was politely declined.

What I hadn't anticipated was the media's reaction to Trump's sudden embrace of birtherism—the degree to which the line between news and entertainment had become so blurred, and the competition for ratings so fierce, that outlets eagerly lined up to offer a platform for a baseless claim. It was propelled by Fox News, naturally, a network whose power and profits had been built around stoking the same racial fears and resentments that Trump now sought to exploit. Night after night, its hosts featured him across their most popular platforms. On Fox's **O'Reilly Factor,** Trump declared, "If you are going to be president of the United States you have to be born in this country. And there is a doubt as to whether or not he was. . . . He doesn't have a birth certificate." On the network's morning show **Fox & Friends,** he suggested that my birth announcement might have been a fake. In fact, Trump was on Fox so much that he soon felt obliged to throw in some fresh material, saying that there was something fishy about my getting into Harvard, given that my "marks were lousy." He told Laura Ingraham he was certain that Bill Ayers, my Chicago neighbor and former radical activist, was the true author of **Dreams from My Father,** since the book was too good to have been written by someone of my intellectual caliber.

But it wasn't just Fox. On March 23, just after we'd gone to war in Libya, he surfaced on ABC's **The View,** saying, "I want him to show his birth certificate. There's something on that birth certificate that he doesn't like." On NBC, the same network that aired Trump's reality show **The Celebrity Apprentice** in prime time and that clearly didn't mind the extra publicity its star was generating, Trump told a **Today** show host that he'd sent investigators to Hawaii to look into my birth certificate. "I have people that have been studying it, and they cannot believe what they're finding." Later, he'd tell CNN's Anderson Cooper, "I've been told very recently, Anderson, that the birth certificate is missing. I've been told that it's not there and it doesn't exist."

Outside the Fox universe, I couldn't say that any mainstream journalists explicitly gave credence to these bizarre charges. They all made a point of expressing polite incredulity, asking Trump, for example, why he thought George Bush and Bill Clinton had never been asked to produce their birth certificates. (He'd usually reply with something along the lines of "Well, we know they were born in this country.") But at no point did they simply and forthrightly call Trump out for lying or state that the conspiracy theory he was promoting was racist. Certainly, they made little to no effort to categorize his theories as beyond the pale—like alien abduction or the anti-Semitic conspiracies in **The Protocols of the Elders of Zion**. And the more oxygen the media gave them, the more newsworthy they appeared.

We hadn't bothered to dignify all this with any sort of official White House response, uninterested in giving Trump a bigger spotlight and knowing we had better things to do. In the West Wing, birtherism was treated like a bad joke, and my younger staffers were heartened by the way late-night TV hosts frequently skewered "the Donald." But I couldn't help noticing that members of the media weren't just booking Trump for interviews; they were also breathlessly covering his forays into presidential politics, including press conferences and travel to the early voting state of New Hampshire. Polls were showing that roughly 40 percent of Republicans were now convinced that I hadn't been born in America, and I'd recently heard from Axe that according to a Republican pollster he knew, Trump was now the leading Republican among potential presidential contenders, despite not having declared his candidacy.

I chose not to share that particular piece of news with Michelle. Just thinking about Trump and the symbiotic relationship he'd developed with the media made her mad. She saw the whole circus for what it was: a variation on the press's obsession with flag pins and fist bumps during the campaign, the same willingness on the part of both political opponents and reporters to legitimize the notion that her husband was suspect, a nefarious "Other." She made clear to me that her concerns regarding Trump and birtherism were connected not to my political prospects but, rather, to the safety of our family. "People think it's all a game," she said. "They don't care that there are thousands of men with guns out there who believe every word that's being said."

I didn't argue the point. It was clear that Trump didn't care about the consequences of spreading conspiracy theories that he almost certainly knew to be false, so long as it achieved his aims; and he'd figured out that whatever guardrails had once defined the boundaries of acceptable political discourse had long since been knocked down.

In that sense, there wasn't much difference between Trump and Boehner or McConnell. They, too, understood that it didn't matter whether what they said was true. They didn't have to actually believe that I was bankrupting the country or that Obamacare promoted euthanasia. In fact, the only difference between Trump's style of politics and theirs was Trump's lack of inhibition. He understood instinctively what moved the conservative base most, and he offered it up in an unadulterated form. While I doubted that he was willing to relinquish his business holdings or subject himself to the necessary vetting in order to run for president, I knew that the passions he was tapping, the dark, alternative vision he was promoting and legitimizing, were something I'd likely be contending with for the remainder of my presidency.

I'd have plenty of time to worry about the Republicans later, I told myself. Same with budget issues, campaign strategy, and the state of American democracy. In fact, of all that was giving me cause to brood that day on the patio, I knew that one thing above all else would demand my attention in the next few weeks.

I had to decide whether or not to authorize a raid deep inside Pakistan to go after a target we believed to be Osama bin Laden—and whatever else happened, I was likely to end up a one-term president if I got it wrong.

CHAPTER 27

OSAMA BIN LADEN'S PRECISE whereabouts had been a mystery since December 2001,
when, three months after the 9/11 attacks that killed
nearly three thousand innocent people, he had narrowly
escaped as American and allied forces closed in on his
headquarters in Tora Bora, a mountainous area along the
border of Afghanistan and Pakistan. The search had
continued in earnest for a number of years, though by
the time I took office, bin Laden's trail had gone cold. He
was still out there, though: As al-Qaeda had slowly reorganized, basing itself in Pakistan's FATA region, their
leader would periodically release audio and video messages, rallying supporters with calls for jihad against
Western powers.

From the very first time I spoke publicly on America's
response to 9/11, opposing the Iraq War at Chicago's
Federal Plaza on the eve of my U.S. Senate race in 2002,
I had advocated for a renewed focus on bringing bin
Laden to justice. I'd returned to the same theme during
the presidential race, pledging to go after bin Laden
inside Pakistan if the government there was unable or
unwilling to take him out. Most of Washington, including Joe, Hillary, and John McCain, had dismissed that

promise as a stunt, a way for a junior senator unschooled in foreign policy to sound tough. And even after I took office, some people undoubtedly assumed I would set aside the issue of bin Laden in order to deal with other matters. But in May 2009, following a Situation Room meeting about terrorist threats, I had brought a handful of advisors—including Rahm, Leon Panetta, and Tom Donilon—up to the Oval Office and closed the door.

"I want to make the hunt for bin Laden a top priority," I said. "I want to see a formal plan for how we're going to find him. I want a report on my desk every thirty days describing our progress. And, Tom, let's put this in a presidential directive—just so everyone's on the same page."

There were the obvious reasons for my focus on bin Laden. His continued freedom was a source of pain for the families of those who'd been lost in the 9/11 attacks and a taunt to American power. Even deep in hiding, he remained al-Qaeda's most effective recruiter, radicalizing disaffected young men around the world. According to our analysts, by the time I was elected, al-Qaeda was more dangerous than it had been in years, and warnings about terrorist plots emanating from the FATA appeared regularly in my briefings.

But I also viewed the elimination of bin Laden as critical to my goal of reorienting America's counterterrorism strategy. By losing our focus on the small band of terrorists who had actually planned and carried out 9/11 and instead defining the threat as an open-ended, all-encompassing "War on Terror," we'd fallen into what I believed was a strategic trap—one that had elevated al-Qaeda's prestige, rationalized the Iraq invasion, alienated much of the Muslim world, and warped almost a decade of U.S. foreign policy. Rather than gin up fears about vast terror networks and feed extremists' fantasies that they were engaged in some divine struggle, I wanted to remind the world (and, more important, ourselves) that these terrorists were nothing more than a band of deluded, vicious killers—criminals who could be captured, tried, imprisoned, or killed. And there would be no better way of demonstrating that than by taking out bin Laden.

A day before the ninth anniversary of 9/11, Leon Panetta and his CIA deputy, Mike Morell, asked to see me. They made a good team, I thought. As someone who'd spent much of his career in Congress before serving as Bill Clinton's chief of staff, the seventy-two-year-old Panetta not only provided steady management of the agency but also enjoyed the public stage, maintained good relationships across Congress and with the press, and had a keen nose for the politics of national security issues. Morell, on the other hand, was the consummate insider, with the meticulous mind of an analyst, and while only in his early fifties he had decades of experience at the agency.

"Mr. President, it's very preliminary," Leon said, "but we think we have a potential lead on bin Laden—the best one by far since Tora Bora."

I absorbed the news in silence. Leon and Mike explained that—thanks to patient and painstaking work, involving the compilation and pattern mapping of thousands of bits of information—analysts had identified the whereabouts of a man known as Abu Ahmed al-Kuwaiti, who they believed served as an al-Qaeda courier and had known ties to bin Laden. They had been tracking his phone and daily habits, which had led them not to some remote location in the FATA but rather to a large compound in an affluent neighborhood on the outskirts of the Pakistani city of Abbottabad, thirty-five miles north of Islamabad. According to Mike, the size and structure of the compound indicated that somebody important lived there, quite possibly a high-value al-Qaeda member. The intelligence community had set up surveillance on the compound, and Leon promised to update me on anything we learned about its occupants.

After they'd gone, I made a point of tempering my expectations. Anyone could be in that compound; even if it was someone with al-Qaeda connections, the likelihood that bin Laden would be staying in a populated urban area seemed small. But on December 14, Leon and Mike were back, this time with an officer and an analyst from the CIA. The analyst was a young man with the polished, fresh-faced look of a senior congressional staffer, the officer a lean, thickly bearded gentleman who was older and with a slightly rumpled, professorial air. He turned out to be the head of the CIA's Counterterrorism Center and the team leader for the bin Laden hunt. I imagined him holed up in some subterranean warren, surrounded by computers and thick manila folders, oblivious to the world as he combed through mounds of data.

The two men walked me through everything that had led us to the Abbottabad compound—a remarkable feat of detective work. Apparently the courier al-Kuwaiti had purchased the property under an assumed name. The compound itself was unusually spacious and secure, eight times larger than neighboring residences, surrounded by ten- to eighteen-foot walls topped with barbed wire, and with additional walls inside the perimeter. As for the people who lived there, the analysts said they went to great lengths to conceal their identities: They had no landline or internet service, almost never left the compound, and burned their trash instead of putting it outside for collection. But the age and number of children in the compound's main house appeared to match those of bin Laden's children. And through aerial surveillance, our team had been able to observe a tall man who never left the property but regularly walked in circles in a small garden area within the compound's walls.

"We call him the Pacer," the lead officer said. "We think he could be bin Laden."

I had a ton of questions, but the main one was this: What else could we do to confirm the Pacer's identity? Although they were continuing to explore possible strategies, the analysts confessed that they weren't hopeful. Given the configuration and location of the compound, as well as the caution of its occupants, the methods that might yield greater certainty that it was in fact bin Laden might quickly trigger suspicion; without us ever knowing it, the occupants could vanish without a trace. I looked at the lead officer.

"What's your judgment?" I asked.

I could see him hesitating. I suspected that he'd been around during the run-up to Iraq; the intelligence community's reputation was still recovering from the role it had played in supporting the Bush administration's insistence that Saddam Hussein was developing weapons of mass destruction. Still, I caught an expression on his face that indicated the pride of someone who'd cracked an intricate puzzle—even if he couldn't prove it.

"I think there's a good chance he's our man," he said. "But we can't be certain."

Based on what I'd heard, I decided we had enough information to begin developing options for an attack on the compound. While the CIA team continued to work on identifying the Pacer, I asked Tom Donilon and John Brennan to explore what a raid would look like. The need for secrecy added to the challenge; if even the slightest hint of our lead on bin Laden leaked, we knew our opportunity would be lost. As a result, only a handful of people across the entire federal government were read into the planning phase of the operation. We had one other constraint: Whatever option we chose could not involve the Pakistanis. Although Pakistan's government cooperated with us on a host of counterterrorism operations and provided a vital supply path for our forces in Afghanistan, it was an open secret that certain elements inside the country's military, and especially its intelligence services, maintained links to the Taliban and perhaps even al-Qaeda, sometimes using them as strategic assets to ensure that the Afghan government remained weak and unable to align itself with Pakistan's number one rival, India. The fact that the Abbottabad compound was just a few miles from the Pakistan military's equivalent of West Point only heightened the possibility that anything we told the Pakistanis could end up tipping off our target. Whatever we chose to do in Abbottabad, then, would involve violating the territory of a putative ally in the most egregious way possible, short of war—raising both the diplomatic stakes and the operational complexities.

By mid-March, in the days leading up to the Libya intervention and my trip to Latin America, the team had presented what they cautioned were only preliminary concepts for an assault on the compound in Abbottabad. Roughly speaking, I had two options. The first was to demolish it with an air strike. The benefits of that approach were obvious: No American lives would be risked on Pakistani soil. Publicly, at least, this option also offered a certain deniability—the Pakistanis would, of course, know that we were the ones who'd carried out the strike, but they would have an easier time maintaining the fiction that we might not be, which could help quell outrage among their people.

As we delved into the details of what a missile strike would look like, though, the downsides were significant. If we destroyed the compound, how would we ever be certain that bin Laden had been there? If al-Qaeda denied that bin Laden had been killed, how would we explain having blown up a residence deep inside Pakistan? Moreover, there were an estimated five women and twenty children living with the four adult males at the Abbottabad compound, and, in its initial iteration, the proposed strike would not only annihilate the compound but almost certainly level several adjacent residences as well. Not long into the meeting, I told Joint Chiefs vice chairman Hoss Cartwright that I'd heard enough: I was not going to authorize the killing of thirty or more people when we weren't even certain it was bin Laden in the compound. If we were going to use a strike, they'd have to come up with a much more precise plan.

The second option was to authorize a special ops mission, in which a select team would covertly fly into

Pakistan via helicopter, raid the compound, and get out before the Pakistani police or military had time to react. To preserve the secrecy of the operation, and deniability if something went awry, we'd have to conduct it under the authority of the CIA rather than the Pentagon. On the other hand, for a mission of this magnitude and risk, we needed a topflight military mind—which is why we had the Defense Department's Vice Admiral William McRaven, head of Joint Special Operations Command (JSOC), in the room to walk us through what a raid might entail.

The chance to work closely with the men and women of the U.S. armed forces—to witness firsthand their teamwork and sense of duty—had been one of the most humbling aspects of my two years in office. And if I'd had to pick one individual to represent everything right about our military, Bill McRaven might have been that person. In his mid-fifties, with a friendly, open face, a deadpan sense of humor, and a plainspoken, can-do demeanor, he reminded me of a sandy-haired Tom Hanks—if Tom Hanks had been a career Navy SEAL. Like his predecessor at JSOC, Stan McChrystal, for whom he'd served as deputy, McRaven had helped write the book on special ops. For his postgraduate thesis eighteen years earlier, in fact, McRaven had studied a series of twentieth-century commando operations—including a 1943 glider rescue of Mussolini ordered by Hitler, and the 1976 Israeli operation to free hostages in Entebbe—examining the conditions under which a small group of well-rehearsed, highly trained soldiers could use stealth to maintain short-term superiority over larger or better armed forces.

McRaven had gone on to develop a model for special

operations that shaped U.S. military strategy around the world. During his storied career, he had personally commanded or carried out more than a thousand special ops in some of the most dangerous settings imaginable, most recently going after high-value targets in Afghanistan. He was also famously cool under pressure. As a SEAL captain, he'd survived a 2001 parachuting accident in which he was knocked semiconscious during a jump and plunged four thousand feet before his chute properly deployed. (The accident broke his back and tore his leg muscles and tendons from his pelvis.) Although the CIA had developed its own internal special ops teams, Leon had wisely chosen to consult with McRaven in mapping out what a raid on Abbottabad might look like. He'd concluded that no CIA operators could match the skill and experience of McRaven's Navy SEAL team and, thus, had recommended an unusual arrangement in which the chain of command ran from me to him to McRaven, who would have complete authority to design and conduct the mission if we decided to go forward with it.

Guided by data collected by aerial photography, the CIA had built a small three-dimensional replica of the Abbottabad compound, and during our March meeting McRaven walked us through how a raid might go: A select team of SEALs would fly one or more helicopters for nearly an hour and a half under the cover of darkness from Jalalabad, Afghanistan, to the target, landing inside the compound's high walls. They would then secure every perimeter entry point, door, and window before breaking into the three-story main house, searching the premises, and neutralizing any resistance they encountered. They would apprehend or kill bin Laden and fly back out, stopping to refuel somewhere inside Pakistan before returning to the base in Jalalabad. When McRaven's presentation was over, I asked him if he thought his team could pull it off.

"Sir, right now we've just sketched out a concept," he said. "Until I can get a larger team together to run through some rehearsals, I won't know if what I'm currently thinking is the best way to do it. I also can't tell you how we would get in and out—we need detailed air planners for that. What I can tell you is that if we get there, we can pull off the raid. But I can't recommend the mission itself until I've done the homework."

I nodded. "Let's do the homework, then."

Two weeks later, on March 29, we reconvened in the Situation Room, and McRaven reported feeling highly confident that the raid could be executed. Getting out, on the other hand, he said, might be a little more "sporty." Based on his experience with similar raids and the preliminary rehearsals he'd run, he was fairly certain that the team could finish the job before any Pakistani authorities caught wind of what was happening. Nevertheless, we considered all the scenarios in which that assumption proved incorrect. What would we do if Pakistani fighters intercepted our helicopters, either on the way in or on the way out? What if bin Laden was on-site but hidden or in a safe room, thus extending the amount of time the special ops team spent on the ground? How would the team respond if Pakistani police or military forces surrounded the compound during the raid?

McRaven emphasized that his planning was built on the premise that his team should avoid a firefight with

Pakistani authorities; and if the authorities confronted us on the ground, his inclination would be to have the SEALs hold in place while our diplomats tried to negotiate a safe exit. I appreciated those instincts; his proposed approach was yet another example of the prudence I'd consistently encountered when dealing with our top military commanders. But with U.S.-Pakistan relations in a particularly precarious state, both Bob Gates and I expressed serious reservations about this strategy. U.S. drone strikes against al-Qaeda targets in the FATA had been generating increasing opposition from the Pakistani public. Anti-American sentiment had been further inflamed late in January when a CIA contractor named Raymond Allen Davis killed two armed men who approached his vehicle in the teeming city of Lahore, setting off angry protests over the CIA presence in Pakistan and resulting in nearly two months of tense diplomatic drama as we brokered Davis's release. I told McRaven and the team that I was not going to risk putting the fate of our SEALs in the hands of a Pakistani government that would no doubt face intense public pressure over whether to jail or release them—especially if it turned out that bin Laden wasn't in the compound. I therefore wanted him to beef up plans to get the raiding party out no matter what—possibly adding two extra helicopters to provide backup for the team in the compound.

Before we adjourned, Hoss Cartwright offered a new, more surgical option for an air strike—one involving a drone that would fire a small, thirteen-pound missile directly at the Pacer while he was taking his daily walk. According to Cartwright, the collateral damage would be minimal, and given the experience our military had developed in targeting other terrorist operatives, he felt satisfied that it could do the job while avoiding the risks inherent in a raid.

The possible courses of action were now in focus. McRaven would oversee the construction of a full-scale model of the Abbottabad compound at Fort Bragg, North Carolina, where the SEAL team would conduct a series of dress rehearsals. Should I decide to authorize the raid, he said, the optimal time to do it would be the first weekend in May, when a couple of moonless nights would provide the SEALs with extra cover. Left unstated were obvious concerns that with each step we took to plan and prepare, and every day that passed, more people were being read into our secret. I told both McRaven and Cartwright that I wasn't yet ready to make a decision as to which option, if any, we'd pursue. But for planning purposes, I said, "Assume it's a go."

ALL THE WHILE, we carried on with business as usual at the White House. I was tracking the situation in Libya, the war in Afghanistan, and the Greek debt crisis, which had flared up again and was once more starting to affect U.S. markets. One day, on the way back from the Situation Room, I ran into Jay Carney, who'd succeeded Robert Gibbs as my press secretary. Jay was a former journalist who'd had a front-row seat for all sorts of historic moments. He'd covered the breakup of the Soviet Union as **Time** magazine's Moscow correspondent and had been on Air Force One with President Bush on the morning of 9/11. Now he was telling me he'd just spent part of his daily press briefing fielding questions about whether my birth certificate was valid.

It had been more than a month since Donald Trump had inserted himself into the national political dialogue. My advisors and I had assumed that, having milked it for all it was worth, the media would gradually tire of his obsession with my birth. And yet, like algae in a stagnant pond, the number of stories on his conspiratorial musings proliferated with each passing week. Cable shows ran long segments on Trump and his theories. Political reporters searched for fresh angles on the sociological significance of birtherism, or its impact on my reelection campaign, or (with barely acknowledged irony) what it said about the news business. A major point of discussion was the fact that the document we'd made available on the internet in 2008 was a "short-form" birth certificate, which was the standard document issued by the Hawaii State Department of Health and could be used to obtain a passport, Social Security number, or driver's license. According to Trump and his fellow birthers, however, the short-form document proved nothing. Why hadn't I produced the original long-form version of my birth certificate? we were asked. Had information on the long form been deliberately omitted from the short form—perhaps some clue that I was Muslim? Had the long form itself been doctored? What was Obama hiding?

Finally I decided I'd had enough. I called in White House counsel Bob Bauer and told him to go ahead and obtain the long-form birth certificate from its home in a bound volume, somewhere deep in the bowels of the

Hawaii Vital Records office. I then let David Plouffe and Dan Pfeiffer know that I planned not just to release the document but to say something publicly as well. They thought this was a bad idea, arguing that I'd just feed the story, and anyway, answering such ridiculous charges was beneath both me and the office of the president.

"That," I said, "is exactly the point."

On April 27, I walked to the podium in the White House briefing room and greeted the press. I began by remarking on the fact that the national TV networks had all decided to break from their regularly scheduled programming to carry my remarks live—something they very rarely did. I observed that two weeks earlier, when the House Republicans and I had issued sharply contrasting budget proposals, with profound implications for the nation, the news had instead been dominated by talk of my birth certificate. I noted that America faced enormous challenges and big decisions; that we should expect serious debates and sometimes fierce disagreements, because that was how our democracy was supposed to work, and I was certain that we had it in us to shape a better future together.

"But," I said, "we're not going to be able to do it if we are distracted. We're not going to be able to do it if we spend time vilifying each other. We're not going to be able to do it if we just make stuff up and pretend that facts are not facts. We're not going to be able to solve our problems if we get distracted by sideshows and carnival barkers." I looked out at the assembled reporters. "I know that there's going to be a segment of people for which, no matter what we put out, this issue will not be put to rest. But I'm speaking to the vast majority of the American people, as well as to the press. We do not have time for this kind of silliness. We've got better stuff to do. I've got better stuff to do. We've got big problems to solve. And I'm confident we can solve them, but we're going to have to focus on them—not on this."

The room was quiet for a moment. I exited through the sliding doors that led back into the communications team's offices, where I encountered a group of junior members of our press shop who'd been watching my remarks on a TV monitor. They all looked to be in their twenties. Some had worked on my campaign; others had only recently joined the administration, compelled by the idea of serving their country. I stopped and made eye contact with each one of them.

"We're better than this," I said. "Remember that."

BACK IN THE Situation Room the next day, my team and I conducted a final review of our options for a possible Abbottabad operation to take place that weekend. Earlier in the week, I had given McRaven approval to dispatch the SEAL team and helicopter assault force to Afghanistan, and the group was now in Jalalabad, awaiting further orders. In order to make sure that the CIA had adequately pressure-tested its work, Leon and Mike Morell had asked the chief of the National Counterterrorism Center, Mike Leiter, to have a fresh team of analysts pore over the available intelligence on the compound and its residents, to see how the agency's conclusions matched up with those of Langley. Leiter reported that his team had expressed a 40 to 60 percent degree of certainty that it was bin Laden, compared to the CIA team's assessment of 60 to 80 percent. A discussion ensued about what accounted for the difference. After a few minutes, I interrupted.

"I know we're trying to quantify these factors as best we can," I said. "But ultimately, this is a fifty-fifty call. Let's move on."

McRaven let us know that preparations for the raid were complete; he and his men were ready. Cartwright likewise confirmed that the drone missile option had been tested and could be activated at any time. With the options before us, I went around the table to get everyone's recommendations. Leon, John Brennan, and Mike Mullen favored the raid. Hillary said that for her, it was a 51–49 call, carefully ticking through the risks of a raid—especially the danger that we could rupture our relations with Pakistan, or even find ourselves in a confrontation with the Pakistani military. She added, however, that considering that this was our best lead on bin Laden in ten years, she ultimately came down on the side of sending in the SEALs.

Gates recommended against a raid, although he was open to considering the strike option. He raised the precedent of the April 1980 attempt to rescue the fifty-three American hostages held in Iran, known as Desert One, which had turned catastrophic after a U.S. military helicopter crashed in the desert, killing eight servicemembers. It was a reminder, he said, that no matter how thorough the planning, operations like this could go badly wrong. Beyond the risk to the team, he worried that a failed mission might adversely impact the war in Afghanistan. Earlier that same day, I had announced Bob's planned retirement after four years as secretary of defense and my intention to nominate Leon as his successor. As I listened to Bob's sober, well-reasoned assessment, I was reminded of just how valuable he'd been to me.

Joe also weighed in against the raid, arguing that given the enormous consequences of failure, I should defer any decision until the intelligence community was more certain that bin Laden was in the compound. As had been true in every major decision I'd made as president, I appreciated Joe's willingness to buck the prevailing mood and ask tough questions, often in the interest of giving me the space I needed for my own internal deliberations. I also knew that Joe, like Gates, had been in Washington during Desert One. I imagined he had strong memories of that time: the grieving families, the blow to American prestige, the recrimination, and the portrayal of Jimmy Carter as both reckless and weak-minded in authorizing the mission. Carter had never recovered politically. The unspoken suggestion was that I might not either.

I told the group that they would have my decision by morning—if it was a go on the raid, I wanted to make sure that McRaven had the widest window possible to time the operation's launch. Tom Donilon walked back to the Oval Office with me, his usual assortment of binders and notebooks tucked under his arm, and we quickly went down his checklist of potential action items for the weekend ahead. He and Brennan had prepared a playbook for every contingency, it seemed, and I could see the strain and nervousness on his face. Seven months into his tenure as my national security advisor, he'd been trying to exercise more and lay off the caffeine but was apparently losing the battle. I'd come to marvel at Tom's capacity for hard work, the myriad details he kept track of, the volume of memos and cables and data he had to consume, the number of snafus he fixed and interagency tussles he resolved, all so that I could have both the information and the mental space that I needed in order to do my job. I'd asked Tom once where his drive and diligence came from, and he'd attributed it to his background. He'd grown up in an Irish working-class family, putting himself through law school and serving on various political campaigns to eventually become a heavy-hitting foreign policy expert; but despite his successes, he said, he still constantly felt the need to prove himself, terrified of failure.

I'd laughed and said I could relate.

Michelle and the girls were in rare form at dinner that night, teasing me relentlessly about what they called my "ways"—how I ate nuts a handful at a time, always shaking them in my fist first; how I always wore the same pair of ratty old sandals around the house; how I didn't like sweets ("Your dad doesn't believe in delicious things . . . too much joy"). I hadn't told Michelle about my pending decision, not wanting to burden her with a secret until I knew for certain what I planned to do, and if I was more tense than usual, she didn't seem to notice. After tucking the girls in, I retired to the Treaty Room and turned on a basketball game, my gaze following the moving ball as my mind ran through various scenarios one last time.

The truth was, I'd narrowed the scope of the decision at least a couple of weeks earlier; every meeting since had helped confirm my instincts. I wasn't in favor of a missile strike, even one as precise as Cartwright had devised, feeling that the gamble wasn't worth it without the ability to confirm that bin Laden had been killed. I was also skeptical of giving the intelligence community more time, since the extra months we'd spent monitoring the compound had yielded virtually no new information. Beyond that, considering all the planning that had already taken place, I doubted we could hold our secret another month.

The only remaining question was whether or not to order the raid. I was clear-eyed about the stakes involved. I knew we could mitigate the risks but not eliminate them. I had supreme confidence in Bill McRaven and his SEALs. I knew that in the decades since Desert One and the years since the Black Hawk Down incident in Somalia, America's special forces capability had been transformed. For all the strategic mistakes and ill-conceived policies that had plagued the Iraq and Afghanistan wars, they had also produced a cadre of men who had carried out innumerable operations and learned to respond to almost every situation imaginable. Given their skill and professionalism, I trusted that the SEALs would find a safe way out of Abbottabad, even if some of our calculations and assumptions proved to be incorrect.

I watched Kobe Bryant launch a turnaround jumper in the paint. The Lakers were playing the Hornets, on their way to wrapping up the first round of the play-offs. The grandfather clock ticked from its spot against the Treaty Room wall. Over the past two years, I'd made countless decisions—on the faltering banks, on Chrysler, pirates, Afghanistan, healthcare. They had left me familiar with, if never casual about, the possibilities of failure. Everything I did or had done involved working the odds, quietly and often late at night in the room where I now sat. I knew that I could not have come up with a better process to evaluate those odds or surrounded myself with a better mix of people to help me weigh them. I realized that through all the mistakes I'd made and the jams I'd had to extract us from, I had in many ways been training for exactly this moment. And while I couldn't guarantee the outcome of my decision, I was fully prepared and fully confident in making it.

THE NEXT DAY—Friday, April 29—was mostly travel. I was going to Tuscaloosa, Alabama, to survey the damage from a devastating tornado outbreak and had an evening commencement address to deliver in Miami. In between, I was scheduled to take Michelle and the girls to Cape Canaveral to see the final launch of the space shuttle **Endeavour** before it was decommissioned. Ahead of leaving, I sent an email asking Tom, Denis, Daley, and Brennan to meet me in the Diplomatic Reception Room, and they found me just as the family exited to the South Lawn, where Marine One awaited. With the roar of the helicopter in the background (along with the sound of Sasha and Malia engaging in some sisterly bickering), I officially gave the go-ahead for the Abbottabad mission, emphasizing that McRaven had full operational control and that it would be up to him to determine the exact timing of the raid.

The operation was now largely out of my hands. I was glad to get out of Washington, if only for the day—to occupy my mind with other work and, as it turned out, to appreciate the work of others. Earlier in the week, a monstrous supercell storm had swept across the south-eastern states, dropping tornadoes that killed more than three hundred people, which made it the deadliest natural disaster since Hurricane Katrina. A single mile-and-a-half-wide tornado fueled by 190-mile-per-hour winds had ripped through Alabama, destroying thousands of homes and businesses.

Landing in Tuscaloosa, I was met by the director of FEMA, a burly, low-key Floridian named Craig Fugate, and along with state and local officials the two of us toured neighborhoods that looked like they'd been flattened by a megaton bomb. We visited a relief center to offer solace to families that had lost everything they owned. Despite the devastation, nearly every person I talked to—from the state's Republican governor to the mother comforting her toddler—praised the federal response, mentioning how quickly teams had been on the ground; how effectively they had worked with local officials; how every request, no matter how small, had been handled with care and precision. I wasn't surprised, for Fugate had been one of my best hires, a no-nonsense, no-ego, no-excuses public servant with decades of experience dealing with natural disasters. Still, it gave me satisfaction to see his efforts recognized, and I was once again reminded that so much of what really mattered in government came down to the daily, unheralded acts of people who weren't seeking attention but simply knew what they were doing and did it with pride.

In Cape Canaveral, we were disappointed to learn that NASA had been forced to scrub the space shuttle launch at the last minute due to problems in an auxiliary power unit, but our family still had a chance to talk to the astronauts and spend time with Janet Kavandi, the director of flight crew operations at the Johnson Space

Center in Houston, who'd come to Florida for the launch. As a kid, I'd been fascinated by space exploration, and while president I'd made it a priority to highlight the value of science and engineering whenever possible, including instituting an annual science fair at the White House at which students proudly showcased their robots, rockets, and solar-powered cars. I'd also encouraged NASA to innovate and prepare for a future mission to Mars, in part by collaborating with commercial ventures on low-orbit space travel. Now I watched Malia and Sasha grow wide-eyed as Kavandi emphasized all the people and the hours of diligent work that went into even a single launch, and as she described her own path from being a young girl entranced by the night sky over her family's cattle farm in rural Missouri to becoming an astronaut who had flown on three space shuttle missions.

My day ended at the graduation ceremony for students at Miami Dade, which, with more than 170,000 students on eight campuses, was the country's largest college. Its president, Eduardo Padrón, had attended the school in the 1960s as a young Cuban immigrant with rudimentary English and no other options for a higher education. After receiving his associate's degree there and later earning a PhD in economics from the University of Florida, he'd turned down lucrative job offers in the private sector to return to Miami Dade, where for the past forty years he'd made it his mission to throw others the same lifeline the school had thrown him. He described the college as "a dream factory" for its students, who primarily came from low-income, Latino, Black, and immigrant families and were, in most cases, the first in their families to attend college. "We don't give up on any student," he told me, "and if we're doing our jobs, we don't let them give up on themselves." I couldn't help being inspired by the generosity of his vision.

In my remarks to the graduates that evening, I spoke about the American idea: what their accomplishment said about our individual determination to reach past the circumstances of our birth, as well as our collective capacity to overcome our differences to meet the challenges of our time. I recounted an early childhood memory of sitting on my grandfather's shoulders and waving a tiny American flag in a crowd gathered to greet the astronauts from one of the Apollo space missions after a successful splashdown in the waters off Hawaii. And now, more than forty years later, I told the graduates, I'd just had a chance to watch my own daughters hear from a new generation of space explorers. It had caused me to reflect on all that America had achieved since my own childhood; it offered a case of life coming full circle—and proof, just as their diplomas were proof, just as my having been elected president was proof, that the American idea endures.

The students and their parents had cheered, many of them waving American flags of their own. I thought about the country I'd just described to them—a hopeful, generous, courageous America, an America that was open to everyone. At about the same age as the graduates were now, I'd seized on that idea and clung to it for dear life. For their sake more than mine, I badly wanted it to be true.

AS ENERGIZED AND OPTIMISTIC as I felt during the trip on Friday, I knew that my Saturday night back in Washington—when Michelle and I were scheduled to attend the White House Correspondents' Dinner—promised to be decidedly less inspiring. Hosted by the White House press corps and attended at least once by every president since Calvin Coolidge, the dinner had originally been designed to give journalists and those they covered a chance, for one evening, to set aside their often-adversarial stance toward one another and have some fun. But over time, as the news and entertainment businesses had begun to blend, the annual gathering had evolved into Washington's version of the Met Gala or the Oscars, with a performance from a comedian, televised on cable, and with a couple of thousand journalists, politicians, business tycoons, and administration officials, plus an assortment of Hollywood celebrities, packing themselves into an uncomfortable hotel ballroom to schmooze, be seen, and listen to the president deliver what amounted to a stand-up routine, roasting rivals and joking about the latest political news of the day.

At a time when people across the country were still trying to figure out how to find a job, keep their homes, or pay their bills in the wake of a recession, my attendance at the black-tie affair—with its clubbishness and red-carpet glitz—had always felt politically awkward. But because I'd shown up the past two years, I knew I couldn't afford to raise any suspicions by skipping out of this year's dinner at the last minute; despite the knowledge that McRaven would soon join the SEAL team in Jalalabad and could likely launch the operation within hours, I'd have to do my best to act like everything was normal in front of a ballroom full of reporters. Fortunately it turned out that the country's leading distraction had been invited to sit at the **Washington Post**'s table that night, and those of us aware of what was going on took odd comfort in knowing that once Donald Trump entered the room, it was all but guaranteed that the media would not be thinking about Pakistan.

To some degree, the release of my long-form birth certificate and my scolding of the press in the White House briefing room had yielded the desired effect: Donald Trump had grudgingly acknowledged that he now believed I was born in Hawaii, while taking full credit for having forced me—on behalf of the American people—to certify my status. Still, the whole birther controversy remained on everybody's mind, as became clear that Saturday, when I met with Jon Favreau and the team of writers who'd prepared my remarks—none of whom were aware of the operation about to take place. They'd come up with an inspired monologue, though I paused on a line that poked fun at the birthers by suggesting that Tim Pawlenty, the former Republican governor of Minnesota, who was exploring a run for president, had been hiding the fact that his full name was actually "Tim bin Laden Pawlenty." I asked Favs to change "bin Laden" to "Hosni," suggesting that given Mubarak's recent turn in the news, it would be more current. I could tell he didn't see my edit as an improvement, but he didn't argue the point.

At the end of the afternoon, I placed a last call to McRaven, who let me know that due to some foggy weather in Pakistan, his intention was to wait until Sunday night to commence the operation. He assured me that everything was in place and his team was ready. I told him that wasn't the main reason for my call.

"Tell everyone on the team how much I appreciate them," I said.

"Yes, sir."

"Bill," I said, not having the words at that moment to convey how I felt. "I mean it. Tell them this."

"I will, Mr. President," he said.

That night, Michelle and I motorcaded over to the Washington Hilton, took pictures with various VIPs, and sat on a dais for a couple of hours, making small talk while guests like Rupert Murdoch, Sean Penn, John Boehner, and Scarlett Johansson mingled over wine and overcooked steaks. I kept my face fixed in an accommodating smile, as I quietly balanced on a mental high wire, my thoughts thousands of miles away. When it was my turn to speak, I stood up and started my routine. About halfway through, I turned my attention directly to Trump.

"Now, I know that he's taken some flak lately," I said, "but no one is happier, no one is prouder to put this birth certificate matter to rest than the Donald. And that's because he can finally get back to focusing on the issues that matter—like, Did we fake the moon landing? What really happened in Roswell? And where are Biggie and Tupac?" As the audience broke into laughter, I continued in this vein, noting his "credentials and breadth of experience" as host of **Celebrity Apprentice** and congratulating him for how he'd handled the fact that "at the steakhouse, the men's cooking team did not impress the judges from Omaha Steaks. . . . These are the kinds of decisions that would keep me up at night. Well handled, sir. Well handled."

The audience howled as Trump sat in silence,

cracking a tepid smile. I couldn't begin to guess what went through his mind during the few minutes I spent publicly ribbing him. What I knew was that he was a spectacle, and in the United States of America in 2011, that was a form of power. Trump trafficked in a currency that, however shallow, seemed to gain more purchase with each passing day. The same reporters who laughed at my jokes would continue to give him airtime. Their publishers would vie to have him sit at their tables.

Far from being ostracized for the conspiracies he'd peddled, he in fact had never been bigger.

I WAS UP early the next morning, before the White House operator's regular wake-up call. We'd taken the unusual step of canceling the public tours of the West Wing for the day, presuming there were important meetings ahead. I'd decided to get in a quick nine holes of golf with Marvin, as I often did on quiet Sundays, partly to avoid telegraphing anything else being out of the ordinary and partly to get outside rather than sit checking my watch in the Treaty Room, waiting for darkness to fall in Pakistan. It was a cool, windless day, and I hacked around the course, losing three or four balls in the woods. Returning to the White House, I checked in with Tom. He and the rest of the team were already in the Situation Room, making sure we were set to respond to whatever might happen. Rather than distract them with my presence, I asked that he notify me once the helicopters carrying the SEAL team were in the air. I sat in the Oval, trying to read through some papers, but got nowhere, my eyes running over the same lines again and again. I finally called in Reggie, Marvin, and Pete Souza—all of whom by this time had been read into what was about to transpire—and the four of us sat down in the Oval dining room to play Spades.

At two p.m. eastern time, two Black Hawk helicopters that had been modified for stealth lifted off from Jalalabad Airfield, carrying twenty-three members of the SEAL team, along with a Pakistani American CIA translator and a military dog named Cairo—the commencement of what was officially known as Operation Neptune's Spear. It would take them ninety minutes to reach Abbottabad. I left the dining room and went back down to the Situation Room, which had effectively been converted into a war room. Leon was on a videoconference line from Langley, relaying information from McRaven, who was holed up in Jalalabad and in continuous, direct communication with his SEALs. The atmosphere was predictably tense, with Joe, Bill Daley, and most of my national security team—including Tom, Hillary, Denis, Gates, Mullen, and Blinken—already seated at the conference table. I was given updates on plans for notifying Pakistan and other countries and our diplomatic strategies in the event of either success or failure. If bin Laden was killed in the raid, preparations had been made for a traditional Islamic burial to take place at sea, avoiding the creation of a pilgrimage site for jihadists. After a time, I could tell that the team was simply covering old ground for my benefit. Worried that I was sidetracking them, I went back upstairs until shortly before three-thirty, when Leon announced that the Black Hawks were approaching the compound.

The team had planned for us to follow the operation indirectly, through Leon, since Tom was concerned about the optics of me communicating directly with McRaven, which might leave the impression that I was micromanaging the operation—a bad practice generally and a political problem if the mission failed. On my way back into the Situation Room, though, I had noticed that a live aerial view of the compound, as well as McRaven's voice, was being transmitted to a video monitor in a smaller conference room across the hall. As the helicopters drew close to the target, I stood up from my seat. "I need to watch this," I said, before heading to the other room. There I found a blue-uniformed air force brigadier general, Brad Webb, seated in front of his computer at a small table. He tried to offer me his seat. "Sit down," I said, putting a hand on his shoulder and finding a spot in a side chair. Webb let McRaven and Leon know that I had changed venues and was watching the feed. Soon the entire team had squeezed into the room.

This was the first and only time as president that I'd watch a military operation unfold in real time, with ghostly images moving across the screen. We'd been following the action for barely a minute when one of the Black Hawks lurched slightly on descent, and before I could grasp exactly what was happening, McRaven informed us that the helicopter had momentarily lost lift and then clipped the side of one of the compound's walls. For an instant, I felt an electric kind of fear. A disaster reel played in my head—a chopper crashing, the SEALs scrambling to get out before the machine caught fire, a neighborhood of people emerging from their homes to see what happened as the Pakistani military rushed to the scene. McRaven's voice interrupted my nightmare.

"It'll be fine," he said, as though remarking on a car

fender bumping into a shopping cart at the mall. "The pilot's the best we have, and he'll bring it down safely."

And that's exactly what happened. I'd later learn that the Black Hawk had been caught in a vortex caused by higher than anticipated temperatures and the rotor's downwash of air getting trapped inside the compound's high walls, forcing the pilot and the SEALs on board to improvise both a landing and their exit. (In fact, the pilot had purposely set the tail of the chopper on the wall to avoid a more perilous crash.) But all I saw in the moment were grainy figures on the ground, rapidly moving into position and entering the main house. For twenty excruciating minutes, even McRaven had a limited view of what was taking place—or perhaps he was staying silent on the details of the room-to-room search his team was conducting. Then, with a suddenness I didn't expect, we heard McRaven's and Leon's voices, almost simultaneously, utter the words we'd been waiting to hear—the culmination of months of planning and years of intelligence gathering.

"Geronimo ID'd . . . Geronimo EKIA."

Enemy killed in action.

Osama bin Laden—code-named "Geronimo" for the purposes of the mission—the man responsible for the worst terrorist attack in American history, the man who had directed the murder of thousands of people and set in motion a tumultuous period of world history, had been brought to justice by a team of American Navy SEALs. Inside the conference room, there were audible gasps. My eyes remained glued to the video feed.

"We got him," I said softly.

Nobody budged from their seats for another twenty

minutes, while the SEAL team finished its business: bagging bin Laden's body; securing the three women and nine children present and questioning them in one corner of the compound; collecting computers, files, and other material of potential intelligence value; and attaching explosives to the damaged Black Hawk, which would then be destroyed, replaced by a rescue Chinook that had been hovering a short distance away. As the helicopters took off, Joe placed a hand on my shoulder and squeezed.

"Congratulations, boss," he said.

I stood up and nodded. Denis gave me a fist bump. I shook hands with others on the team. But with the helicopters still rotoring through Pakistani airspace, the mood remained quiet. It wasn't until around six p.m., when the choppers had safely landed in Jalalabad, that I finally felt some of the tension start to drain out of me. Over a video teleconference line a short while later, McRaven explained that he was looking at the body as we spoke, and that in his judgment it was definitely bin Laden; the CIA's facial recognition software would soon indicate the same. To further confirm, McRaven had a six-foot-two member of his team lie next to the body to compare his height to bin Laden's purported six-foot-four frame.

"Seriously, Bill?" I teased. "All that planning and you couldn't bring a tape measure?"

It was the first lighthearted thing I'd said all day, but the laughter didn't last long, as photographs of bin Laden's corpse were soon passed around the conference table. I glanced at them briefly; it was him. Despite the evidence, Leon and McRaven said that we couldn't be fully certain until the DNA results came back, which would take another day or two. We discussed the possibility of holding off on an official announcement, but reports of a helicopter crash in Abbottabad were already starting to pop up on the internet. Mike Mullen had put a call in to Pakistan's army chief, General Ashfaq Parvez Kayani, and while the conversation had been polite, Kayani had requested that we come clean on the raid and its target as quickly as possible in order to help his people manage the reaction of the Pakistani public. Knowing there was no way to hold the news for another twenty-four hours, I went upstairs with Ben to quickly dictate my thoughts on what I would say to the nation later that evening.

For the next several hours, the West Wing ran at full throttle. While diplomats began to contact foreign governments and our communications team got ready to brief the press, I placed calls to George W. Bush and Bill Clinton and told them the news, making a point to acknowledge with Bush that the mission was the culmination of a long, hard process begun under his presidency. Though it was the middle of the night across the Atlantic, I contacted David Cameron as well, to recognize the stalwart support our closest ally had provided from the very beginning of the Afghan War. I expected my most difficult call to be with Pakistan's beleaguered president, Asif Ali Zardari, who would surely face a backlash at home over our violation of Pakistani sovereignty. When I reached him, however, he expressed congratulations and support. "Whatever the fallout," he said, "it's very good news." He showed genuine emotion, recalling how his wife, Benazir Bhutto, had been killed by extremists with reported ties to al-Qaeda.

Meanwhile, I hadn't seen Michelle all day. I'd let her

know earlier what would be happening, and rather than sit anxiously at the White House, waiting for news, she'd left Malia and Sasha in their grandmother's care and gone out to dinner with friends. I had just finished shaving and putting on a suit and tie when she walked through the door.

"So?" she said.

I gave a thumbs-up, and she smiled, pulling me into a hug. "That's amazing, babe," she said. "Really. How do you feel?"

"Right now, just relieved," I said. "But check back with me in a couple of hours."

Back in the West Wing, I sat with Ben to put the finishing touches on my remarks. I had given him a few broad themes. I wanted to recall the shared anguish of 9/11, I said, and the unity we'd all felt in the days that immediately followed. I wanted to salute not just those involved in this mission but everyone in our military and intelligence communities who continued to sacrifice so much to keep us safe. I wanted to reiterate that our fight was with al-Qaeda and not Islam. And I wanted to close by reminding the world and ourselves that America does what it sets out to do—that as a nation we were still capable of achieving big things.

As usual, Ben had taken my stray thoughts and crafted a fine speech in less than two hours. I knew that this one mattered to him more than most, since the experience of watching the Twin Towers collapse had changed the trajectory of his life, propelling him to Washington with a burning drive to make a difference. It brought back my own memories of that day: Michelle having just taken Malia to her first day of preschool; me standing outside the State of Illinois Building in downtown Chicago, feeling overwhelmed and uncertain after assuring Michelle over the phone that she and the girls would be okay; three-month-old Sasha sleeping on my chest later that night as I sat in the dark watching the news reports and trying to contact friends in New York. No less than Ben's, my own course in life had been fundamentally altered by that day, in ways that at the time I could not possibly have predicted, setting off a chain of events that would somehow lead to this moment.

After scanning the speech one last time, I stood up and clapped Ben on the back. "Good job, brother," I said. He nodded, a jumble of emotions passing across his face before he rushed out the door to get the final edits on my remarks entered into the teleprompter. It was now almost eleven-thirty p.m. The major networks had already reported bin Laden's death and were waiting to take my address live. Celebratory crowds had gathered outside the White House gates, thousands of people filling the streets. As I stepped into the cool night air and started walking down the colonnade toward the East Room, where I'd give my remarks, I could hear the raucous, rhythmic chants of "USA! USA! USA!" coming from Pennsylvania Avenue—a sound that echoed far and wide and would continue deep into the night.

EVEN AFTER THE jubilation quieted down, all of us in the White House could feel a palpable shift in the country's mood in the days immediately following the Abbottabad raid. For the first and only time in my presidency, we didn't have to sell what we'd done. We didn't have to fend off Republican attacks or answer accusations from key constituencies that we'd compromised some core principle. No issues with implementation or unforeseen consequences sprang up. I still had decisions to make, including whether to release photos of bin Laden's dead body. (My answer was no: We didn't need to "spike the football" or hoist a ghoulish trophy, I told my staff, and I didn't want the image of bin Laden shot in the head to become a rallying point for extremists.) We still had to patch up relations with Pakistan. While the documents and computer files seized from the compound proved to be a treasure trove of intelligence, confirming that bin Laden had continued to play a central role in planning attacks against the United States, as well as the enormous pressure we'd managed to put on his network through our targeting of its leaders, none of us believed that the threat from al-Qaeda was over. What was beyond dispute, though, was that we'd dealt the organization a decisive blow, moving it a step closer to strategic defeat. Even our harshest critics had to acknowledge that the operation had been an unequivocal success.

As for the American people, the Abbottabad raid offered a catharsis of sorts. In Afghanistan and Iraq, they'd seen our troops wage almost a decade of war, with outcomes they knew to be ambiguous at best. They'd expected that violent extremism was here to stay in one form or another, that there'd be no conclusive battle or formal surrender. As a result, the public instinctively seemed to seize on bin Laden's death as the closest we'd likely ever get to a V-Day—and at a time of economic hardship and partisan rancor, people took some satisfaction in seeing their government deliver a victory.

Meanwhile, the thousands of families who'd lost loved

ones on 9/11 understood what we'd done in more personal terms. The day after the operation, my daily batch of ten constituent letters contained a printed email from a young woman named Payton Wall, who'd been four years old at the time of the attacks and was now fourteen. She explained that her dad had been in one of the Twin Towers and had called to speak to her before it collapsed. All her life, she wrote, she'd been haunted by the memory of her father's voice, along with the image of her mother weeping into the phone. Although nothing could change the fact of his absence, she wanted me and all those who'd been involved in the raid to know how much it meant to her and her family that America hadn't forgotten him.

Sitting alone in the Treaty Room, I reread that email a couple of times, my eyes clouded with emotion. I thought about my daughters and how profoundly the loss of their mother or father would hurt them. I thought about young people who'd signed up for the armed forces after 9/11, intent on serving the nation, no matter the sacrifice. And I thought about the parents of those wounded or killed in Iraq and Afghanistan—the Gold Star moms Michelle and I had comforted, the fathers who'd shown me pictures of their departed sons. I felt an overwhelming pride in those who'd been part of the mission. From the SEALs themselves, to the CIA analysts who'd pieced together the trail to Abbottabad, to the diplomats who had prepared to manage the fallout, to the Pakistani American translator who'd stood outside the compound shooing away curious neighbors as the raid took place—they had all worked together seamlessly and selflessly, without regard to credit or turf or political preferences, to achieve a shared goal.

With these thoughts came another: Was that unity of effort, that sense of common purpose, possible only when the goal involved killing a terrorist? The question nagged at me. For all the pride and satisfaction I took in the success of our mission in Abbottabad, the truth was that I hadn't felt the same exuberance as I had on the night the healthcare bill passed. I found myself imagining what America might look like if we could rally the country so that our government brought the same level of expertise and determination to educating our children or housing the homeless as it had to getting bin Laden; if we could apply the same persistence and resources to reducing poverty or curbing greenhouse gases or making sure every family had access to decent day care. I knew that even my own staff would dismiss these notions as utopian. And the fact that this was the case, the fact that we could no longer imagine uniting the country around anything other than thwarting attacks and defeating external enemies, I took as a measure of how far my presidency still fell short of what I wanted it to be—and how much work I had left to do.

I set such musings aside for the rest of that week, allowing myself a chance to savor the moment. Bob Gates would attend his last cabinet meeting and get a rousing ovation, appearing, for a moment, genuinely moved. I spent time with John Brennan, who had been involved one way or another in the hunt for bin Laden for close to fifteen years. Bill McRaven stopped by the Oval Office and, along with my heartfelt thanks for his extraordinary leadership, I presented him with a tape measure I'd had mounted on a plaque. And on May 5, 2011, just four days after the operation, I traveled to New York City and had lunch with the firefighters of Engine Company 54/ Ladder 4/Battalion 9, which had lost all fifteen members who'd been on duty the morning of the attack, and participated in a wreath-laying ceremony at Ground Zero. Some of the first responders who had rushed into the burning towers served in the honor guard that day, and I had a chance to meet with the 9/11 families in attendance—including Payton Wall, who got a big hug from me and promptly asked if I could arrange for her to meet Justin Bieber (I told her I was pretty sure I could make that happen).

The next day, I flew to Fort Campbell, Kentucky, where McRaven introduced me and Joe to the SEAL team and pilots involved in the Abbottabad raid. A small-scale model of the compound had been set up at the front of the room, and as the commanding officer methodically walked us through the operation, I studied the thirty or so elite military members seated before me in folding chairs. Some of them looked the part—strapping young men whose muscles bulged through their uniforms. But I was struck by how many of them could have passed for accountants or high school principals—guys in their early forties, with graying hair and understated demeanors. They were a testament to the role that skill and judgment born of experience played in successfully navigating the most dangerous missions—experience, the commander emphasized, that had also cost the lives of many of their colleagues. When the briefing was over, I shook hands with everyone in the room and presented the team with the Presidential Unit Citation, the highest award a military unit could receive. In return, the men surprised me with a gift: an American flag they had taken with them to Abbottabad, now in a frame with their signatures on the back. At no point during my visit did anyone mention who had fired the shot that killed bin Laden—and I never asked.

On the flight back, Tom gave me an update on Libya. Bill Daley and I reviewed my schedule for the month ahead, and I caught up on some paperwork. By six-thirty p.m., we'd landed at Andrews Air Force Base, and I boarded Marine One for the short ride back to the White House. I was in a quiet mood as I gazed out at the rolling Maryland landscape and the tidy neighborhoods below, and then the Potomac, glistening beneath the fading sun. The helicopter began its gentle turn, due north across the Mall. The Washington Monument suddenly materialized on one side, seeming almost close enough to touch; on the other side, I could see the seated figure of Lincoln, shrouded in shadow behind the memorial's curved marble columns. Marine One began to shudder a bit, in a way that was now familiar to me, signaling the final descent as it approached the South Lawn, and I looked down at the street below, still thick with rush-hour traffic—fellow commuters, I thought, anxious to get home.

ACKNOWLEDGMENTS

T HIS BOOK INVOLVED the behind-the-scenes work of many diligent people to whom I am enormously grateful:

My longtime editor at Crown, Rachel Klayman, has stayed the course with me for sixteen years now, bringing her keen intellect, sound judgment, and ferocious eye for detail to every line I publish. Her generosity, forbearance, and dedication have made all the difference. Every author should be so fortunate.

Sara Corbett added editorial expertise and creative vision to this project, coordinating our team, editing multiple drafts, and making critically helpful suggestions throughout. She's also been full of wisdom, encouragement, and good cheer, and made this a far better book than it otherwise would be.

Cody Keenan, who helped me pen some of the best-known speeches of my career, remained a valuable collaborator over the past three years, conducting background interviews, helping to organize my thinking on the book's structure, and contributing thoughtfully to my work in innumerable ways.

Ben Rhodes was not only present for many of the moments described in this book but also supplied key editorial and research support for each draft. More important, our countless hours of conversation and years of friendship have helped to shape many of the insights contained in these pages.

Samantha Power offered rigorous, intelligent, and incredibly useful feedback throughout. I'm thankful for both her integrity and her intensity: She makes me better as a person and better on the page.

I owe a special debt of gratitude to Meredith Bohen, who applied scrupulous standards and an extraordinary work ethic to this endeavor, providing critical research and fact-checking from beginning to end. She was backed up by the considerable talents of Julie Tate and Gillian Brassil, for whose contributions I am also thankful.

Everything I do is fueled by the skill, hard work, and good humor of the smart and energetic people on my staff, many of whom have been by my side for years: Anita Decker Breckenridge worked hard to protect the sanctity of my writing hours and ably steered us through the publishing process. Henock Dory has given to this book in countless ways and with unfailing professionalism, tracking every detail and keeping me moving forward. Emily Blakemore, Graham Gibson, Eric Schultz, Katie Hill, Addar Levi, Dana Remus, and Caroline Adler Morales also helped shepherd us to publication. Thanks as well to Joe Paulsen, Joelle Appenrodt, Kevin Lewis, Desiree Barnes, Greg Lorjuste, Michael Brush, and Kaitlin Gaughran.

I am forever indebted to those who served on my cabinet and staff, whose outstanding work and unswerving ability to stay hopeful made all the difference in advancing my administration's agenda. A number of them have written their own books covering their time in the White House and the issues they worked on, and those accounts have proven to be excellent resources (and fascinating reads).

I'm grateful to the many former staff members and colleagues who took the time to offer their unique perspectives and personal memories as I sorted through my time in office and on the campaign trail, including Admiral Thad Allen, David Axelrod, Melody Barnes, Jared Bernstein, Brian Deese, Arne Duncan, Rahm Emanuel, Matt Flavin, Ferial Govashiri, Danielle Gray, Valerie Jarrett, Katie Johnson, Jack Lew, Reggie Love, Chris Lu, Alyssa Mastromonaco, Marvin Nicholson, Nancy Pelosi, Kal Penn, Dan Pfeiffer, David Plouffe, Fiona Reeves, Harry Reid, Christy Romer, Pete Rouse, Kathy Ruemmler, Ken Salazar, Phil Schiliro, Kathleen Sebelius, Pete Souza, Todd Stern, and Tommy Vietor. And a special thanks to those colleagues who generously read and offered expert feedback on portions of the manuscript: John Brennan, Carol Browner, Lisa Monaco, Cecilia Muñoz, Steven Chu, Tom Donilon, Nancy-Ann DeParle, Jon Favreau, Tim Geithner, Eric Holder, Jeanne Lambrew, Denis McDonough, Susan Rice, and Gene Sperling.

I'm grateful to Anne Withers and Mike Smith at the National Security Council for their review of the manuscript and to Bob Barnett and Deneen Howell of Williams & Connolly, who have been invaluable advisors on the legal front.

I am well aware of and deeply humbled by the hard work and good faith required of many people at Crown and Penguin Random House to put a book like this out, especially during the disruptions of a pandemic.

My gratitude begins with Markus Dohle, who championed the project from the beginning and has enthusiastically mobilized Penguin Random House resources across the globe to make this publication possible. Gina Centrello has been a skilled and steadfast partner, marshalling every department within Penguin Random House U.S. to ensure the book would be well published. Sincere thanks as well to Madeline McIntosh and Nihar Malaviya, whose commitment to this project, and patience as it took longer than anticipated, has been remarkable.

At Crown, the expertise and strategic planning of David Drake and Tina Constable has been essential at every stage. They have not only brought their creativity and insights to bear on publicity and marketing, but have worked hand in glove with their colleagues, my staff, and the foreign publishers of this book to orchestrate the publication process, which was at times dauntingly complex. Moreover, they have shown great respect for their author's literary choices, even when it meant that one book unexpectedly became two. I feel fortunate that my book ended up in their capable hands.

Gillian Blake read the manuscript closely and made astute observations about both structure and content. Chris Brand's vision of this book, as embodied in his designs—from the jacket to the photo inserts to the website—has been inspired. Lance Fitzgerald has sold rights to the book in twenty-four languages and counting, and has been a superb liaison to our U.K. counterparts and other international partners. Lisa Feuer and Linnea Knollmueller went the extra mile to make sure this book was manufactured on time and with craftsmanship and care, working miracles with printers and suppliers. Sally Franklin wrote and tore up innumerable schedules and kept everything on track even when that must have seemed impossible. Christine Tanigawa spent long nights poring over every word and semicolon to stamp out errors and make certain I had said what I meant to say. Elizabeth Rendfleisch ensured that the inside of the book was as handsome as the outside.

Thanks as well to the multitude of other people at Crown and Penguin Random House who pulled together and gave the book their utmost: Todd Berman, Mark Birkey, Tammy Blake, Julie Cepler, Denise Cronin, Kellyann Cronin, Amanda D'Acierno, Sue Daulton, Benjamin Dreyer, Skip Dye, Carisa Hays, Madison Jacobs, Cynthia Lasky, Sue Malone-Barber, Matthew Martin, Maren McCamley, Dyana Messina, Lydia Morgan, Ty Nowicki, Donna Passannante, Jennifer Reyes, Matthew Schwartz, Holly Smith, Stacey Stein, Anke Steinecke, Jaci Updike, Claire Von Schilling, Stacey Witcraft, and Dan Zitt. I'm grateful also to Maureen Clark, Jane Hardick, Janet Renard, Do Mi Stauber, and Bonnie Thompson for excellent copyediting, proofreading, and indexing; to Scott Cresswell for coproducing the audiobook; to Carol Poticny for first-rate photo research; and to North Market Street Graphics for their page-composition accuracy and willingness to work day and night.

Finally, I want to thank Elizabeth Alexander and Michele Norris-Johnson, two top-notch writers who also happen to be dear family friends, for offering their invaluable editorial insights—and for encouraging Michelle to keep putting up with me during the final, especially hectic months of writing and editing.

PHOTOGRAPH CREDITS

INSERT 1

Barack Obama's maternal grandparents, Stanley Armour Dunham and Madelyn Lee Payne Dunham. (Obama-Robinson Family Archives)

Young Barack Obama and his mother, Ann Dunham, on the beach. (Obama-Robinson Family Archives)

Young Barack Obama. (Obama-Robinson Family Archives)

Barack Obama's father, Barack Hussein Obama, Sr. (Obama-Robinson Family Archives)

Barack Obama and his mother, Ann Dunham. (Obama-Robinson Family Archives)

Barack Obama's half sisters, Maya Soetoro-Ng (**left**) and Auma Obama (**right**), with his mother, Ann Dunham, at the Lincoln Memorial in Washington, DC. (Obama-Robinson Family Archives)

Barack Obama with his mother, Ann Dunham (**left**), and grandmother Madelyn Lee Payne Dunham. (Obama-Robinson Family Archives)

Barack Obama and Michelle Robinson at their wedding reception, Oct. 3, 1992, at South Shore Cultural Center in Chicago, IL. (Obama-Robinson Family Archives)

Barack and Michelle Obama and their daughters, Malia and Sasha, at Sasha's christening. (Obama-Robinson Family Archives)

Barack Obama in Chillicothe, IL, during his U.S. Senate campaign, August 2004. (From **Barack Before Obama** by David Katz. Copyright © 2020 by David Katz. Courtesy of HarperCollins Publishers)

U.S. Senate candidate Barack Obama of Illinois delivers the keynote address at the Democratic National Convention, July 27, 2004, Boston, MA. (Spencer Platt/Getty Images)

Barack and Michelle Obama after his keynote address at the Democratic National Convention, July 27, 2004, Boston, MA. (From **Barack Before Obama** by David Katz. Copyright © 2020 by David Katz. Courtesy of HarperCollins Publishers)

Malia Obama watches her father, Barack Obama, during his 2004 U.S. Senate campaign, Aug. 2, 2004. (From **Barack Before Obama** by David Katz. Copyright © 2020 by David Katz. Courtesy of HarperCollins Publishers)

Barack Obama, Michelle Obama, and daughters Malia and Sasha celebrate his Senate victory over Republican rival Alan Keyes, Nov. 2, 2004, Chicago, IL. (Scott Olson/Getty Images)

Sen. Barack Obama on Capitol Hill, Nov. 17, 2005. (Pete Souza/Chicago Tribune/TCA)

Sen. Barack Obama and his chief of staff Pete Rouse. (David Katz)

Sen. Barack Obama in his office on Capitol Hill, January 2005. (Pete Souza/Chicago Tribune/TCA)

Sen. Barack Obama speaks to Congressman John Lewis (**hand outstretched**) outside the White House, Jan. 26, 2005. (Pete Souza/Chicago Tribune/TCA)

Sen. Barack Obama visits a conventional weapons destruction facility in Donetsk, Ukraine, on Aug. 30, 2005. (Pete Souza/Chicago Tribune/TCA)

Kenyans wait for the arrival of Sen. Barack Obama outside a hospital in Kisumu, Kenya, on Aug. 26, 2006. (Pete Souza/Chicago Tribune/TCA)

Sen. Barack Obama arrives for a rally to announce his candidacy for the Democratic nomination for president, Feb. 10, 2007, Old State Capitol, Springfield, IL. (Mandel Ngan/AFP via Getty Images)

Sen. Barack Obama celebrates with his daughter Sasha after a victory in a carnival game at the Iowa State Fair in Des Moines, Aug. 16, 2007. (Scott Olson/Getty Images)

Sen. Barack Obama greets supporters at a rally in Austin, TX, Feb. 23, 2007. (Scout Tufankjian/Polaris)

Sen. Barack Obama leads supporters from a rally to U.S. senator Tom Harkin's Annual Steak Fry in Indianola, IA, Sept. 16, 2007. (David Lienemann/Getty Images)

Supporters wait to hear Democratic presidential candidate Sen. Barack Obama and Oprah Winfrey at a rally at the Hy-Vee Conference Center in Des Moines, IA, Dec. 8, 2007. (Brian Kersey/UPI/Alamy Stock Photo)

Campaign manager David Plouffe and Sen. Barack Obama backstage at the Democratic National Convention, Denver, CO, Aug. 28, 2008. (David Katz)

Democratic presidential nominee Sen. Barack Obama makes a speech in front of the Victory Column in Berlin, Germany, July 24, 2008. (Sebastian Willnow/DDP/AFP via Getty Images)

Republican presidential nominee Sen. John McCain and Democratic presidential nominee Sen. Barack Obama place flowers at the site of the former Twin Towers in New York, NY, Sept. 11, 2008. (Peter Foley/Reuters)

President George W. Bush meets with congressional leaders, including the presidential nominees, in the Cabinet Room of the White House, Sept. 25, 2008, to discuss the financial crisis. **Seated, frsom left:** Chief of Staff Joshua Bolten, Vice President Dick Cheney, Secretary of the Treasury Henry Paulson, Rep. Spencer Bachus, Rep. Barney Frank, House Majority Leader Steny Hoyer, Republican presidential candidate Sen. John McCain, House Minority Leader John A. Boehner, Speaker of the House Nancy Pelosi, President Bush, Senate Majority Leader Harry Reid, Senate Minority Leader Mitch McConnell, and Democratic presidential nominee Sen. Barack Obama. (Pablo Martínez Monsiváis/Associated Press)

Democratic presidential nominee Sen. Barack Obama hugs chief strategist and media advisor David Axelrod on day four of the Democratic National Convention, Aug. 28, 2008, Denver, CO. (Charles Ommanney/Getty Images)

Democratic presidential nominee Sen. Barack Obama at the University of Mary Washington during a rally in Fredericksburg, VA, Sept. 27, 2008. (From **Barack Before Obama** by David Katz. Copyright © 2020 by David Katz. Courtesy of HarperCollins Publishers)

Democratic presidential nominee Sen. Barack Obama speaks at a rally under the Gateway Arch in St. Louis, MO, Oct. 18, 2008. (David Katz)

Barack Obama and his mother-in-law, Marian Robinson, on election night in Chicago, IL, Nov. 4, 2008. (From **Barack Before Obama** by David Katz. Copyright © 2020 by David Katz. Courtesy of HarperCollins Publishers)

Barack Obama, his wife, Michelle, and their daughters, Sasha (**left**) and Malia, at Chicago's Grant Park after his presidential victory, Nov. 4, 2008. (Ralf-Finn Hestoft/Corbis via Getty Images)

People gather around a transistor radio at the Lincoln Memorial to listen to Barack Obama give his election-night speech, Nov. 4, 2008. (Matt Mendelsohn)

President-elect Barack Obama backstage at the U.S. Capitol before walking out to take the oath of office, Jan. 20, 2009. (Pete Souza/The White House)

Barack Obama's hand lies on a Bible as he is sworn in as the 44th U.S. president by Chief Justice John Roberts in front of the U.S. Capitol, Jan. 20, 2009. (Timothy A. Clary/AFP via Getty Images)

President Barack Obama delivers his inaugural address at the U.S. Capitol, Jan. 20, 2009. (Pete Souza/The White House)

President Barack Obama and First Lady Michelle Obama walk on Pennsylvania Avenue during the inaugural parade in Washington, DC, Jan. 20, 2009. (Pete Souza/The White House)

President Barack Obama sits in the Oval Office on his first day in office, Jan. 21, 2009. (Pete Souza/The White House)

President Barack Obama walks down the colonnade at the White House with his daughters, Malia (**left**) and Sasha, Mar. 5, 2009. (Pete Souza/The White House)

INSERT 2

President Barack Obama with White House chief of staff Rahm Emanuel during the White House staff picnic, June 26, 2009. (Pete Souza/The White House)

President Barack Obama with advisors at an economic meeting in the Roosevelt Room of the White House, Mar. 15, 2009. Participants include NEC director Larry Summers, Treasury secretary Timothy Geithner, CEA chair Christina Romer, Chief of Staff Rahm Emanuel, and senior advisor David Axelrod. (Pete Souza/The White House)

President Barack Obama with Senate Majority Leader Harry Reid backstage before his town hall meeting in Henderson, NV, Feb. 19, 2010. (Pete Souza/The White House)

President Barack Obama hugs First Lady Michelle Obama in the Red Room of the White House, with senior advisor Valerie Jarrett, Mar. 20, 2009. (Pete Souza/The White House)

President Barack Obama runs down the East Colonnade with the family dog, Bo, Mar. 15, 2009. (Pete Souza/The White House)

President Barack Obama tours the Pyramids and the Sphinx in Egypt on June 4, 2009. (Pete Souza/The White House)

Palestinians watch a television broadcast of President Barack Obama's speech in Cairo, at their home in the southern Gaza Strip, June 4, 2009. (Ibraheem Abu Mustafa/Reuters)

President Barack Obama talks with Justice Sonia Sotomayor before her investiture ceremony at the Supreme Court, Sept. 8, 2009. (Pete Souza/The White House)

President Barack Obama meets with Denis McDonough, NSC chief of staff, at the Waldorf Astoria hotel in New York, NY, Sept. 23, 2009. (Pete Souza/The White House)

(**From left**) Japanese prime minister Taro Aso, Canadian prime minister Stephen Harper, Italian prime minister Silvio Berlusconi, President Barack Obama, Russian president Dmitry Medvedev, British prime minister Gordon Brown, French president Nicolas Sarkozy, German chancellor Angela Merkel, Swedish prime minister Fredrik Reinfeldt, and head of the European Commission José Manuel Barroso at the G8 summit in L'Aquila, Italy, on July 8, 2009. (Pete Souza/The White House)

President Barack Obama and deputy national security advisor Ben Rhodes in the Oval Office, May 21, 2009. (Pete Souza/The White House)

President Barack Obama and members of the American delegation, including (**from left**) national security advisor General Jim Jones, undersecretary for political affairs Bill Burns, and NSC senior director for Russian affairs Mike McFaul, meet with Prime Minister Vladimir Putin at his dacha outside Moscow, Russia, July 7, 2009. (Pete Souza/The White House)

President Barack Obama leads his daughter Sasha through the Kremlin in Moscow, Russia, July 6, 2009. (Pete Souza/The White House)

President Barack Obama coaches Sasha's basketball team with help from personal aide Reggie Love in Chevy Chase, MD, Feb. 5, 2011. (Pete Souza/The White House)

President Barack Obama jokes with press secretary Robert Gibbs and personal aide Reggie Love (**right**), Oct. 26, 2009. (Pete Souza/The White House)

President Barack Obama reads in the Rose Garden of the White House, Nov. 9, 2009. (Pete Souza/The White House)

President Barack Obama greets a young visitor in the Oval Office, Feb. 5, 2010. (Pete Souza/The White House)

Bob Dylan shakes President Barack Obama's hand following his performance at a concert in the East Room of the White House, Feb. 9, 2010. (Pete Souza/The White House)

At Dover Air Force Base in Dover, DE, Oct. 29, 2009, President Barack Obama and Attorney General Eric Holder (**far right**) attend a ceremony for the dignified transfer of eighteen U.S. personnel who died in Afghanistan. (Pete Souza/The White House)

President Barack Obama delivers a speech on Afghanistan at the U.S. Military Academy at West Point, NY, Dec. 1, 2009. (Pete Souza/The White House)

President Barack Obama greets Cory Remsburg while visiting wounded warriors at Bethesda Naval Hospital in Bethesda, MD, Feb. 28, 2010. (Pete Souza/The White House)

President Barack Obama greets U.S. troops at a mess hall at Bagram Air Base in Afghanistan, Mar. 28, 2010. (Pete Souza/The White House)

Presidential advisors, including (**from right**) Secretary of State Hillary Rodham Clinton; defense secretary Robert Gates; veterans affairs secretary Eric K. Shinseki; Admiral Michael Mullen, chairman of the Joint Chiefs; and General David Petraeus, commander, U.S. Central Command, listen to President Barack Obama's speech on Afghanistan at the U.S. Military Academy at West Point, NY, Dec. 1, 2009. (Pete Souza/The White House)

President Barack Obama and First Lady Michelle Obama talk with Queen Elizabeth II and Prince Philip, Duke of Edinburgh, before they depart Winfield House in London, England, May 25, 2011. (Pete Souza/The White House)

President Barack Obama with Chinese president Hu Jintao at the Great Hall of the People in Beijing, China, Nov. 17, 2009. (Feng Li/Getty Images)

President Barack Obama and Jon Favreau, head speechwriter, edit a speech on healthcare in the Oval Office, Sept. 9, 2009. (Pete Souza/The White House)

President Barack Obama, Vice President Joe Biden, and senior staff react in the Roosevelt Room of the White House as the House passes the healthcare reform bill, Mar. 21, 2010. (Pete Souza/The White House)

President Barack Obama embraces Secretary of Health and Human Services Kathleen Sebelius (**left**) and House Speaker Nancy Pelosi after signing the Affordable Care Act, Mar. 23, 2010. (Pete Souza/The White House)

President Barack Obama is briefed at the U.S. Coast Guard station in Venice, LA, May 2, 2010, about the situation along the Gulf Coast following the BP oil spill. Participants include U.S. Coast Guard commandant Admiral Thad Allen (**seated at left**), Assistant to the President for Homeland Security and Counterterrorism John Brennan, Chief of Staff Rahm Emanuel, and EPA administrator Lisa Jackson (**far right**). (Pete Souza/The White House)

President Barack Obama on the swing set on the South Lawn with daughter Malia, May 4, 2010. (Pete Souza/The White House)

President Barack Obama talks with Ambassador Samantha Power, U.S. permanent representative to the United Nations, following a cabinet meeting, Sept. 12, 2013. (Pete Souza/ The White House)

Nobel Peace Prize laureate President Barack Obama arrives for the award ceremony at Oslo City Hall, Norway, Dec. 10, 2009. (John McConnico/AFP via Getty Images)

President Barack Obama and Vice President Joe Biden on their way to sign the Dodd-Frank Wall Street Reform and Consumer Protection Act, July 21, 2010. (Pete Souza/The White House)

President Barack Obama prepares to deliver an address to the nation from the Oval Office on the end of the combat mission in Iraq, Aug. 31, 2010. (Pete Souza/The White House)

President Barack Obama and Vice President Joe Biden, along with members of the national security team, receive an update on the mission against Osama bin Laden in the Situation Room of the White House, May 1, 2011. **Seated, from left:** Brigadier General Marshall B. Webb, assistant commanding general, JSOC; Deputy National Security Advisor Denis McDonough; Secretary of State Hillary Rodham Clinton; and Secretary of Defense Robert Gates. **Standing, from left:** Admiral Mike Mullen, chairman of the Joint Chiefs; National Security Advisor Tom Donilon; Chief of Staff Bill Daley; Tony Blinken, national security advisor to the vice president; Audrey Tomason, director for counterterrorism; John Brennan, assistant to the president for homeland security and counterterrorism; and Director of National Intelligence James Clapper (**out of frame**). (Pete Souza/The White House)

President Barack Obama, seated between Prime Minister Manmohan Singh (**left**) and President Pratibha Devisingh Patil, at a state dinner at Rashtrapati Bhavan, the presidential palace, in New Delhi, India, Nov. 8, 2010. (Pete Souza/The White House)

President Barack Obama and (**from left**) President Mahmoud Abbas of the Palestinian Authority, President Hosni Mubarak of Egypt, and Prime Minister Benjamin Netanyahu of Israel, in the Blue Room of the White House, check their watches to see if it is officially sunset, Sept. 1, 2010. (Pete Souza/The White House)

President Barack Obama looks out a window in the Blue Room of the White House, Nov. 3, 2010. (Pete Souza/The White House)

President Barack Obama, First Lady Michelle Obama, and daughters Sasha and Malia tour the **Christ the Redeemer** statue in Rio de Janeiro, Brazil, Mar. 20, 2011. (Pete Souza/The White House)

President Barack Obama walks along the West Colonnade of the White House, Jan. 8, 2011. (Pete Souza/The White House)